ANTHROPOCENE
A NEW INTRODUCTION TO
WORLD PREHISTORY

ARCHAEOLOGY AND THE ANTHROPOCENE

1

In *Rapa Nui*, the Hollywood movie of 1994, someone takes an axe to chop down the last tree on Rapa Nui, an island isolated in the southeastern Pacific Ocean. The movie is a story of conflict between two clans, the powerful Long Ears and the oppressed Short Ears, who struggle to feed their families on dwindling supplies, all the while investing hours of labor on constructing monumental stone *moai*. Under escalating demand for ever-larger *moai*, the workers steadily fell trees to create log rollers and rope, leaving behind a devastated and dusty landscape devoid of food and water. As the last palm crashes to the ground, one cannot help but wonder, "What will the living do now?"

For ourselves, we must ask, do we have a choice in making our future world? Rapa Nui has long been held up as one example of humans shaping our environment. In this book, we explore the prehistory of humans and come to understand how our experience of Earth today has been shaped by people of the past. At the core of our story is the Anthropocene, a term that both scientists and the public at large increasingly use to refer to the latest geologic age: with *Anthropos-* ("human") describing the human tenure on Earth, and *-cene*, the geological record we will leave behind. Although most would agree that the presence of humans has considerably changed Earth's environment, scientists continue to debate the specifics of the Anthropocene. When did it start? What defines it? Archaeology has an unique ability to trace the evolution of the Anthropocene, the human choices that shaped it, and our responses to rapidly transforming environments. Archaeology studies human societies of the past through an analysis of what remains of their material culture—that is, their tools, food, buildings, and other artifacts. With the Anthropocene as the conceptual basis for our narrative, archaeology becomes the central toolkit for understanding the processes that shaped human societies and the environments of the past, and demonstrates how the explanatory power of the archaeological record can yield insights into today's problems.

With the Anthropocene as our focus, this book takes on a comparative perspective, moving across the globe in each chapter to explore major themes in world prehistory. Our journey across time and space emphasizes that human history is not a single linear progression (hunter-gatherers to farmers, to states), but rather a cumulative engagement with a range of environments.

This approach explicitly addresses modern existential challenges—increasing global human population, extinction of more and more species, and climate change—by examining them through long-term human history.

What Is the Anthropocene? 10

The Perspective of Archaeology 14

Polynesia and the North Atlantic: Islands as Laboratories 15

Methods: Survey and Excavation 22

How Have Humans Made Their World? 24

Opposite The iconic *moai* of Rapa Nui (Easter Island) in the South Pacific. These figures represent ancestors, and were created and moved by small communities who recognized the statues as their relatives. The *moai* were in place across the island by c. 1450 CE, but were toppled by conflict in later centuries.

Key Concepts

- The Anthropocene: its definition and suggested origins
- The role of archaeology in understanding the human past and human future in the context of the Anthropocene
- Prehistory as a reflection of the diversity of cultural expressions around the world
- The key methods of archaeology: how survey and excavation are used to uncover the past

Our hope is that this will also inspire you to reflect on your own responsibility from the perspective of your place in the long, archaeologically framed trajectory of human engagement with our environment.

WHAT IS THE ANTHROPOCENE?

Human history has unfolded slowly over two geological epochs, known as the **Pleistocene** and **Holocene**. The Pleistocene or Ice Age commenced about 2.58 million years ago, and it was near the end of this epoch that modern humans and their societies evolved, around 250,000 years ago. Pleistocene global temperatures were on average 9–18 degrees Fahrenheit (5–10 degrees Celsius) cooler, and much of the northern and southern hemispheres was covered with glacial ice. Animals and plants adapted to these environments to survive. Some large-bodied animals, known as "megafauna," contended with colder conditions through their sheer size and could be found on every major continent. The Pleistocene's time span was punctuated with fluctuating climate conditions, which included cool and dry periods in which landscapes were covered in sizeable icy glaciers (glacial periods), and warm and wet periods during which the glaciers retreated and sea levels rose (interglacial periods). The Holocene, which followed, began approximately 11,600 years ago and was marked by the retreat of glaciers and the onset of warm and more stable conditions. It was during this epoch that humans came to inhabit places spanning the world: traveling to the American continent and Pacific Islands, developing farming and vast cities, and spreading their civilizations across the planet.

In his Nobel Prize acceptance speech in 2002, atmospheric scientist Paul Crutzen invoked the label "The **Anthropocene**" to highlight humans' role in a new geological age, the age of humankind. Crutzen noted that the nineteenth-century Industrial Revolution had ushered in a period of high consumption of fossil fuels. The consequent high emissions of carbon dioxide and methane marked a threshold in humans' engagement with the global environment, with human activity that has accumulated from across continents and over the decades significantly affecting the makeup of the planet. In other words, humanity has become a geological force in its own right [1.1]. Crutzen's speech led to a heated debate—one that still rages—about the extent to which humans are responsible for the environmental change happening today. If past human activity is the principal cause, when did the Anthropocene begin exactly? Many markers of human-caused or **anthropogenic** change in the environment exist, some more distinct than others. Should we draw the line at the Industrial Revolution, or is there an earlier or later, more accurate date?

Pleistocene Earth's most recent Ice Age, lasting until c. 11,600 years ago.

Holocene The epoch following the Pleistocene, which involved the warming of the planet and retreat of the glaciers, beginning c. 11,600 years ago.

Anthropocene The current geological age, the period during which human activity began to affect the environment.

anthropogenic Human-caused and human-related change.

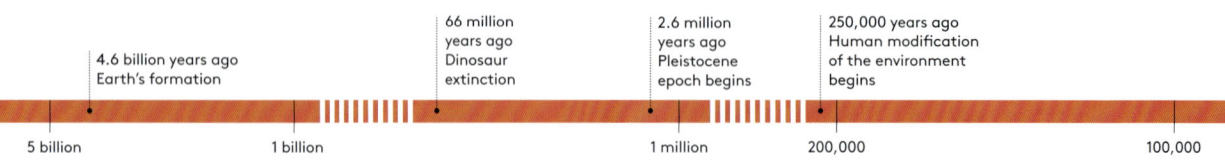

| 4.6 billion years ago Earth's formation | 66 million years ago Dinosaur extinction | 2.6 million years ago Pleistocene epoch begins | 250,000 years ago Human modification of the environment begins |

5 billion | 1 billion | 1 million | 200,000 | 100,000
YEARS AGO

When Did the Anthropocene Begin?

What can be seen as marking the beginning of the Anthropocene? One possibility is the ice-bubbles, calcium carbonates, and other geochemical residues that track rising carbon dioxide and other greenhouse gases in the past three hundred years; another is species die-off, which may leave a sufficient record of diversity loss and mass extinction still visible eons from now. Some consider the nineteenth-century Industrial Revolution's increased use of fossil fuels to be a significant marker—but could the Anthropocene have begun with coal-fueled ironworking in Song Dynasty China (tenth and eleventh centuries) or African iron smelters of the thirteenth century? The geologist Jan Zalasiewicz traces the beginning of the new epoch to June 16, 1945, the date the first atom bomb was exploded. That explosion produced the isotopes cesium 137, and plutonium 239 and 240, which will remain in the environment for thousands of years. In recent decades, awareness about microplastics—tiny, macerated remnants of petroleum products that are filling beaches and oceans—suggests they could be the latest indelible geological signature of our age.

For many, however, including Crutzen, the Anthropocene started with the Industrial Revolution, which marked the beginning of human dependence on fossil fuels, as reflected in increased carbon dioxide (CO_2) levels.

1.1 Artificial islands and a lagoon shaped to resemble a palm tree. Located off the coast of Dubai in the United Arab Emirates, construction began in 2001. Dubai is also building "The Sustainable City," a solar-powered development designed to produce more energy than it consumes.

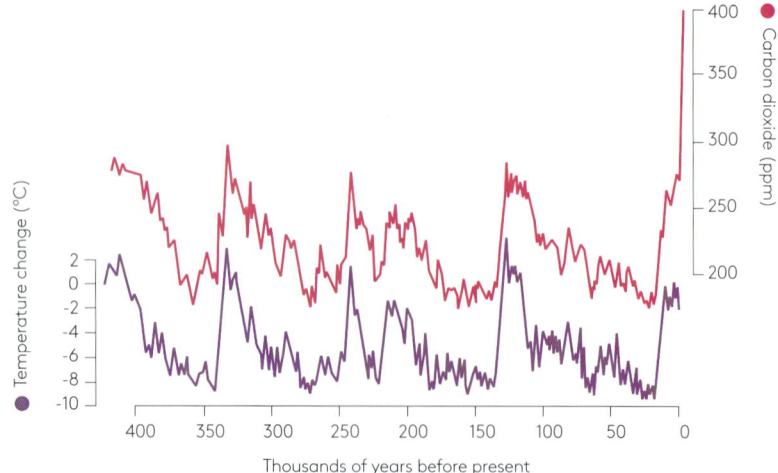

1.2 Carbon dioxide (CO_2) levels over the past 400,000 years. During the glacial and interglacial conditions of the Pleistocene, CO_2 levels in the atmosphere ranged from 180 to 280 parts per million (ppm). Over the last two centuries, CO_2 has steadily risen to more than 415 ppm. Global average temperatures have increased in step with CO_2 emissions, and are projected to rise 3–7 °Fahrenheit (2–4 °Celsius) in the next century.

When the Industrial Revolution commenced, CO_2 molecules numbered about 280 parts per million (ppm) in air. By 1992, that measure had reached 356 ppm, and by 2019, it exceeded 415 ppm at Mauna Loa, Hawai'i, in the relatively pollutant-free mid-Pacific [1.2]. This rate of CO_2 growth over the last two decades is 100 to 200 times faster than what Earth experienced during the transition from the last Ice Age. The increasing levels of CO_2 enveloping our planet are like a blanket that traps solar insolation (heat from the sun), reflecting it back to the planet's surface. This process raises global temperatures. To date, the oceans have absorbed CO_2 in their vast depths, but rising CO_2 levels in the oceans create carbonic acid, and increased acidity in seawater affects the survival of corals and reef life underpinning much of the ocean's food chain. The rate of CO_2 increase in the atmosphere is a human-caused phenomenon and a powerful indicator that we now live in the Anthropocene.

Does the Industrial Revolution, however, mark the moment when greenhouse gases began to accumulate in Earth's air? Levels of methane gas, which are also on the rise, are as significant as carbon dioxide to planetary climate change. The chief contributor has historically been domesticated cattle, the numbers of which, as we will learn in this book, have increased steadily since their initial appearance some 8,000 years ago and which now make up a large percentage of the planet's mammalian life. In addition, the development of metal tools—used for clearing CO_2-absorbing forests—has deep roots in the past.

Yet another marker of the Anthropocene is the direct impact of humans on animal and plant life, with the clearest example being extinctions. The greatest die-off of invertebrates occurred at the end of the Permian period 252 million years ago, followed distantly by the extermination of dinosaurs and other massive reptiles with the famous Cretaceous meteor impact 66 million years ago. In Earth's history, three other colossal extinction phases have since taken place. The so-called sixth extinction is unfolding right now. Each day, dozens of species on Earth disappear forever. Coral reefs in Australia, the Caribbean, and Southeast Asia are dying and, with them, the species dependent on the habitat and food chain they anchor. Diversity-rich rain forests are logged for timber and replaced with miles of rangeland and monocrop, palm-oil plantations. Individuals of endangered species cannot find mates or are isolated in nonviable populations. It is not only the large African fauna, such as rhinos and elephants, that are imperiled or gone: golden frogs in Panama, polar bears in the Arctic, passenger pigeons and little brown bats in the continental United States, Hawaiian honeycreepers, and the Kalimantan orangutan in Borneo may be added to the list. The number and rate of extinctions easily match each of the previous five most significant extinction phases, and there is little doubt that the current global transformation of life on Earth bears the same characteristics as previous transitions from one geologic age to the next, such as that from the Cretaceous to Jurassic period.

The sixth extinction is global in scale and anthropogenic in origin. The roots of the sixth extinction also extend into prehistory, with the disappearance of now extinct animals, such as the giant sloth in South America and the marsupial lion in Australia, coinciding with the first trace of humans.

Underlying many of these anthropogenic changes to the world is the unprecedented rise in the human population [**1.3**]. It took 300,000 years for our species, **Homo sapiens**, to reach 1 billion people and only another century for the global population to double again. Due to the growing human population, the stress placed on the natural world of animals and plants, and the increase in global temperatures, Crutzen would attribute the onset of an Anthropocene era to the past few centuries, but if other forms of anthropogenic transformation are taken into account, the start date of the Anthropocene can be established much earlier. It might even be traced back to when humans initially began to alter their surrounding environment to improve their own chances of survival.

This alteration is what archaeologists refer to as human **niche construction**, the manner in which people have changed their habitat in a way that improves their

Homo sapiens Modern humans. *Homo* describes the genus, and *sapiens* the species.

niche construction The manner in which a species changes its habitat in a way that improves its overall fitness and that of its descendants.

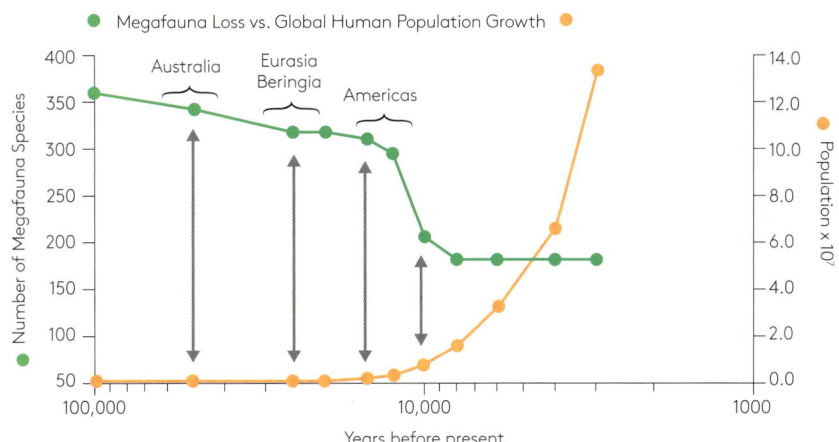

1.3 Dating back to the Pleistocene, large mammal biomass has declined as human populations have increased. Animal domestication began around 10,000 years ago, and now domesticated mammals make up 90 percent of total mammal biomass.

fitness The ability of an individual to contribute viable offspring to the next generation's population.

archaeology The study of past humans through their material remains.

own overall **fitness** and that of their descendants. History is replete with examples of how the environment changed as human populations increased, and how humans, in turn, responded to this change. The Anthropocene might have commenced as early as the first activities of anatomically modern humans approximately 250,000 years ago. Clearing forests, domesticating plants and animals, and building cities are all forms of human niche construction, because such activities modify the environment to best accommodate human survival and advancement. The first signs of this kind of environmental transformation occurred far earlier than the last few hundred years.

Debates about the Anthropocene may be strictly geological (finding its precise age, identified by a fossil as when a new epoch begins), or they might be more exploratory (using the concept to recognize and discuss humanity's long-term effect on the planet). Why does it matter when we believe the Anthropocene began? A relatively late onset for the Anthropocene and its identification with fossil-fueled technologies serve to disconnect humans from our natural condition, suggesting that only modern technologies are to blame for any troubling developments. A longer view of the Anthropocene recognizes our long-term engagement in constructing a planetary niche as a fundamental aspect of human nature. If we accept that humans have significantly changed their environment for thousands of years, it becomes possible to stop looking to the past for who to blame and to understand more fully how people have created dynamics with surrounding plant and animal life: what conditions humans created, and how they have both succeeded and failed in creating a sustainable, resilient environment. Rather than serving as a message of doom, the Anthropocene can be one of hope and choice, inspiring humans to create an ecological niche that will be sustainable for many generations to come.

THE PERSPECTIVE OF ARCHAEOLOGY

Archaeology offers a long-term and global view of how humans have interacted with their environment. The stories across human history are diverse, and a powerful lesson is that no single outcome or save-all solution exists. Examining the past in different locales—how people made choices, and how new niches were made and modified—provides a glimpse into possible plans of action for the future. We can evaluate these examples' relationship to our environments today and use them to inform our choices going forward. The past teaches us that human society and ingenuity can produce successful outcomes—in which humans survive—if we apply a diverse suite of solutions integrating humans with the dynamic natural world.

This book explores the great variety of ways in which humans have constructed the world around them and responded to environmental pressures—some of their own making. As a prelude to how a long-term perspective can help us identify multiple solutions and glimpse possible outcomes, the remainder of this chapter returns to the story of Rapa Nui and compares it to a very different outcome in another part of the world: the North Atlantic.

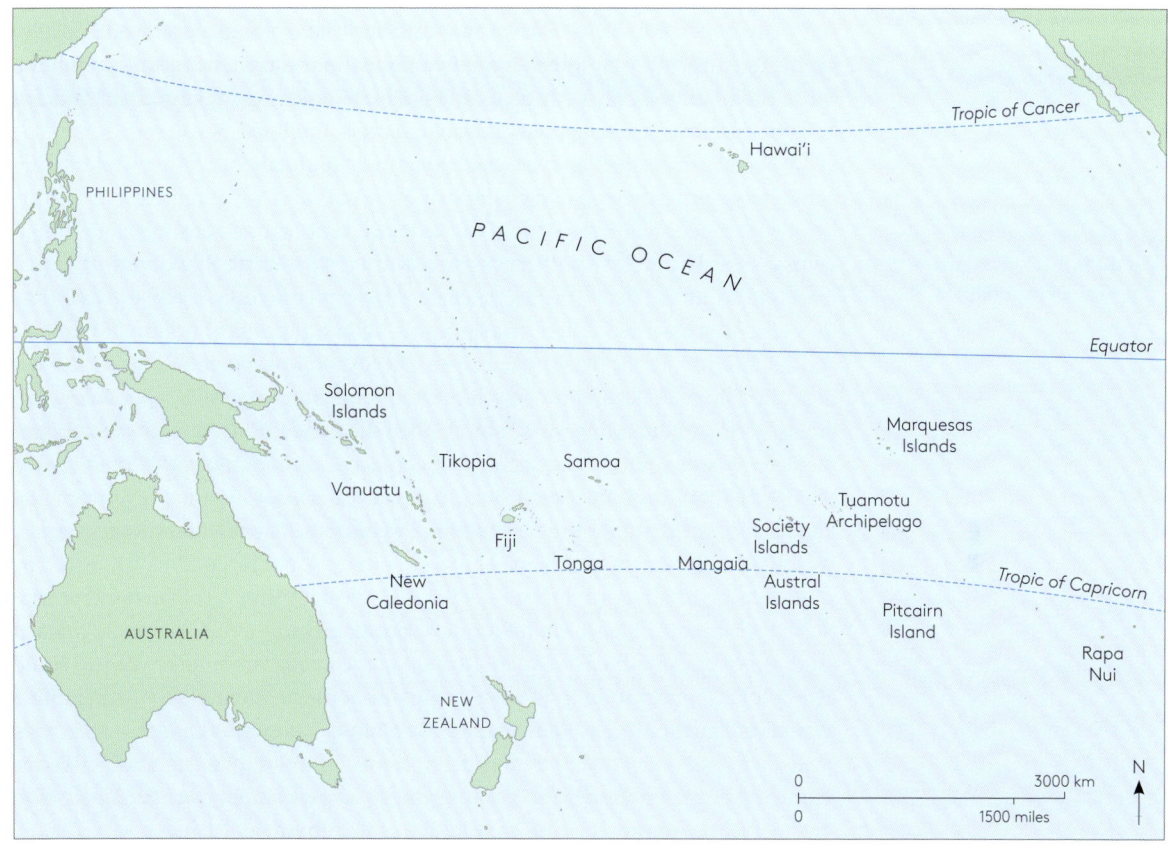

POLYNESIA AND THE NORTH ATLANTIC: ISLANDS AS LABORATORIES

In the recent Hollywood movie *Moana*, a brave heroine leads her people in a dramatic voyage across the Pacific Ocean. In so doing, they reclaim their identity as voyagers who seek a new home. Few viewers of the popular animated film understand that Moana's quest is based on a recorded archaeological mystery: by 800 BCE, her ancestors had indeed settled nearly all the islands of West Polynesia, yet the numerous islands of East Polynesia (including Rapa Nui) remained undiscovered [**1.4**]. "Why did we stop?" Moana implored her grandmother. For seventy-five years, archaeologists have asked this same question.

Archaeological excavations on Manu'a, the easternmost islands of the Samoan archipelago and inspiration for *Moana*'s imaginary island of "Motu Nui," sought the answer. In 1986, archaeologist Patrick Kirch and colleagues conducted a **survey** of the islands. As part of their fieldwork, they walked along the beaches, across the coastal terraces, and up the jungle-covered slopes. Archaeologists use a survey to discover archaeological features, such as isolated artifacts or entire sites, and to

1.4 The South Pacific Islands, homeland of the Polynesian voyagers; includes the islands of Fiji, Tonga, and Samoa, and the many archipelagos of the eastern and western Pacific.

survey Research conducted in the field, including searching for sites and collecting information on the distribution of archaeological objects and features.

excavation The archaeological practice of uncovering and recording remains systematically.

stratigraphic layers Layers of rock or sediment that accumulate over time and can be used to infer the relative age of an archaeological find.

record their locations. In the Pacific Islands, a survey can identify scatters of pottery on the ground and map the extent of surface architecture, including any stone walls and platforms. Survey results thus help determine patterns of past human activities, such as where people gardened, fished, and lived.

Eyeing a trench that had been opened with a bulldozer for a future landfill, the archaeologists discovered a deep deposit of beach sand 6 feet 6 inches (2 meters) below the modern surface. Pottery in the beach sand marked a buried site (called To'aga), so Kirch and his colleagues conducted an archaeological **excavation**, which reached a depth of 11 feet 6 inches (3.5 meters) beneath the surface. While excavating, they carefully recorded eleven **stratigraphic layers**, deposits of sediment that had accumulated at the site over the centuries. The layers closest to the surface had been deposited by such natural processes as wind, rain, and erosion. Deeper below, the deposits contained pottery and marine shell discarded by an unknown people in the distant past, after they had cooked or eaten a meal. Careful excavation revealed that To'aga had been occupied since 800 BCE. This was the outside limit of the Polynesian world at that time. Islands to the east, such as the Marquesas Islands, Society Islands, and distant Rapa Nui, were not explored for another 1,600 years.

Returning to Moana's question: Why did voyaging stop? The answer may be that it did not cease entirely in 800 BCE, but that finding the extremely distant (and relatively small) eastern Polynesian islands took many more centuries of technological innovation in canoe design and noninstrumental navigation. Such a small, isolated island as Rapa Nui was difficult to colonize—it had few resources of its own, and a great deal of modification was required to make it habitable for a growing human population. People on these islands had to construct their own "niches," transforming them from wild places to human landscapes.

The South Pacific Islands are a useful introduction to archaeology and the Anthropocene, as the Manu'a Islands and Rapa Nui have been at the forefront of the "islands as laboratories" view of world prehistory. According to this view, islands are microcosms of human activity and can show the diverse ways humans adapt to and engineer their environment. In the context of the South Pacific Islands, the Anthropocene began when the first canoes slid up onto the sand of a newly discovered beach [**1.5**]. Across the Pacific, the first human colonists founded many island cultures between the years 1500 BCE and 800 CE, each with a similar set of resources to introduce—about twenty-five domesticated plants and such animals as rats, chickens, dogs, and pigs. Courtesy of this "colonist's package," in just about everywhere in the South Pacific, including Rapa Nui, the historical sequence followed a similar pattern: the extinction of many native ground-nesting birds and of palms, enrichment of agricultural land, and expansion of human populations into landscapes across many environmental zones.

The story is not quite that simple, however. On some islands (for example, Tikopia), people cooperated and settled into a relatively egalitarian society with a plentiful breadfruit harvest for all, whereas on others (for example, Hawai'i), conflict led to ruling chiefs and rigid social boundaries. Societies emerged in which some people

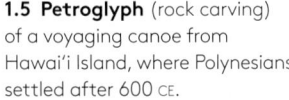

1.5 Petroglyph (rock carving) of a voyaging canoe from Hawai'i Island, where Polynesians settled after 600 CE.

were born to privilege and greater access to resources, and others staked their claims through grisly human sacrifice and warfare. At times islanders became cannibals (such as in Fiji). Where ruling chiefs prevailed, they limited others' ability to procure the most desirable foods (as in Mangaia and Hawai'i). The remotest and poorest islands in terms of soil quality, water, and biodiversity (such as Pitcairn Island) were eventually abandoned by humans as failed experiments. Anthropologists agree that the diversity of island societies and histories suggests no one outcome is ever inevitable.

With the islands as laboratories approach in mind, in the following sections, we explore the Anthropocene from the perspective of two very different island histories: Rapa Nui in the Pacific, and Greenland in the North Atlantic. Both of these histories demonstrate how cultural responses and outcomes can differ, and this teaches us about cultural diversity and the complexity of our own prehistory.

Rapa Nui

The real story of Rapa Nui is fascinating, for not only its tale of colonization but also the later development of an island culture in a precarious environment [1.6]. Archaeological excavations have revealed that Rapa Nui was colonized *c.* 1200 CE by the descendants of people who had recently settled in the Cook Islands, Society Islands, and Austral Islands, located more than 1,243 miles (2,000 km) to the west. Because Rapa Nui was a relatively old volcanic island, its soils were depleted and inadequate for agriculture, with unpredictable rainfall. Imported yam, taro, and bananas barely tolerated the cool, dry conditions, so its colonists eventually came to rely more on sweet potato—mysteriously brought from South America *c.* 1400 CE—as the

1.6 The dramatic stone *moai* of Rapa Nui were placed atop platforms called *ahu*, facing inland. The statues' construction dates to *c.* 1450 CE.

main staple. Rats and chickens, which could survive on native forage, such as palm, became the principal sources of protein.

As their relatives in the rest of East Polynesia did, Rapa Nui islanders hewed iconic, multi-ton monoliths of their human ancestors, called *moai*, from a quarry on the side of a volcanic crater, and transported them to the coast without the assistance of either animals (the largest land animal on Rapa Nui was the domesticated dog) or wheeled carts. Perhaps using a system of ropes to rock the standing statues from side to side, they were moved along prepared roads from the quarry to the coasts. There, the islanders set the *moai* upright on top of stone platforms called *ahu*, and gave them piercing eyes carved from coral so they could watch over their human descendants. *Ahu* and *moai* construction appears to have become widespread on the island by 1450 CE. Archaeologist Jo Anne Van Tilburg and her colleagues have used excavation to determine that the nearly three hundred *moai* and *ahu* were also routinely reconstructed and enhanced.

Life on Rapa Nui was often difficult: the island had a poor reef and offered little hardwood for crafting boats, and crops were vulnerable to drought and failure. Hunger and periods of starvation may have been common, and farmers would have had to work very hard to produce enough food. To retain moisture, gardens were carefully tended in rock-mulched pits, the remains of which still carpet the island landscape. The Pacific rats (*Rattus exulans*) that had come with the first colonists were a good source of scarce protein, but they ultimately exterminated the indigenous palms by nibbling away at their seasonal nuts. Residents also cut down many palms: for the wooden pick handles used for carving *moai*, for cooking fuel, and for the construction of homes. But as the rats continued to eat the palm seeds, the last stands failed to regenerate. Rapa Nui, as a human-engineered niche, had to find a balance.

As a result of the degraded soils and episodic rainfall, human settlement on the landscape was widely dispersed, and people came together locally only for community gatherings centered on the *ahu*. In this way, through a shared tradition, the *moai* shaped social integration (see Chapter 11). Although in later years *moai* were deliberately toppled in conflicts, perhaps as a way of disconnecting people from their ancestors and their ties to the land, little evidence of lethal injuries, fortifications, or deadly weapons survives.

Although the film *Rapa Nui* blames the obsession with creating *moai* for deforestation and destabilization of the island environment, archaeologists now argue that the cultural tradition of constructing *moai* became a unique solution for Rapa Nui's problems. The islanders' response to scarcity was to construct, transport, and install multi-ton stone statues, thus diverting energy that might otherwise have contributed to population growth. Community investment in *moai* construction protected the existing population—artificially constrained in size—from periodic shortfalls that would have resulted in mass starvation. They may not have been aware that their efforts to raise the *moai* actually benefitted them, yet the tight-knit communities who lived to see another day, in turn, passed on this tradition of *moai* building to their descendants to ensure their survival. Archaeology reveals the great impact of anthropogenic change on Rapa Nui in the loss of its palms, the creation of vast areas of rock-mulch gardening, and the extinction of its native sea and land birds. But it also shows how a society cleverly employed technology, ideology, and social connections to survive in a new landscape that humanity had created. Life was difficult, but people persisted.

Greenland

The history of Greenland [1.7], yet another relatively isolated island, speaks to the consequences of different human choices and diverse human cultures. Unlike the Pacific Islands, where vast oceans reduced the force of climate change, Greenland experienced the brief anomaly of a more moderate climate during the medieval warm period (c. 950–1250 CE; 1.8). This coincided with an era of excursions from the northern countries of Europe. From Iceland, the Norse (sometimes referred to as Vikings) sailed west into the cold Atlantic and founded two colonies at the tip of Greenland. Here, they built churches; raised cattle on pasture during a brief grazing season in the summer; cut and stocked hay for the long winters; and ate cheese,

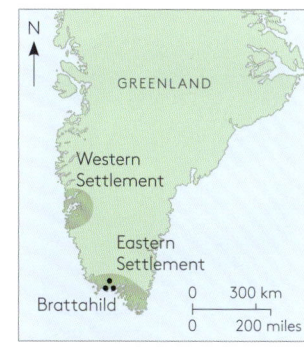

Above: **1.7 The Norse settlement of Greenland.** The Western and Eastern Settlements included many farmsteads and a few churches. The other, more northern, regions of Greenland were populated by Thule Inuit hunters, who maintained a mobile lifestyle.

Below: **1.8 House foundations still stand at Brattahild,** the abandoned Eastern Settlement of the Greenlander Vikings.

1.9 Exquisitely carved bishop's crosier made of whale tooth from the Garðar Settlement in eastern Greenland, radiocarbon-dated to 1246–80 CE. Even at the farthest outpost of Old World civilization, this item reflects the world as the Vikings knew it, with the acanthus-leaf scrolling favored in imagery since the days of ancient Greece and known across the East as far as China.

Thule Ancestors of the Inuit, who rapidly moved across Alaska, Canada, and Greenland from 1000 CE to the thirteenth century.

material culture The tools, food remains, buildings, and other artifacts used by humans.

meat, and fish. Since Greenland had no timbers for their roofs, no metals for their farm tools and cooking pots, and no glass for their church windows, for nearly five hundred years they depended on trading ships to sustain their European-style farmstead communities with both essentials and luxuries. Greenlanders did not even have the local means to brew alcohol.

Over time, the Greenland farmstead lifestyle became unsustainable. As colder climates returned, pastures for cattle began to shrink. The Norse settlers, in response, raised more sheep and goats, which were smaller animals suited to dwindling grass. A study of the chemistry of human bones from local church cemeteries showed that from the mid-thirteenth century on, Norse Greenlanders' diets included greater amounts of seal meat. As the years passed, though, traders stopped journeying to Greenland for walrus hide and ivory [**1.9**]; no new bishop arrived to serve its cathedral; neither timber, iron, glass, mead, nor beer was restocked.

We do not know exactly when and how the last Norse Greenlanders disappeared. The final phase of house abandonment suggests a rapid and desperate departure; among the unsalvaged timbers of one collapsed roof, archaeologists found the remains of butchered hunting dogs—suggesting that they were used for food—and native flies adapted to cold and reduced light. The latest floor levels lacked the fly carcasses of a species abundant in meadow grass, perhaps because the last years' haying had been meager or failed entirely. Many farms showed similar evidence: the carcasses of dogs uncovered in collapsed dwellings open to the sky. Some have suggested that the Norse Greenlanders starved because of the cooling climates, and indeed their skeletal remains indicate that their dependence on dairy products had tapered over time as cattle died off. Other possibilities include an epidemic (for which no archaeological proof exists), the cessation of ship traffic, or even devastation by fifteenth-century pirates from Europe. The only thing that is clear is this: Greenlanders largely stuck to their European cultural habits, even in the face of climate change. Although they attempted to make some limited adjustments—such as eating more seal or fish toward the end of the colony's existence—they failed to construct a sustainable niche on Greenland.

THE THULE The Norse were not the only cultural group that attempted to adapt to Greenland's changing climate. Greenland today is home to the Inuit, an indigenous people who are heirs to the **Thule** culture that from 1000 CE spread rapidly eastward across the Arctic region. Modern-day genetic studies and archaeological **material culture** suggest that Inuit ancestors replaced the preexisting Dorset people in the northern reaches of Greenland [**1.10**]. One theory is that the Thule spread quickly because they were drawn east by the region's scarce and highly desirable meteoric iron; another suggests that they were in pursuit of the resources, especially bowhead whales, who expanded their ranges during the medieval warm period.

Thule cultural practices never seem to have influenced the Greenlander Norsemen. Both the Dorset and Thule peoples practiced hunting strategies and lifestyles wildly different from those of the Norse Greenlanders. Thule traveled throughout the year,

1.10 Mask created by people of the Dorset culture of Canada, 500–1000 CE. This mask was carved from driftwood and used in ceremonies to heal the sick. Other Dorset tools employed the imagery of Arctic animals, such as seals and bears, which were important sources of food and materials.

1.11 A Thule carving from Baffin Island, in the Northwest Territories of Canada, shows a Norse individual in medieval dress. The figurine was found on the stone-paved floor of a Thule house, and its Norse costume suggests contact between the Thule and Norse settlers of Greenland.

relying on sleds, boats, and sophisticated harpoons to hunt seals, walrus, and whales. The Norseman replicated European farming culture, which relied on the raising of sheep, goats, and maintenance of pasture land around settled communities. Archaeology indicates that the two groups were in contact: for example, a Thule Inuit wood carving from Baffin Island in the Northwest Territories of Canada [1.11] depicts a Norse individual in medieval dress, and Norse accounts describe raids against and conflict with the Thule Inuit. Centuries later, the Norse Greenlanders had still not adopted the boats, seal-hunting techniques, bone tools, mobile lifestyle, clothing, open-air living, or other cultural practices that sustained the Thule—perhaps, in the end, the Norse Greenlanders simply joined the Inuit without leaving a trace. If so, not even their genes survive. Genetic studies of modern Greenlander populations have found no evidence of Norse admixture with the Thule people. Had they embraced many Thule Inuit practices, the Norsemen might have adapted to

Greenland's cooling climate. Instead, it seems likely that the young departed for greener shores with the last trade ships, leaving older colonists to bury each other as their farmsteads and churches crumbled into final decay.

Lessons Learned

Through archaeological research, we have learned that the societies of Rapa Nui and Greenland existed in anthropogenic environments: plants and animals were introduced and raised for food, land was transformed into agricultural fields and pastures, and human society adapted to the limitations of the land. In the face of change, however, these two societies exemplify opposite ends of the spectrum of human responses. In Rapa Nui, small communities pooled their efforts to maintain rituals that promoted social integration, and society survived despite episodes of hardship. The Norse Greenlanders, on the other hand, did not adopt Thule-style hunting and gathering as a possible means of survival; instead, they made only modest adjustments in the face of adversity and ultimately perished or chose to abandon their settlements. The Rapa Nui never had the option of leaving and, marooned on their remote island, they found a way to survive.

METHODS: SURVEY AND EXCAVATION

How do we know that Norse Greenlanders altered their farming methods, or that Dorset hunters reached Arctic Greenland about 2,500 hundred years ago? Archaeologists use a variety of methods to build narratives of the past. We will consider each major method in turn throughout the book, but here, we introduce the bare bones of the archaeological method. Archaeologists utilize a survey to find archaeological sites, which can range in size from a single artifact to an entire village or city [1.12]. By walking across a landscape, archaeologists conducting a surface survey are able to document the extent of archaeological remains, which can later be investigated using excavation. Many methods of survey are available, but all of them attempt to take into account the variables that may affect the accurate detection of artifacts and sites, and weigh the costs of human time and labor. Chapter 4 outlines the specifics of an archaeological survey.

The quintessential method of archaeology, excavation, systematically documents the location of artifacts, features, and remains of other aspects of prehistoric and historic life buried in the ground [1.13]. Archaeologists use several techniques to excavate archaeological deposits and minimize the loss of information—such as the disturbance of artifacts from their original location—to determine their context. An artifact's **context** is its association with the other artifacts and features discovered around it. In addition, the context offers clues about the formation of the archaeological record, that is, how artifacts came to be where they were found. If artifacts are uncovered exactly where they were left by humans, then they are **in situ**. Generating information is the true purpose of archaeological excavation;

context The physical association of an artifact with sediment, features, and other artifacts, which indicates how the artifact was used and ultimately deposited in the ground.

in situ The location of an object after it has been discarded; to be in an undisturbed deposit.

1.12 Using image maps developed from satellite imagery of Wadi Sana, in Yemen, Joy McCorriston's team—Tara, Mike, and Nisha— prepares for archaeological survey in planned locations.

1.13 Over the past century, archaeologists have developed a systematic approach to excavation. Here, excavators have sub-divided the floor of an 8,000-year-old goat-herder's house at Ṭabaqāt Al Būma ("owl flats" in Arabic), Jordan. Each section will be wet-screened (using water to rinse off sediment collected in a sieve) to recover tiny artifacts that reveal what the house's inhabitants did in different spots.

finding objects is secondary to the information gathered during the process of excavation. Chapter 5 provides greater detail on the methods that archaeologists employ when excavating.

HOW HAVE HUMANS MADE THEIR WORLD?

In the early twenty-first century, Earth's story is more similar to Rapa Nui's than Greenland's. As in the Pacific Islands, integration and exchange, and the flow of plants, animals, ideas, and technologies, have allowed for the development of human societies in all corners of the world. In exploring the diverse cultures and environments in world prehistory, an important emphasis of this book is how humans have made the world they live in, and most importantly, how humans in the past have transformed the world to suit the needs of their descendants better.

This book outlines the myriad ways humans have practiced niche construction. Along with survival of offspring and genetic transmission, human niche construction may include successfully transferring cultural practices from one generation to the next as equally important for human fitness. The earliest modern humans utilized their unique cognitive abilities to construct symbols—from drawings on cave walls, to monuments and costumes—to communicate human identity and group membership across time and across continents. In turn, these groups allowed a few individuals to explore vast territories, establish new colonies at great distances, and expand human populations across new landscapes. Stone tools (Chapter 3), humanity's most durable technology, allowed humans to hunt the largest mammals on earth, possibly to the point of extinction (Chapters 6 and 7). With the transformation of their ecosystems through extinctions, humans again used tools—this time metal as well as stone devices—to transform forests and fertile river valleys into open spaces that could be populated with domesticated animals, such as goats and sheep, and plants, such as wheat, barley, rice, bananas, and maize (Chapters 3 and 8).

Seven thousand years ago, human-constructed niches existed around the world, and the effects of human activities bled into natural systems. Rural and urban niches within and around human settlements have sheltered most of humanity since then. With the growth of human populations (Chapter 10), those niches have expanded into extensive, managed landscapes, resulting in the systematic control of water, the use of land for food production, and the exploitation of resources and labor.

Throughout these narratives, we come into contact with a diversity of outcomes, driven by not only different environments across the globe but also different choices. We will see how some human choices in the past resulted from the need to optimize current resources for survival; how other decisions were ideologically driven, for instance, in the pursuit of power; and how acts of generating wealth and displaying status have affected the environment for thousands of years. Examining the past in each locale—how people made choices, and how new niches were manufactured and modified—provides a possible plan of action for the future. From these core understandings, we can best evaluate our choices and act accordingly.

Chapter Questions

1. How does archaeology offer insight into the challenges of the Anthropocene?
2. How can comparing cultures in Polynesia and Greenland demonstrate the diversity of cultural expressions around the world?
3. What is the purpose of excavation in archaeology?

Additional Resources

Berglund, Joel. "Did the Mediaeval Norse Society in Greenland Really Fail?," in *Questioning Collapse*, edited by Patricia McAnany and Norman Yoffee, 45–70. Cambridge, UK: Cambridge University Press, 2010.

DiNapoli, Robert J., Morrison, Alex E., Lipo, Carl P., Hunt, Terry L., and Lane, Brian G. "East Polynesian Islands as Models of Cultural Divergence: The Case of Rapa Nui and Rapa Iti," *Journal of Island and Coastal Archaeology* 0 (2017): 1–18.

Hunt, Terry, Lipo, Carl. *The Statues that Walked: Unraveling the Mystery of Easter Island.* New York: Free Press, 2011.

Kirch, Patrick V. *On the Road of the Winds: An Archaeological History of the Pacific Islands before European Contact.* 2nd ed. Oakland, CA: University of California Press, 2017.

Kirch, Patrick V., and Hunt, T. L. (eds). *The To'aga Site: Three Millennia of Polynesian Occupation in the Manu'a Islands, America Samoa.* Oakland, CA: University of California Press, 1993.

Van Tilburg, Jo Anne. *Easter Island: Archaeology, Ecology and Culture.* Washington, DC: Smithsonian Press, 1995.

Easter Island Statue Project, online at: http://www.eisp.org

DISCOVERING DIVERSITY
Modern Human Origins

Twenty thousand years ago, prehistoric people at Lascaux Cave, France, created some of the oldest and most spectacular images in the world. From the 1940s, when the caves were discovered, the paintings on the cave walls drew crowds of tourists—whose very breathing threatened to erase the images. With carbon dioxide levels in the cave rising and mold beginning to form on the paintings, the French government shuttered the cave to the public.

Lascaux had been shut for twenty years when I was a first-year student. Through a radio call-in competition, I was lucky to be offered an exclusive tour of the Grotte de Lascaux. Lively Monsieur Marsal, who had discovered the cave as a teenager, guided my small group through the cave, flipping electric switches to light its passages in sections, drawing attention to each rendering and composition as we made our way through every gallery. As my companions passed ahead, they crossed the light, and the darkened animals seemed to move with the changing shadows. I saw these animals as Paleolithic people saw them, lit with torches. Time collapsed.

We moved into the so-called Hall of the Bulls, the loftiest and widest chamber of Lascaux. We peered closely at one wonderful rendition, then another. The natural bulges and pits of the rock were carefully chosen so as to yield muscles' swells and hollows under the pigment, providing a three-dimensional realism impossible to capture in a photograph. We could see that the animals were laid down one over another, that there were engraved outlines as well as painting, that some images seemed incomplete, and that there were perhaps generations of people who had returned to this cave to revisit the paintings and add to the walls.

Archaeologists have long argued over how to understand the images at Lascaux and the people who created them. From around 75,000 years ago, symbolic expression—either in the form of shell beads, pigment for decorating bodies and objects, or as symbols etched onto stones and other tools—was the hallmark of modern humans. Lascaux has become a symbol of the vivid culture of humans, or *Homo sapiens*, during the Ice Age, but it is only one site within a long, diverse, and exciting narrative of human evolution. This story conveys a wide range of diversity in its cultural expressions, in the challenges people faced and solutions they devised, and in the contexts where humans have lived and shaped their surroundings. This chapter reviews a sample of the cultural remains of ancient humans, as an introduction to prehistory and to discovering our common evolutionary path in a changing world.

2

Diversity of Humans: *Homo sapiens* and Neanderthals 28

Modern Humans 31

Lascaux Cave and the Human Experience of the Ice Age 32

Additional Human Experiences in the Ice Age 37

Human Culture Begins to Shape the Anthropocene 39

Protecting Cultural Diversity 43

Opposite Inside the "Hall of the Bulls" at Lascaux Cave, where images of two wild cattle face each other among those of giant deer and horses encircling the chamber.

Key Concepts

- How *Homo sapiens* crafted symbols, images, and constructions that shaped their natural surroundings
- How the relationship between Neanderthals and *Homo sapiens* demonstrates human diversity and shows that no single outcome of human niche construction is inevitable
- How cultural diversity spans the whole of human existence
- Why protecting archaeological sites is important

Neanderthal Also known as *Homo sapiens neandertalensis*. An early human species that evolved in Europe and became extinct approximately 30,000 years ago.

Archaic humans An overarching category that includes species of the genus *Homo*, Neanderthals among them, who came before *Homo sapiens*.

DIVERSITY OF HUMANS: *HOMO SAPIENS* AND NEANDERTHALS

From the very beginning of human evolution, diversity has existed among humans. The histories of such islands as Rapa Nui and Greenland (see Chapter 1) demonstrate that no single outcome of human niche construction is inevitable: humans reacted to and changed their physical and social environments in a variety of ways. In the Ice Age, or Pleistocene, diversity characterized not only different human cultures but also different human species. Approximately 30,000 years ago, *Homo sapiens* lived alongside other human species—the most famous of which was the **Neanderthal** (*Homo sapiens neandertalensis*). Understanding who the Neanderthals were offers insight into what made the modern human species, *Homo sapiens*, so successful.

Originating in Africa, **Archaic humans** (several species of the genus *Homo* that are not anatomically modern humans) arrived in Central Asia and the Near East perhaps half a million years ago, and their descendants lingered in Gibraltar (southern Spain) and other areas as late as 30,000 years ago. The descendants of Archaic humans in Europe were Neanderthals [2.1], humans with a very robust physique and strong muscles, regardless of sex or age, large noses, and short foreheads. Although they shared some cultural practices, Neanderthals were biologically different from anatomically modern humans (*Homo sapiens sapiens*), who arrived in Europe about 45,000 years ago and in Asia even earlier. Just as humans contributed to an Anthropocene world, Neanderthals also purposely modified their environments. How were Neanderthals different from modern humans? And how were they similar?

The Lascaux paintings were created by *Homo sapiens* approximately 17,000 years ago, but there is increasing evidence that Archaic humans, such as Neanderthals, also explored symbolic expression, for instance, in the wearing of eagle-claw ornaments and perforated shells [2.2]. A recently discovered cross-hatched engraving from Gorham's Cave in Gibraltar, and an enigmatic pair of 175,000-year-old oval rings made of broken stalactites from Bruniquel Cave in France, have archaeologists guessing about the scope of Neanderthal activities and the intention or purpose of their creations. Some cave paintings in southeastern Spain were also completed long before modern humans reached the Iberian Peninsula.

Similarly to other Archaic humans before them, Neanderthals could and did use technology. In the eastern Mediterranean, both Neanderthals and anatomically modern humans utilized variants of the toolmaking technique called **Levallois** to produce a distinctive stone point. This technique prepared a stone cobble by striking off its outer flakes in a specific sequence, a technology that we will discuss in depth in Chapter 3. Because they used such similar approaches to create a stone point,

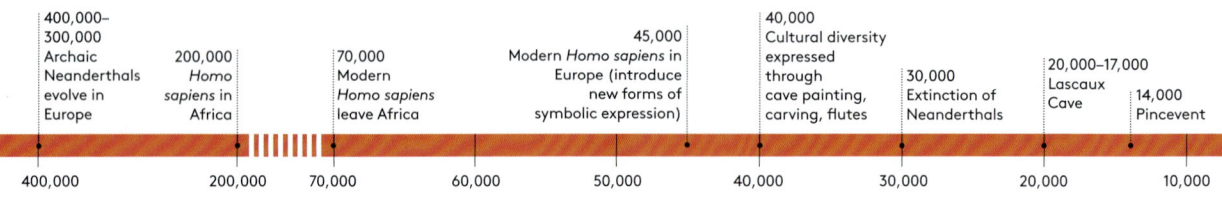

| 400,000–300,000 Archaic Neanderthals evolve in Europe | 200,000 *Homo sapiens* in Africa | 70,000 Modern *Homo sapiens* leave Africa | 45,000 Modern *Homo sapiens* in Europe (introduce new forms of symbolic expression) | 40,000 Cultural diversity expressed through cave painting, carving, flutes | 30,000 Extinction of Neanderthals | 20,000–17,000 Lascaux Cave | 14,000 Pincevent |

400,000 — 200,000 — 70,000 — 60,000 — 50,000 — 40,000 — 30,000 — 20,000 — 10,000

YEARS AGO

2.1 A reconstruction of female *Homo sapiens neandertalensis*, or Neanderthal. Neanderthal faces are distinctive for their large noses and short foreheads. For reasons we do not fully understand, the Neanderthal populations died out around 30,000 years ago as anatomically modern humans—*Homo sapiens*—advanced into Europe.

Levallois A technique for making a stone tool. It involves striking and trimming a stone before completely removing a flake to create a tool that will be sharp on all sides.

2.2 Eagle talons and toe bone from the 130,000-year-old site of Krapina in Croatia. Cut marks and polishing suggest they were strung together on a cord. It is believed that Neanderthals created this as a piece of jewelry.

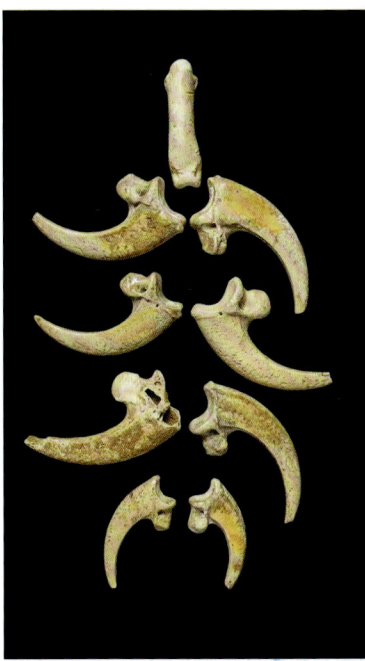

Neanderthals and anatomically modern humans clearly shared some cognitive abilities and learned the specifics from one another.

Neanderthals and anatomically modern humans may have shared information about stone-knapping, but where their populations overlapped, they inhabited different caves and used different strategies to survive. On Mount Carmel in Israel, where large limestone shelters overlook the modern coastal plain, Neanderthal remains have been found at the Tabun, Kebara, and el Wad caves. The nearby Qafzah, Amud, and Skhul caves [2.3, p. 30] contain the remains only of anatomically modern humans. It was once believed that they had simply replaced Neanderthals, but when a new dating methodology called electron spin resonance was developed in the 1980s, for the first time archaeologists were able to date the sediments that had accumulated around hominin burials. This technique suggested that humans had inhabited Qafzah 115,000 to 95,000 years ago. As in Europe, in the Middle East, Neanderthals lived in the same region and eventually disappeared.

When anatomically modern *Homo sapiens* populated West Asia and Europe with Neanderthals, the two groups maintained different lifestyles and experienced different outcomes. They nevertheless had much in common. Neanderthals and humans shared an appetite for big meaty herbivores and plant foods when they could access them. Archaeologists have found buried hearths suggesting that both groups used fire for warmth and food processing, and perhaps to ward off predators. Anatomically modern humans, however, have much closer genetic relationships to one another than to Neanderthals, in spite of the commonalities between the two

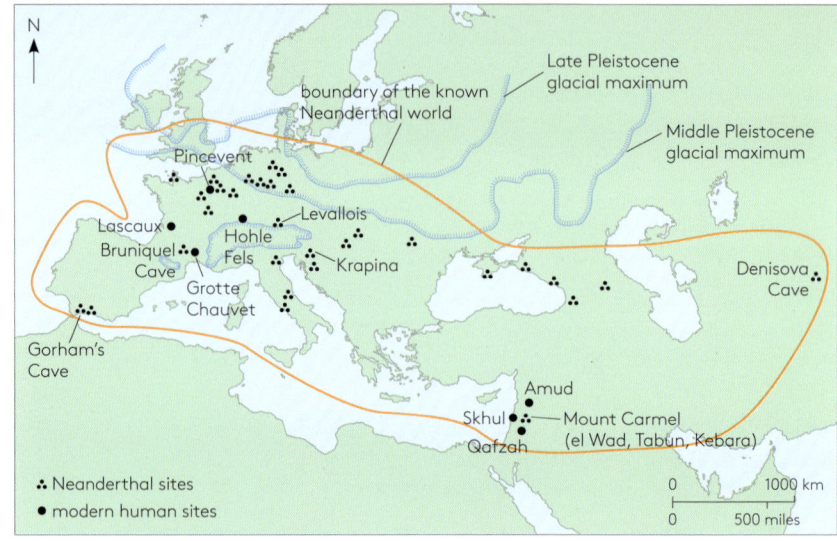

2.3 Map of Eurasia showing the expanse of a Neanderthal presence and its overlap with that of modern humans. The sites shown are not all sites known, but sites discussed in this chapter are indicated.

species. The two populations appear to have lived mostly separate lives. For reasons not yet fully understood, the Neanderthal populations that had existed in Europe for around 300,000 years began to die out as modern humans advanced into the region and colonized it around 45,000 years ago. The timing of their disappearance relatively soon after humans arrived leads us to wonder: Were modern humans responsible for the extinction of our closest relatives? If so, how did that happen? Were our socially connected and communicative direct ancestors just more efficient hunters who out-hunted the Neanderthals? Did the plants and animals on which Neanderthals had relied for millennia also disappear? Did environmental changes widen the gap between the success of Neanderthals and humans in different niches? These questions are all critical to understanding why Neanderthals became extinct, and what role, if any, modern humans played in their extinction. The answers thus far seem to suggest population numbers as a potential reason for their demise: Neanderthals may have never been very numerous, and it is possible the advancing wave of modern humans simply absorbed them.

We do know that sex between anatomically modern *Homo sapiens* and Neanderthals must have occurred; from recent successes in reconstructing, or sequencing, Neanderthal **DNA**, we learned that Neanderthal–*Homo sapiens* hybrids were born, and they passed on their genes to later generations. Small segments of Neanderthal DNA are present in modern, non-African populations (mostly in modern humans who trace their ancestry to Europe). The Neanderthals' extinction—perhaps one of the first extinctions to which modern humans contributed—may have been a unique combination of habitat loss and cultural and biological absorption, to the point that Neanderthals disappeared within the modern human population. What choices made by humans and Neanderthals led to these two vastly different outcomes: on the one hand, global dominance; on the other, extinction?

DNA Acronym for deoxyribonucleic acid, a molecule that encodes genetic information within living cells. DNA can be preserved in bone, teeth, hair, and soil.

MODERN HUMANS

Anatomically modern humans, *Homo sapiens*, appeared throughout Africa as early as 200,000 years ago, with their descendants founding all of modern humanity. By 70,000 years ago, some of these humans had left Africa, taking greater symbolic communication—beads, designs, pigments, and drawings—as well as spoken language with them.

Anatomically modern humans advanced into Europe during the **Aurignacian Period** (45,000–27,000 years ago), probably following the Danube corridor west of the Black Sea region and up the valley of the Rhone. Once there, they began to expand the range of their creative manipulations of the physical world. For example, in caves of southwest Germany along the tributaries of the Danube, archaeologist Nicholas Conard has for more than twenty years been excavating the debris left by modern human predecessors. He has determined that 42,000 years ago humans in Europe produced music on flutes created from bone [**2.4**, **2.5**]. There are now many such flutes in existence, the oldest and most complete one made of mammoth ivory and from Geisenklösterle, a big cave facing a steep valley in the Swabian Jura ("Alps") in southern Germany.

Many anthropologists attribute humans' wide geographic dispersal and impressive demographics to their creative abilities and flexibility. The use of symbolic

Aurignacian Period A period in the Upper Palaeolithic, some 45,000–27,000 years ago, when anatomically modern *Homo sapiens* infiltrated Europe.

2.4 The cave at Hohle Fels in southern Germany contained many important archaeological artifacts from 40,000 to 35,000 years ago, including figurines of animals and humans, and fragments of bone flutes. Under artificial lighting, excavators carefully remove sediments (using sandbags to stabilize unexcavated deposits) and precisely document the location of each fragment.

2.5 The Hohle Fels flute, made by modern humans 40,000 years ago from the wing bone of a vulture. This flute is 8½ in. (21.8 cm) long with a diameter of less than half an inch (8 mm). A replica of this flute has been constructed using modern bone, allowing for experimentation and reproduction of the sounds and music the original may have emitted.

expression, such as body paint and music, may have served—as to some extent it does today—to maintain social cohesion in human groups. Pushing into Neanderthal territory may have been made much easier as a result of well-maintained social networks, which relied on communication to function across distances and between generations. Sculpture, jewelry, and adornment would have served to identify and unify groups, bolstering collective efforts that were needed to sustain the population during times of stress.

LASCAUX CAVE AND THE HUMAN EXPERIENCE OF THE ICE AGE

The cave paintings of Lascaux remain a beautiful window into human history [2.6], the development of human cognition and communication, and the serious challenges archaeologists face in uncovering and understanding the past. Dating back 17,000 years (later than many other forms of image-making in the Palaeolithic, as we shall soon see), Lascaux offers up nearly two thousand figures, including aurochs, stags, bison, and many other animals, including one or two enigmatic humans. The Lascaux complex comprises many caverns [2.7], and no fewer than thirty-seven of these show signs of image-making. When we are confronted with the imagery of this cave, many questions emerge: Were only a privileged few included in the ceremonies that took place inside the cave? Did painters and engravers work alone, or did gatherings occur in the capacious galleries, which are also elaborately decorated?

Other caves provide some clues, because Lascaux is only one of many caverns modified over a span of more than 100,000 years. Richly decorated galleries within these caves offer the best acoustics, and ancient peoples clearly understood this. Lithophones—folded calcite formations that resonate when struck—are found

2.6 Intricate detail of a horse, Lascaux, southern France. Depictions of animals in the cave suggest an intimate knowledge of animals. These details may be related to ritual activities performed in the caves 20,000–17,000 years ago.

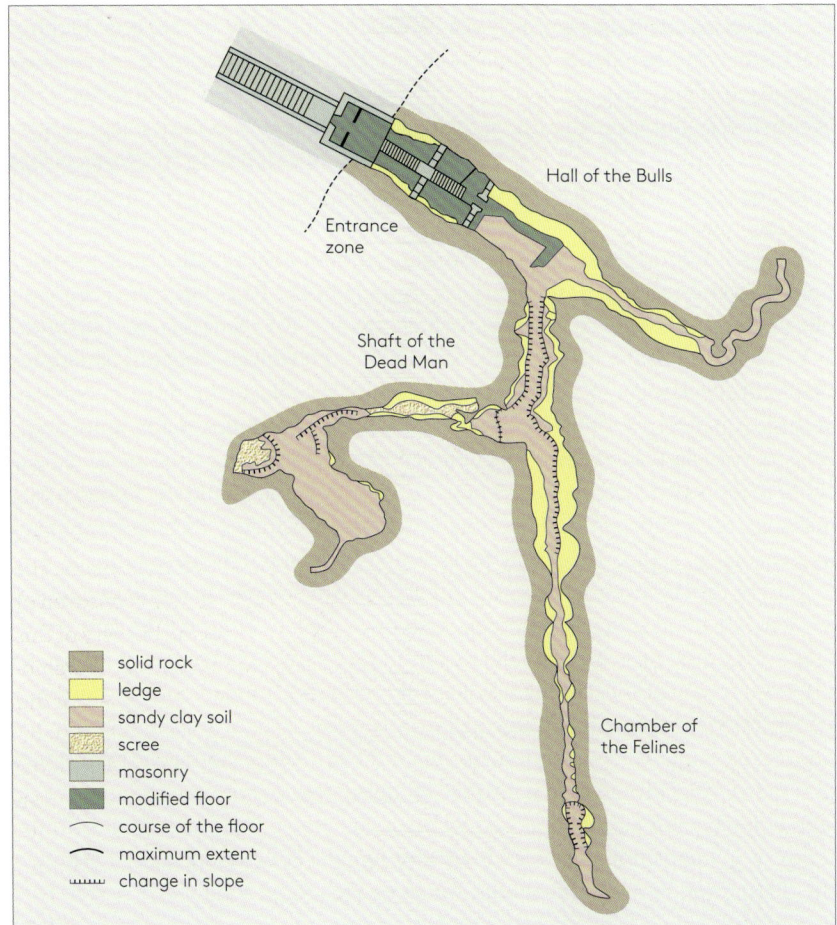

2.7 Plan of Lascaux Cave, showing the Hall of the Bulls, the Chamber of the Felines, and the narrow passageways connecting them.

battered and daubed with paint in large chambers that might have once held audiences. At Grotte Chauvet, a cave discovered in 1994 and carefully preserved, footprints show that children also visited the caves. Children's handprints appear in other caves as well. Some of the images were created in hidden crevices reached only after a difficult entry: a decorated fissure at Pergouset is so narrow that a grown person could not place his or her head inside it. Such images were never intended to be seen, at least not by other humans.

Interpreting Lascaux and Other Caves

Since the discovery of **Paleolithic** "art" in Europe, people have wondered why humans created it. We enclose the word *art* with quotation marks to remind ourselves that we do not know what the images meant to the people who made them. The term *art* evokes a certain response in the modern Western world and suggests

Paleolithic A period in human history that began with the first stone tools, starting 3.3 million years ago. The Upper Paleolithic commenced with the first appearance of anatomically modern *Homo sapiens*. In Europe this was about 45,000 years ago. Upper Paleolithic cultures in Europe include the Aurignacian, Gravettian, Solutrean, and Magdalenian.

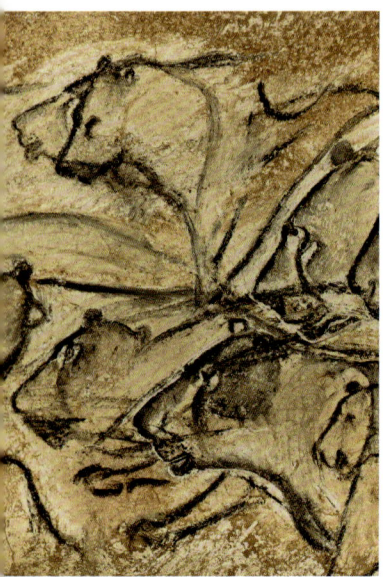

2.8 A pride of cave lions depicted in motion in Grotte Chauvet. The lions are straining in pursuit of prey; lit by flickering torches, they would appear in motion almost as a modern cartoonist might use a simple flip book to make a lion dash.

structuralism A theoretical approach that considers human action to be driven by underlying cognitive frameworks, such as opposition.

ethnographic analysis Understanding human behavior through direct observations and active participation.

an underlying aesthetic that may not be suitable for every image. It is doubtful that medieval Christian iconographers engaged in the spiritual practice of painting considered themselves artists in the same sense that we view them in the early twenty-first century. And there is no reason to assume that Paleolithic image-makers were artists either, at least not as the term *artist* implies today. In an effort to avoid imputing artistic purpose, archaeologists and scholars prefer to call Ice Age images just that: images.

If Paleolithic images are not art as we know it, then what explains their creation? Images in the caves represent various animals in the Paleolithic environment, but not all. Why were some chosen above others? No predators are portrayed at Lascaux—no bears, no hyenas, no cave lions, no wolves—suggesting perhaps that hunting played a role in the choice of animals depicted. In the earlier images at Grotte Chauvet, cave lions do appear [2.8], along with rhinos, mammoths, and a possible volcano. Clearly, temporal-cultural differences influence what image-makers chose to represent. Archaeologists have struggled to understand the function and messages of cave images, and their theories frequently follow the broader changes in archaeological theories of how we view and understand the past.

During the late twentieth century, **structuralism** emerged as a new theoretical approach in archaeology (Chapter 9), and it was used to interpret the cave paintings at Lascaux. Structuralism derives from the study of language and suggests that, as a legacy of the common biology of our brains, humans share a common structural view of the world. One of the most basic structures is binary opposition (for example, cold versus hot, up versus down). André Leroi-Gourhan argued that many Palaeolithic cave paintings followed a pattern of binary opposition, where one type of animal opposed another. He related these oppositions in the imagery to oppositions between male and female. For example, he interpreted the distinction between bison and horse images to be a symbolic representation of that between females and males. In so doing, Leroi-Gourhan perceives the caves (and the activities performed in them) as governed by an underlying structure of gender opposition. The relationships between men and women were restated and renewed in the past when each new painting was added. Although a fruitful avenue for the study of symbols, archaeologists have found that once one exhausts dualism, symmetry, and opposition in studying ancient patterns of culture, a great many questions still linger, and many of the most interesting ones remain unanswered.

There may be more to human thinking than binary opposites. David Lewis-Williams has studied the rock art of modern groups of people (especially the San of South Africa), and his initial commentary on it led him to see the images as products of an altered state of consciousness. If symmetry does not describe the workings of the human brain, the neuropsychology of altered consciousness as a pan-human experience holds some possible clues. **Ethnographic analysis** and laboratory research of what humans claim they "see" in altered consciousness point to a common experience, despite people's culturally specific descriptions of it.

At the beginning of a hallucinogenic state, humans experience entopic phenomena, which are vivid geometric forms and perceptions. People describe these differently according to cultural frameworks: they may perceive wavy lines, or snakes or waves, and interpret such illusions in culturally relevant ways. A fully hallucinatory consciousness sees monsters and strange creatures [**2.9**].

Prompted by common themes in rock art from widely divergent cultures, Lewis-Williams suggested that images in Paleolithic caves were created to record and communicate altered consciousness, a state that many humans around the world have been known to explore deliberately through the ingestion of particular plants, sensory deprivation (such as the utter darkness of caves), and pain. Geometric motifs, similar to the barred, so-called traps and dots at Lascaux, alongside recognizable images of animals, may represent multiple stages of hallucination. David Lewis-Williams sees these as a "neurological bridge to the distant art of Upper Paleolithic Western Europe."

A study of the image-making of modern humans and Neanderthals suggests that the difference between them is one of cognition—not necessarily a difference in the ability to plan or react, but a greater ability to imagine, connect ideas, communicate, and socially integrate with others. It is unlikely that we will ever understand what prehistoric images meant to the people who created them, because archaeology relies on the material remains of the past. Archaeology is a science, and it depends on a body of theory to conceptualize and classify the remains of human activities that have survived until today. Archaeology employs both inductive and deductive reasoning to form and test **hypotheses** [**2.10**, p. 36]. Science works by testing ideas (hypotheses) and eliminating those that do not work. Such archaeological methods as excavation, quantifying and analyzing artifacts, and determining the age of

2.9 The drawings at Lascaux are a dramatic example of material culture that offers us clues about ancient human behavior. The fantastic creature shown here is enigmatic and differs from the faithful representation of other animal images. Its unwieldy, antennae-like horns and sagging pelt are awkward and unconvincingly crude. Monsieur Marsal, who as an adolescent had first happened upon the cave, suggested that the image is a human in disguise. Is this a shaman, a mythical being, or the vision of a hallucination? Whatever its meaning, are you gazing at the disguised, bearded face of a Paleolithic man now dead for two hundred centuries?

hypotheses Ideas about the cause of a particular observation that need to be tested.

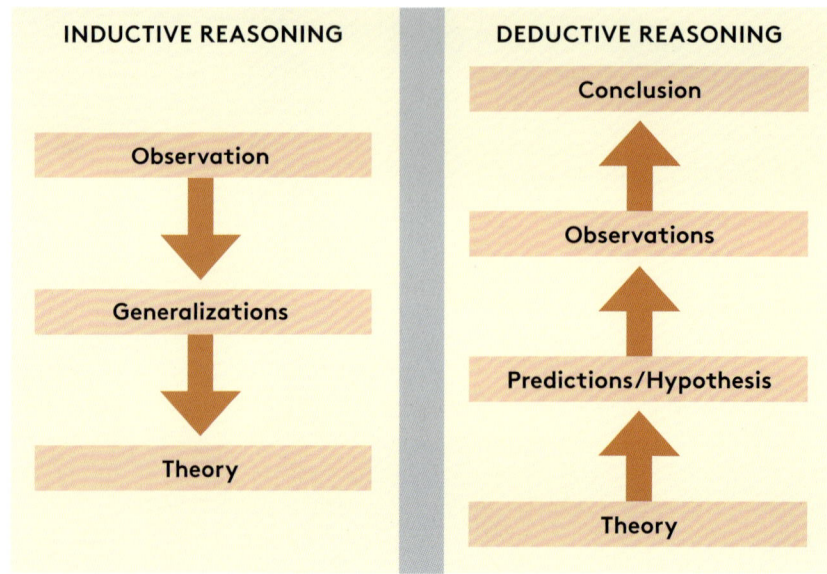

2.10 Inductive reasoning begins with an observation that is used to build a theory. Deductive reasoning begins with a theory or hypothesis that is tested by experimentation.

deposits and artifacts are employed as "tests" to discern if our hypotheses about the past are correct or not.

The deductive process of hypothesis-testing (see 2.10) offers no certain proof, and it works only with ideas that can be tested. Thus far, no one has developed a convincing test to discern what early images may have "meant" to ancient humans. This question is perhaps less important than another one: Why does symbolic expression exist? That query propels us toward an even greater body of questions pertaining to human evolution, the emergence of cognition, and the evolutionary significance of culture to human history and the Anthropocene.

Increasingly, archaeologists have turned to science and the application of scientific techniques to determine how early images were produced. Archaeologists hope to use science to gather better information and to disprove some hypotheses, thus bringing us closer to understanding what role the caves could have served in ancient people's lives. Did humans use the caves for homes, or were they sites for rituals that would integrate the community through shared experience? By various means—analyzing pigments, replicating techniques, dating miniscule samples of organic fats and charcoals, making high-resolution imaging of engravings to match the tools used, conducting precise excavations to document microscopic remains introduced to caves, and most importantly, applying a holistic approach to the Paleolithic era—archaeologists are situating caves in the wider context of the images and symbols that people used, and explaining how early humans lived their lives outside the caves. Understanding the importance of caves to the formation of the "human niche," rather than focusing on their images, provides a fruitful avenue for research and will help answer the questions of what it meant to be human in the Pleistocene, and what it may mean now.

ADDITIONAL HUMAN EXPERIENCES IN THE ICE AGE

After the arrival of anatomically modern *Homo sapiens*, symbolic expression began to appear in a diversity of forms. Once anatomically modern humans began to express symbolic thinking (and probably used language), the material forms of that expression—material culture—started to diverge. Transmission of culture, the successful communication of cultural traits from one individual to the next, was surely amplified by language, as the precision and detail of traits that could be communicated expanded. This transmission allowed greater flexibility in the manipulation of resources and environments. Humans expressed culture in many ways, although only a selection of material culture was preserved.

As we have seen, Lascaux Cave in southern France and quite a few nearby caves (Niaux and Les Trois Frères among them) house many vivid painted and engraved images, and a large number of Cantabrian caves (northern Spain) also offer painted images, albeit with different compositions of animals, and different geometric and hand stencil designs (some with missing fingers). There are no cave images to speak of in the Danube corridor of central Europe. Nor do paintings or engravings grace the walls of the Mount Carmel caves (in Israel). But far to the east, the recently discovered caves of southwest Sulawesi (an Indonesian island) [2.11] revealed 40,000-year-old hand stencils and the image of a *babi rusa*, a native wild boar. In Australia, pigments of ocher and hematite were transported and applied 60,000 years ago, perhaps to adorn bodies as well as rock-shelter walls. Raw pigments have also been found, scratched and abraded, in sites where no rock art even appears.

Rock art is but one form of diverse symbolic expressions: Pleistocene sites in Europe offer mammoth ivory and antler carvings with motifs never before observed

2.11 Images from a cave in southwest Sulawesi (Indonesia). Handprints similar to these have been dated to 40,000 years ago, as old as the paintings from Grotte Chauvet in France. As with their European parallels, the Sulawesi images are a sign of modern humans. In the Sulawesi caves, images of local, fierce animals are somewhat more recent than the handprints.

2.12 Ivory Löwenmensch (in German, "lion man"), which was reassembled from dozens of fragments. This figure is 12 in. (31 cm) tall and approximately 40,000 years old. It provides evidence of human cognition and imagination in its depiction of the hybridization of humans and animals.

on cave walls, including the much-discussed Paleolithic "Venus" figurines of very corpulent women with exaggerated breasts and hips, who undoubtedly symbolize feminine fertility (see 2.13). Among the oldest figures is an Aurignacian era "lion man" [**2.12**], originally found as thousands of fragments at the Hohlestein-Stadel cave in southwest Germany. Like the strange shaman-creature of Lascaux, this figurine offers a glimpse of Pleistocene-era imagination, and perhaps also conception of supernatural or transformed human beings. In a manner similar to the broken fragments of the Hohle Fels flute, the fractured lion man reminds us that the carvings were intended to be interactive—shape-shifting, played, worn, handled, broken—as instruments of culture and communication shaping a human niche.

A few caves preserve evidence of rituals. At the Montespan and Tuc d'Audoubert caves in southern France, bison were sculpted in clay, and the footprints of children on the cave's floor provide mute evidence of some form of gathering. At other sites, engraved and painted stone plaques, some appearing to have been deliberately broken, were recovered. An expert in ancient technologies, Pamela Vandiver, has shown that clay figurines at the eastern European site of Dolní Věstonice were deliberately cast into the fire while wet so that they would shatter—this was not imagery intended to last! The trappings of ceremony are also apparent. Paleolithic specialist Olga Soffer has studied the markings on the female figurine found in Ridaux Cave [**2.13**] to reveal details of bodily ornament and string skirt clothing, likely made of twined and spun plant fibers. Wear on the perforations of shells and other carved bone and ivory items indicates that they were pendants, perhaps worn around the human neck or strung elsewhere. The cave at Qafzah (one of the Mount Carmel caves) contained bivalve seashells with traces of red ocher, possibly the result of the shells having been strung on dyed cords. Mourners also apparently cast red-ocher pigment into burial sites, which probably speaks to the acts associated with burying the dead and ancient rites in the life cycle. All these examples are diverse cultural expressions—the myriad symbolic thoughts of a complex brain—conveying different human emotions and beliefs in a wide range of settings.

2.13 Female figurine carved from mammoth ivory, shown from behind. Discovered in Rideaux Cave near the community of Lespugue in southern France, this rare sculpture is approximately 6 in. (15 cm) tall and dates to 26,000–24,000 years ago, during the Gravettian period.

2.14 The Pleistocene world was colder. Mountain glaciers today, such as these in Glacier Bay National Park in Alaska, are mere vestiges of ice sheets that covered much of the northern hemisphere and high altitudes.

HUMAN CULTURE BEGINS TO SHAPE THE ANTHROPOCENE

In what kind of world did modern humans develop, and how did this landscape come to be? The story of human cognition and communication that is evident at Lascaux is only part of a much older story—one that was dominated by the hunting and gathering of plants and animals across the ages. As part of a long evolutionary trajectory, human ancestors took to upright walking, and the open landscapes of the African savannah became the backdrop for the emergence of that mobile lifestyle, and the communication required to maintain it. By the time modern humans reached Europe, the world that had supported the evolution of the Neanderthals was beginning to change.

The limestone hills of southern France, along the Vézère, Dordogne, and Ardèche rivers, are riddled with tunnels and passages created by ancient underground waters that wore away the seams of softer rock. Today, these hills are covered by a thick, temperate forest of beech, hornbeam, oak, and hackberry, with ash and willow alongside river courses, and Mediterranean scrub oak to the south. Pollen layers at the bottom of European lakes and bogs suggest that the same land was once more open, with grass-mat tundra and few trees. Pollen is a distinctive part of flowering plants and conifers, and pollen grains last for thousands of years; the presence of different types of pollen points to the vegetative conditions that existed when these accumulations formed.

During the **Last Glacial Maximum**—the peak of the most recent glacial period in Earth's history, about 20,000 years ago, ice sheets were at their thickest [**2.14**], Europe was colder and drier, and its northern extremes and alpine heights were

Last Glacial Maximum
The time in the most recent glacial period when ice sheets were at their greatest extent, c. 26,000–20,000 years ago.

locked below thick ice. Underground streams had dried up eons beforehand, and in the frigid years of the final Ice Age, humans used caves for shelter and for other purposes hinted at by musical instruments, sculptures, and painted images.

During the Pleistocene, a foraging and hunting lifestyle kept small groups on the move, probably within familiar and seasonally defined ranges and in pursuit of big game animals. The environment of Lascaux and other caves did not provide enough food for even small groups to remain year-round in one place. At Lascaux and other deep caves, there was no daylight, narrow access, and limited debris; it seems clear that these caves were not where people lived. Daily life took place outside. Although the embellished caves are more visually interesting, Pleistocene open-air sites and rock shelters—overhangs that offered protection and plenty of light—have taught archaeologists a great deal more about the lives of our ancestors and the environments in which they spent most of their days and nights. Working with French colleagues, American prehistorian Margaret Conkey has documented thousands of artifacts that show people crossing and camping in many different landscape zones between the caves. The mineral pigments brought to the caves and used in creating the images at Lascaux and its neighboring caves were transported from at least 25 miles (40 km) away.

During the Pleistocene, which lasted until 11,600 years ago, humans had to be very flexible and adapt to wide fluctuations in temperature and rainfall, not only across seasons but also across decades and a lifetime. Under limited conditions—no agriculture, no domesticated plants, no harvest or stored provisions—it is possible that humans domesticated dogs, or that some groups kept docile wolves at the fringes of their camps. The images of Lascaux offer no suggestion of these activities, but the DNA of modern dogs does indicate that one strain derives from a European domestication that occurred many thousands of years ago. Any early domestication of animals, however, did not offer food security, such as a reliable silo of stored grain for a lean day or an easily available "meal on the hoof" in the form of a domesticated sheep or goat—these would not become part of the human experience for another 7,000 years.

Pincevent: An Ice Age Hunting Camp

Beyond the images of Lascaux, a great range of evidence helps us understand how anatomically modern humans coped with the challenges of living in an Ice Age world. In the Paris Basin, Pincevent (14,000 years ago), a **Magdalenian Period** open-air site, offers one of the best views of a late Pleistocene hunting camp and the ways in which early hunters used available environmental resources. Nearly a hundred hearths, not all used at the same time, were found at the site along with the remains of numerous tent shelters, linked to the dark stains of decayed tent poles that had been arranged in circular patterns [**2.15**, **2.16**]. Painstaking archaeological refitting put back together pieces of chipped stone like a three-dimensional puzzle, revealing the sequence steps the hunters had followed to make tools.

Magdalenian Period A later period in the Palaeolithic, dating 17,000–11,000 years ago.

2.15 A closeup view of a reconstructed hearth from Pincevent shows reddened (oxidized) earth and thermally altered rocks; remnants of charcoal; numerous flakes and chipped stone fragments; and discarded reindeer bones, some of which had been split to extract the fatty marrow.

2.16 A reconstruction of one of the many Pincevent tents. This drawing suggests timber supports, which would have been covered in skins or brush. We know only the circular shape of the base; we do not know the details of upper construction, which long ago decayed. Outside is a hearth where social groups prepared and shared food.

In the refitting analysis, archaeologists could also detect how erosion, plant growth, worm churning, and other soil movement over 14,000 years had shifted and aged materials originally discarded together. Pincevent famously attested to the sharing of food between hearths, and presumably between the prehistoric households that used them, through bones from the same reindeer carcass that showed up at different hearths across the site. We can think of this food-sharing as a common way—as indeed it remains today—for people to make social bonds and to forge the relationships that no doubt helped them organize group hunts or obtain information about the abundance or distribution of resources.

Humans were hunters and foragers dependent on one another to secure and share food, information, and protection. Archaeologists Steven Kuhn and Mary Stiner suggest that the human domestic unit we know as a household came into existence among anatomically modern *Homo sapiens*. By examining the differences in muscle attachments on the bones of males, females, and children, these researchers proposed that early humans habitually performed different tasks that resulted in slightly different development of their muscles. Living in households that shared the output of divided labor, with each member performing a discrete task, is one of the key differences between modern *Homo sapiens* and the other Archaic humans (such as Neanderthals) they encountered and ultimately replaced.

In late autumn, Pincevent would have been occupied by a substantial gathering of small bands of people taking advantage of the reindeer migration through this area. Although the camp stood beside a river, no indications (such as hooks, net sinkers, or fish bones) exist to suggest that fishing was an attraction. Instead, people prized the reindeer for their pelts, meat, and antlers. The images of swimming deer at Lascaux Cave, and a mammoth-ivory carving of a pair of swimming reindeer [**2.17**], hint that this time of year provided human hunters with a perfect opportunity to gain sustenance. Although Pincevent was occupied thousands of years after Lascaux Cave had been painted, the remains of this open-air camp offer a precious glimpse into Pleistocene lifestyles—the foods people prized, the technologies they used to create a comfortable, safe home in a tundra-like environment, and the social bonds of cooperation they formed.

Putting aside the images of Pincevent for a moment, we might consider this related question: What did people eat when they did not have a fresh reindeer kill? Plants are more readily biodegradable than bone and decay easily if not exposed to fire. The remains of plant foods have not been found at Paleolithic sites, which may suggest few edible ones were available. We do find some preservation of charcoal, so archaeologists have been able to learn what substances people burned, such as the juniper wicks recovered from small stone lamps in Lascaux Cave. To better understand what Paleolithic people might have eaten, though, archaeologists rely

2.17 Swimming reindeer carved from the tip of a mammoth tusk, approximately 8 in. (20 cm) long and dated to about 13,000 years ago. This sculpture was recovered in two pieces from a rock shelter in southern France. The reindeer are shown swimming, as they probably did (as we know from their behavior still today) during their annual migration. The hunt that generated the bones of Pincevent may have targeted reindeer during this event.

on environmental reconstructions from pollen cores, climate records, the presence of herbivorous mega-fauna, the geological processes of glaciers, and comparisons with vegetation biomes (communities of plants that dominate ecosystems) present elsewhere in the world today. Indeed, one of Lascaux expert Jean-Philippe Rigaud's scientific activities led him, alongside American archaeologist Lewis Binford, to study how Inuit people survive the conditions of the Arctic tundra (see Chapter 6). As long ago as 1911, the British geologist and anthropologist William Sollas had suggested that the inspirational struggles of modern people in the tundra offered parallels to how people once lived in Pleistocene Europe, and this idea guided the systematic study of modern Inuit subsistence and environment.

Archaeologist Mark Newcomer and his students at the Institute of Archaeology, London, took their analysis beyond observations (e.g., excavation, examination of archaeological artifacts, climate records, and behavioral analogies) with experiments in making stone tools similar to those found at Pincevent. As scientists, they generated data (the facts utilized to test hypotheses and to build theory) using two approaches: observation and experiment. Not content with refitting the ancient pieces (observational science), they attempted to replicate the tools they had found (experimental science), learning in the process how much skill and experience it took to make each piece. Could anyone do this? Easily? Men, women, and children? How much time would be needed before someone became an experienced maker of stone tools? As it turns out, developing this skill requires much practice, and some people are just better at crafting stone than others (see Chapter 3). Because they are the most difficult to make, some of the finest European Paleolithic stone tools are **Solutrean** points, devised by the last Paleolithic people to live in the region of Lascaux Cave. These points are not only hard to create; but they are also distinctive in shape, a cultural marker of Solutrean hunters outside the cave at Lascaux.

The archaeology of Pleistocene Europe provides ample evidence of the unique qualities that defined modern humans: the use of symbolism, and conduct of rituals and activities that would have communicated meaning and also instilled a sense of group cohesiveness. These qualities are what anthropologists call "culture," and culture aided modern humans as they expanded their reach into new and distant habitats. The results were the construction of the human niche, which, as of 20,000 years ago, spanned all of Africa, Europe, Asia, and Australia.

Solutrean An archaeological culture named for a form of tool-making in Europe developed 22,000–17,000 years ago.

PROTECTING CULTURAL DIVERSITY

Lascaux Cave was discovered in the early 1940s, when it was used as a hiding place by local teenagers. Over the next two decades, tourists scuffled through Lascaux, admiring its paintings but also destroying them. The brilliant calcite crust that dazzled the first visitors to the cave has now thickened and spread over a greatly expanded part of the interior. Previously acting as a protective veneer, the calcite crust now threatens to cloak forever from human view the wonderful images of the most dazzling of Ice Age caves. Its formation since the human discovery of Lascaux

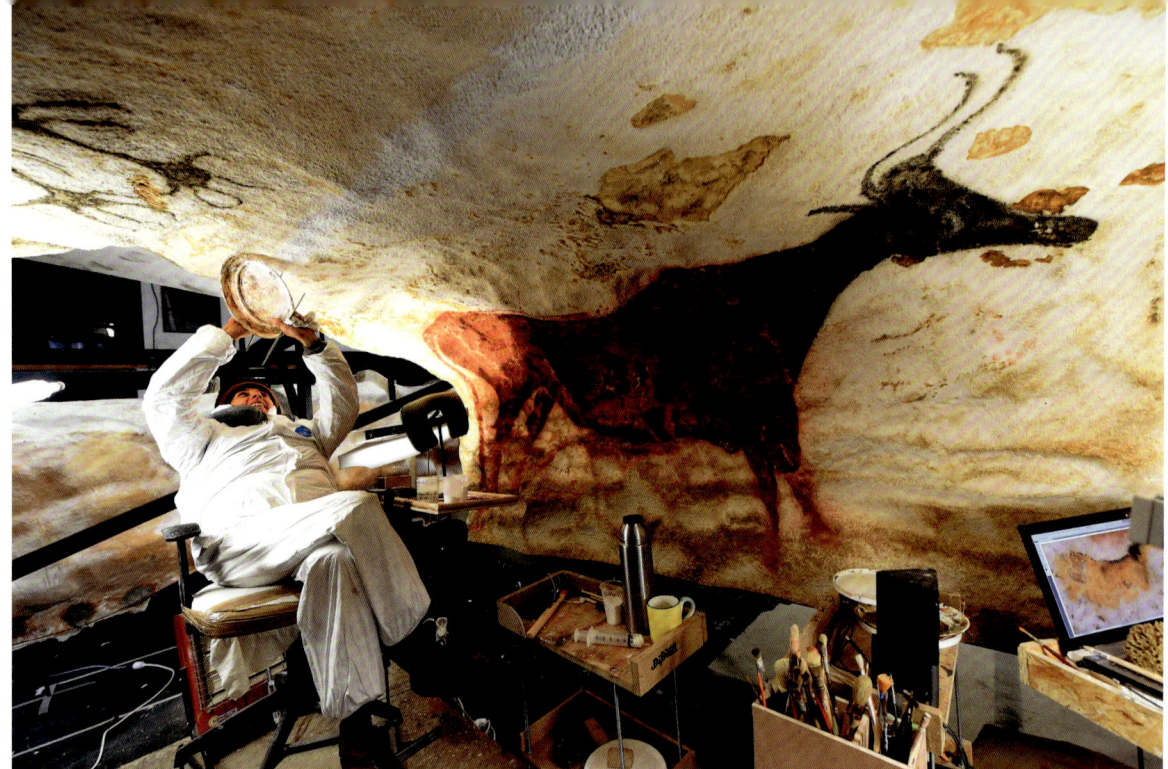

2.18 Following the closure of the original cave, a replica, Lascaux II, opened in 1983, followed by Lascaux III in 2012. The creation of a third replica is shown here. In this latest re-creation, new technologies were used to mold and reproduce the stone wall of the original cave.

stewardship Caring for and maintaining some thing or place for the benefit of all.

has only accelerated, with human exhalations and the atmospheric changes of outside air having compromised the fragile stability of temperature, humidity, and chemistry inside the cave.

In an effort to save Lascaux Cave, the French government closed it to visitors and constructed a replica, Lascaux II [**2.18**], to become the new focus of local tourism. Construction of the replica required many more hours inside the original Lascaux Cave than it could sustain. A green mold began to form on the cave walls, creeping slowly over the images. Technology was reproducing Lascaux, but the process nearly destroyed it. To the technologically innovative use of raman spectroscopy, an instrument that uses laser light to identify molecules, we owe the quick and decisive identification of the characteristics and composition of the mold, but the damage has been done. The cave is now closed to prevent the biochemicals that lead to the growth of mold from forming. Scientists hope that the cave's degradation has been fully arrested, and are working to devise a technique to remove the mold without damaging the underlying ancient images. One important realization lingers, though: we may never see Lascaux I again in our lifetime.

As we consider climate change in its global context, an issue of **stewardship** arises for all of humanity's remains. Lascaux serves as a microcosmic reminder of the challenges that come with atmospheric changes. The human niches that emerged during the Pleistocene, Holocene, and Anthropocene are our homes, and they are delicately and intricately connected to one another. They also are in a constant state of flux. The modern landscape that surrounds Lascaux is predominantly anthropogenic and agricultural, having been transformed by farmers who brought grain and livestock to southern France more than 6,000 years ago. Anthropocene France would be unrecognizable to Neanderthals and early modern humans, yet fragments of their world still remain: remnants of forests dot the valley bottoms, and dark recesses of caves and overhangs preserve ancient sediment and ash. Archaeologists still search for lost fragments of the Pleistocene today, sniffing for cooled updrafts of air rising from cave entrances hidden among the dense bracken-covered slopes of France's southern river valleys.

In 1995, Jean Clottes, who had discovered underwater entrances to dry, painted caverns along the Mediterranean coast, was alerted to the discovery on Christmas Day, 1994 of Grotte Chauvet by Jean-Marie Chauvet and two spelunking (cave-exploring) friends. With the French government mindful of the tragic destruction of Lascaux, the site of Grotte Chauvet Pont d'Arc was kept secret until its entrance could be secured. Footprints of Ice Age adults and children are still visible in the soft floor, with the remains of torches, rope, and artifacts strewn wherever they were dropped. A cave-bear skull still perches atop its pedestal rock, placed there by human hands 40,000 years ago. Whose hands? Those of a ritual observer? A playing child? Did one person, or several, also collect the cave-bear skulls concentrated in a natural hollow around that pedestal?

Chauvet and his fellows were careful stewards of their astonishing discovery. They chose not to walk much on the floor, and indeed much analysis of the cave walls since then has utilized instruments that observe from afar. Some images have not been approached since the last Aurignacian person left the cave. No excavations are planned, so the floor remains undisturbed. This is why few people, even researchers, ever gain entry to Grotte Chauvet. To share its discovery, the French government permitted filming inside and financed an amazing reconstruction. Faithfully recreated to scale, the Caverne du Pont d'Arc lacks only the steady water drip of a real cave. Charcoal lies where it dropped beneath a fluid rendition of racing lions. Bones stick out of the sediments where episodes of flooding left them. They are cave-bear bones, and one can still see the hollows where cave bears curled to sleep out the winter. Humans shared this cave, sometimes engraving over bear scratches, sometimes placing images where waking cave bears had perhaps clawed the walls [**2.19**]. All this has been faithfully reproduced with photogrammetric technology

2.19 On the walls of Grotte Chauvet cave bears reared and scratched, marking their hibernation places. When humans used the cave, they incised images, such as this mammoth, on top of where cave bears had left claw marks. In some spots, the returning cave bears scratched over the human drawings.

(software-based analysis of digital photographs) for the eyes of visitors to Caverne du Pont d'Arc. Technologies of the future may lead to a better understanding of the past, especially if they help us see under Chauvet's surface without destroying it.

Thus, careful stewardship, coupled with advanced archaeological science, has preserved and protected Grotte Chauvet, and also allowed for significant discoveries of ancient human experience in the cave. If the destruction of Lascaux is a warning of the risks our planet now faces, the conservation of Grotte Chauvet stands as a beacon of hope, speaking to our human capacity to recognize and protect our precious resources. Understanding the past in the context of the Anthropocene poses many challenges, but it also promises new insight$_2$ into humanity's past and potential future.

Chapter Questions

1. Why is the history of the relationship between Neanderthals and *Homo sapiens* an effective example of diversity in prehistory?
2. How did anatomically modern *Homo sapiens* differ from other early humans, and how did this contribute to their success?
3. Using Lascaux as an example, how are we culturally and biologically similar to early humans?
4. How has the discovery of Lascaux enhanced our understanding of the need for stewardship of archaeological sites and artifacts?

Additional Resources

Bahn, Paul G. *Journey through the Ice Age.* Berkeley, CA: University of California Press, 1997.

Bahn, Paul G. "Religion and Ritual in the Upper Palaeolithic," in *The Oxford Handbook of The Archaeology of Ritual and Religion*, edited by T. Insoll, 344–57. Oxford, UK: Oxford University Press, 2011.

Conard, Nicholas J., Malina, Maria, and Münzel, Susanne C. "New Flutes Document the Earliest Musical Tradition in Southwest Germany," *Nature* 460, no. 7256 (2009): 737–40.

Leroi-Gourhan, Arlette. "The Archaeology of Lascaux Cave," *Scientific American* 246(6) (1982): 104–12.

Soffer, Olga, and Conkey, Margaret. *Beyond Art: Pleistocene Image and Symbol.* San Francisco, CA: California Academy of Sciences, 1997.

White, Randall. *Prehistoric Art: The Symbolic Journey of Mankind.* New York: Harry Abrams, 2003.

GLOBAL TIMELINE 1: HUMAN ORIGINS AND MIGRATIONS

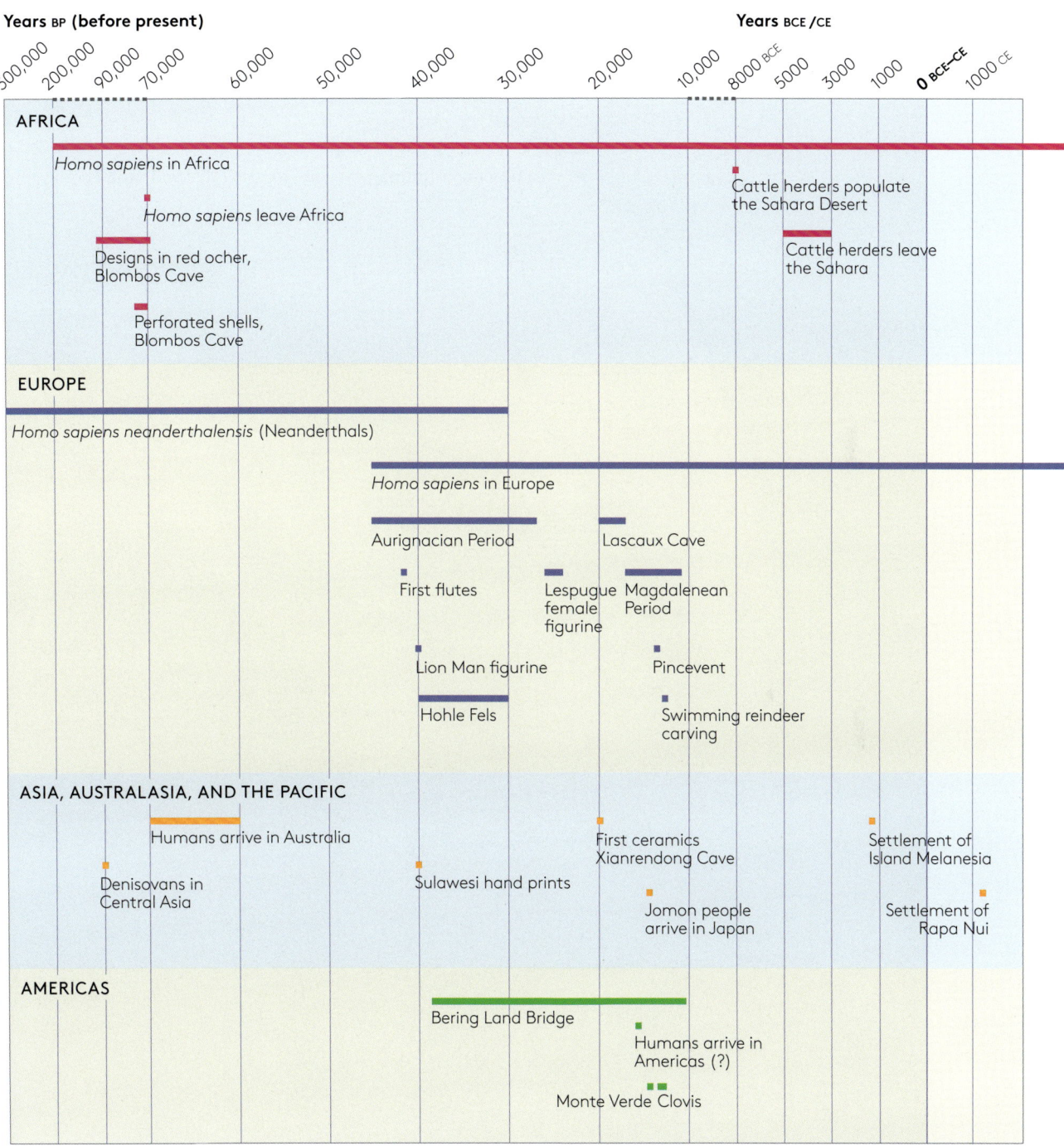

TECHNOLOGY MAKES THE HUMAN
Stone, Metal, and Organic Material Culture

As a student, I once watched Mark Newcomer—a talented experimental archaeologist—make a hand axe. With a practiced left hand, he hefted a knobbly cobble of raw flint, chalky white on the outside with a cloudy gray interior showing where a few pieces had been knocked off. He swung the cobble a few times, and, feeling its weight, he readied his arm to absorb the first blow to the flint.

Symmetry looks easy once you have created it, but Mark had to hit the right place enough times to release the symmetrical core. He had obviously done this hundreds of times to develop an effective technique. Mark's striking arm seemed always to follow the same arc downward. Now he struck first one side, then flipped the stone and struck the other. Quickly, a hand axe began to take shape.

Years later as a new professor teaching my first class, I invited a local flintknapper to demonstrate for us. He was no master, and he warned me of this. Over the course of twenty minutes and to his mounting frustration, he damaged beyond use every facet of the stone he wanted to work on and shattered his three favorite hammerstones. His own tool kit was simple: a hefty chunk of raw stone, a round cobble for striking, and a bit of leather for his knee. Oh, and safety goggles—not a feature of prehistoric toolmaking. He was flustered; I was dismayed; and the students were confused. What I did not recognize was the teachable moment. Making stone tools is difficult. It is a learned skill, not inherited at birth but culturally shared from one generation to the next. It takes long practice (and bloody hands) to learn.

Modern knappers teach us to understand better the complex decisions necessary to create an object as simple as a stone tool. Through close investigation of prehistoric tools and flintknapping debris, archaeologists examine how human cognition developed, from the first toolmakers 2.5 million years ago to the appearance of the first *Homo sapiens*.

Stone tools are also a sign of things to come. The tools themselves mark a moment when hominins began a trajectory that would shape the entire world. Such technologies as bronzeworking and ironworking demanded more elaborate social networks and affected the environment in more significant ways. This chapter on stone tools and technology therefore sets the stage for a long history of cognitive and social development, and—just as importantly—of human niche construction.

Stone Tools and the Discovery of Time 50

The Mechanics of Flintknapping 53

Stone Tools as Evidence of Human Adaptation 56

Metalworking, a New Technology for Communities 60

Perishable Technologies: Revelations from the Iceman 66

Technology, the Environment, and the Anthropocene 70

Opposite This handaxe replicates one of the oldest tools created by humans, first known from pre-human hominins in Africa 1.7 million years ago.

Key Concepts

- The use of technology to discover and define periods in prehistory
- How prehistoric stone tools were made, and what the main components of lithic (stone) tool manufacture are
- How metalworking involves cooperative, integrated tasks that draw on the labor and collaboration of human communities
- The revelation of ancient technologies in perishable materials through the unique discovery of Ötzi the Iceman

STONE TOOLS AND THE DISCOVERY OF TIME

Between the fifteenth and seventeenth centuries CE, Europeans made their first contacts with the inhabitants of the Americas. The "Indians," as Europeans called them, were skilled archers and tipped their arrows with finely made stone points. They also used knives and axes made of stone, and in the case of the Aztecs who battled with Hernán Cortéz in 1521, swords edged with razor-sharp blades of obsidian [3.1].

When Europeans brought some of these implements home as part of curio collections of exotic animals and plants, they made their first analogous link between American stone tools and "fairy stones," which had been collected from caves and quarries across Europe and the British Isles. Fairy stones (also called "dragon tongues" or "lightning stones") were odd, lenticular-shaped stone objects that seemed to have a common shape [3.2]. Scholars of ancient Greece and Rome had suggested that the stones were made by such supernatural beings as leprechauns and fairies, or were perhaps the fossilized tongues of dragons, or the result of lightning strikes, which upon reaching the ground would have left behind a stony imprint in the soil. Explorers in the Americas noted the physical similarities between American stone tools and European fairy stones—they were chipped, triangular in shape, and made from similar sharp, brittle stones. These commonalities could not be explained away as a chance occurrence; the stones had to be part of the same kind of ancient technological tradition: making tools from stone, rather than from metal.

In the European case, the technology to make stone tools had been long forgotten. Tools, such as knives and axes, had "always" been made from metal, at least according to all known written documents. In the sixteenth century came the realization that these fairy stones were actually stone tools. For the first time, evidence

3.1 A depiction in the sixteenth-century Florentine Codex shows Aztec warriors carrying swords edged with obsidian blades.

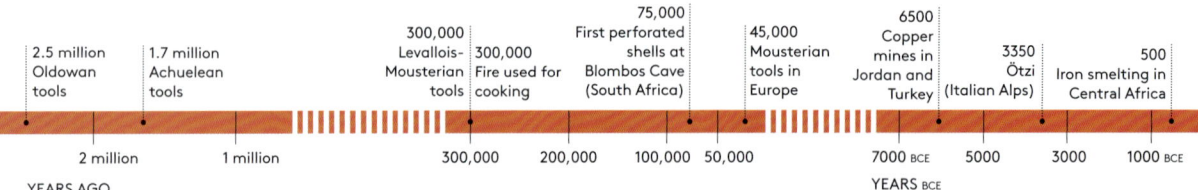

3.2 An ancient tool-kit made of stone. These hand axes are made from flint and measure approximately 6–8 in. (15–20 cm) in length; they are part of the Acheulean tradition of stone-tool manufacture, which began 1.76 million years ago. Until the sixteenth century, Europeans thought these objects were fossilized lightning bolts or the tools of mythical creatures. All known knives and axes by that time were made of metal, and the knowledge to make stone tools had been forgotten.

confirmed a prehistory in Europe that included a stone-based technology. But how long ago was this prehistory, and how did it coincide with the stories of the Bible, or the recollection of Greek and Roman history scholars, who mentioned only metal blades and tools? To suggest that a period of human history earlier than that of the biblical account had existed was heresy (you could, in fact, be burned alive for saying it); few were willing to state openly that there was substantive proof of an ancient world.

Measuring Time with Tools

Scientists did not accept the notion of a pre-biblical world until 1846, when Jacques Boucher de Perthes discovered stone tools and extinct mammal bones mixed together in the gravels of the Somme river in France and suggested they were conclusive proof of human antiquity in Europe [**3.3**, p. 52]. In 1859, several geologists, principally Charles Lyell, validated this claim by confirming the antiquity and sequence of geological strata that contained the artifacts. Although they could not determine the precise age of the tools, bones, and deposits, the geologists were certain that the artifacts represented an era in the distant past—one in which humans, similar in many respects to the native people observed in the Americas, had hunted long-extinct animals. For the next decade, scientific interest in **Antiquity** increased, and "cabinets of curiosity," which contained many gathered examples of stone tools, were examined in detail. Abundant artifacts from the ancient past lived on in Europe, but they remained under lock and key in a confusing state of disorder.

A Danish antiquarian of the early 1800s devoted himself to resolving this confusion. Using the accumulating discoveries of metal troves in Denmark to support his approach, Christian Thomsen adapted a Classical idea (first stated by Greek philosopher Lucretius in the first century BCE) that changes in technology corresponded to changes in time. Thomsen drew on this old philosophy and suggested that humanity had passed through the Stone Age, Bronze Age, and Iron Age (chapter timeline, opposite). (A so-called Golden Age, not a focus of Thomsen's work, produced the political, literary, and philosophical canon of ancient Greece.) Thomsen

Antiquity Originally used to refer to the pre-Christian era in Europe or elsewhere, Antiquity generally means a distant past prior to the ideals and belief systems of modern people.

3.3 William Dyce, *Pegwell Bay, Kent—a Recollection of October 5th 1858*. Dyce's painting represents the growing fascination of wealthy Victorians with the emerging systematic description of nature—and challenges to the biblical account of Earth's creation—in the age of Charles Darwin. It depicts leisurely collectors on a beach, where Jurassic-era fossils crumble from the chalk cliffs at high tide, and a comet overhead (faintly visible in the middle of the sky at the top of the painting) reminds us of the passage of time.

pioneered the use of archaeological data to generate a chronological sequence, and then to date new discoveries by comparing them to that sequence. Thomsen's three-age system has been deeply influential in ordering prehistory. Stone Age, Bronze Age, and Iron Age are still terms we use to name eras of Old World archaeology (the past of Africa, Europe, and Asia), even as archaeologists now understand that many ancient people accessed multiple technologies and materials at many times. As the archaeological record in Europe grew and archaeologists defined a wide range of Old World cultural groups, the three-age system has persisted in name only, a conventional terminology for major periods of human engagement with our environment.

John Lubbock, Lord of Avebury in England, was the first to suggest a temporal sequence for stone and metal tools that was evident in their technological sophistication. In 1865, Lubbock wrote *Prehistoric Times*, a book that vividly illustrated the diverse tools produced in Antiquity, the time before written records. Lubbock called the earliest, least sophisticated period of stone tools the Paleolithic, which spanned the epoch when humans and extinct animals, such as mammoths, coexisted. The later period he called the **Neolithic**, as tools from this period were more finely made and varied in function. Lubbock recognized that stone tools might continue to be popular even as the first, rare tools of bronze became available; likewise, bronze and stone tools were still widely used as the first iron technologies appeared. The hallmark of the Bronze Age and Iron Age, however, was the proliferation of metal-working, which included tools, such as axes and spearheads, and other objects, such as jewelry. The production of metal tools was known to be complex and labor intensive, and this led Lubbock and others to conclude that metals were signifiers of "advanced" cultural and economic development. In truth, metallurgy marked a new technology that fit within preexisting social structures, which already included complicated social and economic arrangements.

Stone tools have been crucial both in realizing the depth of human history and in the first efforts to organize the past into periods—concepts that opened the door to archaeology. Today, the study of stone tools has expanded to include a vast array of research questions, not the least of which was how the making of tools and technological advancement coincided with the growth and development of the human brain. As areas of the brain known to facilitate planning and transmitting information advanced, so, too, did the forms of stone tools. Research moved to reconstructing, step-by-step, how stone tools were made as a way to understand better our own cognitive development through time.

THE MECHANICS OF FLINTKNAPPING

When he first proposed a Paleolithic and Neolithic period, Lubbock suggested that the production of stone tools followed the methods that were common to gunflint-makers of his day. Flint nodules were broken using a hammer, and the shaping of the flint took advantage of the physical properties inherent in the brittle stone. The hammer blows were struck at an angle, producing a fracture and ultimately a **flake** that could be further shaped with additional blows. Lubbock's illustrations of flake-based tools from North America, Africa, Ireland, and Australia, and eye-witness accounts of obsidian tool manufacture in Mexico, bolstered his claim for a near-universal set of techniques for making stone tools in Antiquity. In some parts of the world, this time frame extended well into the nineteenth century.

As all crafts do, **flintknapping** begins with the selection of an appropriate raw material. Making stone tools means finding stone that has a **cryptocrystalline** structure, which when impacted by an external force, reacts in a way that is similar to the response of a fluid. The nearest modern equivalent is glass, which prior to fracturing may ripple just as the surface of a pond does. Flints, **cherts**, and obsidians all have a cryptocrystalline structure. Other stones, such as petrified wood and quartzites, have a coarser crystalline structure and usually a grain that forces breakage in a particular direction [**3.4**, see p. 54].

Neolithic A period in human history that includes the adoption of agriculture and building of monuments, about 9,000 years ago.

flake A piece of a stone that has been struck off through knapping.

flintknapping The act of striking a flint to remove a piece, or a flake, usually to make a stone tool. The people who do this are called flintknappers, or knappers.

cryptocrystalline The microscopic arrangement of crystals in a stone, such as chert, that reacts to a force much as a fluid does, rippling when struck, and breaking to form a sharp edge.

chert A fine-grained rock, frequently used for stone tools; flint is a particular type of chert.

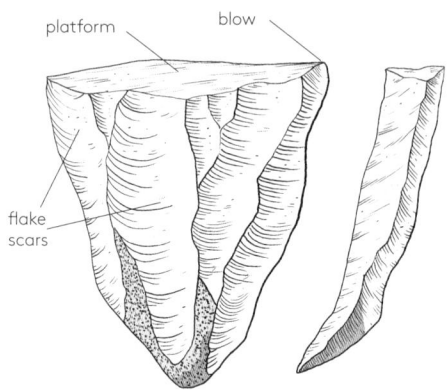

3.4 Features of a core and flake. A single blow at the platform of the core produces a flake. Flake scars on the core indicate where a flake has been removed.

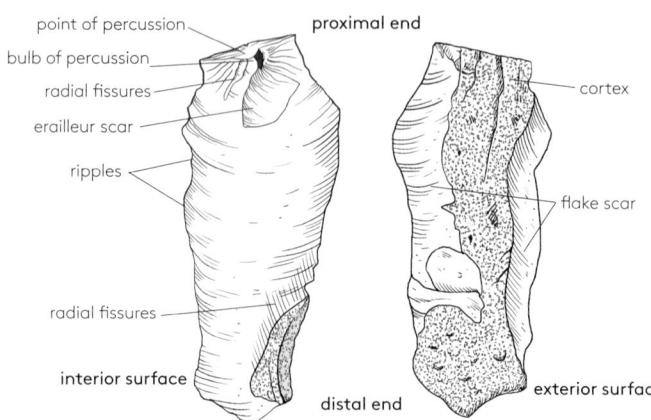

3.5 Key features of a flake, such as the bulb of percussion and ripples, offer evidence of a human purposefully striking the flake from a core. The extensive cortex on the exterior surface shows that this is a primary flake (one of the first struck from raw material).

conchoidal fracture The mechanics of breakage for cryptocrystalline material, such as glass or chert, which produces flakes with smooth surfaces and sharp edges.

primary flakes The first pieces or flakes of a stone that are struck off during knapping.

core A stone trimmed by knapping that can then be cut down into prefashioned flakes or used as a single tool.

striking platform The part of a stone core where the flintknapper strikes to create smaller flakes.

proximal end The point where the flake originated following the strike of the blow; includes the striking platform.

distal end The end of the flake produced by the energy of the blow exiting the stone.

The need for cryptocrystalline material is dictated by the mechanics of flintknapping. Force is applied in the form of blows, which project energy throughout the material. For example, when a sheet of plate glass—such as a window—is struck by a bullet, the force of the impact radiates outward and through it, producing a ringlike wave of energy that exits by forming a perfect cone of glass that pops out from the back of the window. This is called **conchoidal fracture**. All flintknapping employs conchoidal fracture: the blows are directed into the cryptocrystalline structure of the stone at various angles, producing many "cones" of force that break the stone in a predictable way.

To create stone tools, flintknappers must first *find* the raw material they know that they need. Outcrops of stone on hilltops can be broken down into workable cobbles, or rounded pebbles may be found in streams and rivers. Initially, one can strike a stone to create smaller pieces, and these pieces, which are referred to as **primary flakes**, may be further chipped into a shape. Alternatively, a flintknapper can transform the primary stone into a **core**, which is then used to make more flakes or a single tool [**3.4, 3.5**]. A core may be further shaped to create a large flat face, a **striking platform**. The striking platform is the target for striking off flakes, as the force of the blows (which leave a series of small, crushed dents) travels through the body of the core. Where they exit, a part of the core is fractured away, to form a flake. The location at which the flake had been attached to a core is called a flake scar. Flakes have very distinctive features, which are generated as part of the process of fracture: the breakage that occurs when the force of the blow travels outward from its impact through a homogeneous stone.

Most flakes can be oriented according to the direction of the energy that formed them, so the ends that share a portion of the striking platform are the **proximal ends,** and the flake termination is referred to as the **distal end**. Flakes almost always have a small swelling directly below the platform remnant. This is the **bulb of percussion**, made by the force of the energy as it travels outward from the blow.

Conchoidal fracture can also create ripples in the flake's **ventral** surface that are both seen and felt. The **dorsal** surface of a flake may have flake scars or scars at the **cortex** from previous blows to the striking platform. These landmarks on flakes are useful in documenting stone-knapping technology. Students quickly learn to spot the residual edge of the striking platform and a bulb of percussion as the work of human hands. Rocks that have smashed each other in landslides simply do not bear these kinds of landmarks, so they are the signposts of human craftspeople.

Furthermore, one can reconstruct the work that a knapper has done, even in cases where no final tool remains with the debris left for the archaeologist to examine [**3.6**]. Although the terms described above refer to different parts of flakes, they can also be used comparatively to describe the differences between flakes. A primary flake will have a cortex and a secondary flake will not, allowing the archaeologist to understand which part of the knapping process is represented. Did the knapper simply remove the outer part of the raw cobble to make it lighter to carry off? Did he sit at the spot while making a tool? Did she complete the tool, leaving behind the finer, finishing flakes that serrate the cutting edge of a knife or speartip? Different kinds of strokes make different kinds of flakes.

Flintknapping uses three kinds of percussion to create flakes: hard hammer, soft hammer, and indirect percussion. A hard hammer is a round **hammerstone**, which fits into the hand. Soft hammers can be crafted from springy antler, bone, or wood, and they are used to shape thinner, longer flakes. Indirect percussion utilizes a hammerstone and punch, usually created from bone or antler, to break off small flakes. Finer trimming and shaping are done through **pressure flaking**, whereby a pointed object and steady pressure, usually generated by squeezing with the hands, remove tiny flakes from the edge of a tool. The combination of these different techniques can be important in establishing the age of certain flakes. For instance, a flake twice as long as wide with parallel edges is a blade, and the technology for consistently striking blades appeared only 20,000 years ago.

The flintknapping process produces a significant amount of waste and byproducts. Large cobbles are fractured to examine the material, and some of these pieces reduced to create usable cores. Cores can then be shaped to produce blades or further broken down to create flakes of various sizes. A variety of tools may be made from the flakes and blades, which are further shaped with pressure flaking and soft-hammer percussion. The small waste that remains after shaping is generally called **debitage**. Its presence indicates the locus of tool production, as this fine fraction of stone is usually swept from the laps of flintknappers and then falls to the ground. Flakes and tools are often picked up and used again and again; they are thus dispersed well away from the flintknapping locale.

bulb of percussion The bulge below the striking platform of a flake that is produced by the force of the energy passing through the stone.

ventral The interior surface of a flake.

dorsal The exterior surface of a flake.

cortex The outside surface of a stone.

hammerstone A tool used to remove a piece from a stone. Frequently a different, harder type of stone.

pressure flaking Finer flaking of a stone tool using an antler tip, which is pressed against the stone to break off small flakes.

debitage Stone flakes, fragmented stone, and dust (waste materials) produced by knapping a stone tool.

3.6 Exploding flakes. Analysts sometimes practice re-fitting to learn about the knapper's task sequence. This core produced blades, and when reassembled can show where the knapper shifted grip on the core to strike other facets. Such work helps us understand the level of skill, handedness, and intent of individual ancient tool makers.

STONE TOOLS AS EVIDENCE OF HUMAN ADAPTATION

Flintknapping was the first human technology, but it is also the technology that identifies the first humans. The archaeological record of the first flintknapped tools, and of later episodes of technological advancement, coincides with the fossil record of growth and development of the human brain in areas that are known to facilitate planning, communicating, and transmitting information. Physical changes in humans, as well as changes in where they lived, what they ate, and how far they traveled, are all connected to the production of stone tools and the transmission of ideas about toolmaking.

Physical anthropology and biology have clearly articulated, however, that to be human is to also be a primate, and thus our abilities are not solely our own. Our brains are similar to those of other primates, and we share with them a primate heritage that includes intelligence, highly complex social structures, and long-term relationships between adults and offspring. Toolmaking, and the transmission of information on how to make and use tools, are not uncommon in primates. Chimpanzees make tools out of leaves and twigs to extract termites from mounds, and capuchins and macaques use stones to crack open nuts and shellfish. Young primates have been observed watching and attempting to copy their parents and siblings, and ultimately master the most successful techniques. The transmission of techniques over time has also been documented. Archaeological excavations at capuchins' nut-cracking sites in Brazil have revealed that the behavior is more than six hundred years old, likely spanning at least a hundred generations. Transmission of information is perhaps the most "primate" activity of all, and so far on Earth we have been its best practitioners. When we recognize toolmaking techniques repeated over thousands of years, we see cultural transmission of information fossilized in the archaeological record.

Early Hominins, and the Oldowan and Acheulean

At first, stone tool technology was very conservative, with few changes over long spans of time. The first stone tools were made more than 2.5 million years ago in Africa by primates that belonged to the genus *Homo*. *Homo sapiens* (we humans), the only living members of the genus *Homo*, are descended from ancient ancestors that are collectively called *hominins*. In the previous chapter, we discussed anatomically modern humans (*Homo sapiens sapiens*) alongside the Neanderthal (*Homo sapiens neanderthalensis*), which became extinct around 30,000 years ago. Long before *Homo sapiens sapiens* or Neanderthals, the dominant hominins were *Homo habilis*, *Homo rudolfensis*, and *Homo ergaster*. These were the hominins in Africa that began to develop characteristics that we see in modern humans, demonstrating adaptive flexibility and a dependence on material culture.

The fossils of these hominins have been found with broken bones from antelope, zebra, and wildebeest. Scattered among the bones were fractured stones and flakes, all methodically broken. The technique for making these tools was simple handheld

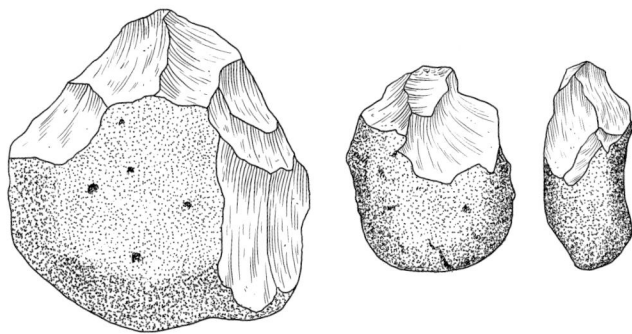
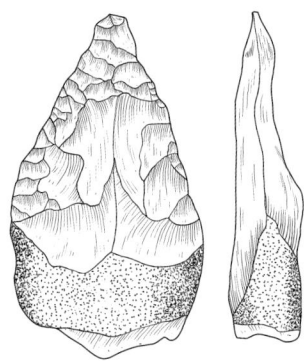

Above left and center: **3.7 These Oldowan tools** were made by our human ancestors in Africa, such as *Homo habilis*, more than 2.5 million years ago.

Above right: **3.8 An Acheulean hand axe,** distinctive for its teardrop shape, used between 1.76 million and 125,000 years ago, and made by *Homo erectus*.

percussion. As a group, these tools are referred to as the **Oldowan** [3.7], named for the location at Olduvai Gorge (Tanzania), where they were first discovered. By "**industry**," archaeologists mean a grouping of tools manufactured in a similar way. Artifacts from a particular site are called an **assemblage**. The presence of dense concentrations of Oldowan tools also serves as an **index fossil**, a temporal indicator for the presence of a particular species—in this instance, the genus *Homo* in Africa.

Experiments with replicated Oldowan tools have demonstrated that their heavy nature made them ideal for cutting tough hide and also breaking through joints and marrow to cut carcasses down to smaller, more portable pieces. It is uncertain how adept our hominin ancestors were at hunting. They may have used wooden spears to kill animals that were drinking at waterholes, but these spears have long since rotted away or burned, leaving no trace of prey. They may also have simply driven off lions, hyenas, and leopards from their kills before the carcasses were consumed. Whichever scenario occurred, the abundance of cutting and chopping tools and animal bones indicates that some members of the genus *Homo* were practiced butchers and meat consumers. The techniques for creating stone tools were observed or directly taught, and the Oldowan industry was transmitted from adult to juvenile, and from peer to peer.

In time, approximately 1.5 million years ago, populations of *H. ergaster* began to colonize the hotter, drier parts of Africa, and by 1 million years ago, a population of *H. erectus*, a species perhaps descended from *H. ergaster*, left Africa and colonized parts of Western Europe, the Near East, Central Asia, South Asia, and East Asia. The fossils of both these hominins have larger brains than their predecessors and leaner bodies, too, which would have better adapted to hot climates. *H. ergaster* and *H. erectus* sites are also associated with stone tools, many of which were manufactured to achieve precise balance and symmetry. The industry of these hominins, the **Acheulean** [3.8], includes a bifacial hand axe that was knapped on both sides, producing a teardrop-shaped blade. The design of these tools would have required

Oldowan The oldest known stone tools made by human ancestors, made more than 2.5 million years ago from simple percussion.

industry A group of tools of similar manufacture, such as the Oldowan.

assemblage Artifacts found at the same site.

index fossil An artifact used to identify the presence of a particular human species.

Acheulean A stone tool industry developed by human ancestors 1.76 million years ago, which included the production of teardrop-shaped hand axes.

an increase in cognitive ability—both to plan their manufacture, and to transmit this information and skill to others. The basic form of the hand axe remained unchanged for more than 1 million years. This may be difficult for us to imagine. In our modern, moment-to-moment, ever-changing human world, the use of the same technology for that length of time is nearly unthinkable. The stability of this tool speaks to its simplicity and broad utility, but also to the limitations of the *H. ergaster* and *H. erectus* minds. A modern human brain was not at work.

A human-like existence, nonetheless, does appear to have formed during this time. Hominins throughout the Old World (Africa, Europe, and Asia) used caves for shelter, and many locations that contained caves became "hominin habitats" occupied by their descendants for more than 1 million years.

Becoming Human: The First *Homo sapiens*

Around 600,000 years ago, brain size in hominins was relatively similar to what it had been 1.8 million years beforehand. Starting 500,000 years ago, though, brain size began to increase, and the hand axes, choppers, and flakes commonly made by hominins started to show more refinement. They were thinner and more symmetrical, suggesting a greater ability to control the flaking process. About this time, a new hominin appeared in Europe and Africa, *H. heidelbergensis*. This hominin was most likely the ancestor of both modern *H. sapiens*, who evolved in Africa, and *H. neanderthalensis*, who evolved in Europe. As mentioned in Chapter 1, *H. sapiens neanderthalensis*, known as Neanderthals, were robust in form, with short limbs and stocky trunks. They were well adapted to the cold conditions of Europe during the Pleistocene (the last Ice Age) and lived in caves. Injuries on the skeletons of Neanderthals suggest that both women and men were involved in violent activities, perhaps caused by ambush hunting of large animals, such as European horses, deer, and rhinoceroses. Neanderthals also produced a stone tool industry known as the **Mousterian** [**3.9**], which was dominated by flake-based tools, such as scrapers, and cutting tools made by **retouching** (sharpening by removing small flakes) along one side (unifacial) and edge of a large flake.

Neanderthals also employed the Levallois technique [**3.10**], whereby a core was carefully prepared so that a single oval or triangular flake with multiple feathered terminations (sharp edges that occur naturally as a product of the stone breaking) could be produced with a single blow. Attempts to replicate this technique revealed that it was a challenging task for a flintknapper, requiring careful planning and precision.

Modern *H. sapiens* appeared throughout Europe, Central Asia, South Asia, East Asia, and Australia, spreading north and east from their ancestral homelands in Africa. Their brains were twice the size of those of *H. ergaster* but somewhat smaller than the brains of Neanderthals. Modern *H. sapiens* also exhibited behaviors that mark them as qualitatively different from all previous hominins. At Blombos Cave in South Africa, perforated shells [**3.11**] and sticks of red ocher incised with designs have been found in deposits 100,000–70,000 years old. These are hints of a social

Mousterian A stone tool industry often associated with Neanderthals.

retouching Further trimming of a stone tool, to produce a sharp edge.

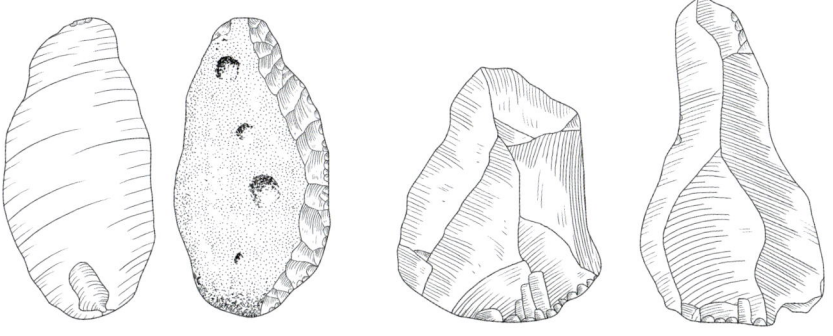

Far left: **3.9 Retouch on a single side of a flake.** One edge of the flake has been trimmed to improve its sharpness, as is typical of Mousterian flake tools made by Neanderthals.

Left: **3.10 Levallois industry flakes.** In this industry, a core is first prepared to make one or more preformed flakes. Levallois points were made by both Neanderthals and anatomically modern *Homo sapiens* more than 40,000 years ago.

consciousness in humans. They are markers of self and perhaps indicative of social roles in a society. Changes in subsistence, with marine animals now included as part of the diet, were also found in other parts of Africa, suggesting a level of cognition and technological skill that had not existed previously. At the Klasies River Caves in South Africa, and at Katanda in the Democratic Republic of Congo, the remains of marine shells and bone harpoons indicate that *H. sapiens* were comfortable in water, and could catch fish and marine organisms.

Modified sources of pigment 300,000 years old even appear in several sites across Africa, suggesting to archaeologist Allison Brooks that human social cognition may have developed rather slowly. By 60,000 years ago, humans at Sibudu Cave (South Africa) were gathering and renewing bedding and reusing hearths, signs of a structured layout to group living. They also used needles, bone points, and glue. These new technological capabilities, plus the ability to communicate and to organize their group-level activities perhaps more effectively, made modern *H. sapiens* the most complex superorganism (an organism composed of many individuals that work together) yet to emerge on Earth.

Wherever modern humans appeared, the preexisting populations of hominins—small to begin with and likely stressed to find mates—melted away. Loss of habitat and declines wrought by disease have been offered as explanations for their extinction, although some evidence exists of their interaction with modern humans. Recent studies of modern human and ancient hominin DNA have revealed that very small amounts (less than 4 percent) of Neanderthal DNA are incorporated in the genomes of some Europeans and Asians. Neanderthals even acquired early

3.11 Shells from Blombos Cave, South Africa. These half-inch (1-cm) shells (of the species *Nassarius kraussianus*) were deliberately perforated and used as ornaments.

STONE TOOLS AS EVIDENCE OF HUMAN ADAPTATION

human DNA, perhaps from interbreeding in the Mount Carmel caves region (Israel), and they then migrated to inner Asia. The DNA of another archaic hominin population called the Denisovans was determined to be present in the genomes of some native Australians. Genetic studies indicate, however, that the rest of humanity is a product of a single, later migration of *H. sapiens* within and out of Africa. Their stone tools also appear to have experienced a revolution, in both design and production. Modern humans invented blades, in which long, linear flakes were struck from prepared cores.

A blade is produced using the same conchoidal fracture as for a flake, but it is also twice as long as it is wide, and typically has parallel edges. Fashioning a blade additionally requires the preparation of a core, not unlike the Levallois core technique, from which multiple blades of similar length and width can be made. Blades were also retouched and shaped into scrapers and spearpoints that could be added to wooden handles. Alternatively, blades could be snapped into segments and then retouched to become barbs. Modern humans thus created the first compound tools, which could be thrown farther and cut more efficiently; their elements could also be easily replaced without remaking the whole tool. These amazing tools provide mute evidence of a newly emerging adaptation: human relationships. To produce these tools required significant training and learning, suggesting a much more developed system of communication. A social structure allowing the young to learn from the experienced would also have been essential to the mastery of this technology.

Just as nineteenth-century historians regarded the first technologies as markers of time, stone tools are now used by archaeologists to mark the important developments in mental planning, cultural transmission, and learning that began with hominins 2.5 million years ago. The development of technology and transmission of culture were the foundation for the successes of humans in adapting to the environment. From these successes, new ideas developed cumulatively, leading to more complex technologies that would require more multifaceted forms of cultural transmission, social networking, and collaboration. The investment would prove to be worth it, as new technologies ultimately added to the triumphs of *Homo sapiens* in creating their own niche in the world and shaping the Anthropocene. We next consider one of these advancements, metalworking, as among the most prevalent and significant technologies developed by humans.

METALWORKING, A NEW TECHNOLOGY FOR COMMUNITIES

Although current flintknappers share information to make the same types of artifact using the same techniques, they are still solitary workers. For a technology transmitted across small bands of mobile humans, as has been the case for 90 percent of our history, solo task technology is unsurprising. But as cognitive archaeologists (archaeologists studying the development of human thinking) have long surmised, our human brains have become increasingly adept at negotiating and forming

3.12 An example of copper-working. A 12-in. (30.6 cm) bird of prey in copper plate from Mound City, Hopewell Culture National Historical Park, Ohio. The perforations on the body of the bird suggest that it may have been worn as a breastplate.

broader social networks. We can work in larger groups for composite tasks in which many people contribute different efforts. Metalworking, which appeared in the Near East and Europe around 7,000 years ago, is one good example.

Metal in the **Chalcolithic Age** (a period before the Bronze Age when copper-making became more common) and in the Bronze Age was extremely rare; everyday items were made from other materials, such as stone, bone, or wood. The initial interest in metal was probably sparked by the bright colors of such copper-oxide ores as malachite (green), azurite (blue), and cuprite (red), which first appear archaeologically as beads and ornaments. Attempts to work these bright copper oxides would have led to experiments with purifying and manipulating copper. Native, or raw, pure copper was rare, but even a small amount could be hammered and worked cold into ornaments, as several Native American groups did in the upper Midwest of North America, using a source from Isle Royal in Lake Superior. The source was later identified in objects found more than 600 miles (1,000 km) away in the Hopewell Mounds of Ohio ([**3.12**]; also Chapter 10). This technology involved few people—just as the stone-knapper acquired her rare flint nodule, so the copper-worker acquired native copper and fashioned it into an ornament or a very soft tool, such as a cosmetic applicator. Only as archaeologists began to find the remnants of technology for mining, **smelting**, and casting copper ore, did we recognize the cooperation involved in metalworking.

To create something out of metal was still an unusual event in the Bronze Age, and would have involved a large number of people. Many people probably participated in the excavation of the copper ore. Similarly, many people would have been required to transport the ore from the quarry and to collect the wood used in heating the fire for smelting. It would take a significant amount of ore to produce a small amount of copper, so the work to produce un-alloyed (pure) copper would have called for many hundreds of hours of labor. Add to that the inclusion of mining and smelting tin to make the copper–tin alloy called bronze. Pure copper bends easily—it may be the ideal substance to craft an animal silhouette, a bangle, or an applicator for eyeliner. But a copper axe or adze (an axe with a cutting edge that

Chalcolithic or Copper Age Refers to Old World cultures after the Neolithic and prior to the Bronze Age. Chalcolithic people used ceramics and some copper tools.

smelting Using heat to melt ore (a rock with dense concentrations of minerals or metals, such as iron) allowing for the extraction of pure metal.

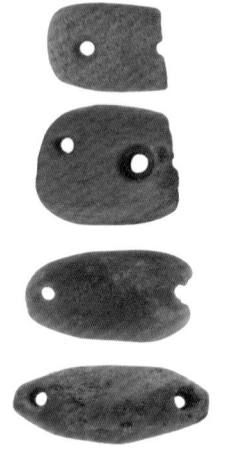

3.13 A selection of green stone beads. People's initial interest in metal was probably sparked by the bright colors of copper oxides. These green beads come from end of Paleolithic and early Holocene cultures in the eastern Mediterranean (modern Israel).

is perpendicular to the handle) wears down quickly when cutting trees or planing wood, let alone working stone. Bronze is tougher.

During the smelting process, additional people would have been required to work the bellows, or to blow on ceramic-tipped tubes, in order to provide enough oxygen to fuel the fire to a temperature hot enough to melt the ore. The molten copper was then poured into a prepared mold, and from that point forward, the work was probably accomplished by a single person—most likely the smith who trimmed the flashings, cast on additional parts, and polished the final piece.

The production of a metal tool involves multiple stages, some requiring cooperation and social networks to assemble and manipulate the resources needed to complete the task. Few ores occur on Earth's surface, so much metalworking requires mining underground; abandoned copper mines in eastern Turkey and southern Jordan show that the process of collective mining was established around 6,500 years ago [**3.13**]. Once mined, ores had to be processed (crushed or separated) to concentrate the oxide, then smelted by heating higher than 2,012°F (1,100°C). A simple bowl furnace—a pit in the ground would suffice—loses a lot of heat and requires cooling after high-temperature smelting. During the smelting process, the metal separates and sinks to form a cooled cake at the base of the pit while lighter slag (glassy and bubbly impurities mixed with the carbon remnants of charcoal fuel) floats and solidifies at the top of the cooled pit. Once it cools, a second process involves chipping off the slag, leaving the metal. At this point, the copper might be reheated to alloy with another metal. It can be worked cold by hammering, with periodic reheating of the emerging object to prevent brittleness.

Alternatively, the metal may be cast, which involves shaping a mold into which molten metal is poured. Such a mold may have a simple open form, but even slightly intricate forms or contours usually require a closed mold, one that can be broken to release the object. The lost-wax method of casting was developed independently in Israel and Pakistan approximately 4,000 years ago, though it was practiced in Asia and South America several millennia later. A craftsperson built up a sculpture in beeswax or plant wax and then encased it in clay, which essentially became the mold. With a few holes cut for the wax to escape, the mold was ready for casting, in which molten metal poured into the mold heated and displaced the wax (hence the lost wax). Once it cooled, the mold could be broken to release the cast object, now ready for smoothing, polishing, and attaching to other cast pieces if so desired.

The resources needed to utilize such metal technology are considerable and imply collective efforts. Labor is involved in the mining, transport, and stoking of fires; it is necessary to reserve charcoal from dense timber during the smelting process; and beeswax, plant wax, and clay are all specialized resources available only in patchy distributions. Finally, time spent in metalworking and accumulating all the resources for it is time lost in gathering food. Someone else will have to compensate for the metalworkers. The arrival of metals thus introduced many social changes, far before the invention of machinery. We will see in Chapter 12 how bronze, in particular, was linked to a significant series of social changes that allowed people to express and bolster their status, beginning the drive for the acquisition, hoarding, and consumption of wealth that lies behind many of the environmental changes we see today.

Central Africa: Iron Smelting

The development of metalworking was not limited to copper and bronze. By the early first millennium BCE, Central African iron smelters in Buhaya (northwest Tanzania), Burundi, and Rwanda were using a particularly efficient, large furnace to smelt iron. These upright furnaces reached high temperatures (2,282°F or 1,250°C) and covered a slag pit around 3 feet (c. 1 meter) across, in which very fluid iron slags cleanly separated from the not-quite-melted iron. By adding green branches to the smelting, smiths introduced more carbon to blend with the iron, forming a steel bloom, a carbon-rich, spongy mass of iron that could be removed once it cooled [**3.14**]. The iron bloom still needed to be forged, a process that involved heating it to a red-hot temperature. This would make it malleable for hammering, which served to squeeze out remaining impurities and create wrought iron. Archaeologists have recovered slag, broken furnaces, and excavated slag pits that may be 2,650 years old, making this controlled iron-smelting technology in Central Africa among the earliest examples of ironworking in the world.

Intense debate surrounds the origins of bloomery iron smelting in Africa. Did the technology travel from the Mediterranean coastal city of Phoenician Carthage (from 2,800 years ago) across the Sahara Desert? Or, did the Romans introduce it via the kingdom of Meroë (2,300 to 1,450 years ago) along the River Nile in northern Sudan? Does evidence exist to support the technology's transmission across the Sahara? As it turns out, the style of the Meroë furnaces is not a convincing precursor for those in

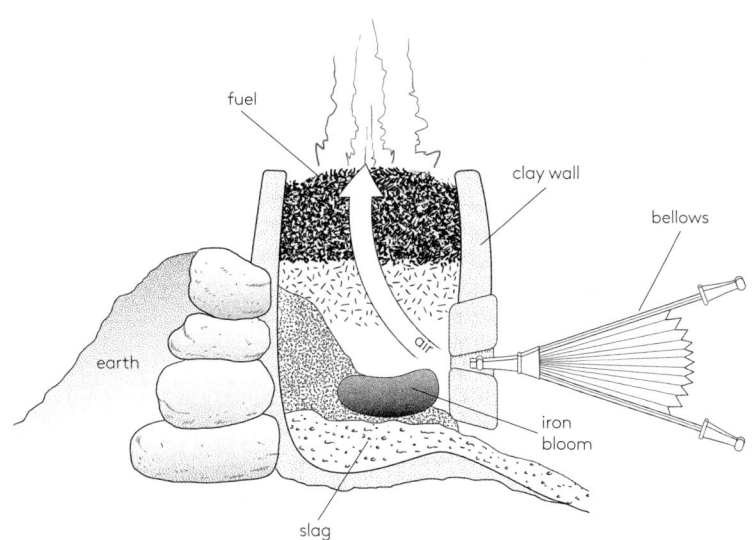

3.14 An iron-smelting furnace in Buhaya, Central Africa. The furnace depicted here could reach a temperature as high as 2,282°F (1,250°C). The addition of iron ore and charcoal, as well as leafy branches, introduced more carbon. The result was a malleable mass called a bloom, which, once forged, produced the metal iron.

Central Africa, and they are also constructed differently from the Central African furnaces, possibly dating to a later period. Instead, Central African iron smelting appears to be a native invention, offering a window into the initial development and spread of metalworking at an archaeologically detectable scale.

The bloomery furnace archaeological sites lie in the lowlands of the African Great Lakes region, a string of large, mostly elongate lakes within the western branch of the Great Rift Valley system of East Africa [3.15]. As a region yielding some of the world's oldest and best-known fossil hominins, the northeastern extent of this system (the area around Olduvai Gorge in Tanzania, and Lake Turkana in Kenya) has long been famous in the annals of human prehistory. It is the last few thousand years of the Holocene, though, during which iron smelting [3.16] appeared, which distinguish this region as the source of a later compelling story—that of a transforming landscape and human innovations—in our narrative of the Anthropocene.

About 6,000 years ago, the Sahara Desert to the north grew increasingly arid, shrinking the marshlands around watering holes and widening the distance between them. This was part of a global, Middle Holocene climate shift. Mobile herders with sheep, goats, cattle, and donkeys moved southward from the increasingly inhospitable Sahara into the African Great Lakes region, arriving in southern Kenya around 4,500 years ago. Here, they encountered highlands still covered in dense tropical rainforest and a deciduous woodland cloaking the lower slopes and lake basins. Humans already lived in this terrain as hunters and foragers. Neolithic herders called the Elmenteitan people maintained low population densities in these environments,

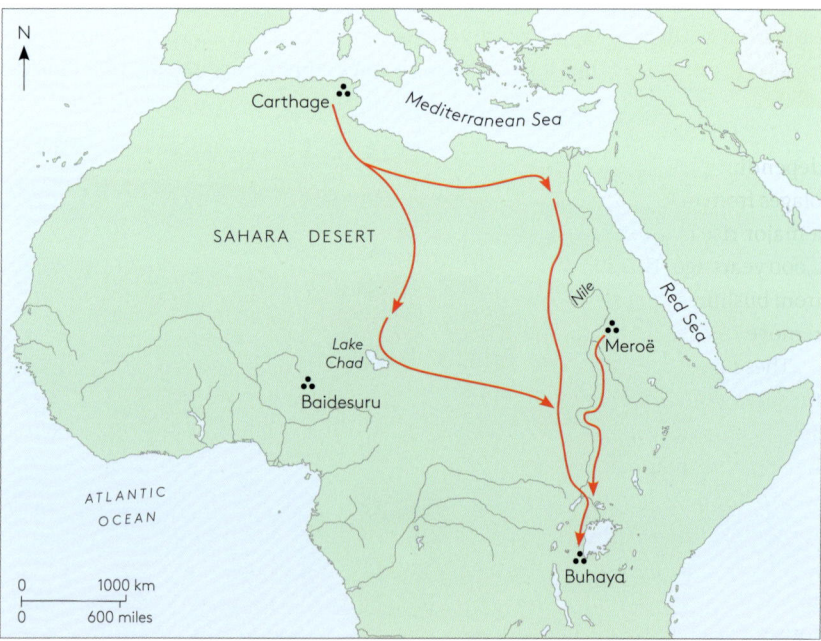

3.15 Map of northeastern Africa showing routes from Carthage or Meroë—along which the technology of bloomery iron smelting possibly traveled—and the Great Lakes region of African bloom furnaces (the site of Buhaya).

3.16 Iron furnaces from the site of Baidesuru, from the Nok culture in West Africa; its population developed iron smelting c. 500 BCE.

depending on available grasslands where their animals could graze. Pollen assemblages from many lakes—Tanganyika, Edward, Albert, Masoko, Victoria—show that a major rise in grass pollens and a shift to modern grassland vegetation occurred 2,000 years ago. This shift coincides with a peak in charcoal flecks (washed into lakes from bushfires) that signal humans' clearing of the landscape to enhance grasslands, remove trees, free fields, and facilitate the production of charcoal.

These developments had important implications for iron smelting. The first iron furnaces were built around this time, within lakeside villages and between village settlements inhabited almost certainly by people who incorporated farming and horticulture (tending mixed gardens and individual plants) in their activities. They were probably the first smiths, and their need for charcoal in smelting contributed to the removal of woodland. Today, the East African grasslands with their wildlife and safari lodges are an icon of the African wilderness, but it is important to remember that it was human technologies—including charcoal-making for iron smelting—that forged these landscapes.

PERISHABLE TECHNOLOGIES: REVELATIONS FROM THE ICEMAN

Metal tools tend to be recycled; unless buried, they are melted down and transformed into other, updated metal objects. Stone tools are therefore the major technology that best survives in the archaeological record, and they were our only durable technology for 90 percent of human history. Human technologies, however, were not limited to stone and metal. Archaeologists often study these materials because they are what remains. The perishable items of daily life, such as clothing, wooden and fiber tools, baskets, furs, skins, and mats, are rarely preserved in sedimentary contexts, and as a result, we know little of them. Did *H. ergaster* wear clothes? Did this hominin use ropes or nets to catch game? We know that wooden spears were in use some 400,000 years ago, as several have been found preserved in waterlogged deposits in Germany. What other ancient technologies had developed by that same time?

Mostly wild speculations are offered about the other ancient technologies. The little that we do know derives from a much later period, and from the possessions and corpse of a single individual, Ötzi, also known as the Iceman, whose remains were discovered in the Italian Alps in 1991 [**3.17**]. In late September of that year, Erika and Helmut Simon were hiking on an alpine trail along the mountainous

3.17 Ötzi's body, as observed by hikers in September 1991.

border between Italy and Austria. Surrounded by melting snow, glacial ice, and boulders, they left the marked trail and descended down a narrow gully. Lying at the bottom of the gully was a pool of meltwater, and within this water they caught sight of a smooth, oblong object. Upon closer inspection, they realized that the object was the upper torso and head of a human body. Believing they had stumbled across the corpse of a lost hiker, they reported their find to authorities. The following day, an Austrian rescue team attempted to remove the rest of the body from the ice using a generator-powered drill. While drilling, they noticed several objects near the body, including an axe made with a wooden handle and a metal blade. At this point, the rescuers concluded that although the remains might be those of a lost hiker, he was also someone who had gone missing for several hundred years, rather than a few dozen.

Over the next several days, the body was freed from the ice and placed in a body bag. New items were then found in the vicinity of the body, including leather, fiber cords, bunches of grass, and a flint dagger hafted with a wooden handle. The body was subsequently transported to the Institute of Forensic Medicine at the University of Innsbruck, in Austria, where the axe was dated to the Late Neolithic–Early Chalcolithic period, around 5,000 years ago. The "Iceman" and his possessions had been preserved by the ice of a glacier that later slid over his body. Soon, he was given the name "Ötzi" [**3.18**], after the Ötztal region of Italy, his likely place of origin (he was actually just a little more than 303 feet or 92 meters inside the border of Italy). Bone from his left femur was sampled for radiocarbon dating (see Chapter 6 for discussion of this technique), and the results indicated that he had lived and died between the years 3350 and 3100 BCE. This made him older than the pyramids of Giza in Egypt, and perhaps also older than the monument Stonehenge in England.

Ötzi's body has been the focus of a series of physical and forensic studies, and his remains have generated a new understanding of the diet and activities of Chalcolithic people in Europe. He came from a small community that practiced farming and herding and lived in relatively small, isolated settlements. He appears also to have been a victim of violence, for injuries to his hands and body indicate he survived an attack shortly before his death. His clothing and tools, which were well preserved, offer perhaps the greatest body of information on technologies to have survived from any ancient society. The technologies Ötzi might have practiced, and that were formative for his community, descended from the technologies of early *H. sapiens* communities in Africa, the Near East, and Europe. All of Ötzi's possessions have been carefully studied and reconstructed, and they reveal what had previously been guesswork with regard to Antiquity: techniques for curing animal hide; weaving fiber; cutting and shaping wood and bark; and sewing soft materials into everyday items, such as coats, hats, and shoes. A full catalog of Ötzi's tools and clothes would fill an entire volume, so we will focus on the strictly perishable materials that offer special insight into the kinds of technologies overlooked in previous reconstructions of much earlier periods.

3.18 A reconstruction of Ötzi, who was aged about forty-five when he died between 3350 and 3100 BCE.

PERISHABLE TECHNOLOGIES: REVELATIONS FROM THE ICEMAN   **67**

Ötzi's Clothing

Ötzi's clothes, which were both expertly and expediently made, suggest that clothing manufacture was a well-established technology in Antiquity [**3.19**]. Ötzi wore a hat made from stitched strips of brown bear hide, which is thick and warm; it was cut to form a half-spherical cap. Two leather strings, tied beneath his chin, would have secured the hat atop his head. The hat's outer surface was made of bear fur, which waterproofed it. Ötzi's outermost garment was a cloak [**3.20a**] made of lengths of grass that had been plaited together, forming a large, waterproof covering. The cloak was fashioned from alpine grass and designed to be draped over his shoulders; it hung down to his knees. Such a cloak could be fabricated seasonally and discarded when the grass fragmented or wore out. One can view it as an early form of the disposable rain poncho.

His shirt [**3.20b**] was fashioned from strips of domestic goat and sheep hide, which had been tanned using smoke and scraped so they would be clean of fleshy tissue. The garment was long, extending down to his knees, and it opened in the front. It had been repaired with animal sinew, using rough stitches, and also with grass thread. The inexpert quality of the stitches suggests that a second person (perhaps Ötzi himself), not the clothesmaker, repaired the shirt at some point.

Although we take them for granted, modern trousers (known as "pants" by Americans) were not commonly worn in Europe until the medieval period. Prior to trousers, humans covered their legs with skirts, or leggings that would have wrapped around each leg individually, and been supported by short suspenders that attached to a belt encircling the waist. Ötzi indeed wore such a garment [**3.20c**]: his leggings were made of domestic goat hide and had been form-fitted to his legs by stitching together small strips of hide. In addition to their upper suspenders, Ötzi's leggings had lower straps that attached his leggings to his shoes, preventing the garment from shifting up on his legs, and perhaps also keeping out any snow or ice. Ötzi's "underwear" was a loincloth, which was a roughly rectangular garment sewn from strips of goat hide. This would have been pulled up between his legs and attached with a belt, with the front and back ends of the hide hanging over his body just as an apron does.

Ötzi wore shoes [**3.20d**] with leather soles made from bear hide. Each of these soles was stitched to a round flap of deer leather that covered the top of each foot; the hairy surface of the flap appeared on the outside of each shoe. A fiber net was attached to this construction; it had been made in the shape of a foot and allowed Ötzi to tie the shoes around his ankles. Dry grass had also been stuffed inside the netting, to give his feet protection from the cold. The laces of his shoes were crafted from cow hide.

Several of Ötzi's clothes, especially the leggings and the shirt, were fitted to his body. This suggests a precise knowledge of tailoring, one that previously was not known to exist in Chalcolithic Europe. Such tailoring may have been a kind of homecraft—something every household could produce—but it still indicates a level

3.19 An artist's reconstruction of Ötzi with full clothing and tool kit.

3.20a Part of cloak

3.20b Shirt

3.20c Leggings

3.20d Grass shoe-stuffing

of mastery and specialization. One can easily imagine Ötzi's tailor, who may have been a woman, such as his wife or daughter, or another man, carefully stitching his clothes by the light of an oil lamp. Modern tailoring directly descends from the techniques visible in Ötzi's clothes. The care shown for these garments, for example the hasty repairs, also suggests that not everyone living in his society had this skill.

Ötzi's clothing and tools also demonstrate an advanced technology for making cured hides (skins that retain their external hair) and leather (skins from which all the hair has been removed). In addition, they indicate an extensive knowledge of and familiarity with animals, both wild and domestic. In Ötzi's possession were objects and clothes created from goat, bear, deer, and chamois (wild mountain goat). The use of these animals appears to have been purposeful: bear hide was chosen for his shoes and his hat, possibly because this hide is thicker and warmer than others. Perhaps generations of people in the Ötzal area had learned from experience that bear hide and hair made the best hats, as these materials were warm and windproof, and shed snow easily. The shirt was crafted from strips of domestic goat hide, perhaps more commonly available for larger garments. Such hide was also more lightweight, so it would have made the shirt more comfortable. The goat hide, because it came from a domesticated animal, probably served as a replacement for another animal hide. Perhaps in generations past, Ötzi's ancestors had made their shirts from deer hide or wild goat. No cloth existed in the Ötzal area in Ötzi's time. Only centuries later did people there fabricate their shirts from wool or flax, rather than tanned hides.

What of everything else in Ötzi's world—the technologies for harvesting, cleaning and storing grain, planing timber, erecting a stockade, or communicating memories?

Other ancient technologies can be discovered only through the trace remains of their activity, and through modern archaeologists' experiments and replications.

TECHNOLOGY, THE ENVIRONMENT, AND THE ANTHROPOCENE

Revealed in the technologies of skins from hunted and herded animals, foods gathered and farmed, and specialized and collective tasks that produced his shoes and his copper axe, Ötzi's possessions emphasize to us that no man is an island. Even Ötzi, a solitary hiker from 5,000 years ago with the blood of others on his clothing and arrows, belonged to a social community of people that used technology to engage with the environment and with one another. That technology allowed him to hike alone into the wilds of the mountains, but it also tied him to his community, a relationship that is still apparent to us today: modern analyses of his possessions and stomach contents connect him intrinsically to the anthropogenic landscapes that constitute the foothills of the Italian Alps.

Developments in technology enabled humans to relate to their environments in different ways. Once early hominins became predators using stone projectiles, and later clubs and snares, they would have altered ecosystems at a local scale. Behavioral shifts in their relationships with other species surely affected the migration routes of animals and the abundance of some species. Evidence for the use of fire by *H. erectus* (around 300,000 years ago) has been discovered only at a handful of sites, but it may have been used for heat, warmth, and cooking, and also as a tool for driving animals and opening up heavily forested areas. This period in human history may mark the earliest beginnings of the "Anthropocene," when hominins became major agents of change in the entire world.

To that end, some archaeologists have argued that the stone tools and chipping debris that carpet vast regions of the Sahara Desert constitute the first anthropogenic landscapes. Estimates from the Messak Settafet escarpment in southern Libya suggest that hominin tool use over 1 million years deposited between 0.5 and 5 million stone artifacts per square kilometer across Africa, the equivalent of 42 to 84 million times the quantity of stone used in creating Khufu's Great Pyramid in Giza, Egypt. And over time, the hominin toolmakers on the Messak Settafet escarpment increased their production of stone tools and associated waste products. In the first millennia of habitation, they made tools requiring 100 separate strokes (for the removal of flakes). By 30,000 years ago, toolmakers' average expenditure of energy had increased to 250 strokes. This change reflected increased effort and decision-making in tool production.

Even as the technologies of the Anthropocene increased in the scale of their impact, they also become more complex over time. By complexity, we refer not only to the increased effort and expenditure of energy for solo toolmakers, but also to the technologies that emerged from cooperative, integrative, and collaborative tasks, such as metalworking. These technologies both imply and support larger social communities of humans. Some researchers have argued that the process of growing bigger brains—called *encephalization*—may be linked to the increasing cognitive load implicit in multilevel social awareness and transactions. Might humans have developed bigger brains while dealing with bigger cognitive demands? Bigger brains appeared deep in human prehistory, concurrent with the first uses of stone tools. Technology might have provided the material support for making us human; it certainly offered a material interface with our environment and the means to make our Anthropocene world.

When Ötzi hiked into the mountains on the day of his death, he left behind his familiar landscape of wheat fields and villages. He was not, however, in a pristine wilderness when he died. The valleys and the passes had been in use by his community for grazing flocks of sheep and goats for generations, a practice that introduced new plants and microbes to the mountain soils. Just as the meadows of the valleys had been transformed into wheat fields, anthropogenic processes were at work in the mountains of Europe. Although his death occurred perhaps 40 miles (60 km) away from his home, the place in which Ötzi died was already part of the Anthropocene.

Chapter Questions

1. How did early historians of the fifteenth through seventeenth centuries understand the past? How has this perception changed?
2. Describe some key aspects of a stone tool, and discuss how archaeologists might study these tools to gain insight into people of the past.
3. How did metalworking change the landscape of Central Africa approximately 2,600 years ago?
4. What kind of technologies and materials were discovered alongside the body of Ötzi? What do these materials reveal about how this individual lived?

Additional Resources

Fleckinger, Angelika, and Steiner, Henry. *The Iceman*. Museo Archeologico Dell' Alto Adige. Bolzano, Italy: La Commerciale Borgogno, 2000.

Jones, P. R. "Experimental Butchery with Modern Stone Tools and Its Relevance for Paleolithic Archaeology," *World Archaeology* 12 (1980): 153–75.

Killick, David. "Cairo to Cape: The Spread of Metallurgy in Eastern and Southern Africa," in *Archaeometallurgy in Global Perspective*, edited by Benjamin W. Roberts and Christopher P. Thornton, 509–27. New York: Springer, 2014.

Trigger, Bruce G. *A History of Archaeological Thought*. 2nd ed. New York: Cambridge University Press, 2006.

Whittaker, John C. *Flintknapping: Making and Understanding Stone Tools*. Austin, TX: University of Texas Press, 2014.

PEOPLING THE WORLD
Human Dispersals to Australia, the Americas, and the Pacific

4

In December 1831, the young Charles Darwin embarked on a five-year round-the-world voyage of scientific exploration. He set sail aboard a British naval vessel—HMS *Beagle*—as a naturalist and gentleman companion to the captain. While in the Galapagos, a chain of islands on the equator some 600 miles (966 km) west of the Pacific coast of South America, he collected specimens of birds and other animals with a range of physical traits. He would later identify, for example, a group of related species of finch with beak sizes that varied according to their diet. This and similar observations of different outcomes in different environments led him to conceive of the idea of "descent with modification," which later became his theory of evolution. The Galapagos finches, in other words, must all have descended from the same ancestor species and over time changed in different ways in response to the specifics of the islands' environment.

As groups of *Homo sapiens* dispersed around the globe, they, too, had to adapt to the varied environments they encountered along the way. In their cases, the adaptations were not solely biological but also cultural. For example, when European sailors reached the scattered islands of the Pacific Ocean, they found them inhabited by people with significant cultural differences who nonetheless shared enough in common with the explorers, particularly the use of language, to suggest that they had all descended from an ancestral people who mastered the ability to navigate safely thousands of miles of open ocean.

In the previous chapters, we traced humans' origins in Africa and their dispersal into Europe and the Near East. Dispersal across the world is one of the most important ways in which humans have transformed the face of this planet. The world would have changed far less if our presence had been limited to only a small island. The migration of humans across the globe led to the movement of many other organisms into new environments. Domesticated pigs, dogs, and cattle were purposefully taken by boat across seas by humans; vermin, weeds, and diseases moved into entirely new ecosystems—many spreading unhampered.

Migration, however, was not easy or simple, and every continent has its own story for how humans arrived, how they adapted and developed diverse cultures, and how they modified the environment. In this chapter, we explore what archaeology can tell us about the great human dispersals to the rest of the world: in particular, Australia, the Americas, and the remote islands of the Pacific.

Inhabiting Australia 74

Human Dispersals in the Americas 81

Inhabiting the Pacific 87

Methods: Archaeological Survey 91

Peopling and the Anthropocene 94

Opposite A *vaka* (traditional sailing canoe) in the waters of Tonga, in the South Pacific Ocean. The double hull provides great stability and can be assembled with traditional ship-building techniques.

Key Concepts

- The peopling of Australia, the Pacific, and the Americas; its history as understood through archaeological evidence
- The archaeological survey methods for discovering evidence
- Archaeology and conflicting claims to ownership of the past

INHABITING AUSTRALIA

While Charles Darwin was back home in England, musing for nearly forty years about the cause of diversity in nature before publishing his theory of evolution by natural selection, young Alfred Russell Wallace was arriving at the same theory, based on his observations of plants and animals in the tropical islands of Indonesia and New Guinea. Among his insights, Wallace noted that islands close to the Asian mainland were populated with distinctly Asian animals, such local species of mammals as tigers, elephants, bears, and apes. Across the sea passages between the islands [**4.1**], however, Wallace observed a change: further east, the Asian mammals were absent, and in their place marsupials, such as kangaroos, and unique species, such as the Komodo dragon (a large, intelligent lizard with a poisonous bite), thrived. The deep waters of the transition zone between these two regions, known as **Wallacea**, acted as a barrier that prevented mammals, with few exceptions, from reaching Australia, even with the low sea level that prevailed during the Pleistocene. One of those exceptions was us—*Homo sapiens*—and it is possible we brought the others (rats and dogs) with us, as companions or stowaways in our boats. We know this

4.1 Map of Wallacea, where *Homo sapiens* traversed the open waters some 65,000 years ago.

Wallacea A zone of islands within a stretch of deep water that has separated Australia from Southeast Asia for 70 million years.

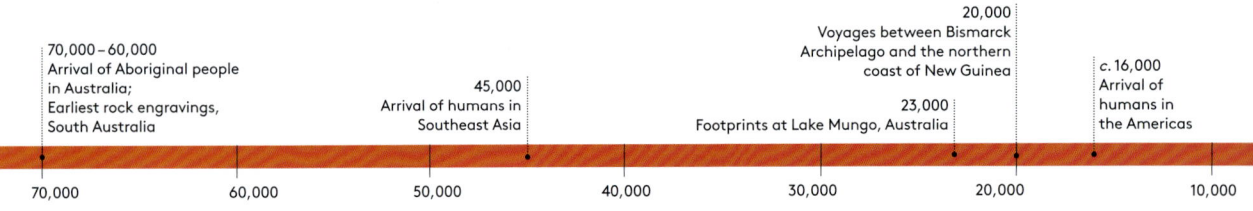

because the earliest artifacts created by *Homo sapiens* in Australia date to around 65,000 years ago, and the only way humankind could have arrived in Australia was by crossing the open waters of Wallacea.

Reaching Australia, and traveling beyond it, would have required boats, or perhaps rafts made from bamboo. We will probably never know for sure if these ancient explorers were accidentally swept to unfamiliar shores, or if, as some speculate, they could see the smoke plumes of natural fires and set out deliberately to encounter new land.

The oldest known site in northern Australia, the 65,000-year-old rock shelter of Madjedbebe, yielded tools made from quartz. These were used for shaping wooden tools, crushing volcanic rock to make heavy axes, and grinding down hematite and ocher, both of which were probably used for making pigment. Residues and the preserved parts of plants also point to the grinding of seeds, which when coupled with the tools indicates a broad range of technologies for hunting and gathering. These skills would have helped the newcomers to disperse rapidly throughout the continent, adapting to new environments as they went, but also transforming them in the process. Humans were a new addition to the ecosystem of Australia, and their entry into this ancient landscape would change it forever.

The First Hunters of Australia

The Australia first encountered by humans [**4.2**, p. 76] was not the Australia of today: it was a rich ecosystem populated with **megafauna**, animals that were considerably larger than their modern descendants. Many giant species, including kangaroos, wallabies, echidnas, and wombats, were found in Australia's varied environments, and these creatures would not have recognized humans as a threat. Over the last 50,000 years, all of Australia's megafauna have become extinct—and archaeologists have long debated the cause. Did such extinctions result from human hunting, or simply the climatic transition from the cool, dry Pleistocene to the warm, wet Holocene? We now know that the story is much more complex than a basic either/or, but humans did play a part. Archaeological sites throughout Australia reveal a rich story of human dispersal, adaptation, and ecological change. Fossils, such as those found at the Tight Entrance Cave in southwestern Australia, suggest that Australia's humans and megafauna coexisted for approximately 13,000 years following colonization. But human presence also brought change, in the form of fires used for hunting. Humans used fire to drive animals from stands of dense vegetation so they could be more easily captured, but the same fires could also burn down thousands of acres of natural habitat. The recent dating of fossils in Australia reveals that giant wallabies and wombats went extinct between 61,000 and 51,000 years ago, and all other megafauna disappeared between 44,000 and 35,000 years ago. These trends do not correspond neatly with paleoclimatic data for climatic changes: earlier periods of cool, dry conditions, or warm, wet ones, were not the catalysts for similar extinctions.

megafauna Large animals especially associated with the Ice Age/Pleistocene.

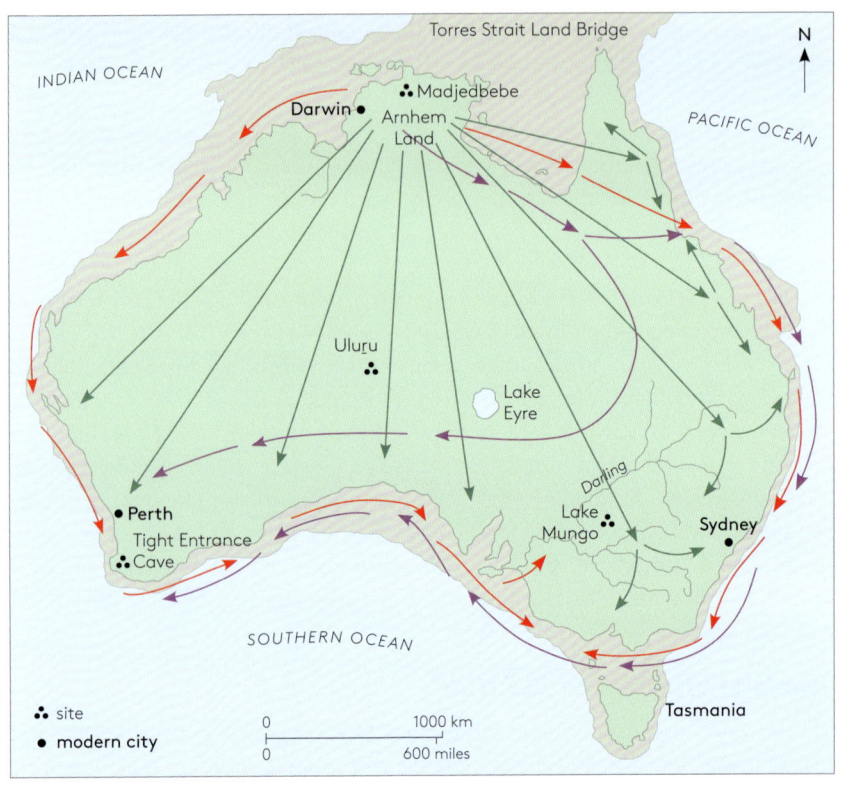

4.2 Map of Australia, *c.* 65,000 years ago, showing Madjedbebe, Lake Mungo, Uluru (Ayers Rock), and multiple possible routes (see arrows in three colors) of human dispersal.

4.3 Lake and marsh landscape, similar to the Willandra Lakes region 40,000 years ago. In contrast to the modern desert currently occupying this region, the lakes and marshes would have provided rich foraging for Australia's hunter-gatherers.

LAKE MUNGO What did cause the extinctions? Local transformations brought about by humans are the likely culprit. Although direct evidence of human hunting of megafauna is rare, ecological change from man-made fires, and humans' wide dispersal throughout Australia, would have fragmented the resources required by the largest animals. The predatory pursuit of megafauna that were slow to reproduce would have also contributed to their slow demise. As the animals disappeared, humans, as evidenced in their tools and food-processing technologies, transitioned to foraging for other, smaller, and more plentiful foods. At Lake Mungo, a site in southeastern Australia, hunters had gathered for millennia. Lake Mungo is a dry lake bed in the Willandra Lakes region of New South Wales [**4.3**]. Today, this region, with its forbidding desert landscape, seems an unlikely site of attraction for ancient humans. Fifty thousand years ago it was an inland region of freshwater lakes teeming with shellfish, crayfish, frogs, and fish and fringed with shady parklands and rich, marshy shores.

geomorphologist A scientist who studies the features of Earth's surface to understand geological processes.

In 1968, Jim Bowler, an Australian **geomorphologist**, was at work in Lake Mungo when he came across a deposit of fragmented, burned bone in the lake's shoreline sediments. Bowler alerted archaeologists at Australian National University to his find, and they quickly began to excavate the site. The bones, they determined, were the remains of a woman who had been cremated 26,000 years ago and buried near a campsite that still exhibited the depressions of a shallow hearth. The camp remains included the shells of mussels, eggshells (from large emu, an ostrichlike ground bird), and charred fish and animal bones; these remnants were surrounded by discarded scrapers and tools used for chopping.

Continuing excavations and study at Lake Mungo revealed numerous campsites of different ages, reflecting varied adaptive strategies and social functions over the past 50,000 years. For example, some were favored places where groups gathered repeatedly, whereas others were one-time camps yielding the remains of a single meal. More burial sites were also found, including some graves that had been sprinkled with red ocher, a pigment that must have come from afar because it is not native to the Willandra Lakes region. During this era, red ocher was used for painting designs on rock outcrops, and it may have also adorned human bodies. Spreading it on the bodies of the dead likely had deep cultural significance.

In sum, the finds at Lake Mungo paint a picture of Ice Age hunters who exploited such marsupials as the rat kangaroo, brown-haired wallaby, and hairy-nosed wombat on the arid plains and returned to the lakeside to net fish and collect mollusks in late spring through the dry summer—a way of life remarkably similar to that of more recent Aboriginal groups.

4.4 Ground-edge axes were probably used for woodworking and clearing brush in Australia shortly after the first human colonists arrived. This fragment, which shows distinctly polished edges, is approximately 44,000 years old.

Ground-edge axes Stone axes that were made by humans in Australia between 49,000 and 45,000 years ago, and which represent the creation of a new technology.

First People The descendants of the first humans to live in Australia and the Americas.

Dispersing through Australia

No one is certain how humans spread from an initial landfall on the Australian continent. Did they follow the coasts to the south, using marine resources familiar to them? Did they spread rapidly into open plains and quickly learn to hunt the big herbivorous marsupials that would have failed to recognize them as predators? Either way, they explored and colonized all of Australia by 50,000 years ago, and had arrived in New Guinea—which was connected to Australia via the Torres Straits land bridge—by 40,000 years ago. Sea-level rise since the end of the Pleistocene has flooded the ancient coastline, so the sites of coastal routes, if they existed, are now lost to us. Sites that were in the interior of Australia, however, have revealed tantalizing clues about diverse strategies for hunting and gathering.

Large marsupials were hunted, and a variety of seeds and nuts collected and processed for consumption. Birds and insects were also trapped and roasted whole. **Ground-edge axes** (**4.4**; stone axes with beveled edges that were ground smooth) emerged as a novel technology in northern Australia at this time. Perhaps used to cut wood, these tools demonstrate how earlier technologies were adapted to the Australian environment. In generating new human niches in Australia, human populations thrived and increased. One of the reasons why more archaeological sites of a later date (20,000–10,000 years ago) exist is that more humans were alive then to create them. Early sites that are older than 40,000 years are rare and difficult to find.

Evidence from the Dreamtime

The Aboriginal people are the **First People** of Australia. They are the direct descendants of the pioneers who crossed Wallacea 65,000 years ago and dispersed throughout the continent. Not surprisingly, they feel a deep connection to the landscape their ancestors inhabited for tens of thousands of years. The Australian past that archaeologists seek to unravel is the Aborigines' past, known as the Dreamtime. And Aboriginals have developed their own account of, and way to access, this time of creation.

Aborigines regard features of the landscape as points of connection with their ancestors, and anchor themselves and their social networks to these places. (See the "Who Owns the Past? Uluṟu" section that follows.) For Aboriginals, Dreamtime ancestors are not only past but also present in the here and now, existing in a parallel, mythical time, which is accessible through the telling and retelling of stories, rock paintings, and forms on the landscape [**4.5, 4.6**]. Ceremonies also imbue physical places with social meaning. Aboriginal groups further understand Dreamtime beings as totemic—linked to specific plants and animals in the natural world. Through them, the living remain in contact with the past.

In tying the past to present, Dreamtime stories may thus encode kernels of information about the arrival and dispersal of humans in Australia. According to one story, the Riratjingu people of Arnhem Land in northern Australia claim to be descended from the great Djankawu, who came from the island of Baralku far

4.5 Aboriginal artists from Warakurna in western Australia collaborate on a painting depicting the Lungarta (Blue Tongue lizard). Artists painting on-country, clockwise from bottom: Dorcas Bennett, Nancy Jackson, Winnie Woods, Molly Yates, Thelma McLean, Polly Butler-Jackson, Eunice Porter, and Judith Chambers.

4.6 Aboriginal rock art in Arnhem Land, Australia, showing a Dreamtime ancestor on the left, and a barramundi (Asian sea bass) on the right.

4.7 Uluṟu (Ayers Rock) is a culturally important location for Aboriginal Australians: it is a sacred site, marking the place where their ancestors first lived and enjoyed the natural world.

across the sea. "Our spirits return to Baralku when we die. Djankawu came in his canoe with his two sisters, following the morning star which guided them to the shores of Yelangbara on the eastern coast of Arnhem Land." From this and other Australian Dreamings, we learn that canoes and passage across the sea are recurrent motifs in Aboriginal traditions.

Who Owns the Past? Uluṟu

One of the most well-known rock formations in Australia is Uluṟu [4.7], a unique sandstone mountain on the flat plains near Alice Springs in the Northern Territory. Rare and richly symbolic, it is the landscape for the stories and sites of the local Aboriginal people, the Aṉangu, and has served as a literal touchstone for Aboriginal histories of, and connections with, the land. According to the Aṉangu, ancestral Mala men ascended Uluṟu upon their arrival in this part of Australia, marking the site as sacred. Rock art images have been uncovered at Uluṟu and its neighbor Kata Tjuṯa; some date to Antiquity, others to more recent times. Along with the regional ecosystem of man-made grasslands, which have been maintained through the traditional practice of frequent burning to provide a habitat for animals and plants, the abundant rock images and other archaeological features attest to a cultural landscape with a long history.

Although Uluṟu is perhaps the most sacred site for many Aboriginal people, it is also a national park that other Australians (who trace their ancestry to nineteenth-century immigrants from other parts of the world) use for hiking, rock climbing, and various leisure activities. For Aboriginals, respectfully maintaining the site is important to preserving their past and is a component of their modern religious life, which includes stewarding the natural resources and stories that link them. In 1987, the Australian government successfully secured a World Heritage Site designation from the United Nations Education, Scientific and Cultural Organization

(UNESCO) that recognized the uncommon geology and natural environment of Uluṟu. (By definition, a World Heritage Site is a site of equal importance to all people of the world, transcending local interest and bringing with its designation an extensive, UNESCO-approved conservation and management plan, media attention, prestige to the sponsoring nation, and tourism.)

Soon after its World Heritage Site designation, even more tourists clambered over Uluṟu. With the Aṉangu's official removal as custodians of the parklands, they became estranged from the places intrinsic to their cultural and social identity. This inevitably led to feelings of disenfranchisement among local communities, leaving many of them alienated and embittered. To address the Aṉangu's grievances, UNESCO in 1994 renamed and expanded the original World Heritage Site as Uluṟu–Kata Tjuṯa National Park. This action recognized the cultural heritage of Aboriginal groups whose narrative of dispersal is literally part of the grasslands, rock art, and native stories of the central Australian landscape.

HUMAN DISPERSALS IN THE AMERICAS

When ice sheets last covered much of the world, their edges teemed with big animals. While humans in France decorated the walls of Lascaux with images of bulls and reindeer around 17,000 years ago (see Chapter 2), the Americas were all but empty of people. The Americas were discovered far later than Australia, Europe, and Asia. Starting perhaps 38,000 years ago, the First Peoples of the Americas arrived in Alaska from Asia during low sea levels, when water was concentrated in glaciers and a vast landmass called **Beringia** connected Russia to the American continent [**4.8**, p. 82]. A rich landscape of its own, Beringia supported human populations who hunted and fed on the resources of lake margins, not knowing that two continents of mountains, plains, forests, and rain forests lay to the east. Only when the glaciers began to melt around 14,500 years ago was the pathway to a new landscape revealed. Between the great **Laurentide and Cordilleran ice sheets** that covered most of the North American continent during the last glacial maximum, an ice-free corridor opened up, offering a direct route into the heart of North America.

It is likely that humans did not move the moment the corridor appeared. A recent study argues that the ice-free corridor between the Laurentide and Cordilleran sheets was too barren to support large game, and hence would not have drawn hunters in pursuit, until 12,600 years ago. By examining the DNA of plants and animals preserved in lake beds at the latest bottleneck to the corridor, the Danish evolutionary geneticist Eske Willerslev and his colleagues determined that the absence of big game and the vegetation needed to support them would have discouraged or failed to attract humans. After 12,600 years ago, grasslands appeared that could have supported mammoths and bison, and eventually trees predominated and sustained elk. Of course, this scenario and its implications for a late human dispersal through the 932-mile (1,500-km) corridor assume that all of its areas were equally barren and that hunters pursued only large game. The presence of lakes inhabited

Beringia A landmass that connected Russia to the American continent during the Ice Age, when sea levels were lower.

Laurentide and Cordilleran ice sheets Massive glaciers that covered North America.

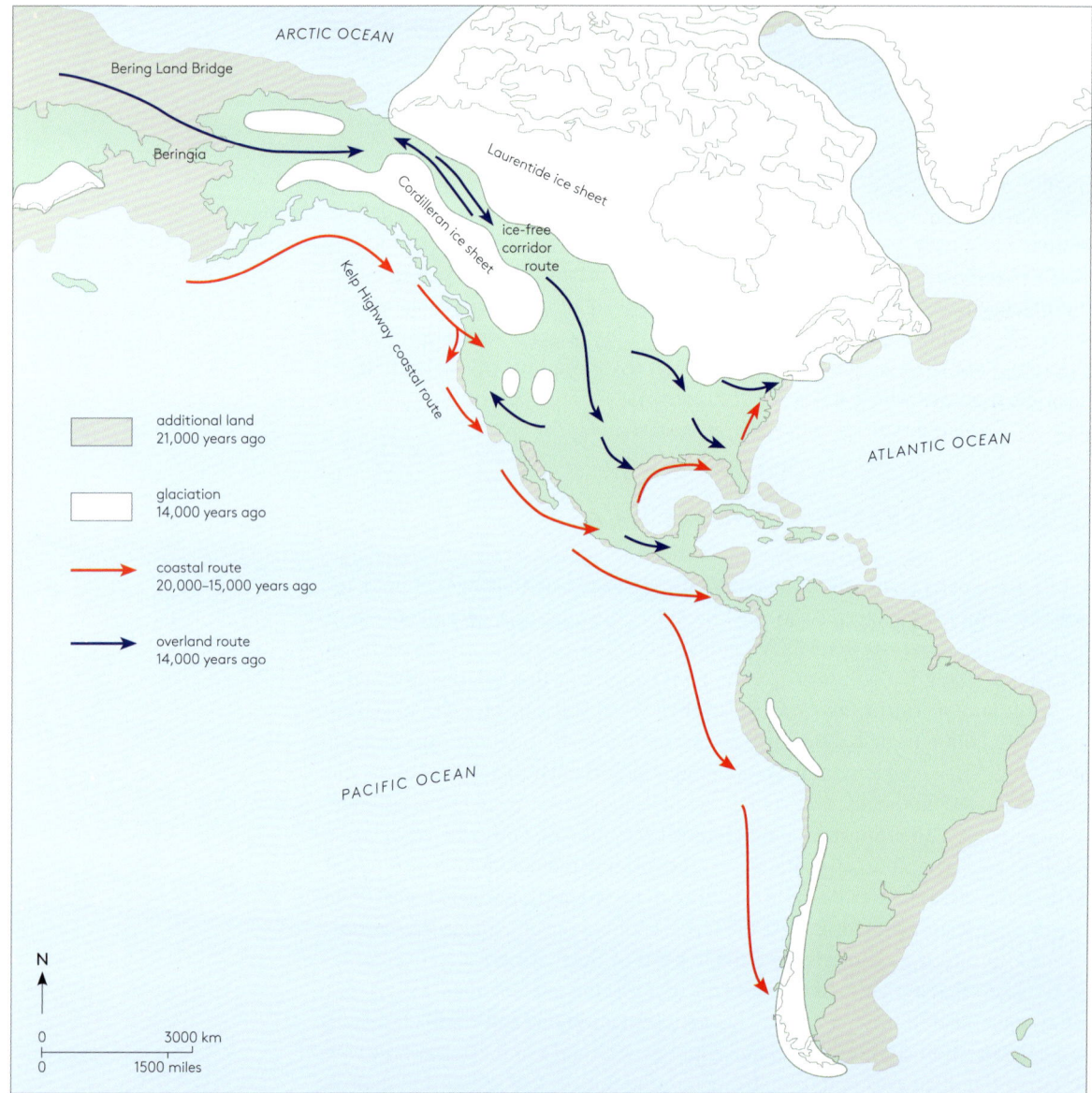

4.8 Map of paleocoastlines and the Bering Land Bridge. Humans entered North America—the New World—at the end of the Pleistocene epoch, as ice sheets were receding, and found there abundant resources for their initially small populations.

by waterfowl and surrounded by stunted sedges could have offered resources for humans using flexible, adaptive technologies that allowed more rapid dispersal into new regions.

The corridor between the Laurentide and Cordilleran sheets may not have been the earliest gateway, however. A coastal route known as the **Kelp Highway** has been proposed as a more likely possibility by some archaeologists. It would have required boats and careful navigation, skirting the edges of the ice in Alaska and

Canada. But given the consistency of the marine environment along the western coast of North America, and also the richness of its kelp beds—an ecosystem that supports significant numbers of plants and animals, including seabirds, seals, whales, and dolphins, and a vast quantity of mollusks, crustaceans, and fish—the Kelp Highway would have offered Pleistocene foragers a secure and swift entryway into the Americas as early as 16,000 years ago.

Whichever route they took, we have no reason to believe these immigrants had an intended destination or plans to colonize. Instead, we imagine mobile, small groups that pursued game—or any readily available resources—with great success, reproducing new family groups in an Ice Age interval of relative warmth and plenty.

The exact time frame for humans' arrival in the Americas is not fixed. It continues to change because of new research and advances in dating technologies. There have, nevertheless, long been hints of early humans' presence in the New World. The underwater sinkhole at the Page-Ladson prehistory site, along the Gulf Coast of Florida, is a long way from either the ice-free corridor or Kelp Highway proposed as the routes of entry to the New World. It would have taken people some time to journey that far. Scuba-diving archaeologists excavated Page-Ladson, and they found stone flakes, charcoal as old as 14,550 years, and a butchered mastodon tusk that had been deposited before a local mastodon die-off. The die-off event was determined via the analysis of fungal spore densities, which sought to measure the amount of dung produced by the mastodons. (Theirs was generally rich in fungus.) The dung and spores had disappeared, as had the mastodons, after 11,000 years ago.

At Meadowcroft Rockshelter [**4.9**] in western Pennsylvania, thin layers of charcoal associated with human occupation yielded radiocarbon dates 14,500 years old; several go back 17,000 years. Such early dates as these have been frequently

Kelp Highway A proposed route from Beringia to the Americas along the Pacific coastline, which followed the distribution of seaweed beds close to shore.

4.9 Archaeologist Jim Adovasio examines some of the deposits (indicated by the round markers) of Meadowcroft Rockshelter in western Pennsylvania. Archaeological evidence includes stone tools and fire hearths, and radiocarbon dating of charcoal suggests human occupation some 17,000 years ago.

Clovis Early hunters of megafauna in North America known by the distinctive point of their speartips, the Clovis point.

disputed, usually because alternative explanations exist for the connection of very old organic materials to stone artifacts. Are artifacts and organics in situ (that is, found where they were discarded), or did they settle together (into an archaeological context) through geological processes? Are samples contaminated by older, natural charcoal, such as that produced when lightning strikes a tree?

The strongest evidence for early dispersal into the Americas has been found at the site of Monte Verde [**4.10**], located in southern Chile. Few agree with excavator Tom Dillehay's analysis that the organic materials lying at the bottom of the site were modified by humans around 33,000 years ago, but the upper levels contain the unmistakable remains of hearths, a wood and hide tent, mastodon meat and hide, and the remains of plants (including seaweed from the distant coast) that had been gathered *c.* 14,200 years ago. Hailed as the most important and securely dated early site in the Americas, Monte Verde provides proof that at least a small population of hunter-gatherers made it all the way to South America's western coast *before* the ice-free corridor opened.

The sites at Meadowcroft and Monte Verde indicate that small numbers of hunter-gatherers had scattered across North and South America more than 14,000 years ago. Known as Pre-Clovis, these populations were later incorporated into a much larger population that swept through the ice-free corridor into North America between 13,100 and 12,900 years ago. Identified by their use of a distinctive, bifacially worked, stone speartip known as the Clovis point, the **Clovis** people (Chapter 6) were swift hunters who appear to have focused on megafauna, such as mammoths, mastodons, and giant sloth. Unlike the human colonization of Australia 65,000

4.10 At Monte Verde, Chile, a semi-circular outline of a former hut preserved the remains of seaweed that had been collected from the coast.

years ago, the arrival of humans in North America at this time does correspond to the warming of the climate at the end of the Pleistocene. Human hunting, as well as local and global environmental changes, coalesced to bring about the extinction of the American megafauna.

Who Owns the Past? NAGPRA and Kennewick Man

In 1990, the United States Congress passed the Native American Graves Protection and Repatriation Act (NAGPRA), giving jurisdiction over burial sites and sacred objects to Native American tribal groups that could show a close affiliation with them. In the case of direct descendants, this legislation was straightforward. For instance, their grandparents' graves and what is in (or on) them are theirs. No matter how valuable any remains might be to science, and irrespective of whether they were buried on public land that the tribes no longer possess, the Native Americans own their relative's remains and have a say in how they will be treated.

In the case of Kennewick Man [**4.11**], a chance discovery in 1996 on public land in Washington State (along the banks of the Columbia River within the city of Kennewick) turned up one of the oldest skeletons in America. He lived after the expansion of Clovis culture in North America and his skeleton was unusual in several regards; this lent support to the hypothesis that he was a descendant of one of the first humans in North America. Shortly after the discovery of Kennewick Man, the managers of the land where he was found—the US Army Corps of Engineers—decided to award his remains to the Native Americans who had historically lived in the area, the Umatilla. The Umatilla wished to rebury him without further study, but a team of archaeologists sued the Corps, arguing that the remains should be available for scientific study because of their possible link to an ancient and unknown American population. They further asserted that because Kennewick Man had lived 9,000 years ago and possessed a unique biology, it would be difficult, if not impossible, ever to link his skeleton to a particular living tribe, as NAGPRA required. Over a period of nine years, the courts ruled that Kennewick Man had no closely affiliated descendant group and allowed enough scientific study to establish the basis for that decision. For years, the Umatilla tribe continued to file legal appeals, insisting that Kennewick Man was their ancestor, and it was thus their legal responsibility to rebury him. No further study of his remains was permitted until 2004, when scientists won their case in a higher court.

In 2015, a new twist developed: Danish geneticists established a direct relationship between the ancient DNA preserved in a bone from Kennewick Man's hand and the DNA of modern Native American tribes from the region. Armed with these results, the Army Corps of Engineers invited Native Americans to file anew their NAGPRA repatriation claim, and in 2016 the US House of Representatives and Senate passed legislation returning the remains of Kennewick Man to the Umatilla. In February 2017, he was reburied in a secret location.

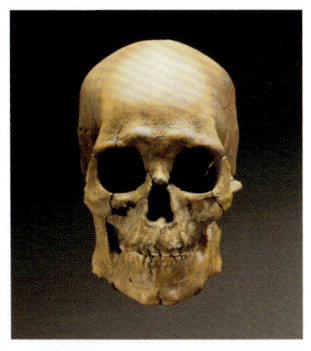

Top: **4.11a Plastic cast of Kennewick Man's skull;** Above: **4.11b Reconstruction of his face.** Referred to as "the most important human skeleton ever found in North America," the Kennewick Man, a 9,000-year-old Native American, was unearthed in 1996 in Washington State. His remains were reburied in 2017.

Archaeological Ethics

People's ethics about the display of the dead have changed over the past century, in part through their understanding that one museum's mummy is someone else's relative. The Egyptian Museum in Cairo no longer displays the mummies of the Pharaohs; native people around the world actively resist the destruction of their ancestors' remains and sacred sites. In turn, archaeologists have been changed. We respect that all humans have an interest in the past and wish to share in its lessons, and must be included in decision-making related to its artifacts. Archaeological ethics are critical to preserving the past for the future.

The following list paraphrases the Society for American Archaeology's (SAA) principles on archaeological ethics:

- **Stewardship:** Archaeologists must preserve and protect the archaeological record by practicing and advancing stewardship for the benefit of all people, and promote public understanding.

- **Accountability:** Archaeologists must acknowledge public accountability, and commit to making every reasonable effort to consult effectively with all groups affected by archaeologists' work.

- **Discouraging Commercialization:** Archaeologists should discourage and avoid activities that enhance the commercial value of archaeological objects, especially those unavailable for scientific study or held privately.

- **Public Education and Outreach:** Archaeologists should reach out to, and cooperate with, others interested in the archaeological record to improve its preservation, protection, and interpretation. They must also cultivate public understanding of how archaeologists do their work.

- **Timely Sharing of Data:** After archaeologists have gained primary access to documents and original materials, they should treat such materials in line with the principles of stewardship, making them available to others in a permanent, accessible repository.

- **Public Reporting and Publication:** Archaeologists should share their knowledge within a reasonable period and as widely as possible through publications or other formats. At the same time, an interest in preserving and protecting in situ archaeological sites must be taken into account when publishing information about their locations and features.

- **Records Preservation:** Archaeologists should work actively to preserve, and provide long-term access to, archaeological collections, records, and reports.

- **Training and Resources:** Archaeologists must ensure they have adequate training, experience, facilities, and other support when conducting any program of research.

INHABITING THE PACIFIC

Given the distances involved, the ecological diversity of the islands that were settled, and the remoteness of their locations, the peopling of the Pacific Islands marks one of the last great dispersals in human history. It is also arguably one of the most remarkable human achievements. Along with sites in Australia and New Guinea, the vast space of Niah Cave in Borneo provides evidence of modern humans' presence in Southeast Asia some 45,000 years ago. Bones recovered from the cave indicate that hunters subsisted on the animals of the woodlands and forests. On the islands to the east of New Guinea, such as New Ireland, mollusks and fish became the staple proteins of island foragers. These islanders were the first maritime foragers of the Indo-Pacific, and by 20,000 years ago they were making routine voyages between the islands of the Bismarck Archipelago and the northern coast of New Guinea.

Between 9,000 and 6,000 years ago, small communities in the western highlands of New Guinea began to cultivate gardens, fostering new human niches that supported the growth of banana (*Musa* spp.) and taro (*Colocasia esculenta*), which later left small fragments of silica from their leaves (known as **phytoliths**) in the soil. These were the beginnings of agriculture in this part of the world, and within a few thousand years, such crops would be incorporated into other agricultural traditions that were expanding beyond Asia. By 2000 BCE, communities of fisher-farmers throughout Island Southeast Asia (maritime Southeast Asia), the coast of New Guinea, and the Bismarck Archipelago were interacting with one another via short sea voyages, and sharing crops, pottery, and genes. By 1350 BCE, a new culture known as **Lapita**, which had a distinctive pottery style (see 7.10, p. 156), had emerged in the region. The Lapita pushed human dispersal to its final limit by journeying into the remote Pacific Ocean, crossing thousands of miles of open ocean, and locating the most distant islands on the planet.

Around 1200 BCE, Lapita communities left the Bismarcks and colonized the archipelagoes of Vanuatu, New Caledonia, Fiji, Tonga, and Samoa, all of which contained islands assembled in wide-ranging arcs. Voyaging to these islands required canoes that were fitted with an outrigger, an extension on the side of the craft that provided stability, and a sail that could be maneuvered to navigate the canoe with or against the wind. Voyaging also required a great deal of knowledge, which more than 60,000 years of inhabiting the island-strewn world of Wallacea, the Bismarcks, and Island Southeast Asia would have undoubtedly generated. Waves and wind direction were used to determine and maintain a vessel's course, and at night the stars and planets allowed for further measurement of direction and distance. Voyages would have lasted for many days or weeks and may have sometimes ended in failure: vessels were lost, or people simply turned around and went back home. The vast number of Lapita sites in Fiji and Tonga, however, suggests that once the location of new islands was determined, colonists arrived in droves. Lapita people brought with them domesticated plants and animals, replicating their home island on each new island they colonized. A new anthropogenic human niche spread across the vast distances of the Pacific Ocean. The period of Lapita discovery continued until

phytoliths Small fragments of silica from plants; can survive for thousands of years.

Lapita An archaeological culture found in the southwestern Pacific Islands, *c.* 1200 BCE.

800 BCE, when the islands of Samoa were finally reached. Further to the east, the small and distant islands of Tahiti, the Marquesas, and Hawai'i would not be discovered for another thousand years. This pause in exploration has been explained as a logistical hurdle—the distances involved were too great, and the islands too remote, to be discovered using the existing technology.

When British explorer Captain James Cook sailed to one of these distant islands, Tahiti, in 1769, he encountered Tupaia, a Tahitian navigator who had retained knowledge of the names and locations of many islands, though he had not visited these places himself. Tupaia even created a map for Cook; it indicated the location of islands more than 1,684 miles (3,000 km) away from Tahiti. At this time, voyaging to very distant places, such as Fiji, had not occurred in a century, but Tupaia's father and grandfather had passed down to him this knowledge of their existence. Tupaia would later voyage with Cook's crew to New Zealand, where he served as an interpreter and was welcomed by the Maori people as an expert navigator.

Cook recognized the importance of Tupaia's knowledge when he encountered the Hawaiian Islands in 1778, which were more than 2,485 miles (4,000 km) to the north of Tahiti. Despite the great distance, the islands were populated by people whose culture and language shared much in common with the Tahitians', indicating that ancient voyages identical to those recorded on Tupaia's map [**4.12**] had once connected these distant people. As Australian Aborigines did, Pacific Islanders

4.12 A map created by Tupaia, a Tahitian navigator who met Captain Cook in 1769. It records Tupaia's knowledge of the location of islands in Tahiti and beyond, as taught to him by his father and grandfather.

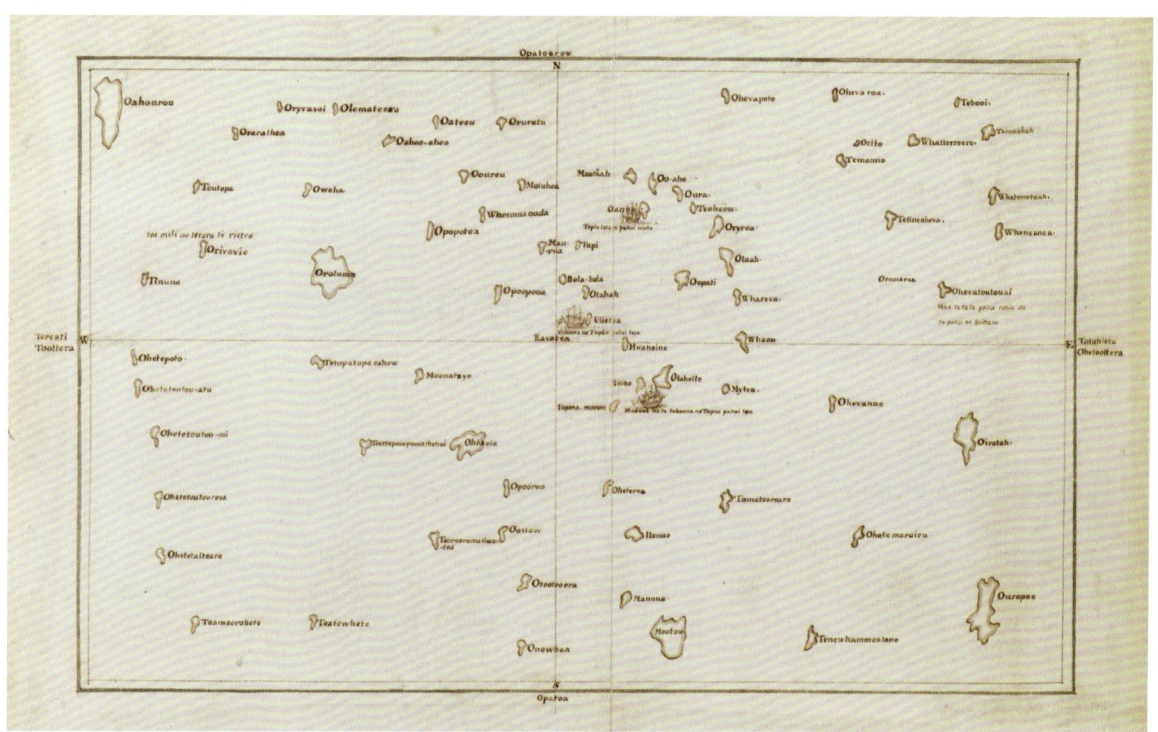

transmitted precious information in their recitations of chants, stories, and genealogies. These oral histories offered the names of people and places, becoming a critical record of the voyages of the past. Narratives of ancestors and their arrivals in new lands are important clues for archaeologists who seek to understand the processes of human dispersals.

One of the great adventurers of the twentieth century, anthropologist Ben Finney, used the clues embedded in oral traditions to develop an experimental study of human dispersals. Scholars studying the colonization of the Pacific Islands had argued that long-distance voyages were something of a fluke, a stroke of good fortune for one of perhaps thousands of flimsy craft that vanished in the open ocean. Finney disagreed, and a team of Hawaiian researchers, informed by oral traditions that recounted great voyages, had greater confidence in Hawaiian ingenuity. In 1973, they founded the Polynesian Voyaging Society, which sought to rediscover and reinvigorate the tradition of long-distance voyaging. By the 1970s, computer models had been developed that suggested a systematic search of the ocean was possible using outbound sailing and return, even if no land was found [**4.13**] The idea of humans' deliberate dispersal across the Pacific gained favor, but how did sailors seek and find land beyond the boundaries of no return?

A bold experiment provided the answer to that very question. Finney and other volunteers at the Polynesian Voyaging Society built a long-distance voyaging canoe,

4.13 Map of the Indo-Pacific region showing the likely routes of island colonization, *c.* 1200 BCE to 1500 CE.

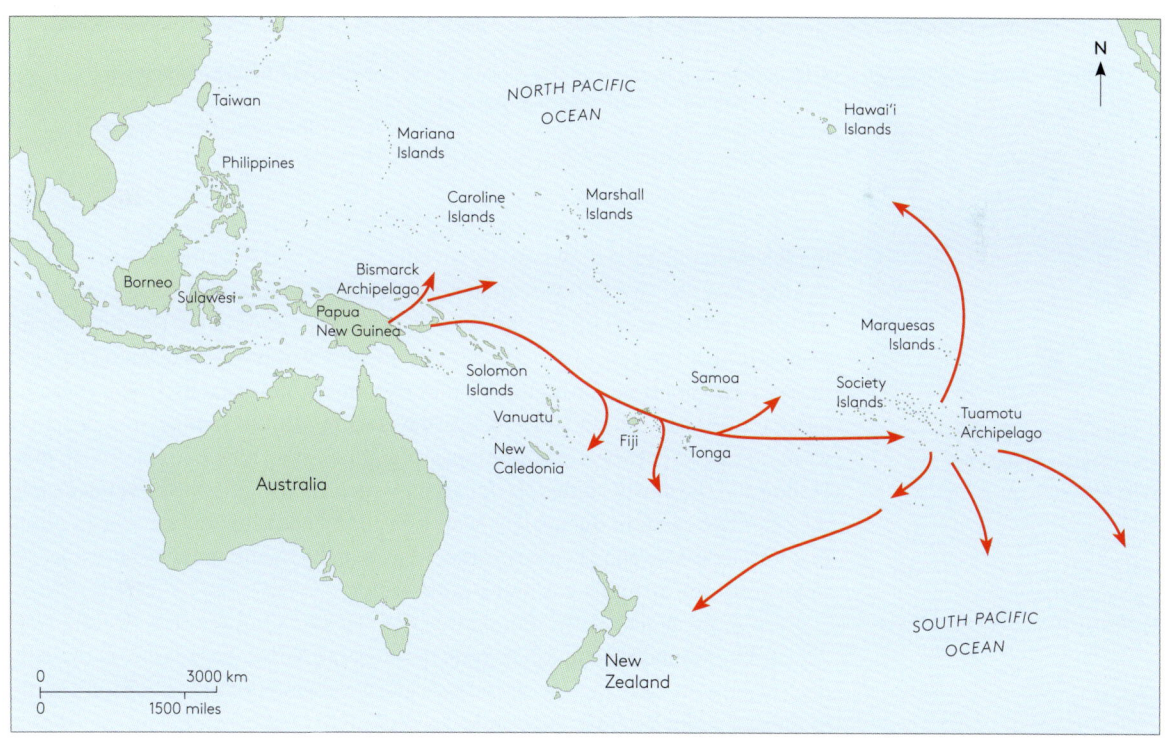

4.14 *Hōkūle'a*, **a modern double-hulled canoe constructed for experiments in ocean voyaging.** The crew of this vessel used the waves, winds, and stars to reach remote islands in the Pacific Ocean, and from 2014 to 2017 they circumnavigated the world. These voyages have inspired a global interest in traditional navigation.

4.15 The pohutukawa tree flowers in summer in New Zealand, signaling the season for voyages from the islands to the north. Just as the oral chants foretold, *Hōkūle'a*'s crew noted pohutukawa flowers in the ocean waters surrounding New Zealand when they arrived in November of 1985.

modeled after historic drawings of Hawaiian canoes and working canoes from the Caroline Islands. They call the canoe *Hōkūle'a* using the Hawaiian name for the star Arcturus, which reaches its zenith directly over the latitude of the Hawaiian archipelago. In an adventure of experimental science, they were joined by Mau Piailug, a master navigator from the island of Satawal in the Caroline Islands, where voyaging using traditional techniques of navigation is still practiced [**4.14**]. Using the stars, wind and wave patterns, and sightings of seabirds returning home to roost, Mau Piailug and the mostly native Hawaiian crew successfully navigated the *Hōkūle'a* to the island of Tahiti in the Society Islands in 1976. Following several oral accounts that linked the Hawaiian people to other islands in the Pacific, the crew later traveled to several more archipelagos in the same area.

Even more significantly, the planners of *Hōkūle'a*'s voyage to southerly New Zealand used modern climate records to select the November season as the only time when cold, rain, high seas, and westerly headwinds would abate sufficiently to allow a canoe to cross 1,600 miles (2,575 km) of cold ocean below the tropics.

Native New Zealand Maori accounts of legendary voyagers specify the lunar month of November as the time of year sages had designated for them to depart from Rarotonga (in the southern Cook Islands). And as the legends also foretold, *Hōkūle'a* arrived among a sea drift of seasonal, scarlet-plumed pohutukawa flowers [**4.15**], thus revealing a sort of botanical code embedded in accounts of long-distance voyaging.

METHODS: ARCHAEOLOGICAL SURVEY

To document the first colonization of an island, archaeologists must find sites, and early sites are rare. Sometimes an outside tip, an accidental discovery, or an oral tradition helps, but archaeologists have also developed a set of survey techniques to locate sites, including unusual or atypical ones.

Archaeologists find sites much the way oceanic explorers found islands, at least in principle, and, as in the instance of long-distance voyagers, we rely on previous information, switch our course depending on what we encounter, and keep careful track of where we have been. Archaeological survey employs both reconnaissance and systematic techniques to gather information, and then uses that information to determine patterns and probabilities of where sites should lie.

For example, it is reasonable to expect that the earliest human settlement of new islands would have occurred in environments most familiar to the colonists—either the coastal areas where fishing techniques and lowland vegetation reminded them of home, or perhaps, for agricultural people, the farming lands most similar to those they left behind. These are the areas to start searching if one is looking for colonization sites. On many of the Pacific Islands, archaeologists have found the earliest sites near the shore, often buried under sediment that washed in as agriculture spread and caused erosion of upper slopes.

An Arabian Example

In the archaeological study of Australia, the earliest sites are frequently located beneath the sea owing to rising sea levels. This problem is not limited to Australia. In Arabia (a peninsula in southwestern Asia that includes Saudi Arabia, Oman, Yemen, and the Persian Gulf States), Joy's research team experienced a similar issue: rising sea levels have submerged the ancient coastal plain. Evidence for early human activities must be located elsewhere. When the team began a survey in Arabia, their research questions were these: When did the Arabian people first adopt and use domesticated plants and animals? Where might these societies have lived?

Survey is an essential part of archaeological work. It is not only something you do before an excavation; it can also be a powerful method in its own right. Systematic survey provides archaeologists with the tools to understand the following: what they have observed and what they might have missed; how rare any recovered remains are; and how thorough their coverage has been. All systematic surveys start with a survey design to plan where archaeologists will go and what they will inventory to understand the relationship of their observations (we call them data) to the entire range of archaeological remains.

In Arabia's Wadi Sana (a wadi is a dried river valley), we opted for a design with several systematic approaches. Wadi Sana is vast, and it would have been impossible to survey the entire region, so a sampling strategy was devised. We designed a survey with intensive coverage of randomly selected strips (transects) across the Wadi Sana [**4.16**, **4.17**], and supplemented it with test excavations, assemblage analysis, and radiocarbon dating to establish a basic sequence of cultural groups through time.

What does it mean to select systematic transects randomly? Our project included an almost 50-mile (80-km) stretch of wadi. In case the middle and far end of the wadi offered very different kinds and distributions of material remains, we did not want to spend all of our time and energy at just one end. It was important that the limited areas that could be surveyed in the time available were representative of all the areas that could not be surveyed. In other words, if the project described a pattern of archaeological remains based on what we observed, such a pattern should also describe the entire wadi. And as the team hoped to find a rare (early) site but had no prior knowledge of where to look, it was important to ensure two circumstances: (1) that as wide a region as possible was considered, and (2) that every site had the same chance of being documented.

With both of those considerations in mind, the transects were randomly selected and systematically surveyed. How did the team refrain from concentrating all the survey transects at one end of Wadi Sana? If the transects were chosen randomly out of all possible selections (each was 328 feet wide, or 100 meters), then could many of them not end up close to one another, with huge gaps between others? A **stratified survey** design was employed to divide the area to be surveyed into sectors, with each sector assigned some of the randomly selected transects. Using convenient artificial sections of latitude, the team imposed additional rules on the random selection process: only one survey transect could be chosen, using random numbers, within each latitudinal band.

Our random, systematic, stratified archaeological survey yielded Manayzah, the earliest site with domesticated sheep and cattle yet found on the Arabian Peninsula. Here, important clues emerged with regard to the identities of the earliest **pastoralists**: they were local South Arabians who used a pressure-flaking technique to make distinctive projectile points. Analysis of the animal bones indicates that these people continued to hunt even as they herded sheep and cattle that originated as domesticates elsewhere. These details suggest that the site was created by a mobile people. At the time of the survey, archaeologists believed that few or no humans inhabited Arabia's interiors, so the pastoralists may have entered a vacant land. The earliest sites with evidence of travelers and their herds would therefore be scarce and difficult to find. Yet, through systematic survey via a random sample, we located one of these sites, which offered new insights into the first food producers of Arabia, who were active 8,000 years ago.

stratified survey A survey technique whereby a landscape is divided into sections before before some of those sections are surveyed.

Pastoralists People who make their living by herding domesticated animals used to produce meat, milk, or wool.

Above: **4.16 An archaeology team begins a survey at Wadi Sana, Yemen.** After establishing an area of the landscape to sample, members of the team walk across it—in a line, to cover the ground with even spacing—and record any objects found on the surface.

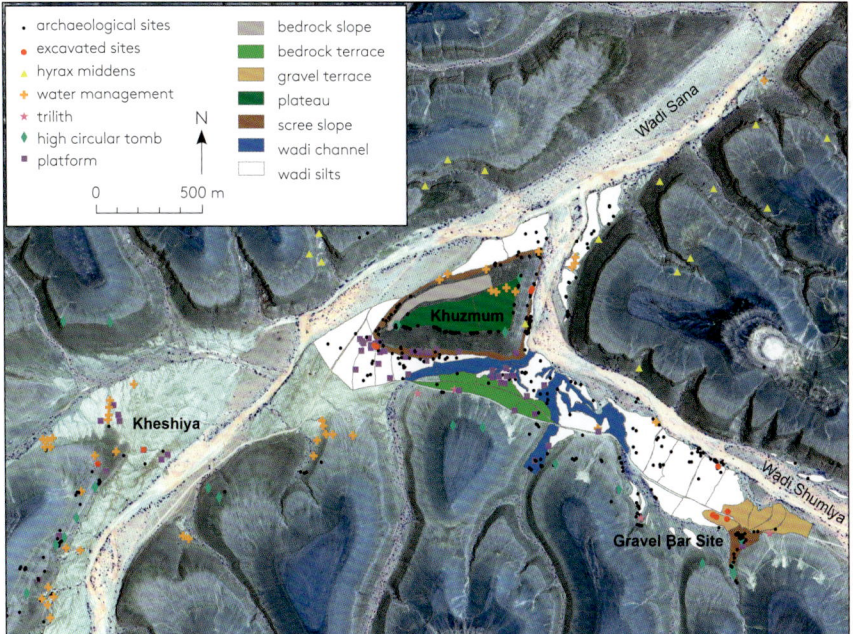

Left: **4.17 An outcome of a survey in Wadi Sana, Yemen.** This image is an overlay of the (colored) areas intensively surveyed by the Roots of Agriculture in Southern Arabia (RASA) Project. The colors indicate types of ground, which help archaeologists better recognize why they find different types of sites in different places.

METHODS: ARCHAEOLOGICAL SURVEY   93

PEOPLING AND THE ANTHROPOCENE

These archaeological examples drawn from the peopling of Australia, the Americas, the Pacific, and Arabia are but a sample of the many episodes of dispersal in our Anthropocene prehistory. Archaeology shows us that humans are mobile and willing to explore and colonize new environments. From the archaeological record, we recognize that people are adaptable, using such technologies as tools, imported plants and animals, and boats to reach new environments as far back as 65,000 years ago.

Colony sites are rare and difficult to find; local informants have thus come to play an important role in understanding dispersals (and in understanding many other aspects of the past, as we will discover later). First Peoples in Australia and the Americas have preserved stories about their colonizing journeys that offer important perspectives; moreover, they are significant stakeholders in the past. One thing that archaeologists, First Peoples, and all others share is the construction of our human niche. As we moved across the globe, our impact on the ecosystems of Australia, the Americas, and the Pacific Islands intensified, changing them dramatically and creating new habitats where humans and other animals might live.

Chapter Questions

1. What archaeological evidence has been used to determine when people first arrived on the Australian continent? How does this peopling narrative compare with the Dreamtime?

2. To what key sites do archaeologists refer to understand the first arrivals of humans to the Americas? What are the principal arguments with regard to the peopling of this continent?

3. Explain the main stages of an archaeological survey, and the benefits and drawbacks of such a survey compared to those of an excavation.

4. What is NAGPRA? How has such a case as the Kennewick Man impacted our understanding of ownership of the past?

Additional Resources

Banning, Edward B. *Archaeological Survey*. New York: Kluwer Academic/Plenum Press, 2002.

Erlandson, Jon M., Braje, Todd J., Gill, Kristina M., and Graham, Michael H. "Ecology of the Kelp Highway: Did Marine Resources Facilitate Human Dispersal from Northeast Asia to the Americas?," *Journal of Island and Coastal Archaeology* (2015): 392–411. doi:10.1080/15564894.2014.1001923.

Finney, Ben. "Myth, Experiment and Polynesian Voyaging," *American Anthropologist* 93 (1991): 383–404.

Smith, Mike. *The Archaeology of Australia's Deserts*. Cambridge, UK: Cambridge University Press, 2013.

Watkins, Joe. "Cultural Nationalists, Internationalists, and 'Intra-nationalists: Who's Right and Whose Right?," *International Journal of Cultural Property* 12 (2005): 78–94.

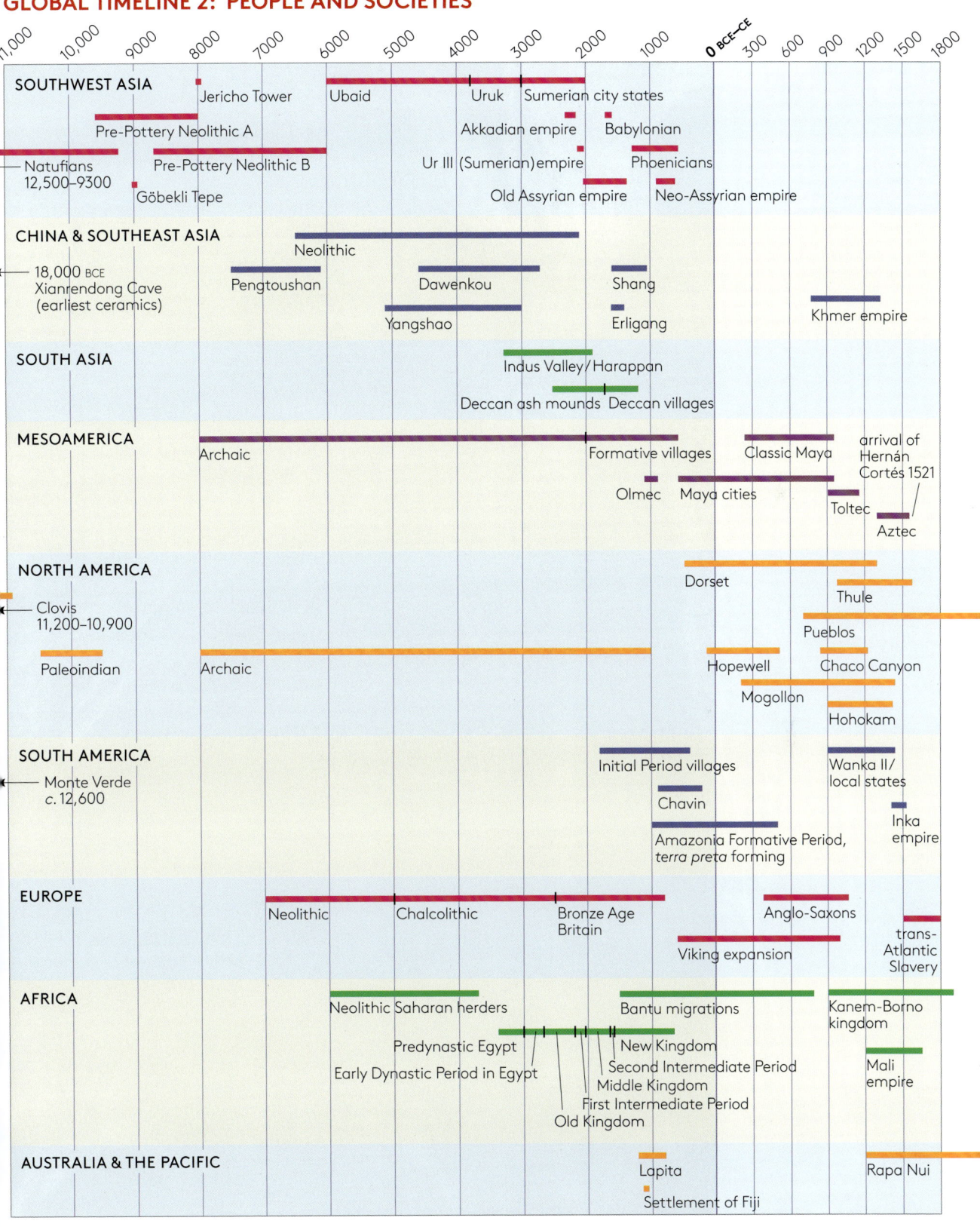

DIGGING IN
Responding to Climate Change in the American Southwest

On a late New Mexico evening one June, I sat within sight of the Zuni Mission Church, hoping to witness the annual dances of the kachinas, the masked deities that are a central component of traditional Zuni religion. Around 2 a.m., a teacher wrapped in a thick overcoat informed those of us waiting in the dark that the dances were about to start. As we approached a window that looked out onto the ancient pueblo street, I began to see several costumed forms dancing inside, their bodies jolting to the steady rhythm of rattles, with deeper tones echoing from the soft thud of pounding feet—sounds that continued to reverberate until dawn.

I'm not exactly sure what I witnessed that night in Zuni. The dancing was but one part of a ritual that was performed largely in private, integral to the Zuni religion and identity, preserving order and balance in the universe. The oral histories of the Zuni speak of their place of origin at Chimik'yana'kya dey'a, a waterfall within the Grand Canyon. The Zuni describe themselves as first emerging from the waterfall as living beings, and after a series of excursions along the river systems that feed into the canyon, then being transformed into humans who became the Zuni people. After further travels, they ultimately reached modern-day Halona Idiwan'a (literally, "Middle Place"). Their annual rituals and ceremonies, which include prayers, offerings, and pilgrimages to sacred sites along the rivers, are still performed to maintain harmony and equilibrium in the cosmos.

The American Southwest has contributed a great deal to the understanding of the interplay between humans and environments. Most importantly, both the rise and decline of societies in that setting may be explained by examining their relationship with the environment. Humans, through their use of farming and foraging, transformed the desert landscape of the Southwest into livable habitats. We will see that these were delicate and temporary arrangements; human societies had to be flexible when the ecological limit of any particular place was reached, ready to abandon one region and start anew in another. Human religion and ritual allowed such communities to stretch the system to its limits. When the population exceeded a reliable source of food, groups simply moved on to establish new communities—a process that was not always peaceful, as we shall discover. It is because of this pivotal relationship between humans and the environment that we introduce the history of the Southwest so early in this book, as a clear window into how humans create their world and respond to the changes their activities have wrought.

5

The American Southwest 98

Methods: Excavation 104

The Colorado Plateau and the Chaco Phenomenon 108

Understanding Ancient Pueblo Society: Broken K Pueblo 115

Other People of the Southwest 118

The Southwest and the Changing Environment 119

Opposite The origin story of the Zuni people of New Mexico identifies the waterfall of *Chimik'yana'kya dey'a* (Ribbon Falls), within the Grand Canyon, as the place where they emerged from the Earth.

Key Concepts

- The prehistory of the American Southwest, as unearthed through the analysis of ancient ceramics, architecture, and patterns of settlement
- The exploration of archaeological sites using excavation
- The formation and abandonment of ancestral Pueblo communities at Chaco Canyon and Sand Canyon
- How people of the ancient Southwest responded to their environment

kiva A subterranean round room found in ancestral Puebloan settlements.

Archaic Period Period in North America from approximately 8000 to 1000 BCE marking the beginnings of agriculture.

pit house A form of house that consists of a shallow pit capped with a timber-and-adobe roof. These houses were constructed in the American Southwest in the centuries prior to the development of pueblos (villages) above ground.

THE AMERICAN SOUTHWEST

The high desert may be chilly at night, but much of New Mexico, Arizona, Nevada, Colorado, and Utah experience hot summer temperatures with warm winters and little rainfall throughout the year. Such rivers as the Colorado, Rio Grande, San Juan, and Gila are crucial for human settlement, and even where little rainfall occurs, summer floods and short-term flow bring essential water to agricultural fields. Juniper trees and piñon pines cover the slopes of high mountains in Utah and Colorado, but many areas of the American Southwest and Mexican states of Chihuahua and Sonora are blanketed in shrubby rabbitbrush, sagebush, and cacti, with cottonwood trees along the streams and many dry washes [**5.1**, **5.2**].

No longer favored, the Navajo word for Ancestral Puebloans, *Anasazi* ("ancient ones"), reflects the abandoned state of most pueblos when Navajo and Apache newcomers moved to these arid lands in the sixteenth century. Ancestral Puebloans were but one of the diverse cultures that had flourished and disappeared in the American Southwest. Their villages were built of stacked stone and adobe (mud plaster), with multiple-story buildings, towers, and underground rooms called **kivas**. Their **Archaic Period** ancestors had adopted maize plants from Mesoamerica by 2000 BCE, and a few thousand years later, they had left traces of settled villages (the Basketmaker culture, see p. 108) with **pit-house** dwellings—a few upright posts holding a timber, reed, and mud roof over a chest-deep, flat-bottomed pit. These structures not only provided warmth and a permanent shelter but also offered a suitable dry place for storing food [**5.3**, **5.4**, p. 100].

Storing food underground in pits secures maize and other seeds for use during seasonal food shortages and encourages cooperation in communities. Such storage is most successful when an "economy of scale" is at play. In a scientific context, this concept advances the idea that the greater the mass of an object is, the smaller in proportion its surface area will be. In the instance of a storage pit, the higher the volume of food stored, the lower the percentage of inevitable spoilage around the edge of the pit, where the grain touches the ground.

In a community where people share pooled resources, they must develop rules to share them. Larger-scale institutions can help resolve individual differences and conflict over resources, and it is in these early pit-house villages that archaeologists discovered the earliest kiva structures. Such ceremonial spaces point to cooperative arrangements among society as a whole—arrangements that were essential for the development of bigger communities with more complex networks of social relationships, methods of exchange, and elaborate rituals.

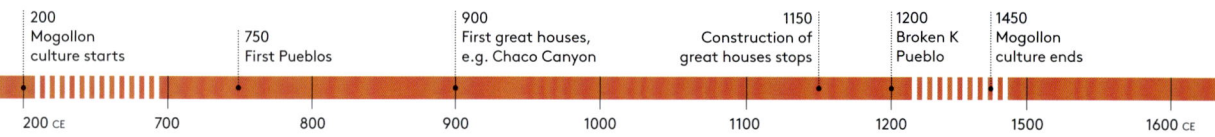

| 200 Mogollon culture starts | 750 First Pueblos | 900 First great houses, e.g. Chaco Canyon | 1150 Construction of great houses stops | 1200 Broken K Pueblo | 1450 Mogollon culture ends |

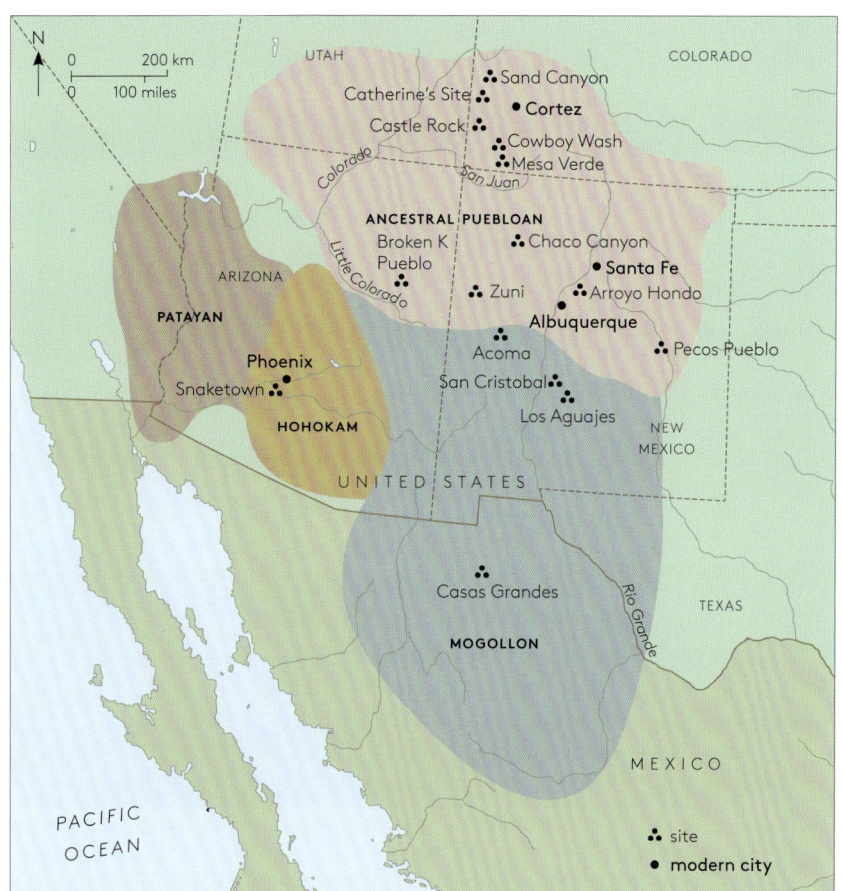

5.1 Map of major Pueblo ruins in the Southwest and modern-day Pueblo communities.

5.2 Sand Canyon as seen from the cliffs above Catherine's Site in southeast Colorado. Excavation of the ruins in the canyon indicated a small community of farmers grew corn in this high desert environment 1100–1290 CE, and then abandoned the area.

THE AMERICAN SOUTHWEST

Above: **5.3 Ruins of Cliff Palace, former home of an Ancestral Puebloan community in Mesa Verde National Park, Colorado.** Although Mesa Verde has undergone major study, conservation, and restoration, many ruins show only minor decay and have hardly been touched since they were abandoned. This pueblo's inaccessible location also protected the community from raids and attacks.

Right: **5.4 "A Corner of Zuni," 1903.** Edward S. Curtis's historic photograph reveals the architecture of Zuni pueblo, similar to that of Ancestral Puebloan archaeological sites of the Southwest.

Early Archaeology in the American Southwest

Native Americans knew long ago that the pueblos of the Southwest existed, and in the early 1900s, Euro-American archaeologists arrived, following the tracks and tales of Western ranchers whose "discoveries" of abandoned settlements had first brought the region's prehistory to the world's attention. Nels Nelson was one such archaeologist, and he pioneered methods of excavation and analysis still crucial in the study of ancestral Pueblo people.

Using a long spade and a set of strings and wooden stakes for measurement, Nelson spent the summer of 1912 digging trenches into the crumbling ruins of the Rio Grande Valley in New Mexico, which spans the vast basin north and south of the modern city of Albuquerque. One of many researchers sent on assignment from the American Museum of Natural History to learn about the ancient and contemporary native cultures of the American West, Nelson was attempting to determine the prehistoric sequence of Pueblo cultures in the region. By 1913, he had surveyed much of the Rio Grande region but was continually disappointed in what he was able to retrieve from the ruins, many of which had been disturbed by "gravediggers," who had looted them in search of pots, bones, jewelry, and other curios. This lack of progress became frustrating for Nelson, who believed that only undisturbed deposits from within the pueblos could indicate the sequences of cultural development that defined Pueblo prehistory. At the ruin of San Cristobal, approximately 200 miles (almost 322 km) east of Zuni, he found a deposit that he believed might provide some answers to his overall question: the related chronology of events. On the river side of the old pueblo was a good-sized refuse heap that consisted of layers of sediment, pottery, stone, and bone. This deposit was nearly 10 feet (about 3 meters) deep and was eroding into the river below. Nelson identified pottery of varying designs and styles in stratified layers—meaning the layers lay one atop the other with evident differences from one layer to the next. Nelson thought these layers, or **strata**, might be indicative of a sequence in time.

Nelson kept track of what lay on top and at different levels in the refuse dump. He was among the first to recognize that the earliest materials rested at the bottom. This proved crucial in his analysis, whereby he divided the pottery fragments from each arbitrary level into types (e.g., "corrugated" or "black-on-white painted" pottery) and created a table in which each row corresponded to a level and each column to a type. In his notes, he described with satisfaction the changing frequency of types across levels. Nelson's careful recording of this sequence demonstrated a phenomenon he recognized as a part of cultural transmission: that ideas were exchanged between peers and passed between generations, resulting in a steady rise, apex, and decline of each design, not unlike the increasing and decreasing popularity of modern clothing styles. These types also gave Nelson a chronological tool. By comparing his pottery sequences to other pottery fragments he had excavated at other sites, such as at Los Aguajes and at the Arroyo Hondo ruins (located nearby, and 80 miles (129 km) to the north), he could determine the relative age of the sites—as either oldest, middle, or youngest—depending on which type of pottery

strata Layers of sediment that are deposited in a sequence; their order records particular events and provides a context for associated artifacts.

5.5 This reconstructed ceramic vessel is an *olla* (storage jar) used to store water. Frequency seriation of the designs on the vessel has been used to identify this style as Black Mesa Black-on-white, which was made in northeastern Arizona 900–1160 CE.

frequency seriation A relative dating method that involves measuring the abundance of a particular design or style of object over time.

traits Specific aspects of an object that archaeologists observe that relate to how it was made or used.

typology Classification of objects according to particular traits, such as color, size, or style.

was present [**5.5**]. This was an early form of **frequency seriation**, a method that would dominate archaeological investigation for the next thirty years.

Following on the heels of Nelson, from 1915 to 1929, Alfred Kidder conducted a series of excavations at Pecos Pueblo, located approximately 20 miles (32 km) west of San Cristobal. Home to the Cicuye people, the pueblo had been occupied for centuries, and the deposits within and surrounding it were deep. Using strata, Kidder identified a series of ceramic "types" that demonstrated the same pattern Nelson had described: over time, the types peaked and declined, marking the deposits as discrete units.

In 1924, Kidder generated the first regional synthesis for the American Southwest [**5.6**]: beginning with cultures that made baskets instead of pottery and resided in pit houses (the so-called Basketmaker cultures, from about 1000 BCE to 750 CE); next the formation of small, single-family masonry pueblos; followed by increasingly complex and large pueblo communities that created elaborate pottery and public architecture, and exchanged goods over long distances (Pueblo Cultures I, II, III, IV, and V spanning 750–900, 900–1150, 1150–1350, 1350–1600, 1600–present day). He also identified the cultural and geographic regions, which today are recognized as the Ancestral Puebloans of the Colorado Plateau, the Hohokam of southern Arizona, the Mogollon in the mountainous areas of New Mexico and Arizona, and the Patayan of northern Arizona.

Classification and Frequency Seriation

Artifact types have been widely used in defining archaeological cultures. Frequency seriation requires that archaeologists define artifact **traits**, such as the shape of arrow points or the decoration of ceramics, and measure the abundance of these traits over time and space, just as Nelson and Kidder classified and ordered pottery in terms of its type [**5.7**]. Functional traits that affect performance, such as the size and weight of an arrow point, or the thermal resistance of a cooking pot, remain relatively stable over time. Hunters would quickly learn to reduce a point that didn't allow an arrow to fly very far, and would pass on that knowledge to the next generation of knappers. Stylistic traits, such as ceramic color, or a shape that does not hamper the flight of the arrow, might come and go, reflecting cultural attitudes about performance rather than physical execution. Distinct differences in the frequency of traits, both stylistic and functional, would be used to indicate breaks in transmission, and these divides would be utilized to refine groups of artifacts into types. Types that were similarly frequent were organized together, producing a **typology**, indicating the extent of various cultures over time and space.

Types and typologies that were produced more than a century ago are still employed as markers to identify cultures and address other cultural questions. Frequency seriations were made by archaeologists to detect the transmission of information across time and space. The widest bands of each type indicate when that particular variation was the most popular. In the nineteenth and twentieth

Region	Culture	Phase	Time period	Sites	Community
Colorado Plateau	Ancestral puebloan	Pueblo V	1600 CE – present	Modern pueblos	Aggregated villages
Colorado Plateau	Ancestral puebloan	Pueblo IV	1350 – 1600 CE		Aggregated villages
Colorado Plateau	Ancestral puebloan	Pueblo III	1150 – 1350 CE	Mesa Verde	Aggregated villages
Colorado Plateau	Ancestral puebloan	Pueblo II	900 – 1150 CE	Chaco Canyon	Aggregated villages
Colorado Plateau	Ancestral puebloan	Pueblo I	750 – 900 CE		Small pueblos
Colorado Plateau	Ancestral puebloan	Basketmaker	1000 BCE – 750 CE		Pit houses
Southern Arizona	Hohokam	Classic	1150 – 1450 CE	Casa Grande	Aggregated villages
Southern Arizona	Hohokam	PreClassic	750 – 1150 CE	Snaketown	Aggregated villages
Southern Arizona	Hohokam	Formative	1 – 750 CE		Small pueblos
Northern Mexico	Mogollon	Mogollon Pueblo	1000 – 1450 CE	Gila Cliff Dwellings	Aggregated villages
Northern Mexico	Mogollon	Late Pithouse	550 – 1000 CE		Small pithouse villages
Northern Mexico	Mogollon	Early Pithouse	250 – 550 CE		Small pithouse villages
Lower Colorado River	Patayan	Patayan III	1500 – 1900 CE		Aggregated villages
Lower Colorado River	Patayan	Patayan II	1050 – 1500 CE		Aggregated villages
Lower Colorado River	Patayan	Patayan I	700 – 1050 CE		Mobile foragers

Above: **5.6 Sequence of prehistoric cultures of the American Southwest,** with associated sites and village types.

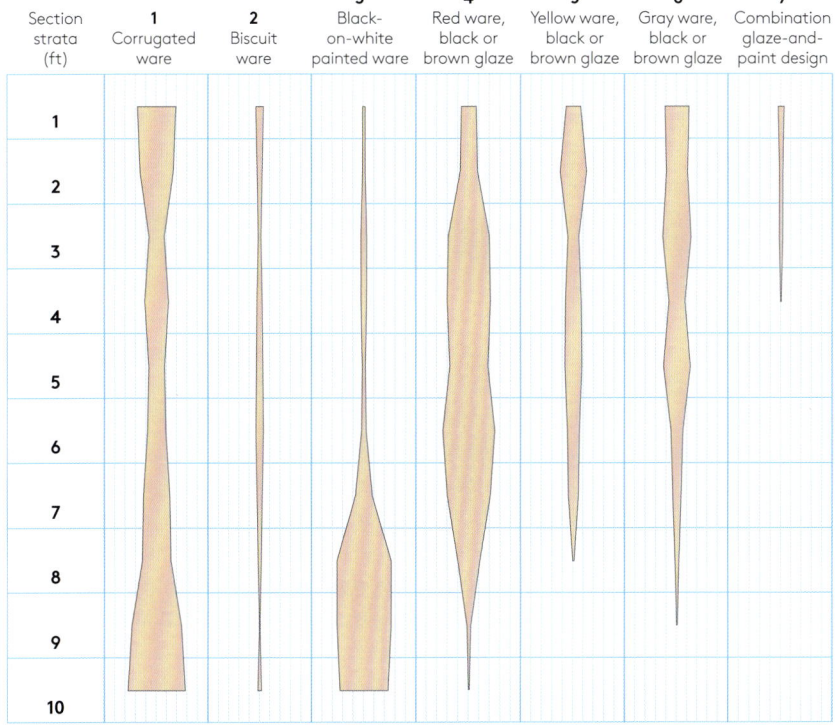

Left: **5.7 Seriation of Ancient Puebloan ceramics** from Nels Nelson's "Chronology of Tano Ruins, New Mexico," 1916. Our diagram converts the number of sherds Nelson recorded to percentages within assemblages. Each 1-foot stratum (row) had an assemblage. (In Nelson's original classification, types 4, 5, and 6 are all Type II ware.)

THE AMERICAN SOUTHWEST

archaeological cultures Specific combinations of artifacts and styles that were produced by a culture in the past.

midden An ancient pile of domestic waste that may contain bone, shell, and pieces of pottery.

centuries, archaeologists argued that the transmission of cultural norms (what to eat, how to dress, how to make tools) emanated from a cultural center, and, much as ripples in a pond do, expanded outward through social transmission (learning and copying). If placed on a map, cultures would look the same as dabs of paint, which are most intensely colored at their centers and fade out to white as one moves further from the center. Similarly, cultural norms would be transmitted through time from parent to offspring, but over time the signal would degrade and slowly disappear altogether. This theory was used to explain how certain traits—such as a particular design on pottery, or the shape of a house's floorplan—often appeared together in time and space. These traits, archaeologists posited, defined **archaeological cultures**: the physical remains of living cultures. Demarcating the boundaries of archaeological cultures in time and space was formerly the only way to identify and organize prehistoric sequences.

METHODS: EXCAVATION

In Chapter 1, we introduced two defining methods of archaeology, excavation and survey, and stressed the importance of context. Here, we reinforce these definitions to explore the role excavation has played in understanding the story of the prehistoric American Southwest.

Archaeological excavation has provided critical information with regard to the construction, occupation, and abandonment of the pueblos of the Southwest. With its arid environment and vast, undisturbed spaces, the region has also uniquely preserved the remains of human activity. Remote pueblos reachable only by determined hikers on rugged treks still offer the most fragile fragments of prehistory: brittle timbers, crumbling basketry, the spat-out quids of chewed plants, a crumpled fiber sandal. With such exceptional preservation, it is not surprising that archaeologists in the American Southwest have regularly pushed the limits of what archaeological excavation can reveal. In the same month as my trip to Zuni in 1989, I participated in my first archaeological excavation with Crow Canyon Archaeological Center in Cortez, Colorado (in the southwest region of that state). The site to which I was assigned, Catherine's Site [**5.8**, **5.9**], was accessible through a crack in the rock, and I climbed gingerly down to arrive at a small pile of rubble, scattered pottery, and not much else.

Or so it looked, to untrained eyes. A masonry house had once stood on the spot, but a heap of stone and mud abutting two large boulders was all that remained. Downhill from the site of the house was the **midden** (the household refuse from the pueblo), which appeared no different from any of the other surrounding hillsides: scattered rocks, sagebrush bushes, and clumps of dry grass. Here and there, a fragment of black-and-white pottery, or a glossy stone flake, revealed itself. The surface of Catherine's Site did not clearly suggest what had once existed there. Nature, in the form of a juniper and piñon forest, had enveloped the remains of a village, leaving little behind that seemed to be the product of human manufacture.

5.8 Catherine's Site excavation. Single 3-feet (1 meter) excavation units revealed a retaining wall (Feature 1) that held sediment and midden, creating a level surface.

5.9 Fragment of pottery with a painted bird design from Catherine's Site. This artifact was a recovered from beneath a stone slab, which was placed deliberately on the floor of a structure prior to its abandonment c. 1290 CE.

The Crow Canyon archaeologists had already planned the excavation at Catherine's Site. Scattered around the edge of the rubble pile and the midden were numerous 3-foot "units" (1 meter square) that had been marked on the ground using wooden stakes and cotton string. Our adolescent minds did not seek to understand how the units might be connected to one another. I and the other students were divided into pairs, and we picked a plot that we found pleasing, in much the same way that campers select a site for their tent. The differences between the units, however, became apparent after a few days of excavation. Students who excavated in the midden found more broken pottery, whereas those excavating nearer to the house uncovered stones that had probably been used to grind maize kernels into soft flour. Within other units, the deposits of pit houses once covered with timber and adobe roofs were discovered.

As the weeks of excavation passed, the archaeologists confirmed that these houses had been purposely destroyed: the wooden beams that had supported the roofs had been intentionally removed, forcing the structures to collapse. At that moment, the apparently random pattern of the excavation units made sense. We were excavating parts of the houses, midden, and other features in order to determine the different activities at Catherine's Site that culminated in the village's eventual abandonment and destruction. That realization led us to two key questions. Why did the people leave their village behind? And how far would they travel, if they were carrying the posts of their former houses with them?

5.10 Excavation with trowels allows for the slow and careful removal of deposits.

Recovering and Recording

My unit at Catherine's Site was located in the midden, and its surface contained a clump of bushes and several rocks. I and the other students were instructed to retrieve several buckets, a pair of trowels, and a pair of dustpans and brooms from the tool locker, and following a brief lesson in excavation from a Crow Canyon archaeologist, we set to work. Archaeologists excavate carefully and slowly. With a trowel, a small amount of sediment is scraped up, usually horizontally across the surface of the unit, and that material is quickly transferred to the dustpan and then emptied into the bucket [**5.10**]. My unit-partner and I started out well but then quickly ran into trouble; tough roots blocked our trowels and, after the first few inches, the sediment became rock-hard. Excavating was not easy, and by the end of the day, hot blisters had formed on our palms. And we proceeded with terrified, agonizing caution. We used measuring tapes to keep track of the depth and frequently called out for help when unsure whether what we were excavating was a rock or an artifact. When our buckets became full, we ran their contents through wire mesh sieves, and any artifacts we might not have spotted while excavating we tried to identify from the pebbles and clods. We hoped to identify some feature unique to the unit—maybe a particular form of architecture, or a deposit from a specific event or activity—but we did not. Instead, over the course of those few days, we uncovered beautiful pottery that had been broken during cooking or cleaning. We took photos of ourselves with the pottery and were completely thrilled.

Although a trowel is indispensable in an archaeological excavation, other tools in a typical toolkit are just as important: a handpick for loosening rocks, plant shears for clipping roots, a line level and string for measuring depths below the surface [**5.11**]. Plastic bags, adhesive labels, pencils, and pens are vital for keeping things

5.11 The archaeologist's excavation toolkit. These tools are essential for clearing vegetation, excavating through rock and soil, measuring depth below the surface, and recording the location of finds.

organized, as all artifacts and samples that are collected must be numbered, marked, and recorded in some way. Archaeological recording in the field also makes use of electronics, such as digital cameras, to capture images of artifacts and sediments in situ. More advanced instruments include mapping systems that employ lasers (a Total Station) that can both pinpoint the location of an artifact in space, or generate a laser scan that can subsequently produce a three-dimensional image of the excavation as it progresses [**5.12**]. These methods are critical to mapping the extent of deposits and artifacts, which aids in determining their origin and later changes.

Excavation, nonetheless, can only be useful to archaeology if it is coupled with a well-designed recording system. It is the location of items, not only the items themselves, that archaeologists use to discern what happened in the past. At Catherine's Site, all recovered artifacts were placed in paper bags that were then carefully labeled with the site's number, our excavation unit number, and the level at which we were excavating, for example 0 to 4 inches (0 to 10 cm) below the surface. This information would later be recorded again, by hand, in a log (these were still the days of paper and pencil), and a third time into a digital database. Only then could the relationships between artifacts, features, and architecture be determined.

A year or two later, the archaeologists at Crow Canyon Archaeological Center used our notes, along with their own and the results of several analyses of the artifacts and deposits, to write a report that detailed the excavation, and to interpret the results within the context of what was already known about the prehistory of the same area. That report is now stored digitally on a website and is freely available to anyone in the world (http://www.crowcanyon.org/researchreports/sitetesting/Text/Ts_11.asp). Publishing archaeological observations and results is the most important step in the research process. As is often said in the field: "If it's not published, then it's not research!"

5.12 A GPS (Global Positioning System) unit can record a site's location using satellite communcations. Here the GPS antenna is on the ground at the base of a tripod (above left) supporting a Total Station. By aligning the Total Station viewfinder to emit a laser beam and detect its reflection from a prism (held atop an ancient site, above right), archaeologists can record precise locations, thus forming the basis of a site map.

THE COLORADO PLATEAU AND THE CHACO PHENOMENON

What archaeologists discovered at Catherine's Site, and also at the nearby ruins of Sand Canyon, Castle Rock, and Mesa Verde, is part of a much bigger story in the American Southwest. It is also one of the best-understood prehistoric sequences in the world, and one that unequivocally shows the dynamic relationships between humans and our planet in the Anthropocene. As Kidder had outlined, around 2,000 years ago, the Basketmaker People who resided in the area were forager-farmers who cultivated maize, beans, and squash and lived in pit houses that had been constructed by digging a wide depression in the ground, and covering that expanse with a timber and adobe roof. Approximately 1,300 years ago (750 CE), Ancestral Puebloan communities built clusters of pit houses and some above-ground homes of stone and adobe, but round subterranean structures, the forerunners of modern kivas, also developed during this same time span. Land was used for farming, and once it grew depleted after a few seasons of cultivation, people regularly moved to new land that was either uncultivated, or had been allowed to lie fallow—that is, unfarmed—for several decades. This kind of residential mobility produced communities that formed and dissolved over time. It marks a period when the Anthropocene comes

5.13 Matching distinctive sequences of growth rings from the inner rings of recent trees to the outer rings of older timbers allows dendrochronologists (scientists who study tree rings to track time) to build a long-term history of yearly events, such as droughts and fires.

108 CHAPTER 5 DIGGING IN • RESPONDING TO CLIMATE CHANGE IN THE AMERICAN SOUTHWEST

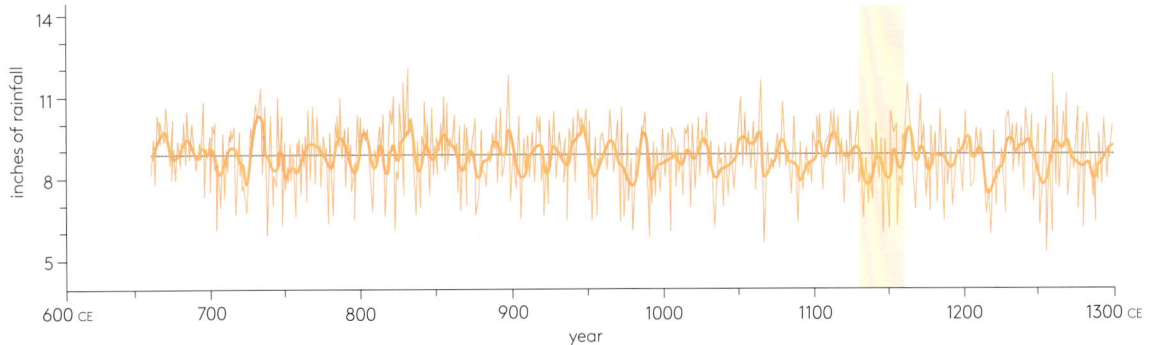

5.14 Drought history of the ancient Southwest. By measuring the growth of dated, annual tree rings and the frequency of fire scars, climatologists have been able to reconstruct a history of rainfall in different regions of the American Southwest. Between 1030 and 1230, more years of drought occurred around Chaco Canyon than in previous centuries. Especially severe and prolonged droughts struck in 1140 and again after 1200; the period indicated here with a colored bar marks the severe drought years of 1130–1160. Construction ceased in the Great Houses around 1150 and the population began to abandon Chaco Canyon.

into focus in the American Southwest, where a dynamic and two-way relationship evolved between humans and local ecological conditions. People used the land and altered it, and, in the years to come, they had to change themselves when the environment demanded as much.

Recent analyses indicate that in addition to soil fertility, climate played a critical role in agricultural production in the Southwest, and that periods of dry and cool conditions made food production impossible. Trees in the Southwest grow very slowly but often live for several hundred years. By measuring the thickness of their annual growth rings, climate scientists have reconstructed local rainfall over the past millennia in the American Southwest [**5.13**, **5.14**]. These reconstructions provide sobering insight into the dynamics of mobile farmer-foragers: people moved because they had to. During the latter part of the Pueblo I period (750–900 CE), the land around Sand Canyon and nearby Mesa Verde was dramatically abandoned; it was not recolonized until approximately 150 years later. This was the first of several significant depopulation events in the region, and it was initially difficult to discern exactly where the inhabitants went. A new clue then emerged some 100 miles (almost 161 km) to the south: Chaco Canyon.

Chaco Canyon

Chaco Canyon is located in a remote part of northwestern New Mexico, and reaching it today requires a drive several hours long across rough dirt roads. The canyon forms part of the southernmost drainage of the San Juan River, but it is, in fact, a very dry place [**5.15**, p. 110]. The landscape is flatter and more open than the high mesas and constricting canyons of Mesa Verde; the scrubland of piñon and juniper is sparse and present only atop the bluffs. The evidence of human manufacture, however, is startlingly grand. Chaco Canyon contains numerous abandoned pueblos that are constructed of masonry and adobe, with multiple floors supported by rows of massive timbers. Some of these pueblos include hundreds of rooms and rise up to four stories in height. The largest pueblos are laid out following a similar design: a series of rooms attached to one another in a curving shape, similar in outline to a large capital "D." Embedded in the sizable crescent-shaped space of the interior were

Above: **5.15 Pueblo Bonito, a "great house," in Chaco Canyon, New Mexico.** The vegetation surrounding Pueblo Bonito in this aerial view of its ruins is shrublike: low, multistem plants typical of the arid canyons in the Southwest. The structural timbers used to build the pueblo came from the distant mountains and were no doubt carried by many people into the sanctuary of the canyon.

Below: **5.16 Re-creation of Pueblo Bonito as it stood c. 1100 CE.** The pueblo had more than 350 rooms on the ground floor, and multiple rooms above, with the highest rooms along the curving wall at the back. Several great kivas measuring almost 33 feet (10 meters) in diameter were hidden beneath the floor of the central plaza.

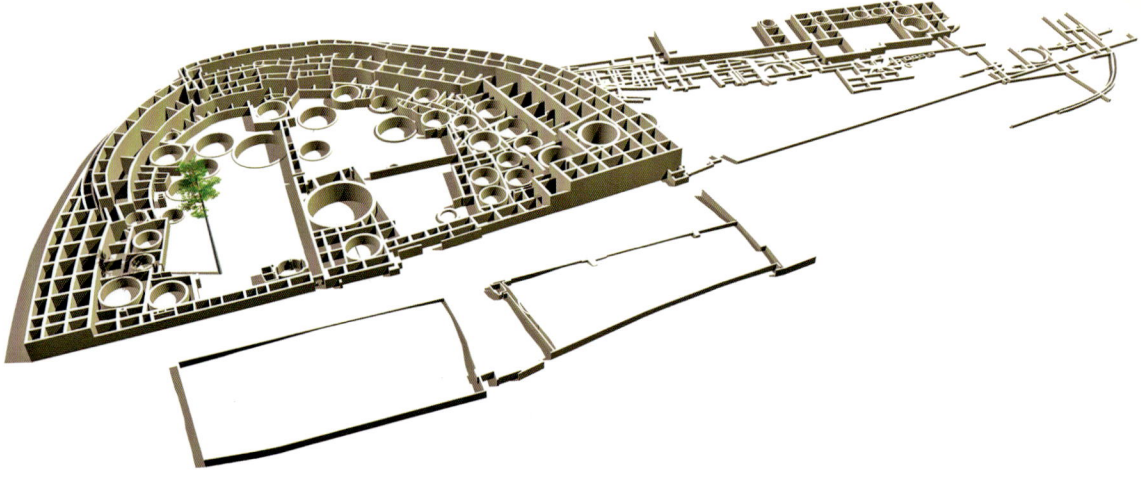

underground kivas. The entire structure suggests a community that was integrated and focused inward, with the kivas and plazas providing mute evidence of the importance of ritual activities performed at the heart of the pueblo.

For over a century, archaeologists have remained conflicted about the origins and logistics of community organization at the canyon. The large D-shaped pueblos or "great houses" [**5.16**] were constructed between 900 and 1140 CE, and would have required an immense effort in terms of labor and supplies. Originally, archaeologists believed that in the past these supplies would have been close at hand, and the canyon was densely forested and verdant, making it an attractive oasis for dispersing populations from other regions. These circumstances now appear *not* to have characterized Chaco Canyon at all. It may have offered some farming opportunities—using ponded stream water and runoff, through the clever manipulation of different soils and patches of land—but a dense forest never existed. Analysis of the timber beams within the great houses indicates that they were imported, frequently from 40 to 100 miles (64 to 161 km) away, and that their use ceased around 1140 CE. Just as the builders of structures at Catherine's Site in distant Colorado did, the Ancestral Puebloans of Chaco Canyon intentionally removed their roof timbers, transporting them over long distances so they might build anew in another location. This suggests that the population initially residing at Chaco may have been a collective one that formed in response to environmental changes affecting population dynamics in other parts of the American Southwest.

Chacoan Communities

The Chacoans were a society vulnerable to climatic fluctuation and environmental changes, some of their own making. Disruptions in food networks, natural cycles of fire, and water flow had important consequences for subsequent generations, on a local and increasingly global scale. It was thus in collectivity, expanded social networks, and the maintenance and manipulation of heritage that the Chacoans were able to adapt and remain successful in the face of climate change. Collectivity is evident from the artifacts recovered in excavations at Pueblo Bonito and other great houses, such as Peñasco Blanco and Una Vida. Archaeologist Deanna Grimstead demonstrated through geochemical analyses of the bone refuse from game, such as deer, that hunting forays often traveled far beyond Chaco Canyon, sometimes reaching the distant mountains to the north and south. Perhaps even more revealing, the analysis of maize cobs from archaeological deposits indicates the crops were frequently grown in locations outside the canyon. Maize was the dietary staple of Puebloans, and its importation suggests that Chaco's great houses drew on a wide network of social relationships farther afield. Less attention has been paid to the smaller pueblos and hamlets in Chaco Canyon, but the significant number of grinding stones and abundant pollen from the outer, heavy husk of maize that were uncovered in the great houses point to prodigious, local processing of the plant. With a wide array of irrigation techniques and soils, local farmers could have cultivated this much maize, but the great houses also incorporated many items that clearly came from elsewhere [**5.17**].

Archaeologists have long proposed that Pueblo communities built and used the great houses of the canyon as part of a newly emerging religion. What beliefs and practices might this religion have espoused? Clues have been unearthed at Pueblo Bonito: copper bells, turquoise beads, seashells, the feathers and bones of scarlet macaws, and cups caked with a residue that has recently been identified as chocolate. All these items would have been imported from distant places—for instance, the chocolate [**5.18**], copper, and macaws likely came from southern Mexico. In addition to being exotic, all had a special visual and sensory presence. The bells would have been both bright and loud; the seashells and turquoise were cut into vivid pieces of jewelry that emulated water animals, such as frogs. The aroma of chocolate, whether savory or sweet, was distinctive and rich (apparently, the Chacoans drank theirs without sugar). The scarlet macaws would have been vividly feathered and perhaps regarded as magical or prescient in their ability to call and converse loudly.

These artifacts, and their origin within a few rooms at Pueblo Bonito, suggest that religious rituals were regularly performed at Chaco. Like the modern dances at Zuni, these rituals may have been public and private, with the vivid ornaments, music, and consumption of exotic products seeking to integrate communities further. Archaeologists have proposed that through participation and shared responsibility, communities from across the Southwest used Chaco Canyon as a kind of integrative

5.17 Chaco Canyon and the other pueblos connected to it.

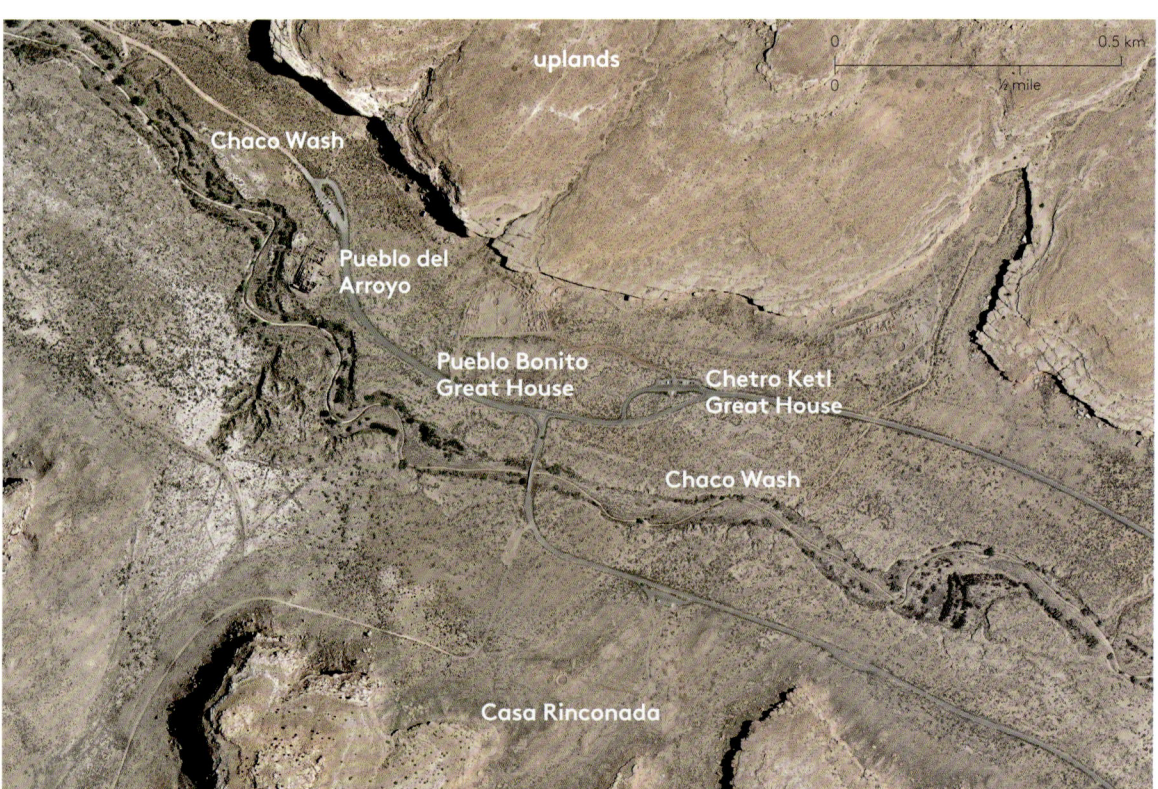

5.18 Cylindrical cups recovered from Pueblo Bonito, Chaco Canyon. The analysis of residues found on fragments of cups similar to these has revealed the presence of theobromine, an alkaloid produced by the cacao plant. These traces indicate that the people of Chaco prepared and consumed drinks made with cacao (chocolate) imported from southern Mexico.

center, which helped them negotiate disputes and cooperate at a regional level. Communities that resided outside of Chaco Canyon during this period displayed their affiliation in the replication of distinctive architectural styles, such as D-shaped buildings, and in dark stripes of sandstone embedded on the exterior walls of their village. Roads leading out of Chaco show little wear but were carefully constructed and appear to form axial connections between Chaco and other communities, and some may have been used in ritual activities.

Were these wide networks maintained to support continuous pilgrimage to Chaco? Some archaeologists suggest that such pilgrimages would have brought only temporary influxes of people, materials, food, and labor, which seems a plausible explanation given that Chaco Canyon had limited resources to sustain permanent large communities. Others suggest that the wide network instead reflects the alliances maintained by a "**house society**," that is, a society that relies on marriage and inheritance to concentrate and conserve wealth, labor, and access to resources within house entities as embodied by material architecture. Even though shared conventions existed—such as how to build a kiva or use maize pollen in ceremonies and medicines—distinct differences appear among the great houses and other pueblos in Chaco Canyon itself. Archaeologist Barbara Mills, indeed, makes a compelling case for recognizing Chaco Canyon pueblos as the architecture of a house society, with houses preserving far-flung social networks and alliances beyond Chaco Canyon itself. The presence of burial sites within Pueblo Bonito—along with its long architectural tradition, rituals of memory and renewal, emphasis on ancestors, and objects of wealth displayed within the great house—are all consistent with the maintenance of property and power in a collectivity organized around an ancestral home.

house society A social organization in which identity, wealth, land, and labor are affiliated with an extended family and a residence, such as a large house or hall.

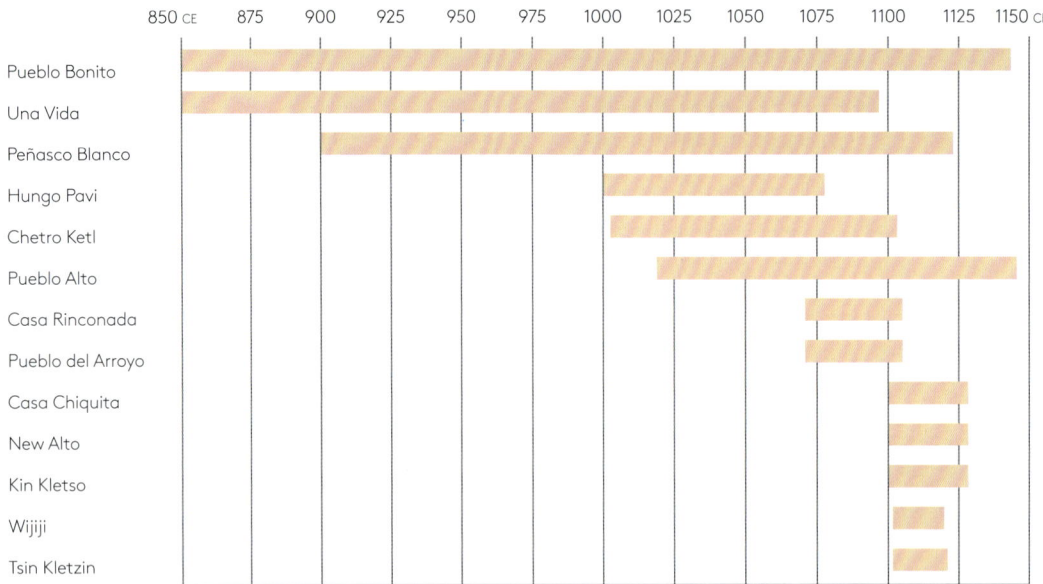

5.19 Calendar dates for the construction of the Chacoan great houses. The construction of new great houses slowed and then stopped in the twelfth century.

Chacoan Dispersion

These clues suggest a Chaco system that resulted from the co-evolution of culture and environment and, for a time, linked-together communities. But just like the depopulation of the Colorado Plateau centuries before, this system ultimately lost its cohesiveness. "Why?" is a question that continues to inspire archaeologists. Paleoclimatic analyses indicate that a severe drought occurred in the Chaco Canyon region during 1130–1180 CE. In spite of the social networks that connected the canyon to other communities, the stress of drought and the long distances required to procure game and maize may have proved too costly. The construction of great houses ceased in Chaco Canyon by 1150 [**5.19**], and within a few decades, new population centers began to emerge to the north, in the Mesa Verde region. People may have simply been "drawn away" as much as "pushed out." The smaller Catherine's Site (where I participated in my first excavation), and the much larger pueblo of Sand Canyon, were also established around this time, perhaps by people who had left Chaco only decades earlier. Some communities lingered, adopting a new masonry style (distinguished by simpler construction and referred to as "McElmo") and building reservoirs to conserve surface water as they reoccupied the buildings that still stood.

Within two centuries of the fall of Chaco Canyon, these communities had also reached a new milestone: villages began to cluster around springs or within the protective alcoves of cliffs. From this same period, evidence also exists of conflict—in the form of weapons, wound marks on skeletons, and possible signs of cannibalism, including cut and burned human bone. The social fabric that connected communities appears to have then frayed and unraveled. Castle Rock Pueblo, which I and my fellow students could see from the vantage point of Catherine's Site, was later revealed by Crow Canyon archaeologists to have been the scene of a massacre around 1280. Severe dry and cool conditions, which spanned 1276 to 1299, provided the backdrop to all these trends. By 1300, the final dispersal occurred, with the population once again abandoning the area. This time, they ventured south to the Rio Grande Valley, to the canyons around Zuni, and to the distant mesas of the Hopi in northern Arizona. There, they started again, founding new societies from the old.

UNDERSTANDING ANCIENT PUEBLO SOCIETY: BROKEN K PUEBLO

How were Pueblo communities and collectives organized? James Hill's excavation of Broken K Pueblo in the late 1960s is a ready-made example of the possibilities of interpretation based on an excavation; it offered some of the first insights into the social organization of ancient Pueblo society. Named for the nearby "Broken K" cattle ranch, the ruined pueblo is located about 80 miles (almost 129 km) west of Zuni, near the Little Colorado River and south of Chaco Canyon. Over several years [**5.20**], Hill and his team excavated 50 percent of the site, treating each room in the pueblo as a single excavation unit. The rooms were selected at random, and after the initial removal of the collapsed roof rubble, he excavated into the floor deposits of each room.

In subsequent analysis, Hill focused on these deposits: the remains of the activities that had occurred in each room, as recorded in the household items that had been discarded on the floors. Among the objects recovered were whole and broken pots, animal bones, and tools for grinding maize. Pollen, some of which was blown in by the wind, was also found on the floors. This was collected and analyzed so that the vegetation around Broken K Pueblo during the time of its occupation could be discerned. Hill and his team also explored beneath the floors and discovered that some rooms had been reused many times, with new floors frequently placed over human burials, earlier structures, and firepits. Newer rooms were additionally built on top of trash (discarded food waste, broken pots, and other debris), indicating that

5.20 Examples of a storage room and a kiva (ceremonial room) at Broken K Pueblo. Storage rooms contained squash and maize pollen on their floors, indicating they were used to store food. Kivas contained artifacts related to tool and ornament manufacture.

the size of the community had increased in the past, requiring new construction. The consensus was that Broken K Pueblo had been abandoned over a period of several years, with a number of the excavated rooms having been abandoned early on and subsequently filled to the brim with trash.

Reconstructing Puebloan Families

James Hill believed he could determine the function of each room based on the presence of different artifacts; such features as stone basins for grinding maize and firepits were used to identify particular activities, for instance, food preparation and cooking. He also utilized some forms of statistical analyses to determine the co-occurrence of specific tools and features, and from these results he created a simple classification of room function. The distribution of activities was then plotted on a plan map for the pueblo. For the archaeology of the day, this represented an exciting advancement: how the society under scrutiny functioned, and how its activities were distributed within the pueblo, became clear. Critics pointed out, however, that Hill's analysis assumed that ceramics and other tools were deposited in the same rooms where they had been created and used. Archaeologists in the American Southwest collectively learned an important lesson from this and other similar criticisms. Excavation can reveal what happened at particular times, but extrapolation beyond that moment must include some uncertainty. The cultural and natural processes that result in deposits being formed have to be understood first.

Hill also hypothesized that it might be possible to reconstruct the ancient social structure of Broken K Pueblo. This too was an exciting proposition for Southwestern archaeology, as it would explicitly connect ethnographic data generated from anthropology to an archaeological case. Using ethnographies from Zuni, Hopi, and Acoma pueblo communities, Hill suggested that the ancient societies may have been organized into family groups, with residence tied to the birthplace of female members (**matrilocal residence**). Ethnographies had also documented the production of pottery, which in modern and historic times has been a household craft performed by women. Mothers taught their daughters how to make pottery, and designs painted on the pots were passed down within families [**5.21**]. Hill surmised that if matrilocal residence occurred in the past, it should also be evident in the distribution of pottery design elements: the frequency of swirls, zigzags, and stripes in pueblo room deposits would identify the residences of particular families.

How did Hill and his colleagues search for these patterns? More than 26,000 pottery fragments were recovered in the excavations, and approximately 6,000 of these came from floor surfaces. With help from an artist, Hill generated a list of 179 design elements and recorded the co-occurrence of designs in each room's pottery (both on the floors and in the trash that had accumulated above them). Using a computer to perform statistical analyses, he determined which design elements were associated with one another. With controls established for the chronology, he produced a map of the pueblo [**5.22**] that showed which rooms had been the homes

matrilocal residence
A residence tied to the birthplace of a female family member.

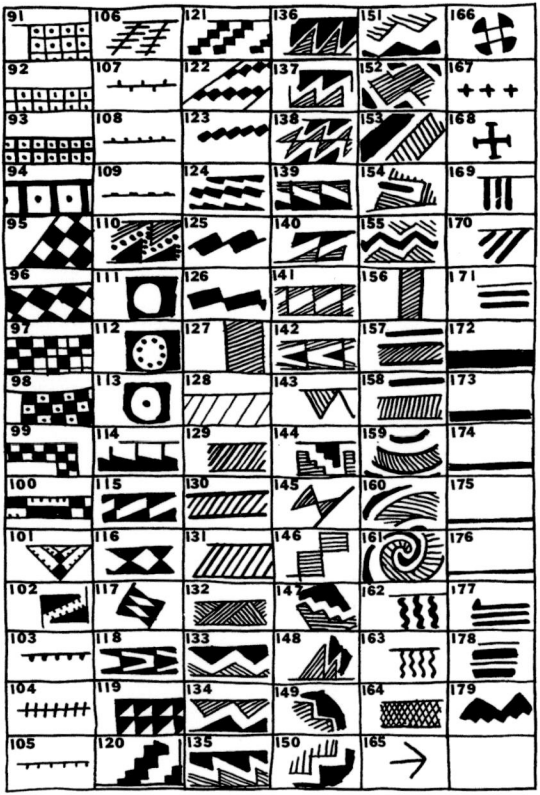

Above: **5.21 Elements of design from painted Pueblo ceramics as identified by James Hill.** Hill assumed that these designs were passed down within families from mother to daughter, and that clusters of designs could thus be used to identify the permanent homes of certain extended families.

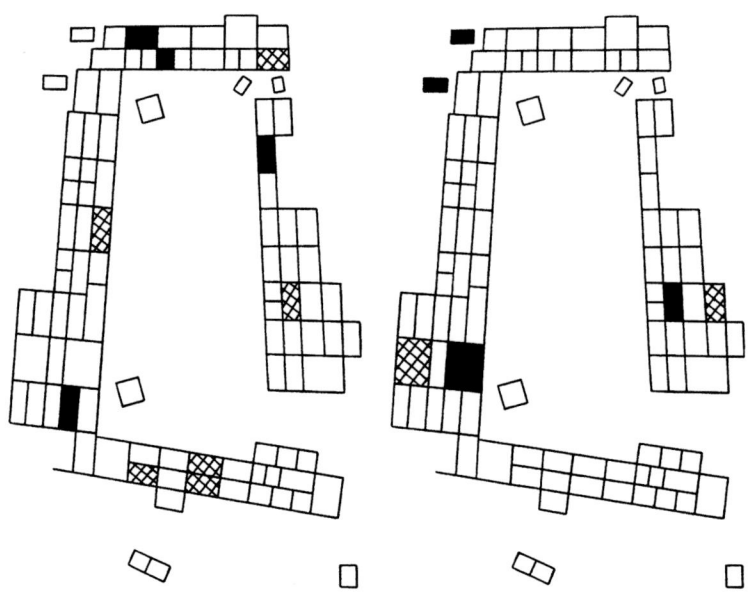

Left: **5.22 Map of Broken K Pueblo generated by James Hill's analysis.** Shaded rooms were identified as the loci for "residence units," or social groups within the community that resided together and were presumably related.

UNDERSTANDING ANCIENT PUEBLO SOCIETY: BROKEN K PUEBLO **117**

of two matrilocal family groups. Hill's findings were groundbreaking for archaeology and truly inspirational. His study and others similar to it portrayed excavation as a powerful tool for detecting social structure down to the family level. In later years, Hill's findings were scrutinized and retested, and not all of the patterns he identified could be replicated. This did not, however, suppress the hopes of archaeologists in the Southwest to explore and understand ancient Pueblo society; rather, it drove them to develop better methods and theory for addressing the limitations.

OTHER PEOPLE OF THE SOUTHWEST

The Chacoans lived among other communities in the Southwest. The ancient people of the Sonoran Desert (also called Hohokam, meaning "those who have gone" in the language of the O'odham people, who currently reside there), roughly contemporary with the dwellers of Chaco Canyon, occupied southern Arizona and parts of northwestern Mexico. They were pioneers in irrigation technologies, developing a series of canals in extensive networks to support their farming settlements along the Gila River in the Tucson–Phoenix Basin. Their communities show extensive contact with southern neighbors in Mesoamerica, from whom the Ancient Sonorans adopted many ceremonial practices, including the construction and use of ball courts and platform mounds. Unlike the early Ancestral Puebloans, Sonoran people cremated their dead. At their largest site, Snaketown (near present-day Phoenix), households clustered around a central plaza, again Mesoamerican-style. It is a pattern that suggests extended kin-groups—bigger than nuclear families—sharing access to common resources in a food preparation space, and perhaps also land and the labor to establish and tend irrigation systems.

The Mogollon people were another Southwestern cultural group that disappeared long before the arrival of Navajo and Apache to the north. The Mogollon occupied the wooded, mountainous regions of southern Arizona, New Mexico, and arid northern Mexico. They also lived in pit houses until about 1,000 years ago, and as the Ancestral Puebloans of the north did, they created subterranean kivas as the foci of their village communities. Farmers and foragers across a diverse set of environments, the Mogollon created and exchanged some of the most aesthetically pleasing ceramics ever made. Over time, their communities constructed pueblo settlements with blocks of rooms and grand ceremonial spaces. In the northern Mexican state of Chihuahua, Casas Grandes [**5.23**], the largest settlement of the Southwest with some two thousand rooms arranged in multiple blocks, remains an engineering wonder. The Mogollon constructed canals throughout the pueblo to provide fresh water and remove waste. Among its ruins, archaeologists found the remains of breeding boxes for the brightly feathered macaw birds and hundreds of their skeletons, attesting to the symbolic importance of this rare species and its probable value in ritual sacrifices.

Casas Grandes and its hinterland network of interconnected communities persisted into the fifteenth century CE, flourishing long after the abandonment of

Chaco Canyon and in an era of conflict and competition for dwindling resources. By the mid-fifteenth century, Casas Grandes had burned down, and the Mogollon had scattered, splintered into smaller social groups dispersed across ever-more precarious environments.

5.23 Ruins of Casas Grandes Pueblo in northern Mexico. The pueblo was made of adobe, and rooms were arranged in a set of blocks with adjacent plazas. A large court used for playing a competitive Mesoamerican ball-game was located on the edge of the pueblo.

THE SOUTHWEST AND THE CHANGING ENVIRONMENT

The rise and decline of societies in the American Southwest offer powerful examples of human ecology. Some of the most creative and advanced computing models in archaeology draw on the vast datasets from the Southwest to re-enact and test the interplay of humans and environments. These data on natural resources—what scientists call **proxy data** from tree rings, fire scars on tree rings, pollen, and various soils' chemistry—combined with the rich archaeological record of ancient people's technologies and behaviors, offer archaeologists, such as Timothy Kohler and Stefani Crabtree, an unprecedented view of human adaptation to changing environments. Increasingly, they and others have used models to test their view of the past, made sharper by computer simulations that project different outcomes as variables are adjusted. These models suggest how and why human societies and the environment were dynamically intertwined in the Southwest, and offer insights into our own Anthropocene human ecology.

Through their farming and foraging, humans transformed the landscape of the Southwest, but these transformations were delicate and temporary, with the landscapes often reaching and surpassing limits of ecological sustainability. Mobility allowed for survival through these periods of drought and exhaustion, and for the

proxy data Types of data used by climatologists to infer climate changes in the past.

cycle of settlement and transformation of the landscape to be repeated. But human religion and ritual were also necessary for communities to persevere. And when the system reached its limits, many groups erupted in violence, as evidenced on some of the human bones that were later unearthed. At Cowboy Wash in southwestern Colorado, archaeologists uncovered incontrovertible proof that the ancestors of famously peaceful Puebloans had consumed their dead enemies. Ancient villagers were massacred, and their skeletons, left unburied, ultimately fragmented. In the center of one abandoned pit house, an invader excreted a human coprolite (fossilized feces) from which scientists extracted the myoglobin protein specific to human muscle tissue. In other words, the last meal was human flesh, eaten sometime after 1150 CE.

The important lessons of the American Southwest link our contemporary world to the challenges faced by Ancestral Pueblo groups and other Southwest people. Using technological innovations—such as the diverse irrigation strategies in Chaco Wash, water conservation in particular soils, and even the modification of field sediments by layering silt and sand for maximum water efficiency—the inhabitants of Chaco Canyon's great houses modified their environment to support large communities. They relied on expanded information and social networks as part of a flexible strategy to supply critical resources not available locally (timber, game, and even maize), sharing their institutions and identity with neighbors near and far. As a house society, the Chacoans also manipulated their ancestral ties and heritage to ensure access to labor and land. Importantly, theirs was a society vulnerable to climatic fluctuation and environmental changes, some of their own making; the subsequent interventions in food networks, natural fire cycles, and water flow had important consequences for later generations, on a local and increasingly wider scale.

Ultimately, the American Southwest is an unequivocal example of resilience during the Anthropocene, and perhaps a cautionary tale for future humans. Although our own rate and scale of contemporary climate change outstrip anything the Ancestral Puebloans ever faced, archaeological knowledge helps us understand human behaviors in the face of anthropogenic change. One warning from the Southwest is that human violence is closely tied to resource scarcity in areas with high environmental instability. Whereas some groups lashed out violently, at other times and in other places ancestral Pueblo people managed to suppress those impulses through cultural institutions that persist among the Zuni and Hopi today. Not all human groups will behave the same way when faced with similar circumstances. On a different note, the long histories and parallel experiences of ancestral Pueblo groups in coping with fluctuating resources and environment show that people will seek alternative environments and contexts to continue doing what they know best—farming maize in cooperative communities—rather than change their fundamental behaviors.

Chapter Questions

1. Describe the seriation methods used by both Nels Nelson and Alfred Kidder to understand the sequence of the Pueblo constructions.
2. What are the main stages of archaeological excavation? How might these stages change given different circumstances?
3. How were Pueblo communities organized? Use Chaco Canyon and Broken K Pueblo as examples.
4. How did the people of Chaco Canyon respond to environmental hardship?

Additional Resources

Billman, Brian R., Lambert, Patricia, and Banks, L. Leonard. "Cannibalism, Warfare, and Drought in the Mesa Verde Region during the Twelfth Century," *American Antiquity* 65, no. 1 (2000): 145–178.

Drewett, Peter L. *Field Archaeology: An Introduction.* New York: Routledge, 2011.

Hill, James N. *Broken K Pueblo.* Anthropological Papers of the University of Arizona No. 18. Tucson, AZ: University of Arizona Press, 1970.

Plog, Steven. *Ancient Peoples of the American Southwest.* London, UK: Thames & Hudson, 1977.

Vivian, R. Gwinn, and Hilpert, Bruce. *Chaco Handbook: An Encyclopedia Guide.* Salt Lake City, UT: University of Utah Press, 2012.

EXTINCTIONS IN THE PAST

6

Extinction is forever. Many can sympathize with the last survivor of a doomed species, whether it be the last branch tip of a rare Hawaiian *Clermontia* grafted to another tree, or the last Tasmanian tiger—a marsupial that once ranged widely over Australia. The last one died in a zoo in 1936. As global climates are warming and human populations increasing at ever-faster rates, the pace and number of species extinctions are rising to set new benchmarks. In 1927, the world human population stood at 2 billion; in 1960, it reached 3 billion, doubling again by 1999; and by the end of this century (2100), it will skyrocket to nearly 11 billion. If you hope to live long into the twenty-first century, yours will be a crowded planet—crowded, that is, with humans living in a poorer natural world.

Many biologists believe that we are currently living through the sixth mass extinction event in Earth's history. Over the past 500 years, about 1 percent of bird species have become extinct and more than 10 percent are severely threatened. By 2100, another 12 percent will surely have gone the way of the dodo, a large flightless bird found on the island of Mauritius in the Indian Ocean in 1598, which was hunted to extinction by 1662.

Are the rates of human population growth and extinctions just another circumstantial episode in the long history of the planet? Or, is the current pace of extinction tied to our cultural condition and just one dimension of the evolutionary context of human ecology? These are key questions that will have key consequences for the future of humanity and other species.

With its long record of our past interaction with other species, archaeology offers significant insight into our engagement with the environment. Through our historic and prehistoric successes as humans dispersed around the world, archaeology allows us to consider whether incurring massive extinctions has always been our nature, and how we responded to these kinds of cataclysmic events in the past. In this chapter, we begin with the "overkill hypothesis," which seeks to answer the long-standing question: Did the actions of Pleistocene hunters generate the massive extinctions of megafauna in North and South America 13,400–11,300 years ago? To understand if human nature is inevitably connected to mass extinctions, we examine the archaeological evidence for natural trends, and the role people play in natural processes. Essential to these arguments is the ability accurately to date human activity as viewed alongside environmental change. Therefore we also describe the technologies commonly used to determine a chronology of events and compare the limitations of these dating techniques.

Big Game Hunters: The Clovis People 124

Radiocarbon Dating 127

The Spread of the Clovis 131

Hunting Megafauna 133

Mastodons and the Role of a Changing Environment 134

South America: The Giant Ground Sloth 137

The Role of Humans in Extinction Events 139

Opposite One of the few photographs of a thylacine, also known as the Tasmanian tiger, a large wolf-like marsupial that evolved in Australia, but is now extinct.

Key Concepts

- Evidence for climate change, or human interaction, as the catalyst for past extinction of megafauna
- The basics of radiocarbon dating
- The Pre-Clovis of South America, who may have tipped the stressors on megafauna, driving extinctions

overkill hypothesis Argues that human activity principally led to the extinction of megafauna shortly after the Ice Age ended.

atlatl A handle that attaches to the butt end of a spear, allowing a person to throw the spear farther and with more force. Predates the bow and arrow.

BIG GAME HUNTERS: THE CLOVIS PEOPLE

In Chapter 3, we examined the first stone tool traditions or industries in Africa and Europe. One of the foremost identifiable stone tool industries in North America is named "Clovis". Crafted more than 12,000 years ago, Clovis points are among the earliest of all technologies to be found in the Americas. The Clovis technology spread briskly across North America as part of one of the most rapid population movements in human history; by some estimates it took just 300 years for Clovis to spread across the entire American continent. In 1929, when Ridgely Whiteman discovered the Blackwater Draw archaeological site outside of Clovis, New Mexico (in the eastern part of that state [**6.1**, **6.2**]), he recognized large points and bone eroding from the banks of a dry stream bed. Careful excavation revealed the bones to be those of huge mammoth, bison, camels, and ground sloths—animals that disappeared from the North American continent starting about 13,400 years ago. Clovis hunters, whose discarded weapons were found in situ among the bones, must also have lived as the megafauna were disappearing. What was the connection between the extinct animals and Clovis? Did humans hunt them to extinction, or were changing climates (especially the onset of warm Holocene conditions) the reason for their sudden decline? This debate, referred to as the **overkill hypothesis**, has remained a critical issue for North American archaeology over the past thirty years.

Clovis people are known for making a distinctive type of stone point, which would have required attachment to a spear in order to propel it toward prey. Archaeologists have examined the technology required to make a Clovis point; it was not a simple tool to craft, calling for extreme skill and experience to manufacture. To make a Clovis point, a stone knapper needed a large piece of fine-grained stone, such as flint, jasper, or chalcedony. One of the most obvious features of these points is that many were enormous, reaching four or more inches in length, even after the shaping and trimming flakes had been removed. Once the point had been effectively thinned and retouched on both edges, its final flakes were removed, leaving a flute, or channel, that ran upward from the base and along the length of the point on each face. Experimental stone knappers have determined that this last step is both difficult and risky—the most challenging strike that cannot go wrong or be fixed without ruining the entire point. The most widely accepted reason for this step is a mechanical one. Fluted points were easily hafted to spears, which could be thrown with great strength and amplified distance from an **atlatl** [**6.3**], which serves as an extension of the hunter's arm. You would need such strength to bring down a mastodon or bison with a stone-tipped spear, as the hair and hide of these animals were dense and several inches thick. Experimentation with modern-day replica points, however, indicates that flutes were not entirely necessary; without

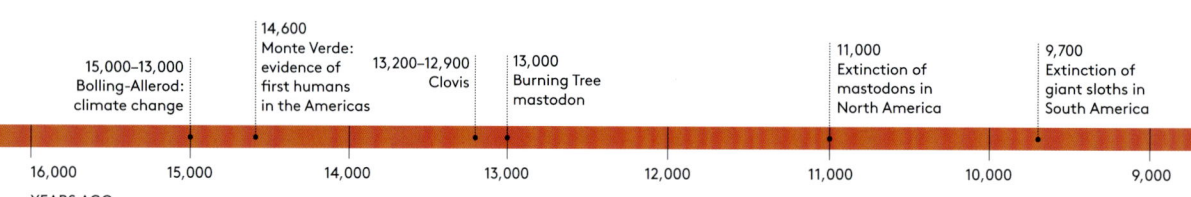

Above: **6.1 Archaeologists excavated Clovis points in situ** among bison and mammoth bones at the Blackwater Draw site in eastern New Mexico. The bone layer is clearly visible in the deposit, which has been preserved under the shelter of a modern museum.

Right: **6.2 Fluted Clovis point from the Vail Site in Maine, dating back 12,000 years.** Clovis points are distinctive for the fluting at their base, which is thought to have allowed for better attachment to a spear.

Below: **6.3 The atlatl works as an extension of the human arm,** allowing a thrower to project a tipped weapon much farther and with greater force than the human arm alone can deliver.

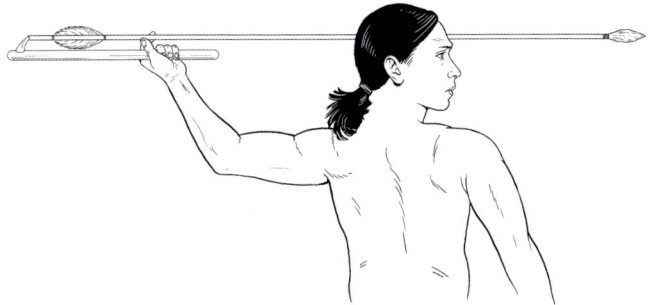

BIG GAME HUNTERS: THE CLOVIS PEOPLE

Paleoindians A general term used to describe the first people who inhabited the American continents.

them, early spears would have worked just as well. Fluting may have been crafted for another purpose then, perhaps acting as a cultural marker for the Clovis people.

Clovis points have been unearthed across North America, south of the Great Lakes, which were still blanketed by ice sheets 13,000 years ago. In rare instances, Clovis points were left behind in caches (a number of finished points buried together in a marked location for future use), but most commonly, they are isolated finds. Many have simply been found on the ground surface, either broken after a hunt or discarded. Clovis people, also known as **Paleoindians**, eventually reached all of North America, and over the next several thousand years, their descendants developed localized and diverse styles of stone tools. That Clovis points appear across North America suggests to archaeologists that initially, and quite rapidly, successful big game hunters dispersed into underpopulated or unpopulated lands.

This movement would explain why Clovis points bearing the same style, made by knappers using the same design parameters and processes to create them, materialized in so many different locations. You need only recall the children's game of "telephone," in which each person whispers a phrase to his or her "neighbor" along a line of people, to imagine how a cultural idea can be transformed over space and time. In a similar way, localized and varied point styles (using techniques that differed across North America) later developed with the transmission of cultural traditions across many generations. Clovis points uncovered thousands of miles apart suggest that their users were nearly contemporary and moved so swiftly into new areas that the knapping technique, with its difficult fluted finish, spread across just a few individuals and generations.

Did Clovis Hunters Cause Extinctions?

What kind of a world did the Clovis hunters encounter? The fossils of mammoths, mastodons, bison, giant ground sloths, camels, and such predators as wolves and lions all support the premise that the Americas in the late Pleistocene was a vast continent of forests, plains, and open parklands. Geologist Paul Martin formulated the prehistoric overkill hypothesis that correlated the disappearance of large mammals—such as mammoths, mastodons, and giant sloths—with the widespread appearance of humans across North America around 13,000 years ago. He proposed that big game hunters fanned out from the limited corridor between the ice sheets, much as a shock wave spreads across a pond. Hunters proliferated rapidly thanks to the supply of easy meat from significantly sized animals not accustomed to humans and unstartled by their presence.

Recent analyses suggest that the population of animals was variable and linked to particular environments, and that dense populations of large animals, such as mammoths and mastodons, would not have existed. Similar to their elephant relatives living in Africa and Asia, these animals reproduced slowly and had expansive home ranges. The megafauna also functioned under a great deal of stress due to the changing climate, which would have reduced the size of their habitat and isolated populations from one another, further impacting their declining birthrates. Did humans, however, cause their ultimate demise? To test this hypothesis, archaeologists and paleoenvironmentalists need to address four crucial questions:

1. Does the timing of Clovis entry into the New World coincide closely with the disappearance of fauna?
2. Were Clovis hunters exclusively focused on megafauna, or did they also consume other animals?
3. Does the scale of extinction (for genera and species) match what would have resulted from the predation of human hunters?
4. Might warming climates at the end of the Pleistocene have affected animal populations in the Americas regardless of humans' entry?

The answers to all four of these questions rely on archaeologists' ability to date the timing of extinctions, and the arrival and circulation of humans into North and South America. They also require a thorough examination of the biogeography of Pleistocene animals, and how these populations may have coexisted with, or become the prey of, the first hunters in the Americas.

RADIOCARBON DATING

The advantages of finding a Clovis point in situ are very apparent when one considers how archaeologists have struggled to generate independent dates for Clovis sites. Such dates are essential to test this hypothesis: that after the Clovis people moved through an ice-free corridor, they spread quickly in a New World of opportunity, focusing their hunting on large animals that would provide the most meat. Unlike stone tools, bone and plant remains can be directly dated in most cases, so their appearance in context with Clovis points affords an indirect method for dating the sites that Clovis people created. One method of dating animal, human, and plant remains is radiocarbon dating. This process estimates the amount of radioactive carbon in artifacts and uses that metric to calculate how many years have passed since the organic material was alive.

How Does Radiocarbon Dating Work?

Such organic materials as charcoal and bone were once living organisms, subject to the biochemical processes of respiration and photosynthesis that characterize all living things. These processes involve the fixing of carbon atoms (the conversion of inorganic carbon to organic carbon) in living tissue. Usually, this process begins with plants. Plant photosynthesis takes in atmospheric carbon dioxide (CO_2) and, in its release of oxygen (O_2), fixes carbon in plant tissue. When animals ingest these plants, the carbon remains fixed in their own tissues [**6.4**, p. 128].

Not all atmospheric carbon is the same. Carbon isotopes vary in the number of neutrons contained in their nuclei. Stable carbon ^{12}C and ^{13}C have six protons and

6.4 Radiocarbon cycle step-by-step. In this process, carbon-14 (^{14}C) is created in the atmosphere and subsequently consumed by plants and animals. Once these living things die, ^{14}C decays at a steady rate into ^{14}N.

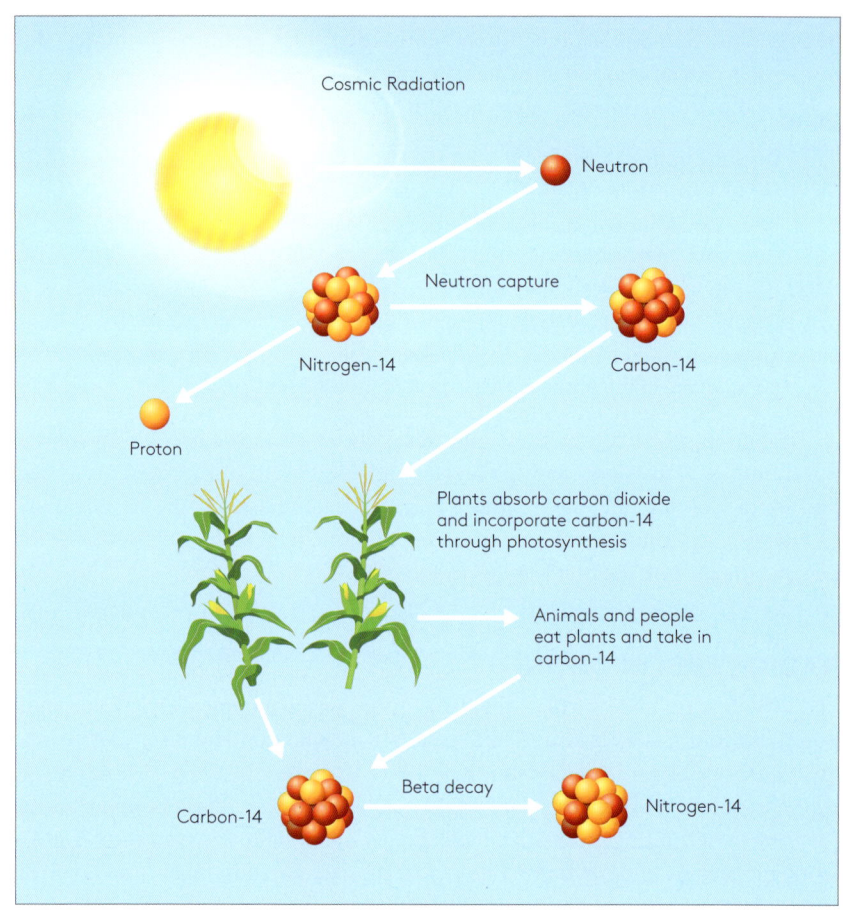

six or seven neutrons, whereas unstable carbon (radioactive carbon or ^{14}C) has six protons and eight neutrons. Radioactive carbon is continuously being created when cosmic rays in the atmosphere knock a neutron into a stable nitrogen atom (^{14}N). This, in turn, knocks a proton from the nitrogen atom, and with this new neutron, the atom becomes ^{14}C.

Importantly, these radioactive ^{14}C atoms are inherently unstable and are continuously decaying (back to stable ^{14}N). As long as plants remain alive, they acquire and fix carbon so that the proportions of ^{14}C to $^{12}C+^{13}C$ in their tissues mirror the proportions of these same atoms in the atmosphere. When plants die, their acquisition of new carbon molecules stops, but the decay of inherently unstable radioactive carbon atoms (^{14}C) in their tissues continues. Thus over time, the proportions of radioactive to stable carbon in dead plant tissues change with the decay of ^{14}C, so an ever-decreasing proportion of ^{14}C to $^{12}C+^{13}C$ occurs. When animals die, their radioactive carbon continues to convert to stable nitrogen, just as in dead plant tissues.

How Is a Radiocarbon Date Calculated?

In the 1940s, Walter Libby recognized the dating potential inherent in a constant rate of decay of radioactive carbon. After 5,730 years, an artifact contains half the amount of ^{14}C that it contained when it was living tissue. This period of time, known as the **radiocarbon half-life**, is a constant used to calculate a radiocarbon date. After 11,360 years (5,730 × 2), the amount of ^{14}C drops to one-quarter of its original amount, and to an eighth after another 5,730 years. If one can determine the current proportion of $^{14}C/^{12}C$ molecules in an artifact, this half-life may be used as a simple calculation of how long it has been since the $^{14}C/^{12}C$ ratio matched the constant atmospheric $^{14}C/^{12}C$ ratios. This result is called a **radiocarbon determination**.

There are several ways to measure the current proportion of $^{14}C/^{12}C$ molecules in an artifact, all of them destructive to the artifact or a portion of it. By burning the artifact and capturing all the gas (CO_2) emitted during combustion, scientists can use a gas scintillation counter to register every ^{14}C decay event over a period of time. That can take quite a while, especially as one awaits decay events in very old specimens with few ^{14}C molecules left. The rate of error can be reduced by counting for a long time, but not eliminated.

Another approach just counts the number of ^{14}C molecules remaining in a sample, without waiting for any of them to decay. It uses an **accelerator mass spectrometer (AMS)**, a machine that detects atoms of specific elements according to their atomic weights and has the distinct advantage of using much smaller samples, as small as a grain of wheat. AMS dating is, therefore, far less destructive to precious artifacts. Its invention means that archaeologists now can date important and unique items, such as an ancient wooden spear shaft that would have been fully destroyed in gas scintillation dating (and therefore ineligible for dating at all). The direct count of ^{14}C molecules usually means more items are available to count, because not just the decay events but all the ^{14}C molecules can now be counted. This expanded range also means that AMS dating allows older material (which may contain very few remaining ^{14}C molecules) to be dated.

The Atmosphere Has Not Always Been the Same

Libby failed to take one major factor into account in his initial calculations. Atmospheric conditions are not constant through time. He realized this when the first atomic bombs set off in the 1940s and 1950s released radioactivity and changed atmospheric carbon ratios through human agency. It turns out that many atmospheric changes also result from solar activity (remember those cosmic rays that bombard nitrogen in the Earth's atmosphere?). If atmospheric carbon isotope ratios ($^{14}C/^{12}C$) fluctuate, then higher or lower atmospheric ^{14}C levels would be fixed in organisms dying off at different times, and this would make the time elapsed since death seem shorter or longer. How can a half-life be used then to calculate a date from a radiocarbon determination? The answer is simple enough: by calibrating the measurement against something of known age.

radiocarbon half-life The time it takes for half the ^{14}C in a sample of organic material to decay, 5,730 years.

radiocarbon determination The calculation of how long it has been since a radiocarbon sample last maintained the same proportion of $^{14}C/^{12}C$ as the atmosphere; usually marks the moment of death of a living organism.

accelerator mass spectrometer (AMS) A machine that detects atoms of specific elements according to their atomic weights.

calibration A method of correcting radiocarbon dates that compensates for fluctuating atmospheric conditions in the past.

dendrochronology The dating of a piece of wood based on an examination of its rings; often involves comparing the ring pattern to those in a larger database.

calibration curve A synthesis of measurements from tree rings and other samples of known age that is used to generate a graph that relates radiocarbon dates to calendar years.

Calibrating Radiocarbon Dating

To account for fluctuating atmospheric conditions, specialists use a correction to radiocarbon date a calculation. This correction is known as **calibration**. Calibration is achieved by acquiring radiocarbon dates on organic material with absolute, fixed calendar dates so that the independent calendar dates can then be used to adjust the radiocarbon dates. Specialists use a method of tree-ring dating, known as **dendrochronology**, to count the annual growth rings from living trees, overlapping the inner (early) living rings with late (outer) rings in older wood (see Chapter 5). By using massive timbers from old buildings, dendrochronologists can build sequences of tree rings over thousands of years, in which each tree ring has an absolutely certain calendar date.

Dendrochronology provided highly accurate dates for the construction and abandonment of Chaco Canyon's great houses and other sites in the American Southwest, where arid conditions had preserved building timbers. With AMS dating of small wood samples from each ring, analysts have built series of radiocarbon determinations linked to calendar dates. Calendar dates (counted on growth rings) on an *x*-axis are then plotted against radiocarbon determinations (from the same growth rings) on a *y*-axis to produce a **calibration curve** [6.5], which winds its way across the graph space. The resulting wiggles reflect the fluctuation in atmospheric conditions, and they also explain why a radiocarbon determination may not precisely match one calendar date. The standard error in counting is also an integral part of a radiocarbon date, so a broad spread of potential calendar dates may exist for a radiocarbon determination.

At death, an organism is in balance with atmospheric radiocarbon levels. Thereafter, the decreased level of ^{14}C in organic material provides a critical clue to its time of death. Radiocarbon dating yields an absolute date for when the plant or animal matter was last alive, an important point every archaeologist must remember

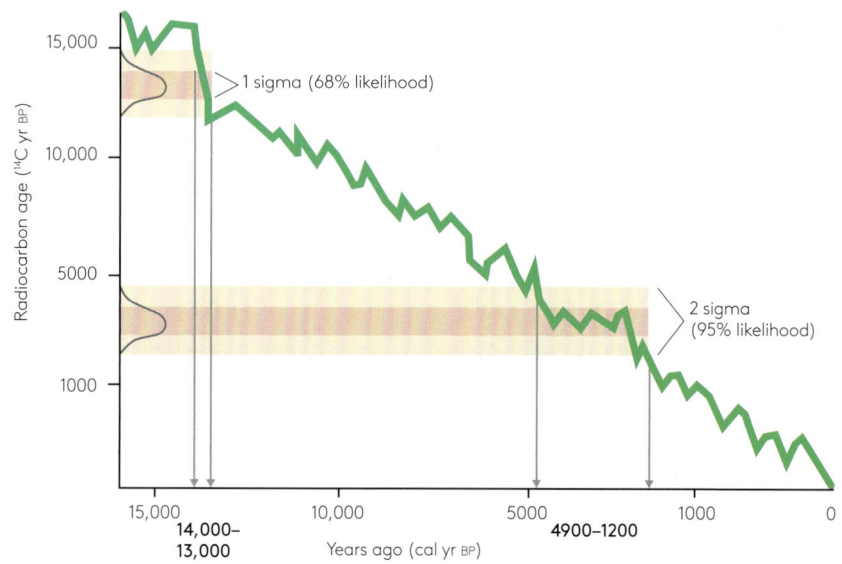

6.5 Determining a calendar date using a radiocarbon-dating calibration curve. The *y*-axis plots the radiocarbon age (^{14}C yr BP, or radiocarbon years before present), and the *x*-axis plots the calendar date based upon the calibration curve (cal yr BP, or calibrated years before present). Where the radiocarbon age strikes the calibration curve indicates the ranges in which the actual age of a radiocarbon sample is likely to lie. The curve wiggles because of inconsistent levels of radioactive carbon in the atmosphere.

when trying to date a stone point found lashed to a wooden shaft. The point itself could be older, or younger than the shaft. A radiocarbon date on the wooden shaft does not date the moment that the stone point was created, but rather, the moment the wood was cut from the tree to make a spear shaft.

THE SPREAD OF CLOVIS

Knowing how archaeologists date ancient artifacts, let us now examine the dissemination of Clovis technology. Around 13,000 years ago, Pleistocene megafauna became extinct in North America. To address whether humans were directly responsible, it is important to establish whether the megafaunal extinction occurred at the same time as the appearance and spread of humans across the continent. Archaeologists still have many questions about the Paleoindian Clovis hunters. How quickly could they adapt to new environments? Could they possibly have dispersed as swiftly as the radiocarbon dates seem to suggest? Archaeologists now question whether Clovis people, in fact, swept rapidly across a landscape hitherto devoid of humans, where megafauna feared no man and were exterminated by reckless hunters. In a recent article, Mike Waters and Thomas Staffords re-evaluated radiocarbon dates associated with Clovis and suggested a narrower and earlier time frame for Clovis culture than was previously ascribed: the newer range is 11,000 to 10,800 radiocarbon years ago, or 13,000 calendar years ago, suggesting either an extremely rapid dispersal of people or an equally accelerated transfer of Clovis technology across existing populations.

One might surmise that the Clovis question could be answered by finding and dating the oldest human skeletons. Alas, very few Paleoindian remains survived, and only a single burial, the Anzick male infant from south-central Montana, is associated with Clovis technology. The bones of this child were directly dated to $10,705 \pm 35$ radiocarbon years ago (approximately 12,707 to 12,556 calendar years ago). Another human skeleton, from Arlington Springs on Santa Rosa Island in Southern California, dates to $10,960 \pm 80$ carbon years ago (about 12,800 calendar years ago). Although the remains of the Arlington Springs Man suggested that people along the Pacific Coast had boats, his burial site did not reveal any evidence of Clovis tools.

With few human remains on which to rely, archaeologists frequently infer the spread of Clovis people from the spread of the Clovis point. The map on p. 132 [**6.6**] shows the distribution of fluted points that have been identified as Clovis or Clovis variants in North America. How does this distribution stack up against the extent of mass extinctions? In the many years since this debate commenced, archaeological evidence has provided ever-more sophisticated and abundant tests of the overkill hypothesis. Although reassessment of the age of Clovis sites suggests an even closer correlation between the arrival of Clovis people and the abrupt disappearance of mammoth and mastodon populations, it also focuses attention once again on another long-standing question: How could a human population reproduce and disperse so quickly that its people reached South America in only 300 years? At the

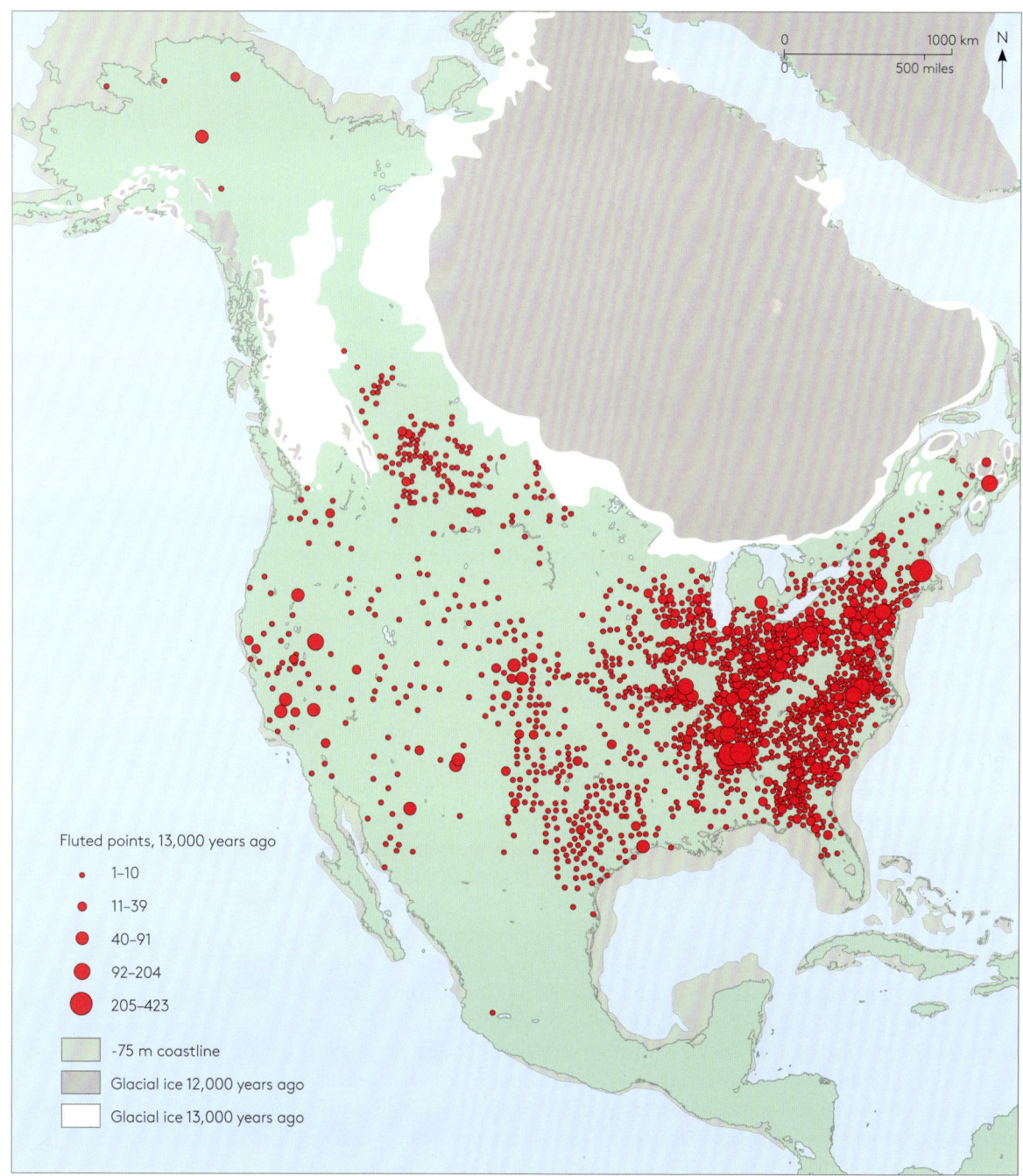

6.6 Distribution of fluted points in North America. Note the higher density in the eastern region than the western region, a pattern still under discussion.

fastest advance of a prehistoric population ever modeled, that of swift hunters who travel 8.5–14.5 miles (14–23 km) per year, a distance of 14,000 miles (approximately 23,000 km) from northern North America to the tip of South America would have taken somewhere between 600 and 1,000 years. And with exceedingly fast dispersal, how could Clovis hunters maintain sufficient population numbers and contacts so that their technology (Clovis points) appeared almost simultaneously across North America and retained stylistic uniformity?

Evidence from other sites—most notably, Page-Ladson (in northern Florida), the Friedkin Site (near Salado, Texas), and Monte Verde (in southern Chile)—now points to a Pre-Clovis population in North America. If a widespread but sparse Pre-Clovis population existed across the Americas, the rapid spread of a new technology among existing groups offers one explanation for the archaeological record: Clovis technology may have radiated in advance of the Clovis people. This more complicated story of the peopling of the Americas could begin to muddy the correlation between the arrival of humans and megafauna extinction.

HUNTING MEGAFAUNA

The timing of megafauna extinction appears to overlap with the arrival of Clovis hunters, although there is some controversy with regard to their first appearance, and what exactly the spread of the Clovis point throughout North America represents. The question to pose in deciphering any connection is whether the Pleistocene people hunted megafauna in great numbers.

The archaeological context of Clovis points indeed suggests a very close association between these weapons and the very largest animals: mammoths and mastodons. Cut-marks on tusks at Page-Ladson and peccary bone at Sheridan Cave (in northwest Ohio), and the caching of mastodon meat at the Burning Tree Mastodon site (in central Ohio), leave little doubt that humans ate these creatures. It also seems likely that humans hunted them, as the bones bear the butchery marks more typical of carcasses hunted than those scavenged.

Based on the few artifacts and occupation sites that have been found, we know the Clovis people moved frequently, but probably lived in semipermanent camps during the winter months. The remains of animal bone have been used to identify the Clovis diet, and it was actually quite varied and not exclusively focused on megafauna. Turkey, deer, sheep, turtles, and rodents have been found in sites across the southern portion of North America, whereas Clovis hunters in the west targeted camels, horses, and mountain sheep. Nuts and seeds were also consumed. Importantly, only five genera of megafauna have been found at Clovis sites: *Camelops* (camel), *Equus* (horse), *Cuvieronius* and *Mammut* (mastodons), and *Mammuthus* (mammoths). Of the several hundred Clovis sites that are known to exist, only fifteen offer evidence of the Clovis-era hunting of megafauna. Clovis points were certainly the tool of choice for hunting megafauna, but it is clear that Clovis hunters foraged more widely. Was their hunting on such a scale sufficient to result in extinction?

disarticulation The chopping up and separation of a corpse or carcass.

anaerobic Conditions without available oxygen, such as wetlands or severe heat and cold.

Below right: **6.7 Burning Tree site near Newark, Ohio, dating back 13,000 years ago.** A mastodon's bones and the contents of its gut were preserved in a swamp, allowing archaeologists to determine the animal's last meal. This image shows the mastodon's skull at the bottom of the excavation.

Below: **6.8 An illustration imagining a mastodon in a woodland habitat.** Long thought to be browsers of coniferous spruce, mastodons could and did consume deciduous trees and grasses, which meant they were able to thrive during climate-driven expansions of such plants.

MASTODONS AND THE ROLE OF A CHANGING ENVIRONMENT

The megafauna in North America became extinct at the end of Pleistocene, and at the same time the climate grew warmer. Could warming climates at the end of the Pleistocene have affected animal populations in the Americas regardless of the arrival of humans?

One site in North America that helps to answer this question is Burning Tree, near Newark, Ohio. Here, extraordinary evidence exists of not only the diet and adaptation of extinct mastodons [**6.7**, **6.8**], but also their exploitation by Paleoindians. Mastodons were an ancient species of elephant that lived in many parts of North America during the Pleistocene. They were smaller than their mammoth cousins, but still 6½ to almost 10 feet (2 to 3 meters) tall and weighing between 4 and 6 tons (around 3½–5½ tonnes).

At the Burning Tree site, no Clovis points or Paleoindian tools could be associated with the remains of a mastodon buried in a bog, but some evidence of **disarticulation** was uncovered. The bones and other parts of the carcass were extraordinarily well preserved by the **anaerobic** conditions of the wetland. This, along with the disarticulation of the remains, suggests that the meat had been "cached" for later consumption. The anaerobic conditions also preserved a cylindrical, reddish mass of partly digested plant material that reeked much as feces do. Microbiologist Jerry Goldstein of Ohio Wesleyan University, and a later team from the Center for Microbial Ecology at Michigan State University, examined the mass and identified species of intestinal bacteria. They also tested the surrounding peat and found

6.9 Gut contents from the Burning Tree mastodon. The contents included moss and grasses, as well as clovers, sedges, pondweed, water lily, and pigweed. This is a far wider range of plants than was expected.

freshwater bacteria but no intestinal varieties. By checking the sediment in which the mastodon was buried, the archaeologists and microbiologists confirmed that both the intestinal bacteria and mass were the remains of a mastodon's gut [**6.9**].

What was in this mastodon's gut? Experts recognized leaves, moss, chewed twigs, and the distinctive flowering (reproductive) parts of grasses, in addition to clovers, sedges, pondweed, water lily, and pigweed. It is the stomach contents of this mastodon that addresses the overkill hypothesis. What interested many was the lack of coniferous needles and twigs in the stomach, which were previously believed to be the major component of a mastodon diet. Paleontologists have argued that changing climate, especially during the **Bolling–Allerod Period** some 15,000 to 13,000 years ago, reduced the spruce woodlands to which mastodons had adapted, which would have threatened their survival. The Burning Tree mastodon, however, does not conform to this picture of the megafaunal tree eater, but instead conjures up the image of an animal grazing grasses and browsing deciduous plants in a location where spruce was widespread. Did Bolling–Allerod climate change really affect the mastodons as seriously as expected?

As paleoecologists develop increasingly sophisticated techniques to understand changing plant communities and the intricacies of climate change, it is apparent that climate changes do not entirely explain the extinctions of North American megafauna, or all extinctions at the end of the Pleistocene elsewhere. In the instance of Burning Tree, the climate may have transformed the forests of North America, but the mastodons still had food to eat. In earlier climatic shifts of the Pleistocene, some quite quick and dramatic in magnitude, mammoths and mastodons nonetheless survived, so their diets may not have been as narrowly defined as once thought.

Bolling–Allerod Period
A period some 15,000 to 13,000 years ago that led to an abrupt warming in the final stages of the Ice Age.

The radiocarbon-dated contents of the mastodon gut indicate that the animal died when Clovis people were present in the area between 11,798 and 11,191 years ago (these are calibrated dates from the site), but were the Clovis hunters really to blame for the megafauna's coming extinction?

Humans or Climate Change?

Critics have argued that the overkill hypothesis (the theory that humans were responsible for the extinction of megafauna) does not account for other animals that did survive the end of the Ice Age in North America. *Bison antiquus*, which is ancestral to the modern bison, endured, even as the climate changed. One argument suggests that the fluctuating population of bison may have had an impact on the ecological structure of the habitats on which other megafauna also relied as the climate changed. Bison are grazers [**6.10**] and closely tied to grassland maintenance, so their numbers affect the vegetation of grasslands and forests.

6.10 Bison in Yellowstone National Park, Wyoming. These bison (*Bison bison*) are the descendants of a species that roamed North America in the Pleistocene. Bison were among the megafauna that did not die out at the beginning of the Holocene.

Smaller species, including large numbers of birds, also became extinct, and these frequently migrated long distances and could escape human predators. Other species that humans valued survived the extinctions too, such as mountain sheep, the butchered remains of which were later found at Paisley Cave, Oregon. Perhaps the strongest alternate hypothesis is that climate change and the rapid disappearance of Pleistocene habitats proved too disruptive for the megafauna. Large animals, such as mammoths and mastodons, were vegetarians that needed access to expanses of plants year-round. The decline and fragmentation of habitats may have forced them to travel greater distances for food, putting additional pressure on their abilities to survive and multiply. In addition, enormous animals tend to reproduce more slowly than smaller ones, making their adaptive response times more sluggish.

The stressors these alternate circumstances created do not exonerate humans from a role in megafaunal extinctions. It is possible that changes in vegetation were amplified with the introduction of grassland fires set as part of human hunting strategies. Another likely scenario is that climatically induced environmental changes narrowed the number of ranges open to mammals and mastodons, pushing them to **refugia** (island-like patches of particular environments) where they could be isolated, easily tracked, and intensively hunted by humans. This scenario helps explain the rapid spread of Clovis culture: if these humans preferentially hunted mammoths and mastodons, then they would have moved from one refugium to the next, skipping past many other ecosystems and resources in between. With the so-called keystone animals (a species considered essential to maintaining an optimum ecosystem) gone, grasslands were transformed by other vegetation, and other fauna dependent on mammoth-maintained plant communities, in turn, experienced existential stresses. Perhaps removal of the mammoths and other big, slow, fearless animals triggered a chain of extinction, a cascading sequence of losses that came to include many species.

refugia Isolated patches of particular environments where animals find refuge.

SOUTH AMERICA: THE GIANT GROUND SLOTH

The question of a possible connection between humans and extinctions is relevant across the world. Recent research in South America provides additional evidence for a complex relationship between humans and megafauna in the Pleistocene and early Holocene. At Campo Laborde in the lush pampas or lowlands of east-central Argentina, stone and bone tool fragments have been associated with the butchered remains of giant ground sloths, which weighed a little more than 13,000 pounds (6,000 kg) and were roughly the size of an elephant. Paleoenvironmental analyses suggest that the landscape had transitioned from cool dry conditions to a marshlike lake, and there humans had hunted the sloths around 9,700 years ago, after many other Pleistocene megafauna had disappeared. Other sites, such as Arroyo Seco 2 (also in the Argentinian pampas), contain the remains of giant ground sloths, and large camels and horses (not megafauna), that were hunted between 14,000 and 13,000 years ago. Although both horses and giant ground sloths [**6.11**, p. 138] eventually

6.11 Reconstruction of a giant ground sloth with its infant. Archaeological evidence suggests that giant ground sloths were hunted up to 9,700 years ago, far later than other species of megafauna that disappeared in the Americas.

6.12 Map of archaeological sites in South America. Evidence from kill sites, camps, and human remains indicates that the first humans in South America, c. 14,000 years ago, pursued a variety of prey animals and collected marine foods.

went extinct in South America, the evidence for hunting across nearly 4,000 years indicates that humans did not necessarily cause their extinction at the outset; declines were variable across species and regions.

In other parts of South America [**6.12**], evidence exists of a Paleoindian diet dominated by marine foods. At the site of Quebrada Tacahuay near Peru's coast, people collected fish, crustaceans, and mollusks from the shoreline as early as 12,850 years ago. These diets were high in protein, and stone tools were not required to procure the marine life: nets and spears were used to collect them. Some 143 miles (230 km) to the north lies another early, seasonal fishing settlement at Quebrada Jaguay (13,200–11,400 years ago). These are among the earliest dated sites in South America; 14,000-year-old Monte Verde in Chile is another (see Chapter 4). The early sites near modern coastlines were several miles inland when sea levels were lower. They may represent only some of the maritime sites of the distant past, perhaps formed as a pre-Clovis population of migrants followed the Kelp Highway into the Americas, via coastal access. If newcomers used familiar marine resources and were quick to adapt to local foods, that strategy would account for rapid dispersal and subsequent expansion inland.

By 12,100 years ago, people were inhabiting highland caves in the Andes. The diverse biome of South America also supported another Pleistocene adaptation: a focus on plants as the main source of calories. Human skeletons at the Lagoa Santa site in central Brazil provide evidence of a varied diet. Dating back some 10,000 to 7,000 years ago, the skeletons' teeth contain a far higher proportion of dental cavities than what is typically found in people who subsist by hunting and gathering. The analysis conducted by Pedro Da-Gloria and Clark Larsen of the Lagoa Santa remains suggests that the cause of their tooth decay was a diet high in carbohydrates, probably local wild tubers. These findings hint at a more complex picture, with not all early humans reliant on hunting big game.

THE ROLE OF HUMANS IN EXTINCTION EVENTS

Since Paul Martin advanced his prehistoric overkill hypothesis, paleoecologists and archaeologists have examined the disappearance of fauna from many continents and islands, weighing the correlation of human dispersals with the geological record of climate changes and faunal extinctions. Assessment of this overkill hypothesis in North and South American contexts, and in Australia, reveals that the role of humans in extinction is both certain and dynamic: many animals of the Pleistocene went extinct and humans played a role, often a devastating one, in their ultimate fate. The great size and diversity of these continents, however, made for many particular trajectories and outcomes.

Other places in the world were transformed when humans entered the scene. For example, on islands where Holocene climates also wrought great environmental changes, many large-animal populations persisted and adapted after the Pleistocene, while their mainland cousins went extinct. The Mediterranean island of Cyprus sheltered pygmy hippos, and dwarf mammoths survived on Wrangel Island in the high Arctic. Then populations disappeared when humans discovered these remote islands. David Steadman's careful studies of bird extinctions on the Pacific Islands have shown a similarly disastrous outcome for the animals: flightless birds, for example the New Zealand moa [**6.13**], were without experience of human predators and very vulnerable to hunters. The very icon of haplessness is the extinguished Mauritian dodo bird. In some cases—such as Rapa Nui—it was not human hunting itself that caused avian extinctions but human-introduced rats that ate the eggs of ground-nesting birds.

Although it is clear that the dramatic climate changes characterizing the end of the Pleistocene would have been responsible for significant environmental changes, the fact is that many animal species also adapted and endured in refugia. In Africa and Europe, the end-of-Pleistocene extinctions seem to owe less to human hunting and more to climatic changes, for fauna in these regions had coexisted with hominin and other carnivorous predators for over 500,000 years (see Chapter 2). The disappearance of megafauna there appears to be gradual and sequential as glaciers retreated and temperate forests covered the continents. A similar case is more difficult to make in North America, South America, and Australia (Chapter 4), where the eradication of many genera of large mammals may be linked to the arrival of new technologies and a new species—human predators bearing enormous weapons and accompanied by trained hunting dogs. Human dispersals undoubtedly contributed to one of the five great extinction events in Earth's history, and it remains to be seen whether our current, unprecedented rate of population increase will cause yet another (which would be the sixth extinction).

6.13 Skeleton of a New Zealand moa. These flightless birds became extinct between 1300 and 1440 CE, not long after humans arrived *c.* 1280.

140   CHAPTER 6   EXTINCTIONS IN THE PAST

Chapter Questions

1. What are the main causes proposed for megafaunal extinction in North America? What forms of evidence have been important in advancing those theories?

2. On what scientific concepts is radiocarbon dating based? What have been the key challenges in ensuring its accuracy, and how have researchers addressed them?

3. Compare the story of megafaunal extinction in South America to that of North America. How are they different, and how might this contribute to the debate surrounding the cause of extinctions?

Additional Resources

Aitken, M. J. *Science Based Dating in Archaeology.* New York: Routledge, 2016.

Haynes, Gary. "The Catastrophic Extinction of North American Mammoths and Mastodons," *World Archaeology* 33 (2002): 391–416.

Politis, Gustavo G., Gutierrez, Maria A., Rafuse, Daniel J., and Blasi, Adriana. "The Arrival of *Homo sapiens* into the Southern Cone at 14,000 Years Ago," *PLoS ONE* 11, no. 9 (2016). doi:10.1371/journal.pone.0162870.

Scott, Eric. "Extinctions, Scenarios, and Assumptions: Changes in Latest Pleistocene Large Herbivore Abundance and Distribution in Western North America," *Quaternary International* 217 (2010): 225–39.

Steadman, David W., Oswald, Jessica A., and Rincón, Ascanio D. "The Diversity and Biogeography of Late Pleistocene Birds from the Lowland Neotropics," *Quaternary Research* 83 (2015): 555–64.

Waters, Michael R., and Stafford, Thomas W. "Redefining the Age of Clovis: Implications for the Peopling of the Americas," *Science* 315, no. 5815 (2007): 1122–26. doi:10.1126/science.1137166.

UNDERSTANDING HUMAN DECISIONS
Evolutionary and Social Theory

7

In archaeology, we may frequently be able to describe the "what," but we must also ask "why." Why did a group of humans choose one strategy or way of life over another? To answer this important question, we will examine how people of the past made their decisions—much as I did when I first traveled to the village of Naduri, on the west bank of the Sigatoka River in Fiji, a remote island nation in the South Pacific Ocean.

Naduri is home to the Tabanivono people, who have resided in Fiji's volcanic mountains for as long as anyone can remember. Their oral histories describe a series of migrations from village to village, one of which was Nokonoko, a hilltop fortification nearby. The chief was absent the day I arrived, but his brothers sat patiently and considered my request to complete archaeological research at Nokonoko. With my promise to return and provide a full report of my findings, they offered their enthusiastic approval, "Bula vinaka, Julie" (Thank you, Julie), followed by a final round of drinks from the bottom of the *tanoa*, the communal kava bowl. The men also gave me some advice: borrow a horse to ascend the steep slope that led to Nokonoko. What they did not explain was why they had chosen to live there in the first place. In such social sciences as anthropology and archaeology, theory—either evolutionary theory or social theory—is used to answer these kinds of questions.

At the core of evolutionary theory is the process of natural selection proposed by Charles Darwin in *The Origin of Species*: that individuals vary in form and behavior, and changes in population are determined by differing rates of reproductive success. Social theory argues that humans act on the basis of shared ideas and conventions, which might validate or limit an individual's choices. These two approaches, in fact, do not stand in opposition to each other; usually, the more accurate interpretations of the past include both.

Archaeology and its view of many outcomes in prehistory offer us an unparalleled array of human choices. In this chapter, we examine different ways to comprehend human decision-making, exploring the bison hunters of the Great Plains and their choices in hunting; communities in Fiji and their choice of conflict; and communal versus individual decisions in St. Kilda, Scotland (the most remote part of the British Isles). Here, as in the chapters that follow, we begin to grasp not only how people's decisions changed the world, but also the reasons why they made those decisions.

Bison Hunters of the American Great Plains **144**

Zooarchaeology **146**

Bison Hunting and Butchering in Context **147**

South Pacific: Conflict and Fortification in Fiji **154**

Europe: Deciding With or Against a Community in St. Kilda **161**

The Amazon: Decision-Making Today **165**

Opposite Preparing and squeezing kava to drink at a traditional ceremony. Wiwi Village, Taveuni Island, Fiji Islands, Pacific Ocean.

Key Concepts

- Evolutionary and social explanations of decision-making in the past
- Concepts underlying the subdiscipline of zooarchaeology
- Both evolutionary and social theory as applied to bison hunting in the American Great Plains, community conflict in Fiji, and decision-making in St. Kilda, Scotland

BISON HUNTERS OF THE AMERICAN GREAT PLAINS

Approximately 2,000 years ago in central Wyoming, a small herd of American bison (*Bison bison*, commonly and inaccurately called "buffalo") grazing on dry grass was suddenly startled. Something had appeared behind the animals, and they abruptly ran forward to escape it. Picking up speed, the bison spurted up the crest of a hill and then headed toward the horizon ahead of them. As they passed several piles of rocks, a number of humans jumped up from behind. The bison then picked up speed and wheeled to the right. It looked as if the dry hills continued for a distance and a clear path lay ahead of them. Instead, the ground dropped out from under their feet and they began to tumble over a low bank into a dry **arroyo**, which was blocked at one end with a high timber wall. The bison surged against the wall, and as more bison piled in from behind, those at the wall were soon pinned against it and then trampled to the ground. They were trapped.

The people who had trapped bison in the arroyo nearly 2,000 years ago established a processing area and camp, and they used ceramic pots to cook meat and fat. They were part of a community that archaeologists named the "Besant" (we do not know what they called themselves), and they hunted bison on the high plains of central Wyoming using corrals (pens) and traps. Their descendants, the Shoshone and Cheyenne, were still hunting bison in the nineteenth century, by which time they had integrated horses into their bison-hunting strategies. The seemingly endless plain of short grass and brush we see now was once home to enormous herds of American bison. It has been estimated that between 30 and 60 million bison lived on the Great Plains in the seventeenth century, prior to Euroamerican settlement and annihilation of the herds for hides, bone, and sport. Bison were so numerous that they expanded across North America much as a hooved ocean would, and it is more accurate to say they constructed the ecosystem of the plains than to say they merely occupied it. Their grazing and dung energized the grasses, and other animals—including birds, deer, and such predators as wolves and coyotes—flourished in their wake. Now the surrounding landscape seems completely empty, nearly two centuries after the bison were eradicated from that part of Wyoming.

arroyo A steep-sided dry creek or stream bed that only flows with water after sufficient rain.

bone bed An archaeological layer that includes a large proportion of bones.

Some 1,800 years after the Besant hunt, the bones of many of these same bison were found eroding from a slope at the Cedar Gap site in central Wyoming among the foothills of the Bighorn Mountain range [7.1]. They were all that remained of a former wooden corral after later floods carved away the sediment. When presented with this **bone bed**, archaeologists had many questions. Would it be possible to determine how these bison had been butchered? How many were killed? During

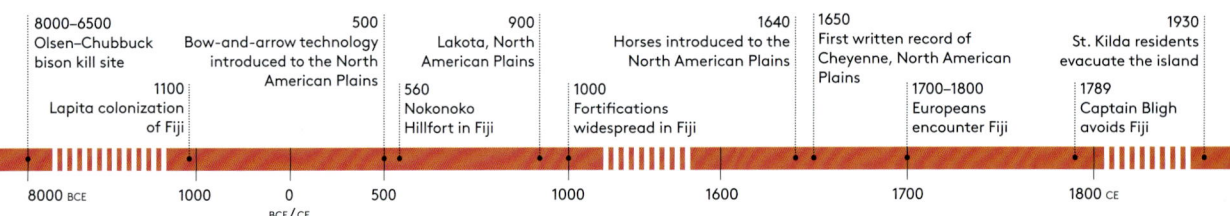

8000–6500 Olsen–Chubbuck bison kill site
1100 Lapita colonization of Fiji
Bow-and-arrow technology introduced to the North American Plains
500
560 Nokonoko Hillfort in Fiji
900 Lakota, North American Plains
1000 Fortifications widespread in Fiji
1640 Horses introduced to the North American Plains
1650 First written record of Cheyenne, North American Plains
1700–1800 Europeans encounter Fiji
1789 Captain Bligh avoids Fiji
1930 St. Kilda residents evacuate the island

7.1 Excavation of the Cedar Gap site, Wyoming. Archaeologists carefully reveal the bones of bison trapped at the site 2,000 years ago. Cord-marked pottery was also recovered from the deposits; it was probably used for cooking the meat.

7.2 Excavation of a bone bed at Hudson–Meng bison kill site, Nebraska. Located at the foot of a steep cliff, this site was used by Paleoindians to kill hundreds of bison, including the extinct *Bison antiquus*, which roamed the grasslands of western Nebraska 10,000 years ago.

what time of year had the slaughter occurred? Would the bones be able to reveal more about how the Besant lived? Both **evolutionary theory** and **social theory** may help answer these questions, but it is first necessary to obtain data, and this is accomplished through excavation, identification, and analysis of the remains [**7.2**].

evolutionary theory Explains human actions in terms of how they may impact fitness (the creation of offspring in the next generation).

social theory Explains human actions in terms of shared ideas and conventions.

BISON HUNTERS OF THE AMERICAN GREAT PLAINS   145

zooarchaeology
A subdiscipline of archaeology that studies past human engagements with animals, usually through the remains of animals at archaeological sites.

reference specimens
The complete set of bones of a particular species that zooarchaeologists use to identify an excavated bone.

taxonomic identification
Identifying to which genus or species a bone belongs.

appendages Limbs of an animal.

axial elements The spine and head of an animal.

ZOOARCHAEOLOGY

Archaeologists regularly encounter the remains of animals in archaeological deposits. A subdiscipline of archaeology, **zooarchaeology** [7.3], seeks to understand how humans have procured and used animals in the past. To serve as a zooarchaeologist, one must have thorough training in comparative animal anatomy and a near-encyclopedic knowledge, both visual and tactile (perceptible by touch), of every element of an animal's skeleton, teeth, or shells, because these are frequently the only part(s) of an animal that are preserved in the ground. **Reference specimens**, the complete sets of bones of particular species, are critical for zooarchaeological study, as they display often subtle differences between the individual bones of different species.

The first step in zooarchaeological analysis is to excavate a bone and transport it to an archaeological laboratory. There, the bone can be analyzed according to element (which part of the skeleton is represented) and then **taxonomic identification**. Taxonomic identification can be quite difficult. For example, the tibia (lower leg bone) of a wolf would be identified as belonging to the family *Canidae* and possibly the genus *Canis*, but beyond that the legs of dogs, wolves, and coyotes are similar. Determining the species (in the case of wolves, *Canis lupus*) often requires the presence of special bones, such as parts of the cranium. Once the most precise taxonomic identification possible for the bones has been determined, bones can be further examined for evidence of human modification. Cutting, smashing, and cooking all leave particular marks on bones that are indicative of butchery and processing. Most butchery focuses on separating the **appendages** from the **axial elements**, and cuts on the bone are usually found near the joints. Large bones can be smashed with heavy stone hammers, allowing the marrow to be extracted.

It is frequently important to understand also how *many* animals have been recovered archaeologically. This is calculated using two different measures. The **number**

7.3 Zooarchaeology in action. A zooarchaeologist uses a reference specimen (left) to compare and identify fragments of bone (right) excavated at an archaeological site. This image shows the maxilla (upper jaw) of a fish.

of identified specimens (NISP) simply counts the number of bones from each taxonomic group (usually genus, but sometimes species) as representative of the total potential individuals. In the case of Cedar Gap, thirty-five bones identified as *Bison bison* (buffalo) would be equated with a herd of thirty-five individuals. This measure certainly overestimates the number of animals in an assemblage (two or more bones may come from a single individual), but it can be useful when comparing the relative proportion of different species in an assemblage.

A second measure is the **minimum number of individuals (MNI)**, which indicates the minimum number of animals required to generate the assemblage. This measures elements that are only found once in one skeleton. In most cases, the most abundant single element from a left or right side can be used to determine the minimum. If the assemblage contains forty-seven right tibiae (the lower bone of the rear leg), then there must have been forty-seven individuals. That is because nearly all mammals (excluding whales and some other marine mammals) only have one right tibia.

Zooarchaeology additionally examines bone **taphonomy**. Animals of different sizes produce bones of varying thickness and length, and local conditions may erode, dissolve, or—in the case of gnawing dogs—crunch and crush bones to the point of destruction. Taphonomy also helps the archaeologist remember that excavations are sometimes biased toward bigger bones, and if large-sized sieving screens are used, the tiny bones of fish, rodents, and birds may be lost. Younger animals, which are often considerably smaller than their parents, may also be more highly fragmented and misidentified as other animals.

Determining the age of animals in the assemblage can also indicate the time of year that the hunt took place. This is done primarily through the analysis of teeth but also by the size and length of limb bones. In all mammals, teeth emerge as the animal grows from juvenile to adult. Older individuals frequently exhibit tooth loss or visible wear and tear on their remaining teeth. In the case of bison, the presence of juveniles and fetuses is the most delicate indicator of time. Calves are born in spring, and cows usually become pregnant in late summer and early fall. If an assemblage contains fetal bison remains but no juveniles, then the hunt probably occurred in late fall after last spring's calves had grown, and the cows were already pregnant again with next year's calves.

BISON HUNTING AND BUTCHERING IN CONTEXT

From analyzing the remains of the bison, it is possible to build a picture of how they were hunted and later butchered. Hunting bison would have been a difficult and complex undertaking for an individual person. Bison were enormous and powerful, not easily intimidated by a single hunter. They also lived in herds, and watched and smelled for any hint of a predator. In addition, bison were intelligent and, as a herd, had intimate knowledge of the vast surrounding landscape. They followed paths and trails that had been tested by their ancestors and found to be safe. How then

---

number of identified specimens (NISP) A total count of the number of bones from each genus or species (e.g., number of bones belonging to the cow family or *Bovidae*).

minimum number of individuals (MNI) A calculation of the minimum number of individuals who could have generated an assemblage of bones, based upon counts of elements that occur only once (such as a left radius).

taphonomy Factors that affect the deposit and preservation of archaeological remains.

were the bison hunted? How did people outsmart them? How did humans determine the best way to hunt and kill an animal so big and so numerous?

For the hunters of the Great Plains, the solution was to work together: take advantage of the bison's numbers and exploit the inevitable confusion that erupts when large groups of animals react to a perceived threat. Based on historical accounts, bison herds numbered in the thousands and migrated across the plains in mega-herds of a million or more. The Great Plains are a large expanse of flat and rolling land, but rivers, canyons, and cliffs snake their way across them. Prior to the introduction of the horse, bison were hunted communally by small groups of people, who drove the prey into box canyons, down steep hills, into arroyos, or off cliffs. In some places, wooden corrals were used to trap smaller herds of bison. These hunts frequently required the use of a decoy (for instance, a human dressed in a bison skin, which the herd would follow out of curiosity) to lure the animals in a particular direction. Then, when the time was right, the remaining hunters would emerge from behind stone cairns (conical stacks of stones) or timber blinds (upright panels) and stampede the bison into the enclosure or over a cliff.

Both archaeological excavations and historic accounts point to what unfolded next. The bison that fell over cliffs often broke their necks or legs; those driven into arroyos and enclosures were crushed beneath the bodies of those running in from behind. Hunters would then face the tasks of slaughtering the injured bison and butchering the dead for meat, hides, and other resources. The number of animals killed was sometimes staggering—from sixty to more than a thousand. The rewards given the expenditure of human effort were enormous, though: the butchering of a single cow could yield approximately 800 pounds (about 363 kg) of meat and fat. When hundreds of animals were slaughtered, the amount of meat might equal more than 100,000 pounds (45,359 kg). This meat could then be cut into strips and dried, allowing it to be stored for months. This method of hunting was clearly efficient. It required the efforts of only a few people and an effective strategy to trap the bison, and the payoff would be plentiful food for a sizable population for quite some time.

This large-scale butchering could also be wasteful, however. In many cases, not all of the meat was used. In 1793, an American trapper witnessed the butchery of bison by Piegan hunters in southern Alberta, Canada. He described the enclosure (what he called a "pound") as being filled with bison "laying 5 or 6 deep one upon the other, all through which in the whole was above 250 buffalo….[W]hen the wind happened to blow from the pound in the direction of the tents, there was an intolerable stench of the great number of putrefied carcasses." Similar cases of waste have been documented at archaeological sites. Eight thousand years ago, at the Olsen–Chubbuck site in eastern Colorado [7.4], a herd of bison became trapped in a narrow gulch (a deep, V-shaped valley). The bison in the lead were crushed beneath the bodies of those rushing from behind, and the bodies soon stacked up three to four deep. The processing of the carcasses indicates both deliberate human choice in terms of which bison were butchered, and an element of efficiency. Only the

7.4 "River of bison bones" at the Olsen–Chubbuck kill site in eastern Colorado. It has been estimated that some 50,000 lbs (22,680 kg) of meat was produced by the kill, but at least forty bison were not butchered at all.

animals on top of the pile were fully butchered, with their bodies stripped of flesh and organs, and their remains scattered widely throughout the gully. Choice body parts were cut away from the buffalo beneath, and the buffalo at the very bottom of the gulch were left untouched. It has been calculated that a total of 50,000 pounds of meat (22,680 kg) were extracted from the kill, although in the end at least forty bison were not butchered. Most likely, the unbutchered carcasses had already started to rot by the time the bison on top of the pile were removed.

Evolutionary Theory and the Bison Hunt

What guides human decisions on hunting? Archaeologists use a variety of approaches to explore this question, one of the most common being evolutionary theory. It argues that natural selection (the factors that determine the survival and reproduction of an animal) shaped many of the choices communities made in the past. Evolutionary theory suggests that individuals adapt because they are self-interested: they eat to live, seek to avoid injury, attempt to reproduce, and will go to great lengths to keep their offspring alive. An organism will also change its habitat in a way that improves the overall fitness of its descendants, forming an ecological niche that is beneficial for future offspring. This explanation can make measuring the fitness of humans difficult as successive generations will need to pass before any sound judgment may be issued on what contributed to fitness and what did not. Because of this, evolutionary biologists utilize the measurement of energy, often expressed as calories, as a proxy indicator of fitness.

At a base level of this theory, "energy," which is food, becomes the main currency in decision-making. Imagine a hungry person stranded on a desert island. Before long, she might begin to wonder if she should spend the next hour gathering snails at the beach, or several hours catching a large fish further from shore. She will then consider the probable rate of success for each strategy—which will yield the most food, the best return, with the least expenditure of energy. Of course, ours is a single-case scenario, but evolutionary approaches suggest that all living creatures with advanced cognitive abilities make these kinds of choices on a regular basis. At this level of hypothesizing, the greatest profit would seem to be the goal of most human activities, but when we delve further into the invested time and effort and measure them against expected returns, the objective instead appears to be efficiency. The people of the Great Plains needed to hunt bison, and they chose to drive bison over cliffs or otherwise entrap them because it was the most efficient means of killing them—and also considerably safer than attempting to hunt them individually with spears or bows and arrows.

Social Theory and the World of the Bison

To describe bison hunting only in terms of sustenance and efficiency would be but one part of the tale, and a somewhat colorless one at that. Bison also played a wider role in the lives of the native people of the Great Plains. Shepard Krech provides a vivid description of their importance. He describes an animal that could be used in its entirety, of which little would be wasted:

> Native people ate an incredible variety of bison parts with great relish: meat, fat, most organs, testicles, nose gristle, nipples, blood, milk, marrow, and fetus. They dried, roasted, boiled, and ate meat raw; pounded bones to make bone grease; and mixed dry, pounded meat with fat to make pemmican.... For people like the Blackfeet, the buffalo provided over one

hundred specific items of material culture. They include robes (hair on) for bedding, gloves, winter clothing, and ceremonial and decoy costumes; hides (hair off) for tipi covers and linings, cups, parfleches, moccasins, leggings and other clothing…the paunch and large intestine as containers; the gallstones for yellow pigment; hoofs as rattles or for glue; the tibia and other bones for fleshers, brushes, awls, and other tools; horns for arrow points, bow parts, ladles, cups, spoons, and containers for tobacco and medicines….From a purely material standpoint, it would have been virtually impossible to be out of sight, touch, or smell of a product fabricated from bison at any time of day or night. The bison was "a tribal department store," as Tom McHugh, a zoologist remarked, a "builders' emporium, furniture mart, and supermarket rolled into one."

What Krech describes is how, with the exception of water, bison offered all the necessary elements for life on the Great Plains of North America. Virtually every part of the bison could be used for food, or to make a tool, item of clothing [**7.5**], or shelter. This is why the animal took on a central role in the religion and ceremonies of Plains people: the bison was the great provider. Hunting the bison would become a sacred task for them, as this creature was so essential to their survival.

An **ideology**, or collection of ideas, emanating from the sacrosanct regard of bison is thus unsurprising given the animal's economic importance in the lives of Plains people. Even as the guiding principles of evolutionary theory render human choices understandable, they may also be explained by social theory. One major social theory, **historical materialism**, identifies an interplay between the economic basis of a society (here, bison hunting) and the ideology that comes to shape social choices. The decisions people reached concerning bison were tied to social expectations and conventions, or **social structure**. This meant religious practices openly referenced bison. The Lakota and Cheyenne people of the northern Plains were known, for example, to perform a bison dance at an annual festival that coincided with the return of the herds; it was sometimes also associated with curing the ill. The people of the Great Plains shared a wide set of conventions that helped them decide when to move camp and how to decipher the signs indicating the approach or direction of nearby bison herds. Even if a pregnant woman might be reluctant to set up a new camp elsewhere, religious ideology and social conventions could persuade her to decide against her reproductive or evolutionary best interest. The choices humans made concerning bison are therefore best understood from both an evolutionary and a social perspective.

Ethnoarchaeology among the Nunamiut

How do archaeologists know so much about the logistics of prehistoric hunting? They have learned a lot from people who still hunt in traditional ways. Beginning in the 1960s, archaeologists put down their trowels and went to the few places

ideology A system of ideas shared by a population that forms the foundation of beliefs and principles.

historical materialism A social theory that relates the economics of a society to its social structure and ideology.

social structure The arrangement of ideas, conventions, and institutions that relate individuals to each other, and make up a society.

7.5 Many objects were made from bison, such as this hide bag (below), decorated with dyed porcupine quills, created between 1790 and 1830 near the Great Lakes. The moccasin shoe (bottom) was found at Promontory Cave, on the north shore of Great Salt Lake, Utah.

ethnoarchaeology The study of modern processes in present-day societies (e.g., how tools are made, how food is prepared) in order to draw conclusions about past societies from their material remains.

where traditional hunting was still being practiced: the plains of northern Alaska, the brush country of Tanzania, and the desert outback of Western Australia. In the 1970s, American archaeologist Lewis Binford went to live with the Nunamiut, who inhabit the interior of northern Alaska and speak a dialect of the Inupiaq language. Other Inupiaq-speaking communities live along the far northern coast of Alaska; they are referred to as the "sea people" because they hunt marine mammals and fish. The Nunamiut [**7.6**] are the "land people," who hunt caribou and other terrestrial (land) fauna. At the time of Binford's visit, the Nunamiut retained much of their traditional lifestyle, as they lived in a remote location and had little contact with outsiders. They clustered in a small village and relied on hunting to provide them with food, clothing, and tools. Binford accompanied them on their hunting trips, recorded the time they spent in each activity, and measured the outcomes: amounts of meat eaten or stored, hides and sinew collected for clothing and tools, the spatial placement of their campfires and heaps of discarded bone. His study and others similar to it generated the new field of **ethnoarchaeology**. The findings produced by ethnoarchaeologists have been used to develop sophisticated models of hunting and foraging, which aid in the interpretation of faunal remains in archaeological deposits.

One of the first developments of ethnoarchaeology was to define how the world looks from the perspective of a forager or a hunter. Both often conceive of space as a series of "patches" that contain a particular resource, such as animals to hunt or foods to gather. Hunters make choices about which patches to try each day, but

7.6 A Nunamiut family moving to a new hunting camp in northern Alaska, using sleds pulled by dogs, c. 1940. In all environments, hunters make decisions about where and what to hunt.

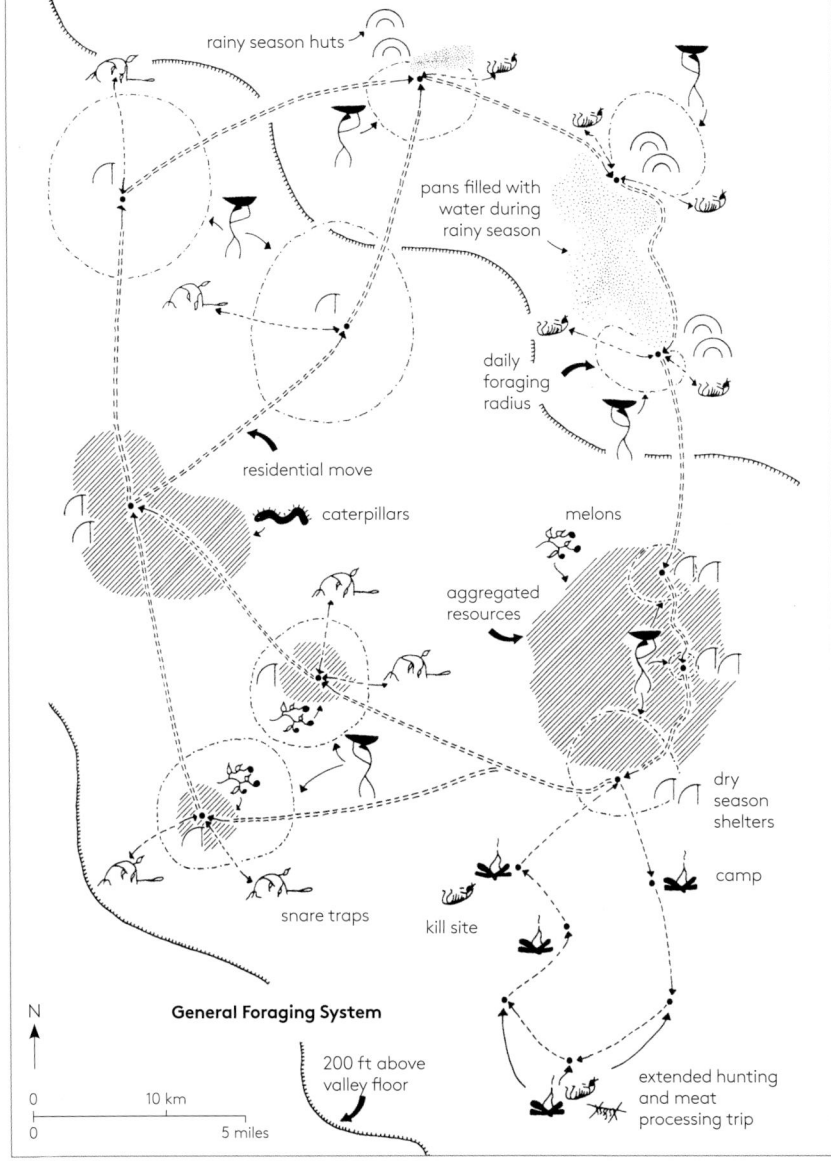

7.7 Lewis Binford's diagram of a foraging subsistence-settlement system. This illustrates how foragers move their residences throughout the year (indicated by the double hashed lines) in order to access different resource "patches," for example concentrations of nuts, melons, and animals that can be captured with snares. Forays out from these residences are indicated by other dashed lines, which show extended trips or daily rounds.

can switch to a new patch if their first choice comes up empty. Their decision to select a new patch must also factor in time and distance: if the new patch is too far away, the hunters may arrive too late to do any practical hunting. They may also need to alter their choice of prey if their preferred animal is not located in enough time. Binford additionally made the point that **settlement systems** (where and how people reside) vary among hunters and gatherers living in different environments [**7.7**]. Some hunters depart from a central place and forage in different directions,

settlement systems The spatial and temporal organization that determines where, when, and how people reside.

returning home each day with their catches. Other communities must move regularly, as the patches around them deplete quickly. For the archaeologist, these two settlement systems would yield very different archaeological deposits.

For the people of the Great Plains, the bison were a large, mobile "patch" with which they had to remain in contact. They moved with the herds and over many centuries observed their movement across different topographic elements, such as arroyos and cliffs. Places that could be transformed into natural traps were augmented with blinds and corrals, and in many instances they were used repeatedly, producing deposits that resulted from several weeks of residence. These groups also timed their hunts to occur in the fall, when the bison had grown their thickest layer of fat and would have provided the most return on the hunters' investment of time and energy. The answer to the daily question of what to hunt would likely not have been rabbit or geese, but rather the bison: "Our traps are prepared. Let us find them."

SOUTH PACIFIC: CONFLICT AND FORTIFICATION IN FIJI

Choices in a community involve not only how to feed your people but also how to interact with those around you. In ancient Fiji, located in Melanesia in the South Pacific, many choices appear to involve conflict. Fortifications were the norm for much of Fijian prehistory. The people whom Europeans encountered in the eighteenth and nineteenth centuries were organized into coalitions of tribes, with high chiefs claiming (and often battling for) control over particular regions. They frequently raided one another's villages, and Fijians had institutionalized violence as a requirement for adulthood: no male child was considered a true man until he had clubbed and killed another person [7.8].

Men kept their clubs tucked in their waistbands in anticipation of ambush or attack. To launch a newly constructed war canoe, chiefs called for "rollers," rows of human bodies over which the heavy hulls would be transported from the beach to the water. Christian missionaries later described how villages rejoiced when their war canoes returned home with a cargo of raided goods and prisoners, many of whom would soon perish in earth ovens (fire pits that were covered with dirt, allowing the meat to roast underground). It was also reported that villagers remained on the lookout for incoming ships exhibiting "birds," the bodies of young children who had been hung by their legs from the masthead. Although it is likely some of these accounts are exaggerated—especially those of missionaries who frequently saw "the devil" in natives' actions—the ghoulishness and brutality of Fijian society were also recounted by other islanders, such as Tongans, who warned European sailors about the dangers of landing on Fiji. Following the mutiny on HMS *Bounty* in 1789, Captain William Bligh and the eighteen crew members set adrift on a launch sailed through Fiji without stopping [7.9], even though the men were in desperate need of rest and supplies. They were terrified of becoming some chief's dinner and unwilling to take any risks. Other islands also had a history of constant warfare and cannibalism, but Fijians seemed to take it to an extreme. Why?

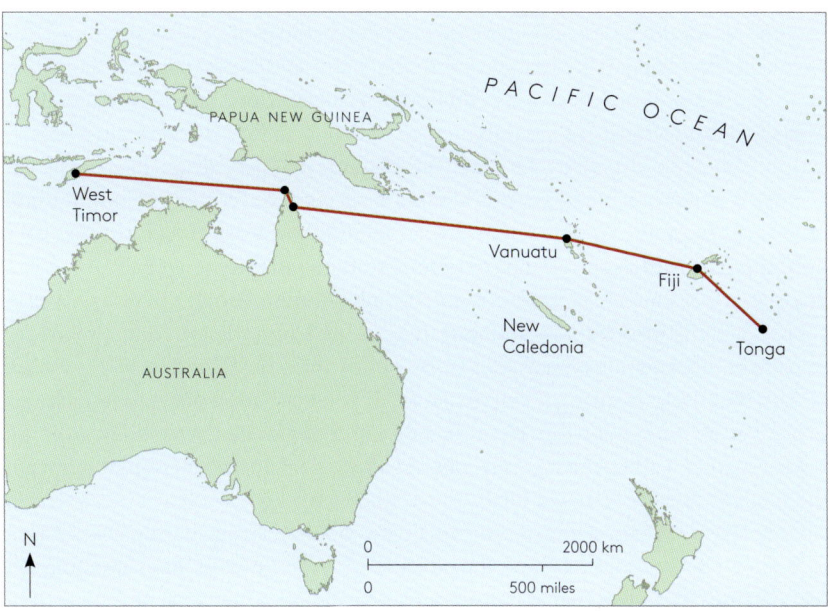

Above: **7.8 Club dance, Fiji.** As depicted by Drayton in 1840, and published in the narrative of the US Exploring Expedition of 1840–43. Conflict was an integral part of Fijian society in the nineteenth century, and hand-to-hand fighting employed heavy clubs. In this image, warriors perform a dance to show off their strength and skill with their clubs.

Left: **7.9 After the mutiny aboard HMS *Bounty*,** Captain William Bligh and eighteen loyalists traversed the seas of the South Pacific, from the island of Tofua near Tonga, to Coupang in Timor, for forty-seven days. Having heard stories of cannibalism and fearing an onslaught, the men did not venture ashore at Fiji.

SOUTH PACIFIC: CONFLICT AND FORTIFICATION IN FIJI

7.10 Lapita pottery, dated to between 1350 and 800 BCE. The Lapita people were the earliest settlers in the Southwestern Pacific, and they voyaged from the Bismarck Archipelago near Papua New Guinea to the Solomon Islands, Vanuatu, New Caledonia, Fiji, Tonga, and Samoa. Their distinctive ceramics were punctuated by geometric designs that have been passed down in traditional Pacific Islands tattooing.

Using an archaeological perspective, we reformulate that question into another: What was the context of conflict in Fijian prehistory? Approximately 3,000 years ago, Fiji was colonized by people adept at sailing long distances. As part of the expansion of the ocean-faring Lapita culture [**7.10**], the first Fijian settlements sprang up on the coast; evidence suggests the population subsisted principally on marine foods. Even so, in their activities the Fijians demonstrated an interest in becoming farmers. In the first 500 years of settlement, they explored and systematically burned the interiors of the islands, removing whole sections of the palm and hardwood forest, and replacing them with open spaces for growing crops, such as taro (*Colocasia esculenta*, **7.11**) and yam (*Dioscorea* spp.). The study of soils and climate throughout the Pacific Islands has revealed that although the isles offer fertile lands, the crops themselves have temporal and spatial limitations. In dry years, and especially after damaging cyclones, the food supplies for an entire region can be wiped out. Little technology exists for storing food in moist, hot climates, making it difficult to maintain a backup supply. These conditions suggest that food producers in Fiji likely ran into consistent problems when seeking to provide adequate sustenance for one community, and often strife became a common, if unsavory, solution to hardship. As revealed in our prior discussion of the kivas and communal storage and ceremony in the American Southwest (see Chapter 5), conflict is not the only solution. People can also choose to cooperate. Why fortifications and warfare remained dominant in Fijian prehistory in spite of other options is a matter worthy of further consideration.

The mountain fortress of Nokonoko [**7.12**] is a very good place to launch our investigation into the history of conflict on Fiji. The forested peak looms over the lower Sigatoka Valley, and it was recorded in historical documents and maps from the 1860s as the site of an old fortification. Rising more than 600 feet (200 meters), Nokonoko is visible from the outskirts of Sigatoka Town. To get there, one is advised to borrow a horse and then follow the ridgeline of the mountains. After climbing 500 feet (152 meters) in less than a mile (or 2 km), the land becomes flat and covered in

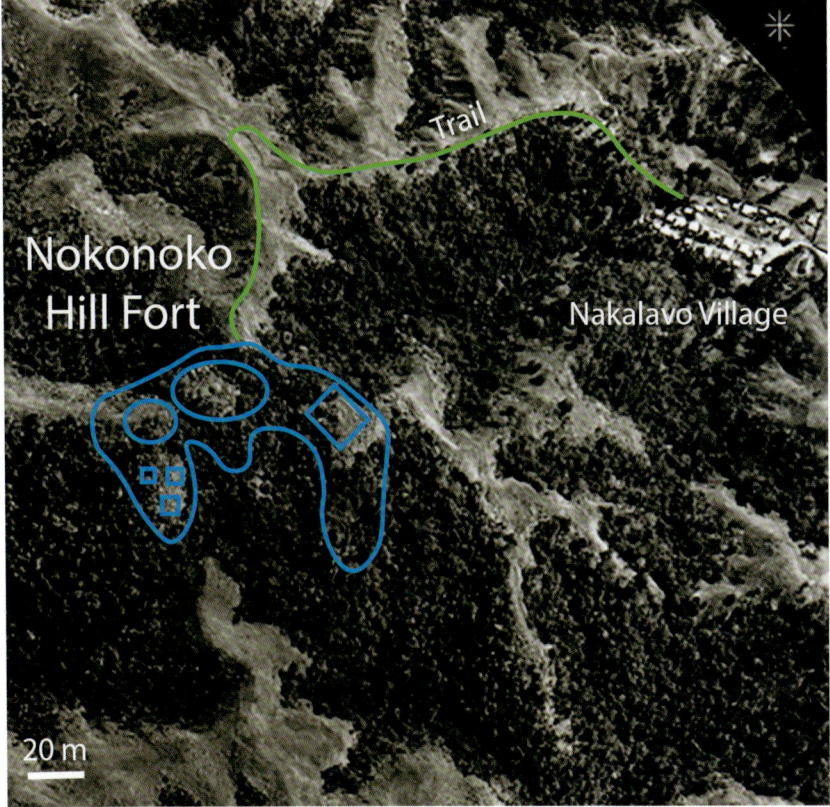

Above: **7.11 A modern-day taro paddy in Waipio Valley, Hawai'i.** The taro (*Colocasia esculenta*) produces a starchy root and nutritious green leaves. Farmers who colonized the islands of the Pacific transformed the landscape to produce these crops.

Left: **7.12 Aerial photograph of the hillfort of Nokonoko, Fiji.** The fortification is very challenging to reach, calling for a climb up steep mountainsides. The access to the site via a ridgeline (green line) crosses several cut trenches that were originally put in place for defense. The mounds on the top of the fortification (light blue line) are prehistoric (500 CE) burials and house foundations.

7.13 View of the Tavuni Hillfort, Fiji. Steep slopes and extensive views defended the inhabitants of Tavuni Hillfort from attack. Many of the hilltops and ridgelines in Fiji were similarly used as fortifications.

low flat-topped mounds. White shell and pottery pieces are visible in the crevices of rocky outcrops. This was Nokonoko, the ancient village of the Tabanivono people. The village counted more than forty mounds, including a high conical mound at its center. The flat mounds are the former foundations of timber and thatched Fijian houses, and the conical mound marks the site of a chief's burial, although the foundation for a home was likely interred at the base. The site is very large by any standard in Fiji, with more houses extending down the surrounding ridgelines. No water exists here, or farmland to grow crops; the nearest stream is back down the trail, over an hour away. As one makes this arduous journey up and across the mountains, it is impossible not to wonder why someone would choose to live here with limited, difficult access to the resources necessary for daily life.

Nokonoko is just one of thousands of fortifications in Fiji [7.13]. Although a complete survey of all the archipelago's peaks has not been made, archaeologists have concluded that fortified villages were the norm for much of prehistory. Either via their location on remote peaks, or through the construction of solid stone, wood, and earth fortifications, Fijians invested great time and effort in making their villages impregnable. They also located them in places honeycombed with caves and kept them stocked with extra food and water, in the event of a lengthy siege. Excavations at Nokonoko revealed that occupation commenced there *c.* 560 CE, and the fortification remained in use as a residence and refuge until 1820. Other fortifications in the Sigatoka Valley were inhabited *c.* 1000. From these data, we may conclude that fortifications and the related behaviors of warfare, such as raids, armed battles, and capture of prisoners, occurred there for at least thirteen centuries.

Why Exist in a Near-Constant State of Conflict?

Evolutionary theory has been used to study conflict in the past. Through warfare, territoriality, or the expansion of an empire, conflict has a very simple goal: capturing resources and driving away rivals. Conflict has both costs and benefits for the individual. It can maximize fitness (i.e., remove rivals or make more food available to ensure offspring and their survival) and reduce risk. In groups, individuals must try to maximize access to resources (or minimize risk to those resources) by competitive and cooperative interaction with other individuals also in the group—usually, family members or members of the community.

Based on ethnographic studies, conflict appears to be linked to ecological variables, in particular, dense and predictable resources. As a simple analogy, an apple tree would constitute a dense and predictable resource, as apples develop every year and are dense on the tree. Conversely, a sparse and unpredictable resource would be wild mushrooms, which occur over a wide area and are closely tied to such variable features as moisture and temperature. Some years are good for mushrooms, others are not. Which scenario would encourage a group of people to behave most competitively? The correct answer is the apple example: the apples promise a large return and occur at a predictable time and place, meaning that people can plan for their collection in the future. It would not make good economic sense for anyone to set aside hours of effort on an uncertain mushroom harvest. Here then is a reason for conflict: to find and maintain access to resources that have **economic defendability** [7.14]. It is thus worthwhile to compete for a resource—you are likely to reap a large return if you own or control it. If you do not, you get nothing.

economic defendability Describes a resource that is worth the energy expended to defend it; usually a resource that is densely distributed in space and predictable in the future.

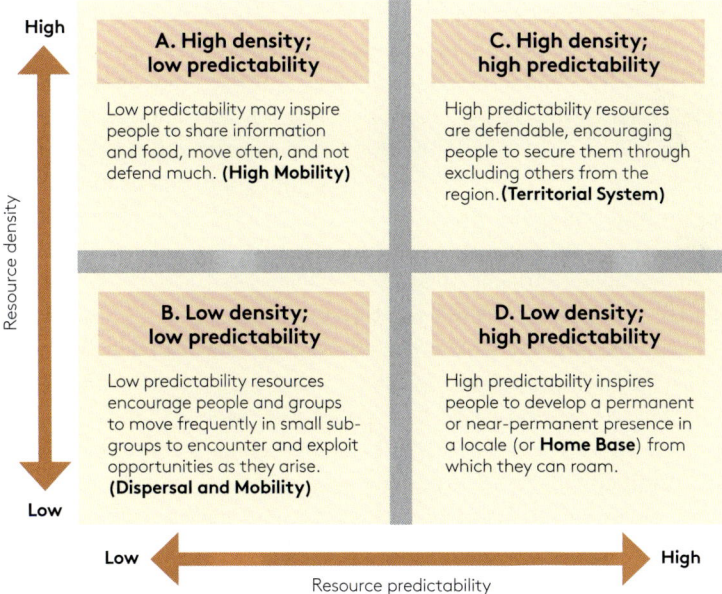

7.14 This diagram models a relationship of resource density and predictability. Different resources may fall in different sectors of the model, so priority resources (for example bison) may guide people's choices. The density and predictability of resources matter greatly when it comes to individual—and group—decisions. Dense and predictable resources inspire territoriality, because they are valuable and will remain so in the future.

Were resources economically defendable in prehistoric Fiji? To answer this question, we need to understand the connection between island ecology, food production, the prehistoric trends in climate, and the distribution of human populations over time and space. Cultivation in the past was limited to land that was well-watered and also of gentle enough slope to be farmed. As a result, only some places offered the right conditions for growing crops year-round. Others could be cultivated for several seasons but would then need to lie fallow (i.e., give the soil a rest from planting and harvesting) to regenerate critical nutrients. In the Sigatoka Valley, certain pockets of land were dense and predictable, and for a farmer, these would have had economic defendability. The choice was either to acquire these and tend them as well as possible in order to grow food, or to rely on lands that were unpredictable.

Defenses as Communal Projects

Fortifications are a marker of economic defendability understood in evolutionary and ecological terms, but they can also be explained in social terms, using social theory. Fortifications stand as a useful venue for the archaeological exploration of social motivations and impact. For one thing, they are durable, frequently preserving the archaeological remnants of many human actions. But first and foremost, they document human investment in a common good: by working together to build walls, ditches, and remote refuges, individuals benefited from the protection provided by the fortification. This sort of investment, though, did come with some costs. An individual had to be willing to sacrifice some of his or her own autonomy to benefit from a group venture. Not every collective project was a defensive fortification, either—societies sometimes used group ventures as a social practice that would bind people together in a community (see Chapter 11). The construction of the *moai* at Rapa Nui (see Chapter 1), the great houses at Chaco Canyon (see Chapter 5), or the tower of Jericho on the West Bank (see Chapter 8) are examples of cooperative projects that had broader social meanings, such as a statement of belonging. They often involved public acts and allowed participating individuals to embrace the greater identity (or message) of the group. Collective projects designed for defense either signaled a group of people's intent to stay and fight, or created a formidable protection that allowed them to do so.

7.15 A dog-tooth pendant and a fragment of a shell bracelet from Tatuba Cave, Fiji.

Archaeologists frequently discuss the rise of fortifications within the context of individuals and groups choosing to cooperate or compete. In Fiji, the system of subsistence that humans utilized to extract food, clothing [**7.15**], and shelter was based on fixed and predictable land. It is no surprise then that human beings there invested in territories—controlling land and controlling access to land—through the use of fortified villages. This decision was in balance with the requirements of the local environment. Archaeological excavations have documented that the relationship dates back a millennium or more, nearly half the time since Fiji was first colonized by humans. Perhaps in those early centuries, the human population had been smaller and enough land was available for all. As the population on the island grew, however, competition escalated between neighbors. As we discovered in Chapter 5, farmers in the American Southwest faced a similar problem: a rapidly growing population and landscape wracked by drought. In that instance, the farmers "voted with their feet" and departed for better conditions elsewhere. On the island of Fiji, there was no place to go. Violence, warfare, and continual fighting erupted and soon became normalized.

EUROPE: DECIDING WITH OR AGAINST A COMMUNITY IN ST. KILDA

On Fiji, people came together to defend their land. In our modern societies, we often face a different kind of choice: Should I make a decision with my community, or reach it on my own? Fortunately, this dilemma is rarely a life-or-death decision, but it is one that can ultimately shape our future society. Making our own decision seems more risky, because we will face the uncertain outcome alone. Is going along with the crowd, though, less risky? It does not appear that this is always the case. Every context is different, and predicting what the future may hold is not possible. Going it alone may indeed result in a better outcome.

One major approach of social theory suggests that social conventions and habits structure the choices individuals make. **Practice theory** argues that people are born into existing structures of social practice—that is, they grow up learning to do things a certain way because that is the custom. Habitual routines are guided by spatial patterns and social conventions; British citizens drive on the left, and they learn to maneuver their family cars, manufactured with the steering wheel on the right-hand side, in this manner. By understanding the ways in which choices are structured, and relating these to evolutionary theory, one can better understand the decisions made by the historical community at St. Kilda.

Approximately 100 miles (161 km) west of the coast of Scotland lie the islands of St. Kilda [**7.16**]. This archipelago consists of two main islands, Hirta and Soay, and a nearby set of sea stacks, which are steep and craggy pinnacles of rock that jut out of the ocean. Archaeological evidence suggests that the St. Kilda group was

practice theory A social theory that explains culture and culture change in terms of the daily and frequent practices that occupy human lives. People repeat what they have learned, and repeat best what they practice often; at the same time, they introduce minor shifts as errors or innovations. Common practices forge institutions, the building blocks of social conformity and social organization.

7.16 Map of St. Kilda, off the northwest coast of Scotland. The island was colonized 2,500 years ago, but officially abandoned in 1930.

colonized 2,500 years ago by people who brought with them domesticated animals and plants, including sheep, dogs, and barley. The islands were, and still are, very remote. Rough seas and winds make it particularly difficult to reach them, and the lack of wood severely limited the islanders' abilities to make boats that could manage the journey back to the mainland. The inhabitants made houses with stone walls and thatched roofs, which provided shelter for both humans and livestock. Both entered through a common door, and the people slept in raised stone niches that were built into the interior walls.

Because of its remote location, the population of St. Kilda was removed from the cultural influence of the Scottish mainland, which absorbed new migrants from England to the south, and Vikings from Scandinavia to the east. The St. Kildans spoke Gaelic and retained religious traditions that were pre-Christian, including the use of rituals involving stone altars and circles. They also maintained an integrated community; each morning, the men of St. Kilda would gather for the "parliament," where they would decide on the tasks for the day. Work was conducted communally, so all the residents would pool their tools and energies to accomplish each daily task. Their way of life included catching seabirds that populated the cliffs during breeding season. The St. Kilda men would snare these birds with ropes and rods, and also rappel down the cliff faces on ropes to collect eggs and chicks. They also farmed the sparse land of their islands, although the cool climate and sea spray made the land particularly unproductive. The first accounts of life on St. Kilda were written by Martin Martin, who visited the islands in 1697. He described the St. Kildans who lived in a village on the island of Hirta [**7.17**]; the population there included approximately 180 people from 27 families. Over the next several decades, the population experienced a series of epidemics of cholera and smallpox, the worst of which occurred in 1729. Prior to that epidemic, 3 adults and 8 boys had traveled to Boreray (a sea stack) to collect seabirds and were unexpectedly marooned there for several weeks. When they returned to Hirta, they discovered that in their absence an epidemic of smallpox had killed every person with the exception of 1 man and 18 children. The population of St. Kilda had declined from approximately 200 to 29 over the course of a few weeks. New settlers from the mainland were brought in to repopulate the island.

Over the next century, the population of St. Kilda hovered around 100 individuals; it then dropped to 74 in 1851 when 36 islanders emigrated to Australia. A third depopulation occurred following World War I, when young men left the island to enlist in the military. Over the next decade, the remaining 37 people struggled to survive. There were simply not enough inhabitants to operate the boats safely, let alone endure days-long journeys to the crags to hunt for seabirds. Only 5 surnames of the original 27 lived on, and more than two-thirds of the people shared the surname of Gillies or MacKinnon. St. Kilda had reached the breaking point: its community was simply too small to survive anymore. Young people lacked prospective husbands or wives, and the island's isolation meant that help was too far away should someone fall sick or become injured.

How might we understand the story of St. Kilda in terms of both evolutionary and social theories? Evolutionary-based explanations suggest that individuals are constantly weighing the costs and benefits of group membership, and that a group remains cohesive only if everyone benefits sufficiently, relative to others in the group. Social theory would imply that when St. Kildans banded together, this permitted them to retain their true identity. By opting to remain in their ancestral home, they were following their traditional system of discussion, decision-making, and cooperation, which had fostered and sheltered them for more than two millennia. Close social connections can also foster altruistic relationships, a kind of intense loyalty whereby individuals do not directly benefit from group cooperation. This pattern is frequently observed in extended families, where adult children support their parents and younger siblings, rather than forming their own families. One could argue that the St. Kilda community of the 1930s had reached a tipping point between individualism and altruism: individuals knew that they would be better off on the mainland, both as a community and as individuals, but anyone who chose to stay behind would perish. Ultimately, their commitments to each other (nearly everyone was related by blood or marriage) and extended families meant that, together, they had to reach the decision to depart. And all had to agree with it. Relocating as a group would ensure that no one was abandoned and each person survived.

After the death of one resident in 1930, the St. Kildans made their momentous decision. The families asked the British government to evacuate them. According to eyewitness accounts, they stoically gathered their possessions and slaughtered

7.17 Ruins of abandoned stone houses at Hirta on St. Kilda. The houses in this community were made of stone and fitted with doors and shutters to keep out the wet weather of the North Atlantic Ocean. St. Kildans stored hay, grain, eggs, and dried seabird meat in the small stone buildings (*cleitean*) in the background; these storehouses were essential for preserving the limited food on the island.

7.18 The St. Kilda parliament in 1879. This community met daily to discuss collective tasks that supported everyone on the island. The parliament included only men from each family, reminding us that a social collective does not imply equal, gender-neutral decision-making.

7.19 The bay and abandoned village of modern-day St. Kilda. It and the nearby islands are now a UN World Heritage Site that preserves the ancient ruins of the abandoned community but also functions as an important habitat for animals native to the North Atlantic.

their dogs (the canines could not be moved due to the chance of spreading disease), and left their homes with the doors unlocked.

Reaching this decision together was also the community's final act [**7.18**]. The cities and towns of the mainland absorbed the St. Kildans, who formed new social connections and communities and adapted to a somewhat different daily routine. All of the evacuees lived the remainder of their lives on the Scottish mainland, and their young children grew up healthy, building businesses and families. The tight-knit community of St. Kilda was gone. Its residents relinquished the cooperative collective that had distinguished them as St. Kildans, but survived as resourceful individuals and proud descendants [**7.19**].

THE AMAZON: DECISION-MAKING TODAY

From the Clovis mammoth hunters to bison-driving on the Great Plains, to Chacoan farmers, to the islanders of St. Kilda, our narrative of the Anthropocene has highlighted societies that made a decision either to access resources or escape conditions that threatened to obliterate their society. The Fijian farmers who fed their growing numbers from the limited resources of their islands had nowhere to go—all the neighboring islands were fully populated—and their resources would ultimately need defending. In the Fijian example, one recognizes a familiar evolutionary pattern: where resources are predictable and locally abundant, they are likely to be defended territorially. By exploring many outcomes in prehistory, archaeology offers a unique catalog of examples and experiments involving human choices, social cooperation, and human conflict.

Our Anthropocene world is an ecological niche. Prior generations of humans altered ecosystems to favor our species and constructed a terrestrial home, where we have since multiplied exponentially. The ancestors of the Lakota set fires on the Great Plains to maintain grasslands that supported vast herds of bison. Fijian farmers created terracing systems and cultivated soils in the island's valleys to grow their crops. By passing such cultural practices from one generation to the next, human societies transmitted not only their genes but also their technologies and institutions. This cultural transmission, which lies at the heart of social theory and the explanations for social consensus and group decision-making, is integral to our biological successes…and to our failures.

The archaeological record shows that our ancestors left us with a world that had to support much larger numbers of people than ever before. In the chapters that follow, we will explore how this development has transformed the world and led to the concept of the Anthropocene. Now we, too, face a planet with predictable, locally abundant resources but nowhere else to go. As those resources face greater demand, we can anticipate escalating human territoriality. Do we have a choice in how we respond to Earth's challenges?

In closing this chapter, we introduce the integrative work of Anna Browne-Ribeiro, one of a new generation of archaeologists determined to use ethnoarchaeology and archaeological results to inform the choices we make in our future. Anna works in the Brazilian Amazon and is among the many scientists deconstructing the recipe for **terra preta**, or Amazonian dark earth [**7.20**, p. 166]. Dark earths are large tracks of soil and sediment in the Amazon that evidence sophisticated manipulation by ancient humans. This manipulation led to the dark earths becoming far more fertile than surrounding soil, allowing for greater numbers of species and more biodiversity.

In the mid-twentieth century, the Amazon was believed to be pristine, its past untouched by humans. Scientists now understand that this vast rain forest has itself been shaped by humans. When megafauna roamed South America's Amazon Basin, they contributed essential nutrients to the soils through their dung. With the animals' extinctions (see Chapter 6), severe changes to phosphorus cycling (when

terra preta Dark earths found in the Amazon that are more fertile than surrounding soils as a result of ancient human activity and enrichment.

plants absorb the organic phosphate needed to grow) followed. Scientists estimate that the lateral flux (or spatial concentration) of phosphorus was reduced by as much as 98 percent, leaving nutrient-poor soils supporting the rain forest canopy.

When the dark earths were discovered, initial explanations attributed them to fallout from volcanoes in the Andes, sedimentation from ancient lakes, or temporary ponds. Archaeologists then determined that the Amazon rain forest was neither empty when Europeans arrived, nor only sparsely populated by small, mobile groups forced to move frequently owing to infertile soils and scarce resources. Instead, humans adapted to the changes wrought by megafaunal extinctions. Large patches of nutrient-rich, carbon-charged soils exist that were created by humans, whose villages and even cities occupied the same locations for 1,000 years. For example, at Upper Xingu sites in southeastern Amazonia, archaeologists documented village plazas on soils rich in charcoal, ceramic chips, and bone, with a higher concentration of carbon and nitrogen than surrounding soils. Suggested dates for these sites vary but could be *c.* 1000 CE.

Pre-Hispanic Native Americans engineered permanent soil changes that left a signature not only in the soil itself but also in the plant communities that grow on *terra preta*, with botanists and forest ecologists finding a higher percentage of plants useful to humans. These discoveries have piqued the interest of ecologists, agronomists, and chemists eager to decode the recipe for dark earth. They still do not know exactly how it accumulated, but they recognize many of its features. *Terra preta* can exhibit seventy times the charcoal and up to three times the organic matter, nitrogen, and phosphorus of adjacent soils. It also has great fertility and stability. *Terra preta* supports genetically distinct communities of archaea (bacteria-like organisms) and a higher diversity of soil microorganisms than adjacent, less fertile soils. These features lead many to believe that the *terra preta* niche is especially suitable for sustained agricultural production.

7.20 *Terra preta*, or dark earths, of the Amazon. These were created from past human cultural activity and are far more fertile than surrounding soils. The *terra preta* is the dark upper soil under which is visible an orange sediment layer typical of Amazonia.

Browne-Ribeiro has been part of the group that passionately argues against the Western notion that the Amazon was mostly empty in the past. The so-called pristine Amazon is a European myth that plays well for the rubber and cattle producers who view the rain forest as underpopulated, underused, and ripe for profit. As the widespread forest clearing and monocropping of fragile and nutrient-poor Amazonian soils have degraded ever-greater stretches of tropical forest ecosystems, the associated release of carbon dioxide into Earth's atmosphere has been recognized as a significant contributor to global warming. As rain forest ecosystems continue to shrink, the question we all face is, "What future use or conservation of the rain forest will humans choose?"

With the ecological research into *terra preta,* the choices for us have widened. Will Brazilian heirs to the ecosystem choose to expand it and safeguard the carbon-rich soils that could sustain more people with less damage to Earth's resources? This is an Anthropocene decision of our day, informed in real time by the international collaboration between Brazilians and foreigners, including archaeologists, anthropologists, soil scientists, geographers, botanists, ecologists, policy and development experts, conservationists—and, one hopes, the traditional farmers of the Amazon. It is an opportunity for cooperative decision-making in our time.

Chapter Questions

1. Define the evolutionary and social theories used to explain change in the past. What differing insights do they offer? Use the Great Plains bison hunters as an example.

2. What kinds of questions do zooarchaeologists ask, and how are they answered?

3. How have social and evolutionary theory been used to explain conflict in Fiji?

4. Do we have a choice as we respond to Anthropocene challenges? Use examples from this chapter to take a stand on this issue.

Additional Resources

Binford, Lewis R. "Willow Smoke and Dogs' Tails: Hunter-Gatherer Settlement Systems and Archaeological Site Formation," *American Antiquity* 45 (1980): 4–20.

Eckles, David G., et al. "Besant-Woodland Artifacts from the Cedar Gap Site (48NA83) in Northwestern Natrona County, Wyoming," *The Wyoming Archaeologist* 56 (2012): 38–48.

Field, Julie S. "Explaining Fortifications in Indo-Pacific Prehistory," *Archaeology in Oceania* 43 (2009): 1–10.

Krech, Shepard. *The Ecological Indian: Myth and History.* New York: W. W. Norton, 1999.

Steel, Tom. *The Life and Death of St. Kilda: The Moving Story of a Vanished Island Community.* London, UK: HarperCollins, 2011.

Woods, William I., et al. *Amazonian Dark Earths: Wim Sombroek's Vision.* Dordrecht, Netherlands: Springer, 2009.

PRODUCING FOOD
Domestication and Its Consequences in Southwest and East Asia

8

When, according to the Bible, the Israelites marched into Canaan, the Promised Land located along the eastern shore of the Mediterranean Sea, the land was already inhabited and had been for many thousands of years. God instructed Joshua (God's appointed leader) to take the city of Jericho by encircling it seven times, bearing the Ark of the Covenant before the Israelites and blowing trumpets. And as the story goes, the walls came a-tumbling down. Jericho's biblical fame inspired more than one archaeologist to dig for its ancient walls. When John Garstang excavated Jericho in the 1930s, he found no walls that dated to the days of Joshua. His most famous discovery was a Neolithic, fine-featured, plaster-covered skull with clamshell eyes, the blind gaze of which still holds the mystery of its purpose.

Garstang's successor at Jericho was Dame Kathleen Kenyon. She understood that the city was ancient and long occupied. She also did not locate a biblical wall, but what surprised her, and everyone since, is that Jericho's earliest wall, connected to a massive stone tower, was built by Neolithic people who appeared to be at the forefront of food domestication and who created one of the first permanent settlements the world has ever known. In this region of the world, we also find evidence of the earliest activities that were domesticating wheat—a development that changed human history and the environment profoundly. Many efforts have been made to explain the emergence of food production in ancient Southwest Asia (the westernmost subregion of Asia). Farming spread to Europe and Central Asia, but food-producing societies also emerged independently in other geographic locales, such as South and East Asia, Central America, Andean South America, sub-Saharan Africa, and East Africa.

In this chapter, we will explore the development of two of the three main staples of human consumption: wheat and rice (we will meet the third staple, maize, in Chapter 10). We will see how the first signs of settlement are often discovered along with evidence for the beginnings of agriculture, but that makes us wonder if agriculture indeed preceded permanent settlement. This leads to a further-reaching question: What are the consequences of agriculture? There have been many. Agriculture affected the possible size of the human population and the ways in which people came to live together; it also dramatically altered the environment and biodiversity, transforming them to become more suitable for human needs.

Southwest Asia: The First Settlements **170**

What Led to the Development of Farming? **178**

Archaeobotany and the Evidence for Food Production **180**

Domestication: A Two-Way Process **181**

China: Independent Domestication and Rice **185**

The Consequences of Farming **189**

The Critical Role of the Community in Food Production **196**

Opposite Plaster figures from Ain Ghazal, Jordan. These 8,500-year-old statues were created for display and may represent mythical figures or gods. They were carefully buried after years of use.

Key Concepts

- Evidence of domestication and permanent settlements in the ancient Near East
- The independent development of agriculture in other parts of the world, notably the development of rice in China
- The contribution of archaeobotany to understanding how people produced, exchanged, and consumed agricultural resources
- The social and environmental consequences of agricultural activities since early farming, and how plants and humans have co-evolved in the Anthropocene

SOUTHWEST ASIA: THE FIRST SETTLEMENTS

Archaeologists still ponder the reasons for humans' shift from a fully mobile lifestyle to a fully sedentary one, yet it is clear that this change accompanied entirely new human technologies and adaptations, and ultimately resulted in momentous environmental repercussions. Throughout most of human history, humans hunted and gathered their food, and this activity ranged over vast areas. Ethnographic studies have revealed that mobility is a strategy closely tied to the density and predictability of resources. If the major source of meat is a migratory animal and few other sources of food exist in the region, humans develop a seasonal pattern of mobility that places them in the right place at the right time; they rely on their knowledge of the environment to predict where food will be. Other environments with few resources that are widely and randomly scattered on the landscape are unpredictable and encourage a strategy of constant movement.

Maintaining a permanent living space represents a major shift away from hunting and gathering. There is abundant archaeological evidence from around the world that hunter-gatherers constructed semi-permanent residences. As part of the mobility strategy described above—what some researchers refer to as a "be there then" approach—these sites were often equipped with tools for processing food, such as grinding basins or heavy mortars, and house foundations that were maintained and reused each season. Plant parts, such as nuts and fruits, were gathered, processed, and consumed. But all these items were abandoned once the fruiting season came to an end, and the people left, sometimes for years, to find food elsewhere. The first true settlements emerged only when humans developed technologies for either producing or obtaining dense and predictable foods. One example was settlements focused on the collection of migrating fish, such as the salmon that return annually to the rivers of western North America. Another was the development of agriculture and pastoralism, which provided an abundant and renewable food source that could be produced nearby. When humans initially recognized the promise of farm-raised plants and that animals could be reared in significant numbers, and with results in the foreseeable future, these realizations transformed the way they lived. The land was no longer a place where food could be found, it was a place where food might be produced. The strategy of "be there then" became "make food here." And this strategy had Anthropocene consequences.

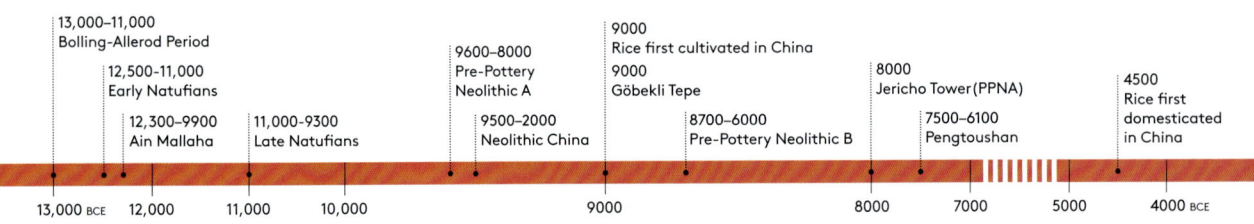

8.1 Map of Southwest Asia, showing the earliest sites associated with food production.

Jericho

How do we know that the earliest settlers in Jericho [**8.1**] grew their own food? We can thank Dame Kathleen Kenyon for this important determination, made in the 1950s. One of the most accomplished excavators of her day, she was scrupulously attentive to minute changes in sediments and deposits, and developed a detailed stratigraphic understanding of the sequence of occupation at Jericho. She named many of the cultural phases still used by archaeologists today, including **Pre-Pottery Neolithic A** (11,600–10,000 years ago) and **Pre-Pottery Neolithic B** (10,700–8,000 years ago). As indicated by the term "pre-pottery," the inhabitants of Jericho at this time did not make ceramic vessels; for shelter they constructed round, semi-subterranean houses that were walled with unbaked clay bricks. The people of Jericho and communities similar to it built hearths both inside and outside their houses, and roasted wild game and seeds, such as wheat and barley. They also worked together to erect larger structures.

Kenyon's excavations dug down more than 65 feet (20 meters), carefully mapping all the architecture and establishing the superposition of the strata (the order in which they were deposited, with the oldest at the bottom) and relative age (how much time it took to deposit each stratum). At the bottom of Trench 1, her workmen discovered a huge stone tower with an internal staircase marked by subsequent human burials [**8.2**, p. 172]. Alongside the tower was the famous, not biblical, stone

Pre-Pottery Neolithic A
A period in Southwest Asia, 11,600–10,000 years ago, when people lived in semi-subterranean houses and relied on foraged plants and animals, but did not use pottery. Also known as PPNA.

Pre-Pottery Neolithic B
A period in Southwest Asia, 10,700–8,000 years ago, when people began to depend more heavily on domesticated plants. Also known as PPNB.

8.2 Plastered skull from Jericho, c. 8700–6000 BCE.
Jericho's inhabitants farmed domesticated wheat and barley after a millennium of gathering wild grain. Ancestors were commemorated by decorating their skulls with plaster, paint, and shells.

wall, with a ditch outside and many trash-filled pits surrounding it. And because Dame Kenyon was a meticulous excavator, she instructed her excavation crew to save some of the tiny charred plant fragments as they scraped through the trash from ancient days. From these charred seeds, it has been possible to identify domesticated plants, which first appeared in the layers after the tower and wall were abandoned. From this evidence, we know that people living in the Pre-Pottery Neolithic B (PPNB) phase of the settlement at Jericho produced plant food.

Many archaeologists have attempted to decipher the purpose of Jericho's wall and tower [**8.3**, **8.4**], and to clarify if the people who built them also used domesticated plants and animals. To this day, no one is certain why Jericho's inhabitants needed to build a wall and tower.

Dame Kenyon excavated at Jericho in the post-World War II years (1952–1958), after British Mandate rule in Palestine had ended but before the Israeli occupation of (then) Transjordan's West Bank. Given the more recent experiences of war and terrorism that followed the partition of Palestine in 1948, and Jericho's biblical reputation as a city with defensive walls, it is perhaps unsurprising that Kenyon regarded the Neolithic wall and tower as a military defense. Later archaeologists have questioned this view, because it is not clear against whom these defenses would have been deployed 10,000 years ago. A posture of defense implies the existence of an attacking army, and organized warfare simply did not exist in the Jordan Valley at that time. In addition, the tower was constructed on the inside of the wall, hardly strategic placement in terms of military defense.

Archaeologist Ofer Bar-Yosef alternatively suggested that Jericho's Neolithic people were beset with major flooding, and the ditch and wall were their attempts to move springtime erosion away from the settlement. This innovation would have represented a reversal of the earlier mobile-forager lifestyle, whereby humans moved whenever flooding occurred.

The Jericho structures hint at entirely new community rules, rules that would support life in a permanent settlement. Geographic relocation to address problems was no longer an option. As other villages (and even a few remaining foragers) soon filled the countryside, one could no longer pick up possessions (or pack up one's family) and storm off. People were obliged to resolve conflict while physically remaining in their communities. New community living meant new rules and strategies to support life. It is thus possible that Jericho's tower stood as a powerful symbol of humans' presence and their claim to a rich oasis and all its resources, many of which had been collected in anticipation of leaner times. The settled villagers now had a strong incentive to cooperate in sharing resources and settling conflicts among themselves. The tower, which may have once had some kind of superstructure and could be readily seen across the oasis, stood as a testament to community effort. No one household would have the labor to build so enormous an edifice.

The need to coexist within large communities was only one consequence of the monumental shift in the lives of the people of Jericho, who had decided to settle there permanently and would eventually adopt farming. In this chapter on the production

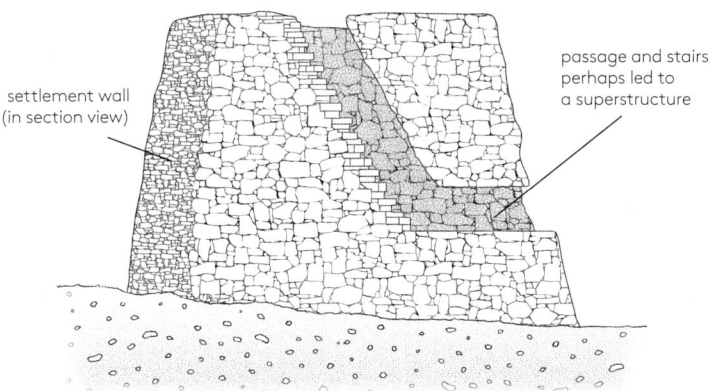

Above: **8.3 The tower of Jericho** is 28 feet (8.5 m) high and contains an inner passageway. At the base of the deepest trench, Dame Kenyon's team uncovered deposits that indicate that the tower and attached wall date to the Pre-Pottery Neolithic A period, about 11,000 years ago.

Left: **8.4 Diagram of the inner passageway and stairs** within the Jericho tower.

of food, we will explore those consequences, both social and environmental. But which came first: permanent settlement or domestication and farming? When placing food production in prehistory within perspective, it is important to understand that no simple sequence can be applied to all people in all places. In Southwest Asia, the stories of the Natufians, the first settlers in Jericho, and of the builders of Göbekli Tepe are stirring examples of human settlement *before* domestication.

SOUTHWEST ASIA: THE FIRST SETTLEMENTS   173

Natufians A late Paleolithic community that gathered and prepared wild wheat and barley in addition to hunting, and adopted a sedentary lifestyle.

commensal Animals that benefit from another animal's behavior without return or harm to the benefactor.

8.5a, b Ain Mallaha: illustration of a house, and site map showing a complex of three houses. Houses were built in shallow pits with stone linings for walls, and each had an ashy hearth ringed with stones near the center. In some houses, ground stone mortars still sat on the floor. A later storage pit was cut down into the wall of the house on the upper left, and once the houses were abandoned, people buried their dead within them. In 8.5a, the side view shows the post-holes and chock stones for timbers, suggesting how these structures were once roofed.

The Natufians: Permanent Settlement before Domestication

In the region of Jericho during the Bolling–Allerod warm interval (15,000–13,000 years ago), foraging communities known as **Natufians** had built stone houses some 3,000 years earlier than Jericho, in the Pre-Pottery Neolithic A (PPNA). This warm interval was a time when plant biomass increased across the Middle East, supporting denser faunal and human populations. The Natufians were hunters who pursued deer and gazelle, but as the climate warmed and the number of people grew, their hunting ranges shrank. Over time, some Natufian communities found themselves restricted by the territorial boundaries of their neighbors and therefore needed to accelerate their hunting of gazelles and exploit an ever-wider pool of plants and animals.

We can see the intensification of both in the early Natufian site of Ain Mallaha (14,300–11,900 years ago; [**8.5a, b**]) between the hills of Galilee and Lake Hula in the Levant. Here, Natufian people built semi-subterranean, stone-lined pit houses, covered with timber and brush roofs. Natufian homes included hearths, and the occupants used such heavy grinding equipment as ground stone mortars and pestles [**8.6**] to prepare plant food, for instance, emmer wheat and barley. These kinds of installations are not conveniently portable, and this suggests that mobility was not important to the Natufians. People apparently lived year-round in such settlements, for the presence of **commensal** animals, such as mice and sparrows, indicates permanent occupation. Although Natufians primarily made do with a broad spectrum of resources, some did episodically depart on hunting or collecting forays into the wild.

Ain Mallaha, as is the case with a number of Natufian sites, lies adjacent to several resource-rich zones, including a lakeside marsh that attracted migratory birds in

a

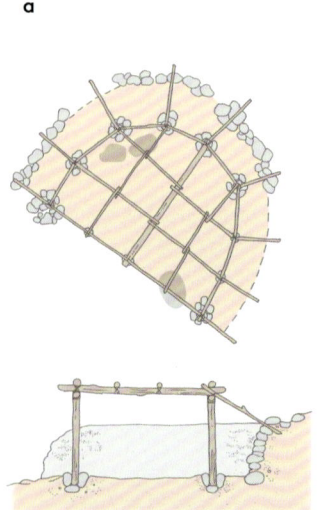

b

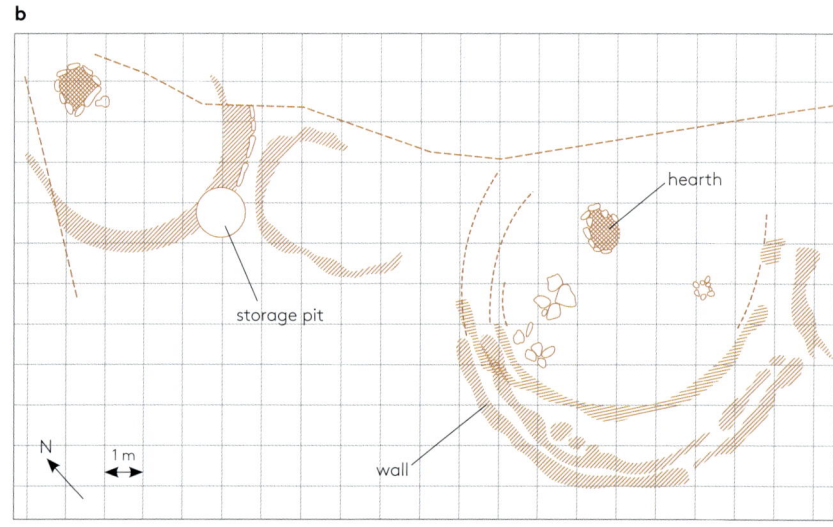

winter, and provided fish, snails, and crabs to supplement gazelle and deer, and seasonally available wild seeds, nuts, rhizomes, and tubers. Archaeologist Brian Byrd has argued that the houses Natufians built in these locations represent a newly strengthened human social unit, the nuclear family household. This social unit implies cooperation across gender and age differences to procure sufficient food for consumption and reproduce the next generation. Households would become the building blocks of village societies and larger communities.

Later, during the **Younger Dryas** period (12,800–11,500 years ago), global temperatures turned sharply colder, posing difficulties for the settled Natufians, who would now have access to less biomass in their immediate vicinity and would therefore need to make new choices about the types of animals they hunted. The game they captured were increasingly smaller (with bigger animals having been overhunted), and Natufians had to work harder to catch quicker, more elusive prey. As a result, people abandoned a sedentary lifestyle as settlers, and returned to mobile hunting and gathering. The change in course on the part of Natufians demonstrates that the development of farming should not be viewed as singular progression from hunting and gathering; rather, these modes can move back and forth in either direction. As for permanent settlement, what potentially govern this decision are resource density and predictability. If one or the other is absent, humans will return to mobility as a means to accumulate adequate resources (Chapter 7). After the Younger Dryas when the warmer, stable climate of the Early Holocene emerged, approximately 11,600 years ago, it allowed for denser and more predictable resources. Villages quickly reappeared, with clusters of houses and, in many cases, community buildings, similar in scale to the tower and wall at Jericho.

8.6 Ground stone fashioned for processing plant food, such as nuts and cereals, c. 9000 BCE. These tools would have been large and extremely heavy: 19½ inches (50 cm) high and weighing 20–30 lbs (10–15 kg). This would make them difficult to transport, which suggests that Natufians lived in permanent settlements, rather than being constantly on the move as mobile foragers.

Gathering and Feasting

Natufians were not the only community that experimented with settled life before farming. Recent excavations in the steppe lands of eastern Jordan have revealed the remains of 20,000-year-old huts built at the height of the last Ice Age, marking some of the earliest constructed habitats in the world. The site at Kharaneh IV documents multiple, repeated occupations by foraging groups who returned, apparently in droves, to re-occupy this rich hunting camp and to bury their dead. Farther away, at Hallan Çemi [**8.7**, **8.8**, p. 176] in the mountains of modern-day southeastern Turkey, Late Pleistocene foragers built round and stone-lined semi-subterranean structures similar to Natufian houses, but much larger, with flagstone flooring and the horns of aurochs (wild cattle) mounted on their walls. Although it is unclear if anyone actually lived year-round at Hallan Çemi, excavators have suggested that the scattered bones of wild animals found outside the structures are evidence of community feasting events there.

Only a few centuries later, around 11,000 years ago, foragers in the same Taurus range in Turkey convened in massive numbers to build an extraordinary set of sunken structures containing T-shaped limestone pillars weighing 3 tons apiece

Younger Dryas A period after post-glacial warming had begun. Between 12,800 and 11,500 years ago, global temperatures dropped sharply, causing significant vegetation changes around the world.

Above: **8.7 The horns of aurochs found on the floor of a house at Hallan Çemi** may have fallen from the interior walls, where the horns were probably hanging as decoration and in memory of a hunt and feast.

Above: **8.8 Excavation at Hallan Çemi in the Taurus Mountains of southeastern Turkey.** The round structures depicted here were made with stone that was capped with wattle-and-daub walls (mud and branches or grass).

and carved with the images of fierce wild beasts. There are at least twenty circular buildings half-sunk into the ground with these pillars, and the hilltop is deep in chipped debris from quarrying the stone. This remarkable site is Göbekli Tepe [**8.9, 8.10**]. Hunting and foraging supported its very large work groups—at least several hundred people would have been needed to construct the complex—but an insufficient water supply precluded permanent settlement. Some of the laborers might have traveled a distance as far as 124 miles (200 km) to reach the site, for the motifs and even the round building style at Göbekli Tepe have been similarly observed in Syria, along the Middle Euphrates River Valley.

From the examples of Kharaneh IV, Hallan Çemi, and Göbekli Tepe, it appears that huge but impermanent gatherings preceded village life and the development of agriculture, and that these gatherings spurred a number of community-building activities, such as feasting and monumental construction. But these were not villages of farming family households as we know them today. To support their villages, people had to enter into a new relationship with plants and begin to farm them.

Above: **8.9 Multiple structures at Göbekli Tepe** were made with stone pillars that served as supports for timber roofs, which have since rotted away. The vast scale of the construction suggests that the site served as a meeting place for communities otherwise separated by huge distances.

Left: **8.10 At Göbekli Tepe, enormous T-shaped pillars** decorated with the images of animals—in this case, vultures and a scorpion—were sometimes half-hidden in dry stone walls. The main purpose of the buildings at this site still remains unknown, but their construction would have required a sizable labor force, subsisting almost entirely on wild foods.

WHAT LED TO THE DEVELOPMENT OF FARMING?

The development of farming is one of the clearest, most transformative, and most enduring examples of the evolutionary relationship between humans and their environments, and it occurred independently across the globe. Why did farming develop? In Southwest Asia where the first villages emerged, archaeology reveals a long chronological backdrop of humans depleting their preferred resources. With their ideal foods dwindling, people utilized a broader spectrum of alternatives, and this, in turn, allowed human populations to expand and form bigger, mostly sedentary communities. There are several indications that even in the early phases of settlement with some community members still practicing seasonal hunting and foraging, people continued to put stress on the local supply of resources. For one thing, the average size of gazelles caught by Natufian hunters became smaller. The evidence suggests that as Natufian hunters skillfully targeted the good-sized, meatiest animals, it was the smaller animals that lived another day to breed, evidently with greater evolutionary success than their hunted companions. Studies show the long-term depletion of large game, such as fallow deer, even as the forest habitat they preferred was expanding [**8.11**].

Humans had been depleting prized resources since the Middle Paleolithic (50,000–30,000 years ago), while reliance on a broader range of resources and

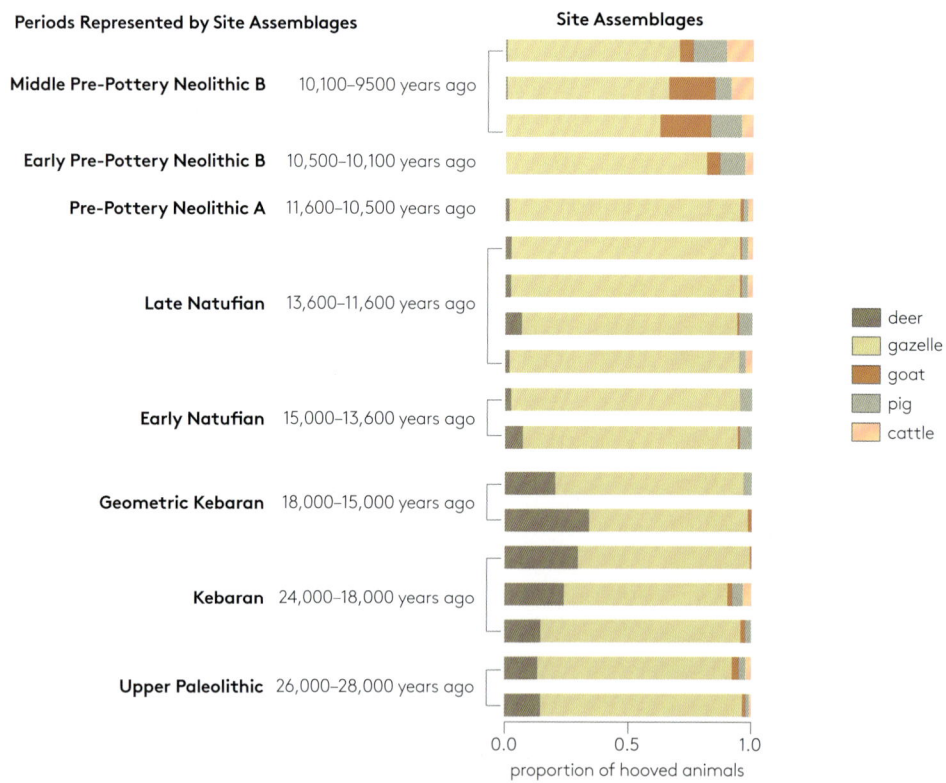

8.11 Through the Natufian period, hunters increased the proportion of gazelles in their prey, even as the average size of gazelles declined. Data from Natalie Munro shows this. Although the forest habitat of deer was expanding in the Early Natufian and in the Neolithic periods, the populations of deer were depleted, so there were few of these animals available and represented in the bone assemblages from archaeological sites. In the Pre-Pottery Neolithic B, domesticated fauna appear in larger percentages, but hunting was still an important source of meat.

smaller animals grew. Zooarchaeologists Mary Stiner and Natalie Munro studied faunal assemblages from Middle and Late Pleistocene (50,000–15,000 years ago) archaeological sites in several Mediterranean regions (including the pre-Natufian Middle East) and found that as the remains of tortoises declined, the remains of hares increased. Tortoises are easy prey—one just picks them up, flips them, and roasts them in the shell. Tortoises also reproduce slowly, and as a result of intensive hunting, their numbers were depleted by the Late Paleolithic period. Snaring a hare or running one down requires quite a bit more energy and creative technologies, but people turned to this food source as populations multiplied and territories became constrained by neighboring foragers. Stiner and Munro argue that this small-meat-packages strategy contributed to population increase and then further resource depletion. Natufians who overhunted gazelles and exploited a wider array of resources than their predecessors simply fit into a long-term trend with evolutionary consequences.

As people's foraging ranges decreased, the catalog of Natufian food resources expanded, becoming a **broad spectrum revolution**—to use an archaeological term—or in other words, a move toward a greater variety of food. A closer look at the innovations of Natufians and other foragers suggests that this "revolution" was as much a social movement as an economic one. True, Natufians were exploiting a wide-ranging list of new foods, such as crabs, water fowl, lizards, fish, and probably small seeds. They were also using new techniques, for example, sickles to cut grasses [**8.12**] and storage bins to keep food. Yet the energy Natufians now invested in constructing and running their homes suggests that the social form of households with pooled family labor and food sharing was being strengthened. In other words, increasingly dense populations at the end of the Pleistocene were deploying new social rules and new social behaviors to cope with expanding populations and competition for resources as much as they were applying new economic strategies, such as the use of new foodstuffs and new technologies to obtain them.

By the late Pre-Pottery Neolithic, the transition to a fully agricultural lifestyle was well under way at Jericho. Foragers who had collected grain from distant fields and spread it to dry inside the village had produced many generations of grandchildren, and these people made new decisions about their food. Rather than range the distant hills every spring to search for the best grains, they sowed and harvested their own grain in nearby fields, and saved grains for next year's planting. Archaeological analysis in this region shows that not everyone practiced this strategy; experimentation and variation were still the norm, and many communities still hunted and foraged. But for the people of Jericho, the production of food was successful enough for them to choose it as a viable alternative to foraging. As the wild game declined and required more energy to find and catch, more land was converted into agricultural fields. The trajectory of such Pre-Pottery Neolithic communities as Jericho was set. The cultural and ecological inheritance from broad spectrum foragers was a critical factor in the decision-making of late Pre-Pottery Neolithic villagers. Future generations would be farmers.

broad spectrum revolution
A process whereby people move toward a wider variety of food, rather than relying on one staple.

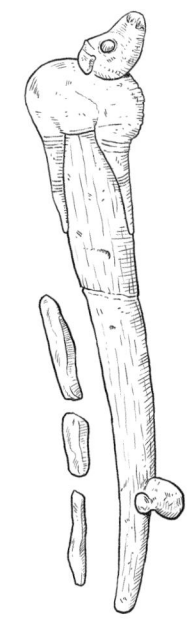

8.12 A Natufian bone sickle from Kebara Cave with bladelets removed; these would have been attached along the shaft using bitumen, a rare natural tar. This composite tool is an efficient technology because it can be repaired with new elements (bladelets). It would have been used to cut reeds and grasses, including wild cereals. Natufians used animal symbolism; this handle is decorated with a carved deer.

WHAT LED TO THE DEVELOPMENT OF FARMING? 179

ARCHAEOBOTANY AND THE EVIDENCE FOR FOOD PRODUCTION

We have already discussed Dame Kenyon's excavations of (post-Natufian) Neolithic Jericho, with its mudbrick houses, wall, and tower where she found the charred fragments of plants. In the same location, archaeologists also found scorched remains from domesticated plants, an innovation that ensured village food supply once the tower and wall fell into disuse. These plant remains, and others from early village sites across Southwest Asia, show that new strategies of plant selection and technologies related to the harvest (such as sickles) resulted in evolutionary changes to plant biology, with new plant forms and species evolving. At Jericho, Kenyon's team uncovered a few examples of charred foodstuffs embedded in plaster, enough for a botanist to recognize the changes in form that mark a domesticated plant. The very earliest of these were cereals, including einkorn, a primitive wheat probably native to the edges of the mountain forest near Göbekli Tepe, and emmer wheat, which also originated elsewhere. Barley was additionally present, and this might have been domesticated from wild barley closer to Jericho itself.

Jericho, however, does not provide many answers for where and how food plants were domesticated and their role in the formation of the earliest village societies. First, with the benefit of accelerator mass spectrometry (AMS) radiocarbon dating (see Chapter 6), archaeologists established that the charred domesticated plants from Jericho came from the Pre-Pottery Neolithic B phase, after the tower, wall, and surrounding pits fell into disuse. Second, although Kenyon's excavations were noteworthy for the time, she practiced few of the techniques now standard, including sieving and sampling. Her excavations simply did not collect a lot of the clues present.

Archaeological sites are perfect places to look for preserved plant remains. Under most circumstances, plants decay after death, but there are exceptions. In villages where people processed, stored, prepared, and consumed food daily, they discarded food refuse, including plant parts they did not eat or plant food that had spoiled. The byproducts of food production thus reflect the routine life of a village. Discarded plant waste nevertheless also decays, unless it is routinely subject to fire, a highly effective agent of preservation. When someone tosses a handful of plant stalks or scrap on the fire, most will burn to ashes. Yet the denser, heavy fragments, such as seeds, will sink into an ash bed, where—deprived of oxygen—they will char incompletely. While they lie buried, charred plant fragments [**8.13**] resist bacterial decay, often for thousands of years.

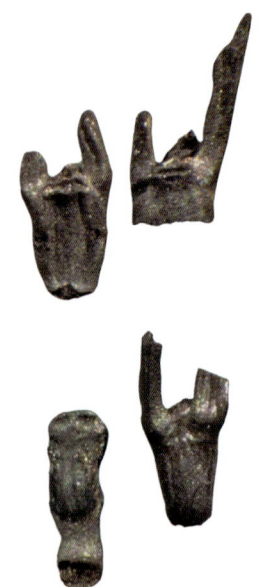

8.13 Charred fragments of cereal stalks. This image shows the remains of wheat, specifically the tough rachis (the stem that attaches the seed to the stalk), that are preserved after being charred in a fire. Fragments of plants allow archaeobotanists to identify fully agricultural communities.

Other kinds of sites also preserve plant food remains. Dry highland caves in Tamaulipas, Oaxaca, and Tehuacàn, in Mexico, contain millions of desiccated plant fragments, some from early domesticated maize and squash. Flooded lakeside villages of the Swiss Neolithic (about 6,000 years old) contain waterlogged wood, seeds, fruits, and stalks that show the activities of their farming inhabitants. But these are rare cases. When faced with an overwhelming abundance of charred plant fragments at thousands of sites, archaeologists have implemented sampling and recovery techniques to generate manageable, representative assemblages of

charred plant remains in the search for early domesticated plants and the patterns of human activity they reflect.

To do so, **archaeobotanists** routinely employ the technique of **flotation**, using the natural buoyancy of charred plant fragments, which are less dense than water. When a sample of excavated sediment is placed in water—whether a simple bucket or an aerated flotation tank [**8.14**]—charred plant fragments (flot) float to the surface, where they can be collected in a sieve, dried, and sent to a laboratory for analysis. In the laboratory, researchers sort flot under a low-magnification (5 to 40×) binocular microscope, recovering each fragment that can be identified, usually by comparison to modern plant specimens in a reference collection [**8.15**]. Not every plant fragment from an excavation can be examined—it would simply take too much time and too many resources to do so—but with careful attention to sampling, an analyzed assemblage should represent the plant economy at the site.

Above left: **8.14 Archaeobotanical samples being processed using flotation.** This system uses water to float the buoyant plant remains into a series of sieves, which collect even tiny fragments for laboratory analysis.

Above: **8.15 After flotation samples arrive at the lab,** archaeobotanists sort through charred plant material and identify botanical elements. In this image, Anna Berlekamp extracts seeds using tweezers.

DOMESTICATION: A TWO-WAY PROCESS

Domesticates are one of the undisputable outcomes of an evolutionary relationship between humans and their environments. A domesticated plant or animal is one that exhibits dependency on humans for its reproduction; without human assistance, it would rapidly become extinct. It also has a mutualistic effect on humans, who rely on domesticates in assuring their own reproduction. One could say that domesticated plants and animals have also domesticated us. Just as a banana plant no longer needs seeds (or has any) because humans spread new banana plantations around the world with vegetative cuttings, so humans need domesticated plants to reproduce. We no longer forage to survive, and few even have the cultural knowledge to do so. This **mutualism**, the cooperation between two species for their mutual benefit, is

archaeobotanists Archaeologists who study the remains of plants from the past.

flotation A method for recovering charred pieces of ancient plants by floating them in water.

mutualism The cooperation of two species for their mutual benefit by enhancing individuals' fitnesses.

morphology The shape and form of an object or species.

seed dormancy The process during which a seed waits for the perfect conditions to sprout.

expressed in behavior and in **morphology**. For example, we humans sow and reap domesticated plants in agricultural fields worldwide as an agricultural behavior. On the plant side, domesticated behavior may be expressed through plant germination in conditions that suit the farmer. For example, domesticated plants have lost **seed dormancy**, meaning that instead of waiting for the perfect conditions to sprout, they do so when the farmer sows them. Under cultivation, seeds that sprouted and therefore ripened at the same time were the ones that yielded collectible, replantable seed. Over generations, seed that remained dormant would contribute fewer seeds to each new population, and those that sprouted would pass on their genes. Over time, only the seeds that would sprout immediately after sowing were left. Natural selection, an evolutionary process, is at work in plant domestication.

Through the same selective processes, plant morphology changed under domestication. For example, a wild cereal, such as wheat or barley, needs a stalk that becomes brittle and shatters once seeds ripen, scattering seeds in their tough seed–leaf wrappers as broadly as possible. If the stalk does not shatter, the ripe seed sits uselessly on the plant until a predator—bird, human, herbivore—comes along and consumes it. That is not beneficial for a wild cereal. Human farmers, on the other hand, need a tough stalk so that ripe cereal grains can be collected efficiently, at one time, and transported for safe storage until some of them are sown the following year [**8.16**]. Unintentionally, then, humans created the first domesticated wheat by "selecting" those with tough stalks. This selection probably came about with the Natufian technological innovation of sickles (a handle with many sharp blades),

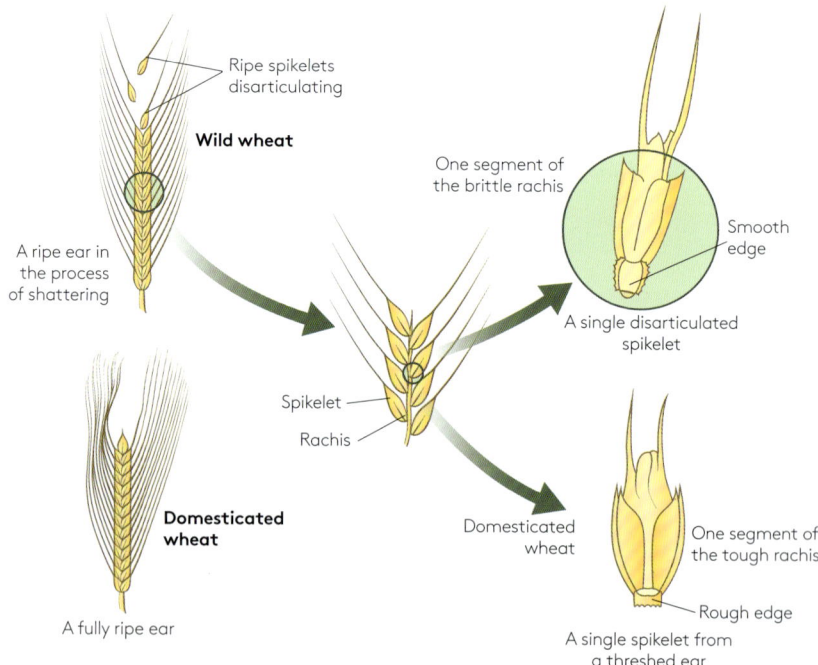

8.16 Comparison of the seeds of wild and domesticated wheat. In wild wheat, the rachis (stem that attaches the seed to the stalk, or spikelet) is brittle, which allows for the seed to fall off the plant naturally, when it is ripe. The domesticated wheat has a tough rachis, which must be manually broken by humans to release the seed.

which continue to be used in some early Neolithic areas. Brittle stalks sawed with a prehistoric sickle would drop their seed, but tough stalks would hold it, ensuring that those seeds were collected by humans, and their genetic code produced the next sowed generation of tough-stalked cereal. In a wild barley patch, a small percentage of stalks are tough because of a recessive mutation, but once that mutation is "selected for" (to use the language of natural selection as intended by Charles Darwin) under cultivation, tough stalks can quickly become dominant. Archaeological and genetic evidence around the world suggests that this process, in fact, took thousands of years, and tough stalks appeared before the emergence of large seeds.

Domesticating Animals

The domestication process in animals follows a remarkably similar pattern to that of plants. Individuals are removed from a wild context, and their reproduction is managed or manipulated by humans. Over the generations, selective breeding produces individuals with different qualities in behavior, body size, or physical features, such as hair length and meatier bodies, or an instinctual need to herd or retrieve objects. Mammals and birds have proven to be the most amenable animals to domestication, as these species naturally bond with a perceived "parent" during infancy. Replacing the mother and extended family with humans allows for the production of an individual that is relatively tame and able to be handled or contained. Around the world, humans domesticated a wide range of mammals, such as dogs, goats, sheep, cattle, and horses, and birds, such as chickens, ducks, and turkeys.

The oldest domesticated animal is the dog [**8.17**], which evolved from several unidentified species of wolves in Europe and Asia. Archaeological remains place dog domestication between 30,000 and 15,000 years ago, when all humans were still enduring the harsh conditions of the last glaciation, and hunting and gathering was the only way of life. The earliest dogs are difficult to identify from archaeological remains, because their bodies are easily confused with those of wild wolves. Subtle changes in the skulls of canids (the family of wolves and dogs)—in particular, the shortening of the muzzle and a reduction in tooth size—have been used to identify the earliest known dogs at the Goyet Caves in south-central Belgium, dating to about 36,000 years ago.

Dogs may have played a role in their own domestication, acting as "camp followers" that searched for scraps at the edges of human camps and producing friendly

8.17 Dog skull from Goyet Cave, Belgium, dated to about 36,000 years ago. Measurement of the 10-inch (25-cm) skull revealed that it had a broader skull and snout, suggesting that it was not a wolf, but instead resembled more recently domesticated dogs.

commensal pathway A path to animal domestication whereby a wild animal is drawn into a human environment and begins to form a mutualistic relationship with humans.

puppies easily adopted by humans. The behavior of wolves and these early dogs was probably what made them attractive domesticates: they could assist in hunting by running down prey, and scent and track other animals for long distances, allowing the hunters more opportunities to make a kill. The hunters, in turn, selected the animals that were not only the best hunters but also the most manageable to breed the next generation. These individuals were the least aggressive toward humans and more receptive to human commands. Over the ages, dog behavior and body characteristics have been further selected to meet the demands of different jobs, from herding to retrieving, fighting, pulling sleds, and even barking at the sound of intruders. The result of 30,000 years of domestication are countless varieties of dogs, today found worldwide in the company of humans.

The Three Paths to Animal Domestication

Zooarchaeologist Melinda Zeder has summarized three pathways by which animals in relationships with humans ultimately become domesticates. The domestication of the dog is a **commensal pathway**. In this form of domestication, a wild animal is drawn into human environments, such as the periphery of a human campsite with its jettisoned food scraps, and begins to forge a mutualistic bond with humans.

Another route to domestication is the **prey pathway**, whereby an animal originally hunted for meat becomes the object of protection and management. Among the earliest animals domesticated for meat were goats [**8.18**] that lived in the central Zagros Mountains of Iran. Excavations at this site, named Ganj Dareh ("Treasure Valley"), and also at Jericho, have recovered the bones of goats that were slaughtered. Another clue about their existence might be the packed deposits of dung, indicating

8.18 Modern-day image of a mixed goat and sheep herd following the herder in northern Mesopotamia (Syria). The process of goat domestication began 10,000 years ago in the Near East, where hunters shifted herd composition by killing young aggressive males for meat and allowing docile females to survive. Here a herder has substituted himself as the leader, and the herd even ignores ripe fields to follow him. Wild sheep and goat naturally follow a leader, making them easier to domesticate.

places where goats were likely penned for short periods. Goat kids, similar to wolf pups, are easy targets for domestication: they stay hidden in brush while their mother goes out to forage, and they can be collected easily and adopted into a human family. Once in the presence of other goats, the animals also display the instinct to herd together, making it easier to keep them under control. The archaeological remains of goats at Ganj Dareh suggest that goat management was under way some 10,000 years ago, and the larger males were routinely culled before they reached adult size. Females were permitted to live longer and probably bred every year to produce offspring that could then be slaughtered and consumed. Maintaining breeding females would have also allowed for their milk to be continuously produced and collected, generating a food supply that could feed human babies, conserve resources (tap, not kill, the animal), and supply a safe liquid for humans when water was brackish (slightly salty) or contaminated.

A final pathway to domestication likely emerged well after commensal and prey pathways; the **directed pathway** describes deliberate intent to bring a wild species under human management. Horses, donkeys, and camels were targets of deliberate human control, and their appearance archaeologically as domesticated animals occurred after about 6,000 years ago, long after people had become the herders and owners of other domesticates.

prey pathway A path to animal domestication whereby humans begin to manage and protect animals that were originally hunted in the wild.

directed pathway A path to animal domestication whereby wild animals are deliberately brought under human management.

CHINA: INDEPENDENT DOMESTICATION AND RICE

The domestication of plants and animals occurred independently in many places across the globe [**8.19**, p. 186]. In the early years of the twentieth century, Russian botanist Nikolai Vavilov traveled the world collecting seeds from little-known strains of crop plants. On the principle that genetic mutations accumulate over time, he reasoned that where one finds the greatest diversity is where a domesticated plant has been evolving for the longest time. Vavilov identified multiple regions where suites of crops expressed genetic diversity; he suggested that crops emerged in these centers of domestication. Archaeological work has followed the road map Vavilov offered, seeking domesticates in the hills of the Near East, the highlands of Mexico and Ethiopia, and the great river valleys of China, where millets and rice, some of the world's most important grains, were first domesticated.

Rice is the staple food of more than two-thirds of today's population. Finding archaeological evidence for rice domestication has been challenging, not least because distinguishing domesticated rice from wild rice relies on examining a very small part of the plant called the spikelet base. This piece is so small it often fell through sieve holes in earlier excavations, before archaeologists knew to look for it. Only very recently have we started to collect samples of rice across Asia to piece together the story of its domestication.

Rice is typically grown in wet conditions, such as paddy fields, which are flooded sections of land. It often requires a huge amount of labor and large quantities of water to irrigate. Two major strains of rice were domesticated in the past: *Oryza*

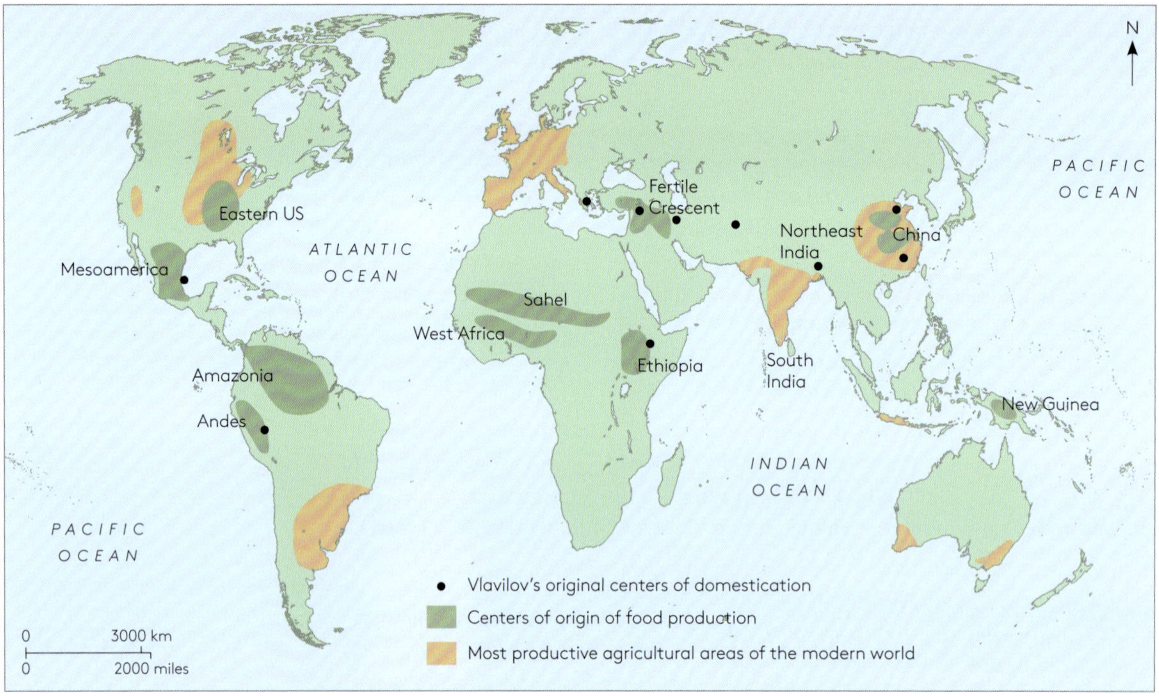

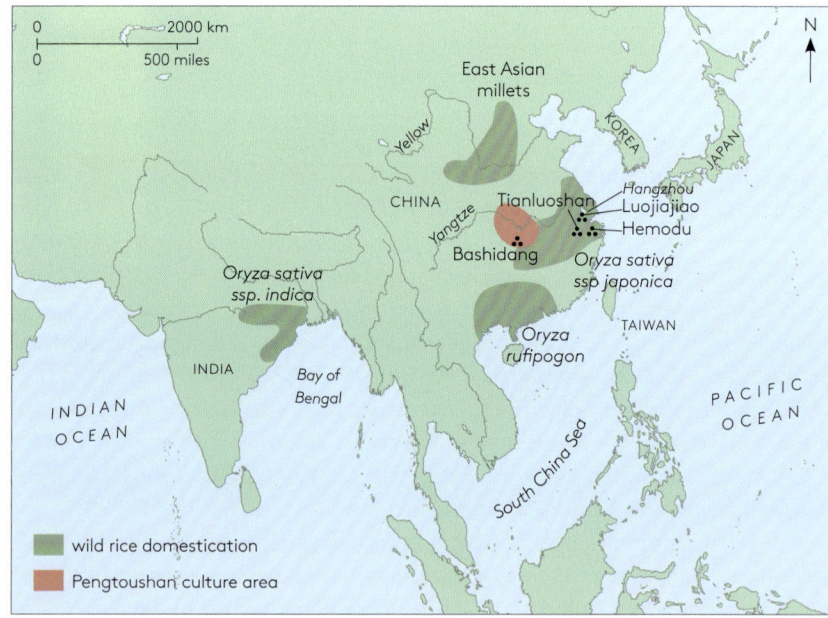

Above: **8.19 Map of Vavilov's original centers of domestication** (from modern crop varieties) with archaeological evidence for centers of origin of food production. These capture many but not all domesticated plants and animals.

Right: **8.20 Map of East Asia** showing where wild rice was first domesticated.

sativa or Asian rice appears in early China [**8.20**], India, Japan, and Southeast Asia, and *Oryza glaberrima* or African rice was domesticated along the Niger River in West Africa (see Chapter 14).

Some of the first traces of Asian rice appeared at the 6,000-year-old Chinese site of Hemodu, located in a humid, subtropical environment on the southern estuary of the Hangzhou River. The site is at the edge of an ancient lagoon, and its deepest layers consist of dark silt holding the wooden pilings that supported wooden buildings at or over the water's edge. From these layers, Swedish and Chinese archaeologists recovered impressive quantities of waterlogged rice, rice stalks and leaves, and the tools for rice processing—a bone spade made from a water buffalo scapula and wooden paddles [**8.21**]. The nearby Neolithic site of Luojiajiao offered similar remains in addition to those of dogs, pigs, and more than twenty species of wild game. Although little doubt existed that these were the villages of early rice farmers, they had cultivated domestic rice in an environment where it could be preserved archaeologically, so researchers did not necessarily believe that either location was the earliest site of rice cultivation.

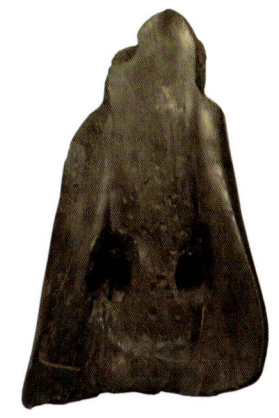

8.21 A bone spade from Hemodu, China, made from the scapula of a water buffalo. Through the central groove and two holes, this blade was attached to a long wooden handle to make a tool useful for shifting mud to level fields and clear irrigation ditches.

The Lower Yangtze River

The Hangzhou estuary of eastern China is not where wild rice, *Oryza rufipogon*, grew in the Pleistocene. Perhaps via the hands of humans, wild rice had spread into this region. Was the estuary where people had first begun to farm rice?

Answering this question would require the expertise of many different researchers bringing together evidence from archaeology, botany, climate studies, genetics, and linguistics. Enter Dorian Fuller, a consummate scientist fond of bright tropical shirts, sandals, black coffee, and collaboration. With students and colleagues across the world, Dorian has been on the track of rice domestication across China and India. He relied on the pioneering work of Zhijun Zhao and Deborah Pearsall, who used microscopic phytoliths, or plant-generated silica deposits, to detect the remains of rice in Neolithic sediments. Phytoliths have distinctive shapes and provided a way to recognize rice even at sites where preservation of plants was poor. Phytolith analysis has shown that rice was in China as early as 11,000 years ago. That is nearly as early as the evidence for wild wheats and barleys in Southwest Asia.

If we know when wild rice was first cultivated, when was it first domesticated? Fuller's team is addressing this question by examining the proportions of nonbrittle rice spikelets (small or secondary spikes). These parts of the plant developed in the domestication of rice following the same principle as the domestication of wheat; the gathering of rice favored the survival of plants that held onto their seeds, rather than plants with brittle spikelets that fell away. Fuller and his team focused on the Neolithic site of Tianluoshan (near Hangzhou) and found that rice domestication was fully under way by 6,500 years ago, and that rice, as wheat and barley do, expressed a tough stalk before selection for grain size. Using genetic and linguistic analysis, Fuller argues that rice was first domesticated in eastern China and spread

Above: **8.22 Rice farming across much of Asia** has shaped our human niche, in terms of: the plants and animals introduced; new physical structures, such as terraces and ditches; and intricate social systems of land access and water management.

Below: **8.23 Rice paddy ecosystems.** Carefully controlled flooding at specific times ensures the highest yield in domesticated rice. In paddy fields, ducks clear algae and pondweed while fish consume mosquito larvae and play a critical role in nutrient cycling. A paddy field yields rice, fowl, and fish for human consumption.

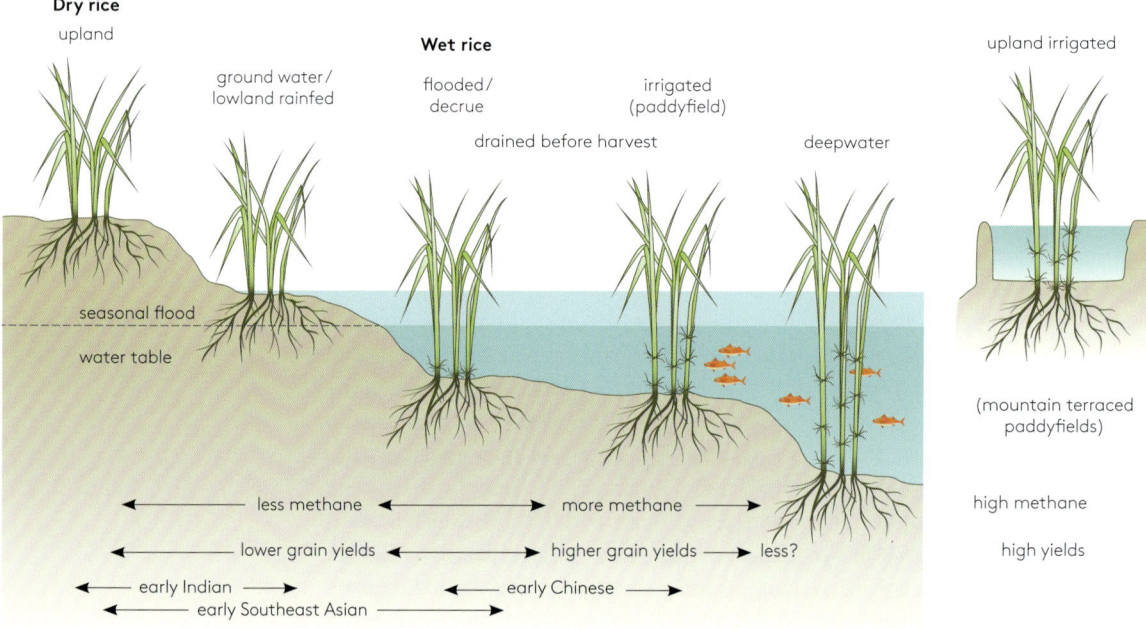

through trade to India, where it hybridized with a different form of wild rice to produce a distinctly Indian domesticated rice in the Ganges Valley 3,000 years ago.

Archaeologists understand relatively little about the lives of early rice farmers. In the middle Yangtze River region, the Neolithic Pengtoushan villages 9,100–6,800 years ago were very small settlements with rare examples of an earthen perimeter wall; many were also enclosed by an encircling ditch, likely for drainage. These villages began to appear as the early Holocene environment shifted to warmer, more humid conditions. Pengtoushan villagers focused much of their activity on the resources of the river. Ceramics were tempered by rice chaff, which left distinct impressions and gave a blackish hue to the pots, which were often decorated. The Pengtoushan people were not focused on rice alone: the remains of wild water caltrop (also known as water chestnut, *Trapa* sp.) and lotus root have also been found. The best-known Pengtoushan site is Bashidang in Hunan Province, which preserved a wide range of organic remains, including wooden and bone spades (possibly used for cultivation in the rice paddies), rope, and bone drills. Apart from the small and diverse sizes of their communities, we can infer little else about the social lives of these Neolithic rice farmers beyond their enduring cultural practices over several thousand years. We can also observe the changes their rice paddies made to the forest of the river floodplain [**8.23**, **8.23**, **8.24**]. Fuller's team is using phytoliths from the species of weeds that developed with rice to detect the kinds of paddies, or fields, in which rice was grown. Using this method, it is possible to trace the shift in farming practices through time, from uncontrolled flooding to managed water levels. Ultimately, this work will help archaeologists to understand the history of rice farming's spread and its contributions to shaping the landscape and creating our Anthropocene niche.

8.24 A rice paddy is an ecological niche for many interdependent species.
Rice farmers prize not only the rice, but also the carp that flourish in the paddies and ditches, eating mosquitoes and other pests. Domestic ducks devour pondweed that could choke rice plants, and they fertilize fields with their waste. Here farmers are removing carp from one field before harvesting the rice.

THE CONSEQUENCES OF FARMING
Demographic

The shift to farming had major consequences. Farming caused humans to live a more sedentary lifestyle, and one result of this was a higher birth rate, leading to population growth. Anthropologists attribute this to multiple factors. Stored crops and domesticated animals afforded a steady food supply, which assured nutrition for the mother through pregnancy and nursing. Access to goat's milk, and, when pottery appeared, wheat or barley gruel (oatmeal), meant that mothers could supplement or replace their breastmilk and wean their babies sooner. Because breastfeeding suppresses ovulation, early weaning of babies enabled mothers to bear another child more quickly, possibly within a year. Becoming less mobile also reduced the need to carry infants and toddlers between hunting camps; mothers could care for much larger families, and childcare could be shared by an extended family.

A farmer's life was nevertheless a hard one. There was greater incidence of disease from contaminated water, higher population density, a narrowed diet, and

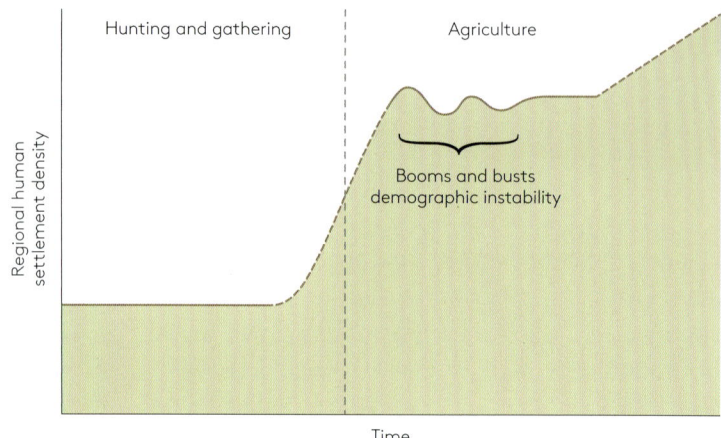

8.25 Population growth in the agricultural niche. Archaeologists have used several proxies of population, including human burials and radiocarbon dates from Neolithic settlements (as implied here in a schematic representation of Stephen Shennan's and Sean Downey's European study) to document a Neolithic demographic transition. Although human populations generally rise when people become farmers, proxy data from regional settlement density suggests that an initial growth is followed by cycles of boom and bust.

closer interactions with animals, including mice, sparrows, and rats that thrive on the environment humans provide. Child mortality rose in early villages, as did the labor requirements in households needing more children to perform agricultural tasks. Recent big data studies of early archaeological sites in Europe reveal that after the introduction of Neolithic farming villages, local populations experienced a boom and then a bust, probably an outcome of resource depletion and the challenges of village life [**8.25**].

Despite the quality of living, and the fact that the dynamics of early agricultural populations are challenging to model, hindsight shows us that early villages composed of household farming units were ultimately highly successful. As village size expanded, some households departed to form new villages on lands never previously farmed. In this way, agriculturalists colonized regions from the Middle East into Central Asia and Europe.

Social

Living permanently in close quarters clearly posed some new social challenges. In the projected near future, human astronauts en route to Mars will struggle with extremely tense group living in cramped space vehicles; NASA scientists consider this as great a challenge as brain swelling, radiation exposure, muscle atrophy, and other biological hazards. Food producers in Neolithic villages faced quarrels over food sharing across households, access to food-producing land, and other new social stressors that could no longer be avoided through the mobility afforded by a change of season. People adopted new technologies that helped them adapt socially to the new environment of village life. For starters, a permanent, physical space—the house—reinforced the household social unit. Strengthened households meant that their occupants recursively drew a stronger sense of social identity in the community.

ÇATALHÖYÜK: LIVING TOGETHER The village of Çatalhöyük [8.26] in Turkey, dating to 8,500 years ago, was one of the largest known villages of its time. Community life took place in extremely crowded conditions. Archaeologists estimate that up to eight thousand people may have occupied the site at its peak. Houses abutted one another, sharing walls and entryways through the roof. Although excavations in the 1960s uncovered dozens of houses, more recent excavations have focused on the detailed studies of just a few. The exhaustive analysis of the artifacts these few houses contained provides an exquisitely detailed view of daily life in this early Neolithic (PPNB) village. House architecture and numerous modifications indicate that houses were occupied over many generations. Over four hundred years, houses in the same spot were built, occupied, and abandoned, with their walls reduced and interior filled to provide a stable base for another house on top. Archaeologists have detected instances of three or four consecutive structures one atop another.

Interior plastering was not the only feature that people introduced: they shifted the locations of sleeping platforms, hearths, bins, and roof entrances; they hid objects for later retrieval; they opened and blocked doorways; and they used space inside and outside according to structured conventions. Living together meant agreeing to unwritten rules. To understand what this involves, think about your own home space. Do you remove your shoes when you enter? Close your door to signal "keep out" to roommates? Shuffle rooms when the room conducive to the best sleep needs a new occupant?

It was common for a single house to be inhabited for more than a century, and over this time the rules, or uses, of the house may have changed. Inside Çatalhöyük,

8.26 House interior at Çatalhöyük, showing the horns of aurochs (wild cattle) embedded in a raised, plastered platform. The rooms of Çatalhöyük employ architectural elements, such as platforms and low walls, indicating that the inhabitants routinely partitioned activities into different spaces.

many houses were coated with dozens of layers of plaster, sealing as many as sixty subfloor burials under sleeping platforms, and obscuring skulls and horns of wild cattle mounted on the walls, or caches of obsidian blades. Archaeologist Ian Hodder has referred to these "memory houses" as repositories for important knowledge. Remembering what was embedded in the house's walls links the occupants to the house and its former occupants. At the same time, it seems likely that the wild beasts embedded in and often painted on plaster also commemorate community-building activities, such as the customary feast following the sacrifice of an animal and the non-edible creatures (e.g., cranes, vultures, or leopards) that became totemic or significant in myth and ideology.

In daily life, clay balls stored near the hearths were used in cooking: after heating them in the fire, people would transfer the hot clay balls to skin-lined baskets to prepare stews (only later in time did they use pottery). Bones found a distance from the houses in refuse heaps at the base of the village mound indicate that some food preparation, such as butchery, took place out in the open, and it was likely that sharing meat—especially wild cattle—among community members strengthened ties beyond a single household [**8.27**]. Roof space was visible to all, and many daily tasks were probably performed there. Although neighbors could see food being prepared on the roof—lentils being sorted, nuts pounded, chaff winnowed, fruits dried—inner storage bins concealed food reserves and how much of these remained.

8.27 The 8,500-year-old site of Çatalhöyük appears as a low hill amidst a flat agricultural plain. It was originally constructed on a low rise within an ancient marsh, and the inhabitants took advantage of the moist soil to cultivate wheat, barley, chickpeas, and lentils. Modern farmers in the region still grow these crops.

Each household was ultimately responsible for its own food production, but some may have been better off than others in this regard.

Charred plant remains show that the settlers of Çatalhöyük were primarily farmers. They raised wheat, barley, and legumes, such as chickpeas and lentils, all staples of early farming villages. These staples were supplemented by a rich and diverse array of resources, for instance, fish, eggs, sedge tubers, nuts, and wild game, including the fearsome but meaty wild cattle. Despite the village's crowded living conditions, archaeologists find little evidence of nutritional stress on human bones and teeth or of physical violence, suggesting that fierce competition for resources did not occur. It appears as if there was sufficient food, and the land to produce it, for all. No contemporary Neolithic village within several days' walk existed, and this is perhaps one of the reasons why the settlement grew so dense. Having many neighbors would assure people of help in times of need—extra hands to process crops quickly—and, importantly, eligible mates for younger household members.

It is clear that Çatalhöyük's inhabitants maintained the external ties that allowed materials to flow over long distances, as evidenced by obsidian, seashells from as far away as the Red Sea, rare precious stones, and imported chert. To this day, no one fully understands why this dense Neolithic community was settled and then flourished in such isolation, but to do so, Çatalhöyük's founders were clearly driven by strong social and perhaps ideological connections to this marshy isolate. The rejuvenating act of plastering rooms appears to have been critical to social cohesion within the village, and it may be that the proximity of marls, a common sediment nearby that was used in plaster, was what fostered the first village. From the earliest times, Çatalhöyük's founders dug deep through the alluvial soils to reach the calcium-carbonate-rich marls, but this effort may have proved too expensive in the long run. Archaeologists note that the original plaster gave way over time to a marl-and-mud mix that was nonetheless an effective agent in community renewal over more than 1,000 years.

Environmental

Domesticated plants and domesticated animals (goats and sheep at first, then the later addition of cattle and pigs) were the economic staples that fed new villages. In terms of human ecology, farming was broadly successful. Farmers exhibited greater fitness, meaning that individuals, on average, produced more offspring, who, in turn, survived also to reproduce. The outcome was significant population growth, with farmers having out-competed foragers in most of Earth's ecosystems. And as farming expanded, so did the farming habitat; a "farmers' niche" was formed. This transition had local effects on plants and animals, and broad impacts on global ecosystems.

FOREST CLEARANCE IN NORTHERN EUROPE From its development in Southwest Asia, farming systems spread into new regions of Europe. In the north, pollen evidence from many peat bogs and lakes speaks to an episode of forest clearance

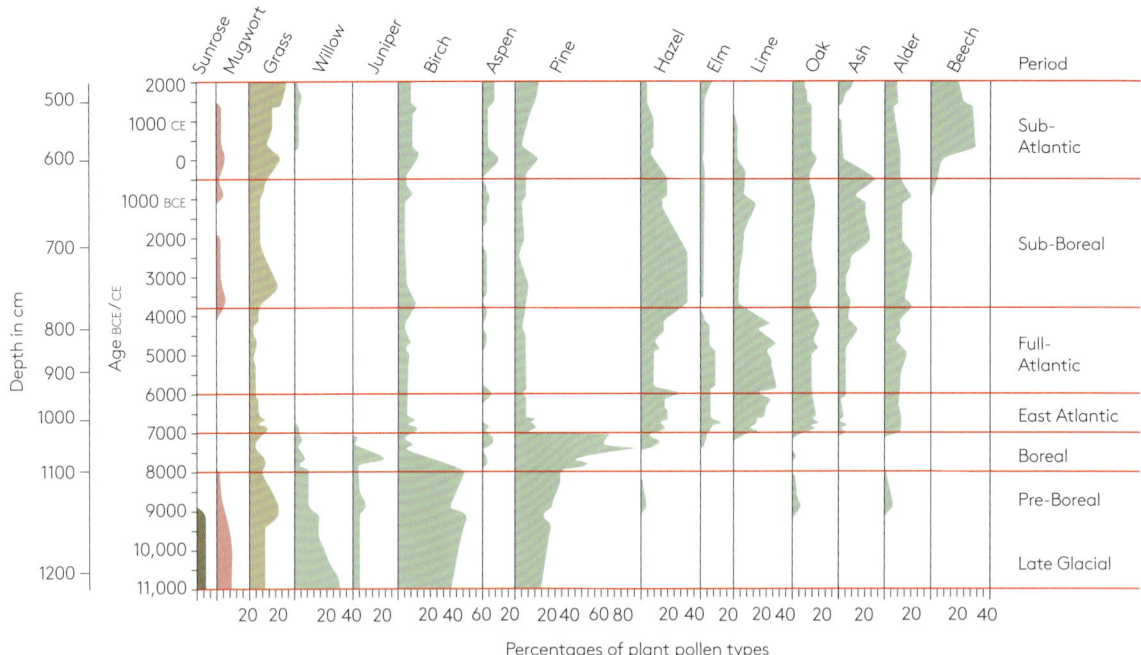

8.28 Pollen diagram from Roskilde Fjord, Denmark. The episodes named on the far right correspond to shifts in pollen abundances noted across many areas. Many shifts in abundance are due to changes in climate, but one shift is the landnam event around 4000 BCE. Note the decline in elm, surge in hazel, and increases in grasses (cereals in fields).

palynology The identification of pollen (created by plants for sexual reproduction) using microscopy and sample specimens.

landnam The clearance of forested land for agricultural purposes.

around 6,000 years ago. By comparing the ratios of pollen from trees and pollen from non-tree taxa (organisms), **palynologists** are able to study the changes in forest cover over time. This approach has generated considerable discussion and refinement, but for fifty years palynologists have generally agreed that they can trace the widespread clearance of forest not attributable to climate change. Anthropogenic in origin, this clearance, or **landnam** (from the Danish for "land occupation"), describes the practice of farmers who upon settling the land cut down forest to make way for the light-loving annual plants that would eventually yield crops.

Following pollen records through time shows an initial clearance phase as the decline of overall tree pollen and increase in grass and herbs when farmers removed forest [**8.28**]. Slow-growing oak then declined. A farming phase followed, resulting in an increase of cereal-type grasses (crops) and weeds. A decline in elm pollen reflects the widespread cutting of leafy boughs to feed domesticated, stalled animals in winter and may be linked to episodes of elm disease that weakened trees. During a subsequent regeneration phase, fast-growing hazel (prized by settlers for making fences and wicker dwellings) increased, but in a regenerated forest phase, this tree fell out of favor because it afforded farmers less light. In many areas of Northern Europe, these pollen-related landnam sequences correspond to the earliest regional archaeology of farming settlements.

WEEDS TAKE OVER IN SOUTHERN CALIFORNIA Also part of the environmental effects of farming and the making of a human niche are the plants that benefited from human presence. Most of the planet is now anthropogenic, modified by humans but also colonized by opportunistic plants. Farming created a very large environment of continuous soil disturbance favorable to weeds. Weeds may be found in any urban environment in the world, but their origins lie at the edges of farmers' fields. Weeds were not always with us. Some weedy plant species have evolved rather recently, within the past 10,000 years, and they have done so as the expanded farming habitat offered new opportunities for plants that reproduce quickly, cross-pollinate (with new mutations and genetic diversity), love light, and mimic crops. Archaeological evidence reveals a history of habitat change and plant adaptation in new farming environments.

In southern California, Native Americans used fire for the last two thousand years to clear patches where small-seeded native annual plants provided wild resources for foragers. When the Spanish friars arrived in 1769 to establish the first Catholic missions, they brought European crops with them, and weeds "hitched a ride." For the first time, tilling and fire suppression were used to control the habitats of California soils. European weeds thrived in the Americas and quickly spread with European farming technologies. In the adobe (mud) bricks of California missions built in the late 1700s, George Hendry found remains of Mediterranean weeds that now proliferate across the grasslands and prairies of the American West: brome grass, wild barley, wild oats, rye grasses, curly dock, thistles, and many others [**8.29**]. These weeds had eight thousand years to adapt to grazing animals in the Mediterranean. In the Americas, they became easy fodder for transplanted populations of horses, sheep, cattle, and goats.

8.29 Tumbleweed, the iconic plant of the American West, blowing across the hills of California. The ancestors of these plants originated in Europe, and journeyed to the Americas in the eighteenth and nineteenth centuries in shipments of other seeds. The weak stalk and rounded form of these plants allow them to break free of the ground and distribute their seeds while tumbling.

OVERGRAZING IN THE MEDITERRANEAN Finally, one must speak of the goats. Goats will eat anything, but unlike cattle and sheep, they are primarily browsers, meaning they consume the leaves of shrubs and trees. It is not uncommon for nimble goats to climb low-branching trees to get at the leaves. The effect of domesticated goats on the Mediterranean woodlands from Jordan and Israel to Spain and Morocco has been evolutionarily profound. Plant ecologist Sandro Pignatti points to the high incidence of thorny and aromatic plants resistant to browsing in the circum-Mediterranean basin as a plant community response to 10,000 years of goat and sheep herding. Rosemary, thyme, savory, and oregano, the zesty herbs of the Mediterranean, developed volatile oils to repel browsers and inhibit other plants from competing for the same open ground. These are the same oils that we humans appreciate in small amounts—as flavorings for our sauces and stews. Spiny plants also resist grazing. Archaeologists have detected this process at work in the Pre-Pottery Neolithic B. At PPNB Ain Ghazal (in Jordan), as farmers cleared the forests for fields and houses, browsing goats ate saplings and tender young plants, selecting for the growth of wild plants that could rapidly mature while being protected by spines, sap that caused itching or burning, toxins, or unpalatable taste. Artichokes, thistles, bitter lettuce, and rue were favored as part of this process, and filled the landscape.

THE CRITICAL ROLE OF THE COMMUNITY IN FOOD PRODUCTION

In the 1920s, archaeologist V. Gordon Childe emphasized the move from foraging and hunting to producing food as a "revolution" in human history. His characterization—based on largely theoretical arguments exciting in his day—led archaeologists to dub the period of first villages a "Neolithic Revolution." It turns out there may be little that felt revolutionary about early food production, at least not in the economic sense that Childe had envisioned. He likened this transformation of human experience to the Bolshevik Revolution of his day (in 1917), when Russian workers and farmers overthrew the government and redistributed land ownership. But archaeology shows us a far more complex picture than a short revolution. One hundred years later, we know now that people lived communally in villages before plants and animals were domesticated. From the vantage point of hindsight, though, we can argue that the changes from gathering to producing food created demographic and social changes that are visible archaeologically in the earliest farming villages [**8.30**].

From the study of charred plant remains, archaeologists can generally determine no morphological changes showing unequivocal domestication until after the Pre-Pottery Neolithic A, about 9,600 years ago, the period when settlers built Jericho's wall and tower and congregants founded Göbekli Tepe. Domesticated plants do not appear in the archaeological record until after villages composed of household units had been in place for at least several hundred years and many generations of foragers had cultivated wild plants. From the end of the Pleistocene

8.30 A cave painting from the Marai-Borda cave in western Egypt shows a herding scene with cows, calves, and herders. Between about 8,000 and 6,000 years ago, cattle were herded across the Sahara Desert in search of grass for grazing, and human societies traveled with them.

onward, growing populations coalesced in large gatherings and participated in massive building projects. Exploiting a broader spectrum of plant and small-animal resources gradually transformed the habitats and resource distributions around such places. Village life and the emergence of food production fit into this longer trend of resource depletion and environmental transformation, taking off in a big way when plants were moved out of their natural habitats.

Manipulation of habitats, the spread of disturbed habitats worldwide, the depletion of wild resources, a narrowed dietary range, and a switch to foods requiring more energy investment to procure are the evolutionary outcomes of human history, perhaps driven by the social characteristics of humans and the possibilities of a stable and predictable warmer Holocene climate. What was revolutionary was social: the emergence of strong household units, the need to commemorate great gatherings and to sustain relationships over longer periods, greater distances, and broader networks. Humans used adaptive technologies, what Ian Hodder has also called "greater material entanglements," to achieve these social changes. Producing food was but one further step in the manipulation of resources to support growing human populations in settled communities, and those changes took a long time. Although Gordon Childe considered food production to be the basis for a Neolithic Revolution with social consequences, the archaeology of domesticating and early food-producing societies now begins to suggest that new social imperatives drove human groups to congregate and establish larger social communities, leading to food production—not the other way around. Whatever the origins of these communities, their impacts have been transformational in shaping human ecology and our global human habitat.

Chapter Questions

1. How do the stories of Göbekli Tepe and the Natufians demonstrate the relationship between domestication and settlement?
2. What processes were involved in the development of domestication in the Near East and China?
3. What kind of information can archaeobotany offer in understanding the development of agriculture in the past?
4. What were some of the Anthropocene (social and environmental) consequences of animal and plant domestication?

Additional Resources

Fuller, Dorian Q. "Pathways to Asian Civilization: Tracing the Origins and Spread of Rice and Rice Cultures," *Rice* 4 (2011): 78–92.

Hodder, Ian. *The Leopard's Tale.* London, UK: Thames & Hudson, 2006.

Kenyon, Kathleen. *Digging Up Jericho.* London, UK: Ernest Benn, 1957.

Miller, Naomi F. "Long Term Vegetation Changes in the Near East," in *The Archaeology of Global Change*, edited by Charles L. Redman, Steven R. James, Paul R. Fish, and J. Daniel Rogers, 130–40. Washington, DC: Smithsonian Books, 2004.

Zeder, Melinda A. "The Domestication of Animals," *Journal of Anthropological Research* 68, no. 2 (2012): 161–90.

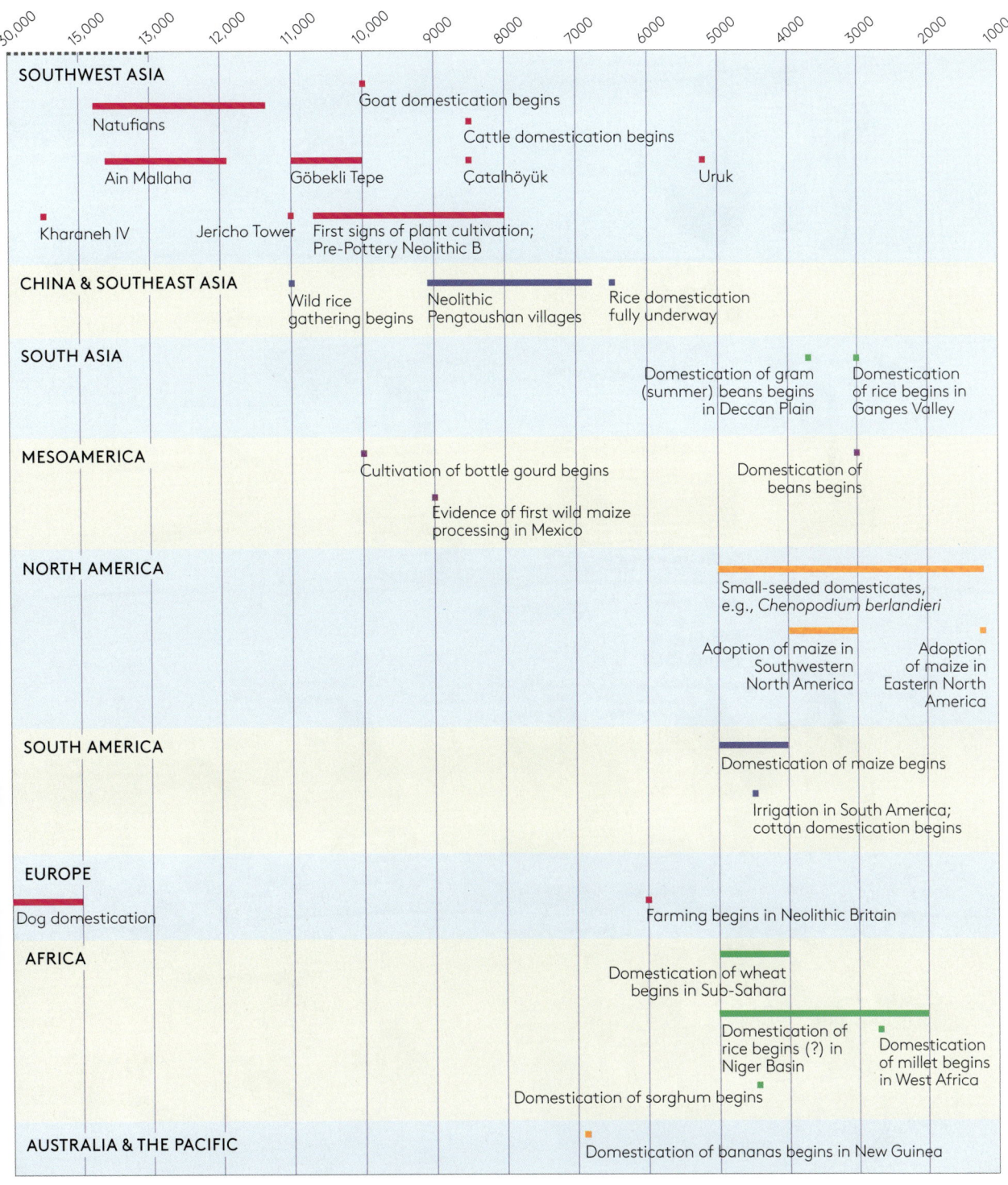

INDIVIDUALS AND IDENTITY
Agency in History

9

How are identities formed? How do they change, and how might an individual's identity affect the kind of power he or she has? Human history is replete with examples of forming and changing identity. Many cultures ritualize the passage between ages. For example, boys of the Sateré-Mawé tribe in the Amazonian jungle must endure the stings of ants as part of a set of rituals that grant them the identity of adult men. Human culture allows us to change our bodies, our names, and our identities—and these identities give us different choices and possibilities in altering the world that surrounds us.

The beginning of a new identity for me began one evening when I met some old friends for dinner. The evening was fun until I felt oddly unwell. My chest tightened, and the room seemed to spin. After several agonizing minutes, the feelings subsided, and I relaxed and began to enjoy my dinner. A few weeks later, other odd symptoms emerged. I felt tired and wanted to sleep all day. I experienced a little nausea, but nothing as bad as the flu or food poisoning. Nothing serious seemed to be wrong. Then one Monday morning while reviewing my online calendar, I noticed I had not circled a day the previous month that I had marked every month on a calendar since I was thirteen years old. That day women around the world dutifully track was shockingly missing. Could it really be true? I was forty years old, and my husband was fifty-one, now facing an unplanned pregnancy.

Nine months later, I was a new, hapless parent. My husband and I were elated, but also confused, frustrated, and totally out of control. Only when I was with other parents did I feel that someone understood me, and I sought a new network of friends in places I had never spent much time before: parks, grocery stores, and schools. Within a few weeks, a new identity completely transformed me. I was suddenly a parent and an active participant in the culture of mothers and fathers.

In this chapter, we will explore how archaeologists examine identities in the past. Just as the new identity of parent overlapped my other identities, we assume that people in the past belonged to a variety of social groups and designations. Some can give the individual more influence or power, whereas others may result in far less freedom and harm the individual. A closer understanding of individuals and identities in the past can show us how a society came together, and how some individuals were able to affect greater change than others.

Studying Identity **202**

Mesoamerica: The Aztecs **203**

Cortés and La Malinché **205**

Textiles, Identity, and Gender **207**

Bioarchaeology **212**

Inequality and Structural Violence in Prehistory **216**

Agency, Identity, and the Anthropocene **219**

Opposite Image from the Codex Mendoza, *c.* 1540. This scene illustrates Aztec views on parenting, which included strict punishments for both boys and girls. From prehistory to modern times, societal structure is replicated in accepted norms for how individuals conduct themselves. An individual's agency can replicate or transform the structure.

Key Concepts

- The history of the Aztecs and the pivotal identity of La Malinché (aka Doña Marina), an indigenous woman of Mexico who aided Hernán Cortés in his conquest
- Through the example of the Aztecs, the importance of artifacts or objects in constructing modern cultural narratives
- The principal methods of bioarchaeology and its ability to reveal the power of individuals in the past
- Archaeology as the voice of inequality in a society

bioarchaeology The archaeological study of bones and other human remains for biological indicators of sex, health, lifestyle, and social status.

structural inequality A societal configuration that results in the oppression of segments of the society.

agency The power of an individual to act within a social structure.

STUDYING IDENTITY

How do archaeologists study identity? Identity can be attributed to both individuals and groups, and used to express the religious, political, private, cultural, or ethnic aspects of one's life. Identity can become a source of cohesion or violence, representing sameness or difference; it may also symbolize an imposition or a choice, singular or fractured, static or fluid. As identity is a difficult concept to grasp or unravel, studying it in the past is not without significant challenges. One method of studying identity is to evaluate historical texts, which can describe what life was like in the past, but even with textual evidence, it is important to understand the context of that information (who is the author of the text, who was the intended audience, and what was its purpose), and recognize that even during historical periods with written records, writing is not accessible to everyone (see Chapter 13).

Archaeologists may also seek to discover the identity of individuals through the study of human remains. **Bioarchaeology** analyzes bones and other remains (including preserved DNA) to determine an individual's age, sex, health, place of residence, and activities in life. These data can be compared with those of other individuals to determine the critical components of human experience, such as relative rates of health and disease. Stress and injuries resulting from activities and occupations are often a direct tie to different individual experiences. Through the study of skeletal populations (such as a group of skeletons excavated from a cemetery), bioarchaeology can explore the different experiences of **structural inequality**, something that can be linked to identity and shape an individual's life.

Whether using textual or archaeological evidence, it is important to develop theoretical tools to comprehend how individuals perceived themselves and others in the wider society. Anthropology and the study of living cultures offer assistance in understanding the social structures that could have conditioned or developed an individual's identity. Chapter 7 introduced the concept of social structure, the overarching rules (be they explicit or implicit) that create society. The other side of the coin is **agency**, the degree that a person has power to create a meaningful life for themselves in accordance with or opposition to the social structure. This concept of agency is not equivalent to personal freedom, but instead identifies the choices available to an individual. Identity is a way for people to realize their agency within a society, and understanding the various identities that comprise a society is a valuable step in building a picture of what life was like in the past, and how things changed.

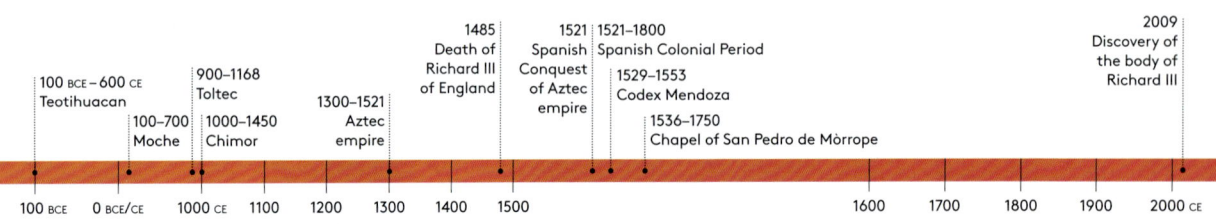

MESOAMERICA: THE AZTECS

The Aztec empire [**9.1**] provides an example of the fluidity of human identity in the past. It shows how the constraints of society coupled with an individual's agency have affected the trajectory of the Anthropocene.

The name *Aztec* was coined by the explorer and geographer Alexander von Humboldt in the eighteenth century, derived from the **Nahuatl** word for the "Aztlan" homeland. The founders of the Aztec empire were a range of Nahuatl-speaking people, including the Mexica, from whom the country of Mexico acquired its name. The Aztec people migrated into the Valley of Mexico, emerging as the last Mesoamerican society in the region prior to the Spanish Conquest led by Hernán Cortés (1485–1547; Chapter 10 describes some earlier Mesoamerican cultures).

The Aztecs integrated some of the social and ideological traditions from earlier civilizations that had developed in the Valley of Mexico. They explicitly constructed their own identity as legitimate Mesoamerican rulers by linking their rituals to the cultural traditions that originated in the previous ancient Toltec society, whose capital center at Tula was in ruins by the mid-twelfth century CE. The massive pyramids, apartment blocks, and civic centers at nearby Teotihuacan (c. 100 BCE–600 CE) were also in ruins, but the iconography of a feathered serpent god and human sacrifice were visible on its walls and statuary, and would be adopted by the Aztecs [**9.2**, p. 204]. The Aztecs forcibly incorporated other ethnic groups into their society and expanded Aztec influence to demand tribute from neighboring cities—the hallmarks of an empire. Sacrifice to the gods, and sacrifice to the Aztec empire, were the dominant themes in the construction of their cultural identity.

Nahuatl A language spoken in the Valley of Mexico, also known as Aztec.

9.1 Map of Mexico showing the extent of the Aztec empire in dark green, with the capital at Tenochtitlán. The cities of Tula and Teotihuacan pre-date the Aztec empire by 500–1000 years.

9.2 Quetzalcoatl, the feathered serpent god. From the pyramid of Quetzalcoatl at Teotihuacan, Mexico.

9.3 Altar of Coyolxuahqui found at the Templo Mayor site—or Temples of Huitzilopochtli and Tlaloc—in Tenochtitlán, now at the heart of Mexico City. According to Aztec stories, Coyolxuahqui was killed and dismembered by her brother, Huitzilopochtli, the warrior god. Her destruction symbolizes the Aztec view of rivals and their place in the universe: the Aztecs were the heirs of Huitzilopochtli, the conquerors, and their rivals must submit or be destroyed. Placing Coyolxuahqui's dismembered image on this altar served as a warning to others, and encapsulated the identity of the Aztec state.

When Cortés, the Spanish, and their Tlaxcaltec allies from the Gulf of Mexico arrived at the Aztec capital of Tenochtitlán (now Mexico City), they found an island city thriving on the tribute of subject people. It was an engineering marvel: surrounded by floating gardens, or ***chinampas***, at the margins of Lake Texcoco, the city center was connected to the mainland by a long causeway. As they entered Tenochtitlàn, the Spaniards wondered at the high population density, the looming central pyramids, the brightly clad feathered warriors, the blood-soaked altars [**9.3**], and the grisly racks displaying the skulls of hundreds of sacrificial victims.

chinampas A Nahuatl word for raised-field agriculture.

CORTÉS AND LA MALINCHÉ

Between 1496 and 1501 CE, about twenty years before the arrival of Cortés, a baby girl known as Doña Marina was born to high-status parents living along the Gulf Coast of Mexico. According to a historic account written many decades later, the girl was given as a child to the Xicalango people and then later, as a young woman as a slave to the Tabasco people. As a result, she spoke Nahuatl, which was the language of the Aztecs, and she also spoke one of the Maya languages of the Yucatan Peninsula.

In early spring of 1519, she and twenty other women were gifted as slaves to Cortés, who had arrived on the northern coast of Mexico with an army of five hundred men, thirteen horses, and several cannons. The Spaniards had sailed from the island colonies of Hispaniola and Cuba, and sought to claim land and riches for themselves and to establish a new colony for Spain in the interior of Mexico. The historical record suggests that Cortés passed the women to his captains. Although some texts imply that the women were servants to these men, they were undoubtedly given as forced sexual partners. The enslaved women were also pressured to convert to Catholicism, which would later allow them to be married in the Church. Doña Marina is the only woman to be identified personally in the Spanish accounts; she is remembered as being outspoken but helpful to the Spanish. As one of the enslaved, Doña Marina was also given to a captain, but Cortés frequently availed himself of her abilities as a translator, and she became his spokesperson and personal representative.

In the weeks that followed, the small Spanish army traveled west toward Central Mexico. As they invaded new regions, Mexican armies met them and several battles ensued, resulting in many deaths. Cortés' strategy was to press on into the territories of tribes that were both the neighbors and enemies of the Aztec empire, and through persuasion or coercion influence them to join the Spanish forces. On numerous occasions, the young Doña Marina spoke for Cortés and convinced the native armies to surrender and serve the Spanish. She also discovered a plot to ambush Cortés and his army while they slept in a supposedly friendly town. After she alerted Cortés of the plan afoot, he had the plotters punished: either their hands or their thumbs were cut off and then delivered to the tribal chiefs as a warning. At each pivotal turn, Doña Marina of Xicalango and Tabasco, who had now assumed

9.4 Cortés and La Malinché (drawing from the Codex Azcatitlan, c. 1540 CE). The image depicts the Spanish troops with Cortés marching to Tenochtitlàn, with La Malinché in the lead in the bottom right. La Malinché wears a *huipil* similar to the one on display at Museo Nacional de Anthropologia de México (see 9.5, p. 208).

the name and identity of La Malinché (literally, "the captains' woman"), proved herself to be a true ally of the Spanish.

In subsequent months, the Spanish forces drew nearer to Tenochtitlán, the capital city of the Aztecs that was home to approximately 100,000 people [**9.4**]. Moctezuma, the ruler of the Aztecs, sent emissaries and gifts to placate Cortés, which were accepted, opening a dialogue between the two forces. With La Malinché's help as an interpreter and confidante, Cortés and his men were able to enter the city peacefully and take up lodging in the royal palace. As Catholics, the Spanish were horrified by the rituals of human sacrifice practiced by the Aztecs. Within a few more months, they took control of the city, and shortly thereafter Moctezuma was killed in a skirmish and the Spanish overthrew the temples. La Malinché survived the battles that ultimately resulted in the destruction of the Aztec state; historians recorded her presence among the Spanish army. After being recognized as an important and identifiable individual by the Spanish, her identity became intimately connected to Cortés, so much so that the term "La Malinché" was frequently used to refer to both of them. Later that year, she gave birth to a son, who was acknowledged as the child of Cortés and the first person of mixed European and Native American ancestry in Mexico.

La Malinché: Choice and Agency

La Malinché made choices that ultimately transformed her identity and that of the Mesoamerican world, though history has not always told her story favorably.

For her role in the Spanish Conquest, she has been called a traitor (even the name "Malinché" colloquially means "cheater"). But she was a slave both to the Aztecs and the Spanish, and her options were few. Did she choose to aid the Spanish invaders, who were completely alien to her, to save her own life? Helping the Spanish would have been a gamble, as Cortés's men were vastly outnumbered, and their victory would not have seemed certain. She could have chosen to defect from her captors, or do nothing. Did she hope that by aiding the Spanish she might escape a life of slavery? The answer to this question is lost to us. No one ever interviewed La Malinché during her lifetime, and her descendants did not recollect or record her point of view.

If we use archaeological and historical sources to view La Malinché from within the context of her society, her decisions seem less those of a conspiring traitor, rather the pragmatic actions of a woman trapped, attempting to negotiate her place within the collision of two powerful societies. She had exchanged one form of slavery for another, but she exercised her agency (the ability to act within or against the structures of one's society) by communicating to both cultures. In turn, her agency contributed to deciding the fates of many people across the Valley of Mexico through the societal upheaval that emerged as a product of the Spanish invasion. The old structures of power and influence that were native to Aztec Mesoamerica evaporated, and even the natural environment of Mexico changed as a result, with new diseases, plants, and animals introduced from Europe.

Though from a young age she did not possess freedom, Doña Marina used her agency to define a new identity for herself, metamorphosing from a slave into "La Malinché." Her actions and identity also served to transform surrounding institutions, creating a new society—one that would possibly keep her safe and provide a home for her future children.

TEXTILES, IDENTITY, AND GENDER

Much of what we know of La Malinché or Doña Marina's life may be learned through historical texts, although none of these records is in her own words. How can we thus explore unspoken and unrecorded identities of the past? What indicators of identity can be gleaned from the archaeological record? Status and identity are perhaps most commonly conveyed in a visual sense by textiles. Anthropologist Annette Weiner has written about the ways in which cloth wealth provided economic and cosmological foundations for rank and hierarchy in Polynesia. She notes that cloth can be hoarded; it can also be culturally enhanced by its maker, by the occasion of its transfer, and by its importance as an heirloom. Just as in the instance of human life spans and political alliances, the duration of cloth is finite, so keeping hold of an ancient cloth can symbolize the continuation of authority and historical tradition, and its decay is akin to death itself. Because textiles can additionally display precious fibers, dyes, painstaking labor, varied designs, and skill, they become a canvas of identity and status.

9.5 Said to have been worn by La Malinché, this *huipil* hangs in the Museo Nacional de Anthropologia de México.

huipil A Nahuatl word for a traditional loose tunic worn by women across Mesoamerica, even today.

    A visit to Mexico City's Museo Nacional de Anthropologia de México will transport you to the world of Doña Marina/La Malinché. Hanging among the Spanish candelabra and crucifixes that illustrate the early history of Mexico as New Spain is a **huipil** with the blazon of a double-headed eagle, a symbol frequently used by Spanish royalty [**9.5**]. Modern *huipil*s in Mexico, Guatemala, and El Salvador have distinctive embroidery, color schemes, and designs specific to a region or even a village—they visibly identify the community to which the wearer belongs. The *huipil* on display at the National Museum, in fact, dates to the eighteenth century, but it is so similar to one depicted in an image of Cortés and La Malinché (see 9.4, p. 206) that it has become associated with her. The double-headed eagle in the border may be evocative of European symbolism, but the warrior clan with its eagle totem was also an established elite class in the Aztec empire. La Malinché played a significant role in binding these two worlds, so it is perfectly understandable that this historic garment has long been identified as hers.

    Huipil garments and the Mesoamerican women who wore them are often beautifully depicted in ancient books —or codices—produced just before and after the Spanish Conquest of the Aztec empire. These books provide some of the best primary sources for Aztec society, richly illustrating diverse aspects of Aztec life and history. A famous example is the Mendoza Codex, created between 1529 and 1553, which details the history of Tenochtitlán's founding and the many conquests of Aztec rulers. One section of the codex illustrates and lists the tributes from each conquered town, and some of these are textiles. Such documents as the Mendoza Codex tell us that the richest, most prestigious clothing was made from the finest raw, white cotton textiles, embroidered and embellished by royal women. Perhaps it seems surprising that the simplest color (white) with the least embroidery, such as La Malinché's *huipil*, would be the most honored. The source for these garments—cotton—originally came from a plant domesticated in Peru, where the Moche, and later the Inka empire, also used fine textiles to convey identity and prestige. Depictions of cloth on human figurines made from stone and wood indicate that the use of highly decorated fabric as a marker of status extends far into Mesoamerican prehistory [**9.6**]. Mesoamerican cloth-making technology remained very simple, with important implications for women's agency in Mesoamerican societies. Ginning cotton (removing seeds and husks from fiber), preparing fibers from maguey (a kind of agave), and spinning to make thread were all very labor-intensive tasks, and dyeing cotton threads and weaving also required handwork. Weavers used a backstrap loom, which presented a simple array of threads tied to a post and around the back of the weaver, whose backward lean created tension in the warp she worked in front of her. Although this practice was widely depicted in ancient imagery, no appreciable archaeological trace of it remains. Women in households could perform simultaneous tasks, too:

9.6 At Yaxchilan, a Maya site in Mexico, a famous image shows a Maya queen magnificently clad in elaborate cotton clothing. She is drawing a thorn rope through her tongue and catching the blood on bark paper to burn as an offering.

spindle whorls Donut-shaped weights of stone, shell, or clay used to spin fiber into thread.

spinning and weaving while engaged in childcare and food preparation. A woman making cloth in excess of household need could exchange it at the market for foods and other goods, but cloth was also required for tribute to Aztec rulers.

Textile Production and Distinct Identities

The Codex Mendoza tells us of towns sending Aztec tribute, but it is the tools of archaeology that locate the very sites of textile production, revealing important clues about who did the work, and even how people communicated distinct identities through their cloth production. In virtually every household, archaeologists have found **spindle whorls**. At the end of a long stick, or spindle, these help a spinner maintain twirling motion, tension, and orientation as he or she twists fiber into thread and winds it for future use. Historical traditions, depictions, and myths suggest that women in Mesoamerica carried out much of the spinning and weaving, as they did when the Spanish arrived. A folio (a page) from the Codex Mendoza shows how spinning was an activity that distinguished boys from girls. Folio 58r [**9.7**] illustrates this in the training of Aztec children. To the left of the page, the Spanish notation identifies the father who is instructing his son, and on the right, the mother is depicted teaching her daughter. The father and son and mother and daughter are shown four times on the same page, with the male or female child appearing a few years older in each drawing. By the time the children reach the age of five (noted by the number of dots next to each), the son is sent out to fetch supplies, while the daughter is seated by her mother and learns to spin thread. Spinning therefore became a means for a young girl to recognize and learn her identity as a female and daughter, as distinct from a male and son.

In addition to offering a picture of the woman's domestic world in Mesoamerican society, the spindle whorl suggests other elements of the spinner's identity. Spindle whorls were somewhat common in household refuse from the period, so archaeologists have been able to assess the status of spinners by examining the size of the houses where spindle whorls were found, whether the houses were finely decorated, and if spindle whorls occurred alongside other indicators of wealth and status. Cloth was produced in homes, with spindle whorls evenly distributed across all kinds of houses. Spinning therefore seems to have been a strictly household activity, not an industry run from one location by specialists. The Aztec empire demanded cloth tribute from the societies it incorporated, but how did the spinners express their agency in this social structure that compelled tribute? Did they make and give willingly, or do signs of resistance or subversion survive? In her study of Aztec women, Elizabeth Brumfiel hypothesized that women from societies conquered by the Aztecs engaged in resistance by providing lesser-quality cloth for tribute. While studying excavated spindle whorls from sites in Mexico, however, she was surprised to find that the size of whorls actually diminished over time in multiple regions, suggesting the women were producing finer cloth after they were conquered by the Aztecs. Although, at first glance, these findings seem to

9.7 Extract from the Codex Mendoza, folio 58r. In Aztec society, older children were expected to become involved in a household's economy. As textiles were an important tribute good, all women in the empire—mothers and their daughters—were expected to contribute to spinning and weaving.

conflict with Brumfiel's expectations, a further review of postcolonial literature helps to explain them.

Women were easily scrutinized by Aztec officials and tribute collectors. Their products were also easily inspected within the usual multiple rounds of tribute collection. Brumfiel explored the possibility that within the structure of Aztec society and its conquered subjects, a woman's identity was so closely linked to her production of cloth that she voluntarily produced fine cloth, even as tribute.

TEXTILES, IDENTITY, AND GENDER   **211**

9.8 **Decorated Aztec spindle whorls of various sizes** to spin thread, both maguey and cotton, for domestic use, not tribute.

The spindle whorls uncovered during archaeological excavations seem to tell a different story, though—one better aligned with the copious postcolonial records of resistance among those compelled to produce tribute. Houses often included two types of spindle whorls: larger ceramic spindle whorls, associated with maguey fiber for the household, and smaller spindle whorls used for tribute. The larger spindle whorls were elaborately incised or molded and painted, whereas the smaller cotton-spinning whorls were plain. The difference in spindle whorl decoration is striking, and it reminded Brumfiel of ethnoarchaeologists' observations that the cultural significance of activities is frequently indicated by the elaborate artistry of artifacts associated with those activities [**9.8**].

The contrast between the spindle whorls noted by Brumfiel speaks to an important difference in how women conveyed separate identities through their textiles while under Aztec rule. The weaver expressed her identity through the high quality of her tribute textiles, but in using plain spindle whorls, she did not connect the output to her wider identity as a member of a home and community. This expression of self was reserved for textiles used domestically and produced with the decorative whorls. This simple act of utilizing different forms of production separated the identity of an Aztec subject and tribute-giver from the identity of a member of a family and home. Examining a spindle whorl in context thus allows us to consider the separate identities—some of which are in conflict with or subvert each other—which any individual woman might maintain.

BIOARCHAEOLOGY

Human bones offer archaeologists a set of comprehensive tools to examine the remains of an individual, an avenue to study his or her identity, agency, and power. Even when historical texts exist, as with the codices and Spanish accounts previously mentioned, an archaeological examination of bones can corroborate or challenge the textual evidence. This was the case with the remains of one of England's most notorious kings, Richard III. Although his is a historical case from a much later period (in prehistory, rarely can we identify the bones of a specific person), it is nonetheless an excellent example of the insight archaeology and the study of burials and bones can offer into how identities were made and then remade in the past.

One of William Shakespeare's earliest plays was *The Tragedy of King Richard the Third*. Throughout the historical drama, Richard is depicted as both a villain and usurper of the English throne, who uses murder, intrigue, and scandal to secure and consolidate power. Richard's elder brother had been king, and it was his children, not Richard, who were the rightful heirs to the throne. By murdering his nephews, Richard takes the crown. To enforce this character's evil dimension, Shakespeare describes him as a hunchback, who can be seen skulking across the stage throughout the play. We can conclude that the history of the playwright's time would have viewed Richard as a morally corrupt individual, one who was born mentally and physically warped. A salient point to remember is that history is often written by the victors, and Richard's death at the battle of Bosworth Field in August 1485 allowed for Henry Tudor to become King Henry VII. When the play was written, Henry VII's granddaughter, Queen Elizabeth I, had already ruled England for thirty-four years. Some of Shakespeare's patrons were also descended from the very lords who had supported Henry VII at Bosworth Field. We can then surmise that Shakespeare's depiction, to a great degree, reflects the political bias acceptable at the time. The body of Richard III had never been studied, or even found, so Shakespeare's descriptions could not be corroborated—until 2009, when a body discovered in a parking lot in central England revealed itself to be Richard. Finally, archaeologists were able to examine it and challenge the identity of an individual principally created through literature and historical texts.

Are These King Richard's Remains?

Bioarchaeologists seek to understand the age, sex, health, lifestyle, and mortuary treatment of an individual through the analysis of physical remains. Usually, these remains are only bone and teeth, but occasionally soft tissues are also preserved. Determining age relies on several physical attributes that develop during a person's life. Because teeth emerge at regular time frames during childhood and puberty, **tooth eruption** can indicate the age of individuals younger than twenty. Tooth wear and loss can be used to estimate the age of someone older than twenty, although this factor is variably accurate. People who consume rougher foods and greater amounts of sugars, or use their teeth for tools, for instance, may exhibit much higher rates of wear, caries (cavities), and loss. Age can also be determined by the analysis of the skeleton, in particular, the fusing of bones and **epiphyses**, the end parts of a long bone that are separate at birth, allowing for growth until adulthood. The epiphyses of different bones fuse at different ages, providing an indicator of age at death.

Osteology is the study of bones, their features, and the variability of a skeleton. Lifestyle and health can be determined by wear on the joints, and other markers that indicate disease, such as lesions on bone that resulted from a long-lived infection. Bones remold themselves throughout life, and people can build bone where the skeleton experiences heavy use and wear. Repetitive action especially, such as

tooth eruption The moment teeth emerge, used to determine the age of individuals younger than twenty years.

epiphyses The end parts of a long bone that initially grow separately from the shaft.

osteology The study of bones, including development and mechanics.

pulling a bowstring or grinding grain in a mortar, can leave patterns of wear and stress in certain skeletal places and across the entire body.

These skills in bioarchaeology and osteology were utilized to examine a body discovered in 2009 beneath a parking lot in Leicester City (in England's East Midlands region). The parking lot stood in the same location as the Church of the Greyfriars, where it was believed Richard III had been buried. The excavation, undertaken by the University of Leicester Archaeological Services Team, revealed a skeleton that had been jammed into a poorly cut grave, located in an area that had once been the choir stalls of the church. The skeleton had a visibly curved spine and damage to its skull, which were the first clues that this could very well be the remains of King Richard III [**9.9**].

When had burial taken place, and did the date match that of Richard's death? In order to assess the age of the skeleton, two fragments of rib bone were sent to two different laboratories for radiocarbon dating (see Chapter 6). The results were very similar, indicating the individual had died between 1455 and 1540 CE. The remains were indeed the correct age to have been Richard III's body. Bioarchaeological analysis of the remains further revealed them to be those of an adult male of very slender build. Based on the analysis of epiphyseal closure and tooth wear, the man was in his late twenties or thirties when he died, which was consistent with the known age at death, thirty-two, for Richard [**9.10**]. The man's spine was also curved by scoliosis, which would have developed as he grew from childhood to adulthood. He would have been approximately 5 ft 8 ins (1.73 m) in height, although the curving of his spine would have considerably reduced his physical stature. In addition, this curvature would have raised one of his shoulders higher than the other, producing a distortion consistent with the "hunchback" condition that has been attributed to Richard III.

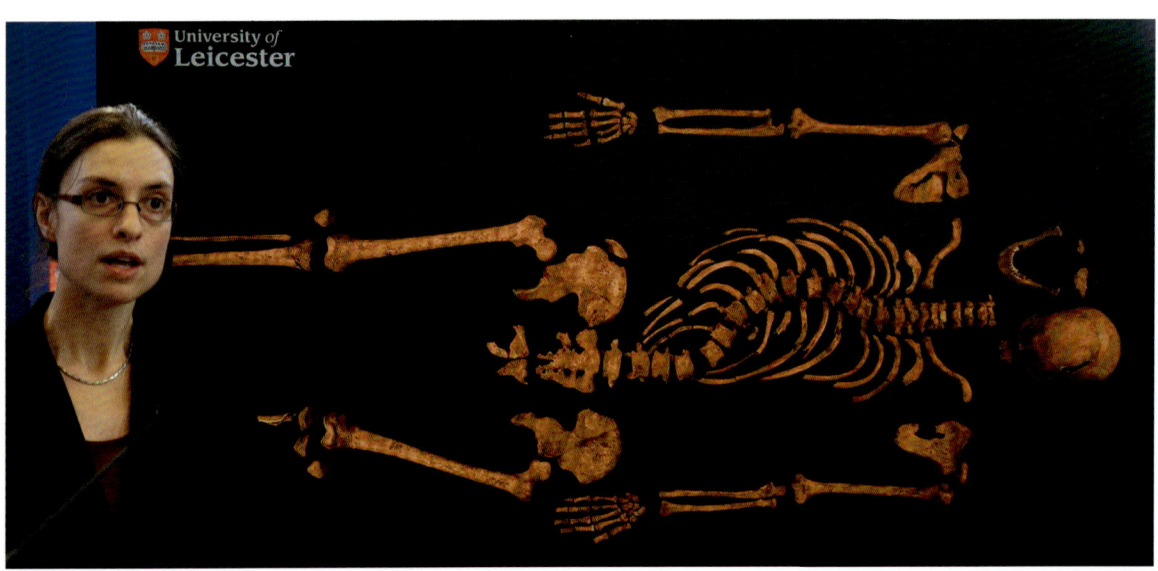

9.9 Images of Richard III's skeleton and the results of the analyses of the remains were presented by osteologist Dr. Jo Appleby in 2013. These analyses were part of a series of studies conducted by the University of Leicester Archaeological Services Team, which determined that the remains were those of Richard, and also determined critical aspects about his life and death.

9.10 Facial reconstruction of Richard III. Careful study of Richard's skull allowed for this reconstruction. Despite his curved spine, in life he would have appeared as a relatively healthy thirty-two-year-old man.

Based on the bioarchaeological analyses of the skeleton, the location of the burial, and the age of the remains, archaeologists concluded that strong evidence supported the hypothesis that this was the body of King Richard III. Conclusive proof of his identity came through the analysis of his preserved DNA. Genealogical research identified two living descendants of Anne of York, who was Richard's older sister. These men, who are members of the Ibsen family residing in Canada, agreed to submit samples of their DNA to the University of Leicester for DNA sequencing. This sequencing focused on **mitochondrial DNA (mtDNA)**, which is inherited through the female line, as the link between Anne of York and the Ibsens. Mitochondrial DNA is passed from a mother to her children and can be used to identify maternal lineages. Anne of York had many descendants, but her mtDNA had been passed down, first to her daughter, and then to subsequent grand-daughters and great-grand-daughters, and ultimately to Michael Ibsen, the eldest of the Ibsen brothers. DNA was extracted from the pulp of one of the skeleton's teeth, and the mitochondrial sequence was compared to that of Michael Ibsen. The sequence was identical: clear proof that Michael Ibsen and the skeleton are descendants of the same woman—in this case, Richard III's mother, Cecily Neville. The skeleton was that of Richard III.

With the unearthing and study of Richard III's body, it was possible to use bioarchaeology to re-analyze the descriptions of this man offered by the Tudor victors. In Shakespeare's play, Richard describes himself as "rudely stamp'd" and "cheated of feature by dissembling nature, deformed, unfinish'd, sent before my time into this breathing world, scarce half made up, and that so lamely and unfashionable that dogs bark at me as I halt by them…," and is called by another character "[a] poisonous bunch-backed toad." In the past, the vision of Richard as a hunchback

mitochondrial DNA (mtDNA) DNA found in the mitochondria of a cell, not the nucleus. This DNA is passed down only from the mother.

might have been regarded as a device used by historians and playwrights to portray the defeated king as an irredeemable villain, but bioarchaeology has demonstrated that at least this portion of his life story is correct, offering us an opportunity to wonder what other aspects of Richard's identity are fact or fiction.

INEQUALITY AND STRUCTURAL VIOLENCE IN PREHISTORY

Archaeology often focuses on the differences that existed between ancient societies (e.g., comparing the Maya to the Aztec), but the study of differences within a society is critical to understanding how it functioned, and how an individual's experience in life may have varied. When groups of skeletons are examined, such as those found buried together in a cemetery, bioarchaeologists are able to generate information about the population as a whole. Bioarchaeology can identify the health-related factors and stressors that affected an individual in life, and also determine injuries or disease that may have contributed to a person's death. General trends in health, diet, and disease that are common in some parts of the population are indicative of shared experiences, which may be tied to social class or gender.

We have talked about social structure as the framework within which an individual lives. When structures suppress a person's agency, and prevent people and groups from reaching their social, economic, and biological potential, the society can be described as having structural inequality. Inequality includes poverty, limited access to resources, and conditions that put a person at risk for higher incidence of disease and injury. In instances where inequality causes direct injury or death to segments of the population, the society manifests **structural violence**. In modern societies, structural violence can persist and even become normalized to the point that injury, illness, and suffering are not recognized. Requiring personal wealth to access health care while excluding large sectors of a population from it is but one contemporary example of structural violence. Similar situations may have existed in the past, especially in hierarchical and patriarchal societies.

Bioarchaeological investigations of structural violence focus on the markers of health and stress. Individuals can experience a variety of stressors that lead to declines in health: poor diets can result in caries (cavities) in the teeth, tooth loss, anemia, and interruptions in early childhood growth. Increased labor produces worn joints and injuries, which often do not heal or are worsened by continued work. Overcrowded housing and poor sanitation can increase rates of contagious disease, which may result in severe infections, lesions, and death for adults and children. In hierarchical societies that foster structural violence, the prevalence of conditions that promote disease, injury, and poor diets (both calorie-poor and nutrient-poor) can also cause women to experience lower birth rates. A study of human remains can therefore offer valuable information about the suppressions and violence within a society, as we will see in ancient Peru.

structural violence Harm done to individuals because of their position in society.

South America: Structural Violence in Ancient Peru

The desert coast of Peru is flanked by the cold, rich waters of the southern Pacific Ocean. By 6,000 years ago, people were congregating in villages and supplying their households with fish, pottery, and textiles. The Moche society emerged in this region, and by 200 CE, they had developed irrigation systems for their crops and traditions of combat and conquest with neighboring societies. Their descendants formed the later society of Chimor (1000–1450), building mud-brick cities called *ciudadelas*. Prior to the influence of the Inkas and the Spanish in the sixteenth century, Chimor society consisted of farmers, craftspeople, and elites [**9.11**].

After the Spanish conquest of the region, the newly established colonial government sought to extract resources from the land (e.g., minerals, gold, and silver from mines), and to transform the native population into Catholics and a tax-paying labor force. Peruvian society emerged as a strict hierarchy of European elites and a Mestizo (of mixed native and European ancestry) middle class who were supported by taxes. The tax-paying native people, who were farmers or employed as miners and laborers for very low wages, made up the rest of society. Throughout Peru, the process of colonialism disrupted the traditional systems of settlement and food production, and many native communities were forced to relocate to poor land that was close to mines or trade routes. These resettlements were extremely crowded and had little or no sanitation, which fostered the spread of infectious diseases.

Bioarchaeologists Haagen Klaus and Manuel Tam sought to investigate the presence of structural violence among native populations of Peru during the Spanish colonial period (c. 1500–1800 CE). They excavated the cemetery at the Chapel of San Pedro de Mòrrope and recovered the remains of 870 individuals who had lived in the area between 1536 and 1750 CE. Their analyses focused on the identification of biological stress, which manifested on individual skeletons in the form of interrupted growth, lesions, and evidence of chronic infections. The fertility of females was also estimated by examining the ratio of individuals older than thirty years of age to those older than five. Klaus and Tam additionally evaluated diet by determining the presence or absence of dental caries, and the incidence and activities of violence by recording degenerative joint disease and traumatic injuries. All these results were compared at the population level to those of the previous Chimor population, who had lived in the region from 900 to 1532 CE.

9.11 Map of South America showing (in dark green) where the Chimor people lived, and the location of San Pedro de Mòrrope.

What Klaus and Tam discovered was that systemic stress had increased significantly during the colonial era. Native people, who were at the very bottom of the social hierarchy in Peru, exhibited high instances of infection and stunted growth during childhood. Degenerative joint disease, especially in the shoulders and arms, increased by more than 200 percent, and dental caries and tooth loss became more prevalent. Indigenous people were forced to work, often to the point of crippling pain and injury, and lived in conditions that resulted in poor diets, more infections, high child mortality, and depressed fertility for women. Historic documents (compiled by the colonials) report on the marginalization of the people buried at San Pedro de Mòrrope and very tellingly express an embedded bias against them: the Catholic

9.12 San Pedro de Mòrrope. Excavation units 10 and 12 from Haagen Klaus's study of colonial-era mortuary practices show a hybridization of Catholic and native practices, such as bundles of elements without coffins. The retention of Peruvian traditions in the face of structural inequality was one way native people used their agency to push back against the structures that oppressed them.

priest of the local church described the Chimor as "savages" and "ignorant brutes." These views reflect the guiding ideology of the social institutions that compelled the indigenous people into this situation [**9.12**]. The colonials viewed the native people as less than human, and enforced upon them lowly identities that normalized the violence that the Peruvians had to endure.

The bioarchaeological study of individuals and groups is relevant to the examination of social structure, identity, and agency, in both the past and the present. Human health is sensitive to the influence of structure, power, and the role of identity in society. What caused suffering and illness in the past can do the same harm today. From archaeological studies, we are able to build expectations for the health of populations experiencing structural violence. More importantly, understanding the history of structural violence is critical to addressing the attitudes and policies that support and replicate it in modern societies.

AGENCY, IDENTITY, AND THE ANTHROPOCENE

In this chapter, we have explored how identities were formed and navigated in the past, but how did this impact the construction of a human niche and the Anthropocene? Humanity is composed of individuals who may make decisions about how to live their lives, but those decisions are framed within a social structure that can enable or limit a person's power. The colonials in Peru claimed identities of power that enabled them to exploit both the native population and the landscape. Social structures do change, however, and some people are able to manipulate them creatively and instigate change. Changes in the past—which broadly included transformations of the natural environment, social structures, even individual habits and choices—were caused by human decisions. Agents of the past contributed to the construction of the Anthropocene, although not everyone had equal power. We are all now a part of this same historic trajectory. As we move forward as a planet of 7.6 billion humans, the balance between structure and agency will matter more than ever, as individual decisions will cumulatively direct change in the future.

Chapter Questions

1. How did the identity of Dõna Marina change with the arrival of Hernán Cortés?
2. What evidence exists to suggest that people subverted the Aztec system of tribute?
3. How does bioarchaeology offer information about the identity of people in the past?
4. How does archaeology offer insight into structural violence in our Anthropocene niche?

Additional Resources

Ashdown-Hill, John. *The Last Days of Richard III and the Fate of His DNA.* Stroud, UK: The History Press, 2013.

Brumfiel, Elizabeth M. "The Quality of Tribute Cloth: The Place of Evidence in Archaeological Argument," *American Antiquity* 61 (1996): 453–62.

del Castillo, Bernal Diaz. *The Discovery and Conquest of Mexico* (1517–1521). Translated by A. P. Maudslay. New York: Farrar, Straus, and Cudahy, 1956.

Klaus, Haagen D. "The Bioarchaeology of Structural Violence: A Theoretical Model and a Case Study," in *The Bioarchaeology of Violence*, edited by Debra L. Martin and Ryan P. Harrod, 29–62. Gainesville, FL: University Press of Florida, 2012.

Ross, Kurt. *Codex Mendoza*. Fribourg, Switzerland: Miller Graphics and Lieber SA, 1978.

Smith, Michael E. *The Aztecs*. 2nd ed. Oxford, UK: Blackwell, 2003.

FEEDING CITIES
Urbanism and Agriculture

10

One spring evening, I got lost in northern Yucatán, in the eastern part of Mexico. Wandering in the twilight, my husband and I passed small farms bursting with crops, followed by dense patches of forests and half-grown fields of weeds and brush. The surrounding landscape was a patchwork of human production: fields no longer under cultivation, a forest that seemed uncut and natural. Archaeologists and anthropologists have long documented this traditional agricultural system of Mesoamerica and determined that it is several thousand years old. That night, the impact of human farming enveloped us, even if at first glance the natural rain forest appeared to dominate.

We had spent our day at Kabah, a ruined city of the Maya. The Maya did not, as popular legend claimed, "disappear," and their descendants live on in the hamlets nearby. As we picked our way along the countryside, we asked a farmer and potter selling his wares, "Who constructed the nearby ruins?"

He spoke of ancient times and two brothers who were dwarf twins with magical powers. They had risen from the earth and moved stones to build the city of Uxmal, now in ruins. It was these twins who had brought forth maize, and people (who were made from maize), from a place of death. Our improbable encounter with the farmer revealed the Maya myth of creation still being passed through oral tradition, 2,000 years later, long after European colonials had burned the last Maya book. This complex story of death-and-rebirth centers on maize, the magical substance at the heart of the mystery of lost Maya cities. The rain forest is now empty of maize, but it had once grown in abundance and fed great cities situated in the forest lands.

This chapter will explain how ancient cities fed themselves. We will explore different types of cities, states, and city states—including Maya cities, Angkor in Cambodia, and cities and states of ancient Egypt and ancient Mesopotamia—illustrating a global pattern in which social complexity emerged repeatedly across the world and depended on environmental circumstances, agricultural technologies, and the possibilities provided by a food surplus. Modern emphases on sustainable agriculture have their roots in the production techniques of these ancient societies. The productivity and resilience of such farming systems, as well as the disasters that came to pass when natural environments were pushed to their limits, are evident in the archaeological record of ancient cities and the anthropogenic landscapes that emerged around them. These long-ago events have implications for our global food production systems that must currently sustain some eight billion people.

Mesoamerica: Discovering the Maya 222

Maize and the Maya 228

The Maya City 230

Southeast Asia: Irrigation and Agriculture at Angkor 234

The State 237

The Environmental Perils of Intensification 240

Cities, Surplus, and the Elite 242

Opposite The hero twins of the Maya, requesting the bones of their father from the maize god. The scene was painted on a ceramic vase produced in Mexico, 600–750 CE.

Key Concepts

- How the domestication of maize fed Maya cities
- The principal characteristics of the city, where food surplus is transported, exchanged, and transformed
- How Maya cities, as compared to Egyptian territorial states, addressed a potential food surplus, its management, and ensuing social complexity
- How human control and transformation of landscapes, such as what occurred at Angkor, and intensive agriculture, contributed to the collapse and lost history of the Maya and ancient Mesopotamia

Maya A pre-Columbian Mesoamerican civilization of the highlands of Southern Mexico, Guatemala, and the Yucatán Peninsula, from c. 1000 BCE.

MESOAMERICA: DISCOVERING THE MAYA

In the mid-nineteenth century, as the Englishmen Charles Dickens and Robert Malthus held literary and economic mirrors to the burgeoning misery of overpopulated European cities, a New York lawyer named John Lloyd Stephens and a talented illustrator called Frederick Catherwood traveled through Yucatán, Chiapas, and the Honduran highlands of Central America, recording one abandoned ruined city after another. As Dickens's novels described the crowded, impoverished, desperate lives of London's urban poor, Catherwood's evocative drawings (published all over Europe and the United States) sparked wonder at cities' ruin and abandonment and the fate that had befallen their peoples [**10.1**]. Was Western civilization headed the same way? The illustrations show ruins half-hidden under strangling roots of the lush vegetation that had reclaimed them. The faces of strange, feathered serpents and the masks of gods were intricately worked into architectural form as doorways, cornices, and altar stones. Stephens and Catherwoods' books sold widely and inspired an interest in the unknown civilizations of Central America, the most remote cities of which are still being discovered today under the canopy and cover of a dense rain forest.

It seemed remarkable that entire cities could be engulfed by trees. As best as archaeologists can determine, the **Maya** first settled in Guatemala and southern Mexico's tropical lowlands around 1000 BCE; approximately 500 years later, they were building cities that would sprawl across the vast lowlands of the Mirador Basin in northern Guatemala [**10.2**]. These Preclassic or Formative cities (c. 1000 BCE to 250 CE) had an urban core, with limestone public buildings constructed on massive platforms. The largest pyramid at a city complex called El Mirador has an earthen and stone core built over a natural hill and is one of the largest pyramids in the world [**10.3**, p. 224]. At Preclassic sites, limestone palaces and royal tombs suggestive of elaborate burial rituals were excavated, along with exotic jewelry made of jade and shell, indicating a distinctive social hierarchy. An extensive network of roads led out of El Mirador and Nakbe, and across the Maya lowlands, facilitating the transport of food and luxuries—all carried exclusively on peoples' backs—and furthering contacts with other cities in the Guatemalan highlands and even Mexico [**10.4**, p. 224]. By 250 CE, the Preclassic cities of the Mirador Basin had been abandoned, and no one is entirely certain why.

After the abandonment of El Mirador, starting in 250 CE, Classic Maya civilization emerged as city-centered states ruled by elite royalty (see 10.2). Across Guatemala's Petén region, Belize, western Honduras, southern Yucatán, and lowland Mexico,

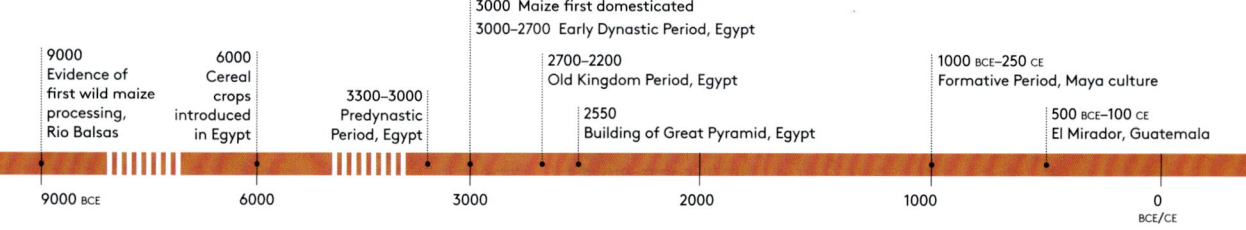

9000	6000	3300–3000	3000 Maize first domesticated		1000 BCE–250 CE
Evidence of first wild maize processing, Rio Balsas	Cereal crops introduced in Egypt	Predynastic Period, Egypt	3000–2700 Early Dynastic Period, Egypt		Formative Period, Maya culture
			2700–2200 Old Kingdom Period, Egypt		500 BCE–100 CE
			2550 Building of Great Pyramid, Egypt		El Mirador, Guatemala

| 9000 BCE | 6000 | 3000 | 2000 | 1000 | 0 BCE/CE |

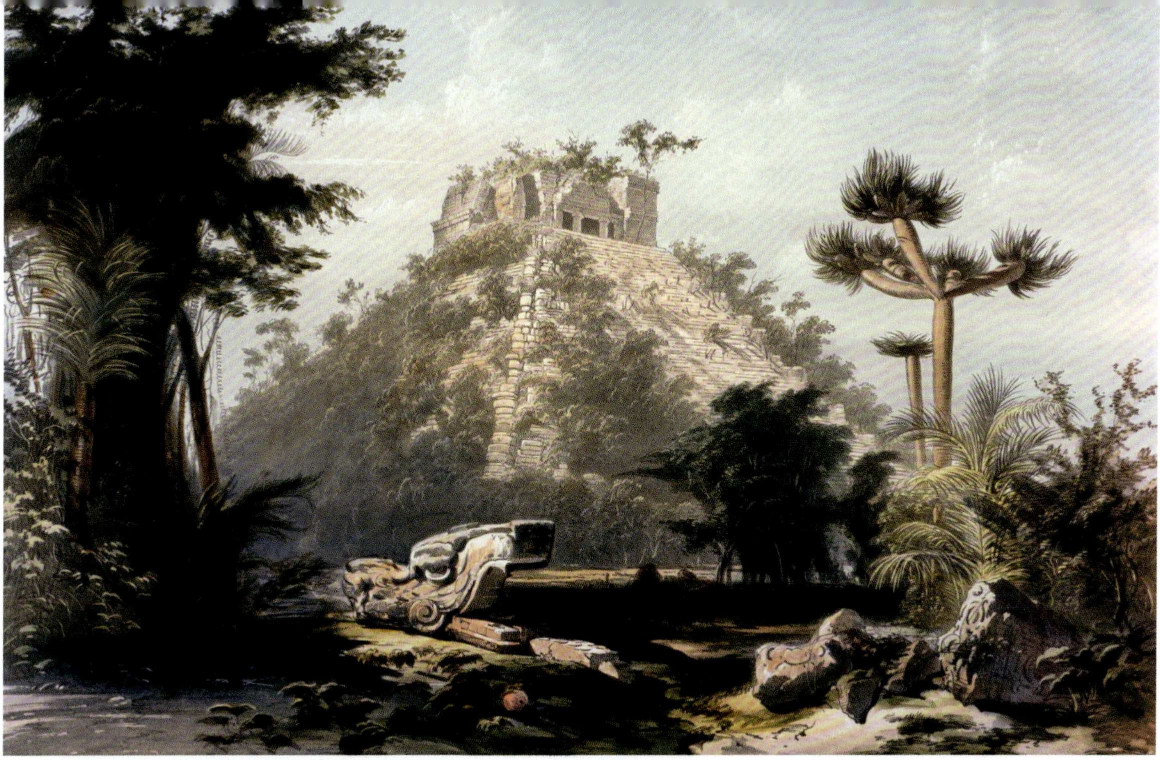

Above: **10.1 The Maya city of Chichen Itza** entangled in forest, as portrayed by Frederick Catherwood.

Left: **10.2 Map of Central America** and its major centers.

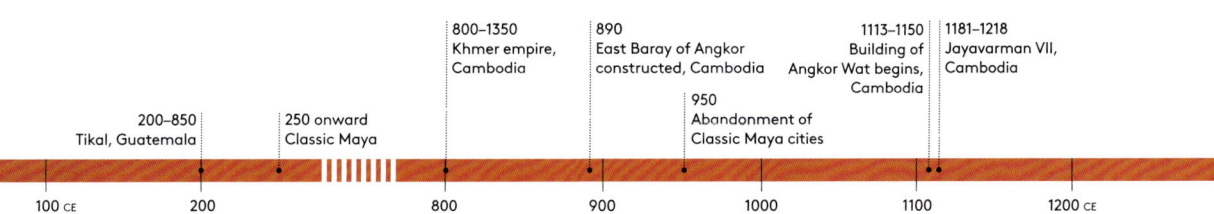

Above: **10.3 Aerial photo of the great pyramid of La Danta** at the Maya site of El Mirador. Even today, this stone structure towers over the forest canopy.

Left: **10.4 Detail of a Maya porter from a mural at Calakmul.** The porter is using a tumpline, which allowed a person to use his or her neck and forehead to support the weight of the load. Maya communities relied upon roads and porters to carry goods from the countryside to the cities.

these states were immersed in fierce competitions and alliances. Maya communities were organized in a hierarchy that included multiple social classes and reflected their access to wealth and to food surpluses. Rulers were on top, with their staff and other elites directly below, and below them, farmers. The Maya also developed extensive **heterarchical** networks at all levels of society: rulers formed alliances and exchanges with other rulers, and commoners were linked through households, professional groups (such as warriors and scribes), and market exchanges with specialized producers.

Much of the dynastic history of Classic Maya rulers may be gleaned from the limestone stelae and altars they commissioned in central plazas at city centers (see Chapter 13), giving us a sense of their power and the societies in which they operated (see Chapter 9). City complexes were often in direct conflict. The two great complexes of Tikal (see 10.13, p. 233) and Calakmul, for instance, became embroiled

in a long-running dispute, with each site ruling a multi-city confederacy, and it concluded with the defeat of Calakmul. Indeed, many of Calakmul's rulers may have ended their lives in ball courts [**10.5**]—rectangular arenas constructed between long platforms—where, later sources suggest, in a ceremonial game they were ordered to re-enact the mythic contest between hero twins and lords of the underworld, with some elites losing the "game" and then their heads.

By 950 CE, the Classic Maya cities had also been abandoned—perhaps because a well-documented drought overwhelmed the already stretched agricultural capacity of these centers, which depended on a steady surplus from farmers to support the complex social roles and activities of city dwellers.

10.5 Monte Alban ball court. This Mesoamerican game was played by two teams, whose players bounced a rubber ball between them using their hips and thighs. In ceremonies, ball-game players re-enacted the mythic contest between the hero twins and lords of the underworld. Monte Alban is a site of the Zapotec civilization, which shared the ball-game tradition with the Maya.

Raised Fields and Agriculture within the Rain Forest

Rain forests typically have nutrient-poor soils, which are quickly and easily depleted. So how were the Maya cities able to feed their dense populations? A region of the rain forest in modern-day Belize called Pulltrouser Swamp [**10.6**, p. 226] helps answer this very question. Aerial photography of the region first revealed outlines of **raised fields** in the wetland areas. Ancient people had created these fertile farm areas by digging up mud from the bottom of the rain forest's swamps—mud that was more nutrient rich than the dry soil—and placing it on mats made of woven

heterarchical A form of social organization based on non-hierarchical organization, where individuals are unranked.

raised fields An agricultural method that grows crops on raised platforms of soil in order to protect crops from flooding.

MESOAMERICA: DISCOVERING THE MAYA   **225**

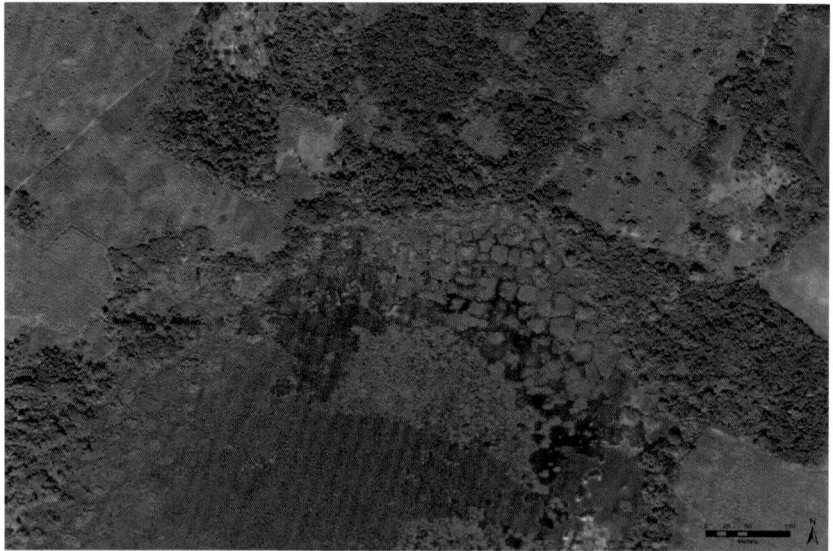

10.6 Archaeological excavation at Pulltrouser Swamp in Belize revealed the construction of abandoned Maya gardens.

reeds 2 feet (more than half a meter) above the water level. The raised fields would have resembled a system of block-shaped islands and canals in the rain forest.

Raised fields were a fragile system requiring constant maintenance. Cultivating crops causes soils to lose nutrients unless new ones are added regularly, and raised fields can fall back into canals over time. Nevertheless, aerial photography shows their basic outlines still visible a thousand years later. The technology of raised-field agriculture was long known in the New World and widespread across cultures. Spanish conquistador Hernán Cortés (1485–1547) and his expedition were stunned by the engineering and maintenance of *chinampas*—raised fields that once fed the vast population of the Aztec city of Tenochtitlàn and continue to flourish in present day-Mexico City (see Chapter 9). Archaeologists investigating the Maya site of Pulltrouser Swamp in 1980 discovered that the raised fields contained pollen traces of such annual plants as maize and cotton, suggesting they were the crops grown there centuries before. This discovery of labor-intensive, raised-field agriculture at Pulltrouser Swamp kindled lingering questions about Maya cities deep within the rain forest.

The rain forest should not be regarded as virgin or untouched; it is the historical outcome of landscape management and modification by many generations of ancient Maya. The Maya cleared immense stretches of forest, cutting it down for fields or leaving behind *pet kot*, or deliberate reserves, where they could harvest wild species (such as tree bark for cloth, dyes, and books, or hardwoods for lintels). The forests never fully recovered, so today's rain forests are oligarchic—dominated by a few successful species that have recolonized the lowlands after the Maya abandoned their cities.

Remote Sensing and Satellite Imagery

The changes to the rain forest are most visible using remote sensing of vegetation rather than land surface. In 2008, IKONOS satellite imagery [**10.7**] succeeded in uncovering a variety of ancient Maya activities in the rain forest. These show up in the differential signatures of the vegetation even in locations where Maya populations abandoned their cities. In particular, the use of limestone blocks and plaster in public architecture and city centers created a different environment for the subsequent regrowth of forest. Because the soil depth, soil chemistry, and soil nutrients vary from those of the surrounding forest, the moisture and nutrients in the canopy also differ, yielding their own distinct satellite readings. In addition, different species are present, possibly relics of trees favored by the Maya.

Remote sensing has not only shown the locations of lost cities, but has also indicated that the Maya built reservoirs, farmed *bajos* (seasonally wet lowlands) and terraces, dug canals, and created high causeways or roads (referred to as *sakbe*, probably piled up from dredged lowlands) that extended for miles beyond city centers. *Sakbe* register as linear features in the satellite imagery.

Digital image analysis can detect subtle differences in vegetation cover that reveal underlying spatial structures. Satellite images are not photographs: they are the digital registry of the level of reflectance of a surface, be it vegetation, ground surface, a body of water, or ice. Digital data are registered spatially so that all reflectance values are pooled within a pixel area. The data themselves, rather than the visual format, are valuable, for they can be manipulated with mathematical filters and algorithms to enhance or detect digital expressions of differences in reflectance [**10.8**]. The data also record infrared light reflectance that is not visible to the human eye, such as that produced by leaves and flowers.

10.7 Image of abandoned Maya cities as visible through IKONOS satellite imagery. The use of infrared light makes the rain forest appear red in the image. The city ruins, which are under thinner vegetation cover, are visible as gray and green geometric shapes.

10.8 The border between Mexico and Guatemala as seen from a Landsat satellite in 1988. The division between the forest (Guatemala) and grazed parkland (Mexico) is clearly visible. Deforestation on the Mexican side makes it easier to discover archaeological sites, but it also contributed to a loss of biodiversity. The stark difference between these countries, and refocused attention on loss of the biosphere, highlight the fragile, nutrient-poor landscapes that made the Maya vulnerable to climate change and natural disasters.

MAIZE AND THE MAYA

The expansion of agriculture led inevitably to the reduction of the rain forest. Although the Maya likely practiced all kinds of growing methods including the cultivation of a diverse array of vegetables, fruit trees, and herbs, and fertilized the land with kitchen refuse and night soils (human manure, food scraps, and other waste), trees were still felled to make room for fields. Into their increasingly deforested and managed environment, the Maya brought maize (which most people today call "corn"). Maya cities could not have flourished where they did without it.

Maize was not native to the rain forest but had been domesticated thousands of years before the Maya settled there. Domesticated maize came from wild annual teosinte grass (*Zea mays* spp. *parviglumis*), mostly native to the lowland Rio Balsas in southeast Mexico [10.9]. Genetic studies of cultivated maize suggest this ancestry, and recent analysis of starch and phytolith grains in grinding stones nearly 9,000 years old from the Rio Balsas also point to the earliest known use of maize.

The original users of maize were mobile, without permanent settlements, and the attraction of the early plant is poorly understood. Early wild forms of maize had much smaller kernels than is now typical, offering far fewer calories compared to other foodstuffs foraged and cultivated at the time, such as squashes and gourds. Not until large cobs appeared approximately 5,000 years ago did maize grain become available as a high-yielding, storable staple [10.10]. Its early uses thus remain speculative: some have suggested that the tiny kernels enclosed in the pod could be popped easily or that the stalk proved a desirable source of sugar, perhaps being the basis for the fermented beverages that were later consumed to establish and maintain community bonds, representing an early form of social drinking (see Chapter 12).

Previously, archaeologists believed that Maya farmers, similarly to the domesticators of maize before them, were highly mobile and depended exclusively on slash-and-burn agriculture, followed by long periods of fallow (not cultivating a piece of land) and regrowth. This theory has since been replaced by an understanding of the underlying Maya **managed mosaic**. Maya farmers practiced different strategies depending on the terrain, but to access the abundant sunlight required to raise maize crops, they cleared forest widely. Whatever the attraction of maize was, its foragers—who also had domesticated squash and gourds available to them—chose to move maize into the new environment of a tropical rain forest and to cultivate it there, removing tree canopy and maintaining adequate soil nutrient levels as necessary to do so.

Maize was also the ideal source of nutrition for Maya cities because it could be stored. As a grain crop, maize can ripen and then dry, losing moisture that might cause starchy particles to rot. Similarly to all annual, large-seeded plants, maize and its wild relatives survive a dry season by packing a large quantity of nutrients around a seed embryo. The parent plant dies, but the embryo has plenty of nutrition to see it through drought until moisture and daylight induce it to germinate. The Maya hastened the process by snapping ripe maize stalks and allowing the cob to dry on the plant, a technique perfectly preserved in the volcanic ash that buried

managed mosaic An agricultural system employed by the Maya that included diverse techniques, such as raised or drained fields, terracing, and a mix of cultivated vegetables and trees.

10.9 Location of the Rio Balsas region, where maize was initially domesticated. Over the next 5,000 years maize was grown throughout Mesoamerica, in environments that ranged from tropical forests to deserts.

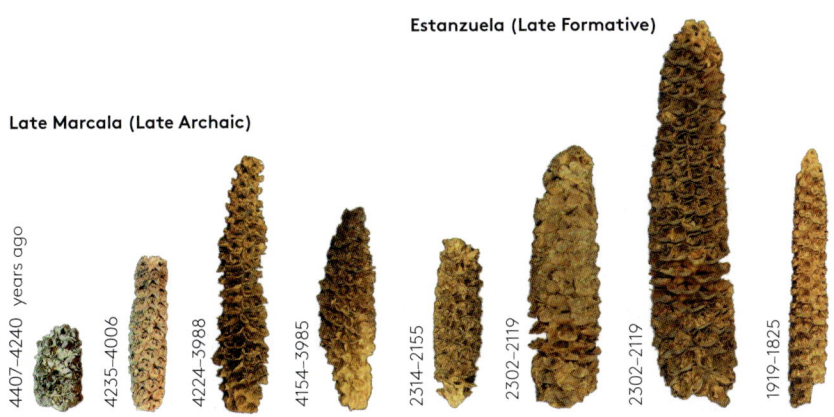

10.10 Early maize cobs from El Gigante rockshelter in Honduras. Over time, morphological changes in maize cobs show increased diameter of cobs, increased rachis diameter, and more rows of kernals—three characteristics associated with increasing yields.

Maya kitchen gardens at Joya de Ceren in 600 CE (in modern-day El Salvador [**10.11**, p. 230]). Just as other domesticated crops are, maize is dependent on humans for survival (see Chapter 8); it no longer relies on the natural dispersal of its seeds for reproduction, but tightly holds onto them until people can disperse the seeds, carefully, into the earth of their farm fields.

10.11 Joya de Ceren is a rare site, sometimes called "the Pompeii of the New World," where the preserved houses are just as the Maya left them—in a great hurry before the entire site was buried by the eruption of the nearby Laguna Caldera in 600 CE. The kitchen gardens are also preserved, so archaeologists can discern the layout of such crops as maize.

THE MAYA CITY

As we have seen, the Maya were involved in complex and intense agriculture that altered the rain forest to cultivate maize. The produce of this labor flowed into the city, where the surplus of maize was managed and distributed. Maya rulers and elites controlled this distribution, which fed the laborers and artisans for public building works, and other professionals who did not, themselves, farm. Specialist works and hierarchies of distribution are distinctive aspects of the Maya city. For example, although densely settled, Çatalhöyük (in Turkey; see Chapter 8) had no public architecture, no visible differentiation of wealth or status, and no craft or religious specialists whose practices kept them from daily farming and food production.

At Çatalhöyük, evidence thus suggests that every household was responsible for its own subsistence. The definitive features of a city—specialization, public works, evidence of an elite—are possible only through the production of surplus food.

Maya cities were fed by the intense agriculture of maize, but where did the surplus maize go? Archaeologists have found no large granaries in which Maya rulers might have stored a surplus of maize in the rain forest cities. Today, the Maya build corncribs of branch slats, mud plaster, and thatch to conserve their harvests close to home. It seems unlikely that the Maya fed cities through vast storehouses which have left no trace: instead, archaeologists point to the existing evidence that surplus maize from each farmer was tapped to meet other needs or converted to other materials. For example, surplus maize fed the Maya laborers who built stone and earthen pyramids and temples, probably no more than a day's walk from their dwellings. Perhaps these labors took place once the harvest was in, or perhaps each farmer owed a labor duty to his or her ruler, in exchange for access to farmland. Evidence also exists of markets, conveniently located in urban centers, where maize and its products could be exchanged for other goods: exquisitely detailed Maya murals uncovered under a pyramid at Calakmul show sellers and buyers of *atole* (maize drink), *tamales* (seasoned maize grits steamed in maize-leaf wrappers), and other items. Maya cities provided a center for exchange so that maize surplus might be traded for cloth, dyes, pots, or such luxuries as obsidian and chocolate.

Markets [10.12] and such public architecture as pyramids, temples, and ball courts (for ceremonial games) defined the urban core of Maya cities. Also present were palaces of carved stone, built by craftspeople whose special skill was supported by maize surplus. Some Maya centers included large, clay-lined reservoirs and *sakbe* leading out into the hinterlands.

10.12 Depiction of a Maya market from a mural in Calakmul. The image shows standing figures lifting vessels, and seated figures drinking or dispensing maize-gruel using dippers.

THE MAYA CITY 231

Opposite above: **10.13 Tikal's pyramids rising above the forest canopy.** This iconic view, which some students will recognize from the *Star Wars* movie series, is visible only because archaeologists have cleared five major pyramid-temple mounds and a central plaza. Other mounds and all the house sites, reservoirs, and plazas remain hidden under the rain forest canopy.

Opposite below: **10.14 LiDAR image of Tikal illustrating the plazas and pyramids that make up the stone center.** Huts of wood, thatch, and matting, as well as gardening areas, would have surrounded this complex. LiDAR technology uses laser beams from aircraft to measure distance, generating a topographic image of a landscape. New studies using LiDAR in the Maya lowlands have revealed a wall around Tikal and seventeen elevated causeways leading from El Mirador.

Tikal

The city of Tikal was one of the largest complexes built during the Classic period. Its population may have been as high as 80,000, numbering some 1,800 people per square mile. Its area was approximately 46 square miles (120 square km), falling within the earthworks that partially surround the center. In this center, large pyramids peek above the jungle canopy [**10.13**, **10.14**]. The tallest is Temple IV, rising to 230 feet (70 meters).

Tikal was the seat of a powerful royal dynasty that formed after the collapse of Preclassic Maya centers, such as El Mirador. All rulers of Tikal looked back to a dynastic founder whose name in hieroglyphs reads Yax Ehb Xook; he ruled around 90 CE. For all of their power, dominating a network extending hundreds of miles, Tikal's rulers were not without rivals. War between the dynasties of Calakmul, Tikal, and their allies raged throughout the seventh century CE, impacting virtually every corner of the Maya lowlands.

Surrounding the Tikal center, most of the Maya landscape was probably a repetitive mosaic of small thatch dwellings on a simple cobble base, surrounded by kitchen gardens, trash heaps, and fields. Looking at Tikal from above, one may have difficulty determining where one city ended and the next began, unless one considers only the limestone urban core. The dense population of Maya had cleared much of the rain forest as far as the eye could see, with the exception of small human-made plantations and unfarmed savannah wastes. As the subjects of Maya rulers and contributors of surplus maize, labor, and other household products, farmers were integral to the functioning of this Maya city.

The concentration of exchange products in central markets, massive public architecture, density of the urban population, and diversity of economic and social activities, align Maya centers with the structure of cities elsewhere. Archaeologists have long considered societies that exhibit a diverse network of economic and social roles to be complex, and cities are a hallmark of such complexity.

The Maya Collapse

Archaeologists have long debated the causes behind the abandonment of Maya urban centers *c.* 850 CE. They have suggested that disease, warfare, overpopulation with demands outstripping potential resources, and the overuse of fragile rain forest soils precipitated a plunge in populations. Paleoclimate experts studying pollen and chemical signatures from lakes in the Maya lowlands have determined that climatic deterioration with a sharp downturn in rainfall occurred around 850, marking a severe drought for the Maya. Farmers already producing at maximum capacity simply could not generate the surpluses needed to sustain urban centers, which then fought for dwindling resources. Living between warring cities may have become a perilous existence, and living in them no longer tenable.

It is clear that today's Maya are descendants of ancestral Maya, and the Maya never truly disappeared. Moreover, the pattern of urban abandonment had

THE MAYA CITY 233

unfolded during several previous eras. One need only look to earlier Olmec centers along Mexico's Veracruz coast (see Chapter 13), and such Preclassic Maya cities as El Mirador in northern Guatemala, which were abandoned when the Classic Maya began to flourish. Following this pattern, the Maya abandoned city life in the central rain forests c. 950 CE, although urban centers did later spring up in Postclassic Yucatán.

SOUTHEAST ASIA: IRRIGATION AND AGRICULTURE AT ANGKOR

Maize fed the people who created the thriving Maya cities, and its cultivation required the regular clearing of the rain forest and treatment of the soil. But the Maya were not alone in altering the rain forest. Remote sensing has revealed water management and irrigation of an almost unimaginable scale throughout the vicinity of Angkor in Cambodia [10.15].

Angkor was the capital of the large **Khmer empire** that spanned much of the Southeast Asian peninsula. To give a sense of comparative scale, so greatly did the city of Angkor dwarf the Maya centers that the entire monumental core of Tikal (60 acres) could fit easily into the ceremonial compound at the heart of Angkor, Angkor Wat [10.16]. From 800 to 1350 CE, Khmer dynasties ruled from the landscape of Angkor, then studded with countless temples and palaces, and now surrounded by Cambodia's lowland rain forests.

Khmer empire A powerful Hindu-Buddhist empire in Southeast Asia (800–1350 CE).

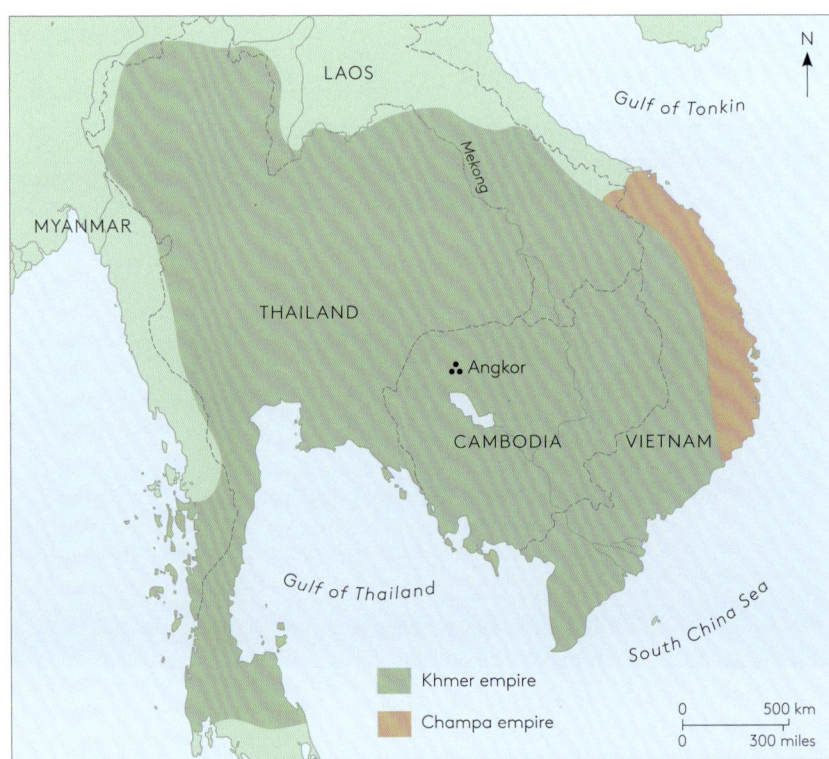

10.15 Map of Southeast Asia showing the extent of the Khmer empire (in mid green) and the Champa empire (in pink), along with the major city of Angkor.

For generations, archaeologists have been drawn to the complex layout of Angkor's enclosures and intricately carved facades. These were constructed over centuries, during which Khmer rulers lost and regained their empire, religious affinity shifted from Hinduism to Buddhism and back again, and power flowed from the Khmer to Champa (on the southern coast of Vietnam) and back again. Throughout these periods of change, temples and palaces were ornamented with magnificent sandstone carvings and what appear to be wooden images that have poorly survived.

Temple motifs included mythological creatures with hybrid human and animal features; *apsaras* (heavenly nymphs, sometimes resembling the wife of the king); youthful female divinities; and cobra and eagle figures from Hindu myth. Enthroned in this pantheon was the king, who doubled as a divinity. This notion of the king as a god is nowhere more apparent than at Bayon, a temple in Angkor, where exquisite and detailed reliefs recount not only historical events and tales from mythology, but also the story of Jayavarman VII, who ruled the Khmer empire around 1200 CE. Among the most distinctive features at Bayon are the serene, carved faces that appear on the stone towers of the upper terraces, which may represent either Jayavarman himself or the Buddha, or a mixture of both. Against this backdrop of the ruler's face in Buddhist guise, sculptural reliefs depict rituals (processions, objects, sacrifices), the life of the court, festivals, and the participation of elites and attendants. Of the artists and farmers that supported this monumental display—not a trace!

10.16 Aerial view of the central temple complex at Angkor Wat. The temples at the center are arranged to resemble mountains, and are richly decorated with sculpture. The entire site is surrounded by a water-filled baray that is 3.5 miles (5.6 km) in length. Angkor Wat is considered by many to be the largest religious complex in the world.

As at Tikal and El Mirador, Angkor was the site of an intricate hierarchy. How was the great complex fed? The Angkor complex maintained absolute control over the landscape and its waterways. A network of highways, causeways, and masonry bridges allowed the easy passage of Khmer armies across a land crisscrossed by extensive public waterworks, including canals and vast reservoirs, known as *baray,* that held water for irrigating the fields. The East Baray commissioned by Yahovarman I in the 890s CE is approximately 5 miles (7.5 km) by 1 mile (1.8 km) and possibly took 6 million manpower days to build. It is an impressive, central symbol of Khmer control of the landscape, a countryside shaped as a niche from which to feed the elites and armies of Angkor [**10.17**].

Hydraulic engineering was not confined to the core of the Khmer empire at Angkor Wat. Because the rain forests surrounding Angkor are today still treacherous with landmines from the Cambodian civil wars of the 1960s and 1970s, archaeologists have used remote sensing by satellite to detect hundreds of reservoirs and canals within a 12.5- to 18.5-mile (20- to 30-km) radius of Angkor. Its roads are lined with evidence of settlement extending from the city center in all directions. These canals would have made the most of the weather in the region. Cambodia's climate is dominated by summer monsoon rains, followed by a dry season during which rice matures for harvest. The management of torrential monsoon rains meant channeling them into depressions and basins from which water could be subsequently spread across the landscape through small ditches.

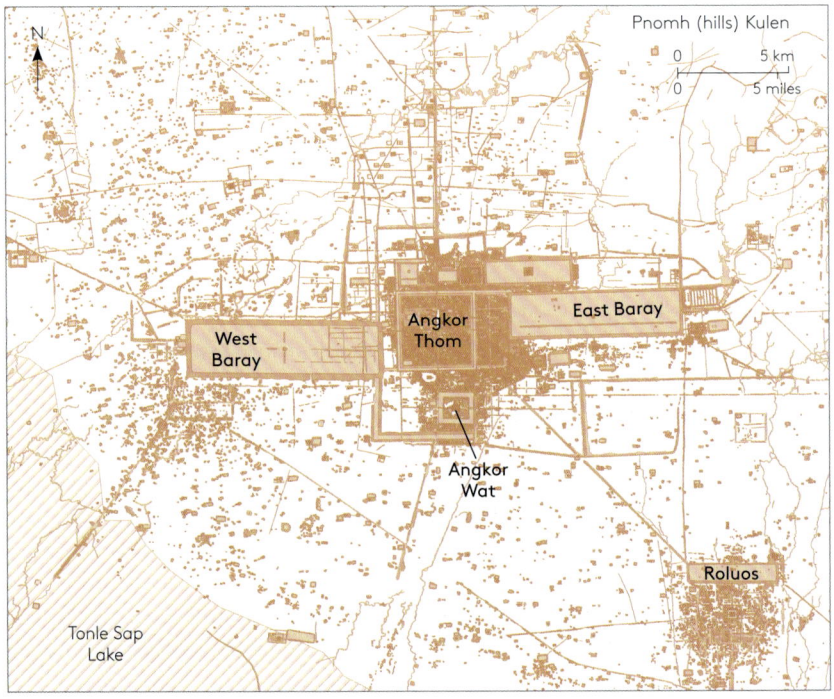

10.17 The core zone around Angkor Wat with immense rectangular artificial lakes (baray) that cluster at temple complexes. The density of smaller shrines, hamlets, field systems, and canal networks extends for hundreds of kilometers between the hills and lake shores. Archaeologists have only fully mapped the site core shown here. Using LiDAR, archaeologists produced regional images, which they then mapped through laborious ground survey. The long, straight features are major canals and roadways that linked the Khmer landscape. Smaller canals and basins are not shown here.

Much of this extensive control of the water resulted from the need to cultivate rice in areas with rainfall that was intermittent but torrential (see Chapter 8). Rice could be dry-farmed, or watered by rainfall, only in hilly regions of the Khmer empire, and hydraulic engineering ensured a reliable, higher crop yield, given the certainty of a controlled water supply and a more consistent distribution of nutrients in the water. For a city that needed a dependable surplus to feed its armies and the builders of its great complexes, and to maintain the prestige of its rulers, irrigated rice offered a steady, storable supply. Surplus production was key to Angkor urban life, and as with maize, the natural seasonal cycle and storage potential inherent in rice made it a product that could be accumulated and exchanged easily.

THE STATE

Cities are locations that demand a surplus of agriculture, to be exchanged and used to feed the builders of public architecture and specialists involved in producing luxury goods. This surplus is often controlled and distributed through the influence of an elite. Cities and city complexes—such as those of the Maya and those in Cambodia—tend to be densely populated, and draw from a defined radius of agricultural land. They are competitive within a network of adjacent cities, and, usually walled, harbor the vast majority of a population. They are home to craftsmen and craftswomen of many trades, and become the locus of markets and exchanges. States also are the structures of complex societies, emerged through much the same processes, whereby elites acquired sufficient authority and power to encourage the production of an agricultural surplus and control its allocation. Territorial states control larger terrain than cities, with bigger populations distributed throughout the countryside and in much smaller centers that house elites and their retinues.

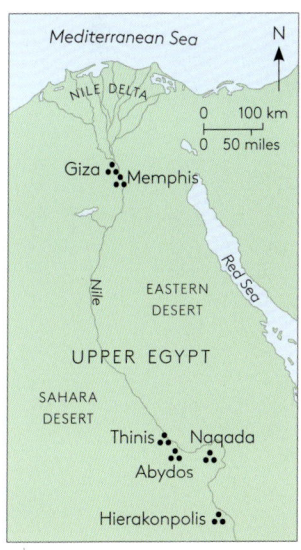

10.18 Map of the Upper Nile showing the Predynastic territories and cities (Thinis, Hierakonpolis, Naqada). Ancient Egyptians considered only the Nile Valley and its inhabitants "Egyptian": from their perspective, "foreigners" occupied the desert to the east and west.

The Ancient Egyptian State

One ancient state with a close connection to, and command of, food production was Egypt. Around 3000 BCE, it appeared as an autonomous, mostly integral territorial state [**10.18**]. Nearly 3,000 years later, Egypt absorbed into its native Pharaonic traditions a Greek dynasty—Cleopatra's Ptolemaic dynasty. Over this long period of time, Egypt experienced many transformations, so this chapter considers only the initial expressions of Egyptian social complexity in the later Predynastic (c. 3300–3000 BCE), Early Dynastic (3000–2700 BCE), and Old Kingdom (2700–2200 BCE) periods.

Just about everyone knows of Egypt's iconic Old Kingdom pyramids, the greatest of which is Khufu's pyramid at Giza (erected c. 2550 BCE). Flanked by the lesser, later pyramids of Khafre and Menkaure, the pyramid complex included a mortuary temple at its base, a temple in the valley, and the packed settlements of pyramid builders who labored for several decades to raise a great limestone tomb for the ruler of all Egypt [**10.19**, p. 238].

THE STATE **237**

10.19 The Great Pyramid (far rear in this image) was commissioned by Khufu. Khafre's smaller pyramid, which retains its outer limestone casing only at the top, appears larger from this angle.

Unlike Maya cities with their relatively small surrounding territories, the Egyptian state had a territorial integrity that allowed its rulers to muster an impressive surplus and mobilize for massive projects, such as the pyramids. Possibly five thousand laborers at the pyramids were full-time craftsmen and specialists skilled in stone-cutting and masonry. These men also managed another fifteen thousand workers (employed on rotation) and their families, who came from all over Egypt to raise the pyramids, the archetypical monuments to the state's social and economic unity (see Chapter 11).

Archaeologists believe that Egypt's potential to develop a staple surplus evolved only once the cereal crops wheat and barley had been introduced, sometime after 6000 BCE. These crops were grown in the rich Nile River Valley, the waters of which flowed through a rainless desert. The only water for agriculture in Egypt comes from the annual rising of the Nile River (in July), which leaves a nutrient-rich, black silt bed as floodwaters recede (in September). Planting and harvest take place after the floods and depend on the abundance of the Nile, which may vary considerably from year to year and, depending on local topography, bunds, and sandbars, from one part of the valley to the next.

After the early construction of small, walled centers that are poorly understood in an archaeological context, Egypt quickly settled into another kind of social and economic order following 3000 BCE. Instead of building competing walled centers, Egyptians consolidated the territory of the Nile Valley into one entity with a single ruling power. Surplus crops were stored in walled compounds that housed only a few wealthy elites and craftsmen whose sole job was to produce luxury goods for the elites, who were headed by a single pharaoh for all of Egypt. Archaeologists have uncovered many of these luxury goods at Egyptian burial sites, which are famous for their rich trappings and preservation in arid environments. Certainly, such luxuries were also used in daily life, but only by the few privileged enough to feed off the surplus of the state's farmers.

Egypt's territorial boundaries were fairly secure from the start, with a desert on all sides that constrained and defined a farming people. Early on, they rapidly formed a complex society with pooled resources integrated and administered by a handful of individuals across a large region. Sir Flinders Petrie (1853–1942), one of the best-known nineteenth-century Egyptologists, excavated part of an archaic walled compound at Naqada (c. 3300–3000 BCE). Inside a mud-brick wall, he found residues of craft specialists at work: chippings from exotic ornamental stone, such as granite and porphyry. He also came across many mud sealings [**10.20**] that speak to the storage and parceling out of goods in ceramic jars or other containers. This ancient administrative technology controlled access to goods in much the same way as the sealing of letters with wax and signet rings controls access to information (as it did in medieval Europe, for example). The finds of sealings also indicate that the stockpiling and accounting of surplus goods, including grain and oil, both of which would have stored well, did take place. In excavated tombs, ivory labels etched with an archaic form of Egyptian hieroglyphics are testament to the control of these goods by elites, who eventually ordered that the name of Pharaoh be scratched on the ceramic jars transported up and down the river.

Outside the Naqada compound and scattered across the terraces of the Nile Valley, Petrie and his successors discovered the cemeteries and ash-covered, pitted surfaces that marked the graves of Egypt's early population of farmers and cattle herders, whose rural lives seldom intersected with the elites. Archaeologists estimate that most of the population of Egypt's early territorial state, about 1.2 million people, lived in rural villages and hamlets of fewer than four hundred people, providing labor and surplus for the maintenance and burial of a wealthy few who lived apart in administrative compounds. Towns were scarce; central markets do not appear to have existed, nor craftsmen who sold their products to a general populace. Egypt also lacked urban spaces flaunting great temples and other public buildings alongside the residences of a wide variety of economic specialists. Although Egypt's territorial state was vast, unlike the dense Maya cities, condensed settlements were few, restricted to such towns as Elephantine, Kom Ombo, Edfu, El-Kab, and Abydos. They were sealed off by thick enclosures and provisioned through a hierarchy of administrative centers that were the capitals of the Egyptian provinces integrated under one pharaoh. Because the administrators of a territorial state could command much greater surpluses from much larger populations on greater expanses of agricultural land, they could support the labor for bigger armies or public projects. True power rested in the ability of Old Kingdom tomb-construction projects to unite the Egyptian people and consolidate the resources of labor, food, and luxury goods.

10.20 Mud sealings that date back to the Old Kingdom period in Egypt. These were used to show that a jar, door, or container had not been opened since the prior sealer pressed his or her imprint into wet clay. This process controlled access to surplus and luxury goods, ensuring that only those authorized to remove or alter them could do so. In the mud sealings with a pilastered palace (bar design), the pharaoh's name is invoked. Where archaeologists find such sealings, they recognize that the control of surplus took place nearby.

THE ENVIRONMENTAL PERILS OF INTENSIFICATION

In spite of the structural differences in scale and in organization between Egyptian, Khmer, and Maya complex societies, their farmers faced a common peril: nutrient depletion and land degradation that can threaten the overly intensive use of farmland. Where farmers are pressed to produce too much surplus from too little land, they need to intensify their efforts to do so. In complex societies, a farmer's yield must include enough for his or her own household, a seed crop, and often a tithe, tribute, or tax to support those involved in nonfarming activities. The tithe may guarantee food from the common granary during a lean year or continued access to such resources as land, water, or farming subsidies. To generate increased yield, farmers may intensify their labor inputs, improve technologies (for instance, the efficiency of sowing, or of water or nutrient delivery), narrow a crop base to a few key plants, expand farming onto new land, or use land more frequently. All these strategies carry risks: instability, crop failure, nutrient loss, and damage to the ecological niche of farming systems. This is clear in the story of the Maya collapse, where the reduction of Mesoamerican rain forests (which have never completely recovered) and a climatic downturn around 850 CE played a role in the widespread abandonment of ancient urban centers in the lowland region of southern Guatemala and Honduras.

Sumerian Civilization in Southwest Asia dating back to 3200–2500 BCE; it included some of the earliest cities in the world. People of the previous Uruk period were also likely to have been Sumerian-language speakers.

Mesopotamia: Sumerian Cities and Intensive Agriculture

As we explore the risks of intensive agriculture driven by the demands of large populations and the need for surplus, the final region covered in this chapter is Mesopotamia [**10.21**], in modern-day Iraq and Iran. We conclude with the story of the **Sumerian** civilization in 3200–2500 BCE, which included some of the earliest cities in the world, because it is the quintessential case of agricultural intensification.

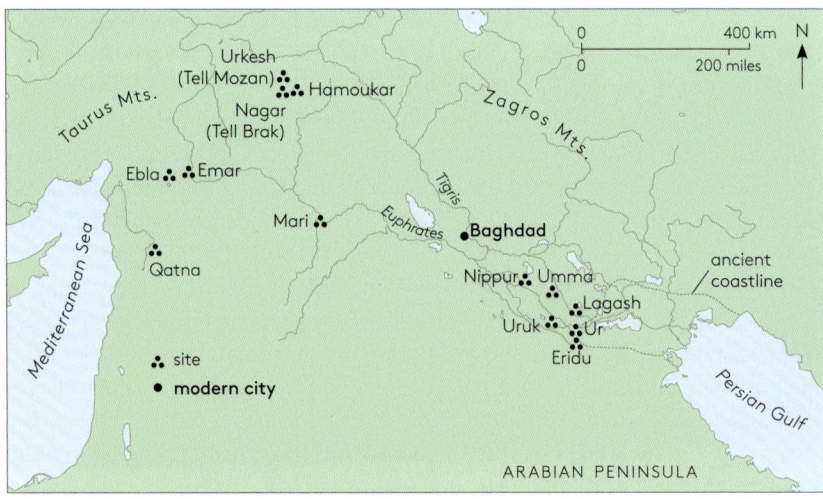

10.21 Map of Mesopotamia and major Sumerian cities.

Similarly to Egypt's population, the inhabitants of the Sumerian cities of Uruk, Lagash, and Ur were dependent on river waters that flowed through desert lands.

Early Sumerians were adept with water: carved stone panels depict how they lived in marshes teeming with wildlife at the juncture of the Tigris and Euphrates rivers in southern Iraq. Close to the sea, they mastered early sailing technology in reed boats caulked with pitch (a petroleum-based material that seeps naturally from sandy deposits), and they plied a wide array of goods up and down the shores of the Arabian/Persian Gulf starting in 5000 BCE. By 3200 BCE, Sumerians had built an enormous urban center at Uruk, where according to ancient texts the legendary Gilgamesh ruled as king. Uruk had a defensive city wall, massive and expensive public buildings, luxury goods, a population with diverse social and economic roles, and major dependence on irrigated wheat and barley.

Irrigation waters in southern Mesopotamia came from floods of the River Tigris in springtime, from snowmelt off the high Zagros Mountains to the east, and from floods emanating from the Euphrates River and Taurus Mountains to the north. These mountains form the outlines of a landscape long called the Fertile Crescent because it is here that the earliest villages, the origins of domesticated wheat and barley, and the irrigated surpluses that fed the first civilizations (the Sumerian cities) may be traced (Chapter 8). Sumerians received no water from rainfall, and spring floods came too late to grow wheat and barley, which need winter watering. Instead, Sumerians relied on canals, cut into the high banks (levees) of the Euphrates River, to lead water across low flatlands to water their fields and drain off the excess from spring floods. A canal system required labor to build and maintain, but it assured farmers of water supplied at the right time in the right amounts. With irrigation, desert soils can be highly fertile, as the Sumerians soon discovered.

Sumerians developed writing on clay tablets to help them keep track of the production of grain (see Chapter 13). These texts record the centralized demand for surplus crops and labor, as called for by the elites, which led to intensified production in ancient Sumer [**10.22**]. The constant pressure associated with such an effort meant that land was not left to fallow (allowed to go uncultivated so it could regain lost nutrients), and the same waters bearing salt leached from the basement rocks of the mountains were directed onto fields each year. As a result, salt accumulated on the surface. Wheat grows poorly in salty ground; barley only marginally better.

Over time, the potential to produce surplus dwindled and, with it, Sumer's great cities. By 2100 BCE, as a result of this declining surplus and a severe drought, the ruling Akkadian dynasty collapsed. Sumer's weakened heartland of cities never again produced the crop yields of its Early Dynastic glory.

10.22 Images of the presentation of food on the Uruk Vase, c. 3200 BCE. This vase displays the worldview of Sumerians. In the lowest register, one sees the crops (cereals and flax) and animals; in the middle (see detail), people bear produce into the temple (they carry what is probably a basket filled with fruits, perhaps pomegranates, and on the left, a ceramic jar perhaps of beer or yoghurt drink); and along the upper part, these worshipers present offerings to the goddess.

THE ENVIRONMENTAL PERILS OF INTENSIFICATION

CITIES, SURPLUS, AND THE ELITE

Across the world, social complexity has emerged repeatedly, driven by population density, environmental change, and the possibilities provided by surplus. Through intense agriculture, complex societies have contributed to the anthropogenic alteration of the Earth. Humans have ploughed its plains, terraced its hill slopes, farmed its forests, and developed cropping systems that have reduced biodiversity in plants and wildlife. Intense agriculture also diversified human societies. This is our human niche.

A comparison of the Maya cities, Angkor, ancient Egypt, and Sumerian cities has highlighted for archaeologists the environment's potential and constraints in supporting surplus production. Here, we also touched on how cities, states, and surplus are connected to the elite. If everyone farmed his or her own food, as at Çatalhöyük, then economic roles would be relatively undifferentiated with little material basis for power in social hierarchies, social networks of exchange, or social factions beyond the household. But if one person or social group holds more surplus than others and converts it to a precious rarity or consumes it in a spectacular way, a material basis for power is created. In the chapters that follow, we will explore the forms this conversion can take: in the building of public works and monuments (see Chapter 11), and through visible or "conspicuous" consumption (see Chapter 12).

Many archaeological approaches and theories have evolved to understand how elite groups rise in societies. Some emphasize control over material resources—the control of the maize surplus by Maya lords being a prime example—but this is not the only way to gain power. Maya lords and Khmer royalty also exploited ideologies, stressing their close relationships to the gods and their intervention in divine affairs, including rainfall and fertility. We will learn more about the manipulation of ideologies and control of information in Chapter 13. The emergence of elites in a social hierarchy supported by storable surplus only highlights the fact that agents drew on both material and ideological resources to press for intensification and the production of even greater agricultural surplus.

Although this chapter explores deforestation of the rain forests in Central America and East Asia, this is also a story about the success of domesticated plants across the world and their introduction in many new habitats. Wheat and rice, staple cereals that fed the first civilizations, are plants of the subtropics that have spread as domesticates deep into temperate zones. As a tropical native, maize has also spread widely. From Mexico, farmers brought maize to the highlands of Andean Peru in South America, to the temperate forests of New England in North America, and by 1600 CE to West Africa and the Ottoman empire of the Eastern Mediterranean (probably from Brazil via the Portuguese). It is a deep irony that the staple crops which fed the first great cities of the Americas prospered widely in later centuries, long after the urban centers that fostered their production had collapsed.

Chapter Questions

1. How did the Maya feed their cities in the middle of a rain forest? Compare their strategy to that of the Khmer.

2. What are some features of a city? How does an urban center differ from a village, for example Çatalhöyük?

3. Compare Maya cities and the ancient Egyptian states. How did they differ? What did they share in the management of surplus?

4. How has intensive agriculture shaped our Anthropocene niche? What have been some of its effects? Use the Maya and Sumerian cities as examples in your response.

Additional Resources

Coe, Michael D. *The Maya.* 7th ed. London, UK: Thames & Hudson, 2005 [1966].

Coe, Michael D. *Angkor and the Khmer Civilization.* London, UK: Thames & Hudson, 2003.

Lehner, Mark. "Villages and the Old Kingdom," in *Egyptian Archaeology,* edited by Willeke Wendrich, 85–101. Chichester, UK: Wiley-Blackwell, 2010.

Redman, Charles L. "Environmental Degradation and Early Mesopotamian Civilization," in *The Archaeology of Global Change,* edited by Charles L. Redman, Steven R. James, Paul R. Fish, and J. Daniel Rogers, 158–64. Washington, DC: Smithsonian Books, 2004.

Trigger, Bruce. *Early Civilizations.* Cairo, Egypt: The American University in Cairo Press, 1993.

BUILDING MONUMENTS, BUILDING SOCIETY
Collective Labor as Social Identity

11

The National Mall, set within Washington, D.C.'s highly symbolic landscape, spans nearly 2.5 miles (approximately 4 km). At its east end stands the Capitol building, and at its west end, the Lincoln Memorial. Within the memorial sits a massive statue of Abraham Lincoln, the sixteenth president of the United States.

In building a monument to Lincoln, the United States established a visual monument to the social order reconstructed after the American Civil War. The Civil War had been the bloodiest conflict up until that point in history. Shattered limbs and severed extremities became metaphors for the state of the nation itself. The Civil War splintered the American Union founded some eighty-seven years beforehand and threatened to fracture it forever.

The memorial—completed in 1922, almost sixty years after the end of the war—is as much a monument to the Union as a national ideal as it is to Lincoln himself. Constructed in the form of a classical Greek temple, the memorial is supported by thirty-six columns, one for each of the thirty-six states in the nation at the end of the Civil War. The Lincoln Memorial and its surrounding landscape symbolize and reinforce a story of social identity: all Americans are joined in an indissoluble union. In an attempt at inclusiveness, that story may gloss over the scars remaining from the conflict and the very issues that provoked it. Although the Civil War ended slavery, African Americans were still denied equality within the Union. But they, too, turned to the memorial as a touchstone symbolic of the struggle for liberation and equality during the March on Washington for civil rights in 1963 and during the 2008 pre-inaugural rally celebrating the election of America's first African American president.

The Lincoln Memorial is not a prehistoric monument; it does not reflect the ideology of archaic people long forgotten; it is not an early step in a global construction of our Anthropocene. It is included here to stress that constructing monuments is a practice societies have followed for at least ten thousand years, and in many parts of the world; the remains of this critical and socially constructive activity may be found also in temperate Neolithic Britain and among mobile groups in the Sahara and Arabian Deserts.

Monuments and Landscapes 246

Ancient Egypt: Building the Egyptian State 247

Monuments among Mobile Communities 257

Stonehenge and the Pastoralist Landscape of Neolithic Britain 261

North America: The Hopewell Earthworks 270

Opposite Photograph of the Lincoln Memorial on the United States National Mall, taken during Dr. Martin Luther King Jr.'s speech, "I Have a Dream," August 28, 1963.

Key Concepts

- How the erection of monuments has unified communities for thousands of years, with the pyramids of Giza, in Egypt, as a prime example

- Monuments are not always monumental, and may be created by mobile communities, not just by large cities and states

- Landscapes can be monumental and can become places of congregation, such as Stonehenge in the UK and the Hopewell Mounds in the US

landscape The perception of a region or environment as a culturally framed and organized space.

monument A structure, the meaning and purpose of which are shared across a social collective.

MONUMENTS AND LANDSCAPES

How and why have humans purposefully shaped their environment to make monuments and landscapes? What exactly is a monument, and what is a landscape? **Landscape** is not the same as one's environment. The environment includes all organic and inorganic components taken together. In archaeology, the term "landscape" is used to describe an environment subject to cultural framing. Chapter 4 introduced an Aboriginal landscape in Australia, where places have associated narratives, meanings, and histories that anchor Aboriginal social groups to the land. No one quite sees the Outback as its Aboriginal inhabitants do.

"Landscape" derives from the seventeenth-century Dutch term *landschap*, which was used then to describe a new style of painting. In *landschap*, nature flows from the worldview of those who commissioned or paid for the artwork. These patrons were emerging capitalists who would drive empires and whose view of the natural world embraced inequality, bourgeois control, and the exploitation of distant people and environmental resources. These seventeenth-century patrons saw nature in certain terms: harnessed and dominated, a setting for the works of "man" (in other words, white, male Europeans). Look to Jacob van Ruisdael's *Windmill at Wijk* [**11.1**] for an example of this dynamic. In the painting, a windmill works to drain soils in the expanding land-reclamation project of the Low Countries. The shipping that projected Dutch power into the colonies is subtly present in the artwork's masts and waterways.

Landscape is a cultural view of the environment, and it differs depending on the viewer and culture. European painters embraced a capitalist political economy with its inherent class-based social order, and they sought to reify and perpetuate that system as the natural state in their depictions of nature. Similarly to European painters, **monument** builders in many cultures shaped a landscape using stone, wood, and earthen berms (mounds) to organize a particular way of seeing the environment.

Within landscapes stand monuments. A monument may be large or small; it may be constructed over a brief period of time or developed through multiple reshapings, additions, effacements, embellishments, or other modifications. What distinguishes a monument from other structures is its meaning and purpose shared across a social collective. Constructing a monument as a group produces and affirms a collective vision. Although one generally expects a monument to be an edifice defined by its significant size, the term also applies to collective action serving a

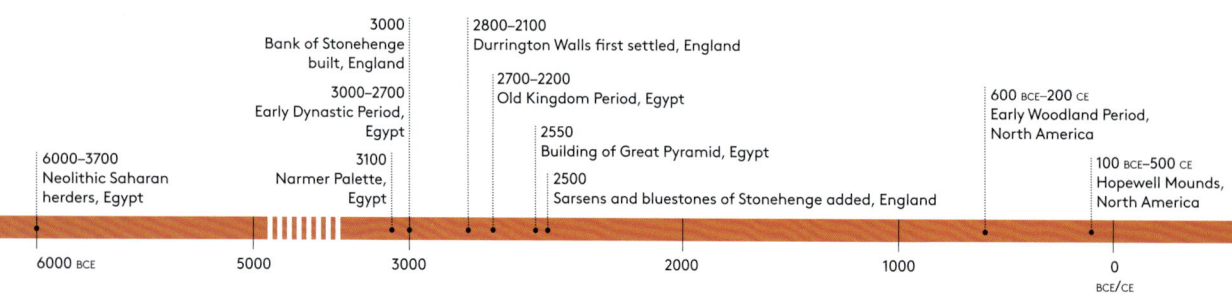

11.1 Jacob van Ruisdael, *Windmill at Wijk*, c. 1670. The artist depicts a landscape that conveys a sense of Dutch colonial power. A windmill, the agent of land reclamation (by draining waterlogged lowlands into canals) dominates the scene and symbolizes the nation's power over nature. Gray clouds loom overhead, but a light from the heavens (perhaps divine blessing?) shines on the windmill through a break in the sky. A simple country scene thus imparts a potent message about Dutch power, the Netherlands' place in the natural order, and heavenly favor for this arrangement.

common purpose. Inherent in a monumental landscape are the labor and collective vision of a society. This includes both the building of a monument and its continued use, which may include the renegotiation and transformation of that monument's meaning over the years.

Monuments usually begin as a grand design: a structure, a reshaped vista, a *bauplan* (a building plan) that conforms to social principles. With the passage of time, an initial installation might be revisited and reimagined. Just as the European painters' embrace of a capitalist social order did, monument builders engage with a specific worldview and re-express it in a magnified way. Similarly to those of early European nations, these collective visions are skewed toward a particular viewpoint, often one shared by the people in power. To illustrate and expand on these concepts, our discussion here will explore a great variety of monuments from very different kinds of societies: Egypt's pharaonic Old Kingdom masses; the loose-knit families of desert-dwelling herders in North Africa; the changing social landscape of Britain's monumental Stonehenge; and the far-flung communities of the great mounds of North America.

ANCIENT EGYPT: BUILDING THE EGYPTIAN STATE

In Chapter 10, we examined the Egyptian state, especially its dependence on intense agriculture. Egypt's Giza pyramids are perhaps humanity's best-known monuments. They are not just the lavish tombs of the pharaohs but also monuments to social unity. Although one cannot see the pyramids from the moon, they loom large over urban Cairo today and endure as perhaps the most iconic manifestation of Egypt's

Old Kingdom Period in Egyptian history from 2686 to 2181 BCE, marking the beginning of the Third Dynasty and end of the Sixth Dynasty. Includes the building of the Great Pyramid during the Fourth Dynasty.

pharaonic past (see **10.19**, p. 238). They also continue to capture the human imagination and spawn a wide range of theories. The pyramids, however, were not built by aliens; or lost Atlanteans; or Hebrew slaves; or Joseph so he might store grain; or mammoths toiling alongside cavemen, as suggested by the movie *10,000 BC*. Egyptians built Giza's pyramids between 2680 and 2180 BCE. Indeed, the pyramids are a familiar example of the symbolic power of monumental construction and the role of monuments in society. In the words of Mark Lehner, who has studied Giza's pyramid landscape for three decades, it is as interesting to understand "how the Pyramids built Egypt as how the Egyptians built the Pyramids."

The Inheritance

The Egyptian state did not emerge perfectly formed, or separately from the African continent, but inherited from previous cultures of the Mediterranean to the north and Sahara to the south, which eventually contributed to the social meaning of the pyramids. Prior to 3000 BCE, Egypt consisted of two lands: Lower Egypt, which included the delta and alluvial plain of the northern part of the Nile River, and Upper Egypt, which extended upriver to the cataracts and canyons of the southern Nile desert ([**11.2**]; see also Chapter 10). The northern society of Egypt had adopted and inherited household social norms and agricultural crops from Neolithic communities in the eastern Mediterranean (see Chapter 8), and southern Egyptian society's cultural roots lay with the Neolithic cattle pastoralists of the Sahara Desert (see below). In disseminating pastoralists' social identities, adorning the body of the living played a deeply important role, especially because the body is a good way for a mobile people (such as cattle-herders) to convey a person's access to, and control of, rare goods—his or her networks and influence—by using jewelry and colorful rare pigments rather than heavy, immobile objects.

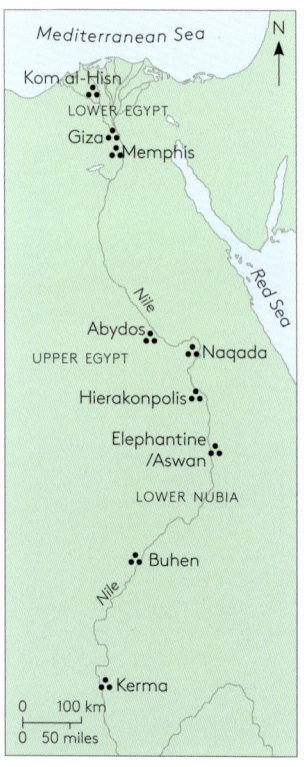

11.2 Map of Upper and Lower Egypt during the Old Kingdom.

Egyptologist David Wengrow has argued that traditions of adorning and manipulating the human body that were important in later Egyptian culture were inherited from earlier African traditions. Just as desert-dwelling pastoralists of the south used the human body as the primary canvas for representing their ideas and symbolic messages, the Egyptian ideal of the state as an indissoluble whole (see Chapter 10) was communicated in the metaphor of a single and indestructible body. Bodies became metaphors for a kind of corporate unity: many people acting as one.

Bodies as symbols, their adornment, and their preservation—all were the pharaohs' cultural inheritance from the social building-blocks of mobile people. By 2700 BCE, two lands, Upper (southern) and Lower (northern) Egypt, were united under one pharaoh, beginning the era of the **Old Kingdom** (lasting until about 2200 BCE; **11.2**). Much of our understanding of this important event derives from Egyptian mythology, which recounts a struggle eventually won by Horus, the totem god of most early Predynastic rulers. Visual representations also appear on palettes of siltstone (a dense rock) that were used for the preparation of cosmetics—more evidence of the importance of communicating via the human body.

A unification of Egypt's regions by force is recorded in the elaborately decorated Narmer Palette [**11.3**]. It shows the king of Upper Egypt conquering the Delta people of Lower Egypt, an event overseen by looming heads of cattle: indeed, the entire palette is in the shape of a cow's head, entwining symbols from Upper Egypt's pastoral past with ideology linked to the formation of the Egyptian state. The Narmer Palette was uncovered in 1897 in the ruins of Hierakonpolis, a bustling elite center in Upper Egypt established by King Narmer, founder of Egypt's dynastic pharaonic tradition in 3200 CE. The image of the king as the pharaoh of a united Egypt provides an index for the new ideology that was emerging at that time: that the state of Egypt was personified in the body of the pharaoh. This was extended into the Egyptian conception of the afterlife, hence the need to preserve the body of the pharaoh in a tomb. In Old Kingdom Egypt, such a monument came to symbolize the unified Egyptian state. Monumental pyramids designed to house the dead were constructed for the next five centuries, representing a political and social unity not unlike that commemorated by Lincoln's Memorial many years later in Washington, D.C., the city built between the Civil War's North and South.

The Old Kingdom lasted about five hundred years and included the Third through Sixth Dynasty of the three-thousand-year Egyptian civilization. Ancient Egypt had some thirty dynasties but was not always politically stable. Although Egyptians conceived of themselves as a united nation and frequently rewrote history to suggest

11.3 Narmer Palette, c. 3100 BCE. The engraved stone tablet is believed to depict the unification of Upper and Lower Egypt under King Narmer. On its reverse side (left), Narmer—wearing the crown of Upper Egypt—slays a dweller of Lower Egypt, with the victim shown naked in defeat at his feet. The god Horus (shown as a falcon) opens the mouth of another resident of Lower Egypt, symbolized by papyrus reeds. Cattle heads, expressive of the lands' pastoral tradition, symbolize the goddess of Upper Egypt as she flanks the name of the ruler in a *serekh*, or icon representing a palace. In the top half of the obverse (right), King Narmer wears the crown of Lower Egypt. With his standards before him, he surveys the headless bodies of his defeated enemies.

ANCIENT EGYPT: BUILDING THE EGYPTIAN STATE   **249**

11.4 Egyptian dynastic history is known with this precision from three principal sources: the kings and their reigns listed 1) by Manetho, a Greek priest in the 3rd century BCE; 2) in the Turin papyrus from the 19th Dynasty; 3) from inscriptions within tombs that marked the cycles of the star Sirius, which have been calculated to modern calendar years.

Egyptian dynastic history

3000–2686 BCE	Dynasties 1 and 2	The Early Dynastic Period
2686–2181 BCE	Dynasties 3–6	The Old Kingdom
2181–2055 BCE	Dynasty 7 to early Dynasty 11	The First Intermediate Period
2055–1650 BCE	Late Dynasty 11 to Dynasty 13	The Middle Kingdom
1650–1550 BCE	Dynasties 15–17	The Second Intermediate Period
1550–1069 BCE	Dynasties 18–20	The New Kingdom
1069–664 BCE	Dynasties 21–25	The Third Intermediate Period
664–332 BCE	Dynasties 26–31	The Late Period

this was always so, some dynasties clashed with each other, fragmenting Egypt into competing territories. These are referred to as the Intermediate Periods between the Old Kingdom, Middle Kingdom, and New Kingdom [**11.4**].

Building the Pyramids

Egyptians located pyramids to the west of the Nile River, in the land of the dead at the edge of the desert, away from precious, limited fertile ground and in the direction of the setting sun. Even today, the small cap of white Tura limestone casing stones on Khafre's pyramid catches the morning sun [**11.5**, **11.6**]. Between about 2680 and 2180 BCE, pyramids dominated the landscape of the Red Land (Western Desert) west and north of Egypt's Old Kingdom capital at Memphis.

The Giza pyramids [**11.7**] were built during a period of relative calm in the Old Kingdom. Each Giza pyramid called for the labor of a generation to construct a massive tomb to house the body of a dead pharaoh and ensure its preservation so that he might enjoy an afterlife. The archaeologist David Wengrow has pointed to the curious paradox of the enfeeblement and decay of the ruler's physical body and the vigor and perpetuation of political power that his body represented. He argues that preserving the body of the ruler preserved the body politic (the nation). Connected to the pyramids were the valley temples, where priests received the pharaoh's body after his last Nile journey. Once he was entombed, the pharaoh's cult continued to honor his memory and preserve his grave. Food offerings were made daily to the pharaoh-god, and these were drawn from all over Egypt. Egyptian texts are scant about what happened to the offerings: we presume that they were presented to the god or to members of the cult. Service in the mortuary temples was a rotating duty, so offerings were distributed widely among the pharaoh's diverse devotees, knitting a community around him, even after death [**11.8**, p. 252].

Although in the provinces mortuary cults for lesser nobles benefited a broad swath of rotating temple staffs, a centralized project of pyramid building engaged thousands of Egyptians across the Old Kingdom. Construction details help us better

Above: **11.5 Pyramids of Egypt atop the Giza Plateau** at the edge of the Western Desert (of the Sahara), where the Egyptians saw the setting sun enter the realm of the dead. This aerial image shows the grand scale of the pyramids, the regular tombs of nobles of the Old Kingdom in the foreground, and the green fields of the Nile Valley to the left.

Right: **11.6 Today this is all that we see remaining** of the brilliant polished limestone that once covered the Giza Pyramids, erected between 2680 and 2180 BCE. The stone was later recycled to build much of al-Fustat, the mediaeval city of Cairo.

Left: **11.7 Perspective view of the Giza pyramids and associated features.** From left to right, the pyramids of Menkaure, Khafre, and Khufu are all fronted by a mortuary temple that was dedicated to the pharaoh's cult. The causeways extended approximately 656 yards (600 m) to the valley temples, which were on the banks of the Nile. Khentkawes Town (to the right of Menkaure's valley temple) and Heit el-Ghurab (the sites at bottom left) were used as residences for the pyramids' many laborers during construction.

11.8 Egyptians believed life continued after death. This detail from the outer sarcophagus of Khonsu shows a jackal-headed (masked?) priest as the god Anubis preparing the body for eternity after death. This image dates to the New Kingdom, 1,500 years after the great pyramids of Giza, when pharaohs' bodies were hidden in secret tombs. Even without pyramids, the Egyptian notion of preserving the body persisted.

11.9 Depiction of how the pyramids of Giza employed encircling ramps, which allowed for the stones to be dragged into place. Wooden scaffolds used for lifting are shown on the corners of the ramps. The internal chambers (shown in yellow), were built into the interior of the pyramid and the entrances hidden following the application of the final layer of limestone. All evidence of the ramps was removed later.

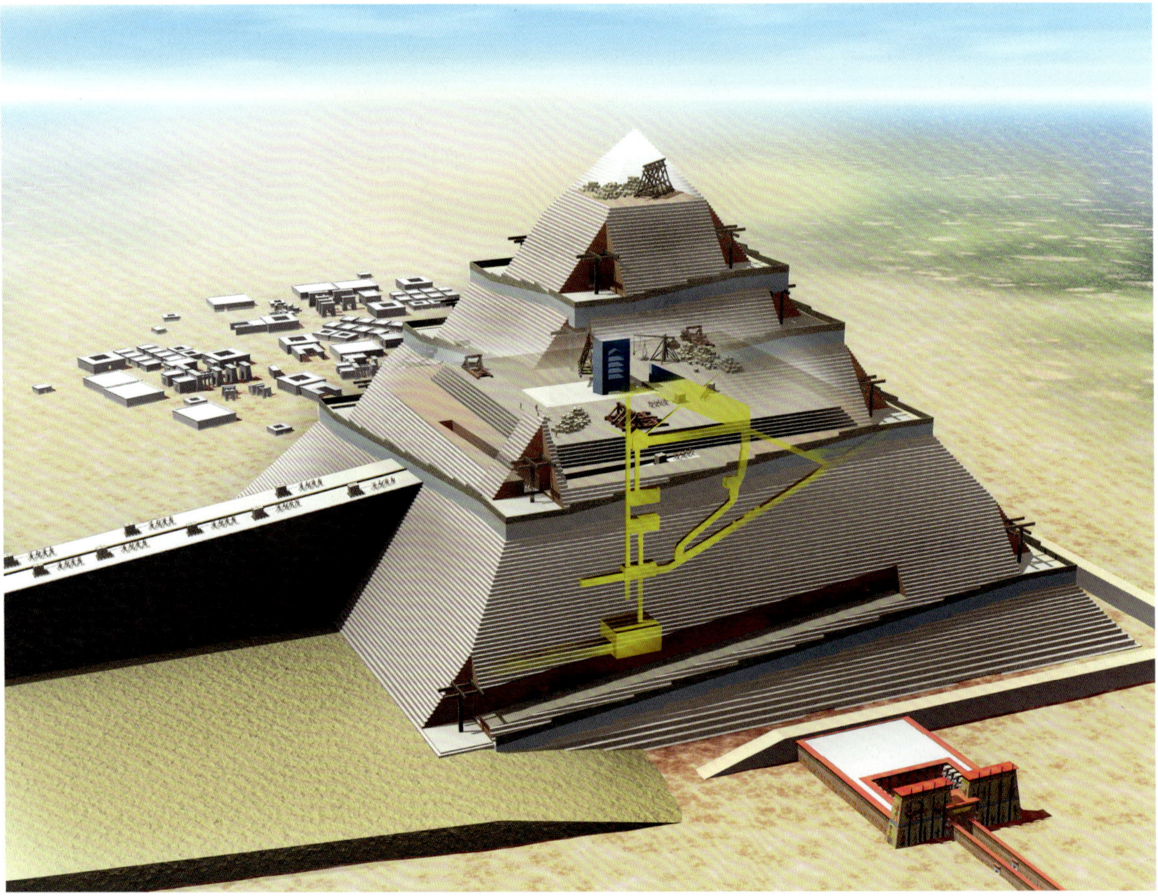

understand the function and meaning of pyramids in ancient Egyptian society. Why did the Egyptians labor for a generation to construct one man's tomb? By deciphering how Egypt mobilized labor, organized work, and supplied it workers, we gain insight into the workings of the Egyptian state, for this was just as much a state-sponsored project as the construction of Lincoln's Memorial was.

With the support of many sponsors, archaeologists, technical specialists, and large teams of students and Egyptian workmen, archaeologists Mark Lehner and Zahi Hawass have uncovered extensive evidence of technical feats that Egyptians accomplished to construct Giza's pyramids. Lehner began his investigations by mapping every inch of the pyramid complex in the old-fashioned way, standing in the hot sun with an optical mapping instrument (a theodolite) and reflector rod. Climbing up and down the huge blocks of Khufu's pyramid, Lehner became interested in the fragments of charcoal and wood in its lime mortar, which led to the first radiocarbon dating of the materials used in pyramid construction. The results were surprisingly old, about four hundred years older than the historical calendar dates previously agreed to by Egyptologists. A compelling explanation exists, however: many hundreds of years after the death of a tree, with its old timbers having been recycled numerous times, valued building and scaffolding materials in the desert were finally burned to make lime mortar. (Chapter 6 on radiocarbon dating discusses other examples of this frequent gap between a target event and a sample's date.) During the days of the Fourth Dynasty pharaohs—Khufu, Khafre, and Menkaure—ancient Egyptians sawed stone with copper tools and grit, using levers and wedges to define and shift great limestone blocks from nearby quarries. They dragged blocks that averaged 2.5 tons in weight on sledges over a specially built, limestone-and-clay path, kept wet to make it slick for the short journey several hundred feet from the quarry. They finished the pyramids with a final layer of polished white Tura limestone quarried across the Nile and floated in on boats, and, working from the top of the pyramid downward, they removed the coiled ramps that had been built into the pyramids' sides, leaving behind a flawless surface [11.9].

THE EGYPTIAN WORKERS' SETTLEMENT Lehner and Hawass also excavated a workers' settlement and adjacent tombs, affording a detailed glimpse of the society of Fourth Dynasty pyramid builders (*c.* 2500 BCE). Workers came from all over Egypt, drawn from an estimated Old Kingdom population of about a million Nile Valley dwellers. Sharply separated from the mortuary complexes by a great wall, a permanent settlement of workers once lived on the Giza Plateau. Known as the Wall of the Crow, it has been clearly visible for millennia, but as is the case with so many features of the Plateau, no one thought much about it before Lehner's Giza mapping project of the 1980s. Both Lehner and Hawass recognized that the sands of the desert had covered mud-brick architecture. In the places where the modern village of Nazlat es-Samaan was expanding, new foundation trenches were turning up Old Kingdom pottery, decayed mud brick, charcoal, and mud sealings that had once secured containers of stored goods (see Chapter 10, p. 239). Their team

11.10 Mark Lehner's map of the work areas and living quarters near the Giza pyramid construction site.

soon discovered a bakery, a fish-processing facility, and the detritus (remnants) of food preparation for thousands of workers, all laid out in a planned town with special-purpose architecture, straight avenues, access to the river, and a cemetery on the rise behind it [**11.10**].

On the walls of their simple mud-brick tombs, pyramid builders inscribed hieroglyphic texts declaring that they had labored in ***phyles***, which were (in the case of pyramid construction) organized work gangs made up of laborers from all over Egypt. The *phyles* system appears to have been a widespread institution in Old Kingdom society, and although it is not comprehensively understood, examples of local *phyles* exist for temple service rotations and other community projects. Young men may have been inducted into *phyles* when they were circumcised, but evidence of similar groups of women having worked at the mortuary temples also survives. Families accompanied the men who labored on construction projects, and they were buried together, with their remains frequently bearing bone deformations and fractures from years of hard labor. Yet these same people had also eaten rich food, including choice cuts of beef, fresh bread, and nutritious beer—not the cheap foodstuff that one would supply to enslaved people or forcibly coerced laborers.

phyles Organized gangs of laborers.

PROVISIONING THE WORKERS To feed up to 20,000 workers at a time, the pharaoh's delegates oversaw a provisioning system that sustained specialists across Egypt, mobilized surplus, and organized its transport to the Giza workmen's town. Archaeologist Robert Wenke directed excavations at Kom al-Hisn, an Old Kingdom regional center in the western Nile Delta region, where extensive, swampy land offered a grassy haven for cattle pasture. In the course of excavations, archaeologists discovered that some of the ceramics at Kom al-Hisn had been imported to the site, as had some foods, such as deep-water fish. The archaeologists also found stamped mud sealings, similar to those at Giza, suggesting that some goods were secured in sealed containers or storage rooms. Studies of both animal remains and charred plant materials point to an emphasis on cattle production. Charred plant remains from Kom al-Hisn included thousands of tiny legume seeds probably grown as animal fodder. The seeds were charred when the Egyptians burned dung—used as a fuel—they had collected from animals confined to stalls, indicating that the seeds had been fed to the animals or crop waste was mixed with dung for fuel. That they were eating crops and weeds, or that fodder crops were grown at all, suggests the supplemental feeding of many animals took place. In other words, the villagers at Kom al-Hisn were raising more animals than their grazing lands could support, so they used some farmland products to feed animals and anticipated imported foods in exchange for surplus cattle.

It is, in fact, the animal bones and their distributions at Kom al-Hisn and Giza that reveal the links between these two Old Kingdom sites [**11.11**]. At Giza, animal remains include a high proportion of meat from cattle, especially their choice cuts. Because the bone assemblage represents only parts of the animal, it appears as if butchering took place at a location separate from Giza, or at least at a facility not yet discovered by archaeologists. The remains of less desirable meats, such as goat and sheep, are more abundant at Kom al-Hisn, although it was an ideal location for raising cattle. Pigs also love swampland, and Kom al-Hisn's inhabitants consumed many of them, more than Giza's inhabitants. With stumpy legs and their constant need for moisture, pigs are unlikely candidates for long-distance transport, and in Egypt's climate, butchery needs to be local. Thus, transporting Kom al-Hisn's cattle to Giza would have been far more practical than shipping pigs. Integrating the data from these excavations offers a glimpse of the complex economy of Old Kingdom Egypt. Bread grains came to Giza from the Nile Valley, cattle from the Delta, and fish from the river.

This economy implies that whether they traveled to Giza to work on the pyramids during the off-season of agricultural fallow—as many did, from all over Egypt—or whether they supplied the workers with surplus food and goods, Egyptians widely supported pyramid construction. In return, they received many benefits. Some were economic rewards, such as the high-quality foodstuffs consumed at Giza or the exchange systems fed by surplus production. Some benefits were political. Egypt under the Old Kingdom pharaoh was united and internally at peace. Except for frontier garrisons and centers for the administrative elite, Old Kingdom Egyptian

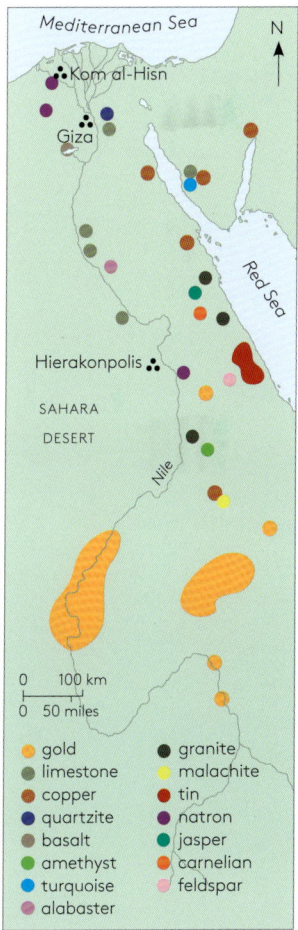

11.11 Map of Giza and the surrounding region indicating the origins of various resources.

11.12 Diorite statue of the Pharaoh Khafre, c. 2570 BCE. This statue is nearly 6 feet (1.8 m) high and originally stood in Khafre's valley temple at the end of the causeway leading up to his pyramid. The falcon, which symbolizes the god Horus as well as a united Egypt, identifies the figure as a pharaoh.

towns had no defensive walls, and most people seem to have lived in dispersed rural settlements in what may have been relative security (in contrast, by this period, 80 percent of the population of Mesopotamia had retreated to walled cities and were in constant conflict with each other). Egypt had ostensibly achieved unity, and pyramid building helped to sustain it.

The greatest benefit of pyramid building was social. A unified Egypt regarded the pharaoh as the "Father of the House of Egypt." His role in raising Nile floods and ensuring fertility was heralded, and ancient Egyptians understood him to be a living god whose bodily manifestation and preservation represented all of Egypt. As the Father, pharaoh also metaphorically assured the continuity of Egypt as a social unit, just as fathers maintain the social cohesion and continuity of households in a patriarchal society. By honoring every pharaoh with a special tomb, Egyptians countered the decay of the very body that manifested the perpetual continuity of Egyptian social order [**11.12**]. Both symbolically and through the practical engagement of Egyptians with each other, the building of pyramids lifted Egyptian society and ensured its preservation.

MONUMENTS AMONG MOBILE COMMUNITIES

Monuments have served to bind together and sustain states running the gamut from ancient Egypt to the American republic, but they may also help to unify other types of society. In Chapter 8, we discussed the Early Neolithic site of Jericho, in the Middle East, which yielded examples of monumental building (the tower and wall) alongside the early signs of agriculture and village life. Communal events and buildings that facilitate and honor social union appear in many shapes and sizes, with some challenging our idea of what is, and is not, monumental. To explore these less familiar forms of monument, we look to a time before the pharaohs in Egypt, to the mobile cattle herders in the Neolithic [11.13]. We will also explore similar communities in India that document both the diverse range of monumental building and the commemoration of community. Although each case is culturally distinct and independent, they nevertheless exemplify a widespread tradition whereby mobile people, not just cities and states, build monuments and shape landscapes to perpetuate their social identities and community.

Sahara: Astronomical Monuments

In the first half of the Holocene era, approximately 10,000 to 6,000 years ago, summer rains brought a flush of new growth across vast swaths of the Sahara and what is now Egypt's Western Desert, bringing grasses, small herbs, and annuals to the drainage bottoms and expanded shorelines of the current silty wastelands of dried lake beds. This plant life could support mobile herders who seasonally led cattle out from the Nile Valley and among various watering holes to graze the late summer growth. Within these Neolithic societies, cattle played a significant role in

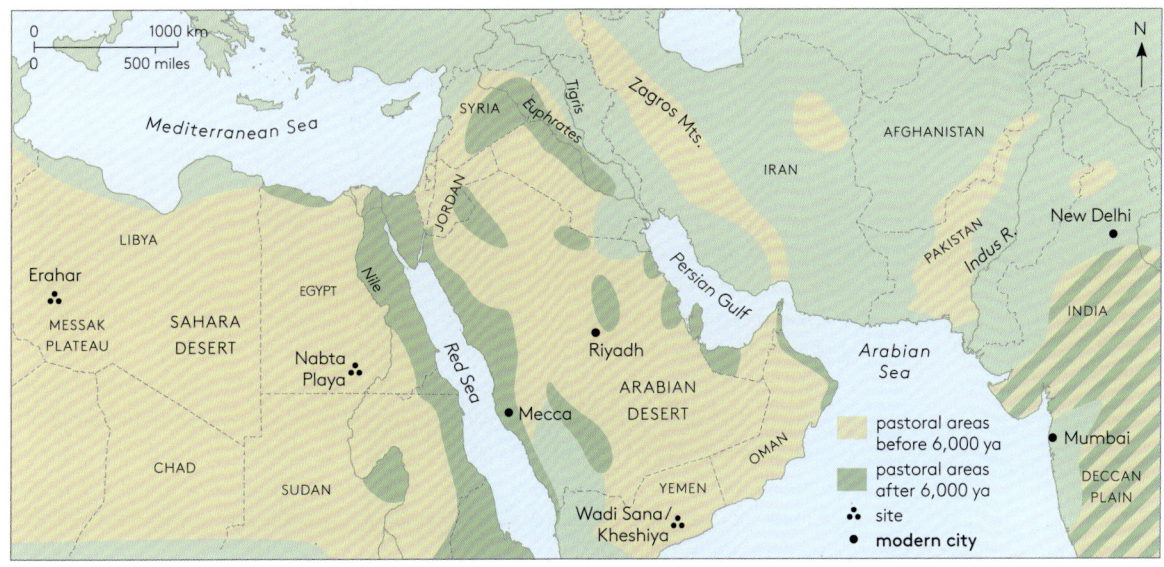

11.13 Map illustrating the extent of herding societies in the Near East and Africa.

tumulus An ancient burial mound.

commemorative practices, whether as the provisions for a great feast that brought together large social groups, with the scene engraved or painted on rocks for posterity, or as sacrifices buried in small-scale stone monuments marking territories for absentee herdsmen.

The Neolithic herders of the Egyptian Western Desert left only scant traces of their campsites, but their elaborate stone monuments survive, aligned to celestial bodies and their movements. The herders deposited markers that referenced a particular time when people were present and signaled to others their presence even when absent. By linking themselves to celestial movements, they acknowledged their own limited human presence across space and time. The Western Desert's Neolithic monuments thus knit events in the heavens with those on Earth.

The construction of megalithic stone uprights at Nabta Playa in Egypt's Western Desert—and their strict alignment with the heavens—required many workers [**11.14**]. Even though these herders were not organized by a pharaoh or provisioned by elaborate institutions of specialized production and exchange, they nonetheless came together for this task. From the resulting congregating and building experiences, their sense of belonging as a community sharing common ground only intensified. Cattle, their sacrifice, and communal meals were clearly important elements of such gatherings as these. Archaeologists found at least one dismembered, sacrificed cow under a Late Neolithic **tumulus** at Nabta Playa [**11.15**]. The sacrifice suggests that people embedded—literally, in this case—the memory of an event within their monuments. The recall of what lies hidden is privileged knowledge, and sharing this knowledge with another person allows for social participation. The Sahara stone uprights and burials demonstrate how monuments can archive memories throughout time; they become useful tools for social connectedness across generations and for the differentiation of insider from outsider in a community constantly on the move.

Constructing a community only begins with building a monument. To stay together and renegotiate social bonds, groups rely on follow-up visits, the retelling of stories, and rituals at the monuments during and after their construction. Archaeologist Savino Di Lernia's team studied the close association between rock art and the burial of dismembered cattle bones on southern Libya's Messak plateau in the central Sahara (Chapter 3 refers to this region as the first anthropogenic landscape). At Erahar, Di Lernia came across three sites of rock art that depicted cattle being sacrificed [**11.16**]. Directly above these carvings on a cliff's edge, his team also discovered the remains of a bull that had been dismembered and burned before being interred in what is called a corbeille monument (a small stone structure). More than forty small-scale stone monuments were found nearby; associated with them were the bones of cattle that had been butchered for meat and marrow, and then buried with flowers and the mace heads used to slaughter them. Erahar demonstrates how the mix of creating rock art and monuments left a lasting memorial to feasts that had taken place 9,000 years beforehand. The archaeological remains reveal a place that people continued to visit, reinscribing themselves into the permanent visible landscape.

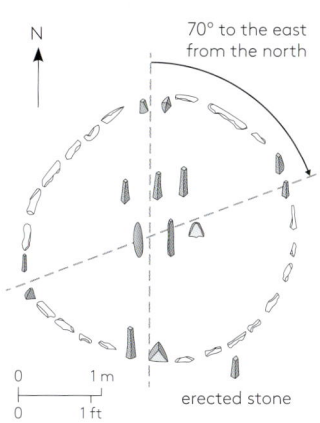

Above, above right: **11.14a, 11.14b Photo and plan of the site of Nabta Playa, an astronomical monument in Egypt's Western Desert.** This monument was created by mobile cattle herders who traversed the savannahs of North Africa *c.* 8000 BCE. The lines of sight align with the summer solstice and the rising of the star Sirius.

11.15 In highland southern Yemen, Joy McCorriston's team excavated a small stone monument (foreground) with a ring of forty-two sacrificed cattle skulls nearby (team measuring in rear). This Neolithic sacrifice and monument construction took place around 4500 BCE, as did its Saharan and Indian analogs.

11.16 Incised rock art at Erahar, Messak Plateau of southern Libya, 7000 BCE. This image spans more than a meter and depicts a bull upside-down (dead) with its head to the right and its horns pointing downward. Incisions to the left and above depict humans in the act of sacrificing the animal.

11.17 **Neolithic ash mounds at Sanganakallu in the Deccan region of South India** were positioned atop natural granitic outcrops, which heightened the mounds' visibility and symbolic value.

South India: Fires and Ash Mounds

In the Sahara, the importance of monuments revolved around the things that were left behind, and the memories of what had occurred, at the associated site. By commemorating feasts and sacrifices, a mobile people created permanent points of reference in the environment and their own cultural landscape.

Ancient mobile communities in southern India appear to have undertaken similar activities. The monuments of Neolithic cattle herders remain prominent along the weathered granite hilltops overlooking the Central Deccan plain. These monuments are not of the expected type; that is, they are not built from permanent rock. Although plenty of stone was available for construction, cattle herders in South India instead formed monumental ash mounds of cattle dung that would be set alight to create great fires [**11.17**].

Archaeologists have long debated the purpose and meaning of these mounds. Some maintain that animals were repeatedly penned near the villages and their waste needed to be torched to quell disease. Although penned cattle are a consistent feature of prehistoric village life in India, only South Indian Neolithic herders created these ash mounds, *c.* 2500 BCE. Dung would have been a valuable fertilizer for the small-grained millets and gram (small summer beans) domesticated by these herders, who were also small-scale farmers. Archaeologist Peter Johansen has argued that by incorporating dung into an ash mound, villagers sacrificed the valuable fertilizer for a common, symbolic purpose. The dung adds to the shared resources needed to create a cultural landscape. Flaring ash fires were an impressive sight, and remnant ash when molded into mounds became a monumental commemoration of such events. Some people even capped the mounds with sterile dirt, sealing previous ash debris (also a potent fertilizer) within them. This example challenges our understanding of what qualifies as monumental, but once its various dimensions are considered—the communal importance of fertilizer, the spectacle of the fires, and the treatment of remains—it becomes quite clear that this activity was a form of monument building.

STONEHENGE AND THE PASTORALIST LANDSCAPE OF NEOLITHIC BRITAIN

Perhaps the best-known archaeological site in the world, England's Stonehenge, has been subject to many interpretations, but it is also a monument that built and sustained a social community [11.18; 11.19, p. 262]. A **henge** is a monument that consists of a circle of stones or timber, and Stonehenge is the grandest of all. Today, its inner ring of **doloritic bluestones**, a metamorphic rock from 124 miles (200 km) away in Wales, stands encircled by an outer ring of upright megalithic limestone blocks known as **sarsen stones**. Some of these sarsens still retain lintels across their tops. The monument would have stood out on the deforested Salisbury Plain where it was located, an area that came to be used for farming and grazing sheep. But is it not surprising that this monument, clearly built by a community, is so often shown without people? Most images of Stonehenge include no humans; in fact, most photographers go to great lengths to avoid showing any. If you exclude people from the picture, it is little wonder that Stonehenge continues to seem "mysterious." But when you put people back into the ancient landscape, as archaeologists do, then the many meanings and practices that characterized Stonehenge societies come into focus.

Stonehenge is part of a large-scale, long-term effort that people in Neolithic Britain (4000–2000 BCE) made to manipulate their surroundings to build and reference a landscape. Over the years, it took much labor to quarry, transport, erect, and

henge A round monument consisting of an earth bank and internal ditch; often includes upright stones or timbers.

doloritic bluestones The inner stones at Stonehenge, brought from the Preseli hills in Wales.

sarsen stones The outer ring of limestone stones at Stonehenge, some of which retain lintels across their tops.

11.18 Stonehenge on the Salisbury Plain of southern England draws a large crowd every year to experience the summer solstice. Its large sarsen stones and lintels (the stones that span the tops) surround smaller bluestones transported from Wales.

reconfigure the standing stones at Stonehenge, the meanings of which also shifted during the passage of time. The monument of Stonehenge began with a pastoral Neolithic people (although even earlier evidence of human interaction with this landscape exists), but once in place, Stonehenge became a touchstone for newer narratives of belonging to a social collective. Such a reframing of Stonehenge's story continues today with neo-Druid ceremonies. If you want to see Stonehenge with people inside—as you should—then visit on Midsummer's Day when huge crowds materialize, or apply for one of the few off-hours visitor passes. As eventually happened at Lascaux Cave (see Chapter 2), the tourists who visit the site pose such a threat to its integrity that English Heritage (the in-trust partner that manages this World Heritage Site) has closed off Stonehenge's inner site to most people, most of the time.

11.19 Excavation of one of the Aubrey Holes of Stonehenge by archaeologist Michael Parker Pearson and his team in 2008. Radiocarbon dates from charcoal in the holes indicate they were part of the first phase of construction at Stonehenge, c. 3100 BCE.

11.20 An early drawing of Stonehenge by William Stukeley, August 1722. Published in 1740 in his book *Stonehenge. A Temple Restor'd to the British Druids*, which popularized his interpretation of the monument as an ancient temple.

Antiquarians Discover Stonehenge

For most of the thousands of years that Stonehenge has stood, it provoked no scientific study. Beginning about four hundred years ago, it caught the interest of gentlemen antiquarians, people with an interest in the sites and artifacts of Antiquity. Possibly the best-known of the seventeenth-century individuals obsessed with the relics of an ancient past was Sir John Aubrey (1626–1697). Aubrey identified a ring of holes that encircle the Stonehenge monument and now bear his name (Aubrey Holes). He was among the first in a series of investigators, including William Stukeley (1719–1740), who identified an avenue leading to or from the standing stones [11.20]. Trenching and digging by various antiquarians led to the discovery of cattle bones, charcoal, and pits dug into the chalk where Stonehenge stood. Sir Flinders Petrie, later famous for his discoveries in Egypt and Palestine, devised a system still in use today for numbering the standing stones. Charles Darwin brought his family for a picnic, dug a few holes, and discovered…earthworms! Earthworm activity raises sediment around stones, contributing to their sinking and burial with the passage of time.

The Building of Stonehenge

By the end of World War II, the field of archaeology stood poised to begin a systematic analysis of Stonehenge, by then many times trenched and probed. Much archaeological study of Stonehenge has focused on how it was built and when. As early as the 1960s, archaeologist Richard Atkinson suggested a construction sequence for Stonehenge [11.21, p. 264]. His sequence assumed that the original builders of Stonehenge had purposely constructed a landscape that might be manipulated

11.21 The Stonehenge we see today is an accumulation of different phases of construction, use, and modification. Initially, Neolithic pastoralists constructed a bank and ditch within which they erected a succession of standing timbers and/or stones. They subsequently shifted these markers and buried the cremated remains of their dead in the left-over "Aubrey holes." A later phase saw another re-location of the bluestones. Finally, the huge sarsen stones were hauled to the site and erected to form the monument we recognize today. These stages took at least six hundred years, but new earthworks, pits, and stone re-arrangements continued long afterwards as later people built their own meanings into Stonehenge.

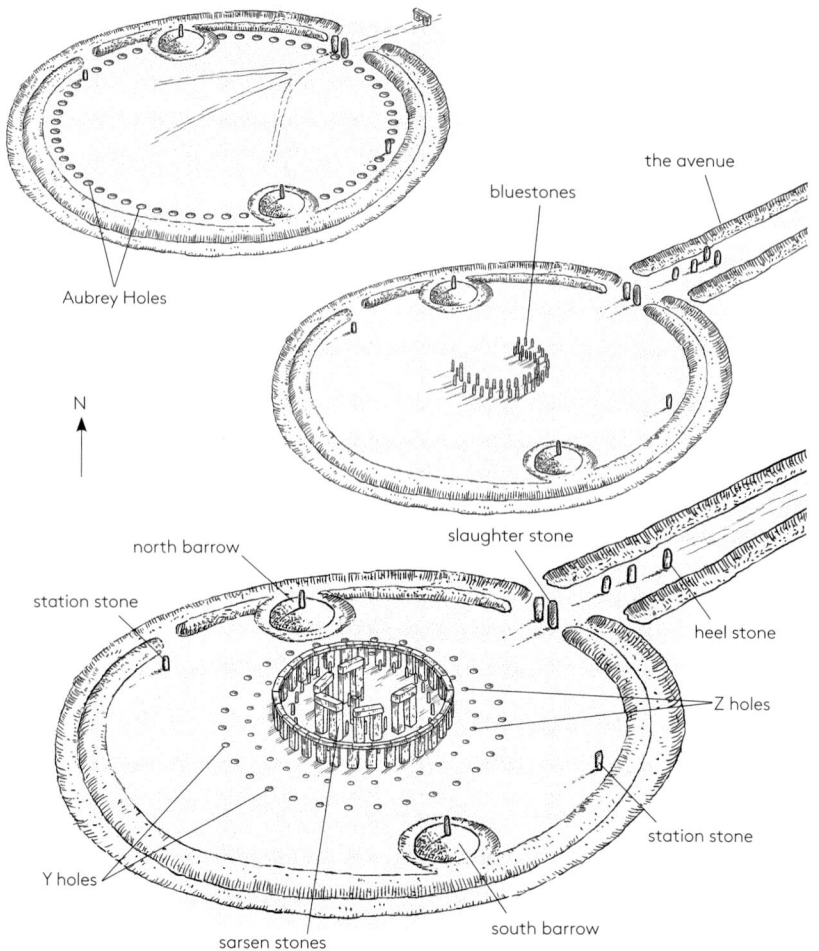

through time, with additions, emplacements, and removals over the course of millennia. Each of these manipulations was linked to social events and the stories that recalled them. Over the last few years, this construction sequence has been further refined with new discoveries. For example, the Stonehenge Riverside Project uncovered a set of pits arranged in a circle by the River Avon. Called Bluehenge, this set of pits may have once held the bluestones now located inside the Stonehenge circle itself.

If the bluestones were indeed moved to Stonehenge, it has proved difficult to date that event; indeed, even dating Stonehenge itself is challenging. If in fact the monument was erected in a single construction, no method exists to date precisely the quarried stones themselves. Radiocarbon dates on organic materials at the bottom of Stonehenge's ancient ditches show that they were dug during Britain's Neolithic period, around 3100 BCE. From one of the holes into which a sarsen stone was set, an antler digging-pick yielded a date of approximately 2500 BCE. Neolithic people, however, were not the first to use the Salisbury Plain: earlier **Mesolithic** pits were possibly used to anchor stones or timbers. Mounds and barrows pre-dating Stonehenge have also left vestiges. One recent discovery is that glaciers carved furrows into the chalk substrate that underlies part of Stonehenge's main avenue, suggesting that this natural orientation along the axis of the summer solstice may have partly inspired the placement of Stonehenge itself, to which perhaps the bluestone ring stones, originally obtained in Wales, were moved.

Experimental archaeology has sought to determine how people at Stonehenge met the challenge of moving massive stones. The quarries from which the stones came have been identified: 30-ton (27 tonne) sarsen stones were from quarries about 8.6 miles (30 km) away, pulled overground with rope-and-timber technology by hundreds of people. Until recently, geologists believed the doleritic bluestone quarries in Wales were close to the ocean and that stones could have been rafted and floated around coastlines and upriver. A study in 2014 of the chemical elements in bluestones now identifies one Welsh source as Carn Goedeg, more than 124 miles (200 km) from Stonehenge and 12 miles (20 km) from the coast. It appears that Neolithic people first transported the bluestones from the quarry to the Bluehenge site near the River Avon. Later, they dug the Aubrey Holes and constructed a ditch and circular bank at Stonehenge itself. Subsequently, the sarsen stones were set in place, the avenue was constructed, and the bluestones brought from Bluehenge to establish an inner ring [**11.22**]. Tiny chips of the bluestones were found in their original sockets at Bluehenge.

Mesolithic The period in Europe falling between the Upper Palaeolithic and Neolithic; refers to the final period of hunter-gatherer cultures before the onset of farming. Its approximate time frame differs across regions.

11.22 Map of Stonehenge and its surrounding landscape. The monument of Stonehenge is connected via the avenue, which turns and intersects the site of Bluehenge beside the River Avon. Further to the east and north lie the settlement of Durrington Walls and monument of Woodhenge. The enigmatic Great Cursus is several hundred years older than Stonehenge and is aligned on the spring and autumn equinoxes. Dozens of barrows (earthen mounds used for tombs) were also raised nearby.

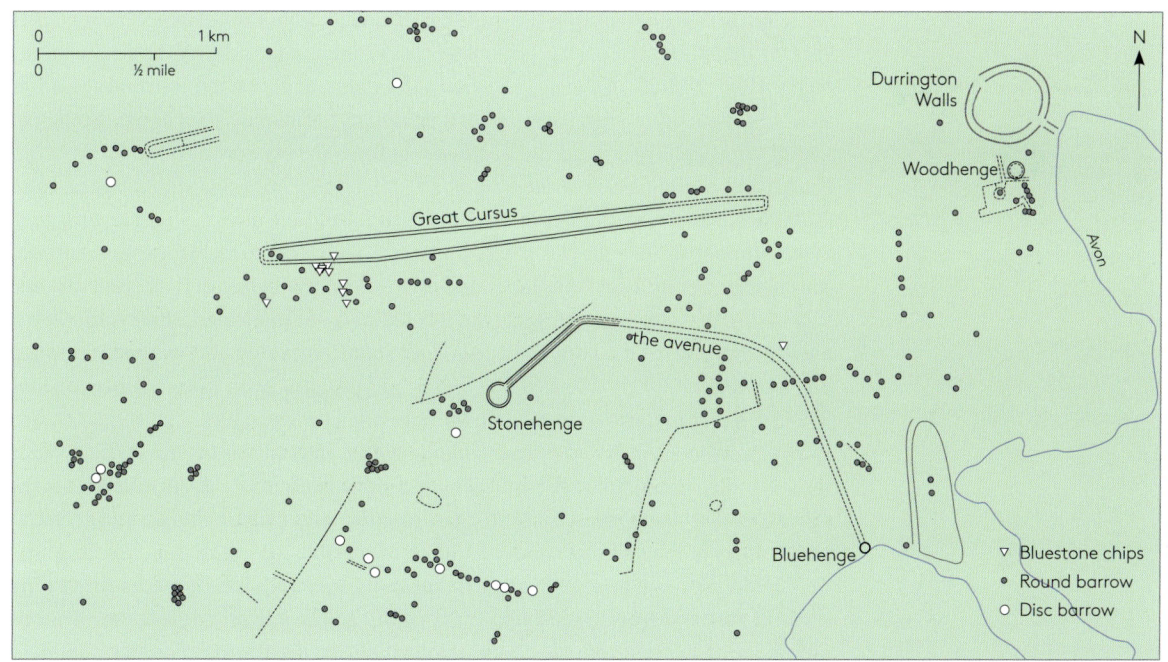

STONEHENGE AND THE PASTORALIST LANDSCAPE OF NEOLITHIC BRITAIN

As it turns out, Stonehenge was part of a complex of sites in the region. Despite its name, nearby Durrington Walls is a relatively flat surface, lacking the permanent monumental aspect of Stonehenge, but its turf and later Iron Age field systems hide some precious clues. Archaeologist Mike Parker-Pearson's team excavating Durrington Walls in 2004 uncovered the stake and wattle (wood and mud plaster) houses of Neolithic people, complete with huge deposits of discarded animal bone, flint cores, and ceramics.

The Neolithic village at Durrington Walls very likely housed Stonehenge's builders. Village occupation began sometime between 2800 and 2100 BCE and lasted no more than 500 years. A close study of the house floors showed that they had been plastered multiple times, perhaps once a season for six seasons. Building the ditch segments around the village took an estimated 220 men, women, and children in each work party. Archaeologists used the stylistic variation of the pottery fragments found in different locales to infer that distinct social groups formed the village of about five thousand people. Individuals from these groups served in cooperative work gangs and built different portions of henge monuments. These kinds of cooperative events were widespread across Britain. New analysis of hundreds of radiocarbon dates for henge monuments suggests that they were constructed very rapidly, appearing over a two-hundred-year period as Neolithic immigrants from Europe further penetrated Britain.

The Purpose of Stonehenge

Stonehenge was built around the same time that Egyptians labored on Khufu's Great Pyramid (*c.* 2580–2560 BCE). Who constructed Stonehenge and why? Since the initial archaeological study of the monument in the 1960s, of greatest importance was the axis of Stonehenge, which consisted of a section of the avenue, a set of parallel banks and ditches leading toward the northeast before curving south to the River Avon. Unearthed in the day of Stukeley, *c.* 1740, the avenue contains the so-called Heel Stone, a sarsen stone that lies on the axis of the summer solstice, when an observer in Stonehenge can see the sun rise in the northeast over the Heel Stone. In the 1960s, astronomer Gerard Hawkins elaborated on these known astronomical observations, suggesting that Stonehenge was constructed as a sophisticated observatory with precise sightings of the summer and winter solstices, spring and winter equinoxes (the sun rises and sets due east and west), and perhaps even lunar eclipses.

Since that time, efforts to explain Stonehenge's function have focused on its use as an astronomical calendar. Several challenges surround this interpretation. What we see today is not what the builders and their immediate descendants always saw. Moreover, the earliest and most popular theories of Stonehenge as a celestial observatory employed little understanding of the archaeological data from the site. Archaeologist Clive Ruggles brought a nuanced appreciation of astronomy to his study of Stonehenge and reasoned that people did not require the huge stone monument to make astronomical observations that could be determined with modest wooden markers. The most important calendrical events marked at Stonehenge were midsummer and midwinter. If Stonehenge is a monument marking these dates, the question remains, why were these dates so important?

Looking to the sky is one way to understand Stonehenge, but archaeologists have broadened their studies to understand better the cultural landscape, including other anthropogenic modifications of the surroundings and careful analysis of the temporal sequence of the monument that still stands. When modern farming encroached very near to Stonehenge's actual ring, some of the earlier observed mounds and banks were displaced, and a World War I airfield flattened part of the surrounding area. Road construction cut through the avenue, severing Stonehenge's connection to the River Avon. Even as new theories emerged to explain the monument's purpose, its broader context within the landscape was in danger of being lost. In recent studies of Stonehenge's wider landscape, archaeologists have discovered a number of new elements and sites.

Stonehenge's landscape includes nearby Durrington Walls [**11.23**], the River Avon to which Stonehenge is linked by a causeway, the Great Cursus monument of earthen banks linking to a number of Neolithic barrows, and other features of the Salisbury Plain. Although many of the barrows, or earthen mounds, that dot

11.23 Floors of wattle-and-daub houses discovered at Durrington Walls. Although the frail walls long ago decayed, the floors appear as darkened soil atop the chalk substrate. Excavators found a charcoal-filled hearth in the center of the house. Around this hearth they recognized the indentations in the floor (visible near the center of this photo as a light-colored square with a pit in its center) caused by the knees of people tending the fire.

the area have long been prominent, many of Salisbury Plain's larger features were recognized only via aerial photography, a remote-sensing technique available since World War I. Crop marks, or differential patterns in agricultural fields, show the clear outlines of ditches and pits invisible on the surface. At Durrington Walls, the earthen embankment and ditch enclose a huge ring of holes that once held circles of upright timbers. Only 230 feet (70 m) to the south is Woodhenge, a smaller circle of postholes for massive timber uprights.

In more recent excavations—the most prominent being the Stonehenge Riverside Project of 2003–2009 and the Stonehenge World Heritage Site Project of 2008–archaeologists discovered new sites in the Stonehenge landscape and were able to tease apart some of the chronological events that explain the remains we see today. To do so, they have used multiple geophysical sensing techniques, such as ground-penetrating radar (GPR), which generates refracted underground waves from a beacon dragged slowly over carefully smoothed ground surfaces. To better understand the Neolithic landscape, Parker-Pearson and his associates launched the Stonehenge Riverside Project. As Parker-Pearson tells it, he was visiting Stonehenge with a Malagasy colleague, Ramilisonina, who was incredulous that Parker-Pearson did not know what the stones represented. Of course, they stood for the ancestors, said Ramilisonina. Stone is for the dead. Wood is for the living. That dichotomy underlies much Malagasy ritual regarding the treatment of the dead, who are regularly memorialized with stone monuments. In the early 1900s, archaeologist William Hawley had uncovered extensive evidence of human cremation while digging around the Aubrey Holes. Re-examination of some of these burials after 2008 showed that men, women, and children were buried at Stonehenge. Cremations disposing of the dead commenced there approximately 3000 BCE, before the standing stones were erected.

Whether Ramilisonina and Parker-Pearson were correct—their assertion was, after all, based on the ethnographic traditions of far-away Madagascar—it led Parker-Pearson and the Riverside team to study Durrington Walls, where people had clearly lived at least part-time and erected huge wooden poles.

Whether 200 or 5,000 people built Stonehenge, a multitude certainly visited there, feasting on pigs and cattle at Durrington Walls, with some traveling a great distance to do so. The chemical analysis of animal teeth [**11.24**] recovered at Durrington Walls points to the diets of ancient cattle and pigs that lived on soils far away from the Salisbury Plain chalklands and likely came from many different herds across the country, then transported to Durrington Walls and consumed there. All the animals were mature, and the absence of young pigs and calves strongly suggests that stockbreeding (the breeding and raising of livestock) was not local [**11.25**].

If the Neolithic people in Britain were pastoralists, then they gathered at Durrington Walls and Stonehenge for feasting. The immediate radius of these sites could not have supported, on a regular or permanent basis, the animal herds required for such large, labor-intensive gatherings. What the British chalklands could sustain, though, was a smaller community anchored at Durrington Walls that welcomed

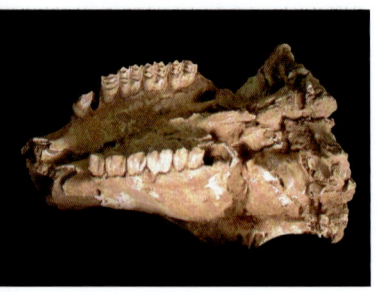

11.24 The age and chemistry of cattle teeth, as seen with this archaeological find, can provide information on herd structure, last diet (microwear on teeth), and life geography of the animal. This cow came from Neolithic Yemen.

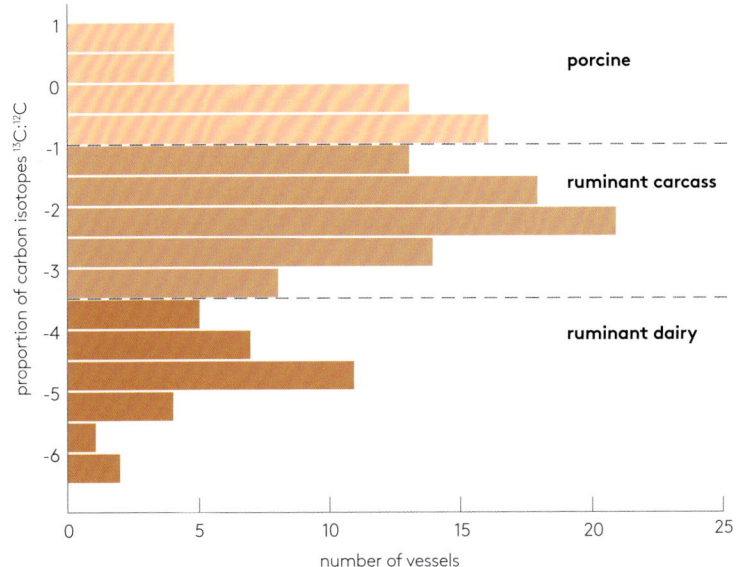

11.25 Isotopic signature of animal fat found on pottery at Durrington Walls. The ratio of carbon isotopes ^{13}C and ^{12}C (see pp. 127–29 and pp. 282–83) reveal where animals consumed their food. Most of the pottery included traces of fat from ruminants (cattle), but porcine (pig) fat and ruminant dairy (cow milk) were also present.

their widespread folk to midsummer and midwinter feasts. At these times, men and women could honor the dead through their communal participation in feasting, in construction projects, in ceremonies, and in reinforcing genealogies that linked the living to the dead and to each other. To fulfill this social need and obligation, Neolithic pastoralists constructed the physical landscape of the Salisbury Plain.

The Stonehenge Landscape through the Ages

The Salisbury Plain of today bears faint resemblance to the Stonehenge landscape of its Neolithic builders. Their memories are long gone, and the surviving stones are markers of newer traditions and later institutions. The timbers of the henges have rotted; the lynchets (long surface mounds delineating fields) bear witness to the traces of Iron Age plows. The ditches of the henges have been filled, enclosures mounded, barrows piled up and eroded, the causeways all but obliterated. The World War I airfield has been dismantled and the old road alongside Stonehenge rerouted. If Stonehenge was, in fact, used to make calendrical-astronomical observations, they are no longer accurate, as the very orbit of Earth has shifted. The Druids—elite Britons from 2,400 years ago who worshiped pre-Roman gods in nature—may have flocked to Stonehenge, but they did not build it.

Stonehenge still remains in use today, primarily as a World Heritage Site (not unlike Uluṟu in Australia's Northern Territory; see Chapter 4) owned and managed by the British government, and by neo-Druids and the environmental movement to which they are linked. In the interests of preservation, most visitors experience the landscape and take in Stonehenge itself from a distance. We can thank Aubrey for the early mistaken identification of Stonehenge as a Druidic creation. He was correct, though, that the builders of Stonehenge preceded the Romans, and in 1660 when he made his determination, no field of archaeology existed to supplement his Classical sources. Neo-Druidic practices venerate nature, and so every year the New Age Druid order converges at Stonehenge for a dawn ceremony to celebrate the summer solstice (Midsummer's Day, June 21). It is but one more expression of the forming and re-forming of Stonehenge, the place's continued history as a communal monument.

NORTH AMERICA: THE HOPEWELL EARTHWORKS

Our final example of a consequential monument brings us back to North America, in Southern and Central Ohio, 350 miles (a little more than 563 km) to the west of the Lincoln Memorial in Washington, D.C. [**11.26**]. Between 1,600 and 2,000 years ago, the Hopewell people built hundreds of mounds in the Ohio region. We do not know for sure how these individuals might have self-identified; the Hopewell Earthworks take their name from a Euro-American landowner, one Mordecai Hopewell, whose property included what came to be known as the Hopewell Mound Group. This parcel

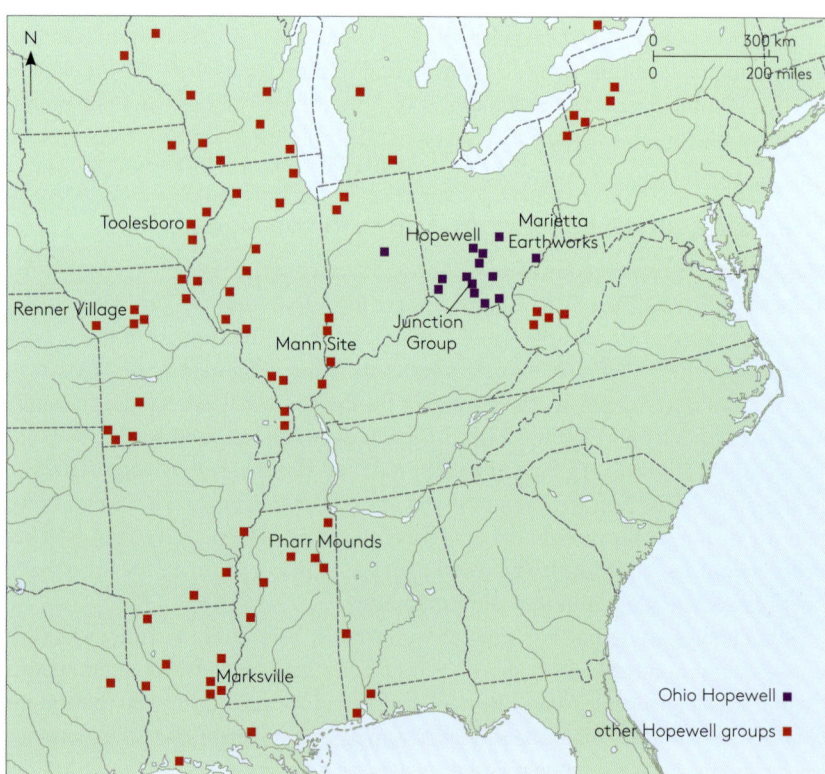

11.26 Map showing the wide distribution of earthworks across eastern North America. The Ohio Hopewell shared similar traditions, such as horticulture with native plants and burials within mounds, with related communities as far away as Canada and the Gulf of Mexico.

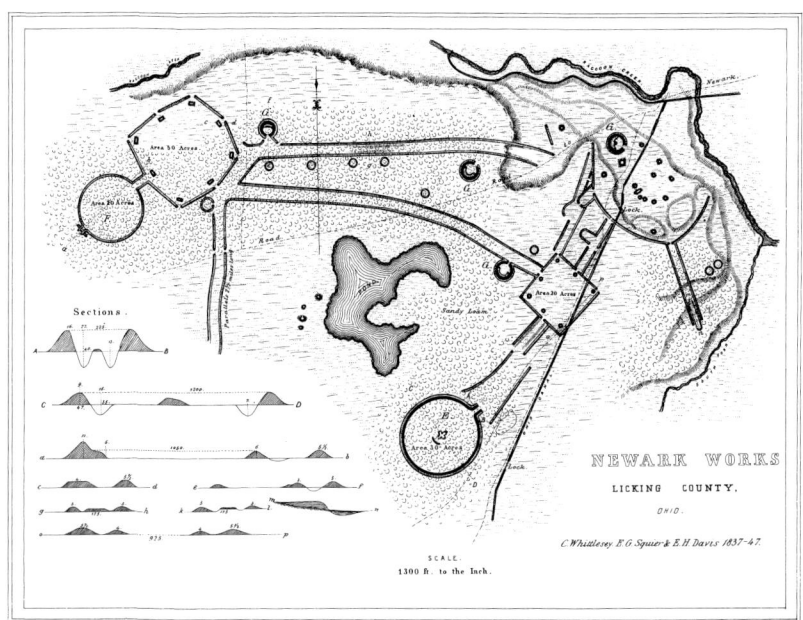

11.27 Map of the Newark Works in southern Ohio from Squier and Davis's *Ancient Monuments of the Mississippi River Valley*, published in 1848.

of land included an enclosure surrounded by more than 2.5 miles (4 km) of earth and stone embankment walls, and more than forty mounds. The ancient builders used silt and gravel from different sources to compile an enclosing wall with distinctly colored layers, and even created a stable feature for holding water. Similar mound groups exist across the Scioto Valley, the Newark area, and the Little Miami River regions of southern Ohio. The Hopewell people had clearly inherited aspects of an earlier tradition, known as Adena, that resulted in the erection of earthen mounds associated with burials in eastern America during the **Early Woodland Period**. Given its impressive style and underlying tradition, the Hopewell Mound Group stands as the most impressive American monument of its day.

Hopewell first entered the world stage in 1845 when Ephraim Squier, an engineer, and Edwin Davis, a medical doctor, produced detailed maps of the mounds. Together, they financed and supervised the rapid excavation of nearly two hundred mounds, collecting artifacts and information for their *Ancient Monuments of the Mississippi River Valley*, the very first publication of the Smithsonian Press in 1848. The book was not a financial success; Squier and Davis disagreed vehemently throughout its publication and parted on bitter terms shortly thereafter [**11.27**]. Yet this seminal work showcased Ohio's Hopewell Earthworks as one of North America's greatest cultural landscapes and simultaneously raised questions about their construction and purpose that remain the focus of archaeological research today.

Following Squier and Davis's excavations, subsequent archaeologists continued to dismantle mounds, recovering burials, often cremations, and offerings that included ornate items made from raw materials brought from distant regions: marine shell

Early Woodland Period
A period of North American ancient history, 2,600–1,800 years ago.

11.28 Hopewell people buried this carved stone tobacco pipe in the shape of a frog in one of the Mound City earthworks. The pipe bowl is in the back of the frog. Other effigy pipes exist in the forms of otters, beavers, felines, and various birds.

11.29 Copper effigy claws, made of cold-hammered copper and recovered from the Hopewell mounds around Chillecothe.

from the southeast, shark's teeth from the Gulf of Mexico, obsidian from the Rocky Mountains, sheet mica from the Blue Ridge Mountains cut into animal, geometric, and anthropomorphic shapes, even copper from the shores of Lake Superior [**11.28**, **11.29**]. The frequency of offerings varies across time but generally shows a steady sequence of construction events. Archaeologist Mark Lynott's analysis of the catalog of radiocarbon dates from all the Hopewell mounds (including the Hopeton Earthworks built on a terrace of the Scioto River in Ohio) suggests that mound groups and earthworks were constructed over a period of several hundred years, a fairly rapid accumulation that nonetheless required several generations to complete. Others argue for a longer time range; the issue remains unresolved.

Excavations inside the region's enclosures and under mounds have uncovered postholes and debris from massive timber structures that pre-dated the mounds. At Mound City (also part of the Hopewell complex in Ohio), James Brown's excavations in 1963 revealed crematory basins with ashes and burnt bone beneath several mounds, and such deposits suggested that Hopewell builders deliberately covered these areas of burial activity with earth—rapidly, it seems, so that no layer of humus formed through exposure before more sediment was added to an individual mound. As archaeological documentation and precision increased, the variety of remains and trenches revealed a general pattern: a layout of paired circles and squared circles (what archaeologists call "squircles") emerged at many monuments [**11.30**]. Alignments of monument groups were visible across the landscape, and enclosure walls, borrow pits, and axis avenues were added as later additions to existing sites. Trenching and mound removal also offered stratigraphic evidence that people had returned to existing mounds and inserted offerings and burials, often many centuries after the original activity.

These revelations led archaeologists then to reconsider another lingering question: Where exactly did the Hopewell people live? New geophysical remote-sensing technologies have sought to detect residences through the nondestructive mapping of the subsurface at many Hopewell sites [**11.31**]. With a magnetometer, changes in soil composition (e.g., the later fill of postholes and ditches, or house floors of clay), and especially the magnetic signature left by a fire, register very clearly as anomalies. This instrument generates large-scale spatial displays that effectively map the subsurface remains of constructed landscapes. Its contribution to Hopewell archaeology has been tremendous: now, strategic test excavations can establish dates and building sequences for the accretive construction of mound groups and determine when mounds were revisited, modified, and remodeled over several centuries. Geophysical techniques themselves have yet to find Hopewell houses, but they have documented monumental wooden architecture—big rectilinear buildings—and more modestly scaled rings of timber uprights, reminiscent of Woodhenge on Salisbury Plain. These represent previously unknown components of Hopewellian monumental landscapes.

Only recently has the work of archaeologists Paul Pacheco, Jarrod Burks, and Dee Ann Wymer unearthed multiple domestic structures in the Hopewell region.

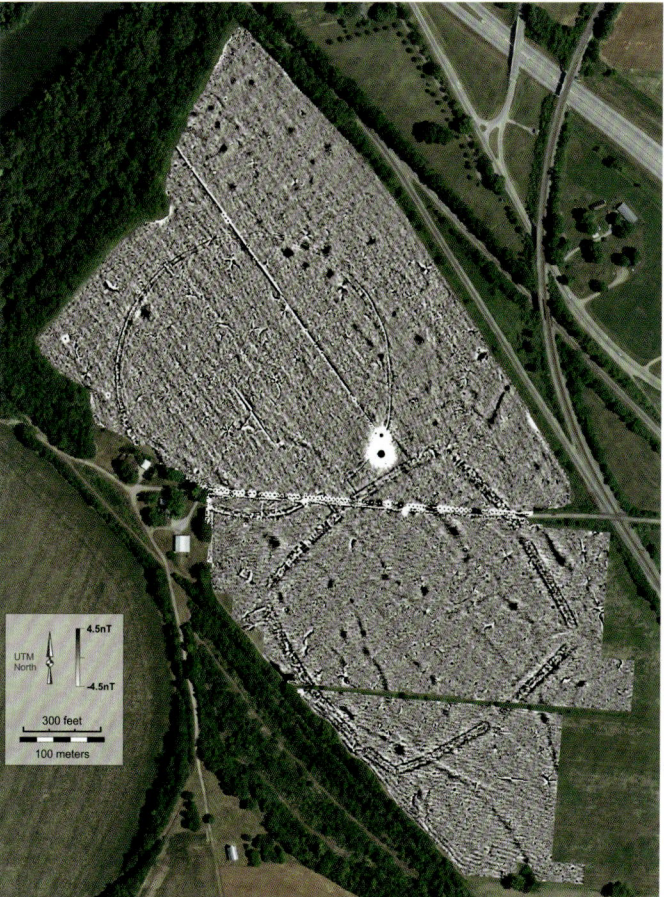

Above: **11.30 The high mound at Seip Earthworks, Chillecothe region.** Like Hopewell, Hopeton, and Newark (see 11.27, p. 271), Seip Earthworks includes a circle and squircle layout. The high mound has been reconstructed after excavations in the early twentieth century revealed at its core a timber chamber with burials.

Left: **11.31 Magnetic gradiometer survey results at the High Bank Works,** a large Hopewell earthwork complex in southern Ohio. The earthwork, a large circle connected to an octagon of similar size, is part of Hopewell Culture National Historical Park.

Domesticated Wild

11.32 Image of domesticated edible chenopodium
(*Chenopodium berlandieri*), one of several crops found at Hopewell sites, as rendered here in a computational image obtained with a microscope. This image uses electron scatter to map the surface of small samples. The domesticated example here is larger and has a thinner seed coat, traits selected for by the Hopewell people.

From the domestic refuse recovered at limited residential hamlets of two to three families, it is clear that the Hopewell people practiced crop cultivation on a modest scale using native crops domesticated in the American Southeast: small barley (*Hordeum pusillum*), chenopodium (*Chenopodium berlandieri* [**11.32**]), sumpweed (*Iva annual*), maygrass (*Phalaris caroliniana*), and sunflower (*Helianthus annuus*). These long served as supplements to gathered foods: acorns and hickory nuts, wild game, fish, and birds. None of these resources offers a food base with sizable and dependable surpluses, though, nor did Hopewell communities build permanent villages around permanent fields or keep livestock. In short, the domiciles found probably housed labor crews living in the Hopewell region on a temporary basis.

Why Did the Hopewell People Build Earthworks?

The Hopewell who built monuments apparently did so as traveling work groups. Few families seem to have lived in nearby hamlets, yet the impressive earthworks of the Scioto Valley, Newark area, and Little Miami River would have required fairly large groups of laborers to build them in a relatively short period. Over several generations, these dispersed people congregated in work groups, scraping away tons of topsoil before erecting giant circles, squared enclosures, berm-flanked causeways, and grand entrances. Archaeologists can calculate how much earth was moved and how many human-hours this kind of effort took; in the earthworks, they can discern deliberate phases of coating in reddish, yellowish, or darkened soil. Some uncovered post and timber structures of significant size could have housed people temporarily, but traces of permanent villages, middens of domestic trash, or storage facilities have yet to emerge.

The newest excavations have revealed the presence of many sizable cooking facilities, for instance, at the Hopewell Mound Group and Steel Group in the region. Given the absence of extensive Hopewell settlements, archaeologists have long assumed that the earthworks served as foci for ceremonies and gatherings after their construction, rendering these earthworks as markers in the landscape—archives—of not only funerary events but also living societies. Enormous earth ovens, meant to steam food sufficient for a feast, would have served significant numbers of individuals who had traveled great distances to comingle. The Hopewell monuments thus served to unite dispersed small communities that forged a strong social bond through their shared experiences: clearing the forest; preparing the ground; building earthworks; burying the dead at, and then revisiting and bringing offerings to, these primarily ceremonial centers.

Similarly to the Neolithic herders at Stonehenge and Egyptian farmers along the Nile, Hopewell people constructed and moved within a cultural landscape shaped by generations, one rich in narratives and meanings of social connectedness. The Hopewell were on the move, foraging diverse resources and cultivating minor crops as they made their way. They depended on the monuments to anchor their lives and to perpetuate their values and rituals in a landscape of their own making. Such a landscape as that created by the Hopewell is a feature of our Anthropocene, for the cultural inheritance it passes along to humans becomes a niche for the success of future generations born into a social world.

Chapter Questions

1. How were the pyramids of Giza built? Who constructed them? In what ways do archaeologists believe the pyramids have shaped the people of Egypt?
2. Discuss several instances of monumental activity by people who were mobile. Use Saharan and South Indian communities as your examples.
3. Explain how Stonehenge has come to be understood in the context of its wider landscape, and how the study of such places as Durrington Walls may help us understand the full role of Stonehenge.
4. Compare the Hopewell Mounds with Stonehenge. Why do archaeologists believe both were places of congregation?

Additional Resources

Hawass, Zahi, and Lehner, Mark. "Builders of the Pyramids," *Archaeology* 50 (1997): 30–43.

Lehner, Mark. *The Complete Pyramid.* London, UK: Thames & Hudson, 1997.

Lynott, Mark J. *Hopewell Ceremonial Landscapes of Ohio.* Oxford, UK: Oxbow Books, 2015.

McCorriston, Joy, Harrower, Michael, Martin, Louise, and Oches, Eric. "Cattle Cults of the Arabian Neolithic and Early Territorial Societies," *American Anthropologist* 114 (2012): 45–63.

Parker-Pearson, Michael, and the Stonehenge Riverside Project. *Stonehenge: Solving the Mysteries of the Greatest Stone Age Monument.* New York: The Experiment, 2014.

Wengrow, David. "Rethinking Cattle Cults in Early Egypt: Towards a Prehistoric Perspective on the Narmer Palette," *Cambridge Archaeological Journal* 11 (2001): 91–104.

CONSPICUOUS CONSUMPTION
Feasts, Burials, and Sacrifice

12

Open any fashion magazine, or watch any ceremony, and you are likely to encounter conspicuous consumption. Consuming rare treats, such as a carefully aged wine from a top vineyard, is often done in public with a great deal of pomp and showmanship. A special vessel, such as a crystal goblet or flute, may be used to serve and display the wine. Prior to drinking it, a designated consumer may remark on its color and smell, and then take only a small sip before remarking on its flavor. Throughout this experience, others observe the drinker and wait for his or her final pronouncement on the wine's quality. If it is declared acceptable, others will be served, and then they, too, can participate in the ritual of drinking the beverage.

This kind of conspicuous consumption is common in many human societies, and it has its roots in the feasting traditions of Antiquity. Exotic animals, uncommon fruits, and dishes that were the result of hours of labor were put on display prior to their consumption. Feasting required the generation of an enormous surplus of food, which could be piled high, stacked, or spread out to convey a sense of abundance and wealth. Unconsumed food also transmitted the secondary message of conspicuous consumption: a society's ability to waste or stockpile food that might otherwise be needed for its very survival.

Over the centuries, the practice of conspicuous consumption included all kinds of objects in addition to rare or lavish food and drink. In Denmark and Britain some 2,400–2,200 years ago, valuable metal wealth was deposited in lakes, rivers, and bogs, as were large quantities of swords, axes, shields, torques, armbands, and other ornaments. Both the mass feasting and disposal of valuable materials are examples of conspicuous consumption—often a method by which elite groups establish and maintain power. Displays of wealth and prestige are important in preserving status, and gift-giving and the hosting of feasts establish a debt or the expectation of reciprocity. But perhaps most significantly, conspicuous consumption is heedless, and frequently deliberately so, to the consequences for sustainability.

Much of the present damage to the environment may indeed be traced back to some form of conspicuous consumption. The archaeological record shows a widespread pattern of wasteful display, with significant impacts on the evolutionary context of human history. Here, we will explore several parallel prehistoric cases in which humans engaged in conspicuous consumption and generated the resources needed to sustain it.

Chiefs and Hoards 278

Feasting 279

Residue Analysis 282

Reciprocity 284

The Ultimate Sacrifice: Human 285

Europe: The Burial of Viking and Anglo-Saxon Ships 290

Is Conspicuous Consumption Inevitable? 293

Opposite The Wandsworth Shield was discovered in the mud of the Thames River, in southwest London, following dredging operations in 1849. The shield was made *c.* 200 BCE and was deposited in the river as part of a ceremonial offering.

Key Concepts

- Feasting, which both forms and maintains important social ties, as an important avenue of conspicuous consumption, and as evidenced in Inka culture

- The archaeological analysis of chemical residues to understand how feasting and food exchange occurred in the past

- The concept of conspicuous consumption as it relates to human sacrificial burials at Ur in Mesopotamia

- How large-scale burials also served as a form of conspicuous consumption in the human past, as evidenced at Sutton Hoo in England

CHIEFS AND HOARDS

At Waldalgesheim, in Germany's Rhine Valley, a farmer accidentally discovered, in 1869, a wooden chamber beneath a burial mound and the remains of a two-wheeled chariot. Also interred with the chariot were jewelry, buckets, and flagons (vessels with a handle and spout) that may have been used to serve drinks. The finest objects recovered were a gold torc (heavy necklace), bracelet, and arm ring, all intricately decorated. The burial was dated to *c.* 330 BCE, and it remains one of the most important discoveries associated with the Early Celtic Period. Why had so much material wealth been buried at the site? Another Celtic burial, unearthed in Ireland in the 1890s and known as the Broighter Hoard, included several pieces of La Tène-style goldwork (characteristic of Celtic artisans), among them a replica of a boat, torques, and a gold bowl. A **hoard**, as its name implies, was something buried as a mass and is perhaps best understood as a sacrifice or votive offering (something offered as part of a promise or vow), as some of the interred implements were never used, and others deliberately ruined before being discarded.

What does it mean to dispose of valuable objects by throwing them in a lake or burying them in a grave? Why would this wealth be discarded? Archaeologist Richard Bradley has long considered the cycles of sacrificing metals in rivers and lakes in Britain, comparing the disposal of weapons during the **Bronze Age** (2,500–800 BCE in Britain) with a similar cycle of metal disposal later in the Iron Age (800 BCE–50 CE in Britain). Bradley has suggested the destruction of metal wealth was a form of conspicuous consumption that had particular social aims. A sacrifice, such as a sword deposited in a lake by a chief, may have been directed to the gods, but it also exhibited the power and ability of the chief to accumulate surplus that he could afford to waste. It is a sign to potential followers: "Stick with me. I can provide enough to trade for luxuries, to waste in sacrifice and burial, and to feed my dependents." In the Thames Valley of Iron Age Britain, these sacrifices were placed at the boundaries of major tribal territories. We previously encountered agricultural surplus in Chapter 10 when discussing the Maya and the Khmer kings from Angkor Wat, where cities and their hierarchical societies were fueled by surplus. Wasting surplus, or the specialized, expensive goods that surplus can buy, is one way to compete with other chiefs for the persuasive power of followers; it became a sort of costly signaling in social competition.

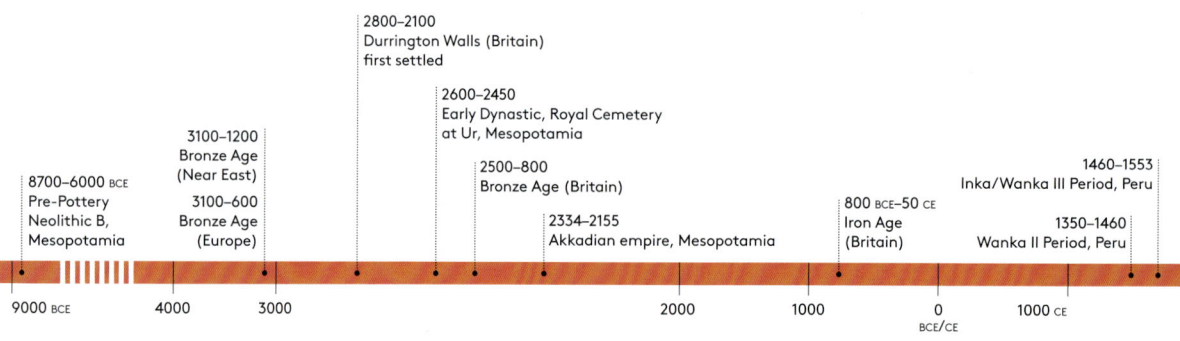

FEASTING

If the emerging elites, rulers, and chiefs of complex societies were able to waste valuable materials in a bid for power, they also conspicuously consumed surplus staples, such as grain and meat. In Chapters 10 and 11, we learned how the Old Kingdom pharaohs used agricultural surplus to feed the builders of the pyramids, but elites also consumed farming surplus directly and in large quantities. Feasts offer strong incentives and support for social gatherings, and the hosts of great feasts can mobilize people to congregate and provide labor for other tasks, as builders, warriors, or political supporters. How can archaeologists detect ancient feasts, events that on their own might not have left behind imposing monuments, conspicuous burial mounds, or treasure?

Chapter 11 introduced us to Durrington Walls, a Neolithic village near Stonehenge (built approximately 2500 BCE) in southern England. Here, archaeologists discovered the still-jointed bones of big meaty animals, such as pigs, cattle, and aurochs (wild cattle), among the ruins of infrequently occupied houses. Because the remains were those of sizable animals that could feed many people at one sitting (unless the meat was preserved) and were discarded with meat still on the bone [**12.1**], the evidence suggests that enormous feasts did take place at this location. This has led archaeologists to envision the landscape of Stonehenge and Durrington Walls as a place for the gathering of widespread folk to feast, and where the dead (both women and men) might be honored. Through this form of conspicuous consumption—and

hoard A mass burial of objects.

Bronze Age A period from 3100 to 600 BCE in Europe; the Near East also had a Bronze Age (3000–1200 BCE). The period when bronze was used widely to make tools, weapons, and other instruments varied from region to region, and in the New World, bronze was never used before the sixteenth century CE (Spanish Conquest).

12.1 Excavation of faunal remains and flint blades from Durrington Walls, southern England. These deposits indicate that animals were butchered and consumed on site, and in great numbers. These bones, and their context as jointed (conjoined) in discard, support the hypothesis of large feasts taking place in association with ceremonies at Stonehenge. Bones still articulated suggest a waste of some meat, a sign of plentiful resources for feasts.

their knowledge and inscribing of the landscape—the people of Salisbury Plain expressed their connectedness. No evidence of a social hierarchy exists, but rather a conspicuous activity the people shared among the entire community.

Faunal remains are by now a familiar type of evidence for past human activities, but additional approaches help detect what people ate and in what form it was consumed. Alcoholic beverages, such as beer and wine, as well as the materials used to produce them, are another critical avenue for the archaeological study of conspicuous consumption.

Alcohol

Feasts mean not only eating and drinking in vast quantities, but also consuming specific forms of food and drink that are expensive to make. Crafting beer requires a lot of grain. Ethnographic studies of traditional grain brewing in West African villages indicate that between 15 and 30 percent of a small farmer's grain harvest is commonly consumed in the preparation for a beer festival [**12.2**]. Enormous quantities of wood are also burned while brewing beer, not to mention the labor in harvesting and processing the grain used to produce it. As described in Chapters 8

12.2 Preparation of millet beer in modern Burkina Faso in West Africa. The millet is first sprouted (malted), then boiled to a mash, to which yeast is added to hasten fermentation. Although creating it is women's work, this beer is mostly consumed by men.

and 10, farming practices cleared away ancient forests and native plants and replaced them with cultivated grains and weeds. Not all farming efforts created food, though; some of them yielded alcohol, which converted otherwise staple food into a highly processed (and costly) beverage. Early Greek and Roman authors, such as Strabo and Pliny, commented on the fermented beverages of the Celts or Gauls at the margins of the Classical world. The latter were famous for their consumption of alcoholic beverages, such as beer, at enormous feasts. Some of these beverages were likely meads made from wheat-and-honey or barley-and-honey; in other instances, grain-based beers were enjoyed.

Today, mead and beer come preserved and packaged for a long shelf life, but in Antiquity, these beverages not only consumed enormous resources in their production but also invited feasting. Traditional beers have less alcohol and more residues remaining from the fermentation process than is the case for modern beer, so they tend to spoil within a few days. Similarly to meat on the hoof, a grain surplus offered much potential as a storable commodity, but once converted to beer, it needed to be quickly consumed. Early alcoholic beverages thus became perfect accompaniments to monumental feasts, parties to herald the efforts of workers, and conspicuous consumption.

chicha A beer that the Inka made from maize.

South America: Maize Beer and the Inka State

At its height in the fifteenth century CE, the Inka empire was the largest sociopolitical entity to have developed in South America, stretching along the Andes Mountains and Pacific coast from Peru to Chile [**12.3**]. From the 1200s, elite groups emerged and secured power in many Andean valleys, conquering and consolidating regional societies into one wealthy empire. The Inka taxed local communities and organized the storage and use of important surplus goods to run their empire, feed their army, and pay for workers in specialized craft industries, such as textiles and gold-working. One well-studied geographic area of the Inka takeover was the Upper Mantaro Valley of central Peru. Here, the shift from the Wanka II Period (*c.* 1350–1460 CE) to Inka or Wanka III Period (*c.* 1460–1533 CE) offers strong evidence for Inka appropriation and control of the means to make maize beer—**chicha**—and then distribute it. The control of chicha and its conspicuous consumption were one means by which the Inka solidified their grip over a vast empire.

Andean archaeologist Christine Hastorf and her colleague Sissel Johannessen studied evidence for the use of chicha in Andean societies. Although many Andean plants provide starches that can be used to brew beer (e.g., potatoes, other tubers, and quinoa), only maize (*Zea mays*) comes from an exotic plant with origins far from South America. Hastorf and Johanessen argue that maize chicha was itself highly transformative. To brew maize beer entailed a metamorphosis: the maize kernels were either sprouted or ground and chewed by women, then cooked, left to settle, separated, fermented, and boiled again before their last fermentation. Maize was also transformative in its power to alter a person's sense of self and

12.3 Map of the Inka empire (shown in darker green)
c. **1450 CE.** The Inka consolidated smaller states along the Andean mountain spine, and they did so in part through incorporating local traditions of feasting into Inka overrule.

12.4 Image of elites using maize beer as part of a ritual. Drawing by Guamán Poma de Ayala, who was born in southern Peru in the 1530s. His travels through Peru allowed him to document many aspects of Andean culture, including the use of beer and feasts by noble families.

residue analysis Analysis of any chemical traces found in a ceramic container.

C4 process the processes of photosynthesis as undertaken by grasses, such as maize or sugarcane.

C3 process the process of photosynthesis as undertaken by herbaceous plants and tubers.

connections with others (real companions or imagined beings, such as spirits and ancestors) through intoxication. Hastorf and Johannessen suggest that the Wanka elite sponsored feasts to consolidate power and incur labor obligations through traditional community activities. Elites chose to dispense chicha at public venues because it aided communication between people and powerful deities, validating the power of those who could amass the surplus grain, labor, and supplies to distribute it for consumption.

Unlike a stone monument, chicha does not endure into the future. It disappears down the drinker's throat, making it a difficult substance to detect in the archaeological record. Hastorf and Johannessen brought together a wide array of archaeological evidence to track the changes in food production and use, including those related to chicha, when the Inka conquered the Wanka state in the Mantaro Valley. From settlement surveys, these archaeologists determined where elites and commoners lived, and evaluated similarities and differences in food preparation and remains around their houses, finding that as elite residences sprang up, so did an increase in the materials utilized to make chicha [**12.4**]. In archaeobotanical remains, from both the Wanka II Period and Inka conquest, they traced the appearance and frequency of large-kernel maize, in addition to the distinctively shaped grinding slabs, hand-stones, and fermentation jars linked to chicha production. One ceramic type (the deep basin used in Wanka II for presentation and feasting) declined in Wanka III elite households, suggesting that the Inka had now appropriated the consumption of chicha at feasts sponsored by the empire's administrators (and held elsewhere than elite homes). Instead, Inka rulers required local elites to craft and supply the brew, and made chicha available at feasts to reward workers and supporters, thereby affirming and consolidating their power.

RESIDUE ANALYSIS

How did archaeologists detect ancient brewing (beer-making)? **Residue analysis** of the isotopic composition of burned organic scrapings on the inside of cooking pots rendered important clues about Wanka and Inka diets, and what foods were cooked or processed, in the Upper Mantaro Valley.

Maize plants process carbon dioxide differently from tuberous plants native to the highland Andes. These differences in photosynthesis (i.e., when a plant takes in atmospheric carbon dioxide (CO_2) and, in its release of oxygen (O_2), fixes carbon in its tissue) yield different ratios of stable carbon isotopes. Maize and other grasses use a chemical process called the **C4 process**; herbaceous plants and tubers use the **C3 process**. In both processes of photosynthesis, carbon is fixed into the plant, in both its ^{13}C isotope and ^{12}C forms. (As described in Chapter 6, ^{14}C is a miniscule and, for stable carbon isotope analysis, negligible percentage of plant carbon.) The C4 process tends to fix more of the ^{13}C isotope than the C3 process. As a result, maize and other C4 grasses include a greater proportion of ^{13}C than do tubers and herbaceous plants. When humans ingest these plants, the different ratios of stable carbon isotopes ($^{13}C/^{12}C$) are deposited in their bone accordingly. By comparing the proportion of each carbon isotope in the bone, it is possible to infer whether a person ate (or drank) mainly maize. Carbon residue also accumulates on pottery during cooking. The only edible C4 plant staple in the highland Andes is maize, so any high proportions of C4-type residues on pots and cups suggest the presence of maize in food or drink. The highest proportion of maize was boiled in stews during the Wanka I Period, before local elites expanded the range of maize types grown to include large-kernel varieties. During the Wanka II Period, the presence of maize in cooking-pot residues declined, but maize consumption was still on the rise: people continued to stew potatoes with it and consume beer, a pattern that Inka rulers amplified by mandating an even greater number of chicha feasts.

Other residues provide chemical signatures from wine and beer. Ceramics first appeared in the ancient Near East around 8,000 years ago, offering the possibility of better storage for fermenting beverages. Prior to ceramics, alcohol was fermented in skin bags, and the origin of the Biblical expression "put no new wine in old skins" comes from thousands of years of human experiments with fermentation. Bubbles put too much pressure on old tough skins, causing them to burst. With ceramic jars, Neolithic people were able instead to use clay stoppers stuffed with cloth, a system that allowed gases given off by fermenting beverages (living yeasts consuming sugars and releasing carbon dioxide) to escape [**12.5**]. Archaeologists have found clay and ceramic stoppers dating back to many periods in the ancient Near East, suggesting that fermentation was widespread. The earliest clues come from the porous ceramics of the Near Eastern Pottery Neolithic (PN), beginning around 8,000 years ago, after the first food producers settled in villages (see Chapter 8).

Unless sealed, fired ceramic is a porous material that traps organic residues, and biochemists have discovered that these pores can preserve the chemical structure of whatever was contained in a pot. Current efforts continue to trace the lipids (milk fats), characteristic of dairying to understand when people switched from herding animals solely for their meat to herding for milk. Milk could be tapped without actually killing the animal providing it, and residues of the substance have been identified in the pores of ceramics in the Near East *c.* 6000 BCE. Butter and whey can be produced inside bags made from animal skin, but to boil milk for infant weaning and make cheese, a ceramic pot would have been very useful to Neolithic people.

Porous ceramics also trap other chemical signatures. In 2017, biochemist Patrick McGovern at the University of Pennsylvania Museum used **infrared liquid chromatography** and wet chemical analyses (which uses such processes as combustion and chemical reaction) to identify the presence of tartaric acid inside a jar embedded in the floor of a Neolithic house in the highland mountains of northwestern Iran, at the site of Hajji Firuz Tepe. There, excavators found the mud-brick wall stumps of a Neolithic village with houses that included living and food-preparation areas, and small storage rooms, rather similar in appearance to the later Neolithic homes uncovered at Çatalhöyük in Turkey (see Chapter 8). In a room identified as a food-preparation area at Hajji Firuz Tepe, five standing jars were hidden in the

infrared liquid chromatography A technique which uses pressure to separate liquids into different chemical components, allowing for the identification of different chemicals and compounds.

12.5 These ancient clay disks with perforations could have held straws to allow escape of carbon dioxide while wine fermented.

RESIDUE ANALYSIS **283**

earthen floor. Inside one, excavators came across yellowish deposits that proved to be the remains of wine, the earliest ever discovered. Grapes are the only source of tartaric acid, so it is certain that the jar once contained grape juice. That it was fermented into wine became clear from two accompanying finds.

On the floor near the jars, excavators found fitted clay stoppers that could seal the jars to prevent the wine inside from turning into vinegar, a process that occurs as wine oxidizes. In a remarkable display of chemical sleuthing, McGovern also detected something else: the unmistakable chemical signature of terebinth resin. Terebinth is the common name for several kinds of *Pistacia* (pistachio) trees that grow naturally in the highland forests of Iran and yield a nontoxic resin [12.6]. From Greek and Roman sources, historians know of the ancient tradition of mixing resins with wine to prevent wine's spoiling. Approximately 7,000 years ago, Neolithic people would have used resins to preserve their wine. Even today, Greeks continue this tradition, using pine pitch to make retsina, their resin-flavored wine. McGovern additionally speculated that the discovery of resin preservatives might be accidental—during the Neolithic period, wild grape and terebinth trees grew in the same environments, so their products might have become mixed during harvesting.

Neolithic people probably coated the interiors of their wine jars with tree resin to seal them. They might have also discovered the resin's preservative properties in this way. Alexa Porter of the British Museum has applied chemical analysis to detect the use of beeswax as a sealant for Iron Age unguent (ointment or balm) jars in southern Arabia, many thousands of years later. Beeswax and resin were acceptable sealants for cosmetics or medicines. Natural tar, or bitumen, was utilized to fix projectile points onto shafts and seal reed boats, but it would have had an unpleasant taste and toxic properties when ingested.

12.6 Yellow terebinth resin preserved inside a sealed Canaanite amphora (a clay vessel used for storage) that was recovered from a shipwreck.

RECIPROCITY

Conspicuous consumption may have also played other roles in the past. Anthropological studies of societies in Papua New Guinea have identified the critical role of gift-giving in the acquisition and maintenance of social status. The Kawelka people of the Mount Hagen region in central mainland New Guinea practice *moka*, a form of extravagant gift-giving based on a system of reciprocity, the human need, and tendency to want, to give something back when something has been received. Individuals who wish to establish themselves in Kawelka society can do so only by providing their competitors with a gift. This gift must be more significant than the one the giver previously received, thus putting the competitor in "debt" and establishing a relationship that in the future will involve repayment. Reciprocity is different from **redistribution**, which occurs in societies that have rulers, or other individuals of high status, who have the right to demand tribute and taxes, but may redistribute this wealth to their supporters and followers to maintain alliances.

The anthropologist Marshall Sahlins described reciprocity as the formal mechanism for political organization in what he called "big man societies," as the great

redistribution The process whereby a leader demands tribute of a population and, under tight controls, then doles it out to supporters and followers.

gift can be obtained only through the construction of a social network of followers. The most important items of wealth in a *moka* exchange are pigs, which are domesticated and fed a diet of sweet potatoes farmed from New Guinea's rocky soils. With the pigs requiring several pounds of sweet potatoes per day, raising many would call for an enormous investment in land and labor by local farmers. People who wish to gain the status of big men must therefore work hard, often for many years, to persuade farmers in their region to raise sufficient pigs for them. When the day of exchange comes, *moka* can mean handing off five hundred or more pigs, plus other livestock and traditional wealth. Hundreds of people also attend the official ceremony marking the *moka*, to witness the exchange between the giver and the receiver, and to participate in feasting, music, and dancing. The structure of society, and the building of social relationships among its members who are widely dispersed across remote valleys, are embraced and rekindled at these events of conspicuous consumption.

THE ULTIMATE SACRIFICE: HUMAN

King Djer was a powerful ruler of the First Dynasty in Upper Egypt, the southern portion of the Nile Valley where the competing cities of Naqada, Abydos, and Hierakonpolis had struggled briefly as rivals some 5,100 years ago. Just a century later, the first pharaohs united all of Egypt as one territory with a single administration (see Chapter 10).

In 1898, British archaeologist Sir Flinders Petrie was excavating the tomb of Djer at Umm el-Qa'ab [**12.7**] when he uncovered hundreds of dead bodies, their open mouths frozen in one final, awful scream, their limbs flexed and neatly placed side by side. Petrie described the gruesome spectacle of a mass burial of human companions for the dead king's final journey to the afterlife. Archaeologists have

12.7 Remains of the tomb of King Djer, Egypt. This elaborate tomb was constructed with many separate cells that were each filled with offerings of food, wine, and human sacrifices, which were meant to accompany the king to the afterlife, 3000 BCE. More than five hundred human bodies were found in and around Djer's tomb.

suggested these individuals might have been initially drugged to prevent resistance as their bodies were carefully bound in the final burial rites for the king. Then, once beer and grain for the king's sustenance had been stockpiled, the incense and chants ceased, and the mud-brick chambers of the tomb sealed, they awoke to the impending moment of their own death, with all physical struggles futile. No greater conspicuous consumption can be imagined than the execution of hundreds in the service of one ruler's burial, and no act more effectively demonstrates power than complete command over so many lives.

For a century, archaeologists have debated the cause of death of King Djer's companions. Some dispute the notion of human sacrifice upon the passing of Egypt's early ruler, suggesting that the gaping expression of Djer's tombmates likely represented the natural relaxing of postmortem muscles. Other evidence points, however, to human sacrifice: carved ivory labels show the throats of bound courtiers being slit. Within the tomb complex, 318 subsidiary burial chambers were simultaneously constructed, holding the remains of some 338 sacrificed retainers. Similar chambers exist in King Aha's tomb (Djer's father) at Abydos, and hundreds were buried with King Den (Djer's grandson), also interred at Umm el-Qa'ab. The pink teeth of some young males point to their death by strangulation. If, indeed, Djer, Den, and Aha were buried among sacrificed retainers, they were not the only rulers to exercise this kind of power in death. The conspicuous consumption of human lives was a feature of many early and emerging societies.

12.8 Sumerian burial artifact from Ur. This exquisite bull's head of gold leaf and lapis lazuli (both rare, exotic substances) decorates the frame of a musical instrument played at banquets (feasts) held by and for Sumerian elites.

Southwest Asia: Royal Burials of Ur

Another example of ancient human sacrifice occurred in Mesopotamia contemporaneous with the burials of the First Dynasty rulers of Egypt. In Chapter 8, we looked at the Sumerians in Mesopotamia and their ultimately doomed intensive agriculture. In the Sumerian city of Ur, Sir Leonard Woolley, the renowned British archaeologist (1880–1960), excavated sixteen shaft tombs (a tomb that is buried deep underground and accessed by a vertical passage) under a palace constructed during the Early Dynastic Period (2600–2450 BCE). Included in the elite burials was treasure: a golden helmet, hair ribbons and wreaths of gold leaves, precious woods inlaid with lapis lazuli (a deep-blue and gold semiprecious stone) and ivory, a minstrel's harp decorated with an ornamental golden-horned bull [**12.8**], a ram statue encrusted in lapis lazuli, gold, carnelian, and lapis lazuli beads, and exotic soapstone boxes that had been carved in far-off Jiroft, a town in the southern mountains of Iran [**12.9**]. All these items were finely made, indicating they were the work of master artisans. The burial of rare materials showing the highest level of craftsmanship represents a staggering consumption of wealth.

The interred elites had consumed more than material wealth, though. Oxen lay slaughtered beside the funerary carts that filled the tomb entry shafts, and dozens of sacrificed retainers accompanied their masters and mistresses in what Woolley

12.9 Map of the Sumer region locating the city of Ur to the south.

called the "Death Pit" [**12.10**, p. 288]. Woolley found their bodies perfectly arranged and bearing no sign of violence (at least none he could see). He suggested that the retainers had gone willingly to the grave, heavily drugged and unable to sense their own imminent deaths. His wife and colleague Katherine pointed to the many cups uncovered nearby and suggested that the retainers had been served a toxic drink beforehand. Sixty-eight women and six men were buried with their weapons, headdresses of gold, lapis lazuli and silver, lyres, cups, and cosmetic pigments. When the site was excavated in the 1920s, it drew international attention as the apparent scene of mass suicide.

We know from their hymns and myths preserved on clay tablets that the Sumerians conceived of the afterlife as a dusty and dismal existence. Unlike Egyptians, they apparently expected no comfort in eternity. Knowing how Sumerians viewed death, archaeologists now speculate that their funerary offerings may have been intended for the gods, or gifts to ingratiate the dead and alleviate a miserable existence in the underworld. However the Sumerians perceived the entombing of goods and people, the so-called Royal Tombs at Ur conspicuously consumed great wealth and much human life.

Moreover, events at the Death Pit may not have played out exactly as Katherine Woolley imagined. One recent analysis performed CT (computerized tomography) scans on several of the skulls that had been preserved for museum display. These scans showed that the retainers died from pointed blows to their skulls, possibly from the spike end of a copper axe, similar to one unearthed in a different grave at Ur. Once the retainers in the Death Pit had perished, their bodies were smoked and sprinkled with cinnabar, a toxic compound of mercury used to preserve corpses in the ancient world. No one disputes that these retainers died with their rulers,

12.10 The Death Pit at Ur (tomb Pg 1237) as drawn by Leonard Woolley in 1928. The tomb was almost 33 feet (approximately 10 meters) long and wide, and contained the bodies of seventy four people, many wearing gold headdresses. Half of the women had cups next to their bodies, which suggested to Woolley that they had consumed drugs or poison. This tomb was located beside the tomb of Queen Pu'abi (tomb Pg 800).

but their participation no longer appears to be suicide but murder. The remains now confirm they were sacrificed.

Another of Ur's so-called Royal Tombs was that of Queen Pu'abi, a woman about 40 years old and outfitted in the highest fashion of her day. Pu'abi entered the afterlife dressed in an elaborate headdress of gold ribbon, crowned with a diadem of gold leaves perhaps fashioned after an exotic tropical tree [**12.11**]. No one is exactly sure how sixteen hundred colorful stone beads came to adorn her dress, but many of these beads were from foreign lands and exhibit skilled craftsmanship. By her right arm was placed a cylinder seal (a carved cylinder that was meant to be rolled across wet clay, producing a unique image of a vivid scene) depicting a banquet in which seated figures sucked beverages from long tubes, and also drank from goblets [**12.12**]. The scene has been interpreted as Pu'abi's feast, where she drank wine and beer. Pu'abi's name intrigues us, too, for among Sumerian speakers, she bore a Semitic name, suggesting perhaps that she and her ethnic kin had made powerful alliances with Sumerians of entirely different origin. Besides the considerable wealth buried

12.11 Reconstruction of Queen Pu'abi of Ur's golden headdress and beaded clothing. These jewels were found on and around the lady's body, and were reassembled by Leonard Woolley. They were manufactured during Ur's Early Dynastic Period (2600–2450 BCE), and incorporated rare and expensive materials from the distant mountains of Iran. The beads were made from carnelian, lapis lazuli, and gold. The headdress is gold, lapis lazuli, and ivory.

12.12 Queen Pu'abi's stone cylinder seal, and its impression on modern clay. This cylinder was a little more than 1 inch tall (approximately 3 cm) and depicted the lady at a feast where she drank beer and wine. The cylinder was perforated, and she probably wore it on a string around her arm or wrist. It was found beside her right arm, indicating she was wearing it as part of her death attire. Seals were used to create a unique imprint on clay documents, similar to a signature.

ziggurats Stepped pyramids found in Mesopotamia.

Rus A Viking group from Northern Europe whose name later came to identify the nation of Russia.

in her tomb, her name and title suggest the existence of a ruling class, the members of which were affiliated through their command of wealth and power, rather than their kin, ancestry, or ethnicity.

Sumerians lived in some of the world's earliest cities, on the seasonally flooded plains between the Tigris and Euphrates rivers of southern Iraq. At the edge of marshland, the ruined heaps of decayed mud brick that were once great cities now conceal the stumps of walls, outlines of palaces and temples, and massive stepped **ziggurats** that Sumerians built as artificial mountains to elevate the houses of their gods above the surrounding plain. It was in these gods' households that scribes labored to account for the intake and outflow of grain surpluses and herd animals, and it was the fruits of this surplus—the gold, carnelian, lapis lazuli, exotic woods, incense, richly colored dyes, copper, pearls, and additional objects of beauty from faraway lands—that Sumerians buried in the graves of their elite. Not only were the first cities dependent on an agricultural surplus (exhausting the land's fertility in the process), but their elite rulers also lavishly consumed this wealth by burying it for ever.

EUROPE: THE BURIAL OF VIKING AND ANGLO-SAXON SHIPS

In Antiquity, other societies burned wealth in a conspicuous display; eyewitnesses recorded these events in their writings. In 922 CE, an ambassador from the court of the Baghdad caliph, then ruler of the Islamic world, traveled far north through foreign lands to reach territory settled by the **Rus**. Once among the Rus, the ambassador, Ibn Fadlan, wrote extensively on what he observed: non-believers (non-Muslims) who drank and washed, in turn, from a single filthy bowl passed from one person to the next; men whose blond hair and hearty physiques astonished him almost as much as the unveiled women; a people who practiced burial rites unlike any he had ever encountered [**12.13**, **12.14**]. Ibn Fadlan, in fact, watched the burial of a Viking ship, and from his tenth-century pen then came our only eyewitness account detailing the consumption of great wealth at the burial of a Viking chief. Were it not for Ibn Fadlan, we might today regard the description of Beowulf's funeral as the stuff of legend (the Anglo-Saxon epic poem of the same name, written in the eighth century, tells the story of a Danish hero of the Viking era who died while slaying a dragon). His tribe, the Geats, burned his body and piled treasure about him in a huge mound. The funeral observed by Ibn Fadlan among the Rus was markedly similar. The following is a portion of his account, as translated:

> They placed him in his grave, which they covered with a roof, and they left him there for ten days, waiting while they finished cutting and sewing his garments….If the dead man was poor, they build him a small boat and place him in it and set it on fire. If he was wealthy, they gather together his fortune and divide it into three parts, one for his family, one to have clothes cut

12.13 Silver cup from a burial at Dollerup, Denmark, first–second centuries CE.

out for him and another to have the *nabidh* [alcoholic drink] prepared that they will drink on the day that his slave girl kills herself and is burned with her master.

When a great man dies, the members of his family say to his slave girls and young slave boys: "Which of you will die with him?" One of them replies, "I will." Once spoken, it is irreversible....

The old woman called the Angel of Death came and put a cord round her neck in such a way that the two ends went in opposite directions. She gave the ends to two of the men, so they could pull on them. Then she herself approached the girl holding in her hand a dagger with a broad blade and [plunged it again and again between the girl's ribs], while the two men strangled her with the cord until she was dead.

Next, [the closest male relative of the dead man] came forward and [took a piece of wood] which he lit at a fire. He then walked backwards towards the boat, his face turned [towards the people] who were there, one hand holding the piece of flaming wood, the other covering his anus, for he was naked. Thus he set fire to the wood that had been set ready under the boat. Then people came with wood and logs to burn, each holding a piece of a wood alight at one end, which they threw on to the wood. The fire enveloped the wood, the man, the girl and all that there was on the boat....

Next at the place where this boat had been drawn out of the river, they build something like a round hill and in the middle they set up a great post of *khandank* wood, inscribed this with the name of the man and that of the king of the Rus. Then they departed.

12.14 An iron sword of Viking type, in use in the ninth to tenth centuries CE. Such weapons were included in the riches buried with Viking chiefs.

Not every ship that was buried was set afire, however. Archaeologists have recovered buried but untorched ships in eastern Sweden and, most famously, under a prominent burial mound at the British East Anglian site of Sutton Hoo [**12.15**, p. 292]. Situated close to the mouth of the River Deben in Suffolk, the Sutton Hoo burial grounds overlook one of the major access routes that were traversed by Germanic traders and migrants in the centuries that followed the withdrawal of the Romans from Britain (410 CE). These were the years during which Anglo-Saxons immigrated to Britain from across the North Sea, displacing speakers of the languages that still persist among some people of the region: Gaelic, Welsh, and Breton. Around 625, an Anglo-Saxon king, probably Raedwald, was buried in an oak chamber, or pavilion, specially constructed in the midsection of a ship almost 89 feet (27 meters) long. In the 1940s, the local landowner at Sutton Hoo commissioned a private excavation by archaeologist Basil Brown that led to the astounding discovery of this burial, a perfect impression in the sand of a rotted ship, with its iron rivets and burial treasure still intact.

Private excavations have been a long tradition in Britain; Victorian picnics frequently included gentlemen's excavations of local barrows and mounds in the hopes of recovering "curiosities." Landowners possessed the legal rights to what they found,

12.15 Outline of the buried ship at Sutton Hoo, eastern England, following its excavation in 1938. The ship was constructed of wood, all of which had rotted away, leaving behind only the iron rivets. The ship was 89 feet long (27 meters) and a man had been buried near its center, atop a wooden platform.

12.16 King Raedwald's helmet from the Sutton Hoo ship burial.

and this was deemed to be the case with the fabulous treasure of Sutton Hoo. Landowner Edith Pretty ultimately gifted the riches to the British people via the British Museum, where one can view the ship's remarkable pieces today. The Sutton Hoo treasure is one of the greatest archaeological discoveries, for it sheds light on the life and practices of Britain's Middle Ages, the texts and artifacts of which have proven highly perishable and are now scant.

King Raedwald appears to have been buried alone; indeed, no body remained in the grave at all. For some time, archaeologists believed the ship, treasure, and mound marked a cenotaph, a memorial grave without a body. Later soil tests revealed high phosphate levels, indicating at least one body that had completely decayed, bones and all, in the acidic earth. Phosphates are concentrated in animal and human tissues and remain fixed as phosphate residues in the soil long after tissues decay. Alongside this body, laid out in the oak pavilion draped with Scandinavian and exotic textiles, was sumptuous wealth. Excavators found an iron sword with a gold-and-garnet scabbard and belt, a bronze-decorated iron helmet [**12.16**], ornate gold and inlaid shoulder clasps, a carved gold belt buckle [**12.17**], silver bowls, traces of textiles and wooden containers, a hoard of Frankish gold coins, and metalwork crafted in Byzantium by highly skilled craftsmen. The treasures came from as far away as Egypt and Syria. King Raedwald—if it was he—took his vast wealth with him to the grave, whether or not he exercised the power of death over sacrificial victims at his funeral. The ship and its contents are yet another example of conspicuous consumption.

King Raedwald's burial and treasure also gave excavators new insight into the considerable extent of trade and influence of elites who had mustered great surpluses during Britain's Middle Ages. They dispatched skins, metals, and slaves in exchange for crafted and precious metals, luxury textiles, wine, and other goods (see Chapter 13). Raedwald's attendants wished for the king's power to be remembered far into the future, far beyond Sutton Hoo. In allegiance, they raised a high earthen mound over his ship's burial, a mound that was visible from the River Deben to all the traders who trafficked on its waterway into Britain.

12.17 Golden belt buckle from the Sutton Hoo boat burial. Made *c.* 600 CE, the buckle is decorated with an intricate interlaced design and inlaid with niello, a mixture of metals and lead. The buckle is just one example of the great wealth buried with King Raedwald.

IS CONSPICUOUS CONSUMPTION INEVITABLE?

In the land of Egypt, there lived a queen (in fact, a woman pharaoh of Greek descent) named Cleopatra, said to be both beautiful and wealthy. Julius Caesar and Mark Antony both fell for her, although it is just as likely that what tempted them was her vast wealth in grain. Egypt was fertile, a breadbasket for the Roman empire. Whoever controlled Egypt controlled the means to feed armies and to gain popular favor. The legends of Cleopatra, at least those that did not concern sex and snakes, revolve around conspicuous consumption. She bathed in donkeys' milk. She once dissolved a priceless pearl in vinegar (probably wine) and drank it. She was the ultimate conspicuous consumer, inheriting a tradition that reached all the way back to Predynastic times and the sacrifice of humans in burials.

tophets Cemeteries of cremated children in ancient North Africa.

Is conspicuous consumption thus inevitable? Not every case of human sacrifice may be linked to conspicuous consumption as a display of power. The Inka consecrated young children as sacrifices to the mountain gods in annual ceremonies, sometimes climbing to the summit of high peaks to place their gifts. In 1995, high on the summits of Ampato volcano, north of Peru's Arequipa city, Andean archaeologists discovered the mummified body of an Inka girl [**12.18**]. She had been wrapped in valuable textiles and probably died of exposure and heavy sedation before her body was deposited. Spanish accounts describe the tradition of Inka people who selected pure young maidens as gifts to the gods and to carry messages into the afterworld. Ancient Aztecs in the environs of modern Mexico City engaged in a similar practice; they treated the children who would later be sacrificed to every luxury and celebrated their passage before they were killed. The conquering Spaniards witnessed the resulting sacrifices and were horrified. These offerings indeed represented the ultimate sacrifice, most certainly for the parents of the children who—willingly or not—made them comply, but they were not intended to exhibit the great wealth or status of elites.

The human sacrifice of a child is often considered a "first fruit" offering (first child, first harvest) to the gods. In Judeo-Christian texts, God required Abraham to sacrifice Isaac and then substituted a ram, hence the symbolic link to first fruits. (For Muslims, Abraham's sacrifice was Ishmael.) The familiar tale then goes on to proclaim that God would no longer require the sacrifice of an eldest child. Another Semitic group, the Phoenicians who settled Carthage, Sicily, Sardinia, Malta, and the Lebanese coast, continued the practice of child sacrifice. At North Africa's Carthage (outside modern-day Tunis) and at Byblos (modern Beirut), archaeologists have recovered the remains of **tophets**, cemeteries filled with the cremated offerings of children. Some accounts suggest that the Carthaginians in their zealous devotion cast their living children into sacrificial flames, but it might be that these descriptions by outsiders are exaggerated because the practice was anathema to them. What

12.18 The "Ice Maiden" is the mummified body of a twelve-year-old Inka girl whose body preserved naturally in the cold, dry temperatures of a Peruvian mountaintop.

is clear from tophet inscriptions is that many Carthaginians willingly sacrificed their own children, and we can only imagine the sadness and pride that must have overcome them as they relinquished their offspring.

The anthropogenic landscape of Antiquity was created to produce products that could be conspicuously consumed, allowing societies to communicate social hierarchy and relationships to future generations. Even as we contemplate modern parallels of conspicuous consumption—converting staple grains to hamburgers via cattle feed, fossil fuel energy for outdoor holiday lights, or shipping wine halfway across the globe—consider also their antecedents. Prehistoric evidence of this behavior survives, and it helps us describe, and understand, the evolutionary pattern that has shaped the world in which we live.

Chapter Questions

1. What benefits do individuals gain from using surplus to hold large feasts or make luxurious food products? Use the Inka as your prime example.
2. What kind of information can archaeologists obtain by examining the chemical residues of ceramics?
3. How does burying wealth, either in hoards or in a human burial, function as a form of conspicuous consumption? What are modern-day equivalents?
4. Compare the burial at Sutton Hoo to the Royal Tombs of Ur. How are they different, and what characteristics do they share?

Additional Resources

http://www.penn.museum/sites/iraq/?page_id=28

https://www.world-archaeology.com/great-discoveries/sutton-hoo/

Bradley, Richard. *Ritual and Domestic Life in Prehistoric Europe.* London, UK: Routledge, 2005. See 145–64, 172.

Carver, Martin H., et al. *Sutton Hoo: A Seventh-Century Princely Burial Ground and Its Context.* London, UK: British Museum Press, 2005.

Hastorf, Christine A., and Johannessen, Sissel. "Prehispanic Political Change and the Role of Maize in the Central Andes of Peru," *American Anthropologist* 95 (1993): 115–38.

Homan, Michael. "Beer and Its Drinkers: An Ancient Near Eastern Love Story," *Near Eastern Archaeology* 67 (2004): 84–95.

Ibn Fadlan, *Ibn Fadlan and the Land of Darkness: Arab Travelers in the Far North.* Translated by Paul Lunde and Caroline Stone. London, UK and New York: Penguin Classics, 2012.

McGovern, Patrick E., and Hartung, Ulrich. "The Beginnings of Wine and Viticulture in the Ancient Near East," *Expedition* 39 (1997): 3–21.

Nairn, Charlie, dir. *Ongka's Big Moka: The Kawelka of Papua New Guinea.* Disappearing World documentary series, Granada Television, London, 1974.

Pollock, Susan. *Mesopotamia: The Eden That Never Was.* Cambridge, UK: Cambridge University Press, 1999.

Wengrow, David. *The Archaeology of Early Egypt.* Cambridge, UK: Cambridge University Press, 2006.

WRITING
A History of Access to Information

13

"*Chan ahaw waxak yaxk'in u oxlajun haab u baahil yik'in chan k'awil yax ho chan kaloomte' k'ujul ahaw mutal....*"

Gesturing with both hands, the man pointed at the looming limestone stela (slab) before us. Streaked grey with mold from the rains, the inscription on the weathered stone appeared indecipherable, an array of mossy crevices flattened by the midday sun. We had to shield our eyes from the noon glare in Tikal's main plaza (in modern-day Guatemala), where Kevin Johnston read aloud the annals of long-dead monarchs. Behind us rose the hulk of a great stone pyramid capped by a small building and a once proudly sculpted roof comb, with images of gods stacked like billowing clouds. Kings had stood there, garbed in quilted cotton, festooned with feathers, and daubed with blood, sometimes their own, in sacrifice to the gods. Kevin read on; as an archaeologist focused on Maya history and culture, he was guiding me through the most famous of Maya cities—his focus on the inscribed text, with his squint directed only at its perceptible hollows and contours. He was reading Maya history, out loud, just as literate Maya orators once did in ceremonial enactments of conquest, ascendancy, legitimation, and authority.

Oration is a powerful tool, especially among the illiterate. Not all the Maya could read—indeed, their glyphic texts are constructed in endless playful variations, at once legible to those who could read, and erudite so as to enhance the appeal of an orator and his authority over his listeners. Texts on stelae were publicly displayed and enigmatic to most, intended to be interpretive tools that only some could wield. They were the technology of authority that allowed those in-the-know to disseminate information to others.

As scripts permit access to and control of information, they become the basis upon which people justify and communicate their choices—including ecological decisions—and then act. The information conveyed may seem intangible, just as the flow of power sometimes does, but it nevertheless plays an important role in shaping human societies and environments, both ancient and modern. In this chapter, we will explore how writing appeared and developed independently in many places across the globe. Although invented on an autonomous basis, many forms of writing involve similar devices, and this can be interpreted as either extending or limiting access to information. By comparing the writing of the Maya with writing in ancient China, Mesopotamia, and the Indus—and examining the later development of alphabetic scripts—we will come to understand how written communication in the past manifested itself in many schema and for more than a single purpose.

Writing in Many Contexts 298

Writings of the Maya 298

Writings of the Sumerians 303

Ancient Chinese Writing 309

Alphabetic Writing 314

Preservation of Writing Systems 316

Without Writing: Systems of Notation 318

North Africa and Arabia: Literacy without Settlement 320

Writing and the Anthropocene 322

Opposite The Great Plaza at Tikal, cleared by the University of Pennsylvania team in the 1950s. Stela 5 (as discussed on this page) sits at the base of the prominent staircase in middle left.

Key Concepts

- How writing systems were invented independently, and in many diverse ways, around the world
- The typical elements of a writing system, including its logographic and syllabographic features
- How some urban societies existed without any form of writing, such as the Inka, who instead used the *khipu* notational system
- The emergence of writing in a society without permanent settlements, such as among Bedouin tribesmen

WRITING IN MANY CONTEXTS

Throughout much of modern human history, marks and symbols have been used as a form of simple communication. Painting and scarring on the human body may have constituted the first form of written communication, conveying to others a message of identity or social status. Perhaps as early as 65,000 years ago (see Chapter 2), humans began to carve, peck, or paint images onto rocks and the walls of caves, and these images likely expressed elements of stories or individual accomplishments. The earliest true form of writing developed in Mesopotamia along the banks of the Tigris and Euphrates rivers approximately 5,000 years ago. It recorded economic transactions, such as the sale or exchange of beer and grain.

While the Sumerians were behind that first form of writing, writing in China evolved 1,500 years later, with Maya writing materializing some 2,500 years after that; all three systems unfolded independently of each other. Regardless of which region is examined first, and in spite of their different contexts and autonomous development, Sumerian, Maya, and Chinese writing systems forged similar general methods for transmitting ideas, words, and sounds [13.1].

WRITINGS OF THE MAYA

On Maya pots and painted murals, you can see scribes sitting cross-legged, holding the bundled instruments of their trade. They were specialists at their craft and likely exempt from the daily toil of growing, grinding, and cooking maize. Seated scribes are shown tallying tribute; it was perhaps scribes who also carved glyphs on stelae, and almost certainly scribes who recited them. With scribal privilege, however, came a price. When King Waxaklajun Ubaah K'awil of Copan was captured by the rival city of Quirigua in 738 CE, he became a public sacrifice to the gods. At the small Maya temple at Bonampak, Mexico [13.2] we learn what happened to scribes captured with their kings. Those who glorified kings had their fingers broken and twisted at perverse angles, and are bleeding profusely. The scribes will no longer serve as propagandists for their king, their technical adeptness having been decisively terminated.

The decision to punish the royal scribes in this brutal manner attests to the power of their writing. In the instance of the Maya, archaeologists have determined some of the uses to which writing was put. Maya texts commonly tell the histories of conquest and succession. Kings extended their influence by ordering the construction of stone stelae and panels to record auspicious births, document dynastic genealogies and alliances, and catalog combat victories and the sacrifice of rival captives. Writing thus reinforced the agency of Maya rulers.

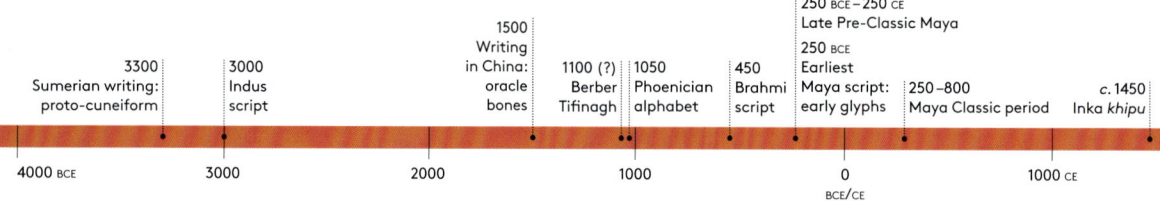

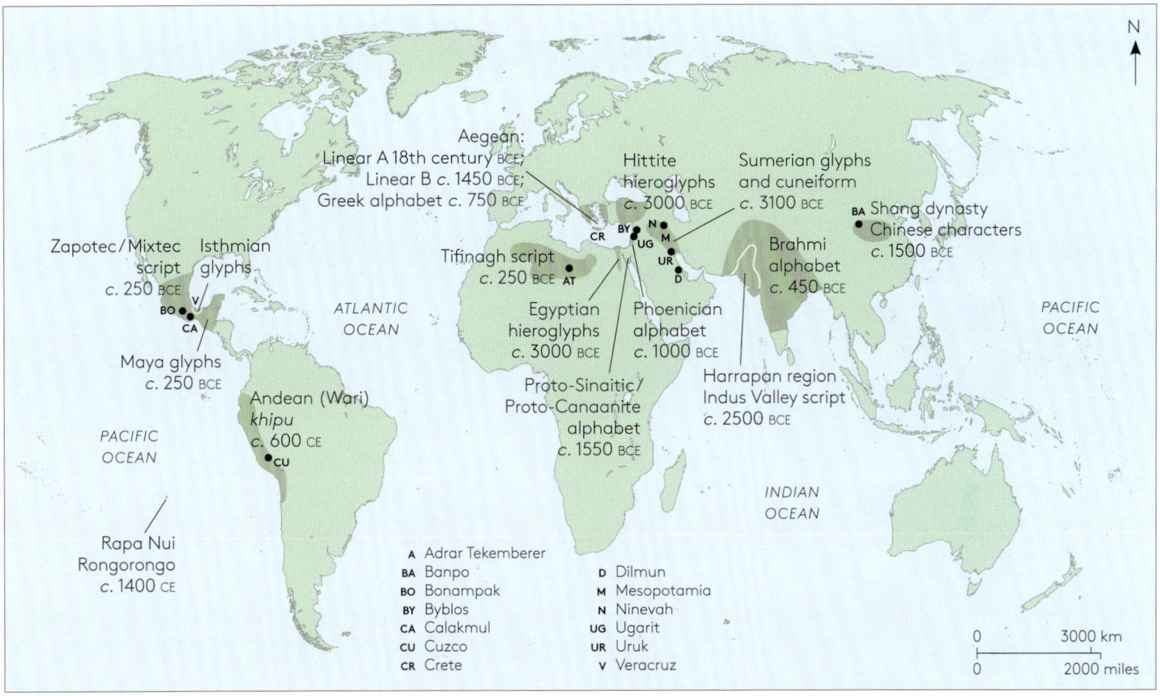

13.1 Map of the world, showing the places where writing was developed in the past.

13.2 Replica of mural from Bonampak, Mexico, depicting the public mutilation of captive scribes who had served the Maya king. Two seated captives in the center-left examine their ruined, bloodied hands. Facing them on the right is another captive with broken fingers, and the captive seated behind him (middle row, to the right) holds a pen (not visible in this reconstruction) the telltale sign of the men's profession.

WRITING IN MANY CONTEXTS 299

13.3 Examples of Maya glyphs.
The upper left example K'AL is a logogram. Below it, both in the first column, B'ALAM and IX/IXIK are pictograms (a form of logogram). In the bottom left register is a logogram with a phonetic compliment (i.e., TE), (a syllobogram). In the middle column, all four glyphs are pictograms. In the third (right-hand) column, multiple syllabograms have been combined to make a multi-syllable word. Notice how the syllabogram for leaf spells the first syllable of the word for house.

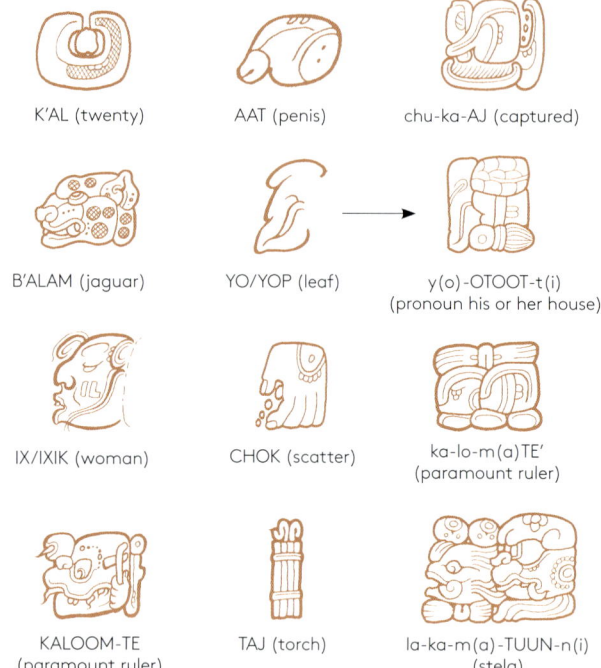

glyph A written symbol within a set of symbols that are used together to represent the elements of a written language.

logogram, logographic An image that stands for a single word. Sometimes a logogram resembles what it stands for (in such cases it is called pictogram), but otherwise it is often stylized.

syllabogram, syllabographic An image that stands for a sound. A phonetic symbol, a series of which can be put together to sound a word.

Anatomy of a Maya Glyph

Most Maya texts date from the Classic Period (250 BCE – 800 CE), and even in its fully developed form, Maya writing exhibits progressive change over time. The Maya used intricate **glyphs** to convey concepts as word signs and sound signs. Maya glyphs are generally square, containing one or more symbols that may represent either an object or idea, or a sound. Often, some glyphs are also fused together, so closely that the individual glyphs may be difficult to recognize. These compound glyphs were not created in a standard way, and combinations of glyph blocks frequently were mixed and substituted freely to make new glyphs. In addition to displaying scribal flexibility, this complexity may have been deliberate, allowing scribes to make it more difficult for others to access information embedded in text.

In early texts, Maya scribes used a single **logogram** in each glyph. A logogram is an image that stands for a word. The reader would need to know the word that each logogram conveys. When the logogram is a picture (or pictogram), for example an eye, it is easy to decipher meaning, but some logograms are highly stylized, such as the logogram for "twenty" [**13.3**]. Over time, Maya scribes included multiple components in many of their glyph blocks. Some of these components were still logograms, but most were phonetic symbols, or **syllabograms**. These syllabograms sometimes provided sounds (syllables) to complement existing words. Occasionally, they built from the existing sound of a logogram, making a new word with an entirely different meaning from the combination of logogram and syllables. For example, a logogram of a stylized root is pronounced *"wi."* When this is attached to the logogram of an animal head that is pronounced *"tzi,"* they can be read together as the word *"witzi,"* which means "mountain." At other times, syllabograms simply clarified meaning and context with grammatical prefixes or suffixes. Frequently, scribes substituted a combination of syllabograms for a logogram. The increased use of phonetic elements over the years led Maya **epigrapher** Stephen Houston to suggest that they reflect the broader scope of literacy—more people could now access information—even as the scribes remained an elite group.

History of Maya Writing

Since Maya texts appear in developed form, it is difficult to discern from them how writing began in that culture. Between 200 BCE and 200 CE, both Maya and another Mesoamerican system of writing called **Isthmian** were fully formed, suggesting that they had been preceded by an ancestral writing system that we have not yet discovered. Few examples of Isthmian script, probably written by people of the Veracruz region in central Mexico, are extant. What remains is one lengthy text from La Mojarra, an etched stone figurine from Tuxtla, and a handful of other inscriptions on smaller objects, such as masks. All the texts are still undeciphered, but similarly to the Maya glyphs, they seem to use syllabograms and logograms linked to an unknown language. The Isthmian script tracked time with **Long Count** dates based on a solar calendar (the days in a year), and began their calendar in the year 3114 BCE, the mythical time of creation. The Long Count calendar records dates that are calculated in cycles of years and months, which were recorded using a numerical system consisting of bars and dots. Using a base 20 system (which generates numerical units based upon the number 20, rather than the 10 that is the basis for modern mathematics), ancient Mesoamericans recorded the dates of specific events, including the birth and death of kings, on commemorative monuments.

Those who wrote in Isthmian glyphs were the descendants of the **Olmec** people, whose ancient culture remains enigmatic. Their civilization began around 1400 BCE, approximately 1,600 years earlier than the Maya Classic Period. Olmec sites exhibit some of the same features that are evident in later Mesoamerican civilizations: they built large mounded monuments topped by temples; and their ceremonial centers feature ball courts very similar to the Maya ones, where rulers ordered the re-enactment of ritual games, frequently sacrificing the losers in the process. The Olmec likely developed a writing system, but archaeologists have examined only one possible text, a poorly dated, undeciphered stone block from Cascajal. By 150 CE, evidence exists of post-Olmec writing in the Isthmian script.

Olmec and Isthmian writing appears only on stone, as do most Maya examples—save for four enduring Maya codices [**13.4**, p. 302]. These are accordion-fold books written on perishable materials, such as thin sheets of tree bark covered with plaster wash, and painted with glyphs (see Chapter 9 for a discussion of Aztec codices). Surely, thousands of Maya codices would have been in circulation in Antiquity.

epigrapher A researcher of ancient writing.

Isthmian A type of Mesoamerican script from the Gulf of Mexico that is related to Maya script.

Long Count A Mesoamerican calendar system that calculates time from a start date in 3114 BCE.

Olmec A Mesoamerican civilization that began approximately 3,000 years ago.

13.4 A page from the Dresden codex, one of the few Maya texts that have endured. This book, which was hand-painted on bark-paper leaves, was obtained by the Royal Library of Dresden, Germany, in 1744. Although it was created in Mesoamerica *c.* 1400 CE, it was transported to Europe between 1500 and 1600 CE.

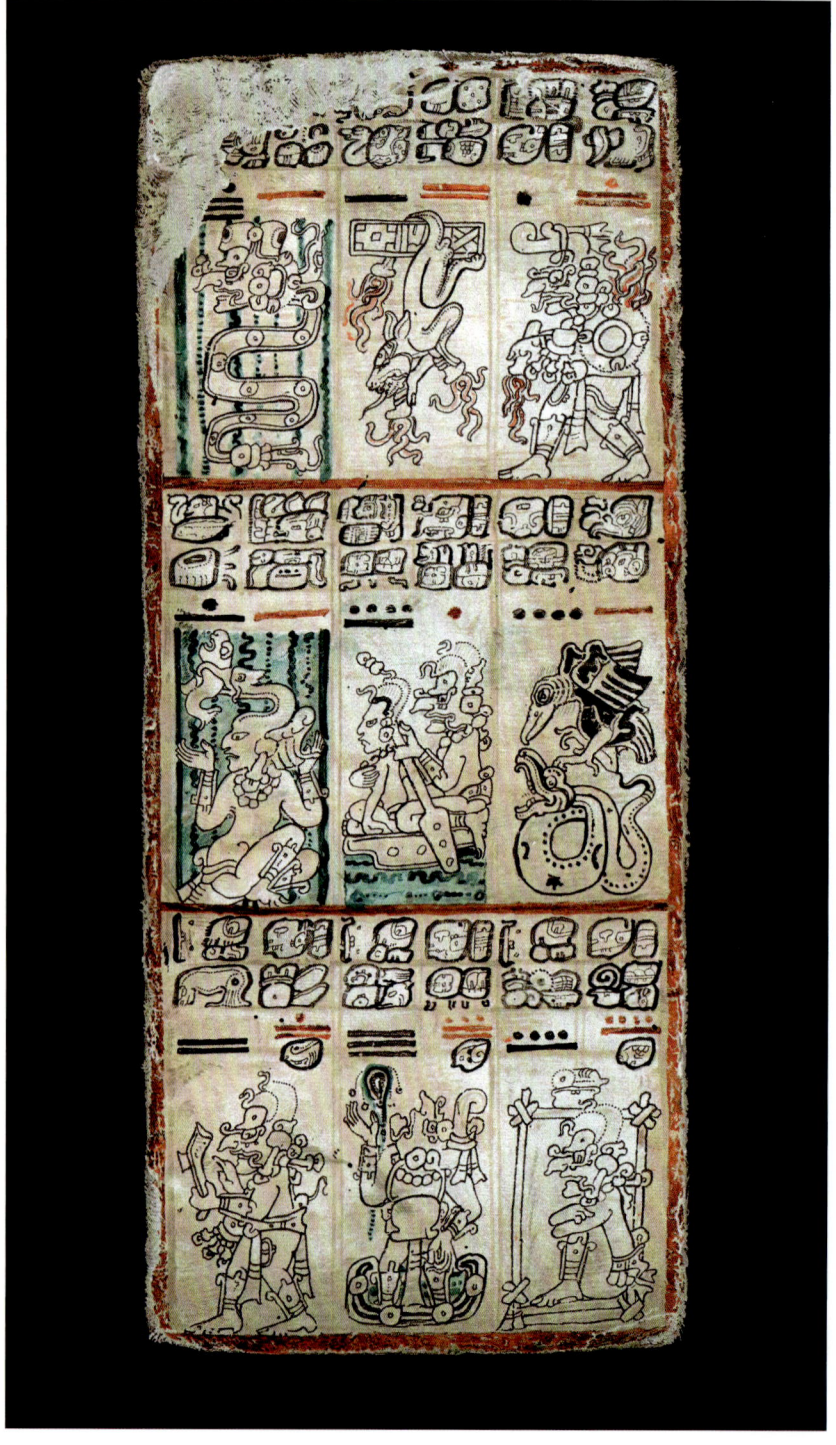

In an utterly apocalyptic *auto da* fé (public bonfire) on July 12, 1562, Bishop Diego de Landa ordered the destruction of all the codified Maya knowledge he could gather. De Landa was a fervent Inquisitor bent on sustaining Catholicism among Maya converts where it had been imposed. Just as the conquistadors arriving in New Spain were, de Landa proved a byproduct of the historical forces playing out in Spain, which included not only the military reconquest of former Moorish lands but also the violent imposition of the Roman Catholic faith and eradication of any rival practices.

At de Landa's order, hundreds of Maya books were tossed into the flames, along with cult images made of wood and fabric. The four codices that survived describe astronomy, almanacs, ceremonies, and prophesies and are heavily mathematical. Named for the cities in which they are preserved today (Dresden, Paris, Madrid), ironically these priceless Maya books survived because they were removed from the damp rain forest where some Maya had hidden them from de Landa's purge. Occasionally, archaeologists (or looters) will encounter the physical traces of another Maya book from within the dank recesses of a tomb, but all that remains is a rectangular pile of white dust and colored paint chips left by the decayed bark backing. Some codices were secreted away long before the Spanish Conquest and hint at a long prehistory of Maya perishable texts. What else might these codices have contained beyond the chronicles of kings?

The rediscovery of Maya codices in the twentieth century was instrumental in deciphering the Maya glyphs that adorn the temples of Mesoamerica. In 1952, Yuri Knorozov's studies concluded that the glyphs were syllobographic, rather than logographic. Beginning in the 1970s, epigrapher Linda Schele and other archaeologists who learned to speak Maya and read these glyphs have since gained key insights into Maya society, and Maya attitudes to power and authority have been distilled and placed into context within the history of rulers and conquest. The study of Maya glyphs—in particular, the determination that the text was composed of both logograms and syllabograms—was especially groundbreaking. Not only was this form of writing encoded with inner meaning, its production and recitation further enhanced the authority of the elites who relied on it for both record-keeping and propaganda.

WRITINGS OF THE SUMERIANS

In the region of modern southern Iraq, ancient Sumerians developed the earliest known writing system; unlike the remnants of Maya writing, which appear fully developed, the archaeological record documents a long development of writing and record-keeping in Sumer. During the **Ubaid Period**, Sumerians inhabited the southern marshlands of Mesopotamia. Their earliest settlements in this area were small hamlets and villages dependent on wheat and barley agriculture and heavily reliant on cattle herding and fishing in the marshes. By the end of this long period, some villages pooled their surplus in large communal granaries and began to demonstrate architectural diversity, such as large houses with differing floorplans

Ubaid Period Stage of development in Mesopotamia, *c.* 6000 to 3800 BCE, when people began to settle permanently.

Uruk Period Stage of development in Mesopotamia, c. 3800 to 3000 BCE, when the first cities were built.

Assyrian A major Mesopotamian kingdom and empire at the juncture of the Tigris and Euphrates Rivers; dates from 2025 (Old Assyrian empire begins) to 609 BCE (end of the Neo-Assyrian empire).

and a shrine at Eridu that remained a sacred site for centuries. In the subsequent **Uruk Period**, the countryside became dotted with settlements of different sizes and the first Sumerian cities emerged (see Chapter 8), including Uruk with its city wall, awe-inspiring size, and legendary king, Gilgamesh [**13.5**].

No version of Gilgamesh's life story was ever written during the Uruk Period, but his hero-king legend lived on [**13.6**]. Originally recorded on twelve clay tablets, the story was rewritten throughout Antiquity, and fragments of the story have been unearthed throughout Mesopotamia. The most complete rendition available to us derives from the library of the Neo-**Assyrian** king Ashurbanipal at Ninevah in northern Iraq, compiled an astonishing 2,400 years later in the seventh century BCE. Ashurbanipal's version speaks of the amazing exploits of Gilgamesh: how he displeased the gods, and persuaded the prostitute Shamhat to tame the wild man Enkidu

13.5 Gilgamesh. Discovered at the palace of Sargon II in modern-day Iraq, this impressive statue, which stands 16.5 feet (approximately 5 meters) high, was carved from alabaster and set in a facade at the entrance to the throne room. The statue dates to the Neo-Assyrian period, and was carved to represent a hero already dead for some 2,400 years.

13.6 Tablet V of the Epic of Gilgamesh. Now housed at the Sulaymaniyah Museum, Kurdistan, Iraq. This tablet was illegally looted from an unknown location in southern Iraq in 2011, but was recognized by museum curators and translated in 2012. It fills in a missing portion of the Gilgamesh story.

with sex and then more sex. After this, Gilgamesh became Enkidu's inseparable best friend, killed the forest demon Humbaba, lost his friend and sought immortality, learned of the great flood from its ark-building survivor Utnapishtim, and claimed a plant that could restore youth, only to be tricked out of it by a serpent. After all these experiences, Gilgamesh returned to Uruk a wiser king. The Judeo-Christian narratives of Noah and Adam were based on these same stories.

In the era of Gilgamesh, writing was in its infancy within Uruk and other Sumerian cities. At the center of the city lay the Eanna precinct, which was sacred to the goddess Inanna for a thousand years. Iraq's greatest archaeological treasures were recovered from this site. Beneath layers of rubble, archaeologists found massive public buildings constructed with elaborate stone cone mosaics (composed of colored stones that were cut into conical shapes and then pressed tip-first into plaster, producing a tiled surface) and limestone walls. In the muddy marshlands, this kind of stone was rare and valuable. Built in the shape of houses but with the expensive décor of temples, these large buildings served as a central focus in urban life. They may have been meeting houses for large cooperative groups, maybe kinsmen convening as landholders, or perhaps they served as temples welcoming all visitors. Discarded cult objects, including the famous stone Uruk Vase (see 10.22, p. 241), show naked worshipers bringing food to the goddess Inanna. To archaeologists, arguably the greatest treasure uncovered was the trove of **proto-cuneiform** tablets discovered in the fill of the Eanna precinct and dating to around 3000 BCE.

13.7 Proto-cuneiform tablet excavated from the Eanna precinct of Uruk. These tablets are the oldest writing in the world, dating to 3000 BCE. Translations indicate they record amounts of grain, wool, and beer. The tablets were likely used to track payments and disbursements by administrators.

13.8 The origin and development of several cuneiform characters through time (in pictograms, logograms, syllabograms). How recognizable are the syllabograms when compared to the pictograms?

proto-cuneiform The oldest known form of writing, traced to Mesopotamia. Because they wrote on clay, Sumerians' early pictographic and numerical notations have been preserved; many of their signs are pictograms and logograms.

pictogram An element of writing that uses a simple symbol emulating an object to convey the word for that object.

cuneiform A writing system developed from proto-cuneiform, but more stylized; named for the wedge shape that the reed stylus made on soft clay.

Along with proto-cuneiform tablets from other nearby cities in Uruk, they represent the oldest writing in the world [**13.7**].

Scribes created proto-cuneiform tablets by incising soft clay preforms with a reed or other stylus. The forms then hardened and preserved the first symbols used in writing: simple drawings that represented objects, the first **pictograms**. After generations of copying, these were transformed into logograms, similar to what occurred with early Maya scripts. The symbols were also arranged in a systematic pattern, organized into a logical sequence by dividing lines carved in the clay. Pictograms include the shape of a ceramic bowl on its side to convey the concept of rations; a head indicates a man, and a triangle is a woman. Only after three centuries of use did Sumerians expand their writing to include events. By this time, the symbols that had once been recognizable as pictures of animals and plants had become highly stylized marks made by pressing the ends and sides of a reed, or ivory stylus, into clay. It is from the wedge-shaped marks thus produced that the writing received its name, **cuneiform**, which is based on the Latin word for a wedge, *cuneus*. The ease and rapidity of reproducing cuneiform writing may account for its transformation into abstract signs, or logograms [**13.8**].

History of Sumerian Writing

Some epigraphers and archaeologists believe that cuneiform tablets developed from an earlier use of tokens, which are small clay cones, spheres, disks, tetrahedrons, and lozenges found scattered among the refuse of villages from 8,000 years ago. Although no consensus exists on the purpose of the simplest, earliest tokens, archaeologists do agree that the appearance approximately 6,500 years ago of so-called complex tokens decorated with incisions and piercings did presage the development of written tally systems. Pierre Amiet and Denise Schmandt-Besserat believe that writing developed from the practice of wrapping these tokens inside a hollow clay ball or **bulla**, which was then stamped on the outside with the seals that people had long used to prevent tampering. In this way, *bullae* and their tokens [**13.9**] became the progenitors of a clay-based record-keeping system.

It is possible that people flattened moist clay to facilitate the imprint of any information inherent in tokens on the clay itself. Although we do not know the meaning of simple geometric tokens, their impressions upon the earliest "numerical notation tablets" noted quantities of goods, such as beer, grain, and oil. Complex tokens and their clay envelopes disappear with the introduction of tablets. These archaic writings include tags with **ideograms** (e.g., an eight-point star for a goddess, or a quartered circle for cattle) and tablets of numerical notation combining numbers and ideographic signs. Only in rare instances did the ideograms in archaic writing also share the shapes of earlier tokens. Numerical notations were arithmetically ambiguous; scribes used different numerical systems for different products, and one might thus write "600" in several ways, depending on whether cattle or beer was being tracked. In ancient Sumer, the consistent theme in the transition to real writing was not a single widespread recording system, but the reason why people used written technologies at all.

Sumerologists recognize that around 5,000 years ago cuneiform began to be used to write the Sumerian language. As with Maya glyphs, a major change evident in cuneiform writing is the transformation of logograms to syllabograms (symbols that represent syllables that are used to make up a word). This transition, referred to as **rebus writing**, allowed for more complex ideas to be expressed. Syllabograms could be combined to create more complicated words. For example, the symbol for *water*, "a," could be combined with the symbol for *ox*, "gu." When combined, the symbols allow one to sound out the word "a-gu," which in Sumerian meant *crown*. Writing emerged from an accounting system that could be used to transfer information regardless of spoken language to a system that reproduced spoken sounds.

Sumerians were the first to use cuneiform signs, but when Akkadian speakers under the leadership of Sargon assumed control of Sumerian cities in 2334 BCE, they took over the administration of authoritative resources; in so doing, they made some important changes. For starters, they began to write the Akkadian language using the sounds of Sumerian syllabograms. To the eventual benefit of archaeologists and epigraphers, Akkadian scribes left behind **lexical lists**, tablets offering lists of Sumerian words and their Akkadian equivalents, both written in cuneiform. Cuneiform writing

13.9 An ancient *bulla* and the tokens contained within it. The *bulla* is approximately 4 inches (10 cm) in diameter, and its outer surface is impressed with symbols that indicated its owner or purpose, and also acted as a seal against opening the *bulla*. The tokens were of various shapes, each impressed or incised with dots, lines, or other marks.

bulla A clay ball used to contain tokens that represented material goods. This method of record-keeping pre-dates writing in Mesopotamia.

ideogram A written character that signifies an idea or concept, but which lacks any indication for the spoken word.

rebus writing A writing system that uses pictograms of objects, the name of which resembles in sound a word or a syllable.

lexical lists Records that indicate words and their equivalents in other languages.

endured for nearly three thousand years as the technology to administer economic resources, with its use ending only when Alexander the Great (a Macedonian king) conquered Mesopotamia in 334 BCE. During that expanse of time, its application expanded to recording hymns; divinations; historical events; diplomatic correspondence; summary judgments and other legal proclamations; dedications; recipes; stories (such as that of Gilgamesh); and multiple languages, including Sumerian, Akkadian, Eblaite, Assyrian, Babylonian, Old Persian, Hittite, and Ugaritic.

Uses of Sumerian Writing

Of the large collections of cuneiform tablets uncovered at Uruk, many deal only with administrative procedures. This was the conclusion drawn by a German team consisting of mathematician Peter Damerow, epigrapher Robert Englund, and archaeologist Hans Nissen, with the three collaborating on the fine-grained analysis of more than five thousand written documents retrieved from the city. In its findings, the German team reported that "not one of [these archaic texts] is clearly related to religious, narrative, or historical topics [except one]...the so-called tribute list." The multiple numerical systems represented in the documents were used for economic purposes, such as tracking beer, grain, animals, and the acreage of fields. Some of the archaic texts also specified the name of the official in charge, an affiliated temple or institution, or associated religious festival. For many decades now, the clay tablets have been looted and sold on the antiquities market, but those found in context, such as the archaeologically excavated hoard at Uruk, come from the precincts of major public buildings. The economic and administrative purpose of writing in Sumer is important because it shows that the texts were primarily used to encode knowledge about the control of resources. This technology was especially utilized by rulers and their administrators in the region, and was exported widely [13.10]. The multiple numerical systems consistently utilized to record tallies for different products suggest that the format for this information was intentionally complicated, so the knowledge would remain restricted. Only those individuals who could read and understand the writing were able to access information that was critical to the lives of people across the society.

13.10 Clay tablet from Ugarit, Syria, c. 1300 BCE. The text describes a sales contract from King Niqmepa V to his servant, Amanichu. Note the impression of a cylinder seal at the top of the tablet, which was rolled across the wet clay to mark the document, similar to the use of mud sealings in Egypt to control surplus and wealth (see Chapters 10 and 11).

The cultural practices of Sumerians—such as the sacred locations of temples, the shape of their houses, the reed boats they sailed, and the foods they produced—had their origins in Mesopotamia 2,000 years earlier than writing. In spite of the resulting cultural continuity, the Sumerian language is not related to any other known language. It is not connected to the Semitic languages spoken across the Near East (including Hebrew, Arabic, and Aramaic, the language of Jesus' Galilee), or to Akkadian, a Semitic language spoken by people who lived among the Sumerians for a thousand years. If language is closely tied to ethnicity, then Sumerians would count as a separate group speaking and writing in their own vernacular. Yet many of those residing in the empire might not have even spoken Sumerian (recall Queen Pu'abi, whom we encountered in Chapter 12, whose elaborate royal tomb was built at Ur; she was likely married to a member of the Sumerian dynasty but was known by an Akkadian name). Rather, Sumerian may have emerged as an artificial construction of the elites that incorporated numerous dialects. Sumerologist Gonzalo Rubio likens the "linguistic picture of early Mesopotamia" to a "fluid and variegated canvas of words traveling together with the objects and techniques they designate." This assessment offers a picture of many languages and dialects contributing to a symbolic repertoire, one that can be accessed only by a select few through writing. By developing an administrative technology to exert greater control over surplus resources (e.g., grain, cattle, land), emerging elites also took control of the power of information in a changing world.

ANCIENT CHINESE WRITING

In Chapter 8, we explored the first signs of rice domestication in China, along the lower Yangtze River, *c.* 7000 BCE. Further north and 3,000 years later, the famous **Shang Dynasty** ruled in regions along the Yellow River Valley. The Shang is traditionally known as the second dynasty of China, succeeding the Xia Dynasty (approximately 2700–1600 BCE), but it is the first dynasty, in fact, supported by archaeological evidence. The Shang Dynasty saw many cultural developments, including bronze casting, the calendar, and writing [13.11].

Shang Dynasty The second dynasty of China, but the first supported by archaeological evidence; dates to 1600–1050 BCE.

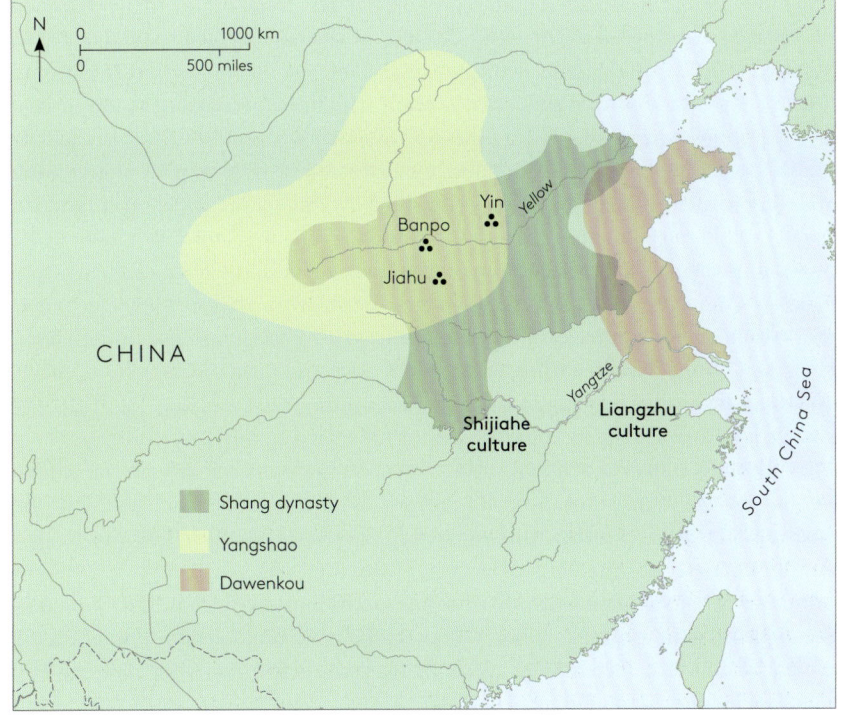

13.11 Map of China showing sites with early forms of writing. Oracle bones and bronze vessels were recovered from sites along the Yellow River, including the ancient Shang dynasty capital, Yin. In the earlier Yangshao and Dawenkou periods, communities at Jihau and Banpo marked their pottery vessels with pictograms that are antecedent to Chinese logograms. The Shijiahe and Liangzhu communities along the Yangtze and Yangzi rivers adopted some of the same components of these writing systems.

13.12 Bronze ritual vessel uncovered in Lady Hao's tomb. Rubbings of the bronze's surface have revealed the presence of an inscription, which has been deciphered to read "Mother Xin," indicating she had many children, and was revered by her extended family.

In the Shang dynastic capital of Yin (near current Anyang), the royal sons of Lady Hao fitted a small, wood-lined underground chamber for her burial. In the chamber, they placed a lacquered coffin with hundreds of weapons, bone ornaments, seven hundred valuable antique jade pieces, cowrie shell money, human sacrifices, and more than two hundred bronze ritual vessels, many with brief inscriptions in the earliest known Chinese writing. Lady Hao was one of many wives to Wu Ding, the first of nine Shang kings. Lady Hao commanded battles, received many gifts, shared King Wu Ding with his other consorts, and presided over many sacrifices. Hers remains the richest Shang Period tomb ever found, and the only royal tomb not looted. She rested under Yinxi (the ruins of Yin) on the Huan River in the northern temperate plains of China. Athough Lady Hao died 3,200 years ago, no one needed to decipher the writing on her bronze cauldrons. Chinese writing came into use in the Shang city states, perhaps even earlier, to record an ancestral form of Chinese language, and this writing and language have been in continuous use and development ever since. Chinese is the oldest continuously used writing system in the world.

When Lady Hao died, she had already borne several sons and at least one daughter. Among the items found in her tomb was a bronze vessel inscribed with the posthumous title of "Mother Xin," indicating she was a revered ancestor for a large family [**13.12**]. It remained buried with her until the tomb's discovery in 1976, but presumably her sons continued to offer her sacrifices above ground every *xin* day, the eighth day in a ten-day week. Other tombs have revealed that many Shang bronze vessels bear the name of an ancestor to whom the food or drink originally contained within is offered.

Oracle Bones and Bronze Vessels

From the era of King Wu Ding and subsequent Shang Dynasty rulers survive the earliest known examples of true Chinese writing. Although some of these early writings are inscribed on jade or bronze weapons, the occasional ox scapula, and pottery, the vast majority occur on two media: river turtle **plastrons** and bronze ritual vessels. More than half the inscribed turtle plastrons (*chia-ku wen*), otherwise known as oracle bones [**13.13**], date from the reign of King Wu Ding (began *c.* 1250 BCE). They were the end-result of a process of divination whereby a turtle shell was hollowed and heated, and the subsequent cracks then interpreted as responses to the diviner's questions. A scribe recorded on the plastron the date and name of the diviner and the question asked. Sometimes the diviner posed multiple queries, or the heating and cracking process was repeated. What seems clear from the writing inscribed after the heating (its characters carefully avoid the cracks generated by the heat) is that writing was necessary to record a successful divination, but was not part of the actual process itself.

Many scorched and cracked turtle plastrons contain no writing; few with writing record an answer to the inscribed query. In the most fully documented examples, such as the birth of Lady Hao's daughter, the diviner who posed the question is named, as are the king (Wu Ding) who interpreted the cracks and the outcome of the divination. Whenever recorded, the outcome is always successful, proclaiming and preserving for posterity the king's success in divination. Many of these oracle bone writings were deeply incised and inlaid with pigments, the cracks made by fire having been carved wider and also inlaid. The results of these divinations were intended to be visible.

The second medium on which Shang writing often occurs is bronze ritual vessels. These vessels were decorated with dragons, birds, and a variety of geometric patterns, and used to provide food and drink (often millet beer) to ancestors. As a long-lived trait of Chinese culture found in Confucianism (a philosophy founded in 600 BCE) and perpetuated by present-day Chinese values, the veneration of ancestors may be traced to the earliest Chinese civilizations of the second millennium BCE. Shang people who could afford fine bronzes commissioned ritual vessels to be inscribed with the names of their ancestors and to contain sacrifices or offerings to them. Often, a dedication was inscribed on the interior of a vessel, where only the ancestral spirit could perceive it.

Shang bronze vessels also generally bear the same characters applied to the oracle bones, but combine them with titles and rank to signify a monogram for the named individual. The title of *prince* accompanies *fish* (pronounced "yu") to identify the owner as *Prince Yu*. Some Shang bronzes carry dedications with symbols elaborately decorated beyond their conventional use in writing, perhaps to render a monogram more visually pleasing. The first evidence of writing from oracle bones and bronze vessels in ancient China differs considerably from the use of writing in ancient Sumer: Chinese writing first appears associated with ritual and ceremony, whereas Sumerian cuneiform was largely a specialist administrative tool.

plastrons The bony panels on the bottom of a turtle shell, used in the divination process in ancient China.

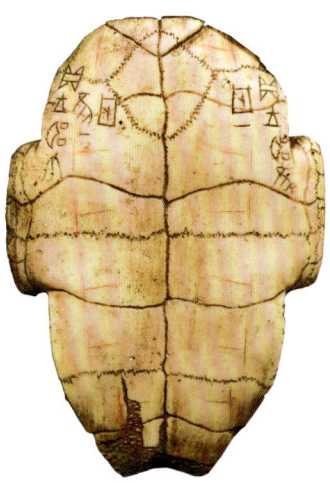

13.13 Oracle bone from the Shang Dynasty, *c.* 1250 BCE. This oracle bone was made from the plastron (belly-plate) of a large river turtle. The inscriptions carved into the shell record the divination of future events, which were indicated by cracks that occurred in the shell when it was heated.

貓頭鷹

"cat"　"headed"　"eagle"

13.14 The Chinese word for owl; translates in English as "cat," "headed," "eagle."

How Did Chinese Writing Originate?

Throughout its history, Chinese script has continued to be logographic (based on symbols that represent individual words). The meaning of each character can contribute to new words. In modern Chinese, there are many thousands of characters, all of which may be combined to form more complex words. For example, the word for owl is a conjunction of three characters: "cat," "headed," and "eagle" [**13.14**].

If writing appeared fully developed in northern China, had it been inspired from elsewhere or was it quickly invented? This remains uncertain, but no similarity exists between Chinese writing and earlier Sumerian, Egyptian, or other script. Something must have preceded the oracle bones, which are linguistically complex and include nouns, verbs, adverbs, and particles in a grammar that is undoubtedly Chinese. Similarly to Maya glyphs on stone, Chinese on bronze and bone is reasonably durable, so these inscriptions survive. These two materials, however, may not be the only ones on which early Chinese scribes wrote. A number of Chinese books survived more than two thousand years, and book-making may date back to an earlier period. These books are a precursor to scrolls, constructed as bamboo slats bound with string into a mat that could then be rolled out or unfurled. They are written in calligraphy, the artistic brush strokes that form thousands of Chinese characters derived from Shang texts. On oracle bones, the logogram for "volume" represents a bundle of tablets, whereas the sign for "writing/picture" is a hand holding a brush and producing a pattern. This suggests that the brush-and-ink technique must be as ancient as the Shang characters themselves. In Shang contexts, calligraphy can be deduced from the brush-written inscriptions on pottery from ancient Yin, hinting that it might have also been applied to other media, maybe bark, bamboo, or leather, that long ago perished.

How old could perishable writing have been? Although hundreds of oracle bones and bronzes may be linked to Yin, no writings endure from north-central China during the preceding **Erligang Period** (1510 to 1460 BCE). Erligang sites occupy the central plains of the Yellow River region, where millet (and later rice and wheat) supported a growing elite and widespread network of exchange. These sites do offer up cast bronze vessels (without inscriptions), created in special workshop areas. Large walled centers may also have been the capitals of competing dynasties named in much later texts (hence, the historical precision of the dates for this ancient time). Some of the centers exhibit a huge investment in labor, with earthen walls more than 65 feet (20 meters) thick. In addition, the wealthy in these early states had rich tombs, replete with the sacrificial offerings of goods and people. Although no firm evidence supports the idea that administrative writing and numerical systems tracked surpluses, indicating a legacy of conspicuous consumption, it is very possible that recovered bamboo slats could have been an important and long-gone corpus of early accounting documents to be understood alongside ritual bronzes and oracle bones.

In their search for clues, scholars have looked to pottery and noted the many and varied marks and signs that appear on Neolithic ceramics in the Yellow River

Erligang Period Culture of farmers that developed along the Yellow River of China c. 1510–1460 BCE; preceded the Shang Dynasty.

region of northern China, long before the earliest cities. A gap of at least six hundred years remains between the most recent Neolithic finds and the oracle bones of the late Shang dynasties, making it problematic to recognize direct development from one to the other. Furthermore, the range of Neolithic signs is in some instances broad and unrepetitive across very few examples. Some highly disputed instances, previously claimed as precursors to writing, include the so-called potter's marks at Banpo, a moated Neolithic village of the **Yangshao culture**, *c.* 5000 BCE, near modern-day Xi'an (Shaanxi). On Banpo pottery rims and occasionally the pots' interiors, archaeologists have identified scratches that might have been originally intended as tallies or identifiers [**13.15**]. These marks, though, bear no affinities with later logograms and are separated by three thousnad years from true writing in Chinese.

Several marks have also been noted on turtle plastrons found at Jiahu near modern-day Wuyang (Henan), that date to 5500 BCE, although analysis indicates the marks may not be as old as the bones. By the Middle–Late Neolithic, both larger- and smaller-sized "culture" villages emerged during the late Dawenkou phase (2800–2500 BCE), and from this period, scholars recognize the earliest pictographic signs antecedent to Chinese logograms. Bigger Dawenkou villages included wealthy tombs with ceremonial pits designed to hold offerings. **Zun jars** found there were used for making or storing wine for the ancestors, and archaeologists have continually associated them with ritual and ceremonial purposes [**13.16**, **13.17**]. These jars show the systematic use of repeated symbols and were recovered across an expanding regional system in which the cultural practices of the Dawenkou spread throughout north-central China's Yellow River area. Some of the same Dawenkou symbols also appear on ritual jade pieces of the Liangzhu culture (3200–2200 BCE)

Yangshao culture A Neolithic culture in Xi'an, China; included the site of Banpo, dating to 5000 BCE.

***zun* jars** Inscribed ceramic vessels made during the Dawenkou phase (2800–2500 BCE) in China, used for ceremonial offerings of wine to the ancestors.

Below left: **13.16 Dawenkou zun jar with incised symbol.** This vessel is 23½ inches (60 cm) in height and would have stood upright either on a stand or embedded in sand. The prominent symbol has been interpreted as "mountain fire-sun," and it was incised on the vessel as a part of the ritual offering of wine to a deceased ancestor.

Below: **13.17 A Dawenkou sign** of a frond-like wand above or emerging from a spool-shaped lozenge; this sign has a Shang meaning that links it to modern "earth" or "south."

13.15 Potter's marks from Banpo were probably not direct antecedents to the formation of Chinese characters.

ANCIENT CHINESE WRITING

centered in the Yangzi River delta to the south and east. Finally, Dawenkou signs and ritual practices clearly influenced the Shijiahe culture (2500–2000 BCE) in the middle Yangtze River area (near Hubei). Here also, *zun* jars bear the same symbols and were utilized in purely ritual contexts.

It seems likely that Dawenkou, Liangzhu, and Shijiahe signs belonged to a system used by several cultural groups interacting, exchanging goods, and engaging emerging elites and rulings families in political–ritual alliances. The signs also appear on ceramics connected to ritual performance, perhaps honoring ancestors. Unlike the inscriptions on Shang bronze vessels, these early signs probably served as the marks of a clan, for they were repetitive and ultimately distributed over a wide area. Alternately (or perhaps additionally), they may have designated the precise purpose of a *zun* jar or jade, whether that purpose was a type of ceremony or its dedication to a named individual.

Despite the many centuries separating the Dawenkou and Shang cultures, continuity emerges between at least some of the Dawenkou signs and Shang characters. Although the Dawenkou signs cannot be read and indeed may not convey a specific language, symbols persist that in a Shang context communicate concepts still inherent in their modern Chinese derivatives. If the origins of Chinese writing truly lie in the control of information by wealthy Dawenkou clan leaders who wished to honor their ancestors with sacrifices, and if they literally carved that command into ritual objects, then the power of Chinese writing is indeed ancient.

The writing of ancient China and Sumer demonstrates that written communication in the past manifested itself in many forms and for more than a single purpose. In the Sumerian case, writing was dedicated to the administration and control of resources. In China, writing appears to vary in its intent: to mark items tied to ritual performances, to relate groups in exchange, or perhaps to record ownership. This diversity of use may originate in the structure of ancient societies and in the need (or lack thereof) to transmit information beyond an immediate community. The technology to harness information that writing offered proved a powerful (sometimes authoritative) resource by which agents could shape the structure of their societies (see Chapter 9). With commanding resources, humans began to control surplus and labor better (see Chapters 10 and 11), and mold our Anthropocene niche.

ALPHABETIC WRITING

Many writing systems use an alphabet, just as you do. Alphabets, which appeared roughly two thousand years after the earliest cuneiform in the Near East, transcend a single language and are widely flexible. "Si je désirais m'exprimer en français, je pourrai communiquer par le même système d'écriture." To read French, you must know the Latin alphabet. Even if you do not understand French, you can passably read aloud the above statement. Put simply, alphabetic systems allow anyone to "decode" words, even if he or she does not know the language the alphabet conveys [13.18].

Brahmi script One of the oldest writing systems, used in ancient India and present-day South and Central Asia from the first millennium BCE.

13.18 Transformation of the alphabetic pictograms, discovered in short inscriptions about 1200 BCE, to the alphabet we know today. The earliest pictograms used images that have an initial sound corresponding to the desired sound; thus a simple house, "bet," corresponds to "b," the second letter of our modern alphabet.

Of course, Latin is not the only alphabetic system. In a Balinese village (in Indonesia), we once bought a bundle of inscribed palm-frond leaflets dried and bound together into the narrowest of books [**13.19**, **13.20**]. In an alphabetic script derived from South Asian Brahmi, incised cursive text flows along the length of the leaves. **Brahmi script** arrived in Southeast Asia with the spread of Hindu religious practices, and it was widely disseminated as an alphabetic system adaptable not

13.19, 13.20 Contemporary palm-frond book pages from a Balinese village, Indonesia. The bookseller displays an elaborately illustrated example.

ALPHABETIC WRITING   **315**

Hittites An ancient Anatolian people who established an empire in Turkey and the northern portions of the Tigris and Euphrates valleys *c.* 1600 BCE.

Phoenician alphabet The earliest systematized alphabet, developed in the ancient civilization of Phoenicia on the eastern coast of the Mediterranean.

Linear A A script used by Minoans in Crete, from 2500 to 1450 BCE, which has never been deciphered.

Minoan A palace culture centered on the island of Crete from 2500 to 1450 BCE.

Harappan A Neolithic culture that developed in the Indus River Valley in Pakistan and India; dates to between *c.* 2600 and 1900 BCE.

only to the Khmer language in Cambodia (see Chapter 10) but also to Old Javanese, Balinese, and the language of neighboring Lombok island. In the tenth century CE, highly literate Arab merchants from the elite families of South Arabia also entered Indonesia, bringing with them the Arabic alphabet used to write the Qur'an. Later, the Dutch claimed much of Indonesia as part of the Dutch empire and imposed a Latin alphabet.

Although they look very different today, both the Arabic alphabet and Latin alphabet derived from the first alphabet, conceived by Late Bronze Age scribes in the coastal city of Ugarit (in modern-day Syria). Ugaritic scribes corresponded with **Hittites** (an ancient Anatolian people) writing in cuneiform and with Egyptians writing in hieroglyphs, a combination of syllabograms and symbols that indicated consonants. Ugaritic scribes applied cuneiform strokes (not cuneiform syllabograms) to create new signs that stood for consonants. Around 1400 BCE, these same scribes committed this system to clay tablets with an order still familiar today—a, b…h…l, m…q, r…t…u. By 1000 BCE, the earliest systematized "alphabet" (named for the first two letters: "aleph" and "beth") entered into use in the ancient civilization of Phoenicia, which was on the eastern coast of the Mediterranean. Evidence of this system is an inscription on the sarcophagus of King Ahiram of Byblos (modern-day Beirut, in Lebanon).

The inscription honoring King Ahiram employs an alphabetic consonantal script—that is, it is composed entirely of consonants, which define the meaning of words in Semitic languages. In Semitic languages, vowels are used to indicate tense, actor, number, or other grammatical–contextual changes in form. Reading a Semitic word is a bit similar to reading a car's vanity license plate: "prty-lvr" would be interpreted as "party-lover." Thus, the Arabic consonant-only word "k-t-b" can be inflected with vowels to: *kātib* ("writer"), *kataba* ("he writes"), *kitāb* ("book"), *kutub* ("books"). The **Phoenician alphabet** was adopted regionally; Paleo-Hebrew, Aramaic, and other derived versions of it therefore evolved. In a few centuries, though, these letters were passed on to the ancient Greeks, who added the vowels a, e, i, o, and u.

PRESERVATION OF WRITING SYSTEMS

Our understanding of the emergence of writing and the roles it played in ancient societies is highly dependent on the writing media used, preservation, and archaeological context. As so many texts on fragile media have perished, many ancient writing systems will remain mysterious. Just as we guess at the range of topics the ancient Maya committed to writing, or ponder whether bamboo-wand scrolls and calligraphy preceded Shang oracle bones, there are cases in which we cannot read ancient writing at all. **Linear A**, a script used in the **Minoan** palaces on Crete until 1450 BCE, has never been deciphered, probably because the Minoan language that it recorded was also lost.

The **Harappan** writing system from the Indus River Valley civilization of South Asia (Pakistan and India) also is indecipherable. Harappans occupied several large

13.21 Harrapan stamp seals from the Indus River Valley. These seals were carved from steatite and are approximately 1 inch (3 cm) wide. In addition to undeciphered script, the seals depict animals and other objects. They would have been pressed into soft clay to mark ownership or indicate transactions.

cities and numerous villages in the Indus Valley floodplain and foothills of Pakistan. When the river floods became more stable approximately 3000 BCE, proto-Harappans devised a system to ensure irrigation and settlement stability in the floodplains, where they grew winter crops, such as wheat and barley, and added summer crops, such as cotton, sorghum, millets, and gram beans. By 1900 BCE, during the Mature Harappan Period, they had developed extensive public architecture in the cities, crafted such specialty goods as copper objects and carnelian beads, and traded widely in an intercultural exchange sphere in the Arabian Persian Gulf. Archaeologists have unearthed numerous Harappan stamp seals, little rectangular buttons of stone with a picture, often of a humped bull (*zebu*), and Harappan script [**13.21**]. The inscriptions are very short, with too few symbols to provide the necessary clues for deciphering them. Are they logograms? Syllabograms? Combinations? Scholars do not even yet know what language or languages they record.

There is reason to believe that Indus Valley civilizations used writing on a broader scale, although corroborating materials have since disappeared. Date palms were common in the Arabian Persian Gulf starting 8,000 years ago, and date sugar was the likely cause of dental decay in many populations that resided in the region during the day of the Harappans. For millennia, the people of the Indian Ocean used date palm leaves to make shelter, to weave baskets, mats, hats, rope, to feed their animals—and to write upon. Balinese artisans also used dried palm leaflets to create books of writing. As early as 500 BCE, Old South Arabian languages, such as Sabaean, Minean, and Himyaritic, were written in cursive texts on the midribs of date palm fronds.

Unlike the inscriptions on limestone and bronze to be found in temples and on public works of the interior deserts of Yemen, these simpler texts record many economic transactions, such as dowries, taxes, contracts, and tithes. As is the case with so many beautifully rendered limestone inscriptions, these fragile texts are

Dilmun An ancient Semitic-speaking culture that developed on the island of Bahrain in the Persian Gulf, *c.* 4000 BCE.

also in peril from looting and the demands of the antiquities market, especially because the current tragic civil war in Yemen has weakened the legal protection of artifacts. We may never fully understand the exact context of palm-stick writing, but we do know that it survived in very arid regions where ancient Arabian kingdoms had built their oases. Harappan texts, if similarly written on palm leaves or ribs, might have perished long ago, but it is also possible that somewhere an undiscovered trove of such documents awaits—perhaps large enough for epigraphers finally to decipher the ancient civilization's writing system.

WITHOUT WRITING: SYSTEMS OF NOTATION

From the archaeological evidence, scholars recognize that writing in Mesopotamia was rooted in an ancient system of notation, but that was not the case everywhere. Just as some writing systems emerged from notation and others did not, we must also recognize that writing systems were not the only means of controlling access to knowledge. Widespread technologies of notation were also used to generate and manipulate surplus and authoritative resources. For example, in 2000 BCE, Harappan merchants shared a common system of measures of weight with their Mesopotamian and **Dilmun** trading partners in the Arabian Persian Gulf. Dilmun was the civilization that developed on what today is the island of Bahrain, and at Dilmun, the ships of Harappans and Akkadians met to exchange wares: carnelian from the Indus Valley cities, copper from Magan (in Oman), steatite vessels from Jiroft (in Iran), and bitumen and textiles from Ur (modern-day Iraq). They spoke different languages, but their use of a standard intercultural system of weights supported by agreed upon measurements represented a framework for notation that required no common language. Beyond communicating meaning, notation can also become a system for developing knowledge through visual thinking. Modern systems of notation include Arabic numerals, algebraic notation, musical scores, dance notation, molecular formulae, and histograms. Notation can be used for a wide variety of communication and may exist separately from a full writing system. The Inka in the Andes are an excellent example of a people who developed a complex notation system without ever developing a system of writing.

Andean *Khipu*

High in the Andes, the Inka empire took shape only centuries before the arrival of Spanish conquistador Francisco Pizarro in 1532 CE, and it was administered through a notational system. At its greatest extent, the Inka empire stretched nearly 3,107 miles (5,000 km) along the coast and mountains of western South America from modern Columbia through half of Argentina. The Inka rulers in Cuzco (present-day Peru) faced a formidable task in administering an empire that not only included ecological zones from the tropical rain forest to the desert, mountain peaks to ocean shore, but also embraced many ethnic groups with different languages. Although

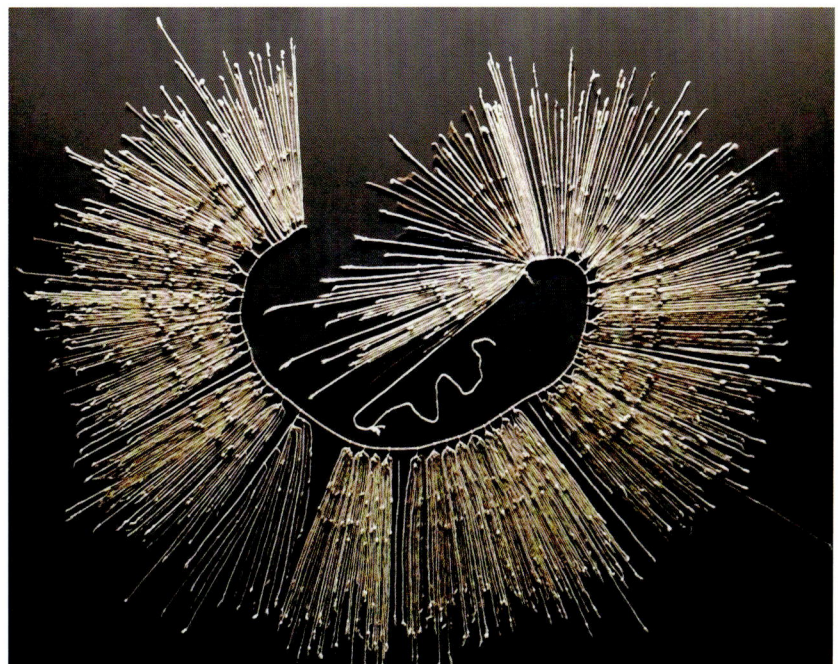

13.22 Andean *khipu* from the coastal region of northern Peru, South America. Khipu were made from knotted cotton and wool and were used to record information via the color of the fibers, how they were twisted into cords, and the position of knots. This *khipu* was made and used *c.* 1430–1530.

Below: **13.23 Inka man holding a *khipu*.** Engraving from Felipe Guamán Poma de Ayala, *c.* 1600 CE.

Quechua was the language of the Inka elites in Cuzco, they needed to find a common means of communication along this lengthy landscape. They did so not through a writing system, but via highly visual imagery supported by a notational system created by **khipu**, or "talking knots" [**13.22, 13.23**]. Almost all *khipu* date to the time of the Inka empire, and it seems likely that the system of notation was used, perhaps amplified, as an imperial elite extended their influence to extract resources from different cultures and ethnic groups.

Khipu were created by people called *khipukamayak*; they are made from colored, spun, and plied threads or strings fashioned from cotton or camel fiber. The cords are arranged so many pendant cords hang from one main cord, called a primary cord. These pendant cords may, in turn, have additional attached cords. The *khipukamayak* would begin by weaving a primary cord, spinning fibers in Z- and S-shaped twists, plying strands together, selecting pendant strands for attachment, and knotting those primary pendant strands using three kinds of knots. From an analysis of today's *khipu*, anthropologist Gary Urton posits that *khipu* construction entailed binary choices (such as S- or Z-shaped twists) at each step of the process. One could compare *khipu* to computer code in which each bit is an on-or-off choice (0 or 1), and in combination (just as bytes do), they convey more complex meaning. Urton suspects two kinds of data are embedded in *khipu*: statistical or numerical records, and sequences of codes that are designed to prompt one's memory.

The evidence for understanding this notational system includes the *khipu* themselves and Spanish Conquest-era accounts of how they were used. Because *khipu*

khipu A system of notation from the Inka empire, *c.* 1450, formed through the tying of knots.

WITHOUT WRITING: SYSTEMS OF NOTATION **319**

are constructed entirely of organic, fragile materials—and may be as old as 5,000 years if authentic—archaeological preservation limits their use to contexts in which they do not readily decay, such as dry deserts. One can only imagine that similarly to most other aspects of Andean cultures, the meanings and roles of *khipu* evolved over time so that something that appears to be an early *khipu* may not, in fact, have functioned in the same way as an Inka-era *khipu*. (The same argument could be made about symbols on Neolithic Dawenkou *zun* jars and monograms on Shang ritual bronzes.) Deciphering *khipu* relies heavily on the accounts of Spanish observers and of local, subjugated people, whose recorded descriptions conform with the expectations and worldview of Spanish overlords.

Spanish accounts of *khipu* indicate that once constructed, they were periodically unfurled, anchored with a foot or toe, and held up to the length of the body. Then, an orator or *harawikuq*, or perhaps their maker, the *khipukamayak*, orally disseminated the encoded information they contained. That specific times were dedicated for this kind of activity suggests that the Inka perhaps followed a calendrical system, maybe even one encoded within *khipu*. According to the Spanish accounts—and these include testimony collected from indigenous people—*khipu* were used to record the census, tribute payment and non-compliance, genealogies, war booty, dispersion of militia, codes of law, historical and mythical deeds, diplomatic correspondence, and even the Inka ruler's address to his people.

In the retrieval of mnemonic information or prompts that *khipu* offered, specialists who could access them had some flexibility in the dissemination of this kind of message. Flexibility was also inherent in the *khipu* themselves, for knots could be undone, strands added or removed, and order rearranged. Indeed, Hernando Pizarro, brother to Francisco Pizarro, described the actions of the *khipu* keepers when the Spanish demanded that they open a storehouse and remove goods: they "untied some of the knots which they had in the deposits section [of the *khipu*], and they [re-]tied them in another section [of the *khipu*]." Since *khipu* have never been fully deciphered by modern-day scholars, it is uncertain whether a single system existed that was universally accessible from one end of the empire to the other, or whether *khipu* were particular to a maker or region. What is certain is that for the Inka empire that followed, *khipu* provided a potentially powerful system of notation and authorization for the extraction of resources.

NORTH AFRICA AND ARABIA: LITERACY WITHOUT SETTLEMENT

Even as true writing emerged in the context of unfolding social complexity, permanently settled scribes and elites fed by agricultural surplus were not the only ones to read and interpret writing. Some of the most broadly literate societies were pastoral nomads who maintained relatively mobile lifestyles across the great deserts of Arabia and Northern Africa and whose networks and limited hierarchies resisted complex social structures. Scholars are not certain what percentage of **Bedouin**

13.24 A script still undeciphered adorns the walls of rockshelters in Dhofar, Oman. The characters, almost certainly alphabetic, appear in vertical lines or columns. Here the exposure to mist and sun has effaced much of the painted text.

13.25 Boulder from the site of Adrar Tekemberet, Algeria, inscribed with Berber Tifinagh script. This script was incised over an earlier panel that depicts a line of giraffes, which had inhabited portions of Algeria prior to the expansion of the desert. The Tifinagh script would have been read by others who were traveling through the region in Antiquity.

tribespeople 2,000 years ago could, in fact, read and write, and many did. From the thousands of desert inscriptions and graffiti written in scripts ultimately derived from the Proto-Canaanite alphabet (i.e., scripts that are ancestral to the Phoenician script), it is clear that a significant number were able to inscribe names, prayers, dedications, curses, place names, and genealogies. For millennia, Bedouin literally "wrote" their presence on the landscape [**13.24**] using scripts that are now called Thamudic, Safaitic, Nabataean, and Hismaic, in the clear expectation that those who followed would choose to access such communication.

Joy's archaeological fieldwork in Oman has spanned a region where a still undeciphered script in an unidentified language (perhaps an antecedent of Mehri or Shehri, both modern-day South Arabian, non-Arabic languages) paints the walls of caves and emblazons rocky surfaces in the desert. Nor was this kind of writing confined to Arabia. A half-dozen scripts were in use across the African Sahara, some as early as 2000 BCE. Perhaps the best known is the Berber alphabetic Tifinagh, inscribed in brief graffiti on rock faces from the third century BCE [**13.25**]. For all these groups,

Bedouin Nomadic people who have historically inhabited the desert regions in North Africa, the Arabian Peninsula, Iraq, and the Levant.

recitation and memory remained the primary means to transmit information, and despite their abilities to read and write in certain scripts, their oral poetic traditions remained the greatest of authoritative resources.

WRITING AND THE ANTHROPOCENE

Writing emerged in multiple instances where societies grew more complex with numerous hierarchies and diverse networks. The ability to communicate information was critical to maintaining social relationships, which facilitated the production of food and transport of goods across long distances. This aided in the transformation of ecological systems into food-producing ones, and allowed for the movement of plants and animals to new environments.

Although the utility of writing and systems of notation is apparent, their meanings are not always clear, with their purpose and cultural context frequently the subjects of much speculation. Importantly, writing systems—whether Maya, Sumerian, or Chinese—were independent inventions in multiple societies. Egyptian hieroglyphic writing also developed separately, as did some lesser-known scripts, such as the undeciphered Rongorongo on Rapa Nui in the South Pacific (see Chapter 1; **13.26**). Moreover, differences in preservation affect our understanding of the uses of early writing. Where scribes used clay in ancient Sumer, the numerical notations and economic purpose of early writing are evident: administrators were keeping records of production and surplus. Early writing occurred also on stone and bone, and maybe on perishable media, such as bark-paper, cured leather, wood slats, palm leaves, beaten papyrus stalks, textiles, and string.

Because writing permitted access to information, it evolved into a technology of power. This may explain why writing emerged with the development of social hierarchy and elites whose power base relied on not only the allocation of resources but also the authority to collect and distribute any surplus. Writing was thus put to many constructive uses—authorizing and recording the collection and distribution of surplus, tribute, exotic materials; documenting contracts, diplomatic exchanges, genealogies, and history; communicating myth and ideology, including codifying and propitiating the gods; transmitting social messages—to name just a few examples.

13.26 Fragment of a wooden panel bearing the Rongorongo script of Rapa Nui. Radiocarbon dating of several panels suggests the script was developed between 1200 and 1600 CE. The script employs stylized animals (such as frigate birds) that would have been present on the remote island.

Writing furthered communication over time and space and was a helpful mnemonic device. It lent itself to agency and was an ideal medium for archaic states in which new classes of people needed to control wealth and consolidate power. As an adaptation that enhanced all these developments, writing became a critical technology in shaping the Anthropocene era.

Chapter Questions

1. Compare the development of writing in the Near East versus China. What are the earliest examples of each, and what do they reveal about the different use of writing in those civilizations?
2. Discuss the elements often found in a writing system, using Maya glyphs as an illustration.
3. Offer an example of a society that existed without a written language.
4. Name several mobile societies that created a system of writing.
5. How has writing aided humans in developing their global niche?

Additional Resources

Bigley, Robert W. "Anyang Writing and the Origin of the Chinese Writing System," in *The First Writing*, edited by Stephen D. Houston, pp. 190–249. Cambridge, UK: Cambridge University Press, 2004.

Dematté, Paola. "The Origins of Chinese Writing: The Neolithic Evidence," *Cambridge Archaeological Journal* 20 (2010): 211–28.

Houston, Stephen D. *Reading the Past: Maya Glyphs*. London, UK: British Museum Press, 1989.

Johnston, Kevin. "Broken Fingers: Classic Maya Scribe Capture and Polity Consolidation," *Antiquity* 75 (2001): 373–81.

Nissen, Hans J., Damerow, Peter, and Englund, Robert K. *Archaic Bookkeeping*. Translated by Paul Larsen. Chicago, IL: University of Chicago Press, 1993.

Postgate, J. Nicholas, Wilkinson, Toby, and Tao Wang. "Evidence for Early Writing: Utilitarian or Ceremonial?," *Antiquity* 69, no. 264 (1995): 459–80.

Schmandt Besserat, Denise. *Before Writing*. Austin, TX: University of Texas Press, 1992.

Urton, Gary. *Signs of the Inka Khipu*. Austin, TX: University of Texas Press, 2003. See especially the quote attributed to Hernando Pizarro, page 3.

EXTRACTING THE MODERN WORLD
Fishing, Mining, and Slavery

14

One June, I was directing an excavation of the interior floor of a Hawaiian *hale* (house), which as far as we could tell had stood in that exact spot on the northern tip of Hawaii Island for the past three centuries. The floor was packed with earth, ash, and debris, and after a few days of excavation, two hearths emerged, side by side and flanked around the edges with flat stones. At the sieving screens, students spent about an hour sorting the contents of each bucket, and the artifacts were so numerous, we could barely keep up with the excavators. Suddenly, one student pulled something out of the sediment from the floor. It appeared to be a portion of a flattened circle, and embossed writing was visible on its edge. After we rubbed off some of the dirt that had adhered to it over time, the object was revealed to be a bronze coin. On its face, "Brasil" was one of the inscribed words. Brazil? In Hawaii?

Later that day, our brief search of numismatic (coin) listings for the seventeenth and eighteenth centuries identified the origins of the coin. It had been struck in Brazil in 1746. The inscription on the coin plainly states its wide-ranging value: "*Pecunia Totum Circumit Orbem*" (This currency has value around the world) [14.1, p. 326]. It certainly did, as is evident from its travels.

The coin was a product of the vast global network of colonies that had been established throughout the world by the start of the eighteenth century. This period marked the beginning of a grand era of extractivism of the seas and the earth, when human societies sought to take resources from one location at little or no financial cost, often at the expense of the environment and human society. Extractivism has accelerated global changes that are part of the Anthropocene, and also contributed to the human diversity of modern-day nations. As early as the ninth century, trafficking in humans had brought thousands of enslaved people from states in West Africa to the cities of the Mediterranean and Middle East. By the seventeenth century, slave-trading was an integrated global enterprise, and colonies throughout North and South America and the Caribbean were founded on the labor of enslaved Africans. All these developments represented the final critical step in the emergence of the modern world since the advent of agriculture and pastoralism 10,000 years ago.

Extractivism, Markets, and the Environment 326

Fishing and Maritime Extractivism 326

Underwater Archaeology 332

Extracted Minerals in the New World 334

Extracting People: The Slave Trade 336

Extractivism and the Anthropocene 346

Opposite Line engraving by Theodor de Bry, 1590, showing enslaved Bolivians and Africans working in the silver mine at Potosi, New Spain (present-day Bolivia). More than 40,000 tons of silver were extracted from the mine using the labor of thousands of slaves.

Key Concepts

- The impact of extractivism on the ecology of oceans and its connection to the emerging Anthropocene
- The earliest evidence of fishing in human prehistory and how that activity compares with whaling in the seventeenth century
- Mining as an example of extractivism
- The history of slavery and the colonial enterprises that supported human extractivism in subsequent centuries

14.1 Brazilian coin fragment from 1746, found inside a post-contact Hawaiian house in the upland leeward Kohala district of Hawai'i island.

extractivism The act of taking resources from the earth or ocean in order to make a product that can be sold or exchanged for other goods.

polis From the ancient Greek for the city-state, or its citizens.

EXTRACTIVISM, MARKETS, AND THE ENVIRONMENT

Extractivism is the process by which value is taken from the Earth to be sold. The term suggests a world market, where resources are exchanged for other goods, or sold for money [**14.2**]. In Chapter 13, we discussed the people of ancient Sumer who had documented the exchange of goods on clay tablets. Their system of accounting did not record the use of money, or of a market, but rather exchanges between individuals. A market is larger, describing a wider community of buyers and sellers. Around the world, markets emerged as a product of some state-level societies, where classes of people dedicated their energies to specialties, such as producing crafts, and exchanged them through simple barter. The creation of surplus products fueled the persistence of markets in urban areas, often in central spaces designed to allow people enough space to display their goods. The earliest known markets, such as the agora of Greece in the fifth century BCE, are some of the first physical spaces to have been investigated archaeologically.

Monetized markets appeared independently in only a handful of places. The first coins were produced in Western Asia and Greece between 500 and 600 BCE, and appear to have been both an instrument of exchange and a form of political power: the likeness of a ruler or the head of a wealthy family could be widely distributed, connecting producers and consumers in a recognizable patron–client relationship. The real power of money and market economies materialized later, as Greek city-states (*poleis*) sought to control the regions surrounding them. Establishing and maintaining the influence of the **polis** required public support, and that came most readily in the form of money. The transition of markets from barter–exchange to coin–exchange traces the influence of state power. Once established, monetized markets became the basis for state and imperial expansion, and by the fourteenth century CE, they were prevalent throughout much of the Old World. These markets required the persistent infusion of goods into the system so that profits could be maintained through a regular rate of exchange. For most of the last millennium, market economies have shaped much of human interaction and laid the foundation for extractivism.

FISHING AND MARITIME EXTRACTIVISM

On land, through the hunting of wild animals, gathering nuts and fruits, or later producing food via the cultivation of seeds, food acquisition and production created a human niche: garden patches supported particular plants and animals,

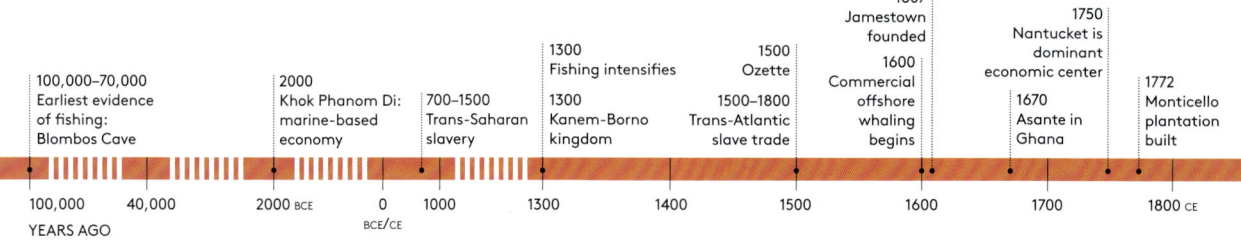

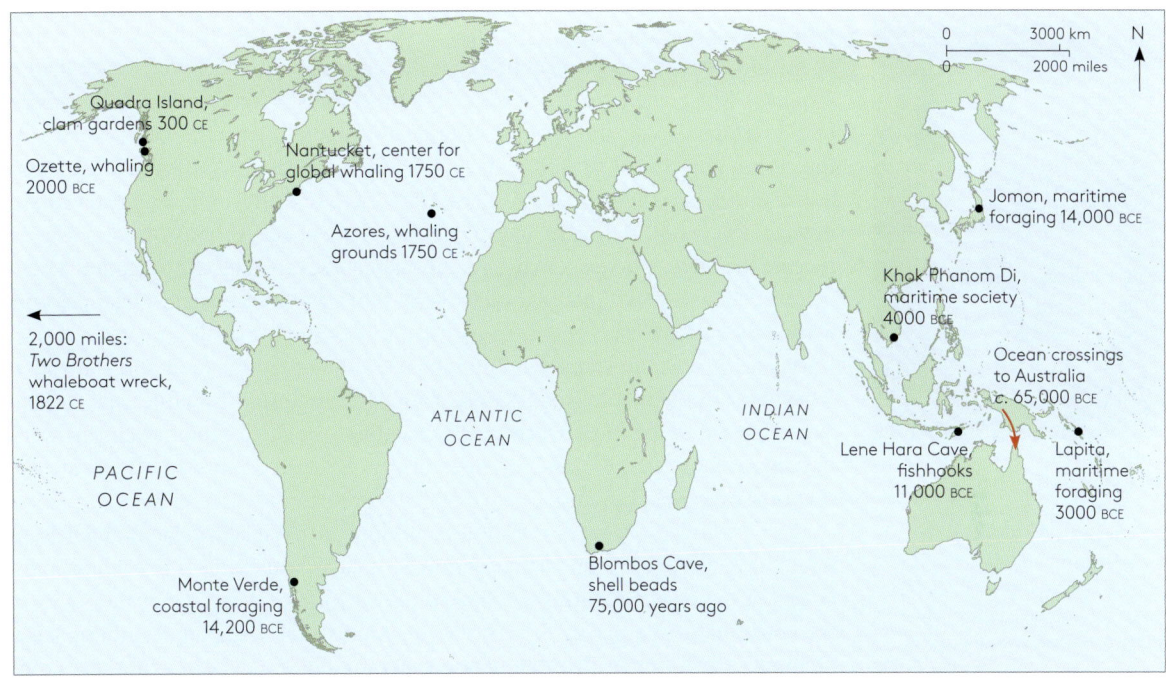

and populations of some wild species benefited from these new environments (see Chapter 8). Humans and animals (both wild and domesticated) co-evolved, creating a new ecological system that was largely self-sustaining and habitable. In contrast to farming the land, fishing is a form of extractivism. Humans collect from shorelines and hunt marine animals at sea, employing nets, boats, and hooks to capture and collect wild animals [14.3]. Organisms are removed from their natural environment and taken back to land for consumption or use; rarely is anything returned to the ocean that is generative. Only in a few rare instances, such as the manufactured clam gardens of Quadra Island in western Canada, which were constructed c. 300 CE, have humans changed or built marine habitats in order to foster the growth of desired populations of fish or mollusks. Throughout all of human history, the ocean has been a place to hunt and gather.

Fishing originated in the Pleistocene, perhaps with the earliest *Homo sapiens* populations. Blombos Cave in South Africa (dating to 100,000–70,000 years ago), the site offering some of the first evidence of red ocher art and shell beads (see Chapter 3), also yielded evidence of the earliest fishing. By 100,000 years ago, humans had discovered that coastlines were rich in marine mollusks and fish, a ready supply of

Above: **14.2 Extraction of maritime resources** occurred around the world and stretches far back in time, beginning in South Africa's Middle Stone Age.

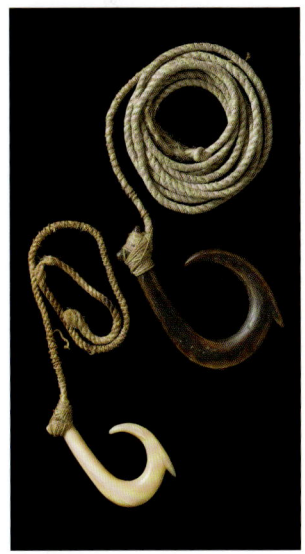

Right: **14.3 Fishhooks** made from whale tooth ivory (left) and sea turtle shell (right) with plant fiber attachments. These 2 cm hooks were made approximately 200 years ago by Pacific Islanders, and would have been attached to a long fiber cord that was held in the hand. The barbs on the bends of the hooks would have prohibited the fish from escaping.

14.4 A shell fishhook as recovered from the early Holocene levels of Lene Hara Cave in East Timor in 2002. This hook is approximately 1½ inches (4 cm) long and made of shell from a marine gastropod. The shape of the hook indicates it would have been used to pull in fish quickly from shallow depths.

Jomon A seafaring culture in Japan, dating back 14,500 years, that also produced some of the world's earliest pottery vessels.

shell midden A dense archaeological deposit composed of clam shells, which is usually generated as a waste product of marine foraging.

protein. Excavated deposits in the Blombos Cave have revealed fishbone and limpet shells, indicating the capture of fish near the shore and the collection of rock-loving mollusks. The presence of giant tuna vertebrae also suggests that the local people had developed some ability to procure deep-water species. Fishhooks, which are the clearest marker of fishing in deeper water, have been found by archaeologist Sue O'Connor in the deposits of Lene Hara Cave in East Timor, an island north of Australia [**14.4**]. Dating to 11,000 years ago, the shell fishhook and associated marine shell remains speak to the evolution of an advanced technology and a new cultural niche: a maritime-focused lifestyle that employed boats, navigation, and fishing for subsistence.

As early as 70,000 years ago, humans used the ocean for food and transport. As evident in the dispersal of people from Africa across the Mediterranean Sea, and eastward to the Indian Ocean, the coastlines provided protein-rich corridors that allowed humans to pass into new regions. By 65,000 years ago, they reached Australia and must have done so using boats or rafts (see Chapter 4).

Over the last 20,000 years, maritime communities that relied on boats and fishing might have dispersed even farther: some of the earliest sites in South America may be linked to people who simply followed the Pacific Ocean rim. Once they skirted the coastline of the Bering Straits, they headed south along an abundant "kelp highway" (see Chapter 4). In the 10,000 years that followed, more sedentary communities that relied on marine resources developed in many locations. In Japan, the long-lived **Jomon** culture (14,000–2,300 years ago) produced some of the world's earliest pottery in conjunction with a hunting-and-gathering system of subsistence that included ocean fishing. The 4,000-year-old site of Khok Phanom Di in Thailand is one of the most amazing examples of a maritime-focused society. Constructed within a mangrove-forested estuary, the society was supported by mollusks and other invertebrates collected from the surrounding mudflats, as well as fish, whales, and sharks caught by boat. In most instances, ancient maritime societies also yielded extensive deposits of marine shell along their coastlines. Known collectively as **shell middens**, these deposits frequently preserve rare household objects and the surfaces for houses, activity areas, and burials.

With the introduction of agriculture, many maritime societies incorporated food production into their livelihoods, or they became fishing specialists who exchanged marine foods for other products. Within the last 3,000 years, some specialists targeted particular species, such as salmon, herring, or cod that bred in seasonal cycles and produced schools of millions of individuals. Fishers also invented new technologies to maximize their returns on the hunting of these species: bigger boats and longer nets could catch more fish in a single expedition, reducing the cost of the trip and the labor needed to bring fish to shore. As fishers became active participants in new market economies, they additionally invented techniques to preserve fish: drying, salting, and packing fish into oil-filled jars allowed them to create a product that could then be stored or traded. Fresh fish, however, commanded the highest price the moment it reached shore. Rotting fish was worth next to nothing. By the fourteenth century CE, the extraction of fish and other marine organisms from the world's oceans was well under way. To keep the industry going, fishers had to keep fishing, and local depletions meant that their boats had to range farther out to bring home a profitable catch.

The human propensity toward extractivism is evident in nearly all societies that developed market economies. Writing is a technology that has aided in extraction, because keeping track of production was critical to planning for the future and for building and managing capital (see Chapter 13). The extraction of fish and animals from the world's oceans, however, has not netted the same reserve of capital. Certainly, the ocean spurred the development of larger and more profitable boats and ports—hence greater wealth—but human extraction has made the ocean environment itself poorer, rather than richer.

The next phase of the Anthropocene is now upon us: it has been projected that as human populations continue to grow and the earth warms, an ecological collapse of the world's oceans will occur over the next century. It is difficult to discern what this will mean for the planet, as the ocean is responsible for so many of the systems that maintain life—the atmosphere, the temperature, the movement of animals and plants. All are connected to the ocean. Human abilities to adapt and transform the world will be pushed to an uncertain frontier.

Whaling: Extracting Light from the Sea

A measure of the impact of extractivism is the story of whaling [**14.5**]. Archaeological deposits and historic documents indicate that many ancient societies took advantage of the mass strandings of whales and dolphins. Either through confusion or disease, large numbers of whales sometimes beached themselves in the shallows of bays and sandspits and, upon discovery, were butchered on the spot. These animals were desirable prey: they were enormous and contained massive amounts of blubber, a thick layer of fat just beneath the skin. This fat is high in calories and can be used for food—and especially for Arctic people, whose diets could count on few plant resources, the fat became a good substitute for meat proteins. Throughout the

14.5 Prime locations for sperm whales (blue) and right whales (dark pink), and major ports for whaling, during the height of the American whaling industry, 1825–49.

Makah A tribe on the Pacific Northwest coast of Washington State who inhabited the ancestral village of Ozette, and who maintain a tradition of whaling.

world, maritime societies would also cut blubber into chunks and use heat to melt it into oil, which might then be used as fuel for simple lamps. In addition, societies with boats and canoes routinely hunted whales and dolphins that came close to shore, customarily using harpoons to capture a whale, and ropes and floats to tire it. Once the whale became exhausted, fisherman could safely approach and lance the animal, causing it to bleed to death. The whale would subsequently be dragged to shore and butchered on the beach. As many species of whales and dolphins migrate along coastlines to reach feeding and breeding grounds, shoreline whaling fisheries developed as seasonal activities.

Ozette, the ancestral village of the **Makah** tribe located on the Pacific Northwest coast of Washington State, is the site of one such fishery. Although the original village was destroyed in a landslide approximately five hundred years ago, several harpoon parts made specifically for hunting whales were preserved. Whaling traditions for the Makah have been maintained in oral histories and modern whale-hunts. In the last century these included a period of seclusion for whalers, devoted to spiritual and physical preparation for the task ahead. Successful whaling also incorporated the efforts of the entire community, who participated in the creation of harpoons, floats, lines, and canoes, and dedicated many weeks to the processing of the whale once it had landed on shore [**14.6**].

With the advent of long-range, sailed vessels in many parts of the world in the fifteenth and sixteenth centuries, whaling transitioned to an offshore pursuit. In Europe and the Americas, the main impetus for this was the production of whale oil for lamps. Before the arrival of gas and electric lighting in the late nineteenth century, oil- and wax-based lamps and candles lit the evening hours, allowing people to work long past sunset. This was particularly important in higher latitudes,

14.6 Carving of a whale cow and calf from the site of Wedding Rocks, near the Makah site of Ozette. This carving is more than 3 feet (1 meter) long and of unknown age, but it depicts a creature that was both culturally and economically important to the Makah people. Archaeologically preserved tools as well as human settlements indicate that reliance on whaling began *c.* 2000 BCE in the Pacific Northwest.

where the hours of daylight could vary dramatically over the solar year. Often, these lamps were a simple reservoir of oil and a wick, but they also included glass lanterns that helped protect the flame and amplify the illumination. Early lamp fuels included animal fats, plant-based oils (such as linseed, palm, and olive), and beeswax, but these materials were never available in sufficient amounts. Whales, however, could provide oil on a massive scale. On average, the processing of a single whale would produce 100 barrels of oil, and each barrel held approximately 31 gallons (a little more than 117 liters). The quantity of oil, which could be sold relatively cheaply, fueled the demand for more whales. As a result, the commercial whaling that emerged in the seventeenth and eighteenth centuries was unlike any other fishing activity up to that time witnessed on our planet: it was far-reaching and highly industrialized, producing oil for a vast global market.

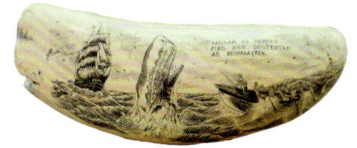

14.7 Engraved tooth of a sperm whale depicting the lancing of a sperm whale during a hunt in the Azores Islands, c. eighteenth century. Although whaling industries targeted all whales for their blubber, sperm whales were valued for the large amounts of spermaceti oil that could be extracted from their heads. The ivory from their teeth was made into buttons and other objects.

Whaling cities emerged on the coasts of Europe and the Americas, and by 1750 CE, the island of Nantucket, located off the coast of Massachusetts, emerged as the dominant economic center for global whaling [**14.7**]. For the next century, Nantucket-based whale ships and sailors dominated the industry; they established whaling grounds in the North and South Atlantic, Indian Ocean, North and South Pacific, and Arctic Ocean. As whale populations were hunted out of an area, the whalers searched further and further out at sea, ultimately setting course on voyages that would last for three to four years. Whaling ships thus became floating industrial factories. Small whale boats manned by rowers would pursue and slaughter a targeted whale with harpoons and lances, and tie the carcass alongside the ship for processing. Using long-handled blades and hooks, experienced butchers would strip the thick layer of blubber from the whale [**14.8**]; it was then cooked on deck in giant cauldrons called try-pots. The rendered oil would be stored in wooden barrels in the hold of the ship, and the boat would return to port only when it

14.8 Engraving of American whalers "cutting in" on a whale, 1874. The layer of blubber was stripped from the whales using a hook and long-handled blades. Once on board, the blubber was heated in iron pots and transformed into oil, which was then stored in barrels. Some whaling voyages spent years at sea collecting oil, and returned to port only when their cargo holds were full.

was full. According to historic records, the year 1853 was the most profitable in the nineteenth century in terms of whale oil production, accounting for the slaughter of some eight thousand whales in a single year.

UNDERWATER ARCHAEOLOGY

Evidence attesting to the long reach of whalers in the eighteenth and nineteenth centuries has been found in shipwrecks located around the world. Maritime archaeology is dedicated to the exploration and recovery of archaeological deposits and artifacts that are underwater. This can include boat wrecks and the remains of docks and ports, but also submerged sites that were inundated by sea-level rise. Being

14.9 A cofferdam excavation. The image above shows the cofferdam exterior, which extends around 10 feet (3 meters) above the surface of Matagorda Bay, in the Gulf of Mexico. The cofferdam is made of reinforced steel, and the water inside it was pumped out to allow the excavation of the ship *La Belle*. This vessel was part of a colonizing expedition from France that ultimately failed, leading to its wreck in 1686. The remains of *La Belle* were excavated in the late 1990s and 2000s.

underwater poses unique challenges for archaeologists. In some cases, sites must be surrounded by **cofferdams**, which create an interior space that can be drained, allowing for surface sediments to be excavated as if they existed on dry land [**14.9**]. When water is too deep, maritime archaeologists must also be trained divers and able to perform all their surveying, mapping, and excavation underwater using diving equipment. The same principles that guide terrestrial archaeology apply to underwater scenarios: archaeologists use datum-points to determine the location of objects, and grids for mapping the location of objects that are visible on the seafloor or river bottom. Excavation methods vary widely, however, and depend on the conditions. In some instances, vacuum systems can be used to suck sediments into a series of sieving screens. At other sites, sediments must be removed manually by brushing.

In 2008, maritime archaeologists working near the French Frigate Shoals, which is part of the Northwest Hawaiian Islands, discovered a site possibly dating back to the height of the nineteenth-century whaling industry. A survey of a nearby reef suggested a whaling ship had wrecked in the surrounding waters. An extremely large metal anchor lay at the bottom of the Pacific, with several metal blubber hooks and iron try-pots strewn along the same stretch. Further surveys of the deep documented the presence of a nineteenth-century ceramic ginger jar and a number of metal harpoon heads. The harpoon heads were identified as "double-fluted" points, which had barbs on both sides of the harpoon's shaft. This exact kind of harpoon was produced for Nantucket whalers in the early nineteenth century, which indicated the wreck had occurred sometime in the early 1800s.

An examination of records for shipwrecks of the period, and the full range of artifacts retrieved, determined that the remains could only come from one ship, the *Two Brothers,* which had sailed out of Nantucket in 1821 [**14.10**]. Bizarrely, the ship's captain had been involved in a prior shipwreck that same year. Captain

cofferdam An airtight enclosure around an underwater archaeological site that can be drained, allowing for surface sediments to be excavated as if they existed on dry land.

14.10 A diver-archaeologist explores the *Two Brothers* wreck on the reef of French Frigate Shoals, in the northwestern Hawaiian Islands, in 2008. Artifacts found on the bottom of the reef corroborated historic accounts that this wreck was the *Two Brothers*.

George Pollard had commanded the *Essex*, which was rammed and sunk by a sperm whale, with his story of struggle becoming the inspiration for Herman Melville's epic novel *Moby-Dick*.

In a few more decades, around 1860, the discovery and production of petroleum-based oils brought about a swift decline in the whale-oil industry, but it did not end whaling. New technologies, such as steam- and diesel-powered engines, explosive harpoons, and factory-ships, ushered in a new era of whaling in the twentieth century. Analysis of catch records delineates that 2.9 million whales were killed between 1900 and 1999, which is perhaps twice as many as those hunted and butchered in the preceding two centuries. Only after 1986 did whaling regulations result in a moratorium on most whaling, but by then the ecological damage may have been too great. After nearly three centuries of industrialized whaling, all whale populations had become a fragment of their former sizes. Genetic analyses of several species suggest that populations have declined by more than 90 percent in that time. Compared to the past, modern oceans are now virtually empty of whales, and many fish stocks show similar horrifying declines. We have extracted huge numbers of fish, whales, and other animals from the ocean, and do not yet know what the future consequences of those actions will be.

EXTRACTED MINERALS IN THE NEW WORLD

The mining of minerals—taking precious metals and stones out of the ground—is a widespread form of extractivism, and has affected the environment in many ways across the world [**14.11**]. In the lofty Catedral de Santa María de la Sede in Seville, Spain, an altarpiece covered in gold reaches several stories to the vault of the ceiling [**14.12**]. Many similar altars exist throughout Spain. Here ended up the extracted wealth of the New World. Spanish galleons transported vast treasure from the Americas to the Spanish Crown, which claimed one-fifth of the spoils of the conquistadors.

One of the legacies of Spanish extraction is the site of Cerro Potosi in Bolivia. Originally a sanctuary dedicated to the Tiwanaku native god Pachacámac (about 1,000 CE), the tiny village attracted little attention from the Spanish until the colonial administrators learned of the silver lodes at the adjacent mountain. Named Cerro Rico ("Rich Mountain") by the Spanish, the mines proved to be the richest in the New World, furnishing the silver for famed Spanish pieces of eight, a currency that made its way around the globe.

A study of nearby Laguna ("Lake") Lobato conducted in the early 2000s has revealed the environmental consequences of extractivism. From the era of the Tiwanaku civilization (1000–1200 CE) in highland Bolivia, native people were already smelting silver from Cerro Potosí: silver largely used for ornaments and display, not as coinage or tools. The smelting produced heavy-metal byproducts—lead, antimony, tin, silver, and bismuth—that hydrolyzed and drifted on the winds to Laguna Lobato, polluting the lake and life around it. Lake cores reveal a heightened level of silver

14.11 This silver pin comes from the Central Andes, before the era of Inka empire. It was likely used by women to fasten clothing. Prior to the arrival of the Spanish, New World metal-working fashioned ornaments, not tools.

Opposite: **14.12 The grand altar of the Catedral de Santa María de la Sede in Seville, Spain.** The altar is almost 120 feet (36 meters) high and made of wood gilded with gold leaf. The gold was extracted from the Andes mountains of South America during the sixteenth century. The altar was completed in the 1550s.

huayrachina An Inka furnace that used the wind as ventilation for the smelting of silver.

byproducts from the Tiwanaku period. When Inka rulers assumed control of the region (1400–1650 CE), silver byproducts decreased. Their technologies that called for smelting in a **huayrachina** (a native wind furnace that stands a little more than 3 feet, or a meter, high) were more efficient and resulted in the loss of less silver, although other heavy-metal byproducts continued to drift into the lake. With the arrival of the Spanish, silver byproducts spiked again as the conquistadors amalgamated—or refined—powdered silver ore with mercury, releasing large quantities of lead. Climate scientists studying the ice in the Quelccaya glacier, almost 500 miles (800 km) away in the highlands of Peru, have detected the clear signature of air pollution with toxic lead and other heavy metals from the two hundred years of Spanish colonial rule, from 1545 to 1821. In local lakes around Potosí, silver byproducts returned to Inka-period levels when colonial administrators re-embraced Inka technology. To this day, the byproducts of arsenic, cadmium, cobalt, iron, manganese, lead, and zinc pollute the adjacent River Pilcomayo. These heavy metals render the water unfit for drinking or agriculture, but have nevertheless infiltrated systems of irrigation and stock watering (used to increase the weight of cattle before their sale). The outcome of extractivism in Bolivia is a landscape no longer fit for humans.

Not only the environment, but also the people of Bolivia, have paid a heavy price for the Spanish extraction of silver. In their eagerness to extract the wealth of New World minerals, colonials enslaved native peoples to coerce the necessary labor. They also brought with them slaves from Africa, and both groups were forced to work the mines, a labor that was taxing and toxic. Perhaps as many as 8 million people died during the centuries of colonial control. One mass grave, unearthed in 2014, is believed to contain the remains of four hundred enslaved miners from the colonial era, whose lives were shortened by the toxic conditions of the smelting process and whose bones document the hardship of their toils. Slavery as a form of extractivism has dramatically altered the shape of our human world.

EXTRACTING PEOPLE: THE SLAVE TRADE

Just as humans have extracted life from the oceans, regarding fish and other creatures as little more than items of value, so, too, have humans extracted other humans from their environments and traded them as commodities. Slavery is the practice of capturing and controlling people, and treating them as property. The trading of slaves has a long prehistory and is a critical marker of extractivism in human economies. Slaves lose their personal liberty and control over their own bodies and fates; they also lose their identity as individuals. Their potential labor and ability to bear children (who will also then become enslaved) are the only considerations in determining their value.

Slavery's origins in Europe, the Near East, Asia, and Africa have been recorded in texts and in the archaeological findings of ancient cities, such as those of the Classical worlds of Greece and Rome. In Europe, while Vikings traded salted cod and Greenlanders sold walrus ivory, they also shipped Slavs from Eastern Europe, people

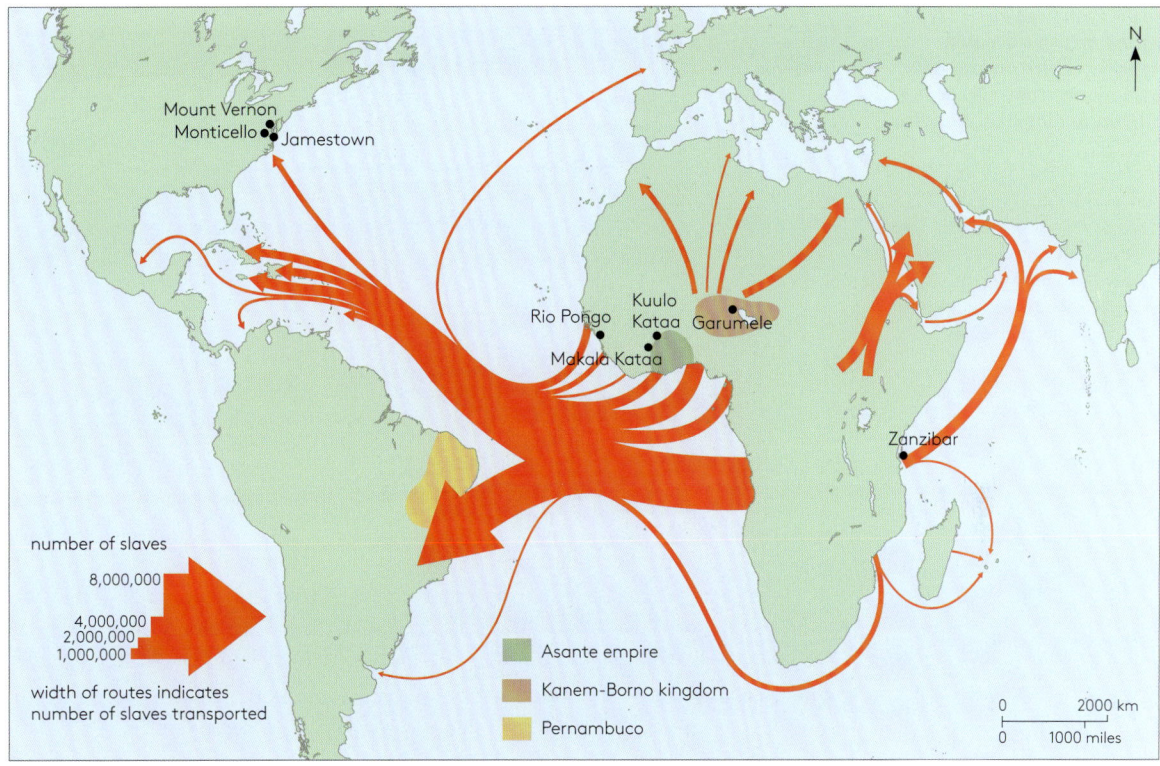

14.13 **Composite map of major slave trade routes**, 1400–1900, including both the Middle Passage (trans-Atlantic) and the Indian Ocean trade.

who had been captured and purchased by the (eastern Viking) Rus (see Chapter 12), to Byzantine Christian and Muslim markets in North Africa, Andalusia, and the Near East. The word *slave*, in fact, originates from "Slav," but the practice itself is much older.

The connection of slavery to the generation of wealth—in particular, trade in luxury goods that were also extracted, such as ivory and gold—is discussed here in the context of sub-Saharan Africa. The trans-Atlantic slave trade expanded this system to colonies in the New World and rim of the Indian Ocean, removing people to lands that were rich in resources but poor in labor [**14.13**].

Slavery in Africa

The emergence of the notorious trans-Atlantic slave trade, which transported West Africans to Brazil, the Caribbean, and eastern North America in the sixteenth through nineteenth centuries, displaced more than 12 million Africans across the Atlantic. The actual number of Africans purchased by traders was considerably higher because passage over the high seas often resulted in a high death rate [**14.14**, p. 338]. This slave industry, by which Portuguese, Dutch, French, Arab, British, and ultimately American ships delivered enslaved Africans to the Americas to work

EXTRACTING PEOPLE: THE SLAVE TRADE   337

14.14 Plan produced in 1788 of the British slave ship *Brookes*, which carried 609 individuals from the coast of Ghana to Kingston, Jamaica. This diagram provides a grim measure of the logistics of the slave trade, which required people to be shackled together in small compartments for a journey of between fifty and seventy days. Nineteen of the 609 people died en route.

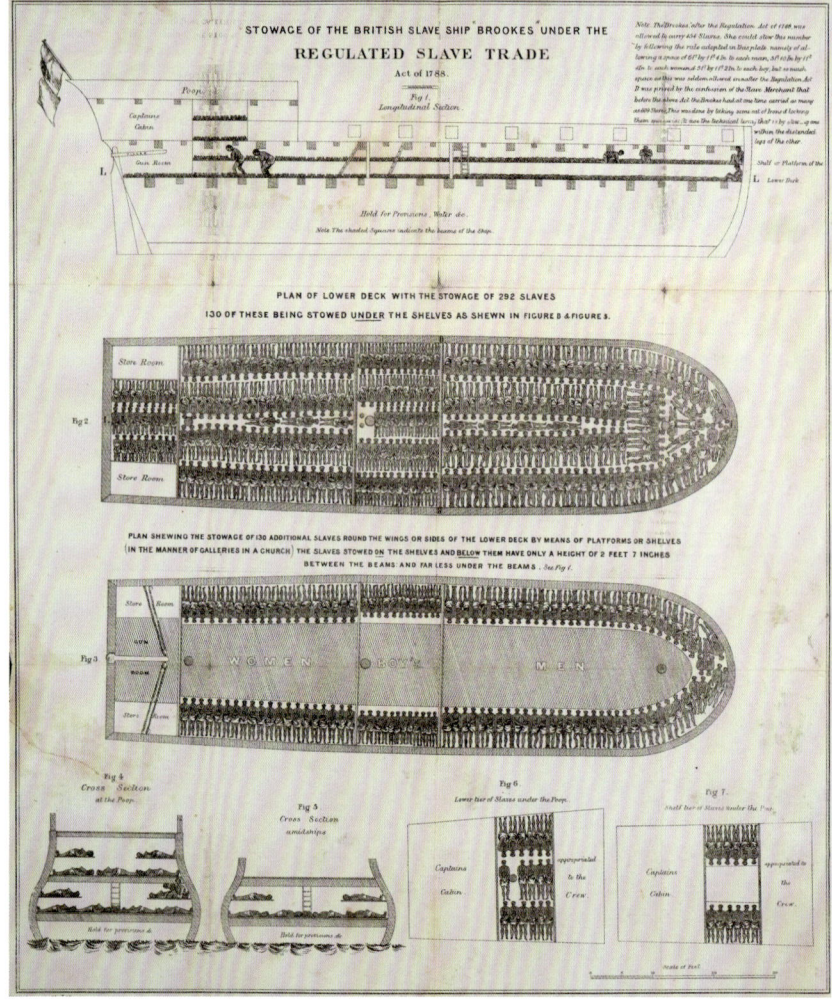

on sugar, rice, tobacco, clove, and cotton plantations, did not develop out of thin air. It grew from the preexisting slave raiding and slaving (the practice of attacking neighboring communities and capturing individuals to be slaves) that had flourished within West Africa since at least 800 CE. The enslaved, along with gold and ivory, were moved northward along trade networks, which helped fuel the rise of African states. A history of African raiding, slaving, and trading does not exonerate European imperialism and its impact on indigenous people, but a broader understanding of slavery's long tradition and integration within the political economy of the continent helps explain its later development and institutionalization.

Slavery systems operate within political economies, which represent the intersection of local, regional, and transregional processes with household production and organization. The term "political economy" implies mutual influence, so a regional change has impact at a household level and vice versa. Because many regions in Africa were land-rich and labor-poor, anthropologists and archaeologists have assumed that control and concentration of labor, not ownership of or control over land, were fundamental to the structure of early African polities. For example, power and prestige might be emphasized through the conspicuous consumption of beer, grown and brewed via the labor of multiple wives and enslaved people (see Chapter 12). Archaeologically, the social compositions of households are difficult to trace, and characterizing the entire African continent in terms of single households would deny its immense diversity. Nevertheless, the issue of scarce human labor remains integral to anthropologists' understanding of the many African political economies that fueled the growth of slavery. A few will be considered here.

TRANS-SAHARAN SLAVERY Slavery existed on a massive scale in much of Africa's Saharan and sub-Saharan regions [**14.15**]. Islamic historical sources suggest that between 700 and 1500 CE around 5.5 million sub-Saharan Africans were enslaved and deported across the Sahara and eastward to the Indian Ocean. This is less than half the estimated 12 million people enslaved in the trans-Atlantic trade after 1500, but the historic numbers point to the long-term significance of the slave trade and its roots.

In the fourteenth century CE, evidence linked to the rise of the **Kanem-Borno kingdom** in the Chad Basin of Central Africa may also be connected with intensified trans-Saharan trade contact. Unlike West Africa, the Chad region did not have gold resources, but it was geographically central to some of the most accessible

Kanem-Borno kingdom
An empire that existed in modern Chad and Nigeria in the fourteenth century CE.

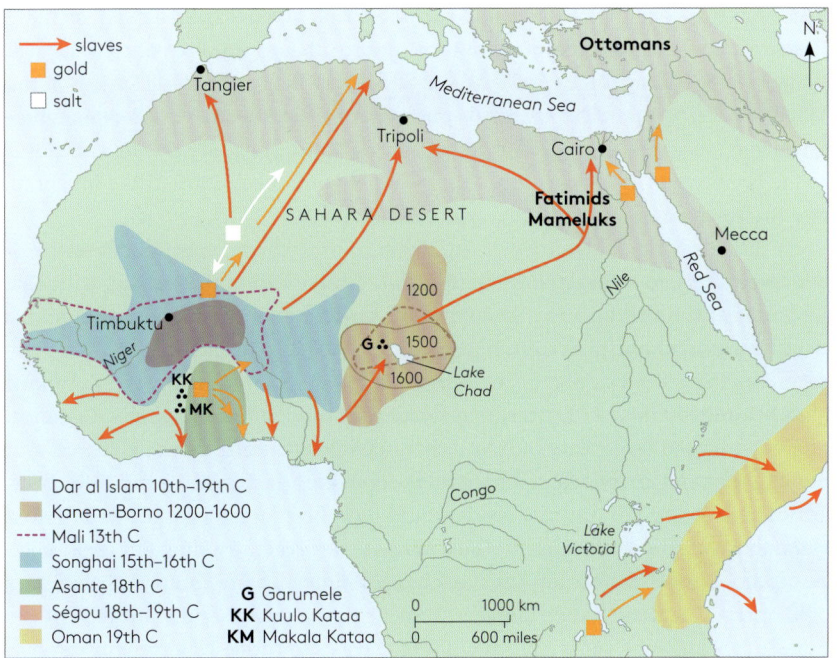

14.15 Map of the trans-Saharan slave trade. Over the centuries many African kingdoms and empires rose and fell. This map shows several, not all of which were contemporaries and not all of which are discussed here. The markets of Islamic and European states absorbed slaves and gold from African kingdoms, making the arduous Saharan trek profitable until the age of sailing ships. Salt, metals, glass, and the practices of Islam also moved along these routes, as did pilgrims headed to Mecca.

14.16 Capture of Hausa-Fulani people in Nigeria during the Kanem-Borno empire. This engraving is from the nineteenth century, but archaeological evidence suggests the routes taken by Kanem-Borno raiders existed as early as the twelfth century, allowing for the transport of slaves through the Sahara Desert to the shores of the Mediterranean sea.

trans-Saharan routes, forming the southern terminus to the Saharan trade route from Tripoli on the Mediterranean coast. For the medieval Islamic world, the inner regions of sub-Saharan Africa housed the largest and seemingly inexhaustible reservoirs of slaves.

Although most accounts of the trans-Saharan slave trade are available through historical texts, significant archaeological markers of slavery also exist: as manifested in changes to settlement patterns and in the appearance of new, foreign traded goods. During this period that coincided with the growth of the Kanem-Borno kingdom, the population expanded southward and westward, with Muslim elites settling in areas offering more fertile agricultural land. These areas were also closer to the homelands of African tribes that were beyond the control of the kingdom, and their people became the targets for slavers [**14.16**].

By the close of the fifteenth century, Kanem-Borno rulers maintained control of a long-established string of oasis settlements from Chad to the Fezzan (southern Libya), thus controlling a key Saharan trade route for goods and enslaved people to be transported north. At Garumele, an archaeological site in Niger that probably served as the walled capital of the Borno kingdom, excavation yielded European glass beads exhibiting a relatively narrow range of production techniques. Chemical analysis allowed researchers to trace these beads to their sources in Venice, and possibly Holland, in the late seventeenth to eighteenth centuries. Because the diversity of source and age of these beads would have been greater if they had filtered through a wide network of multiple exchanges, the presence of any European glass beads at Garumele indicates direct exchanges along a trade route 700–300 years ago. And a direct exchange between Kanem-Borno rulers and traders suggests that Europeans received goods, including slaves, from the Chad region through the trans-Saharan route. Goods obtained from European traders included horses and guns, which would have armed a warrior class at Garumele, whose technical abilities to capture and enslave people fueled not only the local political state but also broader patterns of conspicuous consumption.

Far to the west of Chad, in the Banda area of West-Central Ghana, evidence of such European artifacts as glass beads points to the region's long-distance connection as part of a trans-Saharan slave trade *c.* 1250–1400 CE. The Banda area lies on the forest–savanna boundary, where forest products from the south, such as kola nuts and gold, flowed north, and the northern trade in salt and copper alloys moved south. From the late fifteenth century onward, artifacts then appeared in Ghana that can be associated with the European ship trade in gold, ivory, and slaves along Ghana's southern Gold Coast.

In the seventeenth century, the **Asante** became a powerful polity in the Ghana region. Slavery was a historic tradition in the Asante empire, with captives from enemies in warfare typically enslaved. Throughout this period of Asante expansion, the region of Banda remained relatively undisturbed; the village of Kuulo Kataa, for example, was a fairly large, permanently occupied settlement with rectangular, earthen structures until the end of the seventeenth century. Archaeologist Ann Stahl's excavations at Kuulo Kataa showed the continued local smelting of iron with several furnaces, but also attested to the arrival of other manufactured goods, such as wire and ornaments cast of copper alloy, along with weights for the gold trade, all signs that hint at this remote village's link to the regional processes of extracting gold and people. In Kuulo Kataa's sixteenth- and seventeenth-century deposits, Stahl's team excavated maize phytoliths, the silica deposits that characteristically form in the husks of maize, a New World domesticate (see Chapters 8 and 10). Long before direct European contact, maize filtered along trade networks to inland villages. So did tobacco, another New World crop, as evidenced in hundreds of pipe fragments displaying so much variation in clay composition that the smoking pipes could only have been produced and exchanged widely across the region [**14.17**].

Asante An empire and kingdom in what is now Ghana that flourished during the seventeenth century.

14.17 Glass beads excavated from Garumele, capital of the Kanem-Borno kingdom in Niger. These <1-cm beads were manufactured in Europe from the fifteenth to seventeenth centuries and transported to African markets as part of exchanges that included the sale of enslaved people.

Great African Diaspora The mass dispersion of people from Africa during the trans-Atlantic slave trade.

barracoons Compounds where enslaved captives were held before being transported out of Africa during the seventeenth through nineteenth centuries.

In the eighteenth and nineteenth centuries, the Asante quickly absorbed the Banda region to the north, and it is likely that the Banda people became early Asante captives and were sent south to join the **Great African Diaspora** of enslavement to the New World. The cultural impact of the Asante may be observed in the archaeological findings. In the Banda region, excavations at contemporary Makala Kataa showed new styles of ceramics that appeared during this period, including a rouletted design (impressions made from a disk-shaped stamp that is rolled across the clay) made with maize cobs. The more dispersed production of ceramics was visible, with multiple types now imported to villages instead of being manufactured locally. Some excavators have proposed that the diversity of artifacts in their reconstructed assemblages reflects the diverse backgrounds of Banda villagers who had fled the Asante wars into frontier areas between polities and negotiated new hybrid identities. Oral tradition recounts the disruptive warfare in Asante hinterlands, and the archaeological record at Makala Kataa shows an abrupt abandonment, with ceramics and tools left in situ (see Chapter 6) as occupants presumably fled.

TRANS-ATLANTIC SLAVERY The trans-Atlantic slave trade was responsible for the forced migration of between 12 and 15 million people from Africa to the western hemisphere from the mid-fifteenth century to the end of the nineteenth. African scholars sometimes refer to the trafficking of Africans by major European countries during this period as the Maafa (meaning "great disaster" in Swahili).

Along the Gold Coast of southern Ghana endure the archaeological remains of the Maafa Great African Diaspora that occurred in the eighteenth and nineteenth centuries. European trading posts in Ghana were first established adjacent to the palace compounds of the local elites, who controlled the movements of all foreigners and foreign trade. Europeans thus lived in locally built housing not easily distinguished from that of their hosts. Nineteenth-century independent European trading posts are more visible archaeologically. At several sites associated with trading lodges on the Rio Pongo (Guinea Coast), such exotic items as bottle glass, creamware and pearlware ceramics made in England, Mediterranean beads, and iron cannon attest to a European presence. These outposts included **barracoons** [**14.18**]. Because the compounds might house enslaved people for many months awaiting the seasonal arrival of ships, the support of slavery required stored staple surpluses; locally grown maize became an important crop exchanged for European goods, such as iron bars, cloth, and beads. The enslaved porters who brought rice to the Guinea Coast may have then been sold themselves to Europeans and Americans, for fewer slaves were subsequently needed to transport European exotics inland.

The trans-Atlantic slave trade not only displaced millions of people; it also transformed African and New World landscapes. African rice plantings in the New World, so-called black rice in Brazil and along the Carolinas, speak to the transported knowledge of Africans familiar with this indigenous African domesticate. Nor were slavery-shaped landscapes only a New World phenomenon: to this day, African villages and former village sites are surrounded by garden orchards—maintained

14.18 Engraving of a baracoon in Sierra Leone, 1849. These structures held captives for the trans-Atlantic slave trade. Enslaved people were imprisoned for many months awaiting their final transport to the Americas.

dense and deep and once planted to help villagers escape and hide from mounted, raiding slavers.

By 1637, a Dutch colony founded in northeastern Brazil came across proof of an already established Portuguese plantation landscape at Pernambuco, where Africans farmed rice and other typical African crops, such as okra. Anthropologist Nick Kawa's studies of Brazilian landscapes further demonstrate the entanglement of African peoples and the plants that came with them. These plants, such as castor bean, are used by today's Brazilians as critical medicinal resources. On the opposite, eastern shores of Africa, Portuguese traders in the Indian Ocean were also pioneers in slavery and exchange, bringing such spices as clove from the Moluccas (Indonesia). Clove trees were planted and produced on Omani-run slave plantations in Zanzibar (off the coast of Tanzania), and the valuable spice was transported along trade routes to Europe, Africa, and South Asia. Between the Portuguese and Arabs, slavery expanded through ports along Africa's East Coast, drawing slaves from the interior eastward.

Plantation Slavery around the Chesapeake Bay

The Brazilian coin described in this chapter's introduction linked Hawai'i to a vast global network of colonies established by the beginning of the eighteenth century. One colony was the Jamestown settlement, founded in Chesapeake Bay in 1607 by the English Virginia Company, with the aim of extracting valuable goods, such as gold and silver, from the New World and its native people. These resources were nowhere to be found on the shores of Chesapeake Bay, which were densely forested.

14.19 Called "Jane" by archaeologists, this young English woman (whose face is reconstructed on the right) died during an early winter in the Jamestown settlement. Cut marks on the bone and a postmortem slice from her temple indicate the (successful) efforts to extract her brain. Archaeologists found additional evidence of several likely attempts to eat the dead at Jamestown, a practice to which the historical records attest; though they do not specify who the victims were, and nor do we know who "Jane" really was—her story lives on only through archaeology.

After a few starving winters the Jamestown settlers quickly became planters, turning toward lucrative tobacco for wealth. Tobacco requires labor, which the first settlers procured from indentured servants (people from Europe who had traded a term of future labor for ship passage to the Americas). When tobacco prices fell and Chesapeake land had already been claimed (by Europeans, that is), indentured labor became too costly, and the close-knit plantation families of Virginia turned to the trans-Atlantic slave trade for labor. [**14.19**]

The material conditions of tobacco production and the social world of the closely related plantation families around the southern Chesapeake Bay help explain a political economy dependent on enslaved labor. Plantation families engaged in conspicuous consumption, displaying their wealth in expensive brick housing, ornate architectural elements, and imported glass and tablewares, including wineglasses and plates. At the same time, growing tobacco on these plantations required slash-and-burn agriculture characterized by repetitive and intensive labor easily organized in quarter farms—outlying barrack-style housing for field gangs of enslaved people—with an overseer nearby.

This was the world of American statesman and planter Thomas Jefferson (1743–1826), who at his death owned more than two hundred enslaved people, a far greater number than he ever freed [**14.20**]. Jefferson lived through tumultuous times, distinguished by revolutionary ideas, the independence of colonies in the Americas, and resulting impacts on worldwide trading systems. These changes altered Atlantic markets for tobacco and other crops, leaving such planters as Jefferson to seek new strategies to build and maintain their wealth. Jefferson turned to wheat and diversified crops, which in turn called for the reorganization of slave labor to grow

14.20 Thomas Jefferson as portrayed in the National Museum of African American History and Culture in Washington, D.C. He stands before a wall of bricks, each of which is inscribed with the name of one of Monticello's enslaved people. The display evokes the wealth of America's founding fathers, a prosperity that in some instances is directly tied to the institution of slavery.

Below: **14.21 Dated ceramics, glassware, metal, and other archaeological objects** found at Thomas Jefferson's Monticello plantation show a full range of expensive, imported wares and serve as a reference tool to identify future archaeological finds. Excavations at Monticello began in the 1970s and are ongoing.

these new crops under different conditions and with different tools and techniques around the plantation. This historic shift in agriculture occurred at many plantations.

What became, though, of Jefferson's enslaved labor? Did these people have any control over their living conditions or fate? History gives us their names through Jefferson's accounts and will, and the descendants of Jefferson and Sally Hemings, one of his slaves, share his DNA. Archaeology gives to history the perspectives and agencies of people without a historical voice. History, it is said, is written by the winners. But plantation archaeology offers a divergent perspective, showing in the domestic quarters of enslaved people that a range of African traditions (such as food cooked in stew pots) and non-Christian beliefs or practices (such as the use of amulets) persisted. At George Washington's Mount Vernon plantation, for instance, excavators found an amulet of modified raccoon baculum (or penis bone), and similar items have been unearthed in the slave quarters of other plantations.

Excavations at Jefferson's Monticello plantation since the 1970s have continued to investigate the lives of enslaved people [**14.21**]. From the earliest construction of the plantation in 1772, enslaved people lived in Mulberry Row, a row of wooden houses southeast of the main house. Over time, the size of individual dwellings—especially in the quarter farm outbuildings—shrunk, leaving archaeologists to wonder whether the houses simply crowded the same number of people into smaller spaces, or whether family units of enslaved people succeeded in establishing domestic households. A similar pattern occurred all across the Chesapeake in the late eighteenth century. Clues from subfloor pits provide the critical independent evidence we need to answer this question. The earlier buildings with large rooms have small cellars under their floors. Monticello archaeologist Fraser Neiman suggests that

EXTRACTING PEOPLE: THE SLAVE TRADE

14.22 Reconstructed "t" building on Mulberry Row at the Monticello plantation. The building designation "t" derives from Jefferson's own plan of Mulberry Row and represents one of the smaller, later buildings inhabited by a family household of enslaved people.

the multiple subfloor pits are the outcome of multiple families and/or unrelated individuals being housed in the same room, with little choice over whom they lived with. The pits were a strategy invented by people enslaved in the Chesapeake to bootstrap cooperation among coresidents. Enslaved families dug the pits to store their personal belongings, including food. Others living in the same space knew who owned each pit, and their knowledge, combined with the ease with which access to the pit could be seen by other slaves, helped deter those who might be tempted to remove their contents without the owner's consent.

By the last decade of the eighteenth century, slave houses built at Monticello had a smaller single room; 12 by 14 feet (3.6 by 4.3 meters) was a typical size. The smaller houses had one subfloor pit or none at all. These small buildings housed single families, among whose members kin ties helped ensure cooperation, making the multiple pits unnecessary.

Over time, enslaved people persuaded Jefferson and his overseers to house them as small family units [**14.22**]. Their successful resistance may be connected to the material conditions of the changing political economy, for by then the many new tasks and technologies required in a diversified cropping system made labor oversight more difficult and evasion easier. Jefferson had to entice more than punish to maximize their work.

EXTRACTIVISM AND THE ANTHROPOCENE

Extractivism as a practice has been an essential component of the expansion of modern economies. It has also been an engine of the Anthropocene, reshaping environments and encouraging the creation of profit and wealth at the expense of future recovery, growth, and—as we saw in the Andes, p. 217—health. Slavery is a critical index of the Anthropocene: its emergence may be tied to conspicuous consumption and the desire to create wealth beyond what the immediate environment can provide. In the past five hundred years, the extraction of humans multiplied with the need for labor in colonies that were financial gambles but had the potential to produce extravagant gains. Slavery's persistence in areas that were reliant on other forms of extractivism—such cash crops as tobacco, sugar, and rum shipped around the world—is not coincidental. Slavery and extraction-based production are a yoked pair in any market economy that relies on a low price to maintain high profits, such as the enslavement of Southeast Asian workers in the global seafood supply today.

It is important to note, in closing, that slavery has yet to be completely prohibited in human societies. Although the practice is officially illegal, various organizations and scholars have estimated that between 21 and 46 million people remain enslaved today, held under captivity, threats, and abuse. The extraction of their labor often goes on for decades—and frequently in the case of women and children, for their entire lives. If slavery serves as an index for the Anthropocene, its presence suggests that we have yet to deviate from the path of extractivism.

Chapter Questions

1. Describe the archaeological evidence for the earliest known fishing. How have fishing practices changed?
2. Why did a whaling industry develop in the eighteenth century, and how was it different from earlier forms of whaling?
3. How does the extraction of silver in South America in the seventeenth century continue to affect the environment today?
4. In addition to historical evidence, what kind of material can archaeologists use to understand slavery of the past?

Additional Resources

Catsambis, Alexis, Ford, Ben, and Hamilton, Donny L. (eds.). *The Oxford Handbook of Maritime Archaeology.* New York: Oxford University Press, 2011.

Conrad, Joseph. *Heart of Darkness.* Blackwood's Magazine. 1899.

Cooke, Colin A., Balcom, Prentiss H., Kerfoot, Charles, Abbott, Mark B., and Wolfe, Alexander P. "Pre-Colombian Mercury Pollution Associated with the Smelting of Argentiferous Ores in the Bolivian Andes," *Ambio* 40 (2011): 18–25.

Crosby, Alfred W. *The Columbian Exchange.* Westport, CT: Greenwood Press, 1973.

Dolin, Eric Jay. *Leviathan: The History of Whaling in America.* New York: W. W. Norton, 2008.

Gordon, Stephani, dir. *Lightning Strikes Twice: The Real-Life Sequel to Moby Dick*, 2013. https://vimeo.com/146734532.

Kelly, Kenneth. "Archaeological Perspectives on the Atlantic Slave Trade: Contrasts in Time and Space in Benin and Guinea," in *Slavery in Africa: Archaeology and Memory, Proceedings of the British Academy* 168, edited by Paul J. Lane and Kevin C. MacDonald, 127–47. Oxford, UK: Oxford University Press, 2011.

Lane, Paul J., and MacDonald, Kevin C. (eds.). *Slavery in Africa: Archaeology and Memory, Proceedings of the British Academy* 168. Oxford, UK: Oxford University Press, 2011.

Neiman, Fraser. "The Lost World of Monticello," *Journal of Anthropological Archaeology* 64 (2008): 161–93.

Stahl, Ann Brower. "Entangled Lives: The Archaeology of Daily Life in the Gold Coast Hinterlands, AD 1400–1900," in *Archaeology of Atlantic Africa and the African Diaspora*, edited by Akinwumi Ogundiran and Toyin Falola, 49–76. Bloomington, IN: Indiana University Press, 2011.

Wolf, Eric. *Europe and the People without History.* Berkeley, CA: University of California Press, 1982.

THE FUTURE OF THE ANTHROPOCENE

15

There is an important singular lesson the past can teach us in addressing the looming danger of the Anthropocene: human society with a little ingenuity can produce a successful outcome—one whereby we all survive—if it is open to a diverse suite of possible solutions fully integrated with the dynamic natural world.

THE CHALLENGES AHEAD

In this book, we covered a wide range of examples of anthropogenic change and human niche construction that allowed humans to succeed and spread across the globe. A study of world prehistory and human history allows us to frame the Anthropocene. Understanding how diverse the human species is; how we have expanded our niche through patterns of surplus, consumption, and extractivism; and how our capacity to communicate, to use technologies, and to adjust social institutions to construct and change our niches—all will help us assess and respond to the many challenges ahead.

The methods of archaeology—excavation, survey, experimentation, dating, ethnographic analogy, analysis of human and animal bone, plant remains, chemical residues, and decipherment—show that human societies have great resilience and variability in response to changes and challenges at both the local and regional level. As our human niche has expanded to a global scale, so have the issues that we face. Today, we must confront head-on three major environmental challenges that characterize our modern understanding of the Anthropocene: decreasing diversity of animal and plant species, the rapid rise in the human population, and increased consumption of fossil fuel. These three transformations have had unanticipated consequences that the human species will need to address to ensure a sustainable world.

With the lessons learned from the Anthropocene, it is critical for each of us to consider how he or she might exercise agency to transform the world. In conclusion, we will offer some examples of the ways in which anthropogenic change is improving the world and addressing our three pivotal environmental challenges.

The Challenges Ahead 349

Extinctions and Increasing Diversity 350

Population Growth 352

Fossil Fuel Consumption and Innovation 357

Understand Your Agency 358

Opposite Turning dark into light, this river of solar panels covers a former golf course near the Fukushima nuclear power plant site in Japan. A tsunami-caused radiation leak in 2011 shuttered the nuclear plant and forced residents to re-locate, but the forests have returned and the tainted land has been put to new, sustainable use.

EXTINCTIONS AND INCREASING DIVERSITY

In *African Silences*, author Peter Matthiessen traces the decline of West Africa's great mammalian wildlife: the elephants, hippos, rhinos, wildebeest, and other large animals. This is a modern devastation that may be linked to the global demand for ivory, once a rapacious form of conspicuous consumption (see Chapter 12) and still a potent threat. Poachers with guns and a capacity for rapid strike are not the only threat to African wildlife, for animals compete with expanding human populations and their need for land to grow food and pasture domestic livestock.

As we have learned, the extinction of animals and reduction of biodiversity through human action are not recent phenomena. At least 3,000 years ago, the great East African grasslands of Tanzania and Kenya became a niche managed by fire to increase the food for pasture animals, provide fuel for iron-smelting, and clear fallow land (see Chapters 3 and 8). The population of arid lands by farmers and herders has pushed hunters and their prey to desert margins and remote enclaves, replaced in many areas by monocultures of wheat and barley. The reduction of biodiversity is important, as it is only in a diverse environment that humans have the opportunity to test new solutions, as they have done successfully in the past. To remain adaptable and resilient in the face of climate change, we must replenish biological diversity.

Rewilding and Restoration of Natural Habitats

The need to restore greater biological diversity is the motivation behind the **rewilding** movement. Across the globe, many successful examples of rewilding and restoration projects exist. One took place in the state of Washington and concerned the restoration of the Elwha River. In the early 1900s, two dams, one on the Elwha and the other at Glines Canyon, were built on the river, and although they fueled regional industrial growth, they also blocked the migration of salmon upstream, disrupted the flow of sediment and wood downstream, and flooded the historic homelands and cultural sites of the Lower Elwha Klallam Tribe. After decades of campaigning and planning, the largest dam removal project in US history began on September 17, 2011, first with the removal of the Elwha Dam, and then the Glines Canyon Dam in 2014. Today, the Elwha River once again flows freely from its headwaters, and salmon have returned. Ecologist Michael Scott explains that the free-flowing water will also increase the water and climate resilience of the area. Pooling water in a dammed reservoir leads to more evaporation, reducing the available water in the system. Sending water downstream allows it to sink into the incised basement of the river's channel, and recharge natural aquifers. The Elwha River project demonstrates how restoration of the natural environment is not only good for wildlife but also creates a more stable landscape for humans.

Similar river projects have been under way in other countries. In Croydon, south London, the River Wandle was once heavily polluted by industrial refuse, and portions had been artificially straightened to speed the flow of water away from

rewilding Restoring an area (land or marine environment) to more natural conditions through the removal of human constructions and the replacement or reintroduction of animals and plants.

15.1 A liberated Iberian lynx. In the early 2000s, the Iberian lynx was so endangered that it became the only felid species for which the costly and risky process of captive breeding and reintroduction was essential. This lynx was one of five released in Despenaperros Natural Park in Spain in 2010.

houses and businesses. The natural habitats of the river were gradually killed: the last trout had been caught in 1934. Since 2000, when the Wandle Trust was founded, its members have removed rubbish from the river, built structures to restore its natural shape and flow, negotiated with industries and people whose outflows affect it, and restocked the river with fish. Now, freshwater shrimp and brown trout have returned to the river. It has even become a tourist destination bringing more revenue into the area.

Rewilding has been covered in the news media, too, mostly through stories reporting on the reintroduction of top animal predators, such as lynxes and grey wolves, to the wild. In Spain and Portugal, as of 2018, approximately twenty Iberian lynxes were released in the latest phase of a reintroduction program, helping one species of the world's most endangered cats reclaim their lost habitats [**15.1**]. Once released, the Iberian lynx roam far and wide, and scientists track their movements with radio collars. In 2002, fewer than one hundred Iberian lynx lived in the wild, confined to just two regions in southern Spain. Since then, their population has more than tripled. The Iberian lynx improves biodiversity by controlling the numbers of foxes, mongoose, and genets that would otherwise dominate and, as a unique part of Portugal and Spain's natural heritage, it has become a source of reliable income through ecotourism.

This form of rewilding—restoring ecosystems through the release of top predators—has garnered considerable support in recent years, but it is not without critics. Many farmers fear for their cattle and sheep, and some conservationists express concern that we cannot predict the effects of reintroducing predators on other endangered species.

The rewilding movement nonetheless demonstrates how, given the right motivation and appropriate cultural changes, anthropogenic change can help recover animal and plant species populations. One of the greatest contemporary conservation voices, Nobel Prize winner Edward O. Wilson, estimates that half the Earth's land and half the sea need to become diversity refuges to halt the sixth mass extinction. In his essay "The Global Solution to Extinction," he argues that this critical half "can be put together from large and small fragments around the world…without removing people living there or changing property rights." His is a tall order, but improved public awareness and increased government funding in reimagining our landscape do offer hope.

POPULATION GROWTH

In the midst of global extinctions, our human niche has supported exponential human population growth. The world population has doubled since 1960, and it will double again in this century. With this unprecedented increase in the number of people come the questions of how and if our human niche can expand as populations grow. Will we compete for the last fish in the fisheries of the Great Banks of Newfoundland or the remaining freshwater in the Colorado River? Does our ecological past predict a competition similar to that of the Ancestral Puebloans for scarce resources? Or, will we, through our technologically enhanced ability to transmit culture, solve the problem of resource depletion?

We have seen how people of the past responded to population pressures: by altering their habits of consumption (e.g., transitioning to broad-spectrum resources) or adopting more mobile lifestyles. Human behavioral ecology suggests that we can cooperate (as in St. Kilda, Scotland) and compete (as in Fiji), and that resource distribution and predictability are important factors in understanding which path we choose. Global population growth is an issue too large for any individual to tackle alone, but reducing the environmental impact of each individual so that collectively more people can live sustainably is a goal many people are meeting by assessing their consumption and waste, and by finding more efficient and ecological ways to live together.

The Ecological City

Cities have often had the reputation of being the polluted centers of industrial urban sprawl. Perhaps surprisingly, some leading conservationists see increased urbanization as key to conserving the environment. Joe Walston, director of the Wildlife Conservation Society, argues that urbanization is the biggest driver of environmental progress. Although in the short term more people inhabiting cities will increase consumption as urban infrastructures adapt to high populations, in the long term, urbanization could lead to a reduction in energy consumption per person. Urban dwellers are more likely to use public transportation than those in rural or suburban areas, thus expending less fossil fuel to commute to work;

15.2 The eco-reserve of Zealandia within the city of Wellington, New Zealand. Using extensive fencing to exclude predators, and a reintroduction program, the urban core of Wellington has become a refuge for rare native birds and their native habitat. Human visitors to the park are restricted to trails and other low-impact areas, such as this suspension bridge, in order allow public use but limit disturbance.

their living spaces are typically smaller and clustered in apartment buildings, requiring less energy to heat and cool than larger, freestanding residences. By choosing to live in vertical high-rises, people also use less land, opening up larger wildlife habitats in rural areas. In addition, the concentration of the populace in urban settings can lead to reduced birth rates. For example, in Italy, the population is shrinking (representing −0.2 percent growth), and an overcrowded Japan has similarly experienced negative population growth. Germany, too, has faced historic low or negative population growth, accounting to some degree for its willingness to accept a significant number of migrants in recent years.

Many cities are also the force behind conservation projects and forms of re-wilding. In 1998, the city of Wellington, New Zealand, set aside an area of almost 556 acres (225 hectares) to restore the ecosystem of the Wellington Valley's forest to its original, wild state. Called Zealandia, this urban ecosanctuary is a great example of conservation efforts in close proximity to the city [**15.2**]. The area was completely fenced in order to protect it from destructive introduced species, and eighteen species of native animals have been successfully reintroduced into the area, including some on the edge of extinction, such as the South Island takahē, a bird that was once officially declared extinct [**15.3**].

Many cities also invest in environmental programs, such as bike-sharing and improved infrastructures for cycling. For example, in Denmark, 30 percent of

15.3 The rare South Island takahē, a flightless bird native to New Zealand. A program that focused on captive breeding and the eradication of invasive rodents and deer were required to save the takahē. The birds have been reintroduced to pest-free islands and sanctuaries, but are still a vulnerable species.

Copenhageners ride to work or school along three bicycle superhighways connecting Copenhagen to its outlying suburbs. Twenty-three similar highways are currently in the works. Copenhagen was bicycle-friendly for much of the early twentieth century, but following World War II and well into the 1960s, the city became polluted and congested with car traffic. Citizens eventually pushed back and reclaimed the city for biking. Today, Copenhagen is testimony to what a well-planned bicycle infrastructure can do. Worldwide in 2014, 5.5 percent of urban trips were completed by bicycle.

In yet another initiative, modern cities are beginning to reduce the causes of climate change by looking at the use of fossil fuels. In 2018, the Carbon Disclosure Project (CDP) reported that the number of cities receiving at least 70 percent of their total electricity supply from renewable energy more than doubled after 2015, with 570 cities now on the list. Large urban centers, such as Auckland, Nairobi, Bristol, and Oslo, are among the cities that successfully transitioned away from fossil fuels, and Burlington, Vermont, has reported deriving 100 percent of its power from renewable sources since 2015. Many other cities have opted to participate in the Million Tree Initiative, in which cities set a goal of planting one million trees within urban areas. This movement is aimed at increasing urban forestation and improving air quality by reducing carbon monoxide. As we follow public building works over time, we are beginning to observe increased public awareness and energy, and greater government and private resources, focused on creating new solutions to our Anthropocene challenges.

Reducing What We Leave Behind

Archaeology is often said to be the science of rubbish; archaeologists of the future will examine what contemporary humans leave behind. One related issue of pressing urgency is the proliferation of plastic [**15.4**]. The mass production of plastics began in the 1940s and 1950s, around World War II, when products made of Bakelite (an early form of plastic), and polystyrene and nylon were introduced as synthetic substitutes for wood, metal, paper, glass, and fiber. Plastic is now ubiquitous in modern life, constituting many of our tools, our clothing, and packaging for our food and water. In 2015, the cumulative production of plastic was 7.8 billion tonnes, which is more than one tonne per person on this planet. At present, organizations across the world are working hard to reduce the impact of plastic in the environment. More than 5 trillion pieces of plastic are afloat in the world's oceans, collectively weighing nearly 269,000 tonnes. Many organizations are now committed to reducing their plastic output and the waste that finds its way into the waters of the world. The plastic rings used to hold together a six-pack of beer have become an icon for plastic waste, as they tangle the wings of sea birds and strangle aquatic life. A craft microbrewery in Florida called Saltwater Brewery and a startup named E6PR have addressed this problem by introducing to the manufacturing market six-pack rings made of wheat and barley that will quickly decompose.

Some scientific organizations are also working to remove plastic waste that already exists in the oceans. In 2016, scientists in Japan discovered bacteria that could digest the kind of plastic used to make soft-drink bottles. The bacteria work by secreting an enzyme (a type of protein that can speed up chemical reactions) known as PETase. This splits certain chemical bonds in the plastic molecule, leaving behind smaller molecules that the bacteria can absorb, using the carbon contained in the molecules as a food source. Further research is under way to increase the speed and efficiency of this enzyme. The team of scientists involved have been careful to stress that their discovery is not a complete solution to plastic waste, only one of many projects aimed at reducing non-biodegradable waste present in our environment. Is this kind of intervention simply a technological step beyond domestication (see Chapter 8), breeding better milk cows, or developing GMOs (genetically modified organisms) to secure surplus, storable harvests? With changing technologies and available resources, resilience in our global niche will result in a reorganization of societies and ideas, perhaps even broader popular acceptance of these commitments if new technologies drive down costs and open up opportunities.

Although some scientists are busily devising ways to *remove* plastic from the ocean, many governments have responded to public opinion and pressure from individuals and groups to *reduce* the everyday use of plastic. In 2014, California became the first US state to enact legislation imposing a statewide ban on single-use plastic bags at large retail stores and requiring a minimum charge of 10 cents to shoppers for new recycled paper bags, reusable plastic bags, or compostable bags at certain stores. In 2015, the United Kingdom introduced a mandatory 5-pence charge for plastics bags in supermarkets, and this small change alone has led to an 83 percent drop in the use of plastic bags in major UK chain stores. In 2016, the US government banned microbeads, the tiny balls of plastic used in exfoliation creams; in 2018, the United Kingdom followed suit. Efforts to remove other forms of plastic are ongoing, with plastic bottles and drinking straws at the top of the

15.4 Modern plastic waste is the most common artifact produced by humans today. Overproduction and limited recycling has resulted in global-scale plastic pollution, which contributes to ecological destruction. Community groups, such as these people cleaning up Sanur Beach in Bali on April 13, 2018, are at the forefront of campaigns to restore and protect the ecological systems that sustain life on our planet.

15.5 Orangutan populations have declined by 50 percent over the past century due to deforestation and the establishment of palm oil plantations in parts of island Southeast Asia. Consumer awareness and choice has led to the reduction of palm oil, but rescue programs are still needed to ensure the survival of the species.

list. In fact, as we remove non-biodegradable materials from the environment and reduce their imprint, we may be making the work of future archaeologists that much more difficult!

Inconspicuous Consumption

Crucial in the response to an increasing worldwide population and the resulting environmental impact is altering people's habits of consumption so they will be more sustainable. Just as some companies are concentrating on creating more ecologically friendly packaging, so the transport, fashion, and food industries are exploring more sustainable products. Industry leaders are not motivated to do this out of generosity; they see it as something the consumer wants. Making your own consumer choices known is one of the easiest and most effective ways to instigate change.

The food industry has been a leader in responding to increasing public awareness of the need to be more sustainable. Many innovative foodstuffs continue to appear on the marketplace and make the headlines, such as new Nordic cuisines that offer entirely sustainable gourmet meals, for instance, algae-cake garnished with sea-buckthorn. Although some of these food choices may seem outlandish, others, such as new meat substitutes, have been widely adopted by vegetarians and non-vegetarians alike as an environmentally friendly option. Palm oil, for instance, has captured public awareness in recent years. The palm oil industry is one of the driving forces behind rain forest destruction in Indonesia and Malaysia [15.5].

The oil itself is made from the fruit of African palms. These trees are originally from west and southwest Africa, but were introduced to Indonesia and Malaysia in the late nineteenth and early twentieth centuries. Palm oil is a very profitable crop, but its cultivation is believed to have been responsible for about 8 percent of the world's deforestation between 1990 and 2008. Forests are burned on a massive scale, removing the habitats for such species as orangutans, rhinos, and tigers. The sustainable production of palm oil is possible, but for many years, the food industry would not require the manufacturers of palm oil to offer information on the source of the oil contained in their products. This led many people to boycott palm oil products altogether, pressuring the industry to change its practices. In Europe, palm oil exports decreased by 13 percent in 2018; in India, by 23 percent. Now, some food producers have begun to advertise their products as using only sustainable palm oil.

This new more responsible form of consumption may be viewed as a strong reaction against traditional forms of conspicuous consumption, where consuming in excess is a sign of wealth and prestige. A rising form of prestige now calls for consuming less and consuming more responsibly. Reducing your own conspicuous consumption by purchasing fewer goods and replacing items less frequently, by recycling materials and making conscious decisions about what to buy and when, can contribute to the overall sustainability of humans and the Earth.

FOSSIL FUEL CONSUMPTION AND INNOVATION

In coining the term "Anthropocene," atmospheric chemist Paul Crutzen referred to the increased use of fossil fuels and rise of CO_2 levels as the key markers for an era in which humans are largely responsible for the warming of the planet. Since 2000, CO_2 in the atmosphere has increased at a rate 100 to 200 times faster than in the last Ice Age, and it is leading to warming temperatures and rising acidity in seawater that bleaches coral reefs and can cause toxic algae blooms. The emissions of global warming gases may be traced back to the burning of forestland, the development of metallurgy, and the rearing of cattle, but the largest spike occurred during the Industrial Revolution. Carbon emissions were the result of human innovation (e.g., the invention of the internal combustion engine), but human innovation now works to tackle the ongoing problem they present.

In 1839, the French physicist Alexandre Edmond Becquerel discovered the effect that explained how electricity could be generated from sunlight. He claimed, "Shining light on an electrode submerged in a conductive solution would create an electric current." Renewable energy—solar, wind, hydropower, geothermal, and biofuels—currently makes up 24 percent of global electricity generation. That proportion is expected to rise to 31 percent by 2040. Recently, new technology has given us screen-printed solar cells, a solar fabric that can be used to side a house, even solar shingles to install on our roofs. International markets have opened up, with solar-panel manufacturers playing a key role in the solar power industry. In recent years, the invention and development of LEDs (light-emitting diodes) have changed energy consumption. The first LED dates back to the 1874 invention of the diode, a crystal semiconductor. In 1994, scientists Shuji Nakamura Isamu Akasaki and Hiroshi Amano invented high-brightness LED bulbs, for which they were awarded the Nobel Prize in Physics in 2014. LEDs work much as solar panels do, only in reverse, converting electrons to photons instead of the other way around. They use 90 percent less energy than incandescent bulbs for the same amount of light, and half as much as compact fluorescents, without toxic mercury. On top of that, an LED bulb will last much longer than either of the other types.

UNDERSTAND YOUR AGENCY

Any one of the movements and ideas discussed above, and a myriad more, will benefit from our own agency. Everyone has agency, not just pharaohs and kings. Whether ancient or modern, agency is always shaped by and shaping society, or social structure. Because social structure varies around the world and is perceived differently by different agents, the world offers a rich canvas for your agency. It could take various forms: becoming politically active, voting, building a concerned online community, donating to restoration projects, engaging in efforts to promote sustainable nature or protect heritage sites, backyard bird counting or other ecological monitoring. To protect the Amazon rain forests (see Chapter 7), archaeologists Michael Heckenberger and Wetherbee Dorshow called for a cell phone to be donated to every young person in that region, allowing as many humans as possible to document the loss of trees and thus push back against illegal and unrestricted logging.

Individuals can have a profound impact by simply contemplating innovative ways to help the environment and to incentivize other humans to improve their own habits. In Los Angeles, self-proclaimed bike activist Monica Howe opted to tackle the city's out-of-control car culture by becoming the outreach coordination or spokesperson for the Los Angeles County Bicycle Coalition group. It remapped the city's potholed streets—offering safe bike routes, organizing cycle rallies, helping fledgling cyclists overcome their traffic fears—and challenged the mindset at City Hall, where cyclists tend to be greeted with a certain amount of cynical disbelief. Howe says membership is rising, and cyclists are pedaling into the cityscape as public attitudes, swayed by concerns about air quality, traffic congestion, and global warming, begin to shift.

Even relatively small shifts in one's personal habits can have widespread impact, especially in the age of social media. In 2016, one restaurant in India inspired the public worldwide when it released a video on YouTube in which the owner, Minu Pauline, urges her customers, as well as the larger community, to put their leftover food in a small refrigerator outside the front of the restaurant. The fridge would remain open all day, so anyone in need of food might visit it at any time. In the interview Minu explains, "Money is yours, but resources belong to society. If you're wasting your money, it's your money, but don't waste resources; don't waste food."

Once this story broke across the world, similar refrigerators began to spring up outside many other cafés and restaurants, offering potential participants a way to reduce waste and to help their community. Social media has also helped coordinate volunteer beach cleans along various coastlines. In 2013, surfers and beach lovers Martin Dorey and Tab Parry established the #2minutebeachclean campaign on Twitter, encouraging people to take only 2 minutes from their lives to pick up rubbish at any nearby beaches. After the tweet was posted, thousands of people all over the globe became motivated by the hashtag and soon posted images of their own beach-cleaning activities. These are the stories of individuals who used their own ingenuity and passion to effect change.

World prehistory and archaeology provide the tools for understanding human nature, how human actions have led to significant environmental changes, and how human behavior may evolve going forward. To those who say history repeats itself, we argue that it never does, as our world prehistory unambiguously demonstrates a global and unique human trajectory, the future of which is yet to be decided. You will contribute to that future.

Chapter Questions

1. Will understanding how humans have changed their behavior in the past help us face the challenges of the future?
2. How might rethinking forms of conspicuous consumption improve the environment?
3. How can you exercise your own agency to effect positive change?

Additional Resources

http://www.bbc.co.uk/news/world-europe-33648602

https://beachclean.net/

https://www.drawdown.org

https://greentumble.com/urban-rewilding-concept-successful-examples/

https://www.theguardian.com/environment/2015/may/03/lynx-rewilding-britain-wildlife-countryside

https://www.independent.co.uk/news/world/asia/restaurant-owner-installs-fridge-outside-to-feed-the-homeless-a6963861.html

http://www.monbiot.com/2013/04/26/2642/

https://www.newscientist.com/article/2076921-iberian-lynx-beats-extinction-as-cats-are-released-to-the-wild/

https://www.nytimes.com/2018/01/27/business/mind-meld-bill-gates-steven-pinker.html

https://www.woodlandtrust.org.uk/publications/2017/07/rewilding/

Glossary

accelerator mass spectrometer (AMS) A machine that detects atoms of specific elements according to their atomic weights.

Acheulean A stone tool industry developed by human ancestors 1.76 million years ago, which included the production of teardrop-shaped hand axes.

agency The power of an individual to act within a social structure.

anaerobic Conditions without available oxygen, such as wetlands or severe heat and cold.

Anthropocene The current geological age, the period during which human activity began to affect the environment.

anthropogenic Human-caused and human-related change.

Antiquity Originally used to refer to the pre-Christian era in Europe or elsewhere; generally means a distant past prior to the ideals and belief systems of modern people.

appendages Limbs of an animal.

archaeobotanists Archaeologists who study the remains of plants from the past.

archaeological cultures Specific combinations of artifacts and styles that were produced by a culture in the past.

archaeology The study of past humans through their material remains.

Archaic humans An overarching category that includes species of the genus *Homo*, Neanderthals among them, who came before *Homo sapiens*.

Archaic Period Period in North America from approximately 8000 to 1000 BCE marking the beginnings of agriculture.

arroyo A steep-sided dry creek or stream bed that flows with water only after sufficient rain.

Asante An empire and kingdom in what is now Ghana that flourished during the seventeenth century.

assemblage Artifacts found at the same site.

Assyrian A major Mesopotamian kingdom and empire at the juncture of the Tigris and Euphrates Rivers; dates from 2025 (Old Assyrian empire begins) to 609 BCE (end of the Neo-Assyrian empire).

atlatl A handle that attaches to the butt end of a spear, allowing a person to throw the spear farther and with more force. Predates the bow and arrow.

Aurignacian Period A period in the Upper Palaeolithic, some 45,000–27,000 years ago, when anatomically modern *Homo sapiens* infiltrated Europe.

axial elements The spine and head of an animal.

barracoons Compounds where enslaved captives were held before being transported out of Africa during the seventeenth through nineteenth centuries.

Bedouin Nomadic people who have historically inhabited the desert regions in North Africa, the Arabian Peninsula, Iraq, and the Levant.

Beringia A landmass that connected Russia to the American continent during the Ice Age, when sea levels were lower.

bioarchaeology The archaeological study of bones and other human remains for biological indicators of sex, health, lifestyle, and social status.

Bolling–Allerod Period A period some 15,000 to 13,000 years ago that led to an abrupt warming in the final stages of the Ice Age.

bone bed An archaeological layer that includes a large proportion of bones.

Brahmi script One of the oldest writing systems, used in ancient India and present-day South and Central Asia from the first millennium BCE.

broad spectrum revolution A process whereby people move toward a wider variety of food, rather than relying on one staple.

Bronze Age A period from 3100 to 600 BCE in Europe; the Near East also had a Bronze Age (3000–1200 BCE). The period when bronze was used widely to make tools, weapons, and other instruments varied from region to region, and in the New World, bronze was not used at all before the sixteenth century CE (Spanish Conquest).

bulb of percussion The bulge below the striking platform of a flake that is produced by the force of the energy passing through the stone.

bulla A clay ball used to contain tokens that represented material goods. This method of record-keeping predates writing in Mesopotamia.

C3 process The process of photosynthesis as undertaken by herbaceous plants and tubers.

C4 process The processes of photosynthesis as undertaken by grasses, such as maize or sugarcane.

calibration A method of correcting radio-carbon dates that compensates for fluctuating atmospheric conditions in the past.

calibration curve A synthesis of measurements from tree rings and other samples of known age that is used to generate a graph that relates radiocarbon dates to calendar years.

Chalcolithic or Copper Age Refers to Old World cultures after the Neolithic and prior to the Bronze Age. Chalcolithic people used ceramics and some copper tools.

chert A fine-grained rock, frequently used for stone tools; flint is a particular type of chert.

chicha A beer that the Inka made from maize.

chinampas A Nahuatl word for raised-field agriculture.

Clovis Early hunters of megafauna in North America known by the distinctive point of their speartips, the Clovis point.

cofferdam An airtight enclosure around an underwater archaeological site that can be drained, allowing for surface sediments to be excavated as if they existed on dry land.

commensal Animals that benefit from another animal's behavior without return or harm to the benefactor.

commensal pathway A path to animal domestication whereby a wild animal is drawn into a human environment and begins to form a mutualistic relationship with humans.

conchoidal fracture The mechanics of breakage for cryptocrystalline material, such as glass or chert, which produces flakes with smooth surfaces and sharp edges.

context The physical association of an artifact with sediment, features, and other artifacts, which indicates how the artifact was used and ultimately deposited in the ground.

core A stone trimmed by knapping that can then be cut down into prefashioned flakes or used as a single tool.

cortex The outside surface of a stone.

cryptocrystalline The microscopic arrangement of crystals in a stone, such as chert, that reacts to a force much as a fluid does, rippling when struck, and breaking to form a sharp edge.

cuneiform A writing system developed from proto-cuneiform, but more stylized; named for the wedge shape that the reed stylus made on soft clay.

debitage Stone flakes, fragmented stone, and dust (waste materials) produced by knapping a stone tool.

dendrochronology The dating of a piece of wood based on an examination of its rings; often involves comparing the ring pattern to those in a larger database.

Dilmun An ancient Semitic-speaking culture that developed on the island of Bahrain in the Persian Gulf, *c.* 4000 BCE.

directed pathway A path to animal domestication whereby wild animals are deliberately brought under human management.

disarticulation The chopping up and separation of a corpse or carcass.

distal end In flintknapping, the end of the flake produced by the energy of the blow exiting the stone.

DNA Acronym for deoxyribonucleic acid, a molecule that encodes genetic information within living cells. DNA can be preserved in bone, teeth, hair, and soil.

doloritic bluestones The inner stones at Stonehenge, brought from the Preseli hills in Wales.

dorsal In flintknapping, the exterior surface of a flake.

Early Woodland Period A period of North American ancient history, 2,600–1,800 years ago.

economic defendability Describes a resource that is worth the energy expended to defend it; usually a resource that is densely distributed in space and predictable in the future.

epigrapher A researcher of ancient writing.

epiphyses The end parts of a long bone that initially grow separately from the shaft.

Erligang Period Culture of farmers that developed along the Yellow River of China c. 1510–1460 BCE; preceded the Shang Dynasty.

ethnoarchaeology The study of modern processes in present-day societies (e.g., how tools are made, how food is prepared) in order to draw conclusions about past societies from their material remains.

ethnographic analysis Understanding human behavior through direct observations and active participation.

evolutionary theory Explains human actions in terms of how they may impact fitness (the creation of offspring in the next generation).

excavation The archaeological practice of uncovering and recording remains systematically.

extractivism The act of taking resources from the earth or ocean in order to make a product that can be sold or exchanged for other goods.

First People The descendants of the first humans to live in Australia and the Americas.

fitness The ability of an individual to contribute viable offspring to the next generation's population.

flake A piece of a stone that has been struck off through knapping.

flintknapping The act of striking a flint to remove a piece, or a flake, usually to make a stone tool. The people who do this are called flintknappers.

flotation A method for recovering charred pieces of ancient plants by floating them in water.

frequency seriation A relative dating method that involves measuring the abundance of a particular design or style of object over time.

geomorphologist A scientist who studies the features of Earth's surface to understand geological processes.

glyph A written symbol within a set of symbols that are used together to represent the elements of a written language.

Great African Diaspora The mass dispersion of people from Africa during the trans-Atlantic slave trade.

Ground-edge axes Stone axes that were made by humans in Australia between 49,000 and 44,000 years ago, and which represent the creation of a new technology.

hammerstone A tool used to remove a piece from a stone. Frequently a different, harder type of stone.

Harappan A Neolithic culture that developed in the Indus River Valley in Pakistan and India; c. 2600–1900 BCE.

henge A round monument consisting of an earth bank and internal ditch; often includes upright stones or timbers.

heterarchical A form of social organization based on non-hierarchical organization, where individuals are unranked.

historical materialism A social theory that relates the economics of a society to its social structure and ideology.

Hittites Ancient Anatolian people who established an empire in Turkey and the northern portions of the Tigris and Euphrates valleys c. 1600 BCE.

hoard A mass burial of objects.

Holocene The epoch following the Pleistocene, which involved the warming of the planet and retreat of the glaciers, beginning c. 11,600 years ago.

Homo sapiens Modern humans. *Homo* describes the genus, and *sapiens* the species.

house society A social organization in which identity, wealth, land, and labor are affiliated with an extended family and a residence, such as a large house or hall.

huayrachina An Inka furnace that used the wind as ventilation for the smelting of silver.

huipil A Nahuatl word for a traditional loose tunic worn by women across Mesoamerica, even today.

hypotheses Ideas about the cause of a particular observation that need to be tested.

ideogram A written character that signifies an idea or concept, but which lacks any indication for the spoken word.

ideology A system of ideas shared by a population that forms the foundation of beliefs and principles.

in situ The location of an object after it has been discarded; to be in an undisturbed deposit.

index fossil An artifact used to identify the presence of a particular human species.

industry A group of tools of similar manufacture, such as the Oldowan.

infrared liquid chromatography A technique that uses pressure to separate liquids into different chemical components, allowing for the identification of different chemicals and compounds.

Isthmian A type of Mesoamerican script from the Gulf of Mexico that is related to Maya script.

Jomon A seafaring culture in Japan, dating back 14,500 years, that also produced some of the world's earliest pottery vessels.

Kanem-Borno kingdom An empire that existed in modern Chad and Nigeria in the fourteenth century CE.

Kelp Highway A proposed route from Beringia to the Americas along the Pacific coastline, which followed the distribution of seaweed beds close to shore.

khipu A system of notation from the Inka empire, c. 1450, formed through the tying of knots.

Khmer empire A powerful Hindu-Buddhist empire in Southeast Asia (800–1350 CE).

kiva A subterranean round room found in ancestral Puebloan settlements.

landnam The clearance of forested land for agricultural purposes.

landscape The perception of a region or environment as a culturally framed and organized space.

Lapita An archaeological culture found in the southwestern Pacific Islands, c. 1200 BCE.

Last Glacial Maximum The time in the most recent glacial period when ice sheets were at their greatest extent, c. 26,000–20,000 years ago.

Laurentide and Cordilleran ice sheets Massive glaciers that covered North America during the Last Glacial Maximum.

Levallois A technique for making a stone tool. It involves striking and trimming a stone before completely removing a flake to create a tool that will be sharp on all sides.

lexical lists Records that indicate words and their equivalents in other languages.

Linear A A script used by the Minoans in Crete, from 2500 to 1450 BCE, which has never been deciphered.

logogram, logographic An image that stands for a single word. Sometimes a logogram resembles what it stands for (in such cases it is called pictogram), but otherwise it is often stylized.

Long Count A Mesoamerican calendar system that calculates time from a start date in 3114 BCE.

Magdalenian Period A later period in the Palaeolithic, dating 17,000–11,000 years ago.

Makah A tribe on the Pacific Northwest coast of Washington State who inhabited the ancestral village of Ozette, and who maintain a tradition of whaling.

managed mosaic An agricultural system employed by the Maya that included diverse techniques, such as raised or drained fields, terracing, and a mix of cultivated vegetables and trees.

material culture The tools, food remains, buildings, and other artifacts used by humans.

matrilocal residence A residence tied to the birthplace of a female family member.

Maya A pre-Columbian Mesoamerican civilization of the highlands of Southern Mexico, Guatemala, and the Yucatán Peninsula, from *c.* 1000 BCE.

megafauna Large animals especially associated with the Ice Age/Pleistocene.

Mesolithic The period in Europe falling between the Upper Palaeolithic and Neolithic; refers to the final period of hunter-gatherer cultures before the onset of farming. Its approximate time frame differs across regions.

midden An ancient pile of domestic waste that may contain bone, shell, and pieces of pottery.

minimum number of individuals (MNI) A calculation of the minimum number of individuals who could have generated an assemblage of bones, based upon counts of elements that occur only once (such as a left radius).

Minoan A palace culture centered on the island of Crete from 2500 to 1450 BCE.

mitochondrial DNA (mtDNA) DNA found in the mitochondria of a cell, not the nucleus; passed down only from the mother.

monument A structure, the meaning and purpose of which are shared across a social collective.

morphology The shape and form of an object or species.

Mousterian A stone tool industry often associated with Neanderthals.

mutualism The cooperation of two species for their mutual benefit by enhancing individuals' fitnesses.

Nahuatl A language spoken in the Valley of Mexico, also known as Aztec.

Natufians A late Paleolithic community that gathered and prepared wild wheat and barley in addition to hunting, and adopted a sedentary lifestyle.

Neanderthal Also known as *Homo sapiens neandertalensis*. An early human species that evolved in Europe and became extinct approximately 30,000 years ago.

Neolithic A period in human history that includes the adoption of agriculture and building of monuments, about 9,000 years ago.

niche construction The manner in which a species changes its habitat in a way that improves its overall fitness and that of its descendants.

number of identified specimens (NISP) A total count of the number of bones from each genus or species (e.g., number of bones belonging to the cow family or *Bovidae*).

Old Kingdom Period in Egyptian history from 2686 to 2181 BCE, marking the beginning of the Third Dynasty and end of the Sixth Dynasty. Includes the building of the Great Pyramid during the Fourth Dynasty.

Oldowan The oldest known stone tools made by human ancestors, made more than 2.5 million years ago from simple percussion.

Olmec A Mesoamerican civilization that began approximately 3,000 years ago.

osteology The study of bones, including development and mechanics.

overkill hypothesis Argues that human activity principally led to the extinction of megafauna shortly after the Ice Age ended.

Paleoindians A general term used to describe the first people who inhabited the American continents.

Paleolithic A period in human history that began with the first stone tools, starting 3.3 million years ago. The Upper Paleolithic commenced with the first appearance of anatomically modern Homo sapiens. In Europe this was about 45,000 years ago. Upper Paleolithic cultures in Europe include the Aurignacian, Gravettian, Solutrean, and Magdalenian.

palynology The identification of pollen (created by plants for sexual reproduction) using microscopy and sample specimens.

Pastoralists People who make their living by herding domesticated animals used to produce meat, milk, or wool.

Phoenician alphabet The earliest systematized alphabet, developed in the ancient civilization of Phoenicia on the eastern coast of the Mediterranean.

phyles Organized gangs of laborers used to build the pyramids of ancient Egypt.

phytoliths Small fragments of silica from plants; can survive for thousands of years.

pictogram An element of writing that uses a simple symbol emulating an object to convey the word for that object.

pit house A form of house that consists of a shallow pit capped with a timber and adobe roof. These houses were constructed in the American Southwest in the centuries prior to the development of pueblos (villages) above ground.

plastrons The bony panels on the bottom of a turtle shell, used in the divination process in ancient China.

Pleistocene Earth's most recent Ice Age, lasting until *c.* 11,600 years ago.

polis From the ancient Greek for the city-state, or its citizens.

practice theory A social theory that explains culture and culture change in terms of the daily and frequent practices that occupy human lives. People repeat what they have learned, and repeat best what they practice often; at the same time, they introduce minor shifts as errors or innovations. Common practices forge institutions, the building blocks of social conformity and social organization.

Pre-Pottery Neolithic A A period in Southwest Asia, 11,600–10,000 years ago, when people lived in semi-subterranean houses and relied on foraged plants and animals, but did not use pottery. Also known as PPNA.

Pre-Pottery Neolithic B A period in Southwest Asia, 10,700–8,000 years ago, when people began to depend more heavily on domesticated plants. Also known as PPNB.

pressure flaking Finer flaking of a stone tool using an antler tip, which is pressed against the stone to break off small flakes.

prey pathway A path to animal domestication whereby humans begin to manage and protect animals that were originally hunted in the wild.

primary flakes The first pieces or flakes of a stone that are struck off during knapping.

proto-cuneiform The oldest known form of writing, traced to Mesopotamia. Because they wrote on clay, Sumerians' early pictographic and numerical notations have been preserved; many of their signs are pictograms and logograms.

proximal end In flintknapping, the point where the flake originated following the strike of the blow; includes the striking platform.

proxy data Types of data used by climatologists to infer climate changes in the past.

radiocarbon determination The calculation of how long it has been since a radiocarbon sample last maintained the same proportion of $^{14}C/^{12}C$ as the atmosphere; usually marks the moment of death of a living organism.

radiocarbon half-life The time it takes for half the ^{14}C in a sample of organic material to decay, 5,730 years.

raised fields An agricultural method that grows crops on raised platforms of soil in order to protect crops from flooding.

rebus writing A writing system that uses pictograms of objects, the name of which resembles in sound a word or a syllable.

redistribution The process whereby a leader demands tribute of a population and, under tight controls, then doles it out to supporters and followers.

reference specimens The complete set of bones of a particular species that zooarchaeologists use to identify an excavated bone.

refugia Isolated patches of particular environments where animals find refuge.

residue analysis Analysis of any chemical traces found in a ceramic container.

retouching Further trimming of a stone tool, to produce a sharp edge.

rewilding Restoring an area (land or marine environment) to more natural conditions through the removal of human constructions and the replacement or reintroduction of animals and plants.

Rus A Viking group from Northern Europe whose name later came to identify the nation of Russia.

sarsen stones The outer ring of limestone stones at Stonehenge, some of which retain lintels across their tops.

seed dormancy The process during which a seed waits for the perfect conditions to sprout.

settlement systems The spatial and temporal organization that determines where, when, and how people reside.

Shang Dynasty The second dynasty of China, but the first supported by archaeological evidence; 1600–1050 BCE.

shell midden A dense archaeological deposit composed of clam shells, which is usually generated as a waste product of marine foraging.

smelting Using heat to melt ore (a rock with dense concentrations of minerals or metals, such as iron) allowing for the extraction of pure metal.

social structure The arrangement of ideas, conventions, and institutions that relate individuals to each other, and make up a society.

social theory Explains human actions in terms of shared ideas and conventions.

Solutrean An archaeological culture named for a form of tool-making in Europe developed 22,000–17,000 years ago.

spindle whorls Donut-shaped weights of stone, shell, or clay used to spin fiber into thread.

stewardship Caring for and maintaining some thing or place for the benefit of all.

strata Layers of sediment that are deposited in a sequence; their order records particular events and provides a context for associated artifacts.

stratified survey A survey technique whereby a landscape is divided into sections before before some of those sections are surveyed.

stratigraphic layers Layers of rock or sediment that accumulate over time and can be used to infer the relative age of an archaeological find.

striking platform The part of a stone core where the flintknapper strikes to create smaller flakes.

structural inequality A societal configuration that results in the oppression of segments of the society.

structural violence Harm done to individuals because of their position in society.

structuralism A theoretical approach that considers human action to be driven by underlying cognitive frameworks, such as opposition.

Sumerian Civilization in Southwest Asia dating back to 3200–2500 BCE; it included some of the earliest cities in the world. People of the previous Uruk period were also likely to have been Sumerian-language speakers.

survey Research conducted in the field, including searching for sites and collecting information on the distribution of archaeological objects and features.

syllabogram, syllabographic An image that stands for a sound. A phonetic symbol, a series of which can be put together to sound a word.

taphonomy Factors that affect the deposit and preservation of archaeological remains.

taxonomic identification Identifying to which genus or species a bone belongs.

terra preta Dark earths found in the Amazon that are more fertile than surrounding soils as a result of ancient human activity and enrichment.

Thule Ancestors of the Inuit, who rapidly moved across Alaska, Canada, and Greenland from 1000 CE to the thirteenth century.

tooth eruption The moment teeth emerge, used to determine the age of individuals younger than twenty years.

tophets Cemeteries of cremated children in ancient North Africa.

traits Specific aspects of an object that archaeologists observe that relate to how it was made or used.

tumulus An ancient burial mound.

typology Classification of objects according to particular traits, such as color, size, or style.

Ubaid Period Stage of development in Mesopotamia, *c.* 6000 to 3800 BCE, when people began to settle permanently.

Uruk Period Stage of development in Mesopotamia, *c.* 3800 to 3000 BCE, when the first cities were built.

ventral In flintknapping, the interior surface of a flake.

Wallacea A zone of islands within a stretch of deep water that has separated Australia from Southeast Asia for 70 million years.

Yangshao culture A Neolithic culture in Xi'an, China; included the site of Banpo, dating to 5,000 BCE.

Younger Dryas A period after post-glacial warming had begun. Between 12,800 and 11,500 years ago, global temperatures dropped sharply, causing significant vegetation changes around the world.

ziggurats Stepped pyramids found in Mesopotamia.

zooarchaeology A subdiscipline of archaeology that studies past human engagements with animals, usually through the remains of animals at archaeological sites.

zun jars Inscribed ceramic vessels made during the Dawenkou phase (2800–2500 BCE) in China, used for ceremonial offerings of wine to the ancestors.

Sources of Quotations

Chapter 4, p. 80: Isaacs, Jennifer. *Australian Dreaming: 40,0000 Years of Australian Prehistory*. Sydney: Ure Smith Press, 1992. 20.

Chapter 7, pp. 150–51: Krech, Shepard. *The Ecological Indian: Myth and History*. New York: W. W. Norton & Co., 1999. 127.

Chapter 9, p. 215: Richard III, Act 1, Scenes I and III, The Complete Works of William Shakespeare: http://shakespeare.mit.edu/index.html

Chapter 12, pp. 290–91: Ibn Fadlan, *Ibn Fadlan and the Land of Darkness: Arab Travelers in the Far North*. Translated by Paul Lunde and Caroline Stone. London, UK and New York: Penguin Classics, 2012. 49–54.

Chapter 13, p. 309: Rubio, Gonzalo. "On the Alleged Pre-Sumerian Substratum," *Journal of Cuneiform Studies* 51 (1999): 1–16.

Chapter 15, p. 352: Wilson, Edward O. "The Global Solution to Extinction," *The New York Times*, March 12, 2016.

Sources of Illustrations

a = above; **b** = below; **l** = left; **r** = right

Halftitle © The Trustees of the British Museum; **Frontispiece** Numan Berk Basar/EyeEm/Getty Images; **1.0** Insights/UIG/Getty Images; **1.1** Kurt Saarits/Alamy; **1.2** artwork Peter Bull after Petit et al, 1999; **1.3** artwork Peter Bull after Barnosky, 2008; **1.4** artwork Peter Bull; **1.5** Craig Ellenwood/Alamy; **1.6** Michael Nolan/Robert Harding/Diomedia; **1.7** artwork Peter Bull; **1.8** Werner Forman Archive/Heritage Images/Diomedia; **1.9** photo Christian Bickel; **1.10** Canadian Museum of History, Gatineau (PfFm-1:1728 a, S89-1828-Dp1); **1.11** Canadian Museum of History, Gatineau (KeDq-7:325, S89-1831-Dp1); **1.12**, **1.13** photo Joy McCorriston; **2.0** Sisse Brimberg/National Geographic Image Collection; **2.1** Mark Thiessen/National Geographic Image Collection; **2.2** Croatian Natural History Museum, Zagreb; **2.3** artwork Peter Bull; **2.4** © Universität Tübingen; photo Maria Malina; **2.5** © Universität Tübingen, photo Jensen; **2.6** Sisse Brimberg/National Geographic Collection; **2.7** artwork Peter Bull after Aujoulat, 2004; **2.8** photo courtesy Lionel Guichard-Ministry of Culture and Communication, France; **2.9** Hemis/Alamy; **2.10** no credit; **2.11** image courtesy Maxime Aubert, Griffith University; **2.12** Fine Art Images/Diomedia; **2.13** Muséum National d'Histoire Naturelle, Paris; **2.14** Mark Kelley/Alaska Stock/Diomedia; **2.15** G. Dagli Orti/DeAgostini/Diomedia; **2.16** artwork Peter Bull; **2.17** © The Trustees of the British Museum, London; **2.18** Medhi Fedouach/AFP/Getty Images; **2.19** akg-images; **3.0** photo Joy McCorriston; **3.1** Art Collection 3/Alamy; **3.2** Musée des Antiquités Nationales, St-Germain-en-Laye/Bridgeman Images; **3.3** Album/akg-images; **3.4**, **3.5** artwork Peter Bull; **3.6** photo AKM BW, archive; **3.7**, **3.8**, **3.9**, **3.10** artwork Peter Bull; **3.11** Fine Art Images/Diomedia; **3.12** National Park Service; **3.13** image courtesy Daniella E. Bar-Yosef Mayer, photo Malka Weinberg; **3.14**, **3.15** artwork Peter Bull; **3.16** image courtesy Frankfurt University Nok Project; **3.17** Paul Hanny/Gamma-Rapho/Getty Images; **3.18** Martin Thomas Photography/Alamy; **3.19** © South Tyrol Museum of Archaeology, Bolzano, artwork Sara Welponer/noparking; **3.20a**, **3.20b**, **3.20c**, **3.20d** © South Tyrol Museum of Archaeology, Bolzano; photos Harald Wisthaler; **4.0** Donald Kirkland/Axiom/Diomedia; **4.1**, **4.2** artwork Peter Bull; **4.3** Chris Watson/shutterstock.com; **4.4** from Peter Hiscock, Sue O'Connor, Jane Balme and Tim Maloney, "World's earliest ground-edge axe production coincides with human colonisation of Australia," *Australian Archaeology*, Volume 82 (2016); **4.5** permission courtesy Warakurna Artists, photo Tim Acker; **4.6** Penny Tweedie/Corbis/Getty Images; **4.7** Franck Chaput/Hemis/Getty Images; **4.8** after ML Design; **4.9** photo Kenneth Garrett; **4.10** Tom Dillehay; **4.11** Smithsonian Institution, Washington, D.C.; **4.12** British Library, London; **4.13** artwork Peter Bull; **4.14** © 2015 Polynesian Voyaging Society, photo 'Ōiwi TV/Nā'Ālehu Anthony; **4.15** Vadim Boussenko/Alamy; **4.16** photo Joy McCorriston; **4.17** courtesy Michael Harrower, Johns Hopkins University, Baltimore; **5.0** Patrick J. Endres/Corbis NX/Getty Images; **5.1** artwork Peter Bull; **5.2** courtesy Crow Canyon Archaeological Center; **5.3** Kravka/Alamy; **5.4** Edward S. Curtis Collection/U.S. Copyright Officer/Library of Congress, Washington, D.C.; **5.5** Museum of Northern Arizona, Flagstaff; **5.6** no credit; **5.7** artwork Peter Bull; **5.8**, **5.9** courtesy Crow Canyon Archaeological Center; **5.10** Malcolm Fairman/Alamy; **5.11**, **5.12** photo Joy McCorriston; **5.13**, **5.14** artwork Peter Bull; **5.15** DeAgostini/Getty Images; **5.16** Computer 3D Reconstruction from archaeological data, Pueblo Bonito, Chaco Culture National Historical Park, New Mexico, by Dennis R. Holloway, Architect; **5.17** DigitalGlobe/Getty Images; **5.18** Department of Anthropology, Smithsonian Institution (Catalog numbers A336494, A366499, and A336493), photo James Di Loreto; **5.19** no credit; **5.20**, **5.21**, **5.22** from James N. Hill, *Broken K Pueblo: Prehistoric Social Organization in the American Southwest*, University of Arizona Press, Tucson, AZ: 1970; **5.23** Brigitte Merle/Photononstop/Diomedia; **6.0** Frederick William Bond/Zoological Society of London/Bridgeman Images; **6.1** photo Kenneth Garrett; **6.2** courtesy Maine State Museum (81.1.5581); **6.3** artwork Peter Bull; **6.4** artwork Peter Bull; **6.5** artwork Rowena Alsey; **6.6** artwork Peter Bull after PIDBA; **6.7** courtesy Ohio History Connection, photo Brad Lepper; **6.8** Florilegius/Alamy; **6.9** courtesy Ohio History Connection, photo Brad Lepper; **6.10** Michael Nichols/National Geographic Images Collection/Getty Images; **6.11** Bruce Coleman International/Diomedia; **6.12** artwork Peter Bull; **6.13** Museum of New Zealand Te Papa Tongarewa, Wellington (S.023700); **7.0** Jason Edwards/National Geographic/Getty Images; **7.1** photo Julie Field; **7.2** Skybird Forever; **7.3** Photo J. P. Ruas, Arquivo de Documentação Fotográfica, DGPC; **7.4** Collection of the University of Colorado Museum of Natural History, Boulder; **7.5a** The Picture Art Collection/Alamy; **7.5b** Natural History Museum of Utah, Salt Lake City; **7.6** photo Heige Instad; **7.7** from Lewis R. Binford, "Willow Smoke and Dogs' Tails: Hunter-Gatherer Settlement Systems and Archaeological Site Formation," *American Antiquity*, Volume 45, Issue 1 (1980), 4–20, published by the Society for American Archaeology and reproduced with permission; **7.8** drawn by Joseph Drayton, engraved by Rawdon, Wright & Hatch; **7.9** artwork Peter Bull; **7.10** Stephen Alvarez/National Geographic Image Collection; **7.11**, **7.12**, **7.13** photo Julie Field; **7.14** after R. Dyson-Hudson and E. A. Smith, 1978; **7.15** photo Julie Field; **7.16** artwork Peter Bull; **7.17** Desmond Dugan/ImageBROKER/Diomedia; **7.18** Hulton Archive/Getty Images; **7.19** Tracy Packer Photography/Getty Images;

7.20 photo Nicholas C. Kawa; **8.0 l**, **8.0 r** Bible Land Pictures/Alamy; **8.1** artwork Peter Bull; **8.2** Bible Land Pictures/Alamy; **8.3** Bettmann/Getty Images; **8.4, 8.5a** artwork Peter Bull; **8.5b** artwork Peter Bull after Valla, 1980; **8.6** World History Archive/Alamy; **8.7, 8.8** photo courtesy M. Rosenberg; **8.9** Halil Fidan/Anadolu Agency/Getty Images; **8.10** © DAI, Göbekli Tepe Project; **8.11** artwork Rowena Alsey after Munro et al, 2018; **8.12** artwork Peter Bull; **8.13, 8.14, 8.15** photo Joy McCorriston; **8.16** artwork Peter Bull; **8.17** image courtesy Mietje Germonpré, The Royal Belgian Institute of Natural Sciences, Brussels; **8.18** photo Joy McCorriston; **8.19, 8.20** artwork Peter Bull; **8.21** photo Joy McCorriston; **8.22** Tjeerd Kruse/Alamy; **8.23** artwork Peter Bull; **8.24** The Food and Agricultural Organization of the United Nations (FAO); **8.25** artwork Peter Bull after Sean Downey; **8.26** National Geographic Image Collection/Alamy; **8.27** Images & Stories/Alamy; **8.28** artwork Peter Bull after Schrøder et al, 2004; **8.29** National Geographic Image Collection/Alamy; **8.30** John Zada/Alamy; **9.0** Ann Ronan Pictures/Print Collector/Getty Images; **9.1** artwork Peter Bull; **9.2** ASK Images/Alamy; **9.3** G. Dagli Orti/DeAgostini/Diomedia; **9.4** Photo12/UIG/Getty Images; **9.5** Museo Nacional de Anthropología de México, Mexico City/Instituto Nacional de Antropología e Historia (INAH); **9.6** © The Trustees of the British Museum, London; **9.7** University of California Irvine Libraries; **9.8** photo courtesy Wesleyan University Archaeology and Anthropology Collections, Connecticut; **9.9** Andrew Cowie/AFP/Getty Images; **9.10** Justin Tallis/AFP/Getty Images; **9.11** artwork Peter Bull; **9.12 l**, **9.12 r** photo courtesy Haagen D. Klaus, George Mason University, Fairfax, Virginia; **10.0** Gift of Landon T. Clay/Museum of Fine Arts, Boston/Bridgeman Images; **10.1** SuperStock/Alamy; **10.2** artwork Peter Bull; **10.3** Al Argueta/Alamy; **10.4** Proyecto Arqueológico Calakmul/Instituto Nacional de Antropología e Historia (INAH); **10.5** Rolf Richardson/Alamy; **10.6** photo courtesy Shane Montgomery; **10.7** Space Imaging Inc./NASA; **10.8** Tom Server/NASA; **10.9** artwork Peter Bull; **10.10** from Douglas J. Kennett et al, *High-precision chronology for Central American maize diversification from El Gigante rock shelter, Honduras, PNAS* 114 (34) (2017) 9026–31; **10.11** Cindy Miller Hopkins/Danita Delimont/Diomedia; **10.12** photo Jorge Pérez de Lara; **10.13** Javier Garcia/Alamy; **10.14** courtesy Pacunam LiDAR Initiative; **10.15** artwork Peter Bull; **10.16** R.M. Nunes/shutterstock.com; **10.17** artwork Christophe Pottier, Damian Evans, Pelle Wijker, Sarah Klassen, Roland Fletcher, and the Great Angkor Project; **10.18** artwork Peter Bull; **10.19** Merrydolla/shutterstock.com; **10.20** © 2019 by Ancient Egypt Research Associates; **10.21** artwork Peter Bull; **10.22a** Gianni Dagli Orti/Rex/Shutterstock; **10.22b** photo Scala, Florence; **11.0** AP/Rex/Shutterstock; **11.1** Rijksmuseum, Amsterdam, on loan from the City of Amsterdam (A. Van Der Hoop Bequest) (SK-C-211); **11.2** artwork Peter Bull **11.3 l**, **11.3r** Egyptian Museum, Cairo/Werner Forman Archive/Diomedia; **11.4** no credit; **11.5** Danita Delimont/Alamy; **11.6** Prisma Archivo/Alamy; **11.7** © 2019 by Ancient Egypt Research Associates; **11.8** Alain Guilleux/age fotostock/SuperStock; **11.9** Jose Antonio Penas/Science Photo Library; **11.10** © 2019 by Ancient Egypt Research Associates; **11.11** artwork Peter Bull; **11.12** DeAgostini/Getty Images; **11.13** artwork Peter Bull; **11.14a** Mike P. Shepherd/Alamy; **11.14b** artwork Peter Bull; **11.15** photo Joy McCorriston; **11.16** from S. di Lernia, M. A. Tafuri, M. Gallinaro, F. Alhaique, M. Balasse, L. Cavorsi, et al. "Inside the "African Cattle Complex": Animal Burials in the Holocene Central Sahara," *PLoS ONE* 8(2) (2013) e56879; **11.17** photo Dorian Fuller, Bellary District Archaeological Project; **11.18** Zuma Press/Diomedia; **11.19** photo Adam Stanford © Aerial-Cam Ltd.; **11.20** from William Stukeley, *Stonehenge, A Temple Restor'd to the British Druids*, 1740 (London); **11.21** artwork Peter Bull; **11.22** artwork Peter Bull; **11.23** photo Adam Stanford © Aerial-Cam Ltd.; **11.24** photo Joy McCorriston; **11.25** after Craig et al, 2015; **11.26** artwork Peter Bull; **11.27** from E. G. Squier and E. H. David, *Ancient Monuments of the Mississippi Valley*, 1848 (New York); **11.28** © The Trustees of the British Museum, London; **11.29, 11.30** photo Joy McCorriston; **11.31** image and magnetic survey, Jarrod Burks, in conjunction with the National Park Service, The Ohio State University and the Cleveland Museum of Natural History; **11.32** photo Gary Crawford; **12.0** © The Trustees of the British Museum, London; **12.1** photo Adam Stanford © Aerial-Cam Ltd.; **12.2** Bernard Foubert/Photononstop/Diomedia; **12.3** artwork Peter Bull; **12.4** from Felipe Guaman Poma de Ayala, *Nueva Corónica y buen gobierno*, 1600–1615; **12.5** Brooklyn Museum: Charles Edwin Wilbour Fund (07.447.790a-i); **12.6** Bill Curtsinger/National Geographic Image Collection; **12.7** Mike P. Shepherd/Alamy; **12.8** Granger/Rex/Shutterstock; **12.9** artwork Peter Bull; **12.10** courtesy the Penn Museum, Philadelphia (#8704); **12.11** courtesy the Penn Museum, Philadelphia (#251054); **12.12** © The Trustees of the British Museum, London; **12.13** DeAgostini/SuperStock; **12.14** INTERFOTO/Alamy; **12.15** © The Trustees of the British Museum, London; **12.16** Rex/Shutterstock; **12.17** © The Trustees of the British Museum, London; **12.18** Stephen Alvarez/National Geographic Image Collection; **13.0** Piero M. Bianchi/Getty Images; **13.1** artwork Peter Bull; **13.2** Dennis Cox/Alamy; **13.3** artwork Michael D. Coe; **13.4** Heritage Images/Diomedia; **13.5** G. Dagli Orti/DeAgostini/Diomedia; **13.6** Bible Land Pictures/Alamy; **13.7** The Metropolitan Museum of Art, New York, purchase, Raymond and Beverly Sackler Gift, 1988 (1988.433.1); **13.8** artwork Peter Bull; **13.9** Private Collection; **13.10** INTERFOTO/Alamy; **13.11** artwork Peter Bull; **13.12** The Palace Museum, Beijing; **13.13** Imagine China/Rex/Shutterstock; **13.14, 13.15** artwork Rowena Alsey; **13.16** Asian Art & Archaeology/Corbis/Getty Images; **13.17** photo Joy McCorriston; **13.18** artwork Peter Bull; **13.19** photo Joy McCorriston; **13.20** Luca Invernizzi Tettoni/AGF Foto/Diomedia; **13.21** © The Trustees of the British Museum, London; **13.22** Little Monster/Stockimo/Alamy; **13.23** G. Dagli Orti/DeAgostini/Diomedia; **13.24** photo Joy McCorriston; **13.25** Egmont Strigl/imageBROKER/Diomedia; **13.26** © The Trustees of the British Museum, London; **14.0** Granger/Rex/Shutterstock; **14.1** photo Julie Field; **14.2** artwork Peter Bull; **14.3** Mark and Carolyn Blackburn Collection of Polynesian Art/Bridgeman Images; **14.4** courtesy Professor Sue O'Connor, Australian National University, Canberra; **14.5** artwork Peter Bull after Smith et al, 2012; **14.6** George Ward/Alamy; **14.7** Mauricio Abreu/Alamy; **14.8** DeAgostini/Diomedia; **14.9a** Robert Stanton/AFP/Getty Images; **14.9 b** photo Texas Historical Commission; **14.10** Greg McFall/United States National Oceanic and Atmospheric Administration (NOAA); **14.11** The Metropolitan Museum of Art, New York, gift of Mr. and Mrs. Nathan Cummings, 1964 (64.228.703); **14.12** Wiskerke/Alamy; **14.13** artwork Peter Bull after Eltis and Richardson, 2010; **14.14** Library of Congress, Washington, D.C.; **14.15** artwork Rowena Alsey; **14.16** Granger/Rex/Shutterstock; **14.17** from Peter J. Robertshaw, Marilee Wood, Anne Haour, Karlis Karklins and Hector Neff, "Chemical analysis, chronology, and context of a European glass bead assemblage from Garumele, Niger," *Journal of Archaeological Science* 41 (2014) 591–604. Photo Marilee Wood; **14.18** Chronicle/Alamy; **14.19** Randy Duchaine/Alamy; **14.20** Smithsonian Institution, Washington, D.C.; **14.21** photo Joy McCorriston; **14.22** Danita Delimont/Alamy; **15.0** The Asahi Shimbun/Getty Images; **15.1** Agencia Efe/Rex/Shutterstock; **15.2** Franck Guiziou/Hemis/Diomedia; **15.3** Michael Schwab/Getty Images; **15.4** Ernesto Benavides/AFP/Getty Images; **15.5** International Animal Rescue/Barcroft Media/Getty Images.

Index

Figures in *italic* refer to illustrations

accelerator mass spectrometers 129
Acheulean tools 57–58, *51, 57*
Adena tradition 271
Adovasio, Jim *83*
Adrar Tekemberet *321*
Africa:
  Great Lakes region 64–65, *64*; hominins 56–58; *Homo sapiens* 58–59; megafauna extinctions 140; iron smelting 63–65, *63, 65*; Neolithic herders 257–59, *257, 259*; rice 187, 342; slave trade 337–43, *337, 338, 339, 340, 341, 343*
agency, individuals' 202, 203, 206–7, 209–19, 349, 358–59
agriculture:
  Angkor 234, 236–37; consequences 169, 189–96, *190, 194, 195*; early rice farming 188–89, *188*; intensification 240–41; Maya 225–31; Mesopotamia 240–41; Nile River Valley 238; raised fields and rain forest 225–26; surplus wasting 242, 278, 279–84; urbanism and 221–42; *see also* domestication; farming; specific crops
Aha's tomb 286
Ahiram, king of Byblos 316
ahu, Rapa Nui *18, 17*
Ain Ghazal:
  overgrazing 196; plaster figures *168*
Ain Mallaha, Natufian site 174–75, *174*
Akasaki, Isamu 358
Akkadians:
  cuneiform development 307–8; notation system 318
Alberta, bison butchering 148
alcohol 280–84, *280, 282*
Alexander the Great 308
Alice Springs 80–81
alphabetic writing 314–16, *315*
Amano, Hiroshi 358
Amazon:
  dark earths (*terra preta*) 165–67, *166*; decision-making 165–67; rain-forest protection 358
American Great Plains 144–45, 148, 150–51
American Museum of Natural History 101
American Southwest 97, 98–120; communities 118–19; sequence of cultures *103*; drought history *109*; early archaeology 101–2; environment change 97, 98–103, 119–20
Americas:
  human dispersals into 81–85, *82*; extraction of minerals 334–36; megafauna extinctions 140; paleocoastlines, map *82*; trans-Atlantic slave trade 337–38, *337, 338*; *see also* specific states and regions
Amiet, Pierre 307
Amud cave 29
Anangu people 80–81
Anasazi 98
ancestor veneration:
  Lady Hao 310, *310*; monoliths *see* moai
Ancestral Puebloans 98, 102, 108, 115–18, 120, *100, 103*
Andes:
  chicha 281–82; gold/silver, to Spain 334–36; Inka "ice maiden" 294, *294*; *khipu* 318–20, *319*; silver pin *334*; *see also* Inka empire; Peru
Angkor:
  irrigation and agriculture 234–37; surplus production 242
Angkor Wat 234, *235, 236*
Anglo-Saxon ship burials 290–93, *292*
animals:
  cave painting 33–35, 37, *32, 34, 35, 37, 45*; domestication 183–85; feasting on 175–77, 258–59, 268–69, 277, 279–80; reintroduction of species 351, 353, *351, 353*; teeth, chemical analysis 268, *268*; *see also* megafauna; megafauna extinctions; specific animals
Anne of York 215
Anthropocene 10–14, 349; dispersal journeys 94; extractivism and 346; resources, decision making 165–67; structure/agency balance 219; technologies' impact 24, 70–71; writing and 322–23
Antiquity 51–53, 67–68, 80, 263
Anzick male infant burial 131
Apache people 98, 118
Arabia 91, 320–22
Arabic script 316
archaeobotany 180–81, *181*
archaeological methods:
  context 22; excavation 22–24, 104–7, *23, 106*; survey 22, 91–93, *93*; *see also* specific methods
archaeological theory 9, 14; cognitive 60; ethics 86; structuralism 34–35
Archaic humans 28–30, *29*
Arctic Inuit people 20–22, 329
Arequipa, child sacrifices 294
Arizona 98; Hohokam people 102; Mogollon people 102, 118–19; Patayan people 102
Arlington Springs Man 131
Arnhem Land 78–79, *79*
Arroyo Hondo 101–2, 137
Asante 341–42, *337, 339*
Ashurbanipal's library 304
assemblage analysis 92
Atkinson, Richard 263–64
atlatls 124–25, *125*
atmosphere:
  carbon dioxide (CO_2) levels 11–12, 357, *12*; change 129; methane gas 12
atom bomb, isotopes 11
Aubrey Holes 265, *262*
Aubrey, Sir John 263, 269–70
Auckland 354
Aurignacian period 31–38
Austral Islands 17
Australia:
  Aboriginal First People 78–81, *79, 80*; arrival and dispersals of *Homo sapiens* 74–75, 78, 76; death of coral reefs 12–13; megafauna extinctions 75, 140; Tasmanian tiger 123, *122*; *see also* Lake Mungo; Uluṟu; Willandra Lakes
axes *see* weapons/edge tools
Aztecs 203–12; child sacrifices 294; codices 210, *50, 200, 211*; conquest of 205–7, *206*; empire 203–5, *203*; La Malinché 205–7, *206, 208*; parenting 210–11; spindle whorls 212

babi rusa, Sulawesi cave image *37*
Baffin Island *21*
Baidesuru iron furnaces *65*
Bali, Brahmi script 316
banana cultivation 87
Banda area 341–42
Bar-Yosef, Ofer 172
barley 180
barracoons 342, *343*
barramundi *79*
Bashidang 189
Basketmaker culture 98, 102, 108, *103*
bats 13
Bayon temple 235
beach-clean campaign 359
beads 27, 31, 61, 112, 286, 288, 317, 327, 340–42, *62, 289, 341*
Beagle, HMS 73
Becquerel, Alexandre Edmond 357
Bedouin people, literacy 321
beeswax 62, 284, 331
Belgium, Goyet Cave 183, *183*
Belize:
  Maya cities 222; Pulltrouser Swamp 225–26
Beowulf's funeral 290
Berber Tifnagh script *321*
Bering Straits 328
Beringia 81–82, *82*
Besant people 144–45
Bighorn Mountain range 144
bike-sharing programs 353–54
Binford, Lewis 43, 152–54, *153*
bioarchaeology 212–16
biodiversity reduction, replenishing 350
bird species extinctions 123
bishop's crosier, Garðar *20*
Bismarck Archipelago 87
bison 144–45; artifacts from *151*; Blackwater Draw 124, *125*; butchering 148–49, *145, 149*; Cedar Gap *145*; diet and extinction 136–37; evolutionary theory and 150; Hudson Meng *145*; hunting 81, 124, 126, 147–48; Olsen-Chubbock *149*; social theory and 150–51; Yellowstone National Park *136*
Black Mesa storage jar *102*
Blackwater Draw site 124, *125*
blade production 60
Bligh, Captain William 154, *155*
Blombos Cave 58–59, 327–28, *59*
bloomery iron smelting 63–65, *64*

Bluehenge 264, 265, *265*
Bolivia, silver mine workers 334, 346, *324*
Bolling-Allerod period 135, 174
Bonampak temple 298
bone fragment taphonomy 146–47, *146*
Borneo:
    Kalimantan orangutan 13, *356*; Niah Cave 87
Boucher de Perthes, Jacques 51
Bounty, HMS 154, *155*
Bowler, Jim 77
Bradley, Richard 278
Brahmi script 315–16
Brattahild house foundations *19*
Brazil:
    African crops farmed 343; Amazon decision-making 165–67; coin found in Hawaii 325, 343, *326*
Bristol, transition to renewables 354
British Museum 284, 293
Broighter Hoard 278
Broken K Pueblo 115–18, *115*, *117*
bronze:
    artifacts 53, 62, 63, 293, 310–12, 314, 317, 320, 325, *310*; making 49, 61–62, 309
Bronze Age 51, 52, 53, 61, 67, 278, 316
Brooks, Allison 59
Brown, Basil 291
Brown, James 272
Browne-Ribeiro, Anna 165–67
Brumfiel, Elizabeth 210–11
Bruniquel Cave 28
Buhaya 63, *63*
bullae, Sumerian 307, *307*
Burks, Jarrod 272
Burlington, transition to renewables 354
Burning Tree mastodon site 133–36, *134*, *135*
Burundi iron smelting 63–65
butchery marks 146
Byblos child sacrifices 294–95

Cairo 247
Calakmul:
    and Tikal 224–25; murals *224*, *231*
calibration curves 130, *130*
California:
    European weeds 195; single-use plastic-bag ban 355
calligraphy, Chinese 312
Cambodia *see* Angkor
camels:
    Clovis hunters and 124, 126, 133; domestication 185
Campo Laborde 137
Canaanite amphora *284*
Canada:
    Kelp Highway 82–83; Northwest Territories 21; Quadra Island clam gardens 327
cannibalism:
    Cowboy Wash 120; Fiji 154; Jamestown settlement 344
canoes 16, 80, 87, 89–91, 154, *16*, *72*, *90*
Cantabria caves 37
carbon dioxide (CO_2) levels 11–12, *12*
carbon emissions 357
Carbon Disclosure Project (CDP) 354
Caribbean, coral reef death 12–13
Carn Goedeg 265
Caroline Islands 90
Carthage 63; child sacrifices 294–95
carved objects:
    bone, ivory *38*, *42*, *311*; seals *289*, *317*; stone 18, 176, 258, *16*, *177*, *241*, *259*, *272*, *304*, *306*, *330*; wood 21
Casas Grandes, Chihuahua 118–19, *119*
casting:
    bronze 310, 312, *292*, *310*; copper 61, 62; lost wax 62
Castle Rock Pueblo 108, 114–15
Çatalhöyük village 191–93, 230–31, *192*; house interior *191*; wine remains 283–84
Catherine's Site, Sand Canyon 104–8, *99*; excavation 105–7, *105*; midden 104; pottery fragment *105*; village destruction 105
Catherwood, Frederick 222, *223*
cattle:
    domestication 92; dung ash mounds 260, *260*; herders painting *197*; herding societies map *257*; ritual sacrifice 258, *259*
Cedar Gap site 144–145, 147, *145*
Celts:
    burials 278; fermented beverages 281
Center for Microbial Ecology 134

Central America:
    map *223*; maize cultivation map *229*; *see also* specific countries
Central Asia, Archaic humans 28
ceramics *see* pottery/ceramics
Cerro Potosi silver mine 334–36
Chaco Canyon 109–15, *110*, *112*; communities 111–14, *112*; drought, dispersion 114–15; farming 111–12; great houses 160, *114*; imports 111–12, *113*; roads 113
Chaco Wash 120
Chad, Kanem-Borno slave trade 339–40
Chalcolithic Age 61; Ötzi the Iceman 66–70, 71
Chauvet, Jean-Marie 45–46
chenopodium, domesticated 274
Chesapeake Bay, plantation slavery 343–44
Cheyenne bison hunters 144, 151
Chiapas 222
chicha maize beer 281–82, *282*
Chichen Itza 223
Chihuahua 98, 118–19
child sacrifices 294–95, *294*
Childe, V. Gordon 196
Chile, Monte Verde site 84, 139, *84*
Chillecothe region 272, *273*
Chimor society 217–18
China:
    maps *186*, *309*; writing 298, 309–14, *312*, *313*; rice domestication 185–89, *186*, *188*
cities:
    abandoned/lost 222, 227; and surplus production 242; *see also* Angkor; Egypt; Jericho; Maya cities
ciudadelas, Peru 217
Cleopatra, pharaoh 237, 293
Cliff Palace, Mesa Verde *100*
climate proxy data 119
cloth/clothing:
    Aztec tribute 210; depictions 209, *209*; Ötzi 68, *69*; production and identity 207–12, *208*, *209*; Queen Pu'abi *289*; wealth 207
Clottes, Jean 45
Clovis, New Mexico 124
Clovis people 84, 124–33; diet 133, 139; dispersal 126, 131–33; remains scarcity 131;

sites age reassessment 131; technology dissemination 131–33
Clovis points 84, *125*; distribution 126, 131–33, *132*; making 124–25; radiocarbon dating 127
codices:
    Codex Azcatitlan *206*; Codex Mendoza 208–9, 210, *200*, *211*; Maya 301–3, *302*
cofferdam excavation 332–33, *332*
cognition, Paleolithic art 35–36
cognitive archaeologists 60
Colorado Plateau 102; bison butchering 148; climate 98; drought depopulation 114
Colorado River 98
commensal pathway domestication 174, 184
community labor/roles:
    conflict resolution at Jericho 172; cooperative projects 160–61; food production 196–98; metalworking 60–65; *moai*, building 9, 17–18; Nabta Playa, building 257–59; permanent settlements 172; pyramids, building 250–56; St. Kilda 162; Stonehenge, building 263–66; villages 176
computer simulations 119
Conard, Nicholas 31
conflict theories 159
Conkey, Margaret 39
conquest 225, 281–82; Spanish 203, 207, 208, 210–11, 217, 294, 303, 319–20, 334–36
conspicuous consumption 277–95; environmental damage 277; inevitability 293–94
Cook, Captain James 88
Cook Islands 17
cooking pots 102, 283
Copenhagen, bicycle superhighways 353–54
copper:
    artifacts 70, 253, 272, 287, 290, 317, 318, 341, *61*, *272*; copper-oxide ores 61–62; import 112; working 61–63, *61*, *272*
coral reef, death 12–13
Cordilleran ice sheets 81–82
Cortés, Hernán 203, 205, 226; and La Malinché 205–7, 208, *206*
Cortez, Catherine's Site 104–7, *99*
cotton, domesticated 209

INDEX **367**

Cowboy Wash, cannibalism 120
Coyolxuauhqui altar *204*
Crabtree, Stefani 119
Cretaceous meteor impact 12
Crete, Minoan Linear A script 316
Crow Canyon Archaeological Center 104–7, 115
Croydon, Wandle River restoration 350–51
Crutzen, Paul 10, 11, 13, 357
cultural diversity stewardship 43–46
culture markers 102–4
cultures sequence, American Southwest *103*
cuneiform: administrative applications 306–9; adoptive languages 308; character development 306–8, *306*; Ugarit tablet *308*
Curtis, Edward S. *100*
Cuzco 318–19
Cyprus, pygmy hippos 139–40

Da-Gloria, Pedro 139
Damerow, Peter 308
Danube corridor 31–32, 37
Darwin, Charles 52, 73, 74, 143, 183, 263
dating techniques: fossils 14, 75; plant fragments 180; sequence of tools 50–52; tree-ring dating 130, *108, 109*; *see* radiocarbon dating
Davis, Edwin 271
Dawenkou culture 313–14, *313*
de Landa, Bishop Diego, destroys Maya codices 303
Deccan plain 260, *260*
defenses as communal projects 160–61
Den's tomb 286
dendrochronology 130, *108, 109*
Denisovan genes 60
Denmark: Dollerup burial *290*
Dhofar rockshelters script *321*
Di Lernia, Savino 258
Dickens, Charles 222
digital image analysis 227
Dilmun notation system 318
directed pathway domestication 185
dispersals, human: Americas 81–84, *82*; Australia 75–78, *76*; correlation with extinction events 139, 140; Fiji 143; Pacific 87–90, *89*

Djer's tomb *285*
DNA studies 30, 40, 59–60, 81, 85, 215, 345
dodo extinction 123
dog-tooth pendant *160*
dogs: domestication 39, 183–84; Rapa Nui 18; skull, Goyet Cave 183, *183*
Dolní Vestonice figurines 38
domestication: camels 185; centers map *186*; consequences 169–98; dogs 39, 183–84; donkeys 185; pathways 184–85; plants 180–83, 185–89, *180, 182, 186*; seeds, dormancy 182; sheep/cattle 92; sowing/harvesting 179; two-way process 181–85; *see also* food production
Doña Marina, La Malinché 205–8, *208*
Dorey, Martin 359
Dorset people: Canada mask *21*; Greenland 20–22
Dorshow, Wetherbee 358
Downey, Sean 190
Dreamtime ancestors 78–81, *79*
Dresden codex *302*
drought: ancient Southwest *109*; Chaco Canyon 114; population mobility during 119–20
Dubai artificial islands *11*
Durrington Walls 266, 267–69, 279–80, *265, 267, 279*
Dyce, William, *Pegwell Bay…* 52

Eanna precinct 305
Early Celtic Period 278
Early Dynastic Period 237, 246, 286
Early Holocene period 137, 175, 189
Early Woodland Period 271
earthworm activity 263
East Africa landscape clearance 65
East Asia, rice domestication map *186*
East Timor fishhooks 328, *328*
Easter Island *see* Rapa Nui echidnas 75
ecological city 352–54
ecological research, *terra preta* 167
ecological sustainability 119–20
economic defendability 159–60

Egypt: Djer's tomb *285*; dynastic history *250*; Giza pyramids 237, 247–48, 250–7, *238, 251, 252*; hieroglyphics 316, *239*; map *248*; Marai-Borda cave *197*; province capitals 239; State, building 238–39, 247–56; surplus production 242
Egyptian Museum Cairo 86
Egyptian pharaohs and kings 86, 239, 279, 358; pharaonic tradition 237, 247–58, 279, 285; Aha, King 286; Cleopatra 237, 293; Den 286; Djer 285–86; Khafre 253, *256*; Khufu 253; Menkaure 253; Narmer 249, *249*
Egyptian Western Desert, Neolithic herders 258
einkorn 180
el Wad cave 29
El Gigante, maize cobs 229
El Mirador 234; La Danta pyramid 222, *224*
electron spin resonance 29
Elizabeth I, queen of England 213
Elmenteitan herders 64–65
Elwha River restoration 350
encephalization 71
England: Richard III remains 212–16, *214*; Stonehenge 261–70, *261, 263*; Sutton Hoo burial site 291–93, *292*; Wandsworth Shield *276*; weapons/wealth disposal 277–78
English Heritage 262
English Virginia Company 343
Englund, Robert 308
environmental damage: conspicuous consumption 277; extractivism 334–36; intensification 240–41
environmental impact: farming 193–96, *194*; reduction 352, 357–59
Erahar 258, *259*
Eridu shrine 304
Erligang Period 312
ethics in archaeology 86
Ethiopia, independent domestication 185
ethnoarchaeology, and Nunamiut 151–54
ethnographic studies 34–35, 116, 159, 170, 268, 280, 349

Euphrates River 176, 241
Europe 39–43, 140; forest clearance 193–94; *see also* specific countries
European weeds, California 195
Europeans: Atlantic slave trade 337–42; elites, Peru 217; Neanderthal DNA 30; trading posts, Ghana 342
evolutionary theory 73, 74, 143; and bison hunting 150; on conflict 159
excavation method 22–24, 104–7, *23, 106, 107*; extrapolation uncertainty 116; toolkit 106–7, *106*
extinctions 12–13; human role in 139–40; *see also* megafauna extinctions; specific animals
extractivism 326, *327*; Anthropocene 346; colonization as 325; environmental damage 334–36; fishing 326–29; mining 334, 334–36, *324, 335*; slave trade 336–46, *337, 339*; whaling 329–32, *329, 331*

fairy stones 50
farming: alternating hunting/gathering 175; consequences 189–98; development catalysts 178–79; grain sowing/harvesting 179; managed mosaic 228; *see also* domestication; food production
feasting 279–84; and waste 277
fermentation jars/stoppers 283, 284, *283*
Fertile Crescent 241
Fiji 17, 144; Club dance *155*; conflict and defense 154–61; farmers 165; kava preparation *142*; Lapita dispersal 87
Finney, Ben 89–90
fire use, Neanderthals/humans 29, 70
First People 94; Australia 74–81; Americas 81–85
fisher-farmers, maritime Southeast Asia 87
fishhooks 328, *327, 328*
fishing 326–34; Blombos Cave 327–28; Makah people 330, *330*; migration settlements 170; preservation 328; Quebrada Jaguay 139

flintknapping 49, 53–55, 60, *54*, *55*
floor deposits excavation 115–18
Florida Gulf, Page-Ladson site 83
flotation technique 181, *181*
flutes, bone/ivory 31, *31*
food processing/preparing 102, 170, 174, 283, *175*
food production 169–98; community role 196–98; earliest sites map *171*; evidence 180–81; images on Uruk Vase *241*; *see also* domestication; Jericho
food-sharing 41–42
forest clearance:
  East Africa 65; Northern Europe 193–94; palm oil industry 13, 356–57, *356*; rain-forest destruction 13, 226–28, 242
fossil fuels:
  and rise of CO$_2$ levels 357; use reduction 354, 357–58
fossils dating 14, 75
frequency seriations 102–4, *103*
Friedkin Site 133
Fukushima solar panels *348*
Fuller, Dorian 187–89

Galapagos finches 73
Galilee, Ain Mallaha 174–75
Ganges Valley 188–89
Ganj Dareh site 184–85
Garðar, bishop's crosier *20*
Garstang, John 169
Garumele beads *341*
gatherings/ceremonies 32, 38, 118, *142*; ball games 231, 301, *225*; Dreamtime 78–79; Hopewell 274–75; Durrington Walls feasts 279–80, *279*; kivas *115*; Zuni 97
Gauls 281
Geisenklösterle cave 31
genetic diversity, domesticated plants 185
genetically modified organisms 355
Germany:
  Hohle Fels *31*; negative population growth 353; Waldalgesheim 278
giant ground sloths 124, 126, 137–38, *138*
Gibraltar, Neanderthals 28
gift-giving 284–85
Gila river 98, 118

Gilgamesh, king of Uruk 241, *304*; Epic of 304–5, 308, *305*
Giza pyramids 237, 247–48, 250–57, *238*, *251*; building benefits 255–56; encircling ramps 252; significance 250
Giza region, resources map *255*
Giza workers:
  diet 254–55; town 237, 253–55; work areas map *254*
Glacier Bay National Park *39*
glass 20, 331, 340–342, 344, *341*
Global Positioning System (GPS) unit, using *107*
glyphs:
  Isthmian 301; Maya 300
goats:
  domestication 184–85; herd *184*; overgrazing 196
Göbekli Tepe 196; builders 173; primitive wheat 180; sunken structures 175–76, *177*
gold:
  artifacts 278, 286–90, 293, 334, 337, 338, 341, 343, *286*, *289*, *293*, *335*; mining/making 217, 281, 341
golden frogs 13
Goldstein, Jerry 134
Gorham's Cave 28
Grand Canyon, Zuni people 97, *96*
great houses 160, *114*
Great African Diaspora 341–43
Great Rift Valley 64
greenhouse gases 12
Greenland:
  Dorset people 20–22; Norse settlements 19–22, *19*; Thule culture Inuit people 20–22
Grimstead, Deanna 111
Grotte Chauvet:
  filmed 45–46; images *45*; lions painting 34, *34* Grotte de Lascaux *see* Lascaux Cave
ground-edge axes 78, *78*
Guatemala 227; Maya cities 222, *223*, *224*; *see* Tikal
Guinea Coast trading posts 342

Hajji Firuz Tepe 283
Hall of the Bulls, Lascaux Cave *26*
Hallan Çemi site, houses 175, *176*
hand axes 49, *48*, *51*
Hangzhou River, Asian rice 187
Harappan:
  notation system 318; stamp seals 316–17, *317*; writing system 316–17
hares and tortoises 179
Hastorf, Christine 281
Hawaiian Islands 88, 90; food, conflict and privilege 16–17; island voyaging 88–90, *88*, *89*, *90*; Mauna Kea 12; taro paddy *157*; Brazilian coin found 325, 343, *326*; honeycreepers 13; *Two Brothers* wreck 333–34, *333*
Hawass, Zahi 253
Hawkins, Gerard 266
Hawley, William 268
Heckenberger, Michael 358
Heit el-Ghurab *251*
Hemings, Sally 345
Hemodu Neolithic site 187, *187*
Hendry, George 195
herders 92, 183–85, 196, 283, 350, *184*; Chalcolithic Europe 67; Sahara 64, 248, 257–59, *197*, *257*; South India 260; Stonehenge 268
heterarchical networks 224
Hierakonpolis 249
hieroglyphics 316, 239, *239*
High Bank Works *273*
Hill, James 115–18, *117*
Hismaic script 321
historical materialism 151
Hittite cuneiform 316
Hōkūle'a double-hulled canoe 90
Hodder, Ian 192
Hohle Fels cave *31*; flute 38, *31*
Hohlestein-Stadel cave, lion man *8*
Hohokam people 102, 118
Holocene era 10; environmental changes 75, 139–40; mobile herders 257
hominins, early 56–59
Homo erectus 57–58
Homo ergaster 56, 57–58
Homo genus 28
Homo habilis 56
Homo heidelbergensis 58
Homo rudolfensis 56
Homo sapiens:
  and Neanderthals, diversity 28–30; as complex superorganism 59; population expansion 13; *see also* humans
Homo sapiens neanderthalensis see Neanderthals
Homo sapiens sapiens 28, 29; *see also* humans

Honduras:
  abandoned cities 222; maize cobs *229*
Hopeton Earthworks 272
Hopewell Earthworks 270–75; crop cultivation 274; domestic structures 272, 274; gatherings/ceremonies 274–75; maps *270*, *271*
Hopewell, Mordecai 270
Hopewell Mound Group 274
Hopi people 120
horses, domestication 185
Horus 248
houses:
  Ain Mallaha 174–75, *174*; barracoons 342–43, *343*; Çatalhöyük 191–93, *191*; Durrington Walls *267*; Greenland *19*; Hallan Çemi *176*; Joya de Ceren *230*; Monticello plantation 345–46, *346*; puebloan architecture 98, 109–19, *100*, *110*, *115*, *117*, *119*; St. Kilda *163*; Ṭabaqāt Al Būma *23*; workers' settlement, Giza 253–54, *254*
households 113, 190, 196–98; labor division 42; strengthened 190
Houston, Stephen 301
Howe, Monica 358
Hudson-Meng bison kill site *145*
huipil 208–9, *208*
human niche construction 13–14, 16–19, 18, 20, 24, 28, 30, 36, 38, 43, 44, 60, 78, 87, 94, 150, 165–66, 188–90, 193–94, 195, 240, 242, 314, 326, 349, 352
human sacrifice 17, 203, 205–6, 293–95, 297, 298, 301, 310, 311, 312; child sacrifices 294–95, *294*; as conspicuous consumption 294–95; retainers sacrificed 285–88
humans:
  adaptation, stone tools 56; anatomically modern 28; Archaic 28–30; decision making 143; dispersals 73–94, 89–90; diversity and Neanderthals 28–30, *30*; flexibility, lifestyles 39; groups, symbolic expression 31–32; modern 31–38; role in extinctions 139–40, *13*; *see also Homo sapiens*
Humboldt, Alexander von 203

Hunan Province 189
hunter-gatherers:
    alternating farming 175;
    Australia 75–78; semi-permanent camps 170;
    Pleistocene lifestyle 39–43

Ibn Fadlan 290–91
Ibsen family 215
Ice Age *see* Last Glacial Maximum; Pleistocene
Ice Maiden child sacrifice 294
Iceland 19
Iceman *see* Ötzi
ideograms 307
IKONOS satellite imagery 227, *227*
inconspicuous consumption 356–57
India:
    ash mounds 260, *260*; food-recycling program 358–59; Harappan writing 316–17, *317*; rice domestication 187–89
individuals:
    agency 202, 203, 206–7, 209–19, 349, 358–59; and identity 201–2; environmental impact reduction 352, 357–59
Indo-Pacific region 87, *89*
Indonesia:
    Brahmi script 315–16, *315*; species 74
Indus Valley, Harappan writing system 316–17, *317*
Industrial Revolution 10, 11
inequality, prehistory 216–18
infrared liquid chromatography 283
Inka empire 318, *281*; child sacrifices 294, *294*; diets, residue analysis 282–84; maize beer 281–82, *282*; *khipu* 318–20, *119*
institutionalized violence, Fiji 154–61; *see* structural violence
Inuit people 20–22, 43
invertebrate extinctions 12
Iran 184–85, 283
Iraq:
    Ashurbanipal's library 304; Sargon II 304, 307; *see also* Sumerians
iron:
    artifacts 20, 291, 293, 333, 342, *291*, *292*; smelting/working 11, 20, 53, 63–65, 341, 350, *63–66*
Iron Age 51–53, 266, 269, 278, 284

irrigation:
    Angkor 234–37; Chaco Wash 120; paddy fields 185, *189*; Sumerians 241
islands:
    artificial *11*; as laboratories 15–24; *see also* specific islands
Isthmian writing system 301
Italy, negative population growth 353
ivory 20, 38, 239, 286, 306, 336, 337, 338, 341, 350; mammoth 31, 37, 42, *38*, *42*; whale *327*, *331*

jade 222, 310, 311, 313–14
Jamestown settlement 343–44, *344*
Japan:
    Fukushima solar panels *348*; Jomon culture 328; negative population growth 353; plastic-digesting bacteria 355
Jayavarman VII 235
Jefferson, Thomas, Monticello slave owner 344–45, *345*
Jericho 169, 196; agricultural PPNA and B lifestyle transition 171–80, 196; goat remains 184–85; Natufian people 174–75; plant fragments dating, 180; plastered skull 170, *172*; wheat domestication 169
Jericho tower and stone wall 160, 169–73, *173*; burials 171; inner passageway and stairs *173*; strata superposition 171
jewelry 32, 53, 101, 112, 160, 222, 248, 265, 278, 293, *29*, *289*, *293*; *see also* beads
Jiroft 286
Johannessen, Sissel 281
Johnston, Kevin 297
Jomon culture 328
Jordan:
    Ain Ghazal 196, *168*; goat overgrazing 196; plaster figures *168*; Kharaneh IV site 175
Joya de Ceren village site *230*

Kabah 221
Kalimantan orangutan 13, *356*
Kanem-Borno kingdom, slave trade 339–40, *340*
kangaroos, extinct giant 75
Kata Tjuṯa rock art images 80
Kawa, Nick 343

Kawelka gift-giving 284–85
Kebara cave:
    Neanderthal remains 29; Natufian bone sickle *179*
Kelp Highway 82–83, 139, 328, *82*
Kennewick Man 85, *85*
Kenyon, Dame Kathleen 169, 171, 180
Khafre's pyramid 250, 253, *251*, *256*
Kharaneh IV site 175
Khentkawes Town 251
Khmer empire 234, *234*; Brahmi script 315–16
Khok Phanom Di site 328
Khonsu sarcophagus *252*
Khufu's pyramid 237, 253, *238*, *251*
Kidder, Alfred 102
King, Dr. Martin Luther Jr. *244*
Kirch, Patrick 15–16
kivas 108, 113, 118, 156; Broken K Pueblo *115*; Pueblo Bonito 111, *110*; puebloan homes 98
Klallam Tribe 350
Klaus, Haagen 217–18
Knorozov, Yuri 303
Kohler, Timothy 119
Kom al-Hisn 255
Komodo dragon 74
Krech, Shepard 150
Kuhn, Steven 42
Kuulo Kataa site 341

La Belle (ship) cofferdam excavation *332*
La Malinché 205–7, 208, *206*, *208*
La Tène-style goldwork 278
Lady Hao's tomb vessel inscription 310, *310*
Lagash 241
Lagoa Santa site 139
Laguna Caldera 230
Laguna Lobato 334–36
Lakota people 151
landscapes:
    clearing for grasslands 65; ecological sustainability 119–20; monuments and 246–47
languages:
    Chinese 310; modern humans 31, 37; Hawaiian Islands 88; Nahuatl 203, 205; South Arabian 317, 321; Semitic 308; Sumerian 307–8; *see also* writing

lapis lazuli 286, 287, 290, *286*, 289
Lapita people 87–91, 156, *156*
Larsen, Clark 139
Lascaux cave complex 26, 27, 39, 262, *33*: degradation, closure, and replication 43–44; paintings 28, 32–38, *26*, *32*, *34*, *35*
Lascaux replication projects 43; toolmaking skills 43; Lascaux II and III 44, *44*
Last Glacial Maximum (ice age) 39–43
Latin alphabet 315–16
Laurentide ice sheets 81–82
Lehner, Mark 248, 253
Leicester, England:
    see Richard III, king of England
Leroi-Gourhan, André 34
Les Trois Frères cave 37
Levallois toolmaking technique 28–29, 58, 60, *59*
Lewis-Williams, David 34–35
Liangzhu culture 313–14
Libby, Walter 129
Libya, Messak plateau 258
LiDAR mapping:
    Angkor Wat *236*; Tikal *233*
light-emitting diodes (LEDs) 357–58
Lincoln Memorial 245, *244*
Linear A script 316
linguistic analysis 187–88
lion man 38, *38*
lions 126
Little Colorado River 115
Little Miami River 271, 274
livestock/prey timeline *178*
logograms 300, 306
looters, Rio Grande ruins 101
Los Aguajes ruins 101–2
Los Angeles County Bicycle Coalition 358
lost-wax casting 62
lotus root 189
Löwenmensch see lion man
Lubbock, John (Lord Avebury) 52–53
Lucretius 51
Lungarta lizard painting 79
Luojiajiao Neolithic site 187
Lyell, Charles 51
Lynott, Mark 272
lynx, liberation *351*

Maafa Great African Diaspora 341–43
macaws 118
Madjedbebe rock shelter 75, 76
Magdalenian hunting camp 39–43
magnetic gradiometer survey 273
magnetometer subsurface mapping 272
maize:
    beer 281–82, *282*; Chaco Canyon 111; early cobs *229*; cultivation, Maya 228–30; domestication 180, 228; pollen 111, 113, 115; spread beyond Mesoamerica 242; storage 98
Makah people:
    shoreline whaling 330; carving *330*
Makala Kataa site 342
Mala people 80
Malthus, Robert 222
mammals, large, decline 13
mammoths 124, 126, 131, 133
managed mosaic 228
Manayzah site 92
Mangaia 17
Manu`a, excavations 15–16
Maori people 88, 90–91
Marai-Borda cave 197
maritime archaeology: *see* underwater archaeology
maritime extractivism 326–34, *327*
maritime foragers, Indo-Pacific 87
maritime societies 326–34
Marquesas Islands 16
Marsal, Monsieur 27, 35
marsupials 74
Martin, Paul 126, 139
Massachusetts, Nantucket whaling center 331–32
mastodons *134*; and environment change 134–37; Clovis hunters and 126, 131, 133; diet, non-coniferous 135, *135*; skull, Burning Tree Mastodon site *134*
Matagorda Bay, cofferdam *332*
material culture:
    from bison 150–51, *151*; Inuit people 20–22, *20*, *21*
matrilocal residence 116–18
Matthiessen, Peter 350
Mau Piailug 90
Mauna Kea, Hawaii 12
Mauritian dodo 140

Mauritius 123
Maya cities 222, 224; ball courts 118, 225, 231, 301, *225*; Chichen Itza *223*; conflict 224–25; markets 231, *231*; reservoirs 231; structure 230–32; surplus production 242; urban collapse 232, 234
Maya people:
    hero twins legend 221, 225, *220*; heterarchical networks 224; hierarchies 224; languages 205; maize cultivation 228–29; present-day descendants 232, 234; queen *209*; rain-forest destruction 226–28; Yucatán 221
Maya writing 297, 298–303; codices 301–3; glyphs *300*; scribes, enemy 298, *299*
McCorriston, Joy 91, 259, 321; team 23, *259*
McGovern, Patrick 283–84
McHugh, Tom 151
Meadowcroft Rockshelter 83–84, *83*
Mediterranean, overgrazing 196
Mediterranean weeds, California 195
megafauna 75, *134*, *135*, *138*; and climate change 126–27; and environment change 134–37; hunting 84, 133
megafauna extinctions:
    American 84–85; and human dispersal 127, *13*; Australia 75–78; effect on Amazon 165–67; overkill hypothesis 123–40; rates 139–40; timeline 124
megaliths, Nabta Playa 258, *259*
Melville, Herman 334
Memphis 250
Menkaure's pyramid 253, *251*
Meroe iron smelting 63–65
Mesa Verde National Park 108, *100*
Mesoamerica 200, 202–12, *223*; cloth-making technology 209–10; people 118; writing systems 301–3; *see also* Aztecs, Maya
Mesolithic pits, Stonehenge 265
Mesopotamia *240*; agriculture 240–41; first settlements 170–77; notation system 318; Sumerian burials 286–90; Sumerian writing 298, 303–9; *see also* Sumerians

Messak Settafet, stone artifacts analysis 70
Mestizo class, Peru 217
metals:
    silver-mine workers *324*; mining 61–62, 334–35; tool making 62; *see also* specific metals
metalworking, community labor 60–65
Mexico:
    Aztecs 203–12, *203*; Bonampak temple 298; caves, plant fragments 180; Guatemala border *227*; highlands, independent domestication 185; Maya hero twins ceramic *220*; Mogollon people 118–19; *see also* Maya cities
Mexico City, raised fields 226
microplastics 11, 355
Middle Holocene climate shift 64
Middle Paleolithic, resource depletion since 178–79
migrations:
    animal 42, 70, 137, 148, 170, 174, 330, 350, *42*; Aztecs in the Valley of Mexico 203, *203*; Britain 266, 291; timeline 47; St. Kilda 162; for humans, *see* dispersals; slavery
millets domestication, China 185
Million Tree Initiative 354
Mills, Barbara 113
mineral extraction 334–36
mining 61–62, 334–35, *324*
Minoan Linear A script 316
Mirador Basin 222
mitochondrial DNA analysis, Richard III 215
moai Rapa Nui 9, 18–19, 160, *8*, *17*
Moana (movie) 15
mobile communities, monuments 257–59
mobility, ethnographic studies 170–71
Moche society, Peru 217
Moctezuma 206
Mogollon people 102, 118–19
moka gift-giving 284–85
monetized markets, defined 326
monograms, Shang 311
monoliths, Rapa Nui *see moai*
Montana, Anzick male infant burial 131
Monte Alban ball court *225*
Monte Verde site, Chile 84, 139, *84*

Montespan cave 38
Monticello slaves:
    Mulberry Row quarters 345–46, *346*; NMAAHC memorial display 345, *345*
monuments and landscapes 246–47; mobile communities 257–59
morphology, domesticated plants 182–83, *182*
mortuary cults 250
mounds 246–47; ash mounds, South India 260, *260*; Hopewell 61, 270–75, *270*, *272*, *273*; Fiji 158, *157*, *158*; Çatalhöyük 192, *192*; Stonehenge, Durrington Walls 265, 267, 269
Mount Carmel caves:
    interbreeding 60; no images 37; Neanderthal and human remains 29
mountain sheep 137
Mousterian tool industry 58, *59*
mud sealings, Egypt *239*
Mungo Lake campsites 77–78
Munro, Natalie 179
Museo Nacional de Anthropologia de México 208
mutation, selection and domestication 183
mutualism, domestication 181–82

Nabataean script 321
Nabta Playa megaliths 258, *259*
Naduri, Fiji 143
Nahuatl-speaking people 203, 205
Nairobi, transition to renewables 354
Nakamura, Shuji 358
Nakbe 222
Nantucket whaling center 331, 333, *327*, *329*
Naqada excavation 239
Narmer Palette 249, *249*
National Museum of African American History and Culture 345
Native American Graves Protection and Repatriation Act (NAGPRA) 85
Native Americans:
    copper-working 61, *61*; Kennewick Man 85, *85*; Pre-Hispanic, permanent soil changes 166; tools 50; *see also* Clovis people

INDEX **371**

Natufian people:
　Ain Mallaha site 174–75, *174*; and climate change 175; food resources and hunting, broad spectrum revolution 178–179, *178*; sickles 182–83, *179*
natural selection 143
Navajo people 98, 118
Nazlat es-Samaan village 253–54
Neanderthals 58–60; and *Homo sapiens*, diversity 28–30, *30*; DNA in humans 30, 59–60; extinction 30; larger brains than *H. sapiens* 58; Levallois technique 58, *59*; Mousterian tool industry 58, *59*; physique 28, *29*; remains 28–30; symbolic expression 28, *29*; technology 28–29
Near East:
　see Mesopotamia; Sumerians
Nebraska, Hudson-Meng site 145
negative population growth 353
Neiman, Fraser 345–46
Nelson, Nels 101–3
Neolithic people:
　ash mounds 260; Britain 261–66; Çatalhöyük 191–93; ceramics, Yellow River 312–13; herders 257–59; resins and wine 284; "Revolution" 196–98; rice farming, China 185–89; stonework, Jericho 169; tools 53; *see also* Natufians
Nevada, climate 98
Neville, Cecily 215
New Caledonia, Lapita dispersal 87
New Guinea 87; dispersal to 78; species 74
New Ireland 87
New Mexico:
　Chaco Canyon 109–15; climate 98; Mogollon people 102, 118–19; Zuni people, origin story 97, *96*
New World domesticates, in Africa 341
New Zealand 88; experimental voyage to 90–91, *90*; moa 140, *140*; Zealandia eco-reserve 353
Newark area 271, 274; Works map *271*
Newcomer, Mark 43, 49
Niah Cave Borneo 87
Niaux cave 37
niche construction *see* human niche construction

Niger, Garumele site 340–41
Niger River, African rice domestication 187
Nigeria, Hausa-Fulani people 340
Nile River Valley, agriculture 238
Ninevah, Ashurbanipal's library 304
Niqmepa V of Syria 308
Nissen, Hans 308
Nokonoko fortress, Fiji 143, 156, 158, *157*
nomadic lifestyles 39
non-biodegradable waste reduction 354–55
Norse Greenlanders 19–22, *19*; anthropogenic failure 22; Baffin Island carving *21*; hunting/lifestyles unlike Inuit 20–22; *see also* Vikings
North Africa, pastoral nomads literacy 320–22
North America:
　fish migration settlements 170; human dispersals 81–85; *see also* specific locations
notation systems 318–20; numerical 307
Nunamiut ethnoarchaeology 151–54, *152*

O'Connor, Sue 328
O'odham people 118
Oaxaca caves, plant fragments 180
oceans:
　and CO$_2$ 12; ecological collapse projection 329; *see also* Polynesian Voyaging Society; trans-Atlantic slave trade; whaling
Ohio:
　Hopewell Earthworks 270–75; megafauna butchered remains 133; mounds 270
Ohio Wesleyan University 134
Oldowan tools 56–57, *57*
Olduvai Gorge (Tanzania) 57, 64
Olmec people:
　writing 301; Veracruz coast 234
Olsen-Chubbuck kill site, bison butchering 148, *149*
Oman, Dhofar rockshelters script 321
oracle bones, inscriptions 311, *311*
oral traditions, human dispersals 89–90

orangutan:
　Kalimantan 13; population decline *356*
Oslo, transition to renewables 354
osteology, skeletal analysis 213
Ötzi the Iceman 66–70, 71; clothing 68–69, *68*; discovery 66–67, *66*; photographic reconstruction 67; physical/forensic studies 67
overgrazing, Mediterranean 196
overkill hypothesis, megafauna extinctions 123–40; assessment 139; tests 131
Ozette, Makah people 330

Pacheko, Paul 272
Pacific Islanders 73; conflict and fortification in Fiji 154–58; dispersal 87–91; fishhooks 327; oral histories 88–89
paddy fields 185, *189*
Page-Ladson prehistory site 83, 133; megafauna butchered remains 133
paintings:
　interpreting 33–38; on ceramics 101, 212, *103*, *220*; pigments 27, 37–38, 59, 75, 77, 151; rock art 27–28, 32–34, 37, 40, 42, 43, 45, 77–79, 258, 298, 321, *37*, *79*, *321*
Paisley Cave, Oregon 137
palaces:
　Angkor 234–35; Ghana 342; Maya 222, 231; Minoan 316; Ur 286, 290
Paleoindians *see* Clovis people
Paleolithic:
　art 32–38; diet 41–43; hunting camp site 39–43; toolmaking skills project 43
palm oil industry 13, 356–57, *356*
palynology *see* pollen
Panama, golden frogs 13
Papua New Guinea, *moka* gift-giving 284–85
Parker-Pearson, Mike 266, 268
Parry, Tab 359
pastoral nomads, literacy 320–22
pastoralists, earliest 92; *see also* farming; herders
Patayan people 102
Pauline, Minu 358
Pearsall, Deborah 187
Pecos Pueblo excavations 102

Pengtoushan Neolithic villages 189
Pennsylvania, Meadowcroft Rockshelter 83–84, *83*
Peñasco Blanco 111
Pergouset fissure 33
perishable technologies 67–70, 71
Permian period extinctions 12
Pernambuco 343
Peru:
　Chimor and Inka people, map 217; Cuzco 318–19; shoreline settlements 139; Spanish structural violence 216, 217–18; Upper Mantaro Valley 281–82; *see also* Andes
Peruvians, indigenous:
　poverty/exploitation 217–18
Petrie, Sir Flinders 239, 263, 285
Phoenicians:
　alphabet system 316; child sacrifices 294
phosphorus cycle 165–66
photogrammetric technology 45–46
phyles (work gangs) 254
physical remains analysis 213
phytoliths 187
pictograms 306
Piegan hunters 148
Pignatti, Sandro 196
Pilcomayo River pollution 336
Pincevent hunting camp 40–43, *41*
pit-house dwellings 98, *100*
Pitcairn Island 17
Pizarro, Francisco 318
Pizarro, Hernando 320
Plains 144, 151
plants:
　domestication 180, 182–83, 185, *180*, *182*, *186*; processing stones 174, *175*; remains 75, 180; *see also* archaeobotany; *terra preta*
plastered skull, Jericho 170, *172*
plastic-digesting bacteria 355
plastics:
　microplastics 11; decomposable six-pack rings 354; waste, most common artifact 355; waste reduction 354–55
plastrons 311, 313, *311*
Pleistocene 10, *13*, *39*; carvings 37–38, *38*; Kelp Highway 82–83, *82*; lifestyle 39–43; megafauna extinctions 123–40;

372　INDEX

see also Lascaux cave complex; Neanderthals
pohutukawa tree flowers 91, *90*
polar bears 13
pollen analysis 119, *194*; assemblages, African Great Lakes 65; Europe 39, 43; forest clearance evidence 193–94; Maya lowlands 232; Pulltrouser Swamp 226
Polynesia 15–19, *15*; cloth wealth 207; Lapita culture dispersal 87–91, *89*
Polynesian Voyaging Society 89–91, *90*
Poma de Ayala, Felipe Guamán 282, *319*
population: growth 352, *13*, *190*; mobility 119–20
Porter, Alexa 284
Potosi silver mine workers *324*
pottery/ceramics: classification and seriation 101–3, 266, *102*, *103*; clay balls for cooking 192; design and matrilocal residence 116–18; elements *117*; Lapita *156*; potters' marks 313–14, *313*; residue analysis 269, 282–83, *269*; spindle whorls 212, *212*
practice theory 161
Pre-Clovis people 84, 133
Pre-Pottery Neolithic A and B: Jericho 171–80, 196
Pretty, Edith 293
prey pathway domestication 184–85
primates, toolmaking 56
proto-cuneiform tablets 305–6, 308, *306*
Pu'abi, queen of Ur 308–9; clothing reconstruction *289*; royal tomb 288–90; seal *289*
public education/outreach 86
public transportation 352
Pueblo Bonito: artifacts 111; burial sites 113; cups *113*; re-creation *110*; ruins *110*
Pueblo cultures 98–120; ceramics *117*; Cowboy Wash 120; families, reconstructing 116–18; matrilocal residence 116–18; room functions 115–16, *115*; ruins/modern map *99*; sequencing 101–2; *see also* Chaco Canyon

Pulltrouser Swamp 225–26, *226*
pyramids, Egypt *see* Giza pyramids
pyramids, Tikal city *233*

Qafzah cave 29, 38
Quadra Island clam gardens 327
quartz tools 75
Quebrada Jaguay 139
Quebrada Tacahuay 139
Quetzalcoatl 203, *204*

radiocarbon dating 92; calibration 130–31, *130*; Clovis points with kills 127; data determination 129; domesticated plants remains 180; Meadowcroft Rockshelter 83–84, *83*; principles 127–31; radiocarbon cycle *128*
Raedwald, king, Sutton Hoo burial/hoard 291–93, *292–93*
rain forests: agriculture, raised fields 225–26; destruction 13, 226–28, 242; lost cities/structures 227
Ramilisonina 268
Rapa Nui (Easter Island) 9, 15–16, 17–19, 140; anthropogenic success 22; extinctions 16, 18–19; food scarcity 17–19; *moai* 9, 18–19, 160, *8*, *17*; niche construction 16–19; Rongorongo script 322, *322*
Rapa Nui (movie) 9, 18
Rarotonga 91
rats 18
reasoning, inductive/deductive 36
rebus writing 307
reciprocity 284–85
red ocher designs 75, 77
Red Land (Western Desert) 250
reference specimens 146, *146*
refuse, stratified 101–2
reindeer carving *42*
remote sensing 227
renewable energy 357
reptile extinctions 12
residue analysis 282–84
resources: control 306–8; density and predictability model *159*; depletion 178–79; economic defendability 159–60; sharing, permanent settlements 98, 172
rewilding movement 350–52

rice: genetic analysis 187–88; identification issues 185; phytoliths 187
rice domestication: 185–89; India 188–89; map *186*
rice farming landscape *188*; ecosystems *188*; paddy fields 185, *189*; waterworks, Angkor 236–37
Richard III king of England 212–16, *214*, *215*
Rideaux Cave 38
Rigaud, Jean-Philippe 43
Rio Balsas 228
Rio Grande 98, 101–2
Riratjingu people 78–79
ritual/ceremonial: activities, 80, 97, 98, 111–13, 116, 118, 120, 143, 151, 162, 202, 225, 230–31, 234, 269, 274, 285, 294, 297, 301, 303, 308, 311, 313–15; dances 97, 151, 285, *155*; objects 21, 32, 115, 118, 151, 156, 268, 277, 282, 310–14, *277*, *310*, *313*; kivas 98, 108, 111, 113, 118, *110*, *115*; *see also* sacrifices
rock art *see* paintings, rock art
Rongorongo script 322, *322*
Roots of Agriculture in Southern Arabia (RASA) Project 92–93, *93*
Roskilde Fjord pollen diagram *194*
Ruggles, Clive 266
Rus Viking people 290–91, 336–37
Rwanda, iron smelting 63–65

sacrifices: animal 118, 192, 258, *259*; human 17, 203, 205–6, 285–86, 288, 293–95, 298, 301, 310, 311, 312, *288*, *294*; luxury goods 278, 286–93, 310
Safaitic script 321
Sahara desert: anthropogenic landscapes 70; climate shift 64; Messak plateau 258; mobile communities and monuments 257–59; technology transmission 63–65; trans-Saharan slave trade 339–41, *339*
Sahlins, Marshall 284–85
Salisbury Plain 268
Samoa, Lapita dispersal 87
sampling strategies 92, *93*

San Cristobal ruin, stratified refuse 101–2
San Juan River 98, 109–15
San Pedro de Mòrrope, burial excavations 217–18, *218*
San people, South Africa 34
Sand Canyon *see* Catherine's Site
Sanganakallu Neolithic ash mounds *260*
Santa Rosa Island, Arlington Springs Man 131
Sargon II, King of Akkad 241, 304, 307
satellite imagery: lost cities/structures 227, *227*; maps, using 23
Sateré-Mawé tribe 201
Schele, Linda 303
Schmandt-Besserat, Denise 307
Scioto Valley 271, 274
Scott, Michael 350
scribes, Maya 298, *299*
seals/impressions 284, 288, 308, *289*, *307*
Seip Earthworks *273*
settlements: before domestication 173; consolidated into state 238–39; first permanent *see* Jericho; systems 151–54, *153*; *see also* cities; villages; specific locations
Shakespeare, William 213, 215–16
Shang Dynasty 309–13
sheep domesticated 92
shell middens 328
Shennan, Stephen 190
Sheridan Cave 133
Shijiahe culture 314
ships 20, 73, 87, 330–33, 338, 341, *292*, *331–32*, *338*; burials 290–93, *292*; *see also* whaling
Shoshone 144
Sibudu Cave 59
sickles 182–83
Sigatoka Valley 156, 158, 160
silver: artifacts 287, 293, 343, *334*; Dollerup cup *290*; mining/extracting 217, 334, 336, *324*
Simon, Erika and Helmut 66–67
single-use plastic bags 355
sixth mass extinction event 12–14, 123
Skhul cave 29
skulls 45, 192, 205, 214–15, 259, *134*; human 287, *85*; dogs 183, *183*

INDEX **373**

Slav people, enslaved by Vikings 336–37
slave ship *Brookes*, plan 338
slave trade 337–43; barracoons 342, *343*; extractivism 336–46; routes 339–41, *339*; trans-Atlantic trade 337–43; Vikings Rus trade 336–37
slavery 336; Asante empire 341–42; Bolivians by Spain 336; Chesapeake Bay 343–44; indentured servants 344; Monticello 345–46, *346*; political economies 338–39; trans-Atlantic slave trade 337–43; trans-Saharan slave trade 339–41, *339*
Snaketown site 118
social benefits, pyramid building 255–56
social change, metalworking and 62–63
social consequences, farming 190–93
social identity, collective labor as 245–75
social structure:
  Broken K Pueblo 116–18, *117*; training and learning 60; structural inequality 216–18
social theory 143; bison hunting 150–51; practice theory 161
Society for American Archaeology (SAA), ethical principles 86
Society Islands 16, 17, 90
Soffer, Olga 38
solar cells, panels 357; Fukushima 348
Sollas, William 43
Solutrean points 43
Sonora 98, 188; *see also* Hohokam people
South America:
  archaeological sites map *138*; beer 281–82; giant ground sloths 124, 126, 137–38, *138*; *see also* specific countries
South Arabian languages, cursive texts 317
South Island takahē 353
South Pacific islands 15–19, *15*
Southeast Asia:
  coral reefs death 12–13; fisher-farmers 87; *see also* specific countries
Southwest Asia:
  first settlements 170–79; food production emergence 169, *171*; *see also* specific countries

spade, China 187
Spanish Conquest *see* conquest Spain:
  Andes gold/silver, removal 334–36; Bolivians enslaved by 336; Cathedral altar 334, *335*; Iberian lynx, liberated 351
sperm whale tooth engraving *331*
spindle whorls 212, *212*
squash, domesticated 180
Squier, Ephraim 271, *271*
St. Kilda islands 143, 161–64, *161*, *163*, *164*
Staffords, Thomas 131
Stahl, Ann 341
states:
  and identity 207; as complex society 237–39; consolidation 238–39
Steadman, David 140
Steel Group 274
stelae 224, 297–98, *297*
Stephens, John Lloyd 222
stewardship 43–46, 86
Stiner, Mary 42, 179
stone artifacts analysis 70
stone tools:
  evidence of human adaptation 56; hand axes, Acheulean tradition *51*; quartz, Australia 75; skills replication, hand axe replica *48*; toolmaking techniques 49, 53–55, *54*, *55*
Stonehenge 261–70, *261*, *263*, *264*, *265*; building 263–66; burials 268; dating attempts 264–66; interpretations 266–69; landscape 269–70; Riverside Project 264, 268; World Heritage Site Project 262, 268, 269
stratigraphy 16
structural inequality:
  and identity 202; prehistory 216–18
structural violence:
  bad living conditions 216; ancient Peru 216, 217–18, *218*
structuralism 34–35
structure/agency balance 219
Stukeley, William 263, 266, *263*
subsurface mapping 272, *273*
Sulawesi cave 37
Sulaymaniyah Museum 305
Sumerians:
  agricultural intensification 240–41; burial artifacts, Ur 286–87, *286*; burials 286–90,

289; cities and surplus production 242; irrigation canals 241; language, isolated 308–9; region maps *240*, *287*; Uruk Vase *241*; ziggurats 290; writing development 241, 298, 303–8
surplus production 242; Angkor 234–37; Egypt 237–38; intensification, Mesopotamia 240–41; Maya 224–225, 230–32 survey method 22, 92; Polynesia 15–16; stratified 92
sustainability 14, 119, 221, 277, 349
Sutton Hoo burial site/hoard 291–93, *292*, *293*
Sweden, buried ships 291
sweet potato 17
syllabograms 300
symbolic expression 28, 31–32, *29*
Syria:
  Euphrates Valley structures 176; herding *184*; Ugarit 308

Tabanivono people 143, 158
Ṭabaqāt Al Būma 23
Tabasco people 205
Tabun cave 29
Tahiti 88–89, *88*; experimental voyage to 90
Tam, Manuel 217
Tamaulipas caves 180
taro cultivation 87, 156, *157*
Tasmanian tiger 123, *122*
Tatuba Cave 160
Taurus Mountains 241; structures 175–76, *176*
Tavuni Hillfort 158
taxonomic identification 146
tax-paying 217, 240, 281, 284, 317
technologies:
  stone tools 28–29, 51–60, *51*; metalworking 62–63, *61*, *63*; clothing 66–69, *69*; *see also* specific archaeological techniques
teeth analysis 139, 147
Tehuacàn caves 180
temples Angkor 235, *235*; Aztec 217; Egypt 237; Maya 298–99; Sumerian 290, 308; Tikal 297, *233*
Templo Mayor site 204
Tenochtitlán 208, 226
Teotihuacan 203, 204, 205, 206
terebinth resin 284

terra preta (Amazonian dark earths) 165–67, *166*; plant communities 166–67
test excavations 92
Thailand, Khok Phanom Di site 328
Thames Valley boundary sacrifices 278
Thamudic script 321
Thomsen, Christian 51–52
three-age system 51–52
Thule culture 20–22, *21*
thylacine 123, *122*
Tianluoshan 187
Tight Entrance Cave 75
Tigris River 241
Tikal city 232, 297, *233*, *296*; conflict 224–25
Tikopia 16
time measurement 50–53
Tiwanaku civilization 334–36
Tlaxcaltec Spanish allies 205
To'aga excavation 16
tobacco:
  planters 344; pipes 341, *272*
tokens 307, *307*
Toltec society 203
Tonga 87
tools:
  hand axes, Acheulean tradition *51*; human adaptation 56; metal toolmaking 62; prehistory dating 49–53; quartz, Australia 75; skills replication, hand axe replica *48*; time measurement from 50–53; toolmaking techniques 49, 53–55, *54*, *55*; *see also* weapons and edge tools
Torres Strait land bridge 78
tortoises and hares 179
Total Station mapping systems 107, *107*
trans-Atlantic slave trade 337–43
trans-Saharan slave trade 339–41, *339*
tree-ring dating 130, *108*, *109*
Tuc d'Audoubert cave 38
Tucson-Phoenix Basin 118
Tula 203
tumbleweed 195
Tupaia's Tahitian islands map 88–89, *88*
Turkana Lake 64; Çatalhöyük village 191–93, 230–31, *192*; sunken stone structures 175–76; wine remains 283–84
turtle plastrons 311, 313, *311*

Two Brothers wreck 333–34, *333*
typologies, culture markers 102–4

Ubaid Period settlements 303–304
Ugaritic and cuneiform 316, *308*
Uluṟu (Ayers Rock) sacred site 80–81, *80*; Kata Tjuṯa National Park 81; rock art images 80; World Heritage Site designation 80–81
Umatilla people 85
Umm el-Qa'ab tombs 285–86, *285*
Una Vida 111
underwater archaeology 332–34, *332*, *333*
UNESCO 80–81
United Kingdom: plastic-bags charge 355; microbeads ban 355; *see also* specific locations
United States: extinctions 13; microbeads ban 355; *see also* specific states and locations
Upper Mantaro Valley 282–84
Upper Nile map *237*
Ur king's burial: artifacts 286–87, *286*; chambers 286; conspicuous consumption 286–90; death pit 286–88, *288*
urbanism and agriculture 221–42
Urton, Gary 319
Uruk period 241, 304–7; Gilgamesh, Epic of 304–5; proto-cuneiform tablets 305–6, 308, *306*
Uruk Vase 305, *241*
Utah, climate 98

Vail Site *125*
vaka 72
van Ruisdael, Jacob, *Windmill at Wijk* 246, *247*
Van Tilburg, Jo Anne 18
Vandiver, Pamela 38
Vanuatu 87
Vavilov, Nikolai 185
"Venus" figurines 38, *38*
vessels/bowls/cups 102, 143, 171, 241, 278, 283–84, 290, 306, 310–14, 318, 333, *102*, *231*, *313*
Vikings: iron sword *291*; ship burials 290–91; slave trade 336–37; *see also* Norse
village communities 196–97; climate change 175; farming to support 176

Wadi Sana 23, *93*; sampling strategy 92–93
Waldalgesheim hoard 278
wallabies, extinct giant 75
Wallace, Alfred Russell 74; Wallace islands 74, 78, *74*
Wandsworth Shield *276*
Wanka II Period 281–82; diets, residue analysis 282–84
Warakurna artists 79
Washington, George 345
Washington state: Elwha River restoration 350; Kennewick Man 85, *85*; Makah people 330
waste reduction 354–55
Waters, Mike 131
Waxaklajun Ubaah K'awil king of Copan 298
weapons/edge tools: arrows 102, 151; atlatls 124, *125*; axes, metal 53, 61, 67, 70, 277, 287; axes, stone 49, 50, 57, 58, 75, 78, *48*, *51*, *57*, *78*; helmets 286, 293, *292*; knives 50, 51, 55; points, projectile 43, 84, 92, 124–25, 126, 127, 131–33, *125*, *132*; scrapers 58, 60, 77; shields 277; spears 124, 129, 131, *125*; swords 50, 278, 293, *50*, *291*; weapons 18, 114, 124, 140, 278, 287, 310, 311; *see also* tools
Weiner, Annette 207
Wellington, Zealandia eco-reserve *353*
Wengrow, David 248, 250
Wenke, Robert 255
West Africa: brewing 280–81, *280*; iron-smelting 65; mammalian wildlife decline 350; slave raiding 338
wet-screening 23
whaling: Makah people 330, *330*; Nantucket center 331; oil for lighting industry 330–32; prime locations map *329*; processing *331*; tooth engraving *331*; *Two Brothers* wreck 333–34

wheat: domestication 169; primitive 180; seeds *182*
Whiteman, Ridgely 124
Wildlife Conservation Society 352
Willandra Lakes region 77, *76*
Willerslev, Eske 81
Wilson, Edward O. 352
Wiwi Village, kava preparation *142*
wolves 126; domestication 39, 183–84
wombats, extinct giant 75
women: and Aztec tribute cloth 210–12, *211*; Mesoamerica 209–12; mothers' pottery and residence 116–18; pyramid workers 254; *see also* Lady Hao; La Malinché; Pu'abi, queen of Ur
Woodhenge 268, 272, *265*
Woolley, Katherine 287
Woolley, Sir Leonard 286–87
Wrangel Island, dwarf mammoths 140
writing systems 297–322, *299*; alphabetic 314–16, *315*; ancient Chinese 309–14; and Anthropocene 322–23; Isthmian 301; lexical lists 307; literacy and phonetic elements 301; logograms 300, 306; materials, perishable 317–18; Maya 297, 298–303, *300*; Olmec 301; preservation 316–18; Sumerians 241, 303–8, *306*
Wu Ding, Shan King 310, 311
Wuyang 313
Wymer, Dee Ann 272
Wyoming, bison hunters 144–45

Xi'an, Neolithic village 313
Xicalango people 205

Yangshao culture, Neolithic village 313
Yangtze River 187, 189, 314
Yangzi River, Liangzhu culture 313–14
Yax Ehb Xook 232
Yaxchilan *209*
Yellow River: Neolithic ceramics 312–13, *313*; Shang Dynasty 309–13
Yemen: small stone monument *259*; Wadi Sana sampling strategy 92, *93*

Yin, brush-written inscriptions 312
Younger Dryas period 175
Yucatán 205, 221; abandoned cities 222; Postclassic 234

Zagros Mountains 184, 241
Zalasiewicz, Jan 11
Zanzibar, Omani-run slave plantations 343
Zapotec people *225*
Zealandia eco-reserve *353*
Zeder, Melinda 184
Zhijun Zhao 187
ziggurats 290
zooarchaeology 146–47, 179, *146*
Zun jars 313–14, *313*
Zuni people 97, 120, *96*, *100*